Reading Swift:
Papers from The Third Münster Symposium
on Jonathan Swift

Edited by Hermann J. Real
and Helgard Stöver-Leidig

Edgar Mertner

# Reading Swift:

# Papers from
# The Third Münster Symposium
# on Jonathan Swift

Edited by
Hermann J. Real
and
Helgard Stöver-Leidig

1998

Wilhelm Fink Verlag

Gedruckt mit Unterstützung des Ministeriums für Wissenschaft und Forschung
des Landes Nordrhein-Westfalen

Cover portrait:

The last portrait of Swift, painted around 1740,
by an unknown artist.
Reproduced by kind permission of the
National Gallery of Ireland

Die Deutsche Bibliothek – CIP-Einheitsaufnahme

**Reading Swift:** papers from the Third Münster Symposium
on Jonathan Swift / ed. by Hermann J. Real and
Helgard Stöver-Leidig. – München: Fink, 1998
ISBN 3-7705-3298-8

ISBN 3-7705-3298-8
© 1998 Wilhelm Fink Verlag, München
Satz: Albert Schwarz, Paderborn
Herstellung: Ferdinand Schöningh GmbH, Paderborn

# Contents

# Preface

The Münster Swift industry takes pride in acting swiftly, as a rule. But even our most benevolent critics might be inclined to censure us, however gently, for having been somewhat tardy in the preparation of these twenty-two papers from *The Third Münster Symposium on Jonathan Swift*, held from 30 May to 1 June 1994, for the press. While we are ready to admit the charge, we should also like to plead mitigating circumstances, with the narration of which, however, we would not wish to detain those who like our bill of fare from the diet. In any case, it is a pleasure to thank our contributors not only for their determination to present their essays in the best possible shape but also, again, for all their patience and perseverance. Needless to say, we hope that, as the poet says, all's well that ends well.

Rumour has it that fund-raising has become a difficult venture in these financially desperate days. If it is, the *German Research Council* has disproved the prejudice by responding both generously and efficiently to our application, so much so in fact that we might feel like "trying" it again in the not-too-distant future. Warmest thanks also go to the *Kanzler der Westfälischen Wilhelms-Universität*, and in particular to our dedicated friend, Erwin Löhr. Printing *Reading Swift* has been greatly facilitated by a grant from the *Ministerium für Wissenschaft und Forschung des Landes Nordrhein-Westfalen*. We should particularly like to thank Dr Bergmann for his very active support.

Since 1984, when the first Münster conference on the Dean of St Patrick's was convened, the organizers have emphasized its character as a "symposium," a convivial meeting, that is, not only for intellectual entertainment and stimulating conversation but also for social recreation and good companionship. And since 1984, the elegant ambience of *Schloß Wilkinghege* has been a distinguishing feature, even a hallmark, of the Münster symposia, and as on all earlier occasions we feel the need to record our gratitude to Lubert Winneken, its proprietor, who has turned into a true Prestophile over the years.

Running the three-day event itself is impossible without a team that shares our infectious passion for the great Dean. Alison Turner, B.A., and Dr Michael Düring (now Greifswald), we are sorry to say, no longer work for the Ehrenpreis Center, but we want them to know that their remarkable contribution to *The Third* is all but forgotten. Marlies Thöle, who is something of an old hand at running symposia by now, was at her usual best, dedicated, considerate, and efficient, and so was our "girl guide," Hilde Melian, whose unique knowledge of the Münster geography and its environs proved invaluable. Dr Heinz-Dieter Leidig has many virtues, not the least of which is an uncanny ability to spot printing errors. Last but not least, no Münster symposium would have been what it was without the charm and hospitality radiated by Erika.

On 13 December 1997, Professor Edgar Mertner, whom Irvin Ehrenpreis once justly described as "the architect of the *Englisches Seminar*," celebrated his 90th birthday. Professor Mertner was a co-founder of the Ehrenpreis Center in 1986, and since then he has served as

Vice Chairman of its Friends. Even at ninety, he is an almost daily presence in the library, and always liberal with time and advice. It is for these reasons that the Editors should like to present this volume of essays to Professor Mertner as a mark of their respect, affection, and gratitude.

Münster, February 1998                                                          HJR
                                                                                 HS-L

# Abbreviations

*Prose Works*    [The Prose Works of Jonathan Swift], eds Herbert Davis *et al.*, 16 vols (Oxford, 1939–68; various reimpressions, sometimes corrected).

*Correspondence*    The Correspondence of Jonathan Swift, ed. Harold Williams, rev. David Woolley, 5 vols (Oxford, 1963–72).

*Poems*    Jonathan Swift, The Complete Poems, ed. Pat Rogers (Harmondsworth, Middlesex, 1983).

Ehrenpreis, *Mr Swift*    Irvin Ehrenpreis, Swift: The Man, his Works, and the Age,
*Dr Swift*    3 vols (London and Cambridge, MA, 1983 [1962–83]).
*Dean Swift*

Foxon    D. F. Foxon, English Verse, 1701–1750: A Catalogue of Separately Printed Poems with Notes on Contemporary Collected Editions, 2 vols (Cambridge, 1975).

Teerink-Scouten, *Bibliography*    H. Teerink, A Bibliography of the Writings of Jonathan Swift, 2nd ed., rev. Arthur H. Scouten (Philadelphia, 1963).

Abbreviations of periodicals are those of the "Master List of Periodicals" of the *MLA International Bibliography*.

# I. Early Prose Satires

Hugh Ormsby-Lennon
*Villanova University, Pennsylvania*

# Commonplace Swift[1]

The best Maxim I know in this life is, to drink your Coffee
when you can, and when you cannot, to be easy without it.[2]
Jonathan Swift

COFFEE Induces wit. No good unless it comes through Le
Havre. After a big dinner party, should be drunk standing
up. Drinking it without sugar is very smart: it gives the impression that you have lived in the East.[3]
Gustave Flaubert

ABSTRACT. Swift's fascination with the mechanical operations of nonsense incarnated itself
in two complementary ways: as sense passing itself off as nonsense (portmanteau words, little
languages, codes) and as nonsense passing itself off as sense (clichés, platitudes, polite and
ingenious conversation). Whatever the personal (or Hibernian) sources of the former, the
latter certainly afflicted Swift at Kilkenny School and Trinity College, Dublin, where (as in all
educational institutions for many years thereafter) students were required to transcribe snip-
pets from their reading under the "heads" they had devised for their commonplace books.
From such ragbags of received opinion, trainee writers stitched juvenile masterpieces of intertextual triviality. Prospective lawyers, doctors, and clergymen were also instructed to organize
commonplace books appropriate to their professions. As both writer and divine, Swift burlesqued commonplacing in all its forms and functions. But privately he used what he publicly
disparaged.

# I

Ever since the first pick-up line in Eden – "Madam, I'm Adam" (which doubles as a palin-
drome) – human communication has hinged for its intelligibility upon the formulaic use of
language. Yet to literary innovators, formula and commonplace prove a scandal. What Vic-

---

[1]  I am grateful to Vincent Carretta, Christopher Elrington, Ann Cline Kelly, John O'Neill,
    Barbara Riebling, and James Woolley for their suggestions. I am also grateful to the Folger
    Shakespeare Library for letting me consult its splendid collection of commonplace books.
[2]  Swift to Esther Vanhomrigh, 13 July 1722, *Correspondence*, II, 430.
[3]  Flaubert, *Dictionary of Received Ideas*, trans. Robert Baldick, in *Bouvard and Pécuchet*,
    trans. A. J. Krailsheimer (Harmondsworth, Middlesex, 1976), p. 298.

tor Shklovsky disparaged as "the automatically pronounced word tossed out like a chocolate bar from an automatic machine" becomes an easy mark for revolutionaries and resurrection men determined to "make it new."[4] Against the mechanical operations of language – its automatization – Shklovsky championed the unintelligibility of *zaum*, that "beyonsense" or "transrational" language devised by his friends, the Futurist poets Kruchenykh and Khlebnikov. What makes Swift a Futurist *avant la lettre* was his desire to make language new, if only through word games.

Like these twentieth-century Russians, Swift revelled in portmanteau words and little languages, echolalia and far-fetched etymologies, Babel and Pentecost, gnostic babble and new songs, the language of the birds …[5] Such defamiliarizations certainly shatter the formulaic necessities of ordinary communication. In Anglo-Latinus, for example, spectres of an alternative semantics blanch our normal expectations of how words make sense. From one perspective, Swift's verbal experiments constitute a wearisome exercise in schoolroom tomfoolery; from another, they invite comparison with the schizophrenic's word-salad. Yet like Newton with his alchemy and eschatology, Swift generally confined his Futurist wordplay to the closet in which he kept his manuscripts. In print, by contrast, Swift preferred to castigate, or to mimic, the loss of meaning that mechanical operators inflicted upon language. In "Commonplace Swift," I shall explore not his private forays into "beyonsense" but the grim relish Swift took in watching chocolate bars melt in his hand.

When Swift got up on the wrong side of the bed, he envisioned human communication as a meaningless exchange of prefabricated idioms, an exchange in which nightmare threatens to engulf farce.[6] Unlike the grand academicians of Lagado – dipping into and gesticulating over their cumbersome bundles of things – most of the sublunary folk who move through Swift's works find themselves condemned to swapping trite verbal formulae, a phatic activity that imports little more than the grooming rituals of monkeys as they crack one another's fleas. Swift's hilariously bleak vision of social intercourse as a shuffling of commonplaces has already prompted comparison with Ionesco's *Bald Primadonna* and with Flaubert's *Bouvard and Pécuchet* and *Dictionary of Received Ideas*.[7] Another francophone, Roland Barthes, also assures us that "it is language which speaks, not the author."[8] In the "profound ridiculousness" of "those eternal copyists" Bouvard and Pécuchet, Barthes witnesses "the truth of writing," namely the fact that "the writer can only imitate a gesture

---

4   Shklovsky, "The Connection between Devices of *Syuzhet* Construction and General Stylistic Devices (1919)," trans. Jane Knox, *Russian Formalism: A Collection of Articles and Texts in Translation*, eds Stephen Bann and John E. Bowlt (New York, 1973), p. 48. See also Shklovsky, "The Resurrection of the Word (1914)," *Russian Formalism*, eds Bann and Bowlt, pp. 41–47.

5   For Swift's purported fluency in the alchemystical and shamanic language of the birds, see Hugh Ormsby-Lennon, "Rosicrucian Linguistics: Twilight of a Renaissance Tradition," *Hermeticism and the Renaissance: Intellectual History and the Occult in Early Modern Europe*, eds Ingrid Merkel and Allen G. Debus (Washington, D.C., 1988), pp. 322–23.

6   Temptations to exaggerate Swift's nihilism must be rejected. However gloomy his night thoughts, Swift craved company and celebrated conversation. For a sane account, see Ann Cline Kelly, *Swift and the English Language* (Philadelphia, 1988), pp. 25–36.

7   See Claude Rawson, *Gulliver and the Gentle Reader: Studies in Swift and our Time* (London and Boston, 1973), pp. 95–99.

8   "The Death of the Author," *Image Music Text*, trans. Stephen Heath (New York, 1977), p. 143.

that is always anterior, never original. His only power is to mix writings."[9] I shall not bore you with a litany of the postmodern critic's infinite capacity for deciphering his (or her) own contrivances from Swift's satire, particularly from the *Tub*, but I imagine that commonplace Swift would have found current theories of the "morte d'author" beguiling, if only in his role as a Jack Pudding who inveigles *personae* into the absurdist coils of boa-deconstruction.[10] Indeed, the Tubster concludes his *Tale* with a postmodern "Experiment very frequent among Modern Authors; which is, to *write upon Nothing*; When the Subject is utterly exhausted, to let the Pen still move on; by some called, the Ghost of Wit, delighting to walk after the Death of its Body" (T, p. 208). For, as Michel Foucault explains, "man is in the process of perishing as the being of language continues to shine ever brighter upon our horizon."[11]

"Morte d'author" theorizing has sparked a resurgence of scholarly interest in commonplacers – that is in those eternal copyists who set up commonplace books and engage in commonplacing, the imitation of anterior gestures.[12] For in collections of received ideas, authorial originality may appear to forfeit its authority, retaining merely what Michel Foucault has dubbed the "author function."[13] Such ceremonial moues to postmodernism notwithstanding, we must not forget how writers like E. M. Forster and W. H. Auden have, during our own century, augmented traditions of commonplacing normally associated with earlier writers like John Milton and Thomas Jefferson.[14] In "Commonplace Swift," however, I argue that any exaggerated fealty to the "characteristics of the true commonplace book"[15] – extracts from reading intermingled with some authorial reflections – will obscure the centrality of the commonplace book, more loosely defined, to both the workings of Swift's mind and the makings of his satire. As a student at Kilkenny, Trinity College, Dublin, and Oxford, Swift would have been required to fuss and fiddle with commonplace books; as a young gentleman lately entered into holy orders, he would have been expected to cobble his sermons (or treatises) together from a theological commonplace book; and as an eternal copyist to Sir William Temple – mindlessly transcribing the words of the master or of his

---

9   "The Death of the Author," p. 146.
10  For the contexts of Barthes's essay, see H. L. Hix, *Morte d'Author: An Autopsy* (Philadelphia, 1990), and particularly Sean Burke's incisive *The Death and Return of the Author: Criticism and Subjectivity in Barthes, Foucault, and Derrida* (Edinburgh, 1992). I have used *Tub* as catch-all title for the three works included by Swift in his tripartite satire, *A Tale of a Tub*, eds A. C. Guthkelch and D. Nichol Smith, 2nd ed. (Oxford, 1968 [1958]). References to this edition (T) will appear in the text.
11  *The Order of Things: An Archaeology of the Human Sciences* (New York, 1970), p. 386.
12  In Mary Thomas Crane's *Framing Authority: Sayings, Self, and Society in Sixteenth-Century England* (Princeton, 1993) – astute, thorough, and informative though that volume is – we can trace the scholarly sequelae of "morte d'author" theorizing.
13  See "What is an Author?" *Language, Counter-Memory, Practice: Selected Essays and Interviews*, ed. Donald F. Bouchard, trans. Donald F. Bouchard and Sherry Simon (Ithaca, NY, 1977), pp. 113–38.
14  See Forster, *Commonplace Book*, ed. Philip Gardner (London, 1985); Auden, *A Certain World: A Commonplace Book* (New York, 1970); Milton, "Commonplace Book," *Complete Prose Works of John Milton, I: 1624–1642*, ed. Don M. Wolfe (New Haven and London, 1953), 344–513; Ruth Mohl, *John Milton and His Commonplace Book* (New York, 1969); Gilbert Chinard, ed., *The Commonplace Book of Thomas Jefferson* (Baltimore, MD, 1926); Dickinson W. Adams, ed., *Jefferson's Extracts from the Gospels* (Princeton, NJ, 1963).
15  Mohl, *John Milton and His Commonplace Book*, p. 30.

sister Lady Giffard – Swift came to inhale something of *l'ennui bouvardo-pécuchetien*. Fears of a lifetime condemned to mixing the writings of others petrified the young satirist – before, that is, he came to accept that his originality as a writer sprang, in no small part, from his gift for aping anterior gestures. For the flowering of Swift's genius – we might say – automatization no less than defamiliarization proved the fertilizer.

## II

> Nothing is spoken now but what has been said in former times.
> Terence, as quoted by John Dunton[16]

> Let those who used our words before us perish.
> St Jerome or Aelius Donatus or Anon, as quoted by Samuel Beckett[17]

Swift's mimicry of the commonplace spans his known career – from the platitudinous bombination of his early Pindarics ("SURE there's some Wondrous Joy in *Doing Good*")[18] to the last major work he saw through the press, *A Compleat Collection of Genteel and Ingenious Conversation* in 1738. The origins of *Polite Conversation* may be found during the 1690s when Swift, I hazard, opened a "book of *Drama Common places*" and began to accumulate chic dialogue with an eye to challenging the London triumphs of such *Wunderkinder* from Trinity College, Dublin, as William Congreve and perhaps George Farquhar.[19] Before too long, I conjecture, Swift became disenchanted with this enterprise but saved its word-hoard from oblivion by devising Simon Wagstaff as a mouthpiece. That Wagstaff's *dramatis personae* proves closer to Flaubert's or Ionesco's than to Congreve's or Farquhar's suggests that Swift's intimations of the absurd soon crushed any budding talent for developing plot and character through dialogue. Certainly, pedagogic tedium at Trinity College and long years spent copying and eavesdropping at Moor Park had already sharpened Swift's ear for the formulaic and prefabricated. That Swift's knack for personation was further enhanced during his Grubean rambles the Tubster demonstrates in his fulsome role as "a most devoted Servant of all *Modern* Forms" (T, p. 45). Fully to appreciate Swift's apprenticeship as a commonplacer during the 1680s and 90s, we must first survey its consequences, namely his lifelong impersonation of "the choicest common-places," "A SET of Phrases learn't by Rote," "Phrases battered, stale, and trite," or "A Verse from *Horace*, learn'd by Rote."[20] Swift's career as a satirist comprises a tongue-in-cheek threnody for meaning's demise.

---

[16] Dunton, *The Art of Living Incognito: Being a Thousand Letters on as Many Uncommon Subjects* (London: A. Baldwin, 1700), p. 54 (*i.e.* 44): "*Nihil est jam Dictum quod non Dictum sit prius.*"

[17] For a discussion of this quotation from *Watt* – "pereant qui ante nos nostra dixerunt" – see Christopher Ricks, *Beckett's Dying Words* (Oxford and New York, 1993), p. 101.

[18] "Ode to the King," *The Poems of Jonathan Swift*, ed. Harold Williams, 2nd ed., 3 vols (Oxford, 1966 [1958]), I, 6, l. 1.

[19] On Bayes's dramatic commonplace book as a methodological exemplar, see p. 37 of this essay.

[20] "Phillis, or, the Progress of Love" (1719), l. 49; "The Furniture of a Woman's Mind" (1727), l. 1; "The Journal of a Modern Lady" (1729), l. 112; "Verses on the Death of Dr. Swift" (1731), l. 474; see *Poems*, ed. Williams, I, 223; II, 415, 448, 572.

In contemplating his own "morte d'author," Swift rounds up some commonplaces – ranging from prescribed sentiment to the mundane patois of quadrille – and dragoons them into hudibrastic service:

"The Dean is dead, (*and what is Trumps?*)
"Then Lord have Mercy on his Soul.
"(Ladies I'll venture for the *Vole*.)
"Six Deans they say must bear the Pall.
"(I wish I knew what *King* to call.)

The rest will give a Shrug and cry,
I'm sorry; but we all must dye.
Indifference clad in Wisdom's Guise,
All Fortitude of Mind supplies.[21]

In "we all must dye," Swift registers the vernacular version of "*Mors omnibus communis*," a piece of wisdom flaunted by the Tritical Essayist – despite his detestation of "*stale Topicks and thread-bare Quotations.*"[22] Exhibiting the wisdom of the Tubster – "What tho' his *Head* be empty, provided his *Common-place-Book* be full" (T, p. 148) – the Tritical Essayist diligently stirs the quotidian pot:

THE Mind of Man is, at first, (if you will pardon the Expression) like a *Tabula rasa*; or like Wax, which while it is soft, is capable of any Impression, until Time hath hardened it. And at length Death, that grim Tyrant, stops us in the Midst of our Career. The greatest Conquerors have at last been conquered by Death, which spares none from the Sceptre to the Spade.
      *Mors omnibus communis.*
    ALL Rivers go to the Sea, but none return from it. *Xerxes* wept when he beheld his Army; to consider that in less than an Hundred Years they would all be dead.[23]

If death is the ultimate commonplace – "the one concept that you can't deconstruct" as Morris Zapp remarks[24] – then it is also, as Sibyl and Struldbrugg discover to their chagrin, a commonplace that can prove consoling. After the funeral of his only daughter who had suffered from Down's Syndrome, Charles de Gaulle observed plangently: "Maintenant elle est comme les autres."[25] Thus it was that Swift, *in propria persona*, concluded (or affected to conclude) that "it is impossible that any thing so natural, so necessary, and so universal as death, should ever have been designed by providence as an evil to mankind."[26]

Following the advice of Erasmus in *De Copia*, John Locke opened up a "head" for "Mors" in the commonplace book he began as a youth, whether at Westminster or Christ Church.[27] Yet if Locke himself did not stoop to recording mere tags like "mors omnibus

[21]   "Verses on the Death of Dr. Swift," ll. 228–32, 211–14, *Poems*, ed. Williams, II, 562, 561.
[22]   "A Tritical Essay upon the Faculties of the Mind," *Prose Works*, I, 250, 246.
[23]   *Prose Works*, I, 250.
[24]   David Lodge, *Small World: An Academic Romance* (New York, 1991 [1984]), p. 373. Recent reports in *The New York Times Magazine* indicate, however, that Jacques Derrida is currently contemplating death.
[25]   I quote from memory.
[26]   "Thoughts on Religion," *Prose Works*, IX, 263.
[27]   See Folger Library MS E.A.41, "Commonplace Book c. 1700 which had been originally a Latin notebook of John Locke." An example of the genre of schoolroom essay for which such a commonplace-book was designed may be found in Milton's "Theme on Early Rising," *Complete Prose Works*, I, 1034–39. Foster Watson's remarks on "Theme Writing at the Beginning of the Seventeenth Century with a Note on Erasmus's *De Copia*," *The Eng-*

communis" – his sole entry reads "Quas vita non dat, funus ac cinis dabunt" – other commonplacers enjoyed accumulating the kind of fortitudinous wisdom which today we associate with Chinese fortune cookies or the bottoms of calendars.[28] A Kentish squire, Henry
Oxenden (1609–1670), stockpiled some four dozen "Aphorismes and Apophthegmes" in
Latin: "in vino veritas … ubi amor ibi oculus … occasio non negligenda … pecuniam obe-
diunt omnia."[29] That one of these – "Audentes fortuna iuvat" – resurfaces in the *Dictionary
of Received Ideas* accents the bankruptcy of commonplacing, at least for such mordant observers as Flaubert and Swift.[30] ("Beware of quoting Latin tags," Flaubert drolly advised
commonplacers who wished to load every rift with ore: "they all have something risqué in
them."[31]) Proverbial wisdom – whether in Latin or the vernacular ("A word before is worth
two behind … Rekeless youth makes a goutie age"[32]) – comprised the small change of many
commonplace books; indeed, industrious commonplacers actually took the time and trouble
to transcribe proverbs from printed collections like David Ferguson's.[33] In addition to the
joys of compilation, commonplacers evidently enjoyed garnishing their conversation with
such indifferent wisdom.

"Verses on the Death of Dr. Swift" was, according to its author, "Occasioned by reading
a Maxim in *Rochefoucault*," a maxim he promptly Englished in a hudibrastic couplet: "'In
all Distresses of our Friends / We first consult our private Ends.'"[34] Indeed, if Swift, as he
assured Pope, "really found [his] whole character" in La Rochefoucauld, the higher commonplacing constituted an ideal mode of expression.[35] Yet the differentiation of maxims
(which trade on authorial imprimatur as well as on content) from the commonplace or the
proverbial (which had entered the public domain) proves easier in theory than in practice.
Compiler of the *Polite Conversation* and commonplacer *extraordinaire*, Simon Wagstaff
sneered at the conversational garnish of proverbs – "I utterly reject them out of all ingenious
Discourse" – although he confessed that "a few Sayings" in his thesaurus still betrayed
"a proverbial Air."[36] But even those of his sayings which smack of the proverbial, Wagstaff
explains, "were not originally Proverbs, but the genuine Productions of superior Wits"
which "vulgar Hands" have abraded to "proverbial Maxims."[37] Thus it is that in one commonplace-book tags like "non omnia possumus omnes" and "difficilia quae pulchra" jostle
such a verse from Horace, learned by rote, as "Coelum non Animum mutavit qui trans mare
currit;" each seeds a miniature crop of commonplaces like those in which the Tritical
Essayist embeds "mors omnibus communis."[38]

---

*lish Grammar Schools to 1660: Their Curriculum and Practice* (Cambridge, 1908), pp. 422–39
   may still be profitably consulted.

[28]  Folger MS E.a.41, fol. 10r.

[29]  Folger MS V.b.110, fols 13–14. This folio commonplace book seems to have been compiled
   between 1642 and 1670.

[30]  Folger MS V.b.110, fol. 13. See *Dictionary of Received Ideas*, p. 306, *s.v.* "Fortune" where
   Flaubert gives a slightly different version of the tag: "*Audaces fortuna iuvat.*"

[31]  Flaubert, *Dictionary of Received Ideas*, p. 314.

[32]  Folger MS V.b.300, fol. 77r; a folio compiled 1690–96.

[33]  Folger MS V.b.300, fol. 77r.

[34]  "Verses on the Death of Dr. Swift," ll. 7–8, *Poems*, ed. Williams, II, 553.

[35]  Swift to Pope, 26 November 1725, *Correspondence*, III, 118.

[36]  *Prose Works*, IV, 102.

[37]  *Prose Works*, IV, 102.

[38]  Folger MS V.a.309, fols 34v–35r, 29v, 22v; quarto, c. 1680. The familiarity of the tags re-

As Wagstaff discloses, there is a no-man's land where proverb and maxim, author-function and genuine production coexist uneasily. Here, too, *ipse dixits* collide with platitudes. "It was a saying of Lactantius: That it was ye fate of ill-chosen premisses yt they produced rediculous & absurd conclusions;" "It was Judiciously & advantageously observed by Demosthenes & Quintilian (who were antient schoolmen & great masters of Rhetorick) that there are three kinds of style ["Readers," we recall from the *Tub*, "may be divided into three Classes" (T, p. 184)]."[39] "Riches, said Boethius, Resemble a Dunghill which stinketh when together, but fatneth the ground when spread."[40] "Epicurus sd. of lawes, yt ye were so necessary unto us, yt without them men would enter-devoure one another."[41] "*Plato* lays it down as a Maxim, that *Men ought to worship the Gods, according to the Laws of the Country*."[42] "*Herodotus* tells us, that in cold Countries Beasts very seldom have Horns; but in hot they have very large ones. This might bear a pleasant Application."[43] The last two *ipse dixits* come from Swift, the latter from *Thoughts on Various Subjects* where it functions as a tubbian memorandum.

"Diogenes detested women," we discover – as though an *ipse dixit* could redeem misogyny.[44] With or without such an appeal to authority, antifeminism and bawdry pervade commonplace books since these were, so often, "kept by the sportive male."[45] A jest like the 'gooseberry' riddle, at least as old as the *Exeter Book* of 940 A.D., reappears more often in seventeenth-century commonplace books than it does in print.[46] Indeed, the closest analogues for Swift's scatological poems may well be the ribald or obscene verses on women, particularly loose women, recorded by commonplacers.[47] But even wives, we discover, demand careful handling:

It is of great consequence not to use the Exercise [of lovemaking] too often, for fear of making yr wife too desiorous of that sport, which is too often enough cause of her's search-

corded and the mechanical essays on some of them suggest a schoolboy or student notebook for theme writing. Lodge resuscitates the tag from Horace as an epigraph for *Small World*.

[39] Folger MSS V.b.300, inscribed within the back cover. From Folger MS V.a.399, fol. 41r, we discover that "There be 3 kinde of Sages" and from MS W.a.217, p. 10 that "There are 3 sorts of Atheists."

[40] Folger MS. V.a.255, fol. 22r. Gideon Rutherford's quarto, compiled c. 1690–1725, containing poems, aphorisms, and philosophical maxims.

[41] Folger MS V.a.281; quarto, c. 1650, containing maxims, notes on sermons, and other religious writings.

[42] *Prose Works*, II, 11–12.

[43] *Prose Works*, I, 244. The tubbian and Scriblerian symbolism of asses needs no elaboration.

[44] Folger MS V.a.399, fol. 35v. A quarto commonplace book, c. 1600–1650, which was owned by Charles Shuttleworth in 1691. To a melange of amorous and religious poems, of proverbs, maxims, and riddles, and two facetious sermons in Welsh English, poems by Dryden and Pope were subsequently added.

[45] J. H. P. Pafford, *John Clavell, 1601–43: Highwayman, Author, Lawyer, Doctor* (Oxford, 1993), p. 142.

[46] It can be found, for example, in Clavell's commonplace book (see Pafford, *John Clavell, 1601–43*), twice in the Randle Holme collection (see John Wardroper, ed., *The Demaundes Joyous* [London, 1976], p. 9), and *Wit and Drollery* (London, 1656).

[47] Pafford declares that lines in Clavell's "An epitafe on the scold his wife" are "even coarser than Swift;" *John Clavell, 1601–43*, pp. 145–46. Indictments of prostitution comprise a *topos*; see Clavell's "To the Ladies that use Graies Inn Walkes," *John Clavell, 1601–43*, p. 146, and "Upon the naked Bedlams & spotted Beasts / Brests wee see in Common / Covent garden" in Folger V.a.232, p. 39.

ing else where for releef. For theese Desires are of such a nature, that the more they are quenched the more they kindle.[48]

The future Rector of Middleton in Lancashire, Henry Newcome (1650–1713), picks up the burden in one of the 429 jests he stockpiled in his commonplace book: "A fellow call'd his wife my honey, my Duck, my deer i.e. my sweat, foul, beast."[49] In an epigram, Newcome extends his indictment: "Women were made to helpe men so they doe / Some to diseases, some to greife & woe."[50] The lure of misogyny for clerics may be inferred from the extraordinary vogue of Petrus Alfonsi's *Diciplina Clericalis.*[51] Even Archbishop Sancroft sniped at wives, errant or otherwise, in his manuscript collection of jests: "'How long have you been married, Dr Donne?' R. ''Tis the 7th year of her reign.' But he added not, 'Whom G. long preserve.'"[52] Swift's undertakings "Not to marry a young Woman" and "Not to hearken to Flatteryes, nor conceive I can be beloved by a young woman," first and fifteenth of his "Resolutions 1699 when I come to be old," may usefully be read within this commonplace tradition.[53] Yet his determination "Not to be peevish, or morose, or suspicious" and "Not to boast of my former beauty, or strength, or favor with Ladyes, &c" remain sanguine, and they contrast noticeably with some of Philip Larkin's expectations for his twenty-third year: "To grow sourer and sourer," and "To have nothing to do with women."[54] And the maxim which the poet's father scribbled into his diary – "Women are often dull, sometimes dangerous, and always dishonorable" – highlights a commonplace misogyny long antedating Petrus Alfonsi: "Woman is a pit – a pit, a hole, a watery grave," a Babylonian master instructs his servant: "Woman is a sharp sword of iron that cuts through a man's neck."[55]

Some *dixits* cannot boast much of an *ipse* in the commonplace books: "A certaine Captaine of Grecia was wont to say, if a Lions skinne cannot prevaile adde unto it ye skinne of a foxe: meaning thereby if force cannot, use policy."[56] Other *dixits* have lost their *ipse*: "Nothing is so much admired and little understood as Wit. There are several sorts of false wit ... True wit consists in the resemblance of ideas and false wit in the resemblance of

---

[48]   Folger MS W.a.126, p. 25. This quarto (186 pp., compiled 1700–1725) is chiefly devoted to reflections, maxims, and excerpts involving literature, philosophy, and government. The present quotation comes from the section "Women & Matrimony, Love & Courtship," pp. 17–30.

[49]   Folger MS V.a.232, jest 494 (unpaginated entries started from rear). Newcome began the commonplace book in 1669 (quarto, c. 160 pp.) but many entries date from his years in Lancashire.

[50]   Folger MS V.a.232, p. 36.

[51]   Behind Alfonsi we can glimpse the Arabic *Book of the Wiles and Contrivances of Women.* See Eberhard Hermes, ed., *The Disciplina Clericalis of Petrus Alfonsi* (Berkeley, 1977), p. 7. Alfonsi's blend of proverbs, *ipse dixits*, anecdotes, and jests bears a distinct family resemblance to the commonplace book.

[52]   Quoted by John Wardroper, *Jest upon Jest: A Selection from the Jestbooks and Collections of Merry Tales Published from the Reign of Richard III to George III* (London, 1970), p. 19.

[53]   The new transcription by David Woolley is definitive; see "Miscellanea in Two Parts," *Swift Studies,* 8 (1993), 96–97. Swift's addition of a Latin tag to the resolution about flattery and young women – "Et eos qui herdetetatem [*sic*] captant odisse ac vitare" – underscores the function of "Resolutions 1699" as an astute set of individualized commonplaces.

[54]   Woolley, "Miscellanea," pp. 96–97. Quoted by Andrew Motion, *Philip Larkin: A Writer's Life* (New York, 1993), p. 134.

[55]   Quoted by Motion, *Philip Larkin,* p. 176; quoted by Hermes, ed., *Disciplina Clericalis,* p. 13.

[56]   Folger MS V.a.399, fol.1v.

words."[57] These unattributed insights open the first section – "Of Wit. & Humour, & Satyr" – in what the Tubster would recognize as "a Critick's *Common-Place-Book*" (T, p. 102).[58] They have been filleted, not altogether ineptly, from Addison's *Spectator* papers on true and false wit.[59] Our commonplacer proceeds to pile Pelion upon Ossa's Dike: "The Ancients have term'd Wit a salt; and that it is not fit for food but seasoning; it may be used plentifully in Conversation, moderately in business, but never in Religion;" "Wit is a very good Quality, but then a wise man should always have the keeping of it." "All Humour that is not lineally descended from good sense is counterfeit."[60] What though his Polonian head be empty, provided his commonplace book be full?

Landfall looms here upon those realms of nonsense governed by the Tubster, by the Tritical Essayist, by Wagstaff, and by Swift's other mechanical operators of language. Commonplacers to a man though they be, it is the Tubster who puts the commonplace book through its most varied paces: "*As Wit is the noblest and most useful Gift of humane Nature, so Humor is the most agreeable ... SATYR is a sort of* Glass, *wherein Beholders do generally discover every body's Face but their Own*" (T, pp. 18, 215). Clearly, such tubbian *aperçus* might have popped from the very commonplace books cited. But like *Don Quixote* as copied out by Borges's Pierre Menard, the transcription of received ideas by Swift and Flaubert attains a peculiar novelty, a novelty that is etched in vitriol.[61] Indeed, the Tubster explicitly directs our attention to his sleight-of-hand with the formulaic paraphernalia of beginnings:

> I apprehend some curious *Wit* may object against me, for proceeding thus far in a Preface, without declaiming, according to the Custom, against the Multitude of Writers whereof the whole Multitude of Writers most reasonably proclaims. (T, p. 45)

Such dexterity as he has, the Tubster explains, is attributable not only to "perusing some hundreds of Prefaces" but also to his preservation of "a few Examples" which he promptly inflicts upon us: "One begins thus; *For a Man to set up for a Writer, when the Press swarms with* &c. Another; *The Tax upon Paper does not lessen the Number of Scriblers, who daily pester*, &c. Another; *To observe what Trash the Press swarms with*, &c" (T, p. 45). Thomas Fuller had claimed to "know some that have a commonplace against commonplace books," but Swift, I suggest, contrived a Flaubertian pattern of commonplace books against commonplaces.[62] To fatten up *Bouvard and Pécuchet* and the *Dictionary of Received Ideas*, Flaubert gutted well in excess of 1,500 books, diligently amassing samples of trash in his *sottisier* as he dubbed the *carnets* in which he kept his notes.[63] For Swift, I propose, we can infer

---

[57] Folger MS V.a.126, pp. 1–2.

[58] Note first section.

[59] See *The Spectator*, ed. Donald F. Bond, 5 vols (Oxford, 1965), I, 244–74 (nos 58–63).

[60] Folger MS V.a.126, pp. 4, 10, 3.

[61] See Jorge Luis Borges, "Pierre Menard, Author of the *Quixote*," *Labyrinths: Selected Stories and Other Writings*, trans. Donald A. Yates and James E. Irby (New York, 1964 [1962]), pp. 36–44.

[62] See Fuller, *The Holy State* (Cambridge: J. Williams, 1648), p. 164.

[63] Here I have relied upon Gustave Flaubert, *Le second volume de "Bouvard et Pécuchet:" Le projet du "sottisier." Reconstitution conjecturale de la "copie" des deux bonshommes d'après le dossier de Rouen*, eds Alberto Cento and Lea Caminiti Pennarola (Naples, 1981), and Flaubert, *Carnets de travail: edition critique et génétique*, ed. Pierre-Marc de Biasi (Paris, 1988).

comparable patterns of reading, commonplacing, and composition, particularly during the 1690s.

Those who studied conversation at Will's Coffee-house, Swift complained, found "their Heads filled with Trash, under the Name of Politeness, Criticism and Belles Lettres," but when limbering up for *Gulliver's Travels*, Swift himself consumed an "abundance of Trash," including, as he told Vanessa, "I know not how many diverting Books of History and Travells."[64] The "printed Trash" and "hourly Trash" which swell Swift's corpus[65] achieve postmodern redefinition in Donald Barthelme's *Snow White*. For in justifying their decision to manufacture "plastic buffalo humps," the seven dwarfs explain that the humps

> are 'trash,' and what in fact could be more useless or trashlike? It's that we want to be on the leading edge of this trash phenomenon, the everted sphere of the future, and that's why we pay particular attention, too, to those aspects of language that may be seen as a model of the trash phenomenon.[66]

"The most interesting part" of language, the dwarfs maintain, can be found in its "stuffing," that "endless ... sludge" which endows "verbality" with its "downward pull."[67] Their conviction that "downwardness is valuable" governs their taste in reading:

> We like books that have a lot of *dreck* in them, matter which presents itself as not wholly relevant (or indeed, at all relevant) but which, carefully attended to, can supply a kind of "sense" of what is going on.[68]

Trash and stuffing, sludge and dreck provide commonplace Swift with his working materials: for like Flaubert and the dwarfs, he laboured on the leading edge of his era's trash phenomenon.

Plastic buffalo humps will surface again, for Swift's commonplacing conjures up a postmodern world of endless verbality from which the author has been voided. "We – mankind – are a conversation," Heidegger assures us: "The being of man is founded in language."[69] Ho hum. From avatars of intertextuality like Kristeva and Barthes we discover that "every text builds itself as a mosaic of quotations, every text is absorption and transformation of another text," in short "a multidimensional space in which a variety of writings, none of them original, blend and clash."[70] For like their illusory authors, texts "are never single, complete and identical to themselves, but always plural, shattered," contingent upon "a new articulation of the thetic – of enunciative and denotative positionality."[71] Blah, blah, blah. "There is no such thing as an author," David Lodge explains with deadpan incredulity,

---

64 "Hints towards an Essay on Conversation," *Prose Works*, IV, 90; *Correspondence*, II, 431, 430.

65 "On Poetry: A Rapsody," *Poems*, ed. Williams, II, 643, 652, ll. 93, 356.

66 Donald Barthelme, *Snow White* (New York, 1972 [1965]), pp. 97–98.

67 Barthelme, *Snow White*, p. 96.

68 Barthelme, *Snow White*, pp. 97, 106.

69 Martin Heidegger, "Postscript to 'What is Metaphysics?'" *Existence and Being*, ed. Werner Brock (Chicago, 1970 [1959]), p. 277.

70 Julia Kristeva, *Semiotike: Recherches pour une sémanalyse* (Paris, 1969), p. 146 as translated by Jeanine Parisier Plottel, "Introduction," *Intertextuality: New Perspectives in Criticism*, New York Literary Forum, 2 (1978), p. xiv; Barthes, "The Death of the Author," p. 146.

71 Julia Kristeva, *La révolution du langage poétique* (Paris, 1974) as translated by Margaret Waller, *Revolution in Poetic Language* (New York, 1984), and as reprinted in Toril Moi, ed., *The Kristeva Reader* (Oxford, 1986), p. 111. The definition offered is of intertextuality.

because "there is only production, and we produce our 'selves' in language. Not *'you are what you eat'* but *'you are what you speak'* or, rather, *'you are what speaks you.'*"[72]

The word salad tossed by Barthes and Kristeva wilts under an astringent seasoning from Ben Jonson:

> *Language* most shewes a man: speake that I may see thee. It springs out of the most retired, and inmost parts of us, and is the Image of the Parent of it, the mind. No glasse renders a mans forme, or likenesse, so true as his speech.[73]

Yet Jonson's own voice issues, ventriloquially, from an echo-chamber of commonplaces tagged *"oratio imago animi,"* a head (coming from Menander via Vives) that surfaces elsewhere in commonplace books.[74] "Oratio est animi speculum," records another commonplacer: "Democritus sayth ye wordes of ye tonge are ye shaddowes of ye workes."[75] That Jonson purloins his own resonant sentiments (and vocabulary) from the *Apophthegmata* of Erasmus should come as no surprise; or that the refrain of "Speake that I may see thee!" was taken up by Johann Georg Hamann.[76] "Nullius in verba [On the word of no one]," trumpeted members of the early Royal Society.[77] But in order to mount a resonant challenge to the hegemony of *ipse dixits*, received ideas, and pseudodoxia epidemica, these moderns filched their motto from Horace.[78] "Nothing is spoken now but what has been said in former times," explained the mindless John Dunton, commandeering the words of Terence:

> Nothing pleases the deluded World but the Name and thought of Novelties ... D[ryde]n *stole from Shakespear, and* Shakespeare from *Ben-Johnson* and they all so steal from one another, that there's no Wit in any *Play*, but what we had 50 years ago.[79]

Michel Foucault picks up the intertextual refrain. "I wish I could have slipped surreptitiously into this discourse," he confided at the start of his inaugural lecture at the Collège de France: "I should have preferred to become aware that a nameless voice was already speaking long before me ... a voice behind me which had begun to speak a very long time before, doubling in advance everything that I am going to say, a voice which would say: 'You must go on, I can't go on, you must go on, I'll go on.'"[80] Let us think not on him till tomorrow.

---

[72] David Lodge, *Nice Work: A Novel* (London, 1988), p. 22.
[73] Jonson, "Timber: or, Discoveries," *Works*, eds C. H. Herford, Percy and Evelyn Simpson, VIII (Oxford, 1947), 625.
[74] For Jonson's extensive reliance upon Vives ("imago est animi parentis") and Menander at this juncture of *Discoveries*, see the editors' commentary, *Works*, XI, 270–72.
[75] Folger MS V.a.399, fol. 33v.
[76] See *Works*, eds Herford and Simpson, XI, 272. For Hamann's use, see Harold Stahmer, *"Speak that I may See Thee!" The Religious Significance of Language* (New York, 1968), p. 68.
[77] See, for example, Peter Dear, "Totius in verba: Rhetoric and Authority in the Early *Royal Society*," *Isis*, 76 (1985), 145–61.
[78] See *Epistles*, I, i, 14.
[79] Dunton, *The Art of Living Incognito*, pp. 50, 53, 51. These quotations come from a section devoted to proving that "There is nothing New under the Sun" (pp. 42–56).
[80] Foucault, "The Discourse on Language," *The Archaeology of Knowledge*, trans. A. M. Sheridan Smith (New York, 1972), p. 215.

## III

Autre pays, autre merde.[81]
Patrick O'Brian

Le lion est fait de mouton assimilé.[82]
Paul Valéry

Even if, as has been surmised, no new thing under the sun can galvanize our verbal gambits, we may, none the less, attend the Renaissance gestation of commonplacing. Before the advent of cheap paper and printing, to be sure, authors had kept notebooks into which they set social observations, extracts from their reading, and the makings of their own future works. In the *Topica*, Aristotle maintained that the *topos koinos* or commonplace derived its force from "the majority of the wise;" in the *Rhetoric*, he showed how to organize *topoi* by "heads" under which "a stock of arguments" could be accumulated.[83] The rearticulations of *topoi* as *loci communes* by Roman rhetoricians and medieval philosophers and pedagogues has been traced more reliably by Sister Joan Marie Lechner OSU than by that quirky polymath Ernst Robert Curtius.[84] And in short forms like *sententiae* or the epigram and distich is registered the enduring appeal of works that admitted easy absorption into one's own commonplace book. In anthology, florilegium, and miscellany, moreover, we can discern how private collections entered public currency. How medieval commonplacing may have informed humanist education still invites debate – Sister Joan offers a helpful account of Continental and English theorists – but Erasmus's commitment to *Adagia* and *Copia* as modes of instruction is indisputable.[85] And, like his by-blow Wagstaff, Erasmus wrestled with the contradictory claims of "popular usage" and "novel turns."[86] Certainly, it appears that humanist education depended upon a conversancy with tags and fragments to a degree that we might have found difficult to comprehend – at least, that is, until Barthes and Kristeva ordained that every text comprises no more than "a mosaic of quotations" or "a multidimensional space."

Humanism supposedly ushered in a brave new world of pedagogy. On both sides of the Irish Channel, however, Swift and other seventeenth-century students continued to chip away at scholastic fossils. And – as we know from a chorus of complaints about logic-sodden syllabi – sighs, short and frequent, were exhaled. The Dublin Logic of Narcissus Marsh

---

[81]  O'Brian, *H.M.S. Surprise* (New York, 1991 [1973]), p. 206. The speaker is Jack Aubrey, a naval captain with a merry penchant for butchering his proverbs and Latin tags.

[82]  Valéry, *Tel Quel*, quoted by Plottel, *Intertextuality*, p. xvi.

[83]  Aristotle, *Posterior Analytics* and *Topica*, ed. E. S. Forster (London, 1960), pp. 267–68; *The "Art" of Rhetoric*, ed. John Henry Freese (London and Cambridge, MA, 1967), I, ii, 21–22. See the excellent discussion by Mohl, *John Milton and His Commonplace Book*, pp. 11–13 and, generally, on "The Commonplace Book Tradition," pp. 11–30.

[84]  Lechner, *Renaissance Concepts of the Commonplaces* (New York, 1962), pp. 11–64; Curtius, *European Literature and the Latin Middle Ages*, trans. Willard R. Trask (London and Henley, 1979 [1953]), especially pp. 79–105.

[85]  Lechner, *Renaissance Concepts of the Commonplaces*, pp. 65–226.

[86]  Erasmus defines an adage as "a saying in popular use [*celebre dictum*], remarkable for some shrewd and novel [*novitate*] turn" (*Adagia*, I i 1 to I v 100, trans. Margaret Mann Phillips, ed. R. A. B. Mynors, The Collected Works of Erasmus, XXXI [Toronto, 1982], 4). Quoted by Crane, *Framing Authority*, p. 206.

rematerializes in *Gulliver's Travels*;[87] and ten years after Swift's death Edmund Burke still gagged on scholastic kickshaws. In our reconstructions of curricular tedium at Trinity College, we have tended to highlight scholastic logic at the expense of humanist rhetoric. Yet in struggling with their daily essays in Latin, undergraduates doubtless trawled commonplace books like John Locke's in order to land a formulaic catch. Their weekly declamations from memory demanded comparable skills. In alphabetizing his Latin notebook under "heads" – Adversae Res, Adulatio, Aedificia, Aequabilitas animi, Aequalitas etc. – Locke proved himself another judicious collector. "[A] Student know's of what he Read's," / quipped Samuel Butler, "is not in's own, but under Gen'rall Heads / Of Common Places."[88] "The real difference between [Swift] and the 'judicious collectors,'" Guthkelch and Nichol Smith shrewdly observe, "was that his head and his common-place book were both full at the same time."[89] In "Cadenus and Vanessa," Swift substituted lye for the pap hoarded by students: "'Tis an old Maxim in the Schools, / That Vanity's the Food of Fools."[90]

"For, what tho' his *Head* be empty, provided his *Common-place-Book* be full," the Tubster observes of "*Modern* Wits" on Grub Street, revealing that Butler's pun (still in manuscript) was not unique (T, p. 148). That path from old maxims to Grubean *sagesse* is a short one Wagstaff, Tubster, and Tritical Essayist jointly confirm. Yet as students drudged towards B.A. or M.A., any Erasmian progress in education must have struck them as indistinguishable from those scholastical sow-thistles so exultantly uprooted by humanists. Indeed, the last treatise printed in Locke's *Posthumous Works* was "A New Method of a Common-Place-Book." Although the philosopher apologizes for so "mean a thing" as this "Method," he underscores the personal significance of twenty-five years spent commonplacing and fastidiously details how he takes "a Paper Book of what size I please," rules its pages with black and red lines, selects his heads ("some important and essential Word"), records citations in the fullest detail, and draws up his index.[91] That Locke's new educational methods, like those of Erasmus, appear indistinguishable from commonplacing as advocated by Aristotle lends credence to John Dunton's conviction that "*New Fashions* are but Old fashions reviv'd."[92] In his best-seller, *The Grounds and Occasions of the Contempt of the Clergy*, John Eachard ridiculed the inclination of some divines "to sell all their *Libraries*, and send presently away for a whole *Wagon full of new Philosophy*."[93] But it was upon bad

87 See, most recently, James A. W. Rembert, *Swift and the Dialectical Tradition* (Houndmills, Basingstoke, and London, 1988), pp. 58–59; Kenneth Craven, *Jonathan Swift and the Millennium of Madness: The Information Age in Swift's "A Tale of a Tub"* (Leiden, New York, Köln, 1992), pp. 39–45.
88 "Satyr upon the Imperfection and Abuse of Human Learning," *Satires and Miscellaneous Poetry and Prose*, ed. René Lamar (Cambridge, 1928), p. 72, ll. 167–69.
89 Guthkelch and Nichol Smith, "Introduction to *A Tale of a Tub*," p. lv.
90 *Poems*, ed. Williams, II, 710, ll. 758–59.
91 See Locke, "A Letter from Mr Locke to Mr Toignerd, Containing a New and Easie Method of a Common-Place-Book," *Posthumous Works* (London: A. and J. Churchill, 1706), pp. 314, 316.
92 Dunton, *The Art of Living Incognito*, p. 52.
93 Eachard's work was first published in London in 1670. A sequel, *Some Observations upon the Answer to an Enquiry into the Grounds and Occasions of the Contempt of the Clergy*, came out in the following year. The quotation above is from *Some Observations*, p. 142. Eachard's continuing popularity strongly suggests that neither clerical education nor its parish afterlife changed very much during the Restoration or early eighteenth century. For Eachard's opinions on modern science, see *Grounds*, p. 27; *Observations*, pp. 146–49.

rhetorical habits contracted at the university that Eachard concentrated when indicting Anglican parsons for their wretched performance in the pulpit.

Not only does Eachard – an honorary tubbian (T, p. 9) – shed light upon the commonplacing to which Swift was subjected at Trinity College, Dublin. He also affords a blueprint (of sorts) for *A Letter to a Young Gentleman, Lately Enter'd into Holy Orders* wherein the Dean of St Patrick's offered his mature reflections upon parsonical commonplacing.[94] "An ordinary Cheesmunger or Plum-seller, that scarce ever heard of an University," Eachard declared, "shall write much better sense, and more to the purpose" than the student who warms over "Chicken-broth" and "dainty stuff ... for a *Latin* Entertainment":

> Away he goes presently to his Magazine of collected *Phrases*; he picks out all the *Glitterings* he can find; he hales in all *Proverbs, Flowers, Poetical Snaps*, Tales out of the *Dictionary* ... he falls presently into a most *lamentable complaint of his insufficiency and tenuity: That he, poor thing hath no acquaintance with above a Muse and a half; and that he never drunk above six q. of* Helicon, *and you have put him here upon such a task* (perhaps the business is only, which is the noblest [*sic*] Creature, a Flea or a Louse) *that would much better fit some old soker at* Parnassus, *than his sipping unexperienc'd Bibbership. Alas, poor Child! he is sorry at the very soul that he has no better speech; and wonders in his heart, that you will lose so much time as to hear him: For he has neither Squibs nor Fireworks, Stars nor Glories; the curs'd Carrier lost his best book of Phrases, and the Malicious Mice and Rats eat up all his Pearls and golden Sentences.*[95]

Not only can we here catch formulaic echoes of Chaucer's Franklin, but we can also see prefigured the Tubster's "laborious Collection of Seven Hundred Thirty Eight *Flowers*, and *shining Hints* of the best *Modern* Authors, digested with great Reading, into my Book of *Common-places*" (T, p. 209).[96] Swift's "judicious Collectors of *bright Parts*, and *Flowers*, and *Observanda's*" (T, p. 148) also include the Tritical Essayist and Simon Wagstaff. At the university, of course, techniques of commonplacing were inculcated with an eye to future careers in the Church, and the *Tub* brims with old maxims calculated to douse student enthusiasm ("Credulity is a more peaceful Possession of the Mind, than Curiosity" [T, p. 173]) as well as others inanely Grubean ("*Wisdom* is a *Hen*, whose *Cackling* we must value and consider, because it is attended with an *Egg*" [T, p. 66]). Moreover, the Tubster like Eachard's commonplace student demonstrates his dexterity with the paradoxical encomium (flea or louse).[97] Wherever and however acquired, the habit of commonplacing stuck like a burr, even to Simon Wagstaff who was "proud to own [himself] ... a Man wholly illiterate, that is to say, unlearned." Indeed, it was during the 1690s, when the Tubster was preparing to inflict his best book of phrases upon an unsuspecting public, that Wagstaff claims to have instituted a Grubean system of table books for his "thousand

---

[94] On Swift's use of Eachard in his sermons and *A Letter*, see Louis A. Landa, *Prose Works*, IX, 130–31, and Ehrenpreis, *Dean Swift*, pp. 82–85. See also Robert C. Elliott, "Swift and Dr. Eachard," *PMLA*, 69 (1954), 1250–57.

[95] Eachard, *Grounds and Occasions*, pp. 30–31. Milton's prolusions at Cambridge exemplify, at its best, the genre attacked by Eachard; see *Complete Prose Works*, I, 216–306.

[96] For tropes used by the Franklin in his *captatio benevolentiae* – "I lerned nevere Rethorik, certeyn; / Thyng that I speke, it moot be bare and pleyn. / I sleepe nevere on the Mount of Pernaso / Ne lerned Marcus Tullius Scithero" – see Phyllis Hodgson, ed., *The Franklin's Tale* (London, 1960), pp. 41, 73–76.

[97] For a succinct overview, see Irvin Ehrenpreis, "The Doctrine of *A Tale of a Tub*," *Proceedings of The First Münster Symposium on Jonathan Swift*, eds Hermann J. Real and Heinz J. Vienken (München, 1985), pp. 61–62.

shining Questions, Answers, Repartees, Replies, and Rejoynders" and other "Flowers of Wit, Fancy, Wisdom, Humour, and Politeness."[98]

Shades of the sacred commonplace began to close upon the growing student once he moved from his B.A. towards the M.A. and holy orders. Indeed, the first faltering burps of the pulpiteer were formally known as commonplaces – "Exercises like Sermons, which were delivered in the College Chappel" – a label which registered their humdrum genesis. "Then a head in divinity was to be commonplaced in Latin," Burnet explains, "and the person [was] to maintain *theses* upon it."[99] For an M.A. candidate like Swift during the 1680s, particular reliance upon commonplacing at Trinity College surely rankled.[100] "I paid attention to every word of my teachers in order to observe their ridiculousness," Karl Kraus once remarked, and on the evidence of *Tub*, *Martinus Scriblerus*, and *Gulliver's Travels* we can say the same of Swift.[101] One conduit of student dissatisfaction at Trinity College, as at Oxford and Cambridge, was the Tripos entertainment presented at the Commencement exercises.[102] In 1688, the organizer (or *terrae filius*) was John Jones, a friend of Swift, although it seems probable that his oration and the accompanying skits were "composed by a club of pretended wits," for, as an Oxonian observed, "there must be more Heads than one to write a sensible witty thing."[103] What the manuscripts of the 1685 and 1688 entertainments disclose is that routine governed the students' revue as surely as it did their essays and disputations: spoofs of scholastic logic, lampoons on teachers, antifeminist sallies, and allusions to mutton pies became indispensable as ingredients. It is clear that clubs inherited jokebooks from their predecessors. Even if we do not promote Swift's membership, a seat in the audience would have familiarized him with the club's techniques. Perhaps Swift began to stock a *sottisier* at the same time as he assembled the heads in his commonplace book. If we grant some credence to the eighteenth-century tradition that Swift completed first drafts of the *Tub* while studying at Trinity College, Dublin, then those, too, may have functioned as *sottisiers* as he wrestled with his satire during the following decade.

For the disappointed divine who settled into St Patrick's deanery after 1714, the common round and daily tasks of aspiring or working divines again stood out in dull relief, particularly against the excitements he had experienced during the last four years of Queen Anne. Since the 1680s, moreover, Swift had never been so close for so long to Trinity College and to the pedagogic gauntlet still run by its students. Some of the reflections provoked by this novel professional situation are registered in the *Letter to a Young Gentleman, Lately Enter'd into Holy Orders*, an *ars praedicandi* in which dry wit displaced Eachard's facile

---

[98] *Prose Works*, IV, 118, 100–1.

[99] *Bishop Burnet's History of His Own Time*, 6 vols (Oxford, 1823), I, 60.

[100] "The old rules of the College," J. W. Stubbs explains, "required that a short sermon, or commonplace, on some Scriptural text, should be preached weekly during Term by every resident Master of Arts, although a layman, in the College Chapel;" *The History of the University of Dublin: From its Foundation to the End of the Eighteenth Century* (Dublin, 1889), p. 78. The practice was confirmed in the Laudian statutes and continued until 1836 (p. 98).

[101] Kraus, "The World of Posters," *In These Great Times: A Karl Kraus Reader*, ed. Harry Zohn (Chicago, 1990 [1976]), p. 42.

[102] The best treatment still remains George Mayhew, "Swift and the Tripos Tradition," *Philological Quarterly*, 45 (1966), 85–101.

[103] These quotations about the clubs composing the Act (as the student entertainment was known at Oxford) come from Anthony Wood, *Life and Times*, ed. Andrew Clark, 5 vols (Oxford, 1891–1900), II, 563n9, and Thomas Baker, *An Act at Oxford: A Comedy by the Author of the Yeoman o'Kent* (London: Lintot, 1704), pp. 40–41.

knockabout. Indeed, so frothy was *The Grounds and Occasions* that its detractors compared Eachard's style to that of a *terrae filius*.[104] "I have known men happy enough at ridicule," opined Swift in his *Thoughts on Various Subjects*, "who upon grave subjects were perfectly stupid; of which Dr. *Echard* of *Cambridge*, who writ *The contempt of the clergy*, was a great instance."[105] After his appointment as Dean (if not before), Swift endeavoured to disentangle his roles as priest and jester; yet if he does not cut capers in his *Letter*, he still takes refuge in a *persona*.

By writing as "a Lay-patron," the Dean can claim not only that he recognizes the utility of "Collections of Facts or Cases" – commonplace books maintained by lawyers and physicians – but also that he has "never yet [seen] any written by a Clergyman."[106] Hearsay about clerical commonplacing does not, alas, reassure the Lay-patron. What "every Plowman knows well enough, although he never heard of *Aristotle* or *Plato*," Swift's mouthpiece grumbles, are commonplaced as "eternal Truths" by the parson:

> the Inconstancy of Fortune, the Goodness of Peace, the Excellency of Wisdom, the Certainty of Death [*mors omnibus communis* again]; that Prosperity makes Men insolent, and Adversity humble ... If Theological Common-Place Books be no better filled, I think they had better be laid aside.[107]

To hear parsons regurgitating received ideas in their pulpits did not, in the opinion of Eachard and Swift, edify cheese-mongers, plum-sellers, ploughmen, and other members of their congregations. Worse still, parsons deployed commonplaces in order to justify the unjustifiable. "He had many wholsome maxims ready to excuse all miscarriages of State," Swift writes of Corusodes, his time-serving divine: "*Men are but Men. Erunt vitia donec homines*; and *Quod Supra nos nihil ad nos*. with several others of equal weight."[108]

The Dean's contempt for commonplacing brings into sharper focus the butts of Swift's more youthful satire:

> I have observed in Preaching, that no Men succeed better than those, who trust entirely to the Stock or Fund of their own Reason; advanced, indeed, but not overlaid by Commerce with Books. Whoever only reads, in order to transcribe wise and shining Remarks, without entering into the Genius and Spirit of the Author; as it is probable he will make no very judicious Extract, so he will be apt to trust to that Collection in all his Compositions; and be misled out of the regular Way of Thinking, in order to introduce those Materials which he hath been at the Pains to gather: And the Product of all this, will be found a manifest incoherent Piece of Patchwork.[109]

The Royal Society's motto – "Nullius in verba" – was one to which Swift clearly subscribed,

---

[104] Eachard, *Grounds and Occasions*, p. 37.

[105] "Textual Notes," *Prose Works*, IV, 301.

[106] "The Body of the Civil Law is digested into general Heads, which are like common Boxes," noted Matthew Hale, adding that "I have commended the making and the using of a Common-Place-Book, as the best expedient I know for the orderly and profitable study of the Law" (*Un Abridgment des Plusieurs Cases et Resolutions del Common Ley* [London: A. Crooke *et al.*, 1668], sigs b2r-v, c1r). Greatest of the legal commonplace books that survive is Thomas Jefferson's.

[107] *Prose Works*, IX, 76.

[108] Swift, *Intelligencer*, no 7, Swift and Thomas Sheridan, *The Intelligencer*, ed. James Woolley (Oxford, 1992), p. 97. For Tacitus's "There will be vices so long as there are men" and the pseudo-Socratic "That which is above us does not concern us," see Woolley's excellent notes (p. 99).

[109] *Prose Works*, IX, 76.

although he enjoyed impersonating those who could not. When preaching, he trusted to the fund of his own reason, as the honest kersey rhetoric of his unburned sermons testifies. If the Tubster seems to anticipate the Lay-patron in championing "Parity and strict Correspondence between the Reader and the Author," he exhales not the true genius of authorship but the commonplace spirit of Grub Street. "A perfect Judge will *read* each Work of Wit," Pope asserts, "With the same Spirit that its Author *writ*."[110] A commonplacer concurs: "It is a very just Remark of St. Ev[remond] that few Critics enter into the Beauty & Spirit of an Author."[111] In the *Tub*, reader response criticism entails parity and correspondence not with *peri hupsos* but with *peri bathos*. "How is it possible, we *Modern* Wits should ever have Opportunity to introduce our Collections listed under so many thousand Heads of a different Nature?" the Tubster desperately begs (T, p. 148). Answers loom in "*Systems* and *Abstracts*" where "*Quotations* must be plentifully gathered, and bookt in Alphabet" (T, pp. 145–48). From this grind of commonplacing springs the Grubean Sage. "Allow him but the common Priviledges of transcribing from others, and digressing from himself, as often as he shall see Occasion," urges the Tubster (T, p. 148), and a masterpiece will pop from multidimensional space. Yet in perusing the *Tub* – a work "bookt" by a commonplacer so misled out of regular ways of thinking that he finds himself unable "after five Years to draw, hook, or force into common Conversation, any more than a Dozen" of his pearls and golden sentences (T, pp. 210–11) – we find that an intertextual masterpiece is indistinguishable from an incoherent piece of patchwork.

The Lay-patron's description of the typical commonplace book as "collected" and "headed" in alphabet by a pulpiteer –

> Extracts of Theological and Moral Sentences, drawn from Ecclesiastical and other Authors, reduced under proper Heads; usually begun, and perhaps finished, while the Collectors were young in the Church; as being intended for Materials, or Nurseries to stock future Sermons[112]

– corresponds broadly to the layout of those theological commonplace books still available for consultation.[113] That parsons refer to their utilitarian collections as "commonplace books" reminds us yet again that we should eschew unwarranted rigidity in defining "the true commonplace book."[114] In laying out their pages, compilers often adhere to the finicky stipulations of Locke's "New Method." If the "heads" chosen by Locke typify the requirements of schoolboy essays and undergraduate declamations, then the thousand of heads proliferating in one parson's nursery spoke to the needs of his pulpit:

---

[110] Alexander Pope, "An Essay on Criticism," *The Twickenham Edition of the Poems of Alexander Pope*, I, eds E. Audra and Aubrey Williams (London and New Haven, 1961), 266, ll. 233–34.

[111] Folger MS W.a.126, p. 5.

[112] *Prose Works*, IX, 76.

[113] I have used the following theological commonplace books in the Folger Library: V.b.108 (Henry Fairfax's; folio, 739+ pp., c. 1670; Latin heads; index); V.b.154 (Thomas Hatton's; folio, 520 pp., c. 1680; Latin heads; index); V.b.254 (Etonian allusions; folio, 524 pp., c. 1700; English heads; index); W.a.217 (Matthew Wood's; quarto, 540 pp., c. 1713; English heads). In these volumes, however, will be found relatively few "Extracts" in the sense intended by Swift.

[114] See, for example, V.b.254, p. 1 and inside the front cover; Mohl, *John Milton and His Commonplace Book*, p. 30.

Alchymy ... Alehouse ... Allegiance to Princes
Amphibology ... Anabaptists ... Anagram
Babe ... Babbler ... Backbiting
Buggery ... Building ... Burden
Clown ... Coffin ... Coldness ... Coherence
Hardness ... Harlot ... Harvest ... Harmlessness
Library ... License ... Licentiousness
Shouting ... Shrovetide ... Sibyls.[115]

Entries direct the budding pulpiteer to volumes in his own library where topics are handled at greater length.[116] Another commonplacer's heads reflect an indulgence in that "University Erudition" to which both Eachard and Swift's Lay-patron so strenuously objected: "Motus aetherea regionis ... De Motu Cometum ... De fossibilibus generatione."[117] But most heads register the challenges of sinfulness, whether doctrinal or quotidian: from "Errores de Prae-destinatione" or "Error Pelagianorum" and "Enthusiasm" to the fourteen reasons listed against "drunkenness."[118]

As to when Swift swapped his theological commonplace book for a *sottisier*, we can only guess. One intriguing piece of evidence may survive. After abandoning his first ecclesiastical assignment at Kilroot in order to return to Moor Park, Swift bequeathed some trash – items "not worth the Carriage" – to his successor John Winder. Along with a heap of theological tomes (Foley, Reynolds, Stillingfleet) Swift presented Winder with "the Folio paper book; very good for Sermons or a Receit book for y$^r$ Wife to keep accounts for Mutton, Raisins &c."[119] It was in folios like these that parsons garnered their commonplaces, but one might infer from Swift's letter to Winder that his own was unsullied by such sludge. Partially used theological commonplace books were, of course, continued by others – most notably that of John Jebb which the young Church of Ireland rector began in 1804 at Cashel. Inheriting "Bishop Jebb's Book" from his grandfather (Jebb's chaplain), E. M. Forster announced the "Change of Plan" that would govern his own entries: "I must scrap this awful arrangement by topics, and put down whatever I like."[120] The paper book that Swift gave Winder seems not to have contained any texts of his own sermons which Winder, a moiling pulpiteer, had already "thought fitt to transcribe." These, "the idlest trifling stuff that ever was writt," Swift assured his successor, he had "firmly resolved to burn." What did concern Swift, however, was his "Abstracts and Collections from Reading ... that I would not have lost."[121] "Collections" was a standard term used by commonplacers for excerpts, commentary, and

---

[115] These heads come from individual pages in V.b.254, fullest and most meticulous of the theological commonplace books held by the Folger.

[116] Further *aide-mémoires* direct the user to "my Miscellaneous Book" and the "Catalogue" of the commonplacer's library; see V.b.254, p. 1 and inside front cover.

[117] V.b.108; see also *Prose Works*, IX, 76–77.

[118] V.b.108; V.b.254 (which crossreferences Enthusiasm with Illumination, Inspiration, Sectaries, and Quakers); see also W.a.217.

[119] *Correspondence*, I, 29–30. One assumes that Swift is referring to a "paper book" of the kind recommended by Locke in "A New Method of a Common-Place-Book."

[120] On the provenance, see "Introduction," *Commonplace Book*, ed. Gardner, pp. xiv–xv. Forster's remarks may be found on p. 2. Forster's first entries contain lucubrations on the eighteenth-century novel (including *Gulliver's Travels*) for his Clark Lectures. Of Swift's description of the Struldbruggs, Forster resolves (with Jebbian topicality) to "transcribe this passage into my anthology, under Old Age: here observing that it is Swift at his best" (pp. 10–11).

[121] *Correspondence*, I, 31.

bibliographical citations.[122] The distinctions between the trash Swift had accumulated as a workaday parson and these "parcells of other Papers" seem clear enough.[123] Did one parcel include a *sottisier* of hints for the *Tub*? A conjectural pursuit of Swift's paper trail back and forth across the Irish Channel before 1704 will suggest that there is more to the satirist's exculpatory assertion that he had not been "*Master of his Papers*" than may meet an eye merely tropological (T, pp. 4; 28). In the *Tub*, Swift plays pass the parcel by transforming his own recurrent anxieties about the fate of his manuscripts into running jokes about "*waste Paper and Oblivion*," "*immense Bales of Paper*," and the twenty seven other references to "paper" or "papers" (T, pp. 9, 35). Like Bouvard and Pécuchet, Flaubert also acquired waste paper in bulk, posters, random editions.[124]

In suggesting that Mrs Winder might find "the Folio paper book" suitable for her domestic economy, Swift indicates how easily the commonplace book – an inglorious shot at how the pulpit ought to be – could metamorphose into a housewife's omnium gatherum. Such was the fate of Locke's commonplace book in the Masham household at Oates in Essex where the philosopher died in 1704. Under the head of *Constantia*, we discover how "To make a Cream Tart," under *Virtus* how "To make a Siroop of Viollets," under *Providentia* a remedy "For a Glister" and directions "To make Gilliflower Wine," under *Phylosophia* a remedy for "For the worms," under *Praeceptores* how "To make mirabilis watter." *Causae* affords "A Receipt for a fistula in ye eyes or any part: from ye lady Millme," *Fraus* directions on how "To souce Piggeons like Puffins," *Coniugium* hints on how "To make a salve for all manner of Sores, and an Excellent Searcloth called the Black Plaister." By comparison, "Bishop Jebb's Book" enjoyed a more distinguished fate, although one cannot deny that the Masham ladies appear to have made fuller and more practical use of Locke's Latin notebook than did the young philosopher.

Authorial design rather than some accident of ownership prompted Swift to dose the *Tub* with a bolus of recipes and remedies: "*take fair correct Copies ... distil in* balneo Mariæ, *infusing* Quintessence of Poppy Q.S. *together with three Pints of* Lethe" (T, p. 126). Comparable jests, combining quackery with bookishness, spice the *satura lanx* served up by clubs working on the Tripos entertainment. But with the appearance "*in your Head*" of "*an infinite Number of* Abstracts, Summaries, Compendiums, Extracts, Collections, Medulla's, Excerpta quædam's, Florilegia's *and the like, all disposed into great Order, and reducible upon Paper*" attributable to an "Elixir" (T, pp. 126–27), we also encounter directions for preparing a nostrum which might well have come from Swift's "Folio paper book" had Mrs Winder (like the Masham ladies) pressed it into service as "a Receit book." Such recipes and remedies are often recorded in commonplace books, even when, like Sir Edward Bayntun's, those are primarily dedicated to estate accounts and the transcripts of letters: between notes on leases and bonds, Bayntun jots down "Dr. Wright's medicine for the biting of a mad dog."[125] In the commonplace book of John Clavell, who juggled careers as author and

---

[122] See Bayntun's "Observations and collections out of Nicholas Machiavelli's book called the Art of War," Jane Freeman, ed., *The Commonplace Book of Sir Edward Bayntun of Bromham* (Devizes, 1988), pp. xx, 40.

[123] See *Correspondence*, I, 31.

[124] Flaubert, *Carnets de travail*, ed. de Biasi, p. 766.

[125] Freeman, *Commonplace Book*, pp. 5–6. Recipes and/or remedies may also be found scattered through Folger MSS E.a.1 (compiled by a sixteenth-century family in Hertfordshire);

unlicensed doctor, can be found eighty-one prescriptions (ranging from directions on how "To kill any worms in a man's body" and how "To clear the sight and strengthen it" to details of "A medicine for what scald head soever" and a remedy "For the biting of a mad dog") as well as elegies, prologues, and a medley of other verses.[126] Amidst the Tubster's abstracts and collections from reading may be found his own "admirable Remedy for ill Eyes" as well as Peter's "Sovereign Remedy for the *Worms*" and "his famous Universal *Pickle*" which exempts dogs "from Mange, and Madness, and Hunger" and takes away "all Scabs and Lice, and scall'd Heads from Children." If Peter's prescriptions are "diligently observed, the *Worms* would void insensibly by Perspiration, ascending thro' the Brain" (T, pp. 107, 109–10); Clavell records how he successfully treated a servant to the Lord Deputy of Ireland for "Frenzy. Diarrhea. Epilepsy. Worm in the Head," making "both his ears run matter" and forcing a worm "from his head."[127] From Henry Oxenden's commonplace book, we can distill directions on how "To make excellent Inke" and how "To make Excellent Beer;" another commonplacer offers directions for secret writing and musical glasses.[128] Oxenden provides a remedy "Against a Cough," and the intelligence that "A Bedstead &c made of Yew Tree is said to be an effectual Remedy against Buggs;" "If sugar can preserve both pears and plums," Oxenden muses on his endpapers, "why can it not preserve as well our lungs [?]"[129] What must elude us, then, are sharp distinctions between housewife or househusband pickling in their kitchen and the mountebank blending nostrums on his stage-itinerant; indeed, some iatrochemists styled themselves "Geber's cooks." That "Monsr Ponchart's receit to make leaven Bread," transcribed in Swift's own hand, was pasted to a fly-leaf in the Locker-Lampson *Tub* proves altogether fitting.[130]

    With or without receipts and remedies, many commonplace books present dishes memorably mixed. Quaint and outlandish usages were stockpiled as diligently as proverbs or maxims. In 1669, for example, Henry Newcome began a distinctly untheological common-place book in which he included, alongside smutty epigrams and jests, a list of Lancashire words and their English equivalents as well as comic excursions into Welsh and Scottish dialects.[131] Commonplacers seemed to find Welsh particularly amusing.[132] Henry Oxenden provides an inventory of Kentish names for apples (marigold, bulls, Partridge apple, etc.).[133] And in a commonplace book of the 1690s, we find an assortment of Scottish proverbs, "Some old names of Plants" ("Aders tongue, Ale hoofe, Clowns all Heal," etc.), a list of

        V.a.281 (also contains maxims and notes on sermons), V.a.438 (compiled by a late Elizabethan clergyman); V.a.1683 (also contains weather lore); W.a.341 (Italian).
[126]  Pafford, *John Clavell*, pp. 248, 253, 247. Pafford reprints all of the prescriptions (pp. 237–56) which Clavell entered in the rear of his commonplace book and many of the literary items (141–73). Clavell also used his commonplace books for accounts and for copies of his correspondence.
[127]  Pafford, *John Clavell*, pp. 235–36. Clavell's list of his cures did not, however, appear in his commonplace book.
[128]  See Folger MS V.b.110, p. 8; V.a.399, fol. 43r.
[129]  Folger MS V.b.110, pp. 11, 12, 157.
[130]  For the recipe (and the provenance), see George P. Mayhew, *Rage or Raillery: The Swift Manuscripts at the Huntington Library* (San Marino, CA, 1967), p. 8n9.
[131]  Folger MS V.a.232. The lexicon was begun in the unnumbered pages at the rear of the book. The excursions into dialect may be found (reading from the front) on pp. 34–36.
[132]  See the facetious Welsh sermons in Folger MS V.a.399, fols 5r–6r.
[133]  Folger MS V.b.110, p. 110.

"Words different according to ye severall countries in England," a Latin and English vocabulary for plants, and a list of hard words and etymologies ("Fatiloquy – soothsaying … Scythian in ye Gothick tongue signifieth skilfull Archer").[134] Among sundry entries under "Names, Proper" in his commonplace book, *A Certain World*, Auden evinces a poet's taste for onomastics when he gathers 14 names for the green woodpecker, 12 names for the cuckoo-pint, 20 names of veins in the lead-mining district of Tideswell, Derbyshire, and 45 names for the genitals, both male and female.[135] Lexically unique among Swift's works, the *Tub* may be read fructiferously as a trashcan (or wastepaper basket) for items on word-lists which the satirist had accumulated in his commonplace book since the 1680s, whether the words were hard (like exantlation, spargefaction, tentiginous) or demotic (like pop, twang, snuffle).[136] That Swift compiled a dictionary for Stella's use at Moor Park confirms that he truffled for words during the 1690s.[137]

Commonplace books were gallimaufries, and so was the *Tub*. If the commonplacer embraced characters (for example, a pretender to learning, a critic), so did the Tubster (Section IX concludes with a procession of characters).[138] If commonplacers customized their own "*Compleat Jesters*, and the like," so did the Tubster (the "short Tale" of "*A Mountebank in* Leicester-Fields" conforms to the genre). To be sure, theological commonplace books were dedicated to the production of sermons or works of divinity, but their principle of organization – "booking" under alphabetical heads – engendered some peculiar collisions and juxtapositions, as Folger MS V.b.254 amply demonstrates. Some lay commonplace books, moreover, accommodated both the sacred and the profane: Oxenden found room for passages from Stillingfleet's *Origines Sacrae*, and John Humphrey's *Free Admission to the Lord's Supper*, for some observations "Of Irreligion & Atheism," for ruminations on "The Miserie of the wicked" and "The prosperitie of the Righteous," and for the following unclassifiable item:

And Moses asked and sayd unto the People hath Aaron had his breakefast
    And they answerd no
Then he answered & sayd let Aaron have his breakefast:
    And they sayd what shd that be
    And hee said
A white butter milke posset, a green ginger pudding tyed at both ends with three points Coventry blew, thus endeth the second Chapter of Genesis.[139]

---

[134] Folger MS V.b.300, fols 77r, 76v, 74r, 75r, 49v.

[135] See W. H. Auden, *A Certain World: A Commonplace Book* (London, 1971 [1970]), pp. 268–69.

[136] In addition to holding formulae (beginnings, conclusions, interruptions, digressions) and gnomology (*sententiae*, similitudes, *exempla*), Johann-Heinrich Alsted specified in his *Orator* that commonplace books should also contain a lexicon (rare, barbaric, obsolete words; tropes) and a phraseology (more elaborate phrases, archaisms, and anomalous turns of phrase); see Lechner, *Renaissance Concepts of the Commonplaces*, p. 125. The relevance of these categories both to the *Tub* and to the commonplace books from which I have quoted will be obvious.

[137] The dictionary is now within private hands; see Hermann J. Real, "Stella's Books," *Swift Studies*, 11 (1996), 82n81.

[138] For a collection of characters, see Folger V.b.300, fol. 49r.

[139] Folger MS V.b.110, pp. 177–90, 511, 472, 523, 25.

# IV

*GOOSE, n. A bird that supplies quills for writing. These, by some occult process of nature, are penetrated and suffused with various degrees of the bird's intellectual energies and emotional character, so that when inked and drawn mechanically across paper by a person called an "author," there results a very fair and accurate transcription of the fowl's thought and feeling.*

Ambrose Bierce[140]

By 1711, Swift had achieved fame (or infamy) as an "author," but the bishopric of which he had long dreamed still eluded his grasp. To a divine in such a predicament, Archbishop King's avuncular cluckings surely smacked of indifference clad in wisdom's guise or the "wholesome maxims" mouthed by Corusodes:

Years come on, and after a certain age, if a man be not in a station that may be a step to a better, he seldom goes higher. It is with men as with beauties, if they pass the flower, they grow stale, and lie for ever neglected. I know you are not ambitious; but it is prudence, not ambition, to get into a station, that may make a man easy.

Worse still, King treated England's most scintillating writer as though he were a young commonplacer at Trinity College still alphabetizing his heads:

Say not, that most subjects in divinity are exhausted; for, if you look into Dr. *Wilkins's* Heads of Matters, which you will find in his Gift of Preaching, you will be surprized to find so many necessary and useful heads, that no authors have meddled with. There are some common themes, that have employed multitudes of authors; but the most curious and difficult are in a manner untouched, and a good genius will not fail to produce something new and surprizing on the most trite, much more on those that others have avoided, merely because they were above their parts.[141]

That King touted Wilkins — a virtuoso whom the satirist consigned to a rogue's gallery alongside Sprat, Boyle, and Glanvill — Swift must have found especially galling. And King's trite dithering about the resuscitation of received ideas reminds us of the Tritical Essayist, another moralist-cum-virtuoso like Wilkins. Eschewing "*stale Topicks and thread-bare Quotations,*" the Tritical Essayist boasted that his own "*Thoughts and Observations [were] entirely new,*" his "*Quotations untouched by others.*" Yet he flaunts his Essay "*as a Pattern for young Writers to imitate.*"[142]

"A rare spark this, with a pox!" Swift growled of King's epistolary "Trifles."[143] Swift ignored the Archbishop's advice, unless we choose to read *A Letter to a Young Gentleman, Lately Enter'd into Holy Orders* as a belated response. Of course, the Lay-patron's Flaubertian philosophy of composition — "Proper words in proper Places" — bears scant resemblance to King's "Heads of Matters" and "common themes." To a young writer like Swift in Kilroot, lately entered into holy orders and searching for patterns to imitate, the Archbishop's chicken-broth might just have supplied the base for a sermon. How Swift actually gathered copy for addressing "a Church without a company or a roof" we can only guess.[144] Subsequently, the Lay-patron might disparage extracts and collections, but one suspects that

---

[140] Bierce, *The Enlarged Devil's Dictionary*, ed. Ernest Jerome Hopkins (Garden City, NY, 1967), p. 116.

[141] *Correspondence*, I, 254–55.

[142] *Prose Works*, I, 246.

[143] *Prose Works*, XV, 359; see also *Correspondence*, I, 258.

[144] See *Correspondence*, I, 31.

his creator had once known, like other journeyman preachers, what it was to find himself hurriedly stitching sermons together from a patchwork of heads and hints, thoughts and notes.

When commonplace Swift shifted his satiric attentions from Trinity College, Dublin, to Grub Street during the 1690s, he quickly came to recognize that hacks traded in received ideas and formulaic language with even more alacrity than pulpiteers. Yet Eachard still afforded a blueprint: the commonplace "chyming" which he excoriated — "*Revelation is a Lady: Reason an Handmaid. Revelation's the Esquire: Reason the Page. Revelation's the Sun: Reason's but the Moon. Revelation is Manna: Reason but an Acorn*"[145] — still reverberate in the *Tub* ("*Wisdom* is a *Fox* ... a *Cheese* ... a *Sack-Posset*, a *Hen* ... Is not Religion a *Cloak*, Honesty a *Pair of Shoes*" [T, pp. 66, 78]). Because the *Tub* is a book about beginnings — not least Swift's own first steps as a writer — the Tubster dexterously shuffles the deck of introductory commonplaces. These range from larger forms (epistles dedicatory, prefaces, introductions) to local formulae like those declamations "against the Multitude of Writers" which we have noted. In his "Dedication" to Somers, the Tubster may ostentatiously refuse "to ply the World with an old beaten Story" and "forty other common Topicks" (T, pp. 25–26), but refusal to launch into praise comprises yet another topic of panegyrical commonplacing. Like parsons, Grubean Sages understood how commonplace books sustain automatic writing.

That John Dunton's stable of hacks boasted a clergyman like Samuel Wesley showed Swift that an Oxford M.A. and ordination comprised no preservative against "*a knocking Argument*, hight necessity," as Wesley termed it in *Maggots: or, Poems on Several Subjects, Never before Handled*.[146] The justification Wesley offered for scribbling as another source of income was pragmatic: "*Who knows but my Shoes may want* mending *or my Stockings to be a little out at* Elbows?"[147] Despite his professions of poetic novelty — "*all here are my own* pure *Maggots, the natural Issue of my Brain-Pan, bred and born there, and only there*"[148] — Wesley demonstrates himself a dab hand at the commonplacer's trade. In one epistle dedicatory, Wesley confesses that "I must unavoidably take Refuge at the old thum'd Scrap, *Sic parvis componere magna* — Or, to be more sincere, this seem'd a pretty way of beginning;" in another he dips into his book of critical commonplaces and produces "*somewhat I some time ago* cabbag'd *from* Osborn."[149] Wesley borrows the latter term of art from tailors who habitually bundled up shreds and remnants into a cabbage-like ball under the shop-board: "The Cloth they steal and purloin is called *Cabbage*, which oftentimes affords them Breeches and Wastecoats for themselves, as well as whole Suits for very young and new-

---

[145] Eachard, *Grounds and Occasions*, p. 63.
[146] Wesley, "The Epistle to the Reader," *Maggots: or, Poems on Several Subjects, Never Before Handled* (London, 1685), sig. A6r. One suspects that Dunton himself may have penned much of the prefatory paraphernalia, since they so strikingly resemble his own nervously cachinatory style. *Maggots* was circulated at Trinity College while Swift was a student; its Grubean tropologies of dedication and preface deserve careful comparison with those unspooled in the *Tub*.
[147] "The Epistle to the Reader," sig. A6r.
[148] Wesley, "*To the Honoured Mr. H. D. Headmaster of the Free*-School in D——, in the County of D," *Maggots*, sig. A3v.
[149] "*To the Honoured Mr. H. D.*," sig. A3r; "To the Reader," sig. A6r.

breech'd Boys."[150] Wesley's offhand invocation of "cabbaging" confirms that the term had already entered Grub Street argot even before the Tubster outlined how Sartorist priests "hourly flung in Pieces of the uninformed Mass" into their "*Hell*" beneath the "Altar" (or shop-board) and explained that "the *Taylor's Hell* is the Type of a Critick's *Common-Place-Book*" (T, pp. 76, 102). As a student at Oxford, Swift's snivelling time-server Corusodes, "spent every Day ten hours in his Closet, in Reading his Courses, Dozing, clipping Papers, or darning his Stockings, which last he performed to Admiration."[151] Here we may again discern the analogy between commonplacing and tailoring, for language is the dress of thought.[152] "What is Man himself but a *Micro-Coat*, or rather a compleat Suit of Cloaths with all its Trimmings?" demand the Sartorists (T, p. 78). If we are also what speaks us, then, according to Wesley and the Tubster, we must be no more than intertextual suits, incoherent patchwork, cabbaged together from commonplace books.

"A *Common-place-book*, is what a provident Poet cannot subsist without," declared the Dublin author of *A Letter of Advice to a Young Poet* in 1721:

> for this proverbial Reason, that *great Wits have short Memories* ... a Book of this sort is in the nature of a Supplimental Memory; or a Record of what occurs remarkable in every Days Reading or Conversation: There you enter not only your own original Thoughts, (which a hundred to one, are *few* and *insignificant*) but such of other Men as you think fit to make your own by entring them there.[153]

At worst, this is good pastiche Swift. But to trace the Dean's own hand remains tempting. For as Swift came to terms with his banishment to Dublin, he certainly used his *Letter to a Young Gentleman, Lately Enter'd into Holy Orders* as the cue for a ventriloquial re-examination of his travails in Kilroot, where the realities of an Ulster parish put paid to earlier aspirations as heir to Pindar. "I am Cowley to my self," he had confessed to Thomas in 1692, but the imagery he instantly chose for a qualification – namely that he had "the same pretence the Baboon had to praise her Children" – suggests that even then Jonathan may have glimpsed his own nascent talents in Wesley's "Pindarique on the Grunting of a Hog" rather than in Cowley's "Ode to the Royal Society."[154] The sallies in *A Letter of Advice to a Young Poet* – richly tubbian in their spoof of creativity – not only complement Swift's admonitions to recent ordinands, but they also reflect details in a work of 1720 which only Swift or a close associate could have known, namely the Dean's reflections on his poems as "Collected and Transcribed" by Stella. "A Poet, starving in a Garret," Swift observed, echoing Wesley's ill-shod plight,

> Conning old Topicks like a Parrot,
> Invokes his Mistress and his Muse,
> And stays at home for want of Shoes:

---

[150] I draw my information on cabbaging from Peter Linebaugh, *The London Hanged: Crime and Civil Society in the Eighteenth Century* (Harmondsworth, Middlesex, 1993 [1991]), pp. 245–48. The quotation (p. 246) comes from *A New Canting Dictionary* (1725).

[151] Swift, *Intelligencer*, no 7, ed. Woolley, p. 95.

[152] James Woolley finds the reference to "clipping papers" elusive, but acknowledges that it might well refer to commonplacing. We agree, however, that "clipping" from printed texts (as Jefferson did) appears to be a later phenomenon.

[153] *Prose Works*, IX, 337. For the debate on the authorship of this work, see Ehrenpreis, *Dean Swift*, pp. 135–36.

[154] *Correspondence*, I, 9; Wesley, *Maggots*, p. 21.

*So Maevius*, when he drain'd his Skull
To celebrate some Suburb Trull;
His Similes in Order set,
And ev'ry Crambo he could get;
Had gone through all the Common-Places
Worn out by Wits who rhyme on Faces.[155]

If divines used theological commonplace books as a crutch in the pulpit, then secular writers
– Grubean or otherwise – also crammed paper books in order to sustain themselves as
authors. In Buckingham's *Rehearsal*, Dryden flaunts his "book of *Drama Common places*;
the Mother of many other Plays," explaining how

> I come into a Coffee-house, or some other place where witty men resort, I make as if I
> minded nothing; (do you mark?) but as soon as any one speaks, pop I slap it down, and
> make that, too, my own ... when I have any thing to invent, I never trouble my head about
> it, as other men do; but presently turn over this Book, and there I have, at one view, all
> that *Perseus, Montaigne, Seneca's Tragedies, Horace, Juvenal, Claudian, Pliny, Plutarch's
> lives*, and the rest, have ever thought upon this subject: and so, in a trice, by leaving out
> a few words, or putting in others of my own, the business is done.[156]

Whatever its justice, Buckingham's mockery of Bayes depends upon audience familiarity
with books of drama commonplaces. Certainly, the plays of Wycherley show how dramatists
hoarded the maxims of others as well as honing their own. In *The Tatler*, moreover, Steele
writes jocularly of "having by me, in my Book of Common Places, enough to enable me to
finish a very Sad [Tragedy] ... I have the Farewel of a General ... the Principles of a
Politician ... together with his Declaration on the Vanity of Ambition ... I have all my
Oaths ready, and my Similes want nothing but Application."[157] All this the ploughman
knows well, but Simon Wagstaff's book of drama commonplaces differs from his colleagues'
insofar as he strives neither for Bayes's classical *gravitas* nor for Steele's banal figures of
thought. Of course, Tubster and Tritical Essayist both exhibit Swift's mimicry of pretensions to a literary and philosophical substance unclaimed by Wagstaff. Like Bayes at
Will's, Wagstaff merely snaps up and slaps down unconsidered figures of speech before he,
too, "makes them his own:"

> I ALWAYS kept a large Table-Book in my Pocket; and as soon as I left the Company, I
> immediately entred the choicest Expressions that passed during the Visit; which, returning
> home, I transcribed in a fair Hand ... while the Company little suspected what a noble
> Work I had then in Embrio ... [but now] they shall, as an Instance of Gratitude, on every
> proper Occasion, quote my Name, after this, or the like Manner: *Madam, as our Master*
> Wagstaff *says. My Lord, as our Friend* Wagstaff *hath it*.[158]

Laying claim to author-function, if not to authorship, Wagstaff dreams of a commonplace
apotheosis into an *ipse dixit*.

All the evidence – Wagstaff's patter, allusions in the dialogues, Swift's epistolary references during the 1730s – indicates that *Polite Conversation* was inaugurated before Swift

[155] "To Stella, Who Collected and Transcribed his Poems," *Poems*, ed. Williams, II, 728, 730
(ll. 25–28, 71–76). Probably composed in 1720, this poem was first published in *Miscellanies:
The Last Volume*, 1728.

[156] George Villiers, Duke of Buckingham, *The Rehearsal*, ed. D. E. L. Crane (Durham, 1976),
pp. 5–6 (I, i, 84–86, 115–18, 129–36).

[157] No 22, Tuesday, 31 May 1709, *The Tatler*, ed. Donald F. Bond, 3 vols (Oxford, 1987), I,
176–77.

[158] *Prose Works*, IV, 100, 122, 124.

made his name with the anonymous *Tub*. That a young writer who had already by early 1691 "writt, & burnt and writt again, upon almost all manner of subjects, more perhaps than any man in England" should start a drama commonplace book with which he hoped to emulate Congreve and, just possibly, Farquhar – who had, to his chagrin, matriculated after him at Trinity College, Dublin – should not strain credibility.[159] Indeed, baffled envy as much as righteous indignation surely animates Swift's vision (unpublished) of Congreve's dismemberment by commonplacers:

> The bullion stampt in your refining mind
> Serves by retail to furnish half mankind.
> With indignation I behold your wit
> Forc'd on me, crack'd, and clipp'd, and counterfeit,
> By vile pretenders, who a stock maintain
> From broken scraps and filings of your brain.[160]

Who were these pretenders and cabbagers who forced themselves upon Swift in conversation? In "that saucy and familiar ease" and vile "Gray's-inn grace" displayed by one when bragging of his intimacy with the denizens of Will's – "Wycherly, and you [Congreve], and Mr. Bays" – we may already discern the makings of a trash-filled head later trepanned in *Hints towards an Essay on Conversation*.[161] But in "To Mr. Congreve," I suggest, Swift also hinted disgust with his own evolving book of drama commonplaces wherein *bons mots* filed from Congreve jostled choice expressions gleaned from conversation at Moor Park. Swift's problem was that his gobbets embodied not the repartee of Restoration comedy but what Ionesco registered, in *The Bald Primadonna*, as "the tragedy of language." In contrast to the Restoration stage – where it is the minor, not the major, characters who cannot master (or mistress) the mechanical operations of language – language speaks Wagstaff's characters. "Sounding shells devoid of meaning ... ready-made expressions and the most threadbare clichés ... all that is automatic" define the dramatis personae in *Polite Conversation*.[162] "Emptied of psychology ... talking for the sake of talking" like characters in the Berlitz manuals which Ionesco looted for *The Bald Primadonna*, the Martins and the Smiths, Mr Neverout, Miss Notable and their claque chatter and clatter with "the mechanical routine of everyday life."[163] What Swift began as a book of drama commonplaces, I suggest, metamorphosed into Simon Wagstaff's working materials.

Yet Swift himself steadfastly refuses to dematerialize in a puff of postmodern smoke. For all his delight in aping the commonplace, he never lets us forget that behind the verbal figures of Wagstaffian *politesse* lurk darker impulses and cravings. Body shadows word: "Don't be mauming and gauming a Body so," Miss Notable snaps at Mr Neverout: "Can't

---

[159] See *Correspondence*, I, 4.

[160] "To Mr. Congreve," *Poems*, ed. Williams, I, 45, ll. 52–58.

[161] "To Mr. Congreve," *Poems*, ed. Williams, I, 47, ll. 141, 137, 142. Whether Swift dramatizes an encounter that took place at Moor Park or during one of his trips to London is unclear; his interlocutor, if real, seems to have been a boastful lawyer with literary pretensions.

[162] Ionesco, "The Tragedy of Language," *Notes and Counter Notes*, trans. Donald Watson (New York, 1964), pp. 175–80. See also Johann N. Schmidt, "Talk that Leads Nowhere: Swift's *Complete Collection of Genteel and Ingenious Conversation*," *Reading Swift*, eds Rodino and Real, pp. 159–64.

[163] Ionesco, "The Tragedy of Language," p. 180. For some shrewd distinctions between Swift's and Ionesco's representations of linguistic vacuity, see Rawson, *Gulliver and the Gentle Reader*, pp. 95–97.

you keep your filthy Hands to your self?" For Swift, moreover, the irreducible thinginess of *Directions to Servants* – "Knives, Forks, Spoons, Saltcellars, broken Bread, and Scraps of Meat"[164] – punctured the verbal bladders dispensed by Wagstaff. If Moor Park afforded Swift an entrée into the world of genteel and ingenious conversation, then it also polished his skills as a servant-watcher, particularly if he did indeed sit below the salt.[165] *Polite Conversation* and *Directions to Servants* were "two great works" which complemented each other, as Swift explained to Gay and Pope when contemplating the works' completion during the early 1730s.[166] And the importance of commonplacing emerges yet again in Swift's reliance upon the "head" as a principle of organization in *Directions*. Of the servants' illicit activities, furthermore, not a few revolve around "vailing" and other petty dishonesties comparable to the tailors' "cabbaging" which provided both Swift and the Grubean Sage with metaphors for commonplacing and composition.[167] If counterfeit wits clipped and filed Congreve for their commonplace books, then servants lined their pockets and stomachs more materially. In our readings of commonplace Swift, we should not celebrate intertextuality at the expense of tangibility. Whether manifested as Futurist experimentalism or as Wagstaffian shellgame, Swift's linguistic obsessions were dumbly ballasted by things.

## V

*Truth, whose mother is history, rival of time, depository of deeds, witness of the past, exemplar and adviser to the present, and the future's counselor.*
Miguel Cervantes/"Pierre Menard"/J. L. Borges[168]

TRUTH is eternal, and the Son of Heav'n
Jonathan Swift[169]

In March 1947, Georg Grosz – a great satirist adrift in New York City – ordered eighty books by mail.[170] Titles by Kant and Chekhov were overshadowed by a plethora of those "idiot books" which Grosz had begun to collect: *How to Improve your Conversation, Zoology Self-Taught, Ventriloquism Self-Taught, Hypnotism Made Plain, How to Cane and Upholster Chairs, Facts to Know about Palmistry, How to Throw a Party, How to Psychoanalyse Your Neighbours, Sideshow Tricks Explained, The Magic of Numbers, Reincarnation Explained, Wine, Women, and Song* ... Had Barthelme's disquisition on plastic buffalo humps been available, doubtless Grosz would have added it to his Warholian collection of

---

[164] *Prose Works*, IV, 191; XIII, 21.

[165] On the tradition of Temple's maltreatment of Swift, see A. C. Elias, Jr, *Swift at Moor Park: Problems in Biography and Criticism* (Philadelphia, 1982), pp. 132–54.

[166] See *Correspondence*, III, 493; IV, 31.

[167] For a background to Swift's dishonest servants, see Linebaugh, *The London Hanged*, pp. 250–51.

[168] Borges, "Pierre Menard, Author of the *Quixote*," p. 43.

[169] "Ode to Dr. William Sancroft," *Poems*, ed. Williams, I, 34, l. 1.

[170] See Hans Hess, *Georg Grosz* (New York, 1974), p. 233. All the information in this paragraph is derived from this source.

kitsch and trash.[171] Like Swift and Flaubert (but without their scholarly dedication), Grosz relished the random conjunction of the autodidactic and the commonplace with the charlatanical and the magico-mystical. "I have read far too much in my life," Grosz concluded, shortly after despatching his order: "*Bildung* (education) leads to more *Bildung*, and more *Bildung* leads nowhere."

Swift began his career as a major writer – just as Flaubert ended his – by interring education under a mound of idiot books: "*My New Help of Smatterers*, or the *Art of being Deep-learned, and Shallow-read. A curious Invention about Mouse-Traps. An Universal Rule of Reason, or Every Man his own Carver*; Together with a most useful Engine for *catching of Owls*" (T, p. 130). Such titles display terraefilian or Grubean panache – "quacking" mock titles served both as student jest and as Duntonian gimmick – but Swift, like Flaubert and Grosz, also evinced a keen appetite for genuine (as opposed to simulated) idiocy like that he assimilated for the Partridge papers. As to how and where Swift first contrived his tubbian system for accumulating and voiding trash, we can only guess, but from the 11,000 pages of abstracts, summaries, compendia, extracts, collections, medullas, excerpta quaedams, and florilegia that Flaubert used as a quarry for *Bouvard and Pécuchet* and *The Dictionary of Received Ideas* we may disengage some hints. John Webster's compulsive recourse to his commonplace book also proves instructive – the plays endure as intertextual masterpieces – but Webster set out with no satirical intention of sawing off the commonplace branch upon which he sat.[172] For it was Flaubert who compiled the *ne plus ultra* of commonplace books against commonplaces. In *carnets* and *sottisiers*, he raised a veritable himalayas of every kind of stuffing, sludge, and dreck under the sun. Quacks' bills ("VINAIGRE DE TOILETTE DE L'IMACULÉE CONCEPTION") were squirrelled away with as much diligence as the medical intelligence that fried donkey turd could cure sterility or that a wife's fart in her husband's mouth might prove fatal.[173] Guano represented the foundation stone of Peru's social structure; in *hic jacet* lurked the etymology of *jachere* (fallow or unploughed land).[174] Infanticide in 1860 could be laid at the door of Rabelais; novels caused prostitution even though whores could not read.[175] If the *Tub* showed how "the contrary may almost be proved by uncontroulable Demonstration" (T, p. 34), then Flaubert positively basked in "contradictions littéraires."[176] Specimens of style – scientific, ecclesiastical, periphrastic – were diligently collected.[177] Juxtapositions prove odder than any alphabetized by po-faced commonplacers: a plan to compare Shakespeare's *Coriolanus* with Abeille's (1676) appears on the same page as a note about a notorious water diviner of 1692 and a bibliographical reference to *Histoire naturelle des araignées* (1736).[178] As in the *Tub*, genius is revealed by authorial selections from this midden heap of reading and collection. Flaubert's tongue-in-cheek quo-

---

[171] Hess, *Georg Grosz:* "In earlier years Grosz had made a fantastic collection of absurd postcards: all the trash, Kitsch, jokes, involuntary surrealism, proto-Dada, and the outpourings of the naive mind attracted him. He acquired military, erotic, sentimental absurdities wherever he could find them – in postcards, souvenirs, and advertisements" (p. 233).

[172] See R. W. Dent's splendid study, *John Webster's Borrowing* (Berkeley, 1960).

[173] Cento and Pennarola, eds, *Le projet du "sottisier,"* pp. 13, 19.

[174] See Cento and Pennarola, eds, *Le projet du "sottisier,"* p. 39.

[175] De Biasi, ed., *Carnets de travail*, p. 489.

[176] De Biasi, ed., *Carnets de travail*, p. 489.

[177] Cento and Pennarola, eds, *Le projet du "sottisier,"* pp. 35–186.

[178] De Biasi, ed., *Carnets de travail*, p. 488.

tations from bourgeois authorities remind us how hard it is to separate one man's commonplace book from another's *sottisier*. They also suggest the ways in which the novelist channelled his reading into his satire and thus elucidate Swift's comparable recourse to his own commonplace book.

The lists Flaubert kept of his "gigantesques lectures" — among the 43 titles he "devoured" during the first three months of 1874 were Altairac's *Révélations d'un prétendu fou* (1862), Bienville's *La Nymphomanie, ou traité de la fureur utérine* (1789), Cloquet's *Osphrésiologie, ou traité des odeurs* (bis: 1815, 1821), Debay's *La Vénus féconde et callipédique* (1873), Du Fresnoy's *L'Histoire justifiée contre les romans* (1735), Madsen's *Antiquités préhistoriques du Danemark* (1869–73), Marchangy's *La Gaule poétique* (1819), Maulmond's *Aspirations et réalité* (1874), Passard's *Quarantes milles squelettes humains antediluviens en Europe* (1867), Pomme's *Traité des affections vaporeuses des deux sexes* (1769), Saint-Gervais's *Les animaux célèbres* (1835), Wright's *Histoire de la caricature et du grotesque* (1867) — repay comparison not only with the record Swift himself made for 1697/8 but with the bountiful supplements proposed by modern scholars.[179] Like some of those "Abstracts and Collections from Reading" Swift sought from Winder, the abstracts he made from Cyprian and Irenaeus, Sarpi and Sleidan at Moor Park might well have passed muster in a theological commonplace book. But it is hard to imagine that Swift — so ferocious a scribbler of marginalia — would shield his theological extracts from profane annotations. Some passages that other divines excerpted — for the kind of self-congratulatory citation to which the Lay-patron objects — doubtless went straight into Swift's *sottisier* for future parody. For Swift as for Flaubert, I maintain, commonplace book and *sottisier* became indistinguishable. Yet if *Bouvard and Pécuchet* demonstrates the triumph of a nihilist's Gallic rage for order, the *Tub* exhibits an Hibernian rage for chaos. Of Swift, as of Flaubert, we may say, none the less, that "the task he had set for himself was nothing less than to achieve by labor effects comparable to those of appalling incompetence."[180]

In the Tubster's vertiginous shifts of voice — each so scrupulously personated — we can glimpse Swift delving into his *sottisier*, retrieving stylistic specimens, stale locutions, and received ideas. To envisage both Swift and the Tubster as commonplacers helps us to clarify the conundrum of the *persona*: he is the man with the gigantic commonplace book. Much of the *Tub*'s religious satire acquires its punch from Swift's merger of scatological slapstick (like Aeolist flatulence) with classical and Christian sources (in Section VIII: Lucretius, St Matthew and St Paul, the scholastics, Paracelsus, Olaus Magnus, Pancirollus, etc.), a merger that any system of "heads" surely encouraged. Under "Infallibility," for example, Swift might have entered specimens relating both to the papacy and to mountebankery, a lexical fluke that threads his portrayal of Peter as a charlatan. Some divines could distil

---

[179] De Biasi, ed., *Carnets de travail*, pp. 523–26. For Flaubert's own comments upon his Augean feats, see *Carnets*, pp. 773–74. For "Swift's Reading," see Guthkelch and Nichol Smith, eds, *A Tale of a Tub*, pp. liii–lx, and Hermann J. Real, ed., *"The Battle of the Books": eine historisch-kritische Ausgabe mit literarhistorischer Einleitung und Kommentar* (Berlin und New York, 1978), pp. 128–35 (especially Lyon's transcript for 1697/8). For an incisive overview, see Angus Ross, "The Books in the *Tale*: Swift and Reading in *A Tale of a Tub*," *Proceedings of The First Münster Symposium on Jonathan Swift*, eds Real and Vienken, pp. 209–16.

[180] Hugh Kenner, *The Stoic Comedians: Flaubert, Joyce, and Beckett* (Berkeley, Los Angeles, London, 1962), p. 12.

truth from heresy, but Swift (in the guise of the Tubster) not only managed to extract heterodoxy from Christian doctrine but also converted the Bible into a Grub Street production. Unlike the design that Flaubert imposed upon *Bouvard and Pécuchet*, the way in which Swift cabbaged the *Tub* together comes disconcertingly close at times, I suspect, to the Grubeana he had set out to parody. Doubtless the work went through numerous rescensions but it is to *fortuna gubernans* that we must turn when contemplating what was included and what was not. The satire betrays a haste and desperation that goes beyond the "personation" of a Bedlamite. We can imagine Swift picking (if not always choosing) with habnab abandon from among so many thousand heads of a different nature. Yet much of the *Tub*'s brilliance remains attributable not only to the work's unsettling provisionality but also to what we can intuit of its author's Flaubertian preparations. Swift's first major satire exploded without warning in 1704, whereas Flaubert spent most of his career limbering up for *Bouvard and Pécuchet* and the *Dictionary of Received Ideas*. A cerebral haemorrhage killed the novelist (at the age of 59) as he toiled amongst his *carnets* and *sottisiers* to bring his *magnum opus* to completion. Yet "a work is never *complete*," Valéry reminds us, "but *abandoned*."[181]

"I am never without some great works in View, enough to take up forty years of the most vigorous healthy man," Swift wrote to Pope in 1734: "Although I am convinced that I shall never be able to finish three Treatises, that have layn by me severall years, & want nothing but Correction."[182] Two of these treatises – *Polite Conversation* and *Directions to Servants* – I have already linked to Swift's commonplacing during the 1690s from which the *Tub* also sprang. It is clear that Swift retained a particular affection for compositions which, as he told Pope in 1732, he had "begun above twenty-eight years ago, and [are now] almost finished."[183] If we do not dismiss Swift's precision as mystification, we can certainly date *Polite Conversation* and *Directions to Servants* to the years when the satirist was preparing the *Tub* for the press; I have argued for an earlier date. And their adaptable structure – part commonplace book, part *sottisier* – could easily accommodate expansion and addition. Each is a *magnum opus* designed, idiosyncratically, "for the Universal Improvement of Mankind." And, as Ann Cline Kelly observes, "To read the confidences of the hack writer persona at the end of *A Tale of a Tub* is to read, perhaps, Wagstaff's own history."[184] The projectors entertain fantasies about the systematic implementation of their ideas, but their treatises remain manifest incoherent pieces of patchwork. If other satirists like Bayle, Bierce, and Flaubert shaped their *Weltanschauungen* into Dictionaries, then Swift presented his tubbian dictionary as a dismembered commonplace book, bulging with heads and indexes.[185] If "Dictionary Johnson," then "Commonplace Swift"?

I do not believe, however, that Swift cabbaged from a commonplace book resembling any that have come down to us from the seventeenth century. For his abundant surviving manuscripts suggest that instead of using a "Folio paper book," like the one abandoned in Kil-

---

[181] "Concerning 'Le cimetière marin,'" *The Art of Poetry*, trans. Denise Folliot (London, 1958), p. 140.

[182] *Correspondence*, IV, 262.

[183] *Correspondence*, IV, 31.

[184] "Swift's *Polite Conversation*: An Eschatological Vision," *Studies in Philology*, 73 (1976), 217.

[185] See Umberto Eco, "Metaphor, Dictionary, and Encyclopedia," *New Literary History*, 15 (1984), 255–71.

root, Swift preferred working from parcels of papers. Partly this is attributable to parsimony. "I say again keep very regular accounts in large books and a fair hand," Swift admonished Thomas Sheridan in 1735, "not like me who to save paper confuse every thing."[186] The neatness and organization of Swift's own surviving account books bely this self-criticism,[187] but in a manuscript dating from the 1690s we can glimpse the confusion from which Swift raised the *Tub*. On a sheet of paper which started out as a letter to his mother ("Moor Park – August the 5th 1698 / Dear Mother") Swift jotted notes from Louis Hennepin's discussion of North American Indians, lines from a Latin version of Aristophanes's *Wasps*, a note on the *Memoirs* of Philippe de Comines, neatly inscribed terms for measuring area (possibly a lesson for Stella), and ciphers preparatory to the document's filing.[188] Not dissimilar in form to a heteroclite page in a commonplace book or *sottisier*, Swift's manuscript discloses several hints for the *Tub*. Echoes from Swift's notes on the Indians' use of tobacco and their purported wife-swapping can be heard in *The Mechanical Operation of the Spirit* where modern anthropology and ancient heresiology are melded. And Ehrenpreis conjectures that a related reference to rectal fatiloquy derives from Hennepin, albeit not from this sheet of Swift's notes.[189] Yet Ehrenpreis and Clifford also advance 1724 as another possible date for the manuscript since Hennepin, Aristophanes, and Comines each appears to have influenced Swift's compositions at this later juncture.

A solution to this dating dilemma might be that the notes were made (and partially used in 1698), then filed for future reference, and resuscitated in the 1720s. Expansions to the 1720 edition of the *Tub* indicate that – whatever his perceptions that he confused everything – Swift rescued some manuscripts from the flames and saved them for future use. Some of what did not get included in the first five editions of the *Tub* not only popped up in the 1720 edition but, I hazard, was also cabbaged for the other attacks on England's "*numerous and gross Corruptions in Religion and Learning*" which Swift continued to mount during the first decade of the century (T, p. 4; note date of 1709): their many verbal and thematic continuities suggest that Swift had (like Dunton) already begun to commonplace from notes for, and drafts of, his own works, whether published or unpublished. Several of these works also accumulated in Swift's first *Miscellanies*, in itself something of a writer's commonplace book.[190] Moreover, Swift's word-games, preserved in manuscript at the Huntington and John Rylands Libraries, resemble *nugae* culled by other commonplacers.[191] And the system of "hints" which Swift used when planning new works also sprang from academic and theo-

---

[186] *Correspondence*, IV, 350.

[187] See Paul V. Thompson and Dorothy Jay Thompson, *The Account Books of Jonathan Swift* (Newark and London, 1984).

[188] See the description and analysis by Irvin Ehrenpreis and James L. Clifford, "Swiftiana in Rylands English MS. 659 and Related Documents," *Bulletin of the John Rylands Library*, 37 (1955), 372–75.

[189] On p. 284 of his copy of Guthkelch and Nichol Smith (preserved in the Ehrenpreis Center) Ehrenpreis wrote "? told in Hennepin" alongside Swift's reference to "certain Fortune-tellers in *Northern America*."

[190] See Ann Cline Kelly's persuasive discussion in "The Semiotics of Swift's 1711 *Miscellanies*," *Swift Studies*, 6 (1991), 59–68.

[191] In addition to the linguistic curiosities discussed above (pp. 30–32), see Folger MS M.a. 169, Joseph Wright's *Collectanea quaedam nugalia, alique tamen non perdenda, nec totaliter negligenda*, assembled 1700–1725.

logical commonplacing.[192] This reliance upon "heads" and "hints" when composing the *Tub* Angus Ross and David Woolley have recently linked to Swift's practice as Temple's editor, a comparison which had not escaped William Wotton who objected to "printing Bits of Books" and "loose Apophthegms, Occasional Thoughts, or incoherent Sentences" instead of "Continued Discourses."[193] To pass off the scourings of a commonplace book as a real book does not pass muster with Wotton. Swift's ironies eluded him.

To complain that Swift, as so often, did not practice what he preached would be captious. It is more illuminating to register the ways in which he funnelled his genius through the pedagogic routines and writerly conventions of his age. Yet any invocation of genius within the postmodern dialects of our own fanatic times must call into question both intertextuality and the *morte d'author*. Commonplace Swift would have understood the impasse. "Never any one lieveing thought like you," Vanessa told the Dean, complaining that "no humane creature is capable of geussing at" what passed through his mind.[194] Yet if Swift liberated his unique mentation in futurist experiments with language, he was also convinced that a man should "pass his Life in the common Forms, without any Thought of subduing Multitudes" (T, p. 171). When Swift himself commandeered the common forms of writing, however, it was with the intention of shattering language in all its mechanical operations.

---

[192] See most recently James Woolley's overview in Swift and Sheridan, *The Intelligencer*, pp. 269–75. Swift's use of "hint" (a word spottily covered in the *OED*) deserves careful attention within the commonplace context.

[193] Ross and Woolley, eds, *A Tale of a Tub and Other Works* (Oxford, 1986), p. xvii; Wotton, *A Defense of the Reflections* (1705) in Guthkelch and Nichol Smith, eds, *A Tale of a Tub*, p. 316. Of course, Wotton blamed Thomas rather than Jonathan Swift for the *Tub*.

[194] *Correspondence*, II, 364.

Michael J. Conlon
*Binghamton University, The State University of New York*

# *Performance* in Swift's *A Tale of a Tub*

ABSTRACT. Ideas of *performance* and *person* frame the reader's response to Swift's satire in *A Tale of a Tub*. The distinction between performance as "purposeful action" and perform-ance as "imposture" links the Grub Street author's identification of his text with the "pro-ductions" of the "Stage-Itinerant" to the allegory of the three brothers and their corruption into a life of illusion and spectacle. Performance also informs Swift's use of Hobbes's defin-ition of "person" as "actor" and Swift's creation of a world of public performers who possess neither moral agency nor psychological identity. This "blurring" of world and stage inevitably drives the reader to confront Swift's own personations and performances in the *Tale*.

The word *"Performance,"* John W. Kronik tells us in a recent issue of *PMLA*, "has taken on new dimensions in the current idiom. What once was an event has become a critical category, now applied to everything from a play to a war to a meal."[1] In the seventeenth century, *performance* undergoes less audacious changes, but significant changes nonetheless. By 1665, *performance* includes not only actions and deeds, but also objects of art and literature, paint-ings and written compositions, and the word itself acquires connotations of "illusion and imposture." These new connotations, Jean-Christophe Agnew points out, both "comple-ment" and "subvert" the "word's earlier meaning as the ceremonial execution or discharge of a command or obligation."[2]

In Jonathan Swift's lifetime, *performance* becomes "a significant, binding word" for wide-ly divergent areas of culture and society and a word that both reflects and engages "deep conflicts of value and belief."[3] *Performance* also both binds and divides two sides of Swift's character. He lived his days in the performance of an uncompromising sense of duty to his office as a clergyman: "I look upon myself, in the capacity of a clergyman, to be one ap-pointed by providence for defending a post assigned me, and for gaining over as many en-emies as I can. Although I think my cause is just, yet one great motion is my submitting to the pleasure of Providence, and to the laws of my country."[4] But against this sense of *per-formance* as pure obligation, Swift displays in his writings a *ludic* sense of *performance*,

---

[1]   "Editor's Note," *PMLA*, 107 (1992), 425.
[2]   *Worlds Apart: The Market and the Theater in Anglo-American Thought, 1550–1750* (Cambridge, 1986), p. 83.
[3]   See Raymond Williams, *Key Words: A Vocabulary of Culture and Society* (New York, 1983), pp. 15–23.
[4]   "Thoughts on Religion," *Prose Works*, IX, 262.

creating over the years a gallery of roles, postures, and poses. Both his poetry and his prose disclose Swift's mixed responses of fascination and despair over the popularity, in his time, of mask, costume, entertainment, and spectacle. And in many of Swift's more memorable poems – "A Description of the Morning" and "A Description of a City Shower," for example – he catches his subjects between performance and instinctive response, "momentarily disarmed," in Martin Price's phrase, "their masks slipping if not dropped."[5] *Gulliver's Travels*, too, makes *performance* one of its principal themes, exposing to ridicule the *virtuosi* by showing a series of ironic connections between performances in the sciences and performances on stages and in texts. In rereading Gulliver's story against his letter to Cousin Sympson, moreover, Gulliver's text looks caught and even ratcheted between its original intention as an informative travel narrative and its performative effects as a project to mend the world.

Swift shows a similar preoccupation with *performance* in *A Tale of a Tub* (1704), and this essay explores the question of how connections in the *Tale* between ideas of *person* and *performance* frame the reader's response to Swift's satire. More specifically, the essay looks at three aspects of *performance* in the *Tale*: first, Swift's use of the Stage-Itinerant as a type of the *Tale* itself and as an expression of the Grub Street author's fascination with the mechanical production of learning; second, the allegory of the three brothers and their corruption from the faithful performance of the terms of their Father's Will to a world of imposture and deception; and, third, the connections in the *Tale* between ideas of person and performance and the meaning of Swift's own performance in the *Tale*.

## I  *Performance and The Stage-Itinerant*

Throughout *A Tale of a Tub*, readers witness, in Claude Rawson's words, a "blurring of world and playhouse into unexpected interpenetrations."[6] The engraving of the preaching scene, produced by Bernard Lens for the fifth edition, re-creates a world totally given over to performance. The engraving illustrates the three principal oratorical machines of the Grub Street author's Introduction: the *Pulpit*, the *Ladder*, and the *Stage-Itinerant*. It shows us a series of receding tableaux linking Puritan preacher, tub and audience, in the foreground, with a second scene, viewed through a large window to the preacher's left, that includes two performers on the *Stage-Itinerant*, and slightly to the right of their stage, a ladder and gallows containing the executioner and his charge. Like the engraving, the *Tale* bulges with platforms and stages, and insists on links similar to those in the engraving between preachers, mountebanks, and the Grub Street fraternity. In his account of the typology of the oratorical machines, the Grub Street author identifies his "present Treatise" with the *Stage-Itinerant* or the travelling stage of the Mountebank:

UNDER the *Stage-Itinerant* are couched those Productions designed for the Pleasure and Delight of Mortal Man; such as *Six-peny-worth of Wit*, Westminster *Drolleries*, *Delightful Tales*, *Compleat Jesters*, and the like; by which the Writers of and for *GRUB-STREET*,

---

[5]   *To the Palace of Wisdom: Studies in Order and Energy from Dryden to Blake* (Garden City, NY, 1964), p. 258.

[6]   *Order from Confusion Sprung: Studies in Eighteenth-Century Literature from Swift to Cowper* (London, 1985), p. 166.

The Preacher in his Tub, from Swift's *Tale of a Tub*, fifth edition (1710)

have in these latter Ages so nobly triumph'd over *Time* ... It is under this Classis, I have presumed to list my present Treatise, being just come from having the Honor conferred upon me, to be adopted a Member of the Illustrious Fraternity.[7]

The *Stage-Itinerant*, then, is a type of the *Tale* itself, and it connects the world of quack performers to the world of Grub Street writers. In this regard, Swift anticipates the fascination of the Scriblerians with performance and spectacle, and the tendency of Scriblerian satire to associate modernity with a perverse theatricality. The *Tale* shares with *The Dunciad*, in particular, a world given over to "sights and shows" and "to staring, gaping and gazing" audiences. And in both satires, "the intelligent perception of life and the responsible participation in it are abandoned for the pleasures of sheer mindlessness ... and the diverting flicker of images on the eye."[8]

Swift's presentation of the *Stage-Itinerant* as a type of the *Tale* itself also has the effect of making performance in the sense of illusion and imposture the common activity of mountebanks, Grub Street writers, and fanatic preachers. In the minds of the orthodox, fanatical preachers and mountebanks shared the same stage. As one contemporary attack on enthusiasts in religion and quackery puts it: "The Enthusiast in Divinity, having no sooner acted his part and had his Exit, but on the same stage, from his shop ... enters the enthusiast in Physic."[9] Mountebanks, in turn, advertised their cures and remedies in a variety of printed forms, while members of the Grub Street fraternity, like Swift's mock-author, frequently talked about their "productions" in metaphors drawn from the theatre. John Dunton, for example, mentioned in the *Tale* as a "worthy citizen and Bookseller" (p. 59), who will shortly publish a collection of speeches from the gallows, introduces a work Swift would have known about entitled *The Young Students Library*, published in 1691, by comparing his book to the stage:

> This Book is a kind of a Common Theater where every person may Act or take such Part as pleases him best, and what he does not like, he may pass over, assuring himself every ones Judgment not being like his, another may choose what he mislikes, and so every one may be pleased in their turns.[10]

Dunton's book consists of extracts and abridgements of learned texts, distilled from the originals, so that the young student can know about them without reading them. The entire project seems inspired by Dunton's claim to have found a way of packaging knowledge, which resembles what the mock-author of the *Tale* describes as a "more prudent Method, to

---

[7] Jonathan Swift, *A Tale of a Tub*, eds A. C. Guthkelch and D. Nichol Smith, 2nd ed. (Oxford, 1958), p. 63.

[8] Dennis Todd, "The Hairy Maid at the Harpsichord: Some Speculations on the Meaning of *Gulliver's Travels*," *Texas Studies in Literature and Language*, 34 (1992), 248.

[9] E. Gray, "A Caution to the Wary," Cited in C. J. S. Thompson, *The Quacks of London* (London, 1928), p. 105.

[10] *The Young Students Library: Containing Extracts and Abridgments of the Most Valuable Books Printed in England and in the Foreign Journals, from the Year Sixty Five to this Time. To Which is Added, A New Essay on all Sorts of Learning; Wherein the Use of the Sciences is Distinctly Treated on* (London, 1691), Preface. A. C. Elias, Jr, assures me that Swift knew of this book and points out that Dunton ran advance notices of *The Young Students Library* in his *Athenian Mercury*. In a letter of 14 February, 1691/92, Swift says he had read the first four volumes of the *Mercury*, and Elias believes it is likely that Swift eventually saw a copy of Dunton's book.

[11] *A Tale of a Tub*, eds Guthkelch and Smith, pp. 144–45.

become *Scholars* and *Wits*, without the Fatigue of *Reading* or of *Thinking*."[11] Both Dunton and Swift's Grub Street author glory in the mechanical production of knowledge, and the words "production" and "performance" recur in their writing. Both authors, moreover, show a fascination for spectacle and for the "materialization" of events that art historian, Barbara Maria Stafford, identifies with the theatricalization of culture, in the late seventeenth century.[12]

The metaphor of the *Stage-Itinerant* also provides the appropriate dramatic context for what Swift describes in the *Apology* as those passages in which "*the Author personates the Style and Manner of other Writers*."[13] Swift's "personations" in the *Tale* consist for the most part of persons who, in Richard Poirier's phrasing, are "self-conscious performers," that is, "writers who like to find themselves in acts of composition."[14] In the person of the Apologist, for example, Swift discusses "the author's" intentions, his meanings, his parodies, and threads of irony, together with all the disruptive forces from outside the text that threaten the author's authority – the passages "*blotted* out" (p. 8), the forced interpretations, the accusations of plagiarism, and the disappearance of the author's "Papers" (p. 4). As the Bookseller/Writer of the Dedication "To The Right Honourable John *Lord Sommers*" (p. 23), Swift belabours each step of his passage through a kind of reverse literary check to find the actual person he has dedicated the author's "Papers" to. As the "*freshest Modern*" (p. 130) and "devoted Servant of all *Modern* Forms" (p. 45), he describes the circumstances and genesis of his treatise, what he intended by it, how he wrote it, and how he wishes it to be read. In short, Swift creates for the Tale-as-Stage-Itinerant a troupe of performing writers, commentators, and annotators who persistently reflect upon their methods, distresses, habits, and achievements. And collectively, these personations account for the *Tale*'s "furiously self-consultive" tone and focus.[15]

## II *Performance and Religion*

The Grub Street author's representation of his "treatise" as a performance worthy of the *Stage-Itinerant* contrasts sharply with his initial account of his writing as a performance calculated to divert Hobbes's *Leviathan* and its disciples from "tossing and sporting with the *Commonwealth*."[16] This fundamental contrast between the Grub Street author's use of the word "performance" as purposeful action and the fulfilment of an obligation ("I had the Honor done me to be engaged in the Performance"[17]) and "performance" in the sense

---

[12] In "The Eighteenth-Century: Towards an Interdisciplinary Model," *Art Bulletin*, 70 (1988), Barbara Maria Stafford writes: "Ephemeral spectacle, or the vivid materialization and physical realization of an event, outstripped in popularity the illustration of it in a static medium. During the eighteenth century, not written language, but the theatrical and sensuously involving synaesthetic effect gained ascendancy in the major and minor houses of Europe" (p. 18).

[13] *A Tale of a Tub*, eds Guthkelch and Smith, p. 7.

[14] *The Performing Self* (New Brunswick, NJ, 1992 [1971]), p. 101.

[15] I take this phrasing from Poirier's *The Performing Self*, p. 87.

[16] *A Tale of a Tub*, eds Guthkelch and Smith, p. 40.

[17] *A Tale of a Tub*, eds Guthkelch and Smith, p. 41.

[18] *A Tale of a Tub*, eds Guthkelch and Smith, p. 63.

of entertainment and illusion ("for the Pleasure and Delight of Mortal Man"[18]) reappears in the allegory of the three brothers. And just as the Grub Street author exchanges a conception of performance as duty and obligation for performance as illusion and imposture, the three brothers, whose story enacts the secularization of Christianity, abandon the performance of their faith in favour of a life of fashion and fraud. Throughout the allegory, moreover, Swift appropriates the conventions of seventeenth-century anti-Catholic and anti-Puritan satire and the associations it makes between theatre and performance, Catholicism and Enthusiasm.

Corruptions in religion originate in the brothers' breaking faith and abandoning their obligation to perform the care of their coats according to the instructions in their Father's Will. The coats, like Jesus's tunic described in John (19:23), are made "of very good Cloth," and "so neatly sown, you would swear they were all of a Piece;"[19] "in their original state, they give the brothers the closest resemblance they will ever have, individually and as a group, to God's 'verie Onenesse.'"[20] In the first seven years, the brothers keep "their Coats in very good Order,"[21] but in time they give in to the pressures of the world, and come under the totally secular influence of the tailor-worshippers. The outward and accidental trappings of religion become more important to the brothers than the inward grace they receive through their Father's original coats. The performance of the Father's instructions, therefore, gives way to the performance of fashionable roles, while the brothers' spirituality gives way to the theatricality of the town. In this secular and materialist climate, persons are things or "Suits of Cloaths" that "live, and move, and talk, and perform all [the] Offices of Human Life."[22]

As the allegory proceeds, Peter and Jack become totally preoccupied with matters of appearance and performance. The ornaments of "Popish Worship" promoted by Peter involve his brothers in standards of behaviour determined by actors and fops. In one instance, when "a Player, hired for the Purpose by the Corporation of Fringe-makers, acted his Part in a new Comedy, all covered with Silver Fringe,"[23] making silver fringe the prevailing fashion, Peter cleverly showed his brothers how to circumvent the prohibition against silver fringe in their Father's Will. We learn later that "Peter was also held the Original Author of Puppets and Raree-Shows,"[24] representations in the allegory of the ornaments of Catholic ceremony and worship. In this fashion, the satire on Peter echoes a tradition of anti-Catholic writing extending back to the early fifteenth century that singles out for ridicule the "theatricality" of Catholic worship.[25]

A similar obsession with performance and appearance, however, attends the career of Peter's brother and principal antagonist, Jack, the author of the "renowned Sect of Æo-

---

[19]  A Tale of a Tub, eds Guthkelch and Smith, pp. 81–82.
[20]  Caryn Chaden, "'To Advantage Dress'd': Clothing and Public Identity from A Tale of a Tub to Sartor Resartus," diss., University of Virginia, 1989, p. 35.
[21]  A Tale of a Tub, eds Guthkelch and Smith, p. 74.
[22]  A Tale of a Tub, eds Guthkelch and Smith, p. 78.
[23]  A Tale of a Tub, eds Guthkelch and Smith, pp. 87–88.
[24]  A Tale of a Tub, eds Guthkelch and Smith, p. 109.
[25]  See Jonas Barish, The Antitheatrical Prejudice (Berkeley, Los Angeles, London, 1987), pp. 165–90. Barish discusses the "quarrel between Rome and the reformers" over issues of "visibility" and theatricality.
[26]  A Tale of a Tub, eds Guthkelch and Smith, p. 160.

*lists*,"[26] who cultivate the art of belching:

> To cultivate [this] Art, and render it more serviceable to Mankind, they made Use of several Methods. At certain Seasons of the Year, you might behold the Priests amongst them in vast Numbers, with their *Mouths gaping wide against a Storm.*[27]

The image of "vast Numbers, with their *Mouths gaping*" takes us back to the illustration of the staring, gaping audience seated before the Preacher in his Tub and, in the author's account in his "Preface," of a "huge Assembly" pressing and squeezing before the stage of a Mountebank in Leicester-Fields. Swift repeatedly and ironically identifies the Puritans with various forms of performance, theatricalism, and display rejected by the Puritans in their conduct, but often "adopted" by them in their writing and preaching "as ... metaphor[s] for the condition of sinful man."[28]

By exploiting the connections between Puritan Enthusiasm and theatricalism, Swift reinforces the ironic "resemblance" of Jack to his brother Peter. "Their Humours and Dispositions were not only the same, but there was a close Analogy in their Shape, their Size, and their Mien."[29] Peter and Jack act out the same pattern of corruption Swift presents in his poem, "Baucis and Philemon": that is, "a hypocritical spirituality, proceeding from and degenerating into materialism" that produces in the figure of Philemon a "furbish'd" member of the clergy.[30] In the logic of the *Tale*'s allegory, the original coats show their "virtues" only as long as the brothers keep the faith, acknowledge that they are indeed their Father's sons, and perform according to the instructions of their Father's Will. But Jack and Peter seek to exalt themselves above the world by performing according to the erroneous and materialist premises of the tailor-worshippers. In so doing, they abandon any sense of performance as the fulfilment of one's divinely appointed "role" and reduce their persons to "various 'compositions' of buttons ... cloth" and costume.[31] The allegory, in effect, identifies the abuses in religion with a perverse reduction to the level of self-display and spectacle the trope of *theatrum mundi*, frequently used by orthodox Christians to define performance in relation to divine providence.

## III *Performance and Person*

Swift's deployment of the metaphor of the Book-as-Stage-Itinerant, however, provokes the larger question about the meaning of the word *person* in *A Tale of a Tub*. Near the conclusion of the Bookseller's "Dedication to The Right Honourable John *Lord Sommers*," a parody of Dryden's effusive dedications, the Bookseller observes that "there is no Virtue,

---

27  *A Tale of a Tub*, eds Guthkelch and Smith, p. 153. Phillip Harth discusses the association Swift creates between the Aeolists and the religious fanatics in *Swift and Anglican Rationalism: The Religious Background of "A Tale of a Tub"* (Chicago, 1961), pp. 63–68.

28  *The Antitheatrical Prejudice*, p. 165.

29  *A Tale of a Tub*, eds Guthkelch and Smith, p. 199.

30  See Eric Rothstein, "Jonathan Swift as Jupiter: 'Baucis and Philemon,'" *The Augustan Milieu: Essays Presented to Louis Landa*, eds Henry Knight Miller, Eric Rothstein, and G. S. Rousseau (Oxford, 1970), p. 215.

31  See Chaden, "'To Advantage Dress'd,'" p. 39.

32  *A Tale of a Tub*, eds Guthkelch and Smith, p. 26.

either of a Publick or Private Life, which some Circumstances of [Somers's own life], have not often produced upon the Stage of the World."[32] These words follow from a rambling account of the Bookseller's attempts to find the person who performs the part of the "Worthiest," having discovered on the "Covers of these Papers" the motto *"DETUR DIGNIS-SIMO – Let it be given to the Worthiest."*[33] The Bookseller employs several writers and wits "to furnish [him] with Hints and Materials, towards a Panegyrick upon" Lord Somers. They take whatever they could find "in the Characters of *Socrates, Aristides, Epaminondas, Cato, Tully, Atticus,"*[34] and create a portrait of Lord Somers that may well serve, the Bookseller speculates, as a dedication to another person, indeed, to several persons. Swift's parody, of course, exposes the "mercenary character" of contemporary dedications. But the parody strikes at a deeper issue. The Dedication turns the actual, historical person – John, Baron Somers, the Lord Chancellor of England – into a *construction* of parts: a name on the front of a book in capital letters, hints and materials picked up by hearsay, passages found in the characters of Socrates, Aristides, and other authors "with hard Names," strings of stale, stolen flatteries gleaned from Modern dedications. The dedication makes no attempt, in other words, to disclose and praise a person who lives apart from his public representation.

Persons in the *Tale*, like the Bookseller's version of Lord Somers, do not possess either independent identities or, in Veronica Kelly's phrasing, "continuous psychologies."[35] Rather, as Kelly further suggests, they resemble Thomas Hobbes's notion of person as performer and actor. The word "person," Hobbes says, has been "translated" from "the stage" to mean "any representer of speech and action, as well in tribunals, as [in] theatres. So that a *person*, is the same that an *actor* is, both on the stage and in common conversation; and to *personate*, is to *act*, or *represent* himself, or another; and he that acteth another, is said to bear his person."[36]

Swift personates the voices and roles of a series of public performers: the Apologist, the Bookseller, the Grub Street author, "engaged" – as he puts it – in this "Performance" of the *Tale* by persons representing the Commonwealth. The Grub Street author in turn moves through a variety of roles and poses: the "devoted Servant of all *Modern* Forms," the recently "adopted" member of the Grub Street "Fraternity," the Tale Teller, the favourite of all *"True Modern Criticks,"* and the "Person, whose Imaginations are hard-mouth'd, and exceedingly disposed to run away with his *Reason.*"[37] In these various personations of Moderns Swift chooses to ridicule, he withholds from us any felt sense that they are persons who possess either moral agency or psychological identity. Like William Wotton, they are "Person[s] ... ordain'd for great Designs, as well as Performances,"[38] persons defined wholly by what they perform as representatives of someone else or something else (the Author, the

---

[33]  *A Tale of a Tub*, eds Guthkelch and Smith, p. 23.
[34]  *A Tale of a Tub*, eds Guthkelch and Smith, p. 24.
[35]  "Following the Stage-Itinerant: Perception, Doubt, and Death in Swift's *Tale of a Tub,"* *Studies in Eighteenth-Century Culture*, 17 (1987), 243.
[36]  *Leviathan: or, The Matter, Forme and Power of a Commonwealth, Ecclesiasticall and Civil,* ed. Michael Oakeshott (Oxford, 1955), p. 105.
[37]  See *A Tale of a Tub*, eds Guthkelch and Smith, pp. 45, 63, 103, 180.
[38]  *A Tale of a Tub*, eds Guthkelch and Smith, p. 169.
[39]  *Leviathan*, ed. Oakeshott, p. 105.

Bookseller, the member of the Grub Street fraternity); they are as interchangeable as Hobbes's "*artificial person*."[39] "The *Tale*," therefore, "sets the sheer theatricality of the dramatic personae of the text against any reader's desire to read persons as self-sufficient and continuous psychologies."[40]

The debate of some years ago over whether or not the *Tale* presents us with a consistent, identifiable *persona* reflects in part the frustrations of reading a text consisting of frequent entrances and exits by a cast of persons whose behaviour is fully determined, never free, always rehearsed, and madly discontinuous. Deciding on a single identifiable *persona* like the Hack makes reading the *Tale* all the more tidy and manageable. But in making things manageable, we run the risk of losing sight of one of Swift's most forceful strikes against the Moderns; that is, his creation of a world in which discourse between persons as independent moral agents gives way to the cant of persons of the Grub Street fraternity who behave as interchangeable social constructions. Viewed in this context, the confusion over the question of who speaks in the *Tale* is precisely Swift's point.

Perhaps the most intriguing ambiguities involve the *person* and the presence of Swift himself. Some years ago, the late Frank Kinahan, writing on the subject of voice and theme in the *Tale*, argued that "it is ... impossible to reduce the number of voices in the *Tale* to three or four or fourteen, simply because to do so is to isolate them; and the whole technique of the *Tale* revolves around the fact that its several voices do *not* exist in isolation, that the lines between them cannot be clearly delineated. Indeed, the voices exist *only* in terms of their relation to each other."[41] He gives as an example the following and frequently cited pronouncement by the Grub Street author in his "Digression concerning Madness":

> What Man in the natural State, or Course of Thinking, did ever conceive it in his Power, to reduce the Notions of all Mankind, exactly to the same Length, and Breadth, and Height of his own? Yet this is the first humble and civil Design of all Innovators in the Empire of Reason.[42]

The obvious answer to the question – no man in his right mind would "ever conceive it in his Power, to reduce the Notions of all Mankind" to his own system. But the lines also express the Grub Street author's conception of his own genius; his work, he insists elsewhere, neglects nothing "that can be of Use upon any Emergency of Life."[43] In short, "the lines define genius for the [Grub Street author]" and, at the same time, they "define madness" for Swift.[44] And it would seem virtually impossible to separate the voice of Swift from the voice of the Grub Street author. If we try to reduce these lines to a single *persona* – the voice of the Grub Street author – we have to overlook what the lines actually say.

Kinahan's point is that these lines and many others in the *Tale* prevent us from isolating a single voice. Just when we feel secure that the voice of the Apologist is Swift himself and distinct from the voice of the Grub Street author, we find curious echoes between the two. In the Apology, for example, the Apologist says "*he had endeavour'd to Strip himself of as*

---

40   Kelly, "Following the Stage-Itinerant," p. 243.

41   "The Melancholy of Anatomy: Voice and Theme in *A Tale of a Tub*," *Journal of English and Germanic Philology*, 69 (1970), 279.

42   *A Tale of a Tub*, eds Guthkelch and Smith, pp. 166–67.

43   *A Tale of a Tub*, eds Guthkelch and Smith, p. 129.

44   See Kinahan, "The Melancholy of Anatomy," p. 280.

45   *A Tale of a Tub*, eds Guthkelch and Smith, p. 4.

*many real Prejudices as he could ... because under the Notion of Prejudices, he knew to what dangerous Heights some Men have proceeded."*[45] In Section VIII, we hear these same sentiments: "For, I think it one of the greatest, and best of humane Actions, to remove Prejudices, and place Things in their truest and fairest Light."[46] Our first impulse, perhaps, is to conclude that "the first voice is that of Swift, and he is speaking of 'real' prejudices and a 'real' attempt to rid himself of them; and clearly, the second voice is that of the [Grub Street author], and he is making a fool of himself by claiming to strip away prejudices when in fact he is piling them on."[47] But the two statements on prejudice interact and echo one another. And these ambiguities of voice deepen and take on additional significance in the light of recent accounts of Swift's "Apology" as parody.[48]

Frank Kinahan correctly emphasized the interactive relationship between the *Tale*'s real author and its mock-author. But beyond this, Swift's performance in the *Tale* also frequently locates him between a denial of being another and a denial of *not* being another. His use of the word "personate" in the Apology, in other words, does not suggest simply performing as someone else, but performing in-between identities.

In this regard, much of the action of the *Tale* itself occurs in-between something. The mock-author tells us it was written in "a very few leisure Hours, stollen from the short Intervals of a World of Business." He says, as well, that it was written "during a long Prorogation of Parliament," another "interval" between events.[49] Much of the language and content of the *Tale*, moreover, involve suspensions of consequences, acts of deferral, digressions, diversions, erratic swings into the parenthetical. Performance in *A Tale of a Tub*, then, including Swift's, becomes – like all performances – a paradigm of liminality.

Consistent with this condition of liminality, Swift keeps us on the boundary between what Hobbes defines as two kinds of personation. "A person," Hobbes says, "is he, *whose words or actions are considered, either as his own, or as representing the words or actions of another man ... whether truly or by fiction.* When they are considered as his own, then is he called a *natural person*: and when they are considered as representing the words and actions of another, then is he a *feigned* or *artificial person*."[50]

These two kinds of personation extend to the two meanings of performance singled out at the beginning of this essay – the sense of performance as the pursuit of a personal obligation or duty that constitutes a form of self-fulfilment and performance as "put on" and mimicry. Swift's behaviour in relation to these two meanings of *performance* is far from clear and decidedly mixed. On the one hand, Swift's comments on the *Tale* suggest that he took pride in the performance of his duty to expose the abuses in religion and learning. On the other hand, the *Tale* is a *tour de force*, and by any measure a magnificent *performance*. Indeed, Swift's contemporaries frequently single the *Tale* out for both praise and blame with the word *performance*. It is equally clear that Swift took pleasure in performing what Claude

---

[46]   *A Tale of a Tub*, eds Guthkelch and Smith, p. 161.
[47]   Kinahan, "The Melancholy of Anatomy," p. 280.
[48]   See Judith C. Mueller, "Writing under Constraint: Swift's 'Apology' for *A Tale of a Tub*," *English Literary History*, 60 (1993), 101–3.
[49]   See *A Tale of a Tub*, eds Guthkelch and Smith, p. 30.
[50]   *Leviathan*, ed. Oakeshott, p. 105.
[51]   "The Character of Swift's Satire: Reflections on Swift, Johnson, and Human Restlessness," *The Character of Swift's Satire: A Revised Focus*, ed. Claude Rawson (Newark, London, Toronto, 1983), pp. 80, 64.

Rawson calls his "feats of anarchic mimicry" – even at the risk of appearing to "endorse the language of his speakers."[51] Such double realities of purpose and play, of course, complicate and enrich many of Swift's writings, and in the case of *A Tale of a Tub*, he refuses to sort them out. Indeed, like Ben Jonson in *Volpone*, "it is precisely the uneasy synthesis between a formal antitheatricalism, which condemns the arts of show and illusion on the one hand, and a subversive hankering after them on the other, that lends" to Swift's writing its "precarious equilibrium."[52] Like the classical figure of the *Parodist*, he is always singing beside/against.

---

[52]  *The Antitheatrical Prejudice*, p. 154.

Rudolf Freiburg

*Universität Erlangen-Nürnberg*

# "*Strip, Tear, Pull, Rent, Flay off all*": The Mechanical Reduction of Satire in Swift's *Tale*[1]

How shrunk is every Thing,
as it appears in the Glass of Nature?

ABSTRACT. Critics have often remarked on the enigmatic character of Swift's *Tale* without explaining it convincingly. In the following article, both the techniques of reduction and the principle of semantic gravitation are regarded as explanations for the hermeneutical problems that the text creates. Based on the assumption that Swift's use of devices such as "formal reduction," "reduction of mind to matter," "reduction of matter to nothing," as well as "*reductio ad absurdum*" contribute to the obscurity of the satire, these techniques are disclosed as self-referential. Swift's *Tale* is consistently interpreted as a self-effacing construction. In a world of extreme semantic gravitation, even norms are doomed to collapse. Turning the Hack's predilection for syllogisms against himself, satire and irrationality prove to be forms of reduction. To put it succinctly, satire is tantamount to madness.

Describing Swift's *Tale*, Samuel Johnson strictly censures Swift's base "delight in revolving [*sic*] ideas," but his comment on this famous satire on the errors in religion and learning displays a considerable degree of both admiration and amazement:

> His *Tale of a Tub* has little resemblance to his other pieces ... It is of a mode so distinct and peculiar, that it must be considered by itself; what is true of that, is not true of anything else which he has written.[2]

It is precisely a satiric device, namely semantic gravitation combined with three modes of reduction, to which the *Tale* owes its uniqueness.[3] In a world of "semantic gravitation,"

---

[1] For the linguistic support that I received for this article, I would like to thank my friend and former colleague John Coates, Seminar für Englische Philologie, Georg-August-Universität, Göttingen. I am also obliged to Evelyn Werner-Kretschmar and Jackie Wittig for typing parts of this article.

[2] Samuel Johnson, "Jonathan Swift (1667–1745)," *Lives of the English Poets*, ed. L. Archer-Hind (London and New York, 1968 [1925]), II, 267. For further reactions to Swift's *Tale*, see Donald M. Berwick, *The Reputation of Jonathan Swift, 1781–1882* (New York, 1965 [1941]), pp. 35–38; 68–71; 105–8; 143–48.

[3] As early as 1969, Joseph Bentley, in a brilliant essay on the techniques of reduction, "Semantic Gravitation: An Essay on Satiric Reduction," *Modern Language Quarterly*, 30 (1969), 3–19, showed the importance of "semantic gravitation" for satire, and almost ten years later, Werner v. Koppenfels analysed the impact of *meiosis* in the use of metaphors

Swift's *Tale of a Tub* adopts the role of a black hole, sending gravitational waves through a cosmos of folly, destroying planetary systems of learning that spin round dead suns such as Aristotelian philosophy, Gnosticism, or arcane learning, and rearranging the galaxies of religion. In assigning a unique character to the *Tale*, Johnson anticipates the awkward attempt of modern mathematicians to describe the state of black holes as a "state of singularity" in which all conventional rules of physics and mathematics break down.[4] For the universe, or rather the bipartite "duoverse" of Swift's satire,[5] singularity means that the wonted principles of his satire are no longer valid.

I

Like other artists, the writer strives to adopt the role of an *alter deus* longing for the realization of unity and harmony, symmetry and proportion in his own artificial or literary universe.[6] Renouncing these principles by favouring the paradoxical concept of a "formless form," the author gives up the role of *alter deus*. Being of divine origin, the word serves as a minimal emblem of sense, displaying a bipartite structure consisting of both matter and mind that mirrors the whole universe as a cabbalistic "physico-theological" concoction of not-God and God, of substance and idea, of physicality and spirituality, of time and timelessness, of decay and sublimity. These ideas portray the universe as a state of inherent Manichean dichotomies,[7] as a blend of sublimity and grossness, even of good and evil,[8] or, to put it in the familiar terms of the Elizabethans, as a combination of both superlunary and sublunary forces.[9] The literary nature of the universe is most appropriately expressed in the formula of God's two books, the Bible on the one hand and the "Book of Nature" on the other.[10] Interpretations of both the Bible and the "Book of Nature"

---

in Swift's *Tale*; see "Swifts *Tale of a Tub* und die Tradition satirischer Metaphorik," *Deutsche Vierteljahrsschrift für Literaturwissenschaft und Geistesgeschichte*, 51 (1977), 27–54.

[4]  See Stephen Hawking, *A Brief History of Time: From the Big Bang to Black Holes* (London, 1990 [1988]), p. 49.

[5]  This idea, of course, refers to the "A-B structure" of formal verse satire; see Mary Claire Randolph, "The Structural Design of the Formal Verse Satire," *Philological Quarterly*, 21 (1942), 368–84; see also Howard D. Weinbrot, "The Pattern of Formal Verse Satire in the Restoration and the Eighteenth Century," *Publications of the Modern Language Association of America*, 80 (1965), 394–401.

[6]  See Martin C. Battestin, *The Providence of Wit: Aspects of Form in Augustan Literature and the Arts* (Oxford, 1974), pp. 141–63.

[7]  See also Philip Pinkus, *Swift's Vision of Evil: A Comparative Study of "A Tale of a Tub" and "Gulliver's Travels," I: A Tale of a Tub* (University of Victoria, 1975), 57–68, who presents a brief but informative sketch of Gnosticism.

[8]  See Paul Watzlawick, *Vom Schlechten des Guten oder Hekates Lösungen* (München und Zürich, 1991 [1986]).

[9]  See E. M. W. Tillyard, *The Elizabethan World Picture* (Harmondsworth, 1972 [1943]).

[10]  For information on the metaphor of the "Book of Nature," I am deeply indebted to Professor Ernst Friedrich Ohly, Münster. See also Erich Rothacker, *Das "Buch der Natur:" Materialien und Grundsätzliches zur Metapherngeschichte* (Bonn, 1979), and Hans Blumenberg, *Die Lesbarkeit der Welt* (Frankfurt/M., 1981). See also the survey of the metaphor's history in Ernst Robert Curtius, *Europäische Literatur und lateinisches Mittelalter* (Tübingen und Basel, 1993 [1948]), pp. 306–52. Besides Paracelsus (p. 325), who deeply influenced Swift's *Tale*, Curtius mentions Bacon, John Owen, and Sir Thomas Browne (p. 326) as well as Donne, Milton, Vaughan, Herbert, and Crashaw (p. 327) as authors who favoured the metaphor.

to a certain extent try to invert the process of creation, of turning matter into mind, endeavouring to discover God's intention as expressed in biblical stories and the hieroglyphics of creation. On the whole, writing and hermeneutics are sustained efforts of refinement, sublimation, and purification,[11] attempts to slough off the terrestrial burden of physicality of both words and bodies.[12] Especially in biblical exegesis, the doctrine of the three spiritual meanings of a word,[13] "allegorical," "tropological," and "anagogical,"[14] demonstrate the persistent attempt to attain the sublime state of Platonic ideas. In the mode of literary alchemy, nature is transformed into spirit, physicality into spirituality. In an act of interpretation that reveals both faith and optimism, the "Book of Nature" is subjected to an essential transubstantiation.

As an Anglican divine, Swift was well read in ancient poetics. He was not only familiar with the patristic tradition of the *ars interpretandi*; he also borrowed its technical terms.[15] But the absence of a "concept of nature" in Swift's *Tale* is amazing. Nature gives way to artificiality. With Swift, the concept of a "Book of Nature" is replaced by the "nature of the book." The optimism inherent in the spiritual interpretation of the world yields to cynicism and skepticism, as well as to an attempt to vex the world, to a satiric pessimism of Augustinian rather than Augustan origin. By way of an anagram, the *Tale of a Tub* may be interpreted as the tale of an everlasting "But," as a denial of belief in the inherent meaning of existence. Swift's favourite tool of destroying the false optimism of a Pelagean shape is semantic gravitation combined with reduction.[16] Swift shows a predilection for three modes of reduction: reduction of form, reduction of mind to matter, and logical reduction or *reductio ad absurdum*.[17]

---

11  These ideas were also cherished by Gnosticism; see Ronald Paulson, *Theme and Structure in Swift's "Tale of a Tub"* (New Haven, 1960), pp. 96–122.

12  See, for example, the logic of Metaphysical Poetry, with Donne's "The Ecstasy" as a case in point. See also the inspiring chapter "Mirror of Creation" in A. J. Smith, *Metaphysical Wit* (Cambridge, New York, Melbourne, 1991), pp. 7–20. David Nokes in his *Jonathan Swift: A Hypocrite Reversed* (Oxford, 1985), p. 49, defines Swift's puns as "incarnations, a constant process of words becoming flesh and spirit becoming substance." See also Thomas E. Maresca, "Language and Body in Augustan Poetic," *English Literary History*, 37 (1970), 374–88.

13  See Everett Zimmerman, *Swift's Narrative Satires: Author and Authority* (Ithaca and London, 1983), pp. 39–60; Zimmerman lists useful sources of information on "biblical exegesis" on p. 44n4.

14  See Friedrich Ohly, "Vom geistigen Sinn des Wortes im Mittelalter," *Schriften zur mittelalterlichen Bedeutungsforschung* (Darmstadt, 1977), pp. 1–31.

15  See Jonathan Swift, *A Tale of a Tub: To which is added, The Battle of the Books, and the Mechanical Operation of the Spirit*, eds A. C. Guthkelch and D. Nichol Smith (Oxford, 1973 [1958]), p. 61; all quotations are taken from this edition. For the meaning of "type" in biblical interpretation, see Friedrich Ohly, "Halbbiblische und außerbiblische Typologie," *Schriften zur mittelalterlichen Bedeutungsforschung*, pp. 361–400.

16  According to John Traugott, "A Tale of a Tub," *The Character of Swift's Satire: A Revised Focus*, ed. Claude Rawson (Newark, London, Toronto, 1983), p. 122, Swift reduces "sublime pretensions to their elemental coprology." In his *Swift and Anglican Rationalism: The Religious Background of "A Tale of a Tub"* (Chicago, 1961), Phillip Harth meticulously analyses the analogies between reductive systems and "enthusiasm;" see, for instance, pp. 64, 65, 78.

17  I shall not concentrate on the reduction of wholes to particulars; the technique of employing a part for the whole (*pars pro toto*) though frequently to be observed in the *Tale* is not an important aspect of "semantic gravitation."

## II

The simplest mode of reduction in the *Tale* is formal. Instead of conveying the impression of unity, coherence, or proportion, the *Tale* seems to be a hodge-podge of diversities,[18] a super-conceit of heterogeneous ideas and themes "yoked by violence together."[19] The Hack praises the advantages of rambling in one of his numerous digressions;[20] reducing coherence to "amorphy" makes sense[21] since the Moderns prefer "diversion" to "instruction." He compares the *Tale* to a "*Soup*," an "*Ollio*," a "*Fricassée*" or "*Ragout*,"[22] insinuating that this is the only food fit for the stomachs of his intellectual *gourmands*.[23] The form of formlessness cheats any expectations since the heuristic function of literary genre ceases to work.[24] Essayistic in structure, the *Tale* lacks formal teleology and logic, causality and clear chronology. The amorphous structure, characterized by a high degree of primitive enumeration and addition, mirrors a stream of reduced consciousness that might best be described as meandering.[25]

By simply imitating literary conventions, in particular the rhetorical *topoi* of his day,[26] Swift manages to ridicule them. In this case, reduction consists of a process of denuding texts of their meaning.[27] By mechanically enumerating apology, forewords, and dedications, he renders them stale; no generic purpose is to be detected; they lack teleology or sense.[28] In his own words, the Hack is unable to deliver anything that "is to the Purpose."[29] Swift's

---

[18] The *Tale* thus discloses an "anti-Ciceronian" nature, an "order-in-disorder" and a structure comparable to that of an encyclopaedia; see Paulson, *Theme and Structure in Swift's "Tale of a Tub*," pp. 233–34.

[19] See Johnson, "Abraham Cowley," *Lives of the English Poets*, I, 11. For Swift's technique of eclectically reducing anti-Quaker propaganda to pointed ingredients of his satire, see Hugh Ormsby-Lennon, "Swift and the Quakers (I)," *Swift Studies*, 4 (1989), 34–62.

[20] See *Tale*, p. 144.

[21] For the idea that the *Tale* "is the literary approximation of chaos," see Battestin, *The Providence of Wit*, p. 230.

[22] For a discussion of the parallels between Swift's *Tale* and the seventeenth-century anatomies of Nash, Burton, and Browne, see Paulson, *Theme and Structure in Swift's "Tale of a Tub*," pp. 1–34.

[23] See *Tale*, pp. 143–44.

[24] Genre governs understanding; see Klaus W. Hempfer, *Gattungstheorie: Information und Synthese* (München, 1973), and the concept of "genre" in E. D. Hirsch, Jr, *Validity in Interpretation* (New Haven and London, 1967), pp. 68–126.

[25] Claude Rawson talks of "centrifugal energies of the form;" see "Order and Cruelty: A Reading of Swift (with some Comments on Pope and Johnson)," *Modern Critical Views: Jonathan Swift*, ed. Harold Bloom (New York, New Haven, Philadelphia, 1986), p. 105. Everett Zimmerman interprets the *Tale* as "energy without form;" see *Swift's Narrative Satires: Author and Authority*, p. 60.

[26] See *Tale*, p. 45.

[27] Swift probably criticizes mechanical writing and "mechanical preaching;" see Eugene R. Hammond, "In Praise of Wisdom and the Will of God: Erasmus' *Praise of Folly* and Swift's *A Tale of a Tub*," *Studies in Philology*, 80 (1983), 254.

[28] For an analysis of the relationship between mechanical behaviour and comedy or satire, see John M. Bullitt, *Jonathan Swift and the Anatomy of Satire: A Study of Satiric Technique* (Cambridge, MA, 1953), pp. 123–57, who bases his arguments on Bergson's theory of laughter. Writing without purpose furthermore ridicules the Baconian principle of "utilitarianism;" see Miriam Kosh Starkman, *Swift's Satire on Learning in "A Tale of a Tub"* (Princeton, NJ, 1950), p. 66.

[29] *Tale*, p. 144.

achievement lies in the fact that the Hack goes out of his way to show off his originality, but ironically ends up in reducing literary conventions to hackneyed clichés already dead at birth.[30] These texts are not able to conjure any spirit, neither in any ordinary nor in any extraordinary sense.[31] They seem to be castrated, purged of any genuine intention, and lay bare a fairly mechanical mode of introducing books.[32]

Even before the *Tale* starts with an apology, a list of titles allegedly written by the author is presented that covers treatises ranging from "characters," "essays," "histories," "voyages" to "descriptions" and "defences." The treatises again are formally reduced to titles. The "Annotations upon several Dozens," which the Hack promises, shrink to "a few Hints."[33] When the Hack, in his introduction to the *Tale*, proclaims that the author of alchemical treatises, the *Adeptus Artephius*, worked "wholly by *Reincrudation*," the same is true of himself.[34] According to *A Short Lexicon of Alchemy*, "*reincrudation*" is "the retrogradation of a substance which has reached a certain degree of perfection to a degree of a lower order."[35] In other words, *reincrudation* works hand in hand with semantic gravitation. Reduction here pays a satirical tribute to the impoverished intellectual capacities of modern scholars, who are only capable of learning with "little time and form," preferring a quick if superficial glimpse of a book instead of reading it. Indirectly, scholarship is identified with the mechanical repetition of titles and indexes, or to quote the mildly obscene view of the Hack, in which he burlesques Bacon's principle of *ordine retrogrado*:[36] "Thus Men catch Knowledge by throwing their *Wit* on the *Posteriors* of a book, as Boys do Sparrows with flinging *Salt* upon their *Tails*."[37]

Predilection for reductive systems of information induce the Hack to recommend "large *Indexes*, and little *Compendiums*," "*Quotations*," "*Lexicons*," "*Flowers*" and "*Observanda*."[38] With regard to books, reduction and condensation work hand in hand.[39] Again, the Grub Street sage portrays his obsession with all forms of arcane learning when he applies his forms of reduction to books. It is the idea of a literary philosopher's stone that sets the alchemical process of *reincrudation* going. The ideal that is inherent in this process and typical of modern lethargy is the general reduction of systems to *quintessentia*, to an essence that renders all sustained studies of theories redundant. In his "Digression in the Modern

---

[30] There is an interesting contrast between the Hack puffed up to "a kind of gigantism" and the deflative processes of reduction at work in the *Tale*; for the interpretation of the Hack as a "giant," see Peter Steele, *Jonathan Swift: Preacher and Jester* (Oxford, 1978), p. 73. Note also John R. Clark's observation that the Hack proves to be a disciple of Horace by pretending to develop an anti-Horatian poetology; see *Form and Frenzy in Swift's "Tale of a Tub"* (Ithaca and London, 1970), p. 229.

[31] See Hugh Ormsby-Lennon, "Swift's Spirit Reconjured: das Dong-an-sich," *Swift Studies*, 3 (1988), 9–78.

[32] This device helps to alienate the book as book; see William Kinsley, "Le 'mock-book,'" *Études Françaises*, 18 (1982), 43–60.

[33] *Tale*, p. 68.

[34] *Tale*, p. 68.

[35] "Notes on 'Dark Authors,'" *Tale*, p. 354.

[36] See Clark, *Form and Frenzy* in Swift's "*Tale of a Tub*," p. 210.

[37] *Tale*, p. 145.

[38] *Tale*, pp. 147–48; for a comparable recommendation of the using of extracts and epitomes, for instance by John Dunton, see Starkman, *Swift's Satire on Learning*, pp. 82–83.

[39] In his digressions, the Hack reduces "themes" to "fragments of themes;" see Starkman, *Swift's Satire on Learning*, p. 145.

Kind," the Hack dreams of reducing "an universal System in a small portable Volume, of all Things that are to be Known, or Believed, or Imagined, or Practised in Life."[40] The alchemical reduction of complex theories to essential substances is broadly documented throughout the *Tale*. A case in point is the Receipt, or *Nostrum*, which the narrator found in the papers of a late philosopher of *O. Brazile*:

> YOU take fair correct Copies, well bound in Calfs Skin, and Lettered at the Back, of all Modern Bodies of Arts and Sciences whatsoever, and in what Language you please. These you distil in *balneo Mariæ*, infusing *Quintessence of Poppy Q. S.* together with three Pints of *Lethe*, to be had from the Apothecaries. You cleanse away carefully the *Sordes* and *Caput mortuum*, letting all that is volatile evaporate. You preserve only the first Running, which is again to be distilled seventeen times, till what remains will amount to about two Drams. This you keep in a Glass Viol *Hermetically* sealed, for one and twenty Days. Then you begin your Catholick Treatise, taking every Morning fasting, (first shaking the Viol) three Drops of this *Elixir*, snuffing it strongly up your Nose. It will dilate it self about the Brain (where there is any) in fourteen Minutes, and you immediately perceive in your Head an infinite Number of *Abstracts, Summaries, Compendiums, Extracts, Collections, Medulla's, Excerpta quædam's, Florilegia's* and the like, all disposed into great Order, and reducible upon Paper.[41]

The alchemical production of quintessential knowledge is self-descriptive, providing a key to the understanding of *A Tale of a Tub*. One might of course argue whether a reduction like this comes under the category of "reduction of form;" but it seems indisputable that formal aspects like "weight," "bulk," "length" of a book are alluded to.[42] Formal reduction does not stop here.[43] The Hack even reduces "wit" to a typographic signal boasting "that whatever word or Sentence is Printed in a different Character, shall be judged to contain something extraordinary either of *Wit* or *Sublime*."[44] Numbers favoured by Gnostic and cabbalistic arithmetic,[45] in particular the number "three,"[46] provide other conspicuous systems of reduction.

Whereas reductive systems like those described by alchemy condense substance, others split language and meaning. The best example presented in the *Tale* is the attempt, by one of the brothers, to bring the Father's will into line with new developments in fashion. The

---

[40]  *Tale*, p. 125.

[41]  *Tale*, pp. 126–27; for the parallels between this passage and the doctrine of the Rosicrucians, see Starkman, *Swift's Satire on Learning*, p. 53.

[42]  The insinuation is, of course, that "scribblers are waste-makers above all;" see Pat Rogers, *Hacks and Dunces: Pope, Swift and Grub Street* (London and New York, 1980 [1972]), p. 181. See also Frances Deutsch Louis, *Swift's Anatomy of Misunderstanding: A Study of Swift's Epistemological Imagination in "A Tale of a Tub" and "Gulliver's Travels"* (London, 1981), pp. 66–67, and Angus Ross, "The Books in the *Tale*: Swift and Reading in *A Tale of a Tub*," *Proceedings of The First Münster Symposium on Jonathan Swift*, eds Hermann J. Real and Heinz J. Vienken (München, 1985), pp. 209–16.

[43]  Even the syntax of several passages in the *Tale* displays the reduced musicality of a staccato rhythm; see the similar observation by Steele, *Jonathan Swift: Preacher and Jester*, p. 36.

[44]  *Tale*, pp. 46–47.

[45]  Numbers play a vital role in ancient and medieval literature; see Curtius, *Europäische Literatur und lateinisches Mittelalter*, pp. 491–98. For the idea that "mysticism … is merely a subtler form of materialism," see Battestin, *The Providence of Wit*, p. 232.

[46]  For the meaning of *gematria* as a method of interpreting letters as numbers and vice versa, see Harold Bloom, *Kabbalah and Criticism* (New York, 1975), p. 46. See also Papus, *Die Kabbala*, trans. Julius Nestler (Wiesbaden, 1991 [1980]), pp. 66–73.

first stage in the linguistic reduction process is expressed by the Latin term *totidem verbis*. As the words in the testament, however, do not serve the intended interpretative purposes, they are reduced to syllables, *totidem syllabis*. Since even the syllables do not enable the brothers to provide the desired effect, they, too, are reduced to letters, *totidem litteris*, which are then subjected to sophisticated techniques of finding anagrams.[47] In the *Tale*, even these shrivel into insignificance. Mind is turned into matter, and matter is liable to dissolve into air.[48]

What is true of the testament should, according to the Hack, also be applied to the *Tale*. Playing with the sexual connotations of the term "spirit" and the letter "O," which like Shakespeare's "zero" or "No-thing" symbolize the female pudenda, the Hack recommends this interpretative technique for the *Tale*:

> AND therefore in order to promote so useful a Work, I will here take Leave to glance a few *Innuendo*'s, that may be of great Assistance to those sublime Spirits, who shall be appointed to labor in a universal Comment upon this wonderful Discourse. And First, I have couched a very profound Mystery in the Number of O's multiply'd by *Seven*, and divided by *Nine*. Also, if a devout Brother of the *Rosy Cross* will pray fervently for sixty three Mornings, with a lively Faith, and then transpose certain Letters and Syllables according to Prescription, in the second and fifth Section; they will certainly reveal into a full Receit of the *Opus Magnum*.[49]

Any number "multiply'd by zero" will remain nil. And indeed, formal reduction in the *Tale* ends with nothing. Even a cursory reader will stop at the many footnotes of the text. Here whole treatises are reduced to simple formulae, presented in annotations that sometimes leave the reader uninformed. The marginal notes, too, provide but elliptical information. Even words are abbreviated, and treated as linguistic cripples unfit for peripatetic communication. Phrases like "*Hiatus in MS.*" or "*Hic multa desiderantur*,"[50] allegedly added by the editor, symbolize the reductive communication system of the *Tale*. Formal reduction ends in a gap. This, of course, is the reason for the plethora of blanks in the *Tale*.

## III

Next to formal reduction of books to titles, and titles to footnotes, words to syllables, syllables to letters, and these to nothing, the *Tale* is conspicuous for its reduction of the world of mind to a world of matter.[51] Literalization of metaphors is a sure sign of Swift's

---

[47] See *Tale*, pp. 83–84.

[48] In his chapter "Satiric Materialism in *A Tale of a Tub*" of his *Satire in Narrative: Petronius, Swift, Gibbon, Melville, and Pynchon* (Austin, TX, 1990), pp. 39–63, Frank Palmeri argues that Swift attacks both techniques of allegory and literalization. See also Martin Price, *Swift's Rhetorical Art: A Study in Structure and Meaning* (New Haven and London, 1953), pp. 89–90.

[49] *Tale*, pp. 186–87.

[50] *Tale*, pp. 62, 170.

[51] I owe much of this discussion to Louis, *Swift's Anatomy of Misunderstanding*; see also her quotation of Pascal, *Pensées*: "All philosophers confuse ideas of things, speaking of material things in terms of spirit and of spiritual things in terms of matter" (p. 106). Metaphysics are mechanized, prepared for the anatomist's table; see Starkman, *Swift's Satire on Learning*, p. 30. See also Harth, *Swift and Anglican Rationalism*, who refers to Cudworth's description of the "Atheist's Madness" as "*Pneumatophobia.*"

style.[52] Swift reduces "wit" to a "razor," "criticism" to "bad breath," "satire" to "a tennis ball;" he takes the metaphor of a "mirror" verbatim and literally analyses the meaning of a "brain on a rack."[53] Examples of this form of reduction in the *Tale* are legion. By blurring the line between physicality and spirituality, Swift manages to render even abstract ideas vulnerable. As in the "Voyage to Laputa,"[54] he reduces words to *signifiants*, eliminating their immaterial *signifié*. Reducing mind to matter, he bestows weight and bulkiness on concepts, doctrines, ideas, and systems, thus mischievously subjecting them to the laws of semantic gravitation.[55]

Even more important is his inversion of traditional techniques of philology. Instead of using language as a vantage point to set the mind free, language with Swift serves as a kind of intellectual trap, fixing the errant mind and binding it by gravitational laws.[56] Patristic interpreters, for example, employed the analysis of "proprieties" in order to show a way out of the "prison house of language,"[57] endeavouring – in the words of the Hack – to "exalt" them, to spiritualize and refine them "from the Dross and Grossness of *Sense* and *Human Reason*."[58] Swift's analysis, however, only examines the proprieties of doctrines and ideas in order to confer the nature of materialism to them, so that they can easily be pulled down to the sublunary realm where they become susceptible to physical decay and transitoriness.[59] The Hack ties weights to the heels of philosophical systems and religious beliefs,[60] forcing them to sink to the centre of his black hole where they are to be anatomized.[61] Displaying

---

[52] For a discussion of literalization, see, for instance, Michael V. DePorte, *Nightmares and Hobbyhorses: Swift, Sterne, and Augustan Ideas of Madness* (San Marino, 1974), p. 70; Maurice J. Quinlan, "Swift's Use of Literalization as a Rhetorical Device," *Publications of the Modern Language Association of America*, 82 (1967), 516–21. For the epistemological importance of metaphors, see Hans Blumenberg, "Paradigmen einer Metaphorologie," *Archiv für Begriffsgeschichte*, 6 (1960), 1–142.

[53] See *Tale*, pp. 49, 52, 103, 114; see also the concrete metaphors for "Truth": "Fox," "Cheese," "Hen," "Sack-Posset," and "Nut;" *Tale*, p. 66.

[54] See *Prose Works*, XI, 185–86 (III, v, 19–23).

[55] See Ormsby-Lennon, "Swift and the Quakers (I)," p. 41: "Throughout the *Tub*, we can glimpse Quaker principles grossly embodied in lubricious or scatological physicality; as always in his satire, Swift reduces doctrinal nicety and theological subtlety to their lowest common denominator."

[56] Swift lays snares even for his readers; see Brian McCrea, "Surprised by Swift: Entrapment and Escape in *A Tale of a Tub*," *Papers on Language and Literature*, 18 (1982), 234–44.

[57] I employ this term as a translation of the German "Proprietätenanalyse"; see Ohly, "Vom geistigen Sinn des Wortes im Mittelalter," *Schriften zur mittelalterlichen Bedeutungsforschung*, pp. 1–31.

[58] See *Tale*, pp. 61–62.

[59] For the importance of the theme of "corruption" in Swift's thinking, see Deborah Baker Wyrick, *Jonathan Swift and the Vested Word* (Chapel Hill and London, 1988), pp. 36–37. See also the interpretation of "decay" as an attack on the idea of progress by Starkman, *Swift's Satire on Learning*, pp. 8–9.

[60] See *Tale*, p. 32; the religious problems are explained by Harth, *Swift and Anglican Rationalism, passim*; Harth's position has been slightly modified by Roger D. Lund, "Strange Complicities: Atheism and Conspiracy in *A Tale of a Tub*," *Eighteenth-Century Life*, 13 (1989), 34–58. See also Irvin Ehrenpreis, "The Doctrine of *A Tale of a Tub*," *Proceedings of The First Münster Symposium on Jonathan Swift*, eds Real and Vienken, pp. 59–71.

[61] For the role of anatomy in the *Tale*, see Louis, *Swift's Anatomy of Misunderstanding*, pp. 7–8. Angus Ross believes that the satire of the *Tale* is placed "within the context of an 'Anatomy Lesson;'" see "*The Anatomy of Melancholy* and Swift," *Swift and his Contexts*, eds John Irwin Fischer, Hermann J. Real, and James Woolley (New York, 1989), p. 150.

a smattering of alchemical knowledge in "The Preface," the Hack illustrates the reductive process at work in the *Tale* when he compares "wit" to "mercury" which the *Moderns* attempt to "fix":

> The *Moderns* have artfully fixed this *Mercury*, and reduced it to the Circumstances of Time, Place and Person. Such a Jest there is, that will not pass out of *Covent-Garden*; and such a one, that is no where intelligible but at *Hide-Park* Corner.[62]

Reducing abstracts like wit to place and time is typical of modern frenzy.[63] This form of reduction mirrors the satire of a staunch hermeneutic belief of the time, expressed in Pope's *Essay on Criticism*, where the poet recommends:

> A perfect Judge will *read* each Work of Wit
> With the same Spirit that its Author *writ*.[64]

The sanity of this advice is burlesqued by semantic gravitation since Swift supersedes Pope's "spirit" by a materialized version of the hermeneutic conditions of understanding:

> Whatever Reader desires to have a thorow Comprehension of an Author's Thoughts, cannot take a better Method, than by putting himself into the Circumstances and Postures of Life, that the Writer was in, upon every important Passage as it flow'd from his Pen.[65]

And the reader learns that the ingenious author wrote the *Tale* in bed, was extremely hungry, had taken medicine, and was suffering from poverty. It seems as if the word "Condition" had really "descend[ed] to the very *bottom* of all the *Sublime*,"[66] distorted by the forces of gravitation.

In his physico-logical scheme, which reforms the erroneous notions of regarding words as "types, emblems, shadows, and symbols,"[67] the Hack sets out to prove the materiality of both air and words.[68] In his analysis of "Oratorial Machines," he insinuates that words are mechanically produced by machines, denuded of spirituality, reduced to the bulk and weight of matter. "Wit," "Passions," "Conceits," "Bombast," and "Buffoonry" are interpreted in terms of "Gravity," some of them sinking down to the centre of the earth, some of them soaring up.[69] It is only consistent that the Hack recommends judging books, which may justly be considered tubs of material letters, according to their "Weight and Number."[70]

Alchemical transformation of mind into matter also takes place in the tale proper. Here Jack plays the role of the *adeptus*, considering his Father's will to be not of an immaterial

---

[62] *Tale*, p. 43.

[63] For the affinity between wit, satire, and London topography, see Rogers, *Hacks and Dunces*, pp. 1–17.

[64] Alexander Pope, "An Essay on Criticism," ll. 233–34, *Pastoral Poetry and An Essay on Criticism*, eds E. Audra and Aubrey Williams (London and New Haven, 1961), The Twickenham Edition of the Poems of Alexander Pope, I, 266.

[65] *Tale*, p. 44.

[66] *Tale*, p. 44.

[67] See *Tale*, p. 61.

[68] The emblem itself can be considered a highly reductive system by which complicated theological and philosophical theories are simplified and distorted; see Thomas Stephen Kingston, "Hieroglyphs, Characters, and Concepts: The Emblematic Imagery in Swift's *Tale* Satires," diss., Northwestern University, 1980, pp. 37; 48–49.

[69] See *Tale*, pp. 60–61.

[70] *Tale*, p. 64; see also Section VI, p. 140, where arguments are judged in terms of "*Levity*" and "*Gravity*."

kind but of "deep" and "dark matter" waiting to be transformed. He even looks upon it as a *panacea* or *Philosopher's Stone*:

> He had a Way of working it into any Shape he pleased; so that it served him for a Night-cap when he went to Bed, and for an Umbrello in rainy Weather. He would lap a Piece of it about a sore Toe, or when he had Fits, burn two Inches under his Nose; or if any Thing lay heavy on his Stomach, scrape off, and swallow as much of the Powder as would lie on a silver Penny, they were all infallible Remedies.[71]

Nowhere does Swift demonstrate his talent of inverted transubstantiation,[72] his alchemical skill of transforming mind into matter, more convincingly than in his description of Aeolism.[73] The Aeolist system with its reduction of each and every thing to wind,[74] of pulling down the lofty ideals of religion to the tangible sphere of materialism, serves as a case in point of satirical alchemy. Mirroring the tradition of deflating the *alazon*, the inflated Aeolists serve as perfect butts for satirical strategies of *meiosis*.[75] Semantic gravitation deflates the children of the wind, who would otherwise blow themselves out of existence. It is not only the level of materialism to which Swift chains them by way of semantic gravity; he also impels them to descend to the level of putrid matter. Whatever functions scatology in other works by Swift may serve,[76] in the *Tale* it symbolizes a state of matter in decay,[77] of fetid substance and offensive waste. This is the reason why Swift makes his narrator reduce alleged religious messages to the art of belching:

> Upon these Reasons, and others of equal Weight, the Wise *Æolists*, affirm the Gift of BELCHING, to be the noblest Act of a Rational Creature ... At certain Seasons of the Year, you might behold the Priests amongst them in vast Numbers, with their *Mouths gaping wide against a Storm*. At other times were to be seen several Hundreds link'd together in a circular Chain, with every Man a Pair of Bellows applied to his Neighbour's Breech, by which they blew up each other to the Shape and Size of a *Tun*; and for that Reason, with great Propriety of Speech, did usually call their Bodies, their *Vessels*.[78]

It is not only life that shrinks to "breath;" so does wind in its various forms of "*Forma Informans*," "*Spiritus*," "*Animus*," "*Afflatus*" or "*Anima*."[79] Alluding to the widespread doctrine of the humours, the Hack associates venerable phenomena like inspiration with the

---

[71] *Tale*, pp. 190–91.

[72] For a similar use of this theological term, see Nokes, *Jonathan Swift*, p. 51.

[73] See *Tale*, pp. 150–61.

[74] Swift here obviously refers to the pre-Socratic reductive philosophies of Heraclitus, Thales, and especially Anaximenes; see Harth, *Swift and Anglican Rationalism*, p. 66. For the relationship between Aeolism and the Eulysian Mysteries, see William Kupersmith, "Swift's Aeolists and the Delphic Oracle," *Modern Philology*, 82 (1984–85), 190–94.

[75] See Bentley, "Semantic Gravitation: An Essay on Satiric Reduction," pp. 356–61. See also Hugh Ormsby-Lennon, "Swift and the Quakers (II)," *Swift Studies*, 5 (1990), 53–89.

[76] In Swift's view, "bodies" and their scatological aspects are highly comical; see Jean-Paul Forster, *Jonathan Swift: The Fictions of the Satirist* (Bern, Frankfurt/M., New York, 1991), pp. 125–94; 214.

[77] Treating mind and words as excrement displays a deconstructive allegory of writing; see Wyrick, *Jonathan Swift and the Vested Word*, pp. 119–20; 121: "Whereas excrement is an externalized inside of physical bodies, words are the externalized inside of textual bodies." For a drastic description of this particular state of words, see Carol Houlihan Flynn, *The Body in Swift and Defoe* (Cambridge, New York, Melbourne, 1990), pp. 88–109; 207.

[78] *Tale*, p. 153.

[79] Swift's doctrine of Aeolism was influenced by occult books like Thomas Vaughan's *Anthroposophia Theomagica*; see Starkman, *Swift's Satire on Learning*, pp. 44–47.

sordid gases produced by the human body, in particular belching and flatulence.[80] With him, even soaring spirits, capable of conquering a kingdom, are likely to "conclude in a *Fistula in Ano*."[81] Furthermore, the description of the Aeolists bristles with sexual innuendoes. Spiritual ecstasy is confounded with carnal ecstasy,[82] and the mechanical reduction of flatulence by attaching a machine to the "Posteriors" of an Aeolist priest can hardly be called innocent. But besides deflating Puritan zeal and enthusiasm by associating them with corporeality and sexuality,[83] Swift reduces both religion and learning to nil. In a preposterous syllogism, the narrator demonstrates the ontological vacuity of learning and religion: "*Words are but Wind; and Learning is nothing but Words*; Ergo, *Learning is nothing but Wind*."[84]

Critics have often remarked not only on the predominance of materialism in the *Tale*, but also on the narrator's obsession with surface.[85] In celebrating surfaces, another form of reduction becomes manifest. The tale proper of course exemplifies the importance of this theme. With the universe treated as a piece of cloth or "micro-coat," the sartorial metaphor is turned into an instrument which illustrates the significance of appearance and surface. Sartorial philosophy takes the world at face value, reducing its depth to a state of shallow existence. Any form of metaphysics is turned into physics, paying tribute to the "tyranny of facts."[86] In the *Tale*, texts are dressed according to the common vogue in "Types" and "Fables,"[87] displaying beautiful externals without serving the end to teach any longer. Modern obsession with delight is illustrated by the ambition to polish surfaces. The Horatian twin-formula of "*prodesse et delectare*" is reduced to its hedonistic element. The paradoxical inversion of outward and inward, the ludicrous claim that a man's outward appearance is his soul, demonstrates that the Grub Street philosopher endeavours to grasp nothing but the appearance of things. In his distorted view, religion is reduced to a "*Cloak*," "Honesty" to a "*Pair of Shoes*," "Self-love" to a "*Surtout*," "Vanity" to a "*Shirt*," and "Conscience" to a "*Pair of Breeches*."[88] This infatuation with surface, the Hack leaves no doubt, has epistemological and eudemonological consequences. Reduction guarantees hap-

---

[80]  See Ehrenpreis, *Mr Swift*, p. 198. The myth of illumination is reduced "to epidemic indigestion;" see Kenneth Craven, *Jonathan Swift and the Millennium of Madness: The Information Age in Swift's "A Tale of a Tub"* (Leiden, New York, Köln, 1992), p. 199; see also DePorte, *Nightmares and Hobbyhorses*, pp. 60–66.

[81]  *Tale*, p. 166.

[82]  See *Tale*, p. 157.

[83]  For the general meaning of "association" in satire, see James W. Nichols, *Insinuation: The Tactics of English Satire* (The Hague and Paris, 1971), pp. 90–98. The tradition of Puritan satire is copiously documented by William P. Holden, *Anti-Puritan Satire, 1572–1642* (New Haven and London, 1954). See also C. M. Webster, "Swift's *Tale of a Tub* Compared with Earlier Satires of the Puritans," *Publications of the Modern Language Association of America*, 47 (1932), 171–78.

[84]  *Tale*, p. 153.

[85]  It is the "modern conceit" of "ordering surface information into rational systems rather than mining for wisdom;" see Craven, *Jonathan Swift and the Millennium of Madness*, p. 7. The whole discussion of "surfaces" in the *Tale* is influenced by the opposition of "curiosity" *versus* "credulity;" see, for example, Clark, *Form and Frenzy in Swift's "Tale of a Tub*," pp. 3–36; Richard Burrow, "Credulity and Curiosity in *A Tale of a Tub*," *Interpretation*, 15 (1987), 309–21, and Richard Nash, "Entrapment and Ironic Modes in 'Tale of a Tub,'" *Eighteenth-Century Studies*, 24 (1991), 415–31.

[86]  See Louis, *Swift's Anatomy of Misunderstanding*, p. 27.

[87]  *Tale*, p. 66.

[88]  *Tale*, p. 78.

piness, one of the *Tale*'s messages proffering deception as the definition of felicity. According to the Hack, reality should be reduced to its appearance because trying to peep behind the scenes would inevitably lead to disappointment and melancholy:

> Last Week I saw a Woman *flay'd*, and you will hardly believe, how much it altered her Person for the worse. Yesterday I ordered the Carcass of a *Beau* to be stript in my Presence; when we were all amazed to find so many unsuspected Faults under one Suit of Cloaths: Then I laid open his *Brain*, his *Heart*, and his *Spleen*; But, I plainly perceived at every Operation, that the farther we proceeded, we found the Defects encrease upon us in Number and Bulk.[89]

Although the means the Hack recommends in order to remedy the deficiency of an impaired outward appearance seem to run counter to the argument of this essay since he advises philosophers and projectors to practise the art of "patch[ing] up the Flaws and Imperfections of Nature," this recommendation is only a subtle form of reduction: in reality a human being is reduced to corporeality and mere appearance. Though the Hack's eudemonology claims to be modern, paradoxically it is anti-Baconian; it is a triumph of those very idols of which Bacon in his *Advancement of Learning* had endeavoured to purge philosophy. The Hack's definition of happiness, as "*a perpetual Possession of being well Deceived*," and as "the Serene Peaceful State of being a Fool among Knaves," may be considered a belittlement of modern achievements in philosophy since it paradoxically tries to usher in a pre-Baconian age of modernism.[90]

# IV

To list all evidence of *reductio ad absurdum* in the *Tale* would be an absurd enterprise in itself.[91] The *Tale* teems with absurdities of minor and major importance.[92] Seen as a whole, it displays the features of an absurd artefact with its innumerable contradictions, fallacies, and paradoxes. Most of the quotations that have been listed under the categories of "formal reduction" and "reduction of mind to matter" could also be classified as reduction to the absurd. One funny example of absurdity is the egotistic interpretation of the Latin phrase, "*DETUR DIGNISSIMO*,"[93] a stock phrase of dedications, as an honour the Hack is inclined to attribute to himself. Precision, usually the hallmark of serious scholarly work, is rendered grotesque when the Hack in his "Preface" restricts the number of Wits in England to precisely "nine thousand seven hundred forty and three Persons,"[94] of which he himself, we may

---

[89] *Tale*, pp. 173–74; Swift probably found the idea of a "flay'd woman" in Burton's *Anatomy*. A source for Burton was Chrisostom; see Prem Nath, "The Background of Swift's Flayed Woman," *Forum for Modern Language Studies*, 20 (1984), 363–66.

[90] See *Tale*, pp. 171, 174. – One satirical butt of this definition is Shaftesbury's philosophy; see Craven, *Jonathan Swift and the Millennium of Madness*, pp. 85–108; especially p. 89.

[91] For the general meaning of *reductio ad absurdum* in satire, see Nichols, *Insinuation*, pp. 85–86.

[92] Even the narrator is absurd, a figure reduced to the absurdity of Lilliputian nature. He can hardly be considered reliable, since he has given up his authority; see, for instance, Zimmerman, *Swift's Narrative Satires*, p. 40.

[93] *Tale*, p. 23.

[94] *Tale*, p. 41. – For the Gnostic and cabbalistic meaning of numbers, see Papus, *Die Kabbala*, p. 66.

be sure, is one. Semantic gravitation starts to work when the Academy, which is to be estab-lished according to the example of Bacon's *House of Solomon* and the Royal Society, is described as consisting of different schools, of which the "*Pederastick* School, with *French* and *Italian* Masters" is the first. Authorial intention is reduced to absurdity when the author declares, that "something ... profound" is to be expected whenever he is not understood.[95] There is no need to prove the ironical absurdity of the Hack's confession that he lacks a satirical vein and would rather embark on the project of praising the world in a treatise entitled *A Panegyrick upon the World.*[96] The sartorial philosophy of confounding Body and Soul, of inward and outward clothing, can only be accepted if the principle of a "willing suspension of disbelief" is carried to its extreme.[97] The reader cannot help laughing when he hears of the Hack's modest proposal that a true, that is mechanical, critic should commit suicide,[98] nor can he avoid identifying the tongue-in-cheek definition of the critic as a col-lector of mistakes who ends up presenting the "Quintessence of what is bad" in his own writing as "the thing that is not." The reduction of Moderns to Ancients is a bizarre stroke of genius worth quoting:

> These [Noble *Moderns*] have with unwearied Pains made many useful Searches into the weak sides of the *Antients*, and given us a comprehensive List of them. Besides, they have proved beyond contradiction, that the very finest Things delivered of old, have been long since invented, and brought to Light by much later Pens, and that the noblest Discoveries those *Antients* ever made, of Art or of Nature, have all been produced by the transcending Genius of the present Age.[99]

Just as in cosmic singularity caused by black holes, time loses its character,[100] chronology in the *Tale* is inverted. Small wonder, then, that the Hack suspects the Ancients to have imi-tated the Moderns.[101]

A brilliant example of absurdity is Lord Peter's project to insure "Tobacco-Pipes," "Mar-tyrs of the Modern Zeal," "Volumes of Poetry," "Shadows," and "Rivers" against Fire.[102] Absurdity of this (blasphemous) kind burlesques the theological concept of transubstan-tiation, referred to in the definition of "*Beef*" as the "*King of Meat.*"[103] Still other absurd-ities, to mention but a few, are the indictment of Homer for a lack of knowledge that he

---

[95] *Tale*, pp. 41; 46.

[96] *Tale*, p. 53.

[97] See *Tale*, p. 79.

[98] See also Starkman, *Swift's Satire on Learning*, pp. 87–105.

[99] *Tale*, p. 96.

[100] See Hawking, *A Brief History of Time*, pp. 81–98.

[101] See *Tale*, p. 97; for a discussion of the famous fray between the Ancients and the Moderns, see Joseph M. Levine, *The Battle of the Books: History and Literature in the Augustan Age* (Ithaca and London, 1991); see also Elke Wawers, *Swift zwischen Tradition und Fortschritt: Studie zum ideengeschichtlichen Kontext von "The Battle of the Books" und "A Tale of a Tub"* (Frankfurt/M., Bern, New York, 1989). See also Hermann Josef Real's introduction to his edition of Jonathan Swift, *"The Battle of the Books": eine historisch-kritische Ausga-be mit literarhistorischer Einleitung und Kommentar* (Berlin und New York, 1978), pp. XVII–XXXV.

[102] See *Tale*, p. 108; the satire attacks the Office of Indulgences; see Hermann Josef Real's commentary on the *Tale* in Jonathan Swift, *Ein Tonnenmärchen*: Übersetzung von Ulrich Horstmann (Stuttgart, 1994), p. 227n318.

[103] See *Tale*, p. 116.

could not have,[104] paradoxical collocations such as the *"Art of being Deep-learned, and Shallow-read,"*[105] the definition of labour as the seed of idleness, and darkness as illumination.[106] The climax of reducing logic to absurdity is reached towards the end of the book when the Hack announces his latest project:

> I am now trying an Experiment very frequent among Modern Authors; which is, to *write upon Nothing*; When the Subject is utterly exhausted, to let the Pen still move on; by some called, the Ghost of Wit, delighting to walk after the Death of its Body.[107]

Absurdity has come full circle. The Hack's new project mirrors the gradual reduction of words to syllables, to letters, to blanks. *Nothing* is the theme and purpose of his further writing. This looks like madness.[108]


# V


In the *Tale*, the technique of reduction and the theme of madness are closely linked. Madness, as it was seen throughout the eighteenth century,[109] is an imbalance in the faculties of the mind: memory, judgement, and imagination. It is imagination that due to its ability of rearranging data stored in the memory is susceptible to fits of hallucination, to use a modern term. As Bacon had warned, imagination cut loose from reason and judgement was bound to produce chimerical notions and absurd worlds of fantasy.[110] To put it even more clearly, the reduction of reason and judgement enhances the impact of the imagination to a degree that it borders on madness:

> But when a Man's Fancy gets *astride* on his Reason, when Imagination is at Cuffs with the Senses, and common Understanding, as well as common Sense, is Kickt out of Doors; the first Proselyte he makes, is Himself, and when that is once compass'd, the Difficulty is not so great in bringing over others; A strong Delusion always operating from *without*, as vigorously as from *within*.[111]

Like "wit" without "learning" in Johnson's fable in *The Rambler*, no 22, unchecked imagination is bound to lead men astray.[112] Imagination leads man to madness, introduces him to that dark region of the mind where mind becomes matter,[113] where Height and Depth

---

[104] See *Tale*, pp. 127–30.

[105] *Tale*, p. 130.

[106] See *Tale*, pp. 146 and 186.

[107] *Tale*, p. 208.

[108] For an analysis of the traditional link between "poets" and "madness," see Curtius, *Europäische Literatur und lateinisches Mittelalter*, pp. 467–68. Defoe is considered the first to have interpreted Swift's *Tale* in terms of madness; see Robert M. Philmus, "Mechanical Operations of the Spirit and *A Tale of a Tub*," *English Studies in Canada*, 10 (1984), 393–94.

[109] For a discussion of madness in (iatro-)mechanical terms, see Starkman, *Swift's Satire on Learning*, p. 26.

[110] This is the meaning of "Converting Imagination;" see Bullitt, *Jonathan Swift and the Anatomy of Satire*, pp. 134–48.

[111] *Tale*, p. 171.

[112] See *The Rambler*, eds W. J. Bate and Albrecht B. Strauss (New Haven and London, 1969), The Yale Edition of the Works of Samuel Johnson, III, 121–25.

[113] In Swift's attack, both forms of madness, taking mind for matter and matter for mind, are ridiculed. The eccentricities of Paracelsus and the absurdities of Royal Society virtuosi are

meet, where straight Lines are drawn by their own Length into a Circle, and where Fancy after having soared too high falls down like "a bird of paradise." Faculty psychology is a vehicle for the understanding of the precise function of semantic gravity in the *Tale*. Gravity prevents birds of paradise from flying too high, it prevents fancy from soaring into regions of thin air, and it helps imagination to seek reorientation by attaching itself to the principles of judgement. But here an inherent paradox is revealed. Gravity, as we have seen throughout this essay, reduces form to atoms, mind to matter, logic to absurdity. With its forces of reduction, it prevents the Bird of Paradise from soaring into Nothing, and it forces the narrator to stumble on his way to fame.[114] But reduction is also one of the main symptoms of madness.[115] Reducing the world to one's favourite ideas is just another form of creating delusions or, to use the Baconian term, of re-establishing idols. Reduction is unnatural. As the Hack says:

> For, what Man in the natural State, or Course of Thinking, did ever conceive it in his Power, to reduce the Notions of all Mankind, exactly to the same Length, and Breadth, and Height of his own?[116]

It is precisely in this aspect that Swift's *Tale* differs from almost all of his other satires. The technique of reduction, it is true, no matter whether in the mode of *meiosis*, or reduction of mind to matter, or *reductio ad absurdum*, is a genuine and legitimate tool of satire.[117] Juvenalian and Horatian satirists have frequently made use of it in order to create a topsy-turvy world that could then be measured against the yardstick of their critical norms. In the *Tale*, however, reduction is not only a technique of satire but also its butt. Satire is not exempt from the forces of gravitation. Black holes, as their names imply, do not let the light of "satiric truth" emerge.[118] Formal unity reduced to "amorphy" violates Dryden's recommendation of concentrating satiric attacks on one vice or one individual only.[119] In the *Tale*, the sheer quantity of themes and targets runs counter to this recommendation. The reduction of mind to matter applied to satire leads to a conception of satire as a war-machine praised for its random shots. The technique of *reductio ad absurdum* inherent in both the logic and the structure of the *Tale* eventually delivers the *coup de grâce* to its satire: Defining reduction as a symptom of madness also means that the reductive satirist is mad. Measuring

---

equally subjected to criticism; see also Craven, *Jonathan Swift and the Millennium of Madness*, pp. 172–73.

[114] For the idea of "madness in the narrator," see DePorte, *Nightmares and Hobbyhorses*, pp. 66–78.

[115] The traditional view is that Swift lashes both the corruptions of Scholasticism and the aberrations of mechanical Cartesian philosophy that reduces "mankind to soulless machines;" see Ehrenpreis, *Mr Swift*, p. 193.

[116] *Tale*, p. 166.

[117] For a survey of the meaning of the term "satire," see Jürgen Brummack, "Zu Begriff und Theorie der Satire," *Deutsche Vierteljahrsschrift für Literaturwissenschaft und Geistesgeschichte*, 45 (1971), 275–327; see also Hermann Josef Real, "An Introduction to Satire," *Teaching Satire: Dryden to Pope*, ed. Hermann Josef Real (Heidelberg, 1992), pp. 7–19.

[118] For the terminology of "satiric truth," see Edward W. Rosenheim, Jr, *Swift and the Satirist's Art* (Chicago and London, 1963), pp. 179–238.

[119] See John Dryden, "A Discourse Concerning the Original and Progress of Satire," *Essays*, ed. W. P. Ker, 2 vols (Oxford, 1926 [1900]), II, 15–114.

life and its errors against the standard of satiric norms is madness.[120] Normative systems are reductive systems.[121] In a syllogism that might remind one of the Hack's logic, I am bold enough to claim that in Swift's *Tale* Satire is reductive; madness is reductive; ergo: Satire is Madness.[122] The force of semantic gravitation even causes the bipartite structure constitutive of satire to break down: deficiency becomes a norm, and norms are synonyms of a deficiency; in other words, they are reduced to absurdity. In the wake of gravitational energy, even norms as the foundations of the Augustan age are mechanically reduced, causing bewilderment among those critics who concede "the *Tale of a Tub* to be a masterpiece" without quite seeing why.[123] Black holes do not let the light of truth emerge. Thus the *Tale* can no longer be considered to be an ordinary form of satire with either implicit or explicit norms, clearly a case of singularity. The gravitational pull is strong enough to let the tub rotate, drawing some of its critics into its vortex.

---

[120] In his letter of 29 September 1725, Swift says: "I never will have peace of mind till all honest men are of my Opinion: by Consequence you are to embrace it immediately and procure that all who deserve my Esteem may do so too" (*Correspondence*, III, 103).

[121] For the problem of norm in satire, see DePorte, *Nightmares and Hobbyhorses*, p. 83, and Helmut Markus, "Der bleibende Nutzen der Satire: Überlegungen zum Problem der satirischen Norm," *Anglistik & Englischunterricht*, 9 (1979), 131–58.

[122] For the idea of "Swift in idiotic guise" and "the satirist as a great fool," see Traugott, "*A Tale of a Tub*," pp. 102; 104.

[123] See Clark, *Form and Frenzy in Swift's "Tale of a Tub*," p. x.

Hermann J. Real
*Westfälische Wilhelms-Universität, Münster*

# A Taste of Composition Rare:
# The *Tale*'s Matter and Void

It is a tale
Told by an idiot, full of sound and fury,
Signifying nothing.
Shakespeare, *Macbeth*

ABSTRACT. Swift's attitude towards Lucretius reflects the same ambivalent and paradoxical stance that is distinctive of the New Science in general. In the one camp, Lucretius appeared as one of the founding fathers of modern science; in the other, he was a mad modern whose teachings on the structure and origin of the world were "never to be reconciled with reason." In the *Tale*, as a result, the many references to the *De rerum natura* have to be seen both as a means of characterizing a mad modern philosopher and also as tools in Swift's attack on the archetypal exemplification of the spirit that always says "no," Grub Street. Utilizing the two most important principles of Lucretian physics, Swift explodes the inventions of modern technology. Modern authors are shown to be "makers" of physical objects consisting of matter and void.

In 1657, Josua Poole, the compiler of *The English Parnassus: or, A Helpe to English Poesie*, defined "Epicurean" as synonymous with "godless, voluptuous, sensuall, brutish, bestiall, beastly, irreligious, ungodly, loose, dissolute, intemperate, vitious, wallowing, swinish, insatiate, gluttonous, gurmandizing, self-pampering, self-pleasing."[1] A collection of "choice epithets" like this is usually indicative of violence in intellectual controversy; in this case, it is indicative of a violence which is acrimonious by any standards: "Few philosophies," one historian writes, "can have endured such hostility, neglect, or sheer misrepresentation through the centuries as Epicureanism; few can have more deliberately provoked their opponents into violent and emotional counter-propaganda."[2] Indeed, it is no exaggeration to say that, until the middle of the seventeenth century, the reception of Epicurus and his followers, most notably that of Lucretius, is little more than a chronicle of calumny and denunciation; a chronicle that is, worse still, no better than a case history of reliance on unsupported testimony.[3]

---

[1]  Josua Poole, *The English Parnassus: or, A Helpe to English Poesie* (London, 1657), p. 89.
[2]  Peter Green, *Essays in Antiquity* (London, 1960), p. 76.
[3]  I have presented a great deal of the evidence in my *Untersuchungen zur Lukrez-Übersetzung von Thomas Creech* (Bad Homburg v. d. H., Berlin, Zürich, 1970), which also sum-

Poole's list falls easily into two parts. Each of these points to a verdict by which professional rivals (like the Stoics) and Fathers of the Church endeavoured to ostracize the Philosophy of the Garden as atheistic in character and hedonistic in intent. Harking back to Cicero's dictum (repeated verbatim by his Christian namesake, Lactantius, and echoed by many others) that Epicurus "actually abolished the gods, although professedly retaining them" (*Epicurus re tollit oratione relinquit deos*),[4] no less an authority than Calvin, in one of the more infamous volleys of his *Institutio christianae religionis*, berated "the blasphemous sayings of [that] filthy dogge Lucretius,"[5] and the highly regarded French friar, Marin Mersenne, followed suit by branding him *Atheorum princeps*, "prince of atheists," in his commentary on *Genesis*.[6]

In like manner, Horace's jocular self-portrayal, *Epicuri de grege porcus*, "swine from Epicurus's herd," in his letter to Tibullus,[7] inspired the custodians of his fame into converting the joke into a polemical formula with which to combat the whole gang of "voluptuous Epicures and cursed Atheists ... liuing in this world like brute beasts, & like dogs and swine, wallowing in all sensuality."[8] Throughout the century, the Epicurean creed, or, more precisely, its ethics and theology, continued to arouse the passions of pamphleteers such as Robert Hobson, who declaimed against "the Divels Swine, these sonnes of Beliall, Hogs of Epicurus stye,"[9] and Alexander Ross, who insisted that it was fitting "[to call] a wanton Atheist an Epicure," the Epicurean philosophy, Ross maintained, being but a system of which "*Tobacco*-suckers and *Wine*bibbers [would] hardly admit."[10] And as late as 1682/83, when Thomas Creech scored a sensational success with the first complete translation of the

---

marizes earlier research on the subject; see, in particular, pp. 11–19, 49–62, 75–85. See also Bernhard Fabian, "Lukrez in England im siebzehnten und achtzehnten Jahrhundert: einige Notizen," *Wolfenbütteler Studien zur Aufklärung, VI: Aufklärung und Humanismus*, ed. Richard Töllner (Heidelberg, 1980), pp. 107–29.

[4]  *De natura deorum*, I, xliv, 124; see also Lactantius's "Epitome divinarum institutionem," *Opera omnia*, CSEL, XIX, pt 1, ed. Samuel Brandt (Prag, Wien, Leipzig, 1890), 706, 31; [Robert Parsons], *A Booke of Christian Exercise* (London, 1594), p. 465; [Charles Wolseley], *The Unreasonableness of Atheism Made Manifest* (London, 1669), p. 39; and Thomas Creech in the "Notes" on his translation of *Titus Lucretius Carus: His Six Books of Epicurean Philosophy, Done into English Verse*, 3rd ed. (London, 1683), p. 2.

[5]  The quotation is from Thomas Norton's translation; see *The Institution of Christian Religion* (London, 1578), fol. 9v. There were two editions of the *Institutio christianae religionis* in Swift's library, one of which (Geneva, 1553) was acquired before 1715; see LeFanu, *Catalogue*, p. 15.

[6]  *Quaestiones celeberrimae in Genesim* (Paris, 1623), cols 1439–40. For the meaning of the "hydra-headed term" atheism in the seventeenth century, see, among others, Samuel I. Mintz, *The Hunting of Leviathan: Seventeenth-Century Reactions to the Materialism and Moral Philosophy of Thomas Hobbes* (Cambridge, 1962), pp. 39–41; Michael Hunter, *Science and Society in Restoration England* (Cambridge, 1981), pp. 162–70; and David Wootton, "New Histories of Atheism," *Atheism from the Reformation to the Enlightenment*, eds Michael Hunter and David Wootton (Oxford, 1992), pp. 24–32.

[7]  *Epistles*, I, iv, 16; see also Eduard Fraenkel, *Horace* (Oxford, 1966 [1957]), pp. 254–56.

[8]  Thomas Beard, *The Theatre of Gods Judgements* (London, 1597), p. 139.

[9]  *The Arraignement of the Whole Creature, at the Barre of Religion, Reason, and Experience* (London, 1631), pp. 178, 327.

[10]  See *Arcana Microcosmi: or, The Hid Secrets of Mans Body Disclosed* (London, 1651), p. 256; and *The Philosophicall Touch-Stone* (London, 1645), p. 53.

*De rerum natura* to be published in England, the "[notorious] Wantonness of the *Epicureans*" was still taken for granted.[11]

Yet by the 1680s, Creech was flogging a seriously ill, if not dead, hog. By then, more sober spirits like Sir Thomas Browne and Thomas Stanley, not to mention Pierre Gassendi and Walter Charleton, had assigned the "Disrepute," into which the Philosophy of the Garden "as the Source of all Vice and Immorality" had been brought, to linguistic errors.[12] By then, more significantly, the New Science was firmly established.

In fact, many "natural philosophers," scientists and theologians alike, sensed that a "paradigm change" was imminent as early as the 1640s. While, in 1651, the Moravian educational reformer, Jan Komenský (Comenius) still demanded that "*Aristotle [was] not to be tolerated in Christian schools as the onely Master of Philosophie*" any longer,[13] some twenty years later Meric Casaubon and Richard Burthogge, among many others, testified that the change was complete: The once abominated Epicurus had "now become the *Saint* of many Christians," and "Lucretius [was] as much consulted as Moses."[14]

This shift, in the course of which Aristotle was declared to be "an Asse to Epicurus" (as the anonymous "Ballad of Gresham Colledge" would have it),[15] was not a mere caprice of intellectual fashion but the outcome of historical logic. Its most momentous significance lies in the fact that Epicurean atomism, the "*Atomical Hypothesis*,"[16] superseded the Aristotelian-Ptolemaic synthesis and went on to become the predominant philosophy of the age: "Surely, if it is rightly examined," John Webster, for one, ruled in the *Academiarum Examen* of 1654, "[the Epicurean Philosophy] will prove a more perfect, and sound piece, than any the Schools ever had, or followed."[17]

Epicurean atomism posits two ontological principles, matter and void. Ultimate existence is an infinite number of infinitely small, indivisible particles, or atoms, "contained" in an infinite void. The atoms, which are invisible and as indestructible as they are eternal, fall through space not on account of divine intervention but by mechanical causation. Since they digress, or swerve, in their downward path, they collide and coalesce into compound bodies, so that the perceptible world, in the final analysis, is built up from a fortuitous conflux of atoms. In the infinity of space, there is an infinite number of (inhabited) worlds. There may

11  "Notes upon the First Book," p. 1. On Creech's impact, see, in addition to Real, *Untersuchungen*, pp. 141–53, Cosmo Alexander Gordon, *A Bibliography of Lucretius* (London, 1962), pp. 169–80.

12  See Sir Thomas Browne's *Pseudodoxia Epidemica*, ed. Robin Robbins, 2 vols (Oxford, 1981), I, 599; Thomas Stanley, *The History of Philosophy*, 3rd ed. (Hildesheim and New York, 1975 [1701]), sig. c2r. The first edition came out, in three volumes, in London, 1655–60. See also Walter Charleton, *Epicurus's Morals* (London, 1656), sigs A3r–e1r, Leonard Lessius, *The Temperate Man: or, The Right Way of Preserving Life and Health* (London, 1678), p. 159, and, in particular, Pierre Gassendi, *De vita et moribus Epicuri libri octo* (Lyons, 1647), pp. 79–106.

13  *Naturall Philosophie Reformed by Divine Light* (London, 1651), sig. a6r.

14  Meric Casaubon, *Of Credulity and Incredulity in Things Natural, Civil, and Divine* (London, 1668), pp. 200–1; Richard Burthogge, *Tagathon: or, Divine Goodness Explicated and Vindicated from the Exceptions of the Atheist* (London, 1672), sig. A4v. See also Danton B. Sailor, "Moses and Atomism," *Journal of the History of Ideas*, 25 (1964), 3–16.

15  Dorothy Stimson, "'Ballad of Gresham Colledge,'" *Isis*, 18 (1932), 109 (5).

16  Joseph Glanvill, *Scepsis Scientifica: or, Confest Ignorance the Way to Science* (New York and London, 1978 [1665]), pp. 107–8.

17  *Academiarum Examen: or, The Examination of Academies* (London, 1654), p. 78.

be room for gods in the infinity of space, in the "interspaces between the worlds" – peaceful abodes where the gods live in everlasting tranquillity and self-sufficient happiness – yet there is none for divine interference, of whatever kind, in man's affairs. The human soul, which is composed of rarefied if material elements, is mortal and dies, or rather dissolves into its component parts, with the body. Nothing is ever created out of nothing by divine power (will), and nothing is ever destroyed into nothing. The terrors of "religion" and the fear of death, therefore, have no foundation.[18]

To some extent, the philosophical and theological problems which the atomic model of the universe entailed resulted from the course the history of science took since the middle of the sixteenth century; in particular, from the idea of an infinite universe as propagated by followers of Copernicus like Thomas Digges and Giordano Bruno;[19] from the debate on the plurality of worlds in an unbounded cosmos as initiated by the teachings of Bruno and the discoveries of Galileo;[20] by the much ado about nothing following the demonstration of a vacuum by Evangelista Torricelli, Galileo's pupil and secretary,[21] and, last but not least, from the belief in the existence of atoms, or rather what seventeenth-century virtuosi took to be atoms,[22] ever since the revival of Epicurean physics by Pierre Gassendi and its subsequent legitimation by Walter Charleton and Robert Boyle in England.[23] In each of these cases, the New Science had corroborated the ancient teachings of Epicurus.

To an even greater extent, however, the theological and philosophical problems inherent in the atomic model followed from the distinctive structure of the Epicurean system. As the Epicurean Torquatus explained in Cicero's *De finibus bonorum et malorum:*

---

[18] See, in particular, *Titi Lucreti Cari De rerum natura libri sex*, ed. Cyril Bailey, 3 vols (Oxford, 1963 [1947]), I, 51–72; see also S. Sambursky, *The Physical World of the Greeks*, 2nd ed. (London, 1963 [1960]), pp. 105–31; and Alfred Stückelberger, "Vom Atomon der Antike zum Atom der Neuzeit: zur Geschichte der Materievorstellung," *Antike und europäische Welt: Aspekte der Auseinandersetzung mit der Antike*, eds Maja Svilar und Stefan Kunze (Bern, Frankfurt/M., New York, 1984), pp. 187–207.

[19] See, in addition to Francis R. Johnson, *Astronomical Thought in Renaissance England: A Study of the English Scientific Writings from 1500 to 1645* (Baltimore, 1937), Alexandre Koyré's by now classic *From the Closed World to the Infinite Universe* (Baltimore and London, 1976 [1957]).

[20] See, in addition to Grant McColley, "The Seventeenth-Century Doctrine of a Plurality of Worlds," *Annals of Science*, 1 (1936), 385–430, the more recent and comprehensive account by Stephen J. Dick, *Plurality of Worlds: The Origins of the Extraterrestrial Life Debate from Democritus to Kant* (Cambridge, 1984 [1982]), particularly pp. 44–105.

[21] See, in addition to Charles Singer, *A Short History of Scientific Ideas to 1900* (Oxford, 1972 [1959]), pp. 269–70, Edward Grant, *Much Ado about Nothing: Theories of Space and Vacuum from the Middle Ages to the Scientific Revolution* (Cambridge, 1981), pp. 182–255; see also Max Jammer, *Concepts of Space: The History of Theories of Space in Physics* (Cambridge, MA, 1954), pp. 51–92.

[22] See Cyril S. Smith and John G. Burke, *Atoms, Blacksmiths, and Crystals: Practical and Theoretical Views of the Structure of Matter in the Seventeenth and Eighteenth Centuries* (Los Angeles, 1967).

[23] See, for example, Robert Hugh Kargon, *Atomism in England from Hariot to Newton* (Oxford, 1966), pp. 63–105; Sabina Fleitmann, *Walter Charleton (1620–1707), "Virtuoso": Leben und Werk* (Frankfurt/M., Bonn, New York, 1986), pp. 212–74. I would also like to recommend, even if with reservations, the richly documented and densely argued account of Gassendi's atomism and its domestication in England by Richard W. F. Kroll, *The Material Word: Literate Culture in the Restoration and Early Eighteenth Century* (Baltimore and London, 1991), pp. 113–79.

In physicis plurimum posuit. Ea scientia et verborum vis et natura orationis et consequentium repugnantiumve ratio potest perspici; omnium autem rerum natura cognita levamur superstitione, liberamur mortis metu, non conturbamur ignoratione rerum, e qua ipsa horribiles exsistunt saepe formidines.

Natural Philosophy he deemed all-important. This science explains to us the meaning of terms, the nature of predication, and the law of consistency and contradiction; secondly, a thorough knowledge of the facts of nature relieves us of the burden of superstition, frees us from fear of death, and shields us against the disturbing effects of ignorance, which is often in itself a cause of terrifying apprehensions.[24]

Physics, then, is the foundation and origin of all philosophy. It is the investigation into the laws of the physical world, not aprioristic speculation, which may enlighten man about the teleology, or purposelessness, of the creation, the providence, or indifference, of (the) gods, and the immortality, or mortality, of man. In the Epicurean view, theological and ethical positions are *epi*phenomena, mere concomitants, secondary accidental consequences following from, and on, the inquiry of the *prima causa*, Nature: "Die Philosophie Epikurs war wesentlich eine Therapie der menschlichen Beunruhigung durch die Erscheinungen der Natur."[25]

The implication was obvious: If the New Science merely confirmed what Epicurean mechanistic materialism had anticipated, it was natural as well as logical to conclude that what had been deduced from these mechanistic and materialist premises for theology and ethics was as "true" as the premises themselves, two thousand years of denunciation and vilification notwithstanding. Any seventeenth-century advocate of Epicurean atomism, therefore, was in danger of being associated with atheism and libertinism, Epicurean physics being, as the anonymous author of *Remarques on the Humours and Conversations of the Town* (1673) noted, "the principle of their grandest debauchments."[26] The dilemma seemed inescapable: For convinced atomists "to give up atomism" would have been tantamount to giving up "any serious pretension of studying natural science," but at the same time atomists "recognized that they were playing with fire in championing a philosophy that had once stood in opposition to their fundamental religious beliefs."[27] It is for this reason that the intensity of contemporary polemics against the Philosophy of the Garden never seriously abated. Even virtuosi like Charleton and Boyle, who were so instrumental in reconciling Epicurean atomism with the Christian creed, were only able to do so by inserting a few "pious alterations" which made all the difference.[28] "I have never yet found out any justifiable ground, why *Atoms* may not be regarded *Mundi materies*, the Material Principle of the Universe," Charleton, for one, maintained, "provided that we allow, that God created that first *Matter* out of *Nothing*."[29]

---

[24] I, xix, 63; see also Lucretius, *De rerum natura*, I, 147–49; II, 58–60; III, 91–93; VI, 38–40.

[25] Hans Blumenberg, *Die Legitimität der Neuzeit* (Frankfurt, 1966), p. 107.

[26] *Remarques on the Humours and Conversations of the Town* (New York and London, 1974 [1673]), pp. 73–74.

[27] Richard S. Westfall, *Science and Religion in Seventeenth-Century England* (Ann Arbor, MI, 1973 [1958]), p. 108; see also Hunter, *Science and Society in Restoration England*, pp. 170–77.

[28] See Kargon, *Atomism in England*, p. 89.

[29] *The Darknes of Atheism Dispelled by the Light of Nature* (London, 1652), p. 44; see also Robert Boyle, *About the Excellency and Grounds of the Mechanical Hypothesis* (London, 1674), pp. 3–4.

When Swift first encountered the Philosophy of the Garden at Sir William Temple's in the 1690s,[30] the image of Lucretius (and/or Epicurus, for that matter) was still as ambiguous and inconsistent as that of the virtuosi. On the one hand, Lucretius remained what he had always been, an atheistical monster and the "Secretary of Hell;"[31] on the other, he was hailed as a "profound oracle of wit and sense."[32] In the one camp, the ancient philosopher-poet, or *Lucretius redivivus*, appeared as one of the founding fathers of modern science;[33] in the other, he was a mad modern whose teachings on the structure and origin of the world were "never to be reconciled with Reason."[34] Even critics who were by no means hostile to the Sage of the Garden, such as the early deist, Charles Blount, "esteemed the *Epicurean* Philosophy ... even when manag'd with the greatest Art and cunning, to be but a rational kind of madness."[35] In this context, critics would often refer to the apocryphal tradition in Lucretius's biography according to which the poet suffered from fits of madness, and that he composed the six books of his *De rerum natura per intervalla insaniae*, "in his lucid intervals."[36] Luckily for the adherents of "orthodoxy," if there was method in the system, there was also madness both in the system and the man.


# II


Swift's attitude towards Lucretius reflects the same ambivalent and paradoxical stance that is distinctive of the seventeenth century. Most significantly, perhaps, Epicurus and Lucretius, "great Introducers of new Schemes in Philosophy" that they are, people "the *Academy* of *Modern Bedlam*" in "A Digression concerning Madness."[37] And as late as January 1728, when he came to write the character of Mrs Johnson on those sorrow-stricken nights before and after her funeral, the Dean remembered the authors whom he had directed Stella to

[30] See the brief but delightful account of Temple's Epicureanism in the Introduction to *Five Miscellaneous Essays by Sir William Temple*, ed. Samuel Holt Monk (Ann Arbor, MI, 1963), pp. xviii–xxiv. The most thorough discussion is that by A. C. Elias, Jr, even though for reasons that will appear later I do not agree with all of it; see *Swift at Moor Park: Problems in Biography and Criticism* (Philadelphia, 1982), pp. 157–72 and *passim*.

[31] Charleton's phrase; see *The Darknes of Atheism Dispelled*, p. 158. For a more contemporary view, see Theophilus Gale, *The Court of the Gentiles*, 2nd ed., 2 pts (Oxford, 1670–72), II, 440–48.

[32] Thomas Shadwell, *The Virtuoso*, eds Marjorie Hope Nicolson and David Stuart Rodes (London, 1966), p. 9 (I, i, 1–6).

[33] See Alfred Stückelberger, "Lucretius reviviscens: von der antiken zur neuzeitlichen Atomphysik," *Archiv für Kulturgeschichte*, 54 (1972), 1–25.

[34] William Bates, *Considerations of the Existence of God, and of the Immortality of the Soul: For the Cure of Infidelity, the Hectick Evil of the Times* (London, 1676), p. 52; see also Ross, *Arcana Microcosmi*, pp. 263–67; Matthew Hale, *The Primitive Origination of Mankind, Considered and Examined according to the Light of Nature* (London, 1677), pp. 257–58; and George Berkeley, *Three Dialogues between Hylas and Philonous* (London, 1713), p. 76.

[35] *Anima Mundi: or, An Historical Narration of the Opinions of the Ancients concerning Man's Soul after this Life* (London, 1679), p. 72; see also Thomas Burnet, *The Theory of the Earth*, 3rd ed. (London, 1697), pp. 200–3, and Karl-Josef Walber, *Charles Blount (1654–1693), Frühaufklärer: Leben und Werk* (Frankfurt/M., 1988), pp. 73–90.

[36] Creech, "The Life of Lucretius," sig. A3r. For a careful and balanced consideration of the evidence, see Bailey's "Prolegomena" (I, 1–8).

[37] *Prose Works*, I, 104–5.

read and study with care: "She understood the Platonic and Epicurean philosophy, and judged very well of the defects of the latter."[38] As a priest in the Church of England, Swift was bound to share the widespread prejudice against the Philosophy of the Garden, its materialist account of the universe, its denial of divine participation in it, as well as its categorical dismissal of life after death.[39] Some kind of orthodoxy is to be expected from the ordained, after all. And yet, for Swift, there was more to the Epicurean philosophy than errors to refute.

During his great reading period in 1697/98, Swift read Lucretius no less than three times in a single year; incidentally, the only title he read three times, Florus's epitome of Roman history excepted.[40] The Latin gloss, *ter*, "three times," which Swift added to the name, suggests that he did not study Lucretius in Creech's translation, with which he was also familiar,[41] but that he tackled the formidable *De rerum natura* in the original.[42] It seems that the Dean found the experience enjoyable enough. In 1721, he returned to Lucretius with two of his students, George and John Rochfort, the sons of Lord Chief Baron Rochfort:

> Thalia, tell in sober lays,
> How George, Nim, Dan, Dean, pass their days.

---

[38]  *Prose Works*, V, 231.

[39]  See Max Armin Korn, *Die Weltanschauung Jonathan Swifts* (Jena, 1935), pp. 15–36; Roger D. Lund, "Strange Complicities: Atheism and Conspiracy in *A Tale of a Tub*," *Eighteenth-Century Life*, 13, no 3 (1989), 34–58; and the more recent discussion by Michael DePorte, "The Road to St Patrick's: Swift and the Problem of Belief," *Swift Studies*, 8 (1993), 5–17, which emphasizes the blend of anarchical and orthodox elements in Swift's views of religion.

[40]  See Jonathan Swift, *"The Battle of the Books": eine historisch-kritische Ausgabe mit literar-historischer Einleitung und Kommentar*, ed. Hermann J. Real (Berlin und New York, 1978), pp. 128–32.

[41]  The evidence for Swift's familiarity with Creech's translation may be found in the footnotes added to the fifth edition of the *Tale*. It is certain that "Swift had a hand in the unsigned notes, if he did not write them all" (*A Tale of a Tub, to which is added, The Battle of the Books, and the Mechanical Operation of the Spirit*, eds A. C. Guthkelch and D. Nichol Smith, 2nd ed. [Oxford, 1958], p. xxiii). For quotations from Creech's translation in the *Tale*, see pp. 60, 100; see also *Prose Works*, IV, 37. There is no trace of its having been on Swift's shelves, though.

[42]  Swift owned two editions of Lucretius, published at Amsterdam, 1631, and Cambridge, 1675, both of them insignificant and unannotated; see LeFanu, *A Catalogue of Books*, p. 23, and Harold Williams, *Dean Swift's Library: With a Facsimile of the Original Sale Catalogue* (Cambridge, 1932), item 30 in the sale catalogue. One of these, the one published at Amsterdam, was acquired in April 1699 and "bears all the marks of having been read with great care, if we may assume that the frequent pencil points in the margins throughout the whole of the five books and the occasional pointing fingers were made by Swift" (*Prose Works*, V, xxxi). In any case, this cannot have been the edition Swift studied in the previous year. Given the unsatisfactory information about Sir William Temple's library, it is impossible to state with precision (*pace* Everett Zimmerman, *Swift's Narrative Satires: Author and Authority* [Ithaca and London, 1983], p. 85) whether Swift knew any of the major editions by Lambinus, or any of the later annotated editions; see, for these, Gordon, *Bibliography of Lucretius*, pp. 78–93. As Sir Harold Williams said, "it might have been expected that Lucretius would have been better represented" (p. 43n2).
        The view that Lucretius is "difficult" is as old as Quintilian (see *Institutio oratoria*, X, i, 87). For more contemporary *testimonia*, see Milton's *Of Education* (1644) (*Complete Prose Works, II: 1643–1648* [New Haven and London, 1959], 349–95n122), and the collection in Thomas Pope Blount's *Censura celebriorum authorum* (London, 1690), pp. 39–40.

> Begin, my muse, first from our bowers,
> We sally forth at different hours;
> At seven, the Dean in night-gown dressed,
> Goes round the house to wake the rest:
> At nine, grave Nim and George facetious,
> Go to the Dean to read Lucretius.[43]

Swift remembered his reading of the *De rerum natura* so well that he was able to quote from, and allude to, the poem throughout his life: "The thought borrowed from Lucretius," is a characteristic growl commenting on somebody's plagiarism in 1727/28.[44] The Dean was not even averse to utilizing Lucretian material for his own good purposes, as becomes evident from Corinna's anxiety dream in *A Beautiful Young Nymph Going to Bed* (1734), for example.[45] And a few years earlier, the epigraph to *Gulliver's Travels*, like that to *A Tale of a Tub* in 1704, had come from the *De rerum natura*.[46]

All this evidence points to a reader who while not a disciple of Epicurus was a student of Lucretius, the master's most passionate propagandist. Paradoxically, Swift was addicted to a poet-philosopher of whom he was, and had to be, censorious. In that respect, his attitude towards Lucretius resembles his stance towards another materialist philosopher, Thomas Hobbes, by whom Swift also felt attracted and repelled at the same time.[47] Swift knew a genius, however devilish, when he saw one. That early stroke of wit, *A Tale of a Tub*, is a case in point.

III

The Tale-teller is an iridescent, multi-faceted figure who has been called many names: a *persona*, whether distinct from Swift or Swift throughout; a mask whether Swift's *alter ego* ("Swift") or his voice; a "character," or impersonation, variously labelled the Hack, the Madman, the Gnostic, the Fool(s), the *Ingénu*, and the Critic.[48] Like the chameleon, which

---

[43] *Poems*, p. 235, ll. 1–8.

[44] *Prose Works*, V, 335; XIV, 33. See also the Index to *Prose Works*, XIV, 231, *s.v.* Lucretius; *Correspondence*, II, 312; and Irvin Ehrenpreis, "Four of Swift's Sources," *Modern Language Notes*, 70 (1955), 98–100.

[45] See Hermann J. Real and Heinz J. Vienken, "'Those odious common Whores of which this Town is full': Swift's 'A Beautiful Young Nymph Going to Bed,'" *Arbeiten aus Anglistik und Amerikanistik*, 6 (1981), 248–50; see also John F. Sena, "Swift as Moral Physician: Scatology and the Tradition of Love Melancholy," *Journal of English and Germanic Philology*, 76 (1977), 350–51.

[46] See Charles Scruggs, "Swift's Use of Lucretius in *A Tale of a Tub*," *Texas Studies in Literature and Language*, 15 (1973), 40–41; and Richard H. Rodino, "'Splendide Mendax': Authors, Characters, and Readers in *Gulliver's Travels*," *Reading Swift: Papers from The Second Münster Symposium on Jonathan Swift*, eds Richard H. Rodino and Hermann J. Real, with the assistance of Helgard Stöver-Leidig (München, 1993), pp. 172–73.

[47] See Irvin Ehrenpreis, "The Doctrine of *A Tale of a Tub*," *Proceedings of The First Münster Symposium on Jonathan Swift*, eds Hermann J. Real and Heinz J. Vienken (München, 1985), pp. 62–69; see also Frank Palmeri, *Satire in Narrative: Petronius, Swift, Gibbon, Melville, and Pynchon* (Austin, TX, 1990), pp. 40–48.

[48] It is neither possible nor desirable to list all the literature on the subject here. See, in addition to John Traugott's memorable *bravura* performance on "the giddy speaker" ("A Tale of a Tub," *The Character of Swift's Satire*, ed. Claude Rawson [Newark, London, Toronto, 1983], pp. 83–126), Edward W. Rosenheim, Jr, *Swift and the Satirist's Art* (Chi-

changes its colour on a whim, the Tale-teller changes his profile as fancy takes him, perpetually voicing views he never knew he had. Like Proteus, who knows everything, the Tale-teller is in the habit of assuming different shapes in order to escape being questioned.

In addition to being all that, the Tale-teller asserts himself as a mad follower in the footsteps of Lucretius, who, unlike his idol, however, composed his *spiel* not "in his lucid intervals" but during bouts of insanity: "The whole Work was begun, continued, and ended, under a long Course of Physick."[49] As it turns out, his tale/*Tale* is studded with references to the *De rerum natura*, too. Few of these references seem accidental, the odd quotation used as an incantational formula ("*Quod procul à nobis flectat Fortuna gubernans*")[50] or as an affirmation excepted,[51] and most of them evoke central parts of the poem. Like Lucretius, the Tale-teller, his modern proselyte, feels impelled by the same mission:

> ———— *Juvatque novos decerpere flores,*
> *Insignemque meo capiti petere inde coronam,*
> *Unde prius nulli velarunt tempora Musæ.*
>
> Tis sweet to crop fresh flowers, and get a Crown
> For new and rare Inventions of my Own,[52]

as well as by the same utilitarian *telos*:

> WE whom the World is pleased to honor with the title of *Modern Authors*, should never have been able to compass our great Design of an everlasting Remembrance, and never-dying Fame, if our Endeavours had not been so highly serviceable to the general Good of Mankind. This, O *Universe*, is the Adventurous Attempt of me thy Secretary;
> ———— *Quemvis perferre laborem*
> *Suadet, & inducit noctes vigilare serenas.*
>
> Yet for respect of You with great delight
> I meet these dangers, and I wake all night,
> Labouring ... [53]

---

cago and London, 1963), pp. 138–39; Jay Arnold Levine, "The Design of *A Tale of a Tub* (With a Digression on a Mad Modern Critic)," *English Literary History*, 33 (1966), 200–1; Gardner D. Stout, Jr, "Speaker and Satiric Vision in Swift's *Tale of a Tub*," *Eighteenth-Century Studies*, 3 (1969–70), 175–78.

[49] *Prose Works*, I, 27.

[50] See *Prose Works*, I, 95. The quotation is from Lucretius, V, 107 (line numbering after Bailey's edition). I have checked all quotations from the *De rerum natura* in the *Tale* against the two editions known to have been in Swift's library (see n. 42) and have noted the differences. For an account of the line's function in the *Tale*, see Traugott, "A Tale of a Tub," p. 111.

[51] See *Prose Works*, I, 61. The quotation is from Lucretius, VI, 786–87. The Amsterdam edition of 1631 reads "retro" instead of "tetro". However, it is misleading to conclude that Swift here made "an intentional misquotation" from Lucretius (Ronald Paulson, *Theme and Structure in Swift's "Tale of a Tub"* [New Haven, 1960], pp. ix, 118–19). The variant "tetro" is common in seventeenth-century editions of the poem. For a stimulating survey and account of the Lucretian elements in the *Tale*, see Thomas E. Maresca, *Epic to Novel* (Ohio State University Press, 1974), pp. 148–56.

[52] The epigraph as quoted on the title-page (see *Prose Works*, I, xxxix). The quotation is from I, 928–30; repeated in the proem to Book IV, 3–5 (for a discussion, see Bailey, II, 756–61). All English translations are from the third edition of Thomas Creech's *Titus Lucretius Carus: His Six Books of Epicurean Philosophy, Done into English Verse, with Notes* (London, 1683); see p. 29, ll. 935–39.

[53] *Prose Works*, I, 77. The quotation is from Lucretius, I, 141–42. For the translation, see Creech, *Titus Lucretius Carus*, p. 6, ll. 172–73; see also William Bragg Ewald, Jr, *The Masks of Jonathan Swift* (New York, 1967 [1954]), p. 32.

In like manner, the Tale-teller echoes the famous Lucretian complaint about the poverty of the Latin tongue ("the Narrowness of our Mother-Tongue"),[54] and he endorses the two principles of Lucretian physics which flew in the face of Christian providential theism and which were deemed the most risible, "contrary to all *sense* and *reason*," by seventeenth-century Christian virtuosi: the doctrine of the *clinamen*, or "swerve,"[55] and the account of the world as caused by "undesigning impetuous chance."[56] Utilizing the time-honoured macrocosm-microcosm analogy,[57] this "most devoted Servant of all *Modern* Forms" at one stage even goes so far as to describe his own creation, the literary microcosm of *A Tale of a Tub*, as an amorphous, incoherent jumble of parts whose composition was subject to the same "laws" of fortune that determine the design of the universe:

> THE Necessity of this Digression, will easily excuse the Length; and I have chosen for it as proper a Place as I could readily find. If the judicious Reader can assign a fitter, I do here empower him to remove it into any other Corner he please.[58]

Not to mention the Aeolist system, whose bipartite structure mirrors the division of the Epicurean arguing, as it does, its moral and theological (or rather demonological) principles from physical and cosmological premises ("THE Learned *Æolists*, maintain the Original Cause of all Things to be *Wind*"),[59] the part of the Epicurean philosophy that comes most to the fore in the Tale-teller's argument is its sensualist epistemology. Epicurean sensualism holds not only that the senses are the sole source of knowledge, in fact, the only guarantee of truth, but also that knowledge is created by sense "impressions," literally by contact between the person perceiving and the atoms (*simulacra*, or "idols") emitted from the ob-

---

[54]  *Prose Works*, I, 105; see Lucretius, I, 136–39. In the Amsterdam edition of 1631, the text is as follows:
Nec me animus fallit Grajorum obscura reperta
Difficile inlustrare Latinis versibus esse:
Multa novis verbis præsertim cum sit agendum,
Propter egestatem linguæ & rerum novitatem.

[55]  See *Prose Works*, I, 105; Lucretius, II, 216–93 (for a considerate and balanced discussion, see Bailey, II, 837–42). For a seventeenth-century assessment, see Creech, "Notes," p. 21.

[56]  *Remarques*, p. 74. A similar criticism was put forward by Edward Stillingfleet, *Origines Sacræ: or, A Rational Account of the Grounds of Christian Faith*, 4th ed. (London, 1675), p. 404, a title which was in Swift's library (see LeFanu, *Catalogue*, p. 29). See *Prose Works*, I, 105 and I, 246–47; see also I, 36, where the Tale-teller subscribes to the Epicurean doctrine of sound.

[57]  See *Prose Works*, I, 46–47; for the idea of the poem as literary microcosm, see S. K. Heninger, Jr, *Touches of Sweet Harmony: Pythagorean Cosmology and Renaissance Poetics* (San Marino, 1974), pp. 364–97.

[58]  *Prose Works*, I, 94. See also Scruggs, "Swift's Use of Lucretius," p. 44. Some of the Tale-teller's more recent readers have endorsed this self-assessment. "Formally, [the *Tale's*] characteristic is not unity and a coherent design, but disintegration; not an organic wholeness, but a jumbled multiplicity of discrete parts and fragments," one critic writes (Martin C. Battestin, *The Providence of Wit: Aspects of Form in Augustan Literature and the Arts* [Oxford, 1974], p. 230). See also Pat Rogers, "Form in *A Tale of a Tub*," *Essays in Criticism*, 22 (1972), 142–60; Frances Deutsch Louis, *Swift's Anatomy of Misunderstanding: A Study of Swift's Epistemological Imagination in "A Tale of a Tub" and "Gulliver's Travels"* (London, 1981), p. 46.

[59]  I have explained this idea in greater detail in my commentary on Jonathan Swift, *Ein Tonnenmärchen: Übersetzung von Ulrich Horstmann* (Stuttgart, 1994), pp. 240–41n452.

jects perceived and entering the perceiver's nose, ear, or eye.[60] As the Tale-teller correctly states, in the Epicurean view perception and knowledge depend on "the *Films* and *Images* that fly off upon [a person's] Senses from the *Superficies* of Things."[61]

It is hardly a cause for surprise that Epicurean sensualist epistemology should come under heavy fire during the seventeenth century. For one thing, it became associated with that favourite bogeyman of the age, Thomas Hobbes, in whose material system sensation was also due to contact, or impact.[62] For another, since knowledge is gained only through the perception of the "idols" coming from the surface of physical objects, it is difficult to account for the existence of meta-physical objects, or beings like God. As Stillingfleet unmistakably put the case in *Origines Sacræ*: "If then our *knowledge* of *truth* comes in by our *senses*, and *sensation* doth wholly depend upon the *impression* of outward *objects*, what becomes of all *common Notions* and of the *Prolepsis* of a *Deity*?"[63] Finally, if sensation as the supreme arbiter of truth rests upon effluences, that is to say, tiny atomic conformations coming off from the *surface* of objects, atomists are hard put to explain how man, in what investigation soever, can ever hope to penetrate further than the outside. That is why the modern proselyte of Lucretius who tells the *Tale* presents himself as an idiot who praises ignorance, the state of "not seeing *through*," as the source of happiness:

> He that can with *Epicurus* content his Ideas with the *Films* and *Images* that fly off upon his Senses from the *Superficies* of Things; Such a Man truly wise, creams off Nature, leaving the Sower and the Dregs, for Philosophy and Reason to lap up. This is the sublime and refined Point of Felicity, called, *the Possession of being well deceived*; The Serene Peaceful State of being a Fool among Knaves.[64]

Never has a reversal of the Epicurean system, in which enlightenment held out the promise of happiness, after all, been more complete.

It is important to realize that in all of these references to the *De rerum natura* the Epicurean philosophy is, first and foremost, a *means of characterization*. It is a *device* of characterizing a mad modern philosopher; it is not a/the satirical *butt*.[65] If it is a satirical butt, it

---

[60] See Lucretius, IV, 26–215; 469–521; and the précis of this position by Bailey, I, 52–53, and III, 1179–81, 1237–39, as well as by Sambursky, *The Physical World of the Greeks*, pp. 118–19.

[61] *Prose Works*, I, 110; see also I, 36. I find it difficult to see in this a "travesty" of Lucretius's exposition; see, for this view, Zimmerman, *Swift's Narrative Satires*, pp. 102–3.

[62] See *Leviathan*, ed. C. B. Macpherson (Harmondsworth, Middlesex, 1986 [1968]), pp. 85–87.

[63] *Origines Sacræ*, p. 386.

[64] *Prose Works*, I, 110. See also Martin Price, *Swift's Rhetorical Art: A Study in Structure and Meaning* (New Haven and London, 1953), pp. 93–94, and Louis, *Swift's Anatomy of Misunderstanding*, pp. 60–62, although the connection with Lucretian epistemology is not explicitly made. See, however, Maresca, *Epic to Novel*, p. 143. From what has been said, it follows that I regard Robert C. Steensma's account as misleading; see his "Swift and Epicurus," *Bulletin of the Rocky Mountain Modern Language Association*, 17, nos 1–2 (1964), 10–12. I also disagree with A. C. Elias's interpretation that "Swift's definition of happiness" is an attack on Temple (see *Swift at Moor Park*, pp. 157–65), and with Kenneth Craven's recent suggestion that it is a dig at Shaftesbury (see his *Jonathan Swift and the Millennium of Madness: The Information Age in Swift's "A Tale of a Tub"* [Leiden, New York, Köln, 1992], pp. 95–99, 142–44).

[65] See also Rogers, "Form in *A Tale of a Tub*," p. 154; J. A. Downie, *Jonathan Swift, Political Writer* (London, Boston, Henley, 1985 [1984]), pp. 94–95.

is only by indirection, on account of its traditional and contemptible allegiance with (theological) atheism and (philosophical) madness, which *serves* to drive the satiric points home. Yet, we remember, Swift felt repelled *and* attracted by Lucretius at the same time. In *A Tale of a Tub*, the cause of the attraction lies in the two ontological principles of Epicurean physics, matter and void. These turned out to be admirable tools for Swift's clash with what he regarded as the archetypal exemplification of the spirit that always says "no," Grub Street.[66]

IV

Grub Street was made possible by the new technology of print. Throughout the sixteenth and seventeenth centuries, the Moderns, in their war of the words with the Ancients, never tired of citing the invention of the triad, gunpowder, the compass, and printing, as evidence of the fact that the virility of Nature and the creativity of man had never "degenerated" in the course of history. "His tribus tota antiquitas nihil par habet," the Italian humanist and encyclopaedist, Girolamo Cardano, whose *Opera omnia* were in Swift's library, enthused in 1552.[67] Among the three, printing was easily regarded as the supreme modern accomplishment.[68] There was nothing in the whole of antiquity, one paean claimed, that compared "to the wonderfull inuention, vtility and dignitie of printing."[69] The printing press was widely considered a "divine art," an invention "of a higher and diviner order" than the arts taught humanity by the gods of old,[70] and in "auncient times," one eulogist declared, Johann Gutenberg of Mainz, "to whom the Christian world is vnder God most beholding for this sacred Art, might haue beene a God of higher esteeme" than Mercury himself.[71]

Significantly, however, the invention of printing was celebrated not only as a triumph of modern ingenuity, not only as a heroic feat of modern man's mind, but also because of its beneficial consequences and effects, whether economic or religious, cultural or educational.[72]

---

[66] See in particular Pat Rogers, *Grub Street: Studies in a Subculture* (London, 1972), pp. 218–35.

[67] See *Opera omnia*, 10 vols (Stuttgart-Bad Cannstadt, 1966 [1663]), III, 609. See also *Prose Works*, I, 242, and LeFanu, *Catalogue*, p. 15, as well as Richard Foster Jones, *Ancients and Moderns: A Study of the Rise of the Scientific Movement in Seventeenth-Century England*, 2nd ed. (St Louis, 1961), pp. 12–13, 36–37, 130–31 *passim*; Elizabeth L. Eisenstein, *The Printing Press as an Agent of Change*, 2 vols (Cambridge, 1979), I, 20–21; and Michael Giesecke, *Der Buchdruck in der frühen Neuzeit: eine historische Fallstudie über die Durchsetzung neuer Informations- und Kommunikationstechnologien* (Frankfurt/M., 1991), pp. 147–56.

[68] See Roy S. Wolper, "The Rhetoric of Gunpowder and the Idea of Progress," *Journal of the History of Ideas*, 31 (1970), 589–98.

[69] See R. H. Bowers, "Some Early Apostrophes to Printing," *Papers of the Bibliographical Society of America*, 54 (1960), 113–15; see also John Amos Comenius, *A Patterne of Vniversall Knowledge* (London, 1651), p. 31.

[70] See Eisenstein, *The Printing Press as an Agent of Change*, I, 249–50; Giesecke, *Der Buchdruck in der frühen Neuzeit*, pp. 159–66.

[71] Thomas Jackson, *A Treatise Containing the Originall of Vnbeliefe* (London, 1625), p. 128.

[72] See, for these aspects, Harvey J. Graff, *The Legacies of Literacy: Continuities and Contradictions in Western Culture and Society* (Bloomington and Indianapolis, 1987), pp. 108–37, 151–63.

Echoing the views of the Reformers who were aware that the printing press had been con-ducive to their cause, Meric Casaubon, for one, was convinced that without the discovery of printing "that *reformation*, which God intended in his Church," would not have been pos-sible.[73] "By this *excellent Invention*," Joseph Glanvill summarized a lengthy debate in his *Plus Ultra* of 1668, "*Knowledge* is advantageously *spread* and *improved*,"[74] and the Dis-senting minister, Richard Baxter, in 1673 took comfort in the thought that "Good Books [were] a very great mercy to the world."[75]

But the Ancients were nobody's fools. Even if it was difficult for them to deny the facts of modern inventiveness and creativity, they were quick to realize that the (Baconian) prin-ciple of regarding the consequences and effects of discoveries was double-edged.[76] After all, it could be argued, the Reformation meant schism (necessary though it may have been), and that first and "famous *Rupture*" had engendered more schisms, the printing press "(that *villanous* Engine)," fanning and spreading the fire of religious controversy all the while:

> When *Lucifer* no longer could advance
> His works on the false ground of Ignorance,
> New Arts he tries, and new designs he laies,
> Then, his well-study'd Master-piece he plays;
> *Loyola, Luther, Calvin* he inspires
> And kindles, with infernal Flames, their fires,
> Sends their fore-runner (conscious of th' event)
> Printing, his most pernicious Instrument:
> Wild Controversie then, which long had slept,
> Into the Press from ruin'd Cloysters leapt.[77]

Moreover, critics of the printing press would point out, the ubiquity of Grub Street, that "multitude of Scriblers, who daily pester the World with their insufferable Stuff,"[78] showed if anything that ignorance remained as epidemic as it was endemic, and, finally, the advent of the printed book, in particular of the portable and cheap printed book produced in mas-sive numbers, resulted in the (re)production of mass and the proliferation of matter. As Sir William Temple put it: "The invention of printing has not ... multiplied books, but only

---

[73] *A Letter to Peter du Moulin, D. D.* (Cambridge, 1669), p. 26; see also Eisenstein, *The Printing Press as an Agent of Change*, I, 304–6.

[74] *Plus Ultra: or, The Progress and Advancement of Knowledge since the Days of Aristotle* (1668), ed. Jackson I. Cope (Gainesville, FL, 1958), pp. 77–79; see also William Wotton, *Reflections upon Ancient and Modern Learning* (London, 1694), pp. 170–71.

[75] See David L. Ferch, "'Good Books are a very great mercy to the world': Persecution, Private Libraries, and the Printed Word in the Early Development of the Dissenting Aca-demies, 1663–1730," *Journal of Library History*, 21 (1986), 350–61; see also Marcus Walsh, "The Superfoetation of Literature: Attitudes to the Printed Book in the Eighteenth Cen-tury," *British Journal of Eighteenth-Century Studies*, 15 (1992), 151–61.

[76] See the thorough and instructive survey by Giesecke, *Der Buchdruck in der frühen Neu-zeit*, pp. 168–91.

[77] Sir John Denham, "The Progress of Learning," *The Poetical Works*, ed. Theodore Howard Banks, 2nd ed. (Archon Books, 1969), p. 118, ll. 139–48; see also Andrew Marvell, *The Rehearsal Transpros'd and The Rehearsal Transpros'd the Second Part*, ed. D. I. B. Smith (Oxford, 1971), pp. 4–5.

[78] John Dryden, "Discourse concerning Satire," *The Poems*, ed. James Kinsley, 4 vols (Ox-ford, 1958), II, 605.

the copies of them."[79] Perhaps, the view was not amiss that Heaven permitted the invention of printing for the sins of the learned and the unlearned.


# V

There are numerous echoes of this thought in Swift. In fact, "rampant and promiscuous publication" and the "sheer quantity of detritus conveyed in Grub Street's disemboguing streams" is one of the *Tale*'s leitmotifs.[80] Yet profusion of matter not only surrounds the *Tale*; it also composes it. As critics have noted, the effect is one of "thinginess."[81] This effect is due, first of all, to the maze of dedications, prefaces, and introductions, supplemented later by an apology, a postscript, and a commentary, not to mention *The History of Martin, A Project, for the Universal Benefit of Mankind,* and *The Kingdom of Absurdities*.[82] All, or most, of this is *vox et praeterea nihil,* auditory matter, as it were. Musing on the requirements "for obtaining Attention in Publick," the Tale-teller visualizes himself in the "Introduction" addressing his audience from "*a superiour Position of Place*":

> But, altho' this Point be generally granted, yet the Cause is little agreed in; and it seems to me, that very few Philosophers have fallen into a true, natural Solution of this *Phænomenon*. The deepest Account, and the most fairly digested of any I have yet met with, is this, That Air being a heavy Body, and therefore (according to the System of *Epicurus*) continually descending, must needs be more so, when loaden and press'd down by Words; which are also Bodies of much Weight and Gravity, as it is manifest from those deep *Impressions* they make and leave upon us; and therefore must be delivered from a due Altitude, or else they will neither carry a good Aim, nor fall down with a sufficient Force.
>
> *\*Corpoream quoque enim vocem constare fatendum est,*
> *Et sonitum, quoniam possunt impellere Sensus.* Lucr. *Lib.* 4.
>
> AND I am the readier to favour this Conjecture, from a common Observation; that in the several Assemblies of these Orators, Nature it self hath instructed the Hearers, to stand with their Mouths open, and erected parallel to the Horizon, so as they may be intersected by a perpendicular Line from the Zenith to the Center of the Earth. In which Position, if the Audience be well compact, every one carries home a Share, and little or nothing is lost.[83]

When the "tale" proper begins, about a third of the book has been wasted on "hot air." The French moralist, Jean de La Bruyère, whom Swift read and annotated in 1697/98,[84]

---

[79]  *Five Miscellaneous Essays,* ed. Monk, p. 38. This is of course a traditional complaint; see, for example, Henry Peacham, *The Complete Gentleman, The Truth of our Times, and The Art of Living in London,* ed. Virgil B. Heltzel (Ithaca, NY, 1962), p. 189.

[80]  See *Prose Works,* I, 266; XI, 147; and Daniel Eilon, "Swift Burning the Library of Babel," *Modern Language Review,* 80 (1985), 269–71. See also John R. Clark, *Form and Frenzy in Swift's "Tale of a Tub"* (Ithaca and London, 1970), pp. 134–35.

[81]  Downie, *Jonathan Swift, Political Writer,* p. 93; see also Angus Ross, "The Books in the *Tale*: Swift and Reading in *A Tale of a Tub*," *Proceedings,* eds Real and Vienken, pp. 214–15.

[82]  See *A Tale of a Tub and Other Works,* eds Angus Ross and David Woolley (Oxford and New York, 1986), pp. xi–xix.

[83]  *Prose Works,* I, 36. The quotation is from Lucretius, IV, 526–27. For the translation, see Creech, *Titus Lucretius Carus,* p. 118, ll. 547–48.

[84]  See LeFanu, *Catalogue,* p. 22, and Hermann J. Real and Heinz J. Vienken, "'Not in Timon's Manner': La Bruyère and Swift," *Notes and Queries,* 230 (1985), 203–4.

remarked on the "superficial formality" of such "prefatory self-congratulation" that the remaining number of pages scarcely sufficed to merit a volume the title of a book.[85]

The theme that the Tale-teller's *spiel* is not a book but rather a non-book, or congeries of matter, is taken up again in the Digressions, Lucretian "swerves," as it were, which Hobbes considered to be signs of madness, symptoms of "a Man's Fancy *astride* on his Reason."[86] All of these appear to be afterthoughts,[87] appended to the main body of the work, the religious allegory or "tale" proper, in no recognizable order (or at least in no easily recognizable order),[88] and they tend to become increasingly self-referential.[89] At the end of the "*Digression in Praise of Digressions*," which is suitably digressive itself, the Lucretian Tale-teller, upholding the belief in "the Infinity of Matter," envisages a future generation of authors capable of producing "books" which are mere physical objects:

> [They] will desire no more Ingredients towards fitting up a Treatise, that shall make a very comely Figure on a Bookseller's Shelf, there to be preserved neat and clean, for a long Eternity, adorn'd with the Heraldry of its Title, fairly inscribed on a Label; never to be thumb'd or greas'd by Students, nor bound to everlasting Chains of Darkness in a Library.[90]

It is not surprising under the circumstances that among the "wonderful Advantages" preserved for modern readers in books (such as the *Iliad*) is not rich spiritual nourishment but material dainties like "a Nut-shell in an Iliad."[91]

But then, as mere matter never composes the Epicurean universe, so sheer physicality does not constitute the Lucretian microcosm of *A Tale of a Tub*: "In a Lucretian world, everything is a tale of a tub – everything that exists is a container that contains nothing."[92] Both literally and metaphorically, the *Tale* is full of emptiness. Paradoxically, the emptiness is made visible. It comes to the fore, for example, in the (in)significance of the *Tale*'s title,[93] in the lack of a key to the religious allegory,[94] in the loss of all linguistic and hermeneutical stability,[95] and, not to forget, in those numerous *lacunae* and *hiatus* ("chasms"), those dashes

---

[85] See Ehrenpreis, *Mr Swift*, p. 204; see also Battestin, *The Providence of Wit*, p. 228, and Harald Stang, *Einleitung – Fußnote – Kommentar: fingierte Formen wissenschaftlicher Darstellung als Gestaltungselemente moderner Erzählkunst* (Bielefeld, 1992), pp. 23–29.

[86] See *Leviathan*, ed. Macpherson, p. 136; *Prose Works*, I, 108. See also Michael V. DePorte, *Nightmares and Hobbyhorses: Swift, Sterne, and Augustan Ideas of Madness* (San Marino, 1974), pp. 66–78.

[87] See Ehrenpreis, *Mr Swift*, p. 187.

[88] See, for example, Levine, "The Design of *A Tale of a Tub*," pp. 214–15.

[89] See Frank A. Palmeri, "'*To Write upon Nothing*': Narrative Satire and Swift's *A Tale of a Tub*," *Genre*, 18 (1985), 158.

[90] See *Prose Works*, I, 93; see also I, 143–44; and Battestin, *The Providence of Wit*, pp. 234–35; Louis, *Swift's Anatomy of Misunderstanding*, pp. 65–66, 80–82.

[91] *Prose Works*, I, 90.

[92] Maresca, *Epic to Novel*, p. 159.

[93] I have summarized the results of the debate in my notes on Swift, *Ein Tonnenmärchen*, trans. Horstmann, p. 191n1; see also David P. French, "The Title of 'A Tale of a Tub,'" *Notes and Queries*, 196 (1951), 473–74.

[94] See *Prose Works*, I, 17, and Sir Roger L'Estrange, *Fables of Æsop and Other Eminent Mythologists: With Morals and Reflexions*, 4th ed. (London, 1704), sig. A4v: "*An* Emblem *without a* Key *to't, is no more than a* Tale of a Tub."

[95] See, for this thought, Clive T. Probyn, "'Haranguing upon Texts': Swift and the Idea of the Book," *Proceedings*, eds Real and Vienken, pp. 187–97; see also Terry J. Castle, "Why the Houyhnhnms Don't Write: Swift, Satire and the Fear of the Text," *Essays in Literature*,

and blanks, those *Desunt-nonnulla-* and *Desunt-caetera* pointers that pervade the *Tale* almost from beginning to end.[96] In perpetrating one of the "chasms," *Hic multa desiderantur,* "Here, much is missing," Swift explodes "the inadequacy of the Modern's materialistic philosophy, which can account for nothing," in one devastating pun: "Here much is to be desired."[97]

Above all, however, the *Tale's* "mighty-sounding nothings" assert themselves in two sections which bracket the main body of the work, the "tale" proper, in "The Epistle Dedicatory, to His Royal Highness Prince Posterity," and "The Conclusion."

In the "Dedication to Prince Posterity," Swift rewrote one of the sacred formulas employed by the Moderns in their quarrel with the Ancients throughout the sixteenth and seventeenth centuries, *Veritas filia temporis,* "Truth is the daugher of time." This modern motto, which is in fact of ancient origin,[98] was frequently inscribed on coins and title-pages; it occurred in collections of proverbs as well as in those of emblems,[99] not to mention woodcuts, engravings, and paintings.[100] Even if interpretations naturally differed, many of these representations picture Father Time (from Greek Kronos/Saturn, later identified with *Chronos,* "Time")[101] as an old man with a scythe in his hand raising his daughter Truth from the cave (or well) in which she is being held prisoner. In one reading, Time appears as the friend of the Moderns, who having promoted the recognition of Truth are gaining authority "in proportion as the truth which it embodies is the result of the ripening power of time."[102]

Not surprisingly, in Swift's (in)version of the apophthegm, Time, Prince Posterity's Governor, recalls the more ancient emblem of Time the Destroyer, inherent in the sinister,

---

[7] (1980), 33–37; Carol H. Barnett, "The 'Children of the Brain' and 'All Devouring' Time: Swift on Books," *CLA Journal,* 32 (1989), 504–5.

[96] See, in particular, *Prose Works,* I, 37–38, 43, 51, 52, 60, 67, 74–75, 104, 107, 111, 113, 128. For a different though not mutually exclusive account of these *lacunae,* see Clark, *Form and Frenzy in Swift's "Tale of a Tub",* pp. 166–67. I have also found some inspiration in W. B. Carnochan, "Swift's *Tale:* On Satire, Negation, and the Uses of Irony," *Eighteenth-Century Studies,* 5 (1971), 122–44.

[97] See *Prose Works,* I, 107, and Clark, *Form and Frenzy in Swift's "Tale of a Tub",* pp. 47–48.

[98] In Swift's edition of Pindar's *Olympia, Pythia, Nemea, Isthmia* (Saumur, 1620), the editor, Joannes Benedictus, writes in his commentary on the first Olympian ode: "Vnde Gellius admonet quenda[m] veterum poëtarum *Veritatem* temporis filiam vocasse" (p. 14; see also p. 186). Benedictus was referring to Aulus Gellius, *Noctium Atticarum libri XX* (XII, xi, 7), of which Swift owned an edition published at Leyden in 1706. See LeFanu, *Catalogue,* pp. 18, 26.

[99] See, in particular, W. von Leyden, "Antiquity and Authority: A Paradox in the Renaissance Theory of History," *Journal of the History of Ideas,* 19 (1958), 485–91. See also Geoffrey Whitney, *A Choice of Emblemes and Other Devises* (Leyden, 1586), p. 4; Henry Peacham, *Minerva Britanna: or, A Garden of Heroical Devises* (London, 1612), p. 134; and Donald Gordon, "'Veritas Filia Temporis': Hadrianus Junius and Geoffrey Whitney," *Journal of the Warburg and Courtauld Institutes,* 3 (1939–40), 228–40.

[100] See Fritz Saxl, "Veritas Filia Temporis," *Philosophy & History: Essays Presented to Ernst Cassirer,* eds Raymond Klibansky and H. J. Paton (New York, Evanston, London, 1963 [1936]), pp. 197–222.

[101] See, in particular, Erwin Panofsky, "Father Time," *Studies in Iconology* (New York, 1967 [1939]), pp. 73–81. For an instructive example from Swift's library, see Ben Jonson's "Hymenæi," *Works,* eds C. H. Herford, and Percy and Evelyn Simpson, VII (Oxford, 1952 [1941]), 233. See LeFanu, *Catalogue,* p. 21.

[102] von Leyden, "Antiquity and Authority," p. 485; see also Hans Blumenberg, *Lebenszeit und Weltzeit,* 2. Aufl. (Frankfurt/M., 1986), pp. 153–62.

cannibalistic, and cruel figure of Kronos (Saturn), who can only "fulfill the office of unveiling Truth [by destroying spurious values]":

> It were endless to recount the several Methods of Tyranny and Destruction, which Your *Governour* is pleased to practise upon this Occasion. His inveterate Malice is such to the Writings of our Age, that of several Thousands produced yearly from this renowned City, before the next Revolution of the Sun, there is not one to be heard of: Unhappy Infants, many of them barbarously destroyed, before they have so much as learnt their *Mother-Tongue* to beg for Pity. Some he stifles in their Cradles, others he frights into Convulsions, whereof they suddenly die; Some he flays alive, others he tears Limb from Limb: Great Numbers are offered to *Moloch*, and the rest tainted by his Breath, die of a languishing Consumption.[103]

In Swift's rewriting, Time triumphs over fame: *Vacuitas filia temporis*, "Posterity's offspring is Emptiness;" or: Time's daughter is Void.

Not coincidentally, "The Conclusion" ends upon "an Experiment very frequent among Modern Authors; which is, to *write upon Nothing*"[104] (if nothing can be concluded, that is). At the end of the book, the Tale-teller continues what he has been doing all along, talking on about the nothing he knows (or the something he does know without saying anything about it) and putting together "a treatise on Nothing ... from the trivial and ridiculous productions of the human spirit." While this treatise on Nothing may well be a paradoxical encomium "on man's Bedlamite achievements" in its own right,[105] nothing, we remember, is also a prerequisite for fashioning a Lucretian cosmos (whether literary or otherwise), which consists of matter *and* void. From this point of view, Swift parries the modern claim to be able to *print* books by the counter-argument that Moderns are not even able to *write* books. The best Moderns can do is to *make* books. Literalizing the old metaphor of poets as "makers," as inventors and creators, who do create *ex nihilo*,[106] Swift describes modern authors as makers of physical objects consisting of matter and void.

In the satirical scene of the *Tale*, the arts of writing and printing have been entirely lost. It will not do, therefore, to call the *Tale* "a parody of the book as a book," emphasizing "to the point of grotesqueness exactly those features which distinguish the printed book *per se*, the printed book as technological artifact, from a human document."[107] The *Tale* cannot be a parody of the book as a book for the simple reason that it never is a book in the first place.

Writing, Socrates urges in Plato's *Phaedrus* (274a–277a) is inhuman because

> first, it pretends "to establish outside the mind what in reality can be only in the mind. It is a thing, a manufactured product."
> Second, "writing destroys memory. Those who use writing will become forgetful, relying on an external resource for what they lack in internal resources. Writing weakens the mind."[108]

---

[103] See Panofsky, *Studies in Iconology*, p. 93; and *Prose Works*, I, 20.

[104] *Prose Works*, I, 133.

[105] Stout, "Speaker and Satiric Vision in Swift's *Tale of a Tub*," pp. 194–95; see also Clark, *Form and Frenzy in Swift's "Tale of a Tub"*, pp. 189–91, as well as the introductory remarks on Fielding's "Essay on Nothing," *Miscellanies*, I, ed. Henry Knight Miller (Oxford, 1972), xxxviii–xxxix.

[106] See Heninger, *Touches of Sweet Harmony*, pp. 287–324.

[107] Hugh Kenner in *Jonathan Swift, A Critical Anthology*, ed. Denis Donoghue (Harmondsworth, Middlesex, 1971), pp. 264–65; endorsed by Peter Steele, *Jonathan Swift: Preacher and Jester* (Oxford, 1978), p. 38.

[108] I am indebted for this idea to Walter J. Ong, *Orality and Literacy: The Technologizing of the Word* (London and New York, 1982), pp. 78–81.

"*Memory* being an Employment of the Mind upon things past, a Faculty, for which the Learned, in our Illustrious Age, have no manner of Occasion,"[109] this passage, with due apologies to Plato, will now have to be rewritten:

Printing, Swift urges in *A Tale of a Tub*, is inhuman because

> first, it pretends "to establish outside the mind what in reality can be only in the mind. It is a thing, a manufactured product."
> Second, "printing destroys memory. Those who use printing will become forgetful, relying on an external resource for what they lack in internal resources. Printing weakens the mind."

In the *Tale*, Swift utilizes (the) two (most important) principles of modern science, which, for good paradoxical measure, were of ancient provenance, to explode the inventions of modern technology. Where/if nothing is held, nothing is produced.[110] As Lucretius had said: *nihil ex nihilo fit.*

---

[109] *Prose Works*, I, 84.

[110] Michael Seidel, *Satiric Inheritance: Rabelais to Sterne* (Princeton, NJ, 1979), pp. 187–91. In a more recent essay, Michael DePorte writes that the *Tale* "affords extensive ... support for the view ... that civilization itself depends on memory" ("From the Womb of Things to Their Grave: Madness and Meaning in Swift," *University of Toronto Quarterly*, 58 [1988–89], 377).

Ann Cline Kelly
*Howard University, Washington, D. C.*

# Swift's *Battle of the Books*: Fame in the Modern Age

ABSTRACT. The clash between the Ancients and the Moderns in the *Battle of the Books* dramatizes Swift's choices as a novice author. Allegiance to the Ancients affirmed the timeless perfection of the classical canon, the élite vocation of the writer, and a nostalgic vision of a hierarchical society. Allegiance to the Moderns affirmed an aesthetics of inclusion, the importance of innovation, and topicality. Swift is poised intellectually and emotionally between these two visions – the one rooted in the aristocratic order of the pastoral landscape, the other generated by the democratic chaos of the market-place. The battle Swift depicts in St James's Library is caused by Bentley's use of Gabriel Naudé's idea that texts should not be organized by chronology or format, but by subject, a radical proposal that puts Ancient and Modern authors in the same category.

Although *The Battle of the Books* is read primarily as Swift's defence of Sir William Temple, Swift had something more personal at stake. In *The Battle of the Books*, Swift explores an issue of great concern to him as an author beginning his career: whether he and his writings will be remembered by Posterity.[1] By 1704, Swift had published several things – the "Ode to the Athenian Society," the editions of Sir William Temple's letters, and *Contests and Dissensions* – yet he was still almost totally unknown, even though his name had appeared on all the publications except the *Contests and Dissensions*. In his early writings, and particularly in *The Battle of the Books*, Swift begins the "trial of ideas" that Lawrence Lipking suggests is part of an author's way of shaping "some sort of career, some sort of destiny or vocation."[2] Of crucial interest to Swift were the possibilities of Fame in the Modern Age.

In the 1690s, when Swift begins writing, the traditional path to the Temple of Fame had become a cul-de-sac. Formerly, those with literary ambitions affected an ethereal distance from everyday bourgeois concerns – the poet invoked the Muse to inspire him, an aristocratic patron to sponsor him, and a heavenly tribunal to award him Fame. After the Civil Wars, when reading material became a broadly produced and distributed commodity in English society, the writer had to lower himself to the market-place to realize his ambitions. The print market-place was a Hobbesian war of "each against all," in which the honoured writers of the past had no inherent advantage. Issues and authors cycled rapidly to satisfy the demand for news and novelties. Was "eternal fame" now impossible? At this time, the "unique

---

[1]   See Ehrenpreis, *Dr Swift*, p. 381.
[2]   Lawrence Lipking, *The Life of the Poet: Beginning and Ending Poetic Careers* (Chicago, 1981), p. xii.

explosive power" of print, according to Jürgen Habermas, redefined the "public sphere" less as the domain of a privileged few, and more as an inclusive arena that previously marginalized citizens could enter.[3] And, as Leo Braudy points out in *The Frenzy of Renown: Fame and its History*, publication, rather than political and military action, was "defining itself as the new prime place of fame."[4] That opened the possibilities of Fame, such as could exist in modern times, to the lower links of the Great Chain of Being, now fast becoming an anachronistic paradigm. The print market-place was thronged by authors of all persuasions jostling for the attention of an expanded reading audience.

Some relished the passing of the Old Order, and some regretted it, a clash of visions that reflected an epic struggle for power. The debate between the relative virtues of the Ancients and the Moderns in the 1690s was a shadow play of this struggle. Allegiance to the Ancients affirmed the perfection of the classical canon, the élite vocation of the writer, and a nostalgic vision of a hierarchical society – in other words, an aesthetics of exclusion that preserved feudal values. Allegiance to the Moderns affirmed an aesthetics of inclusion, the importance of innovation and contemporaneity, the middle-class impatience with the *status quo*, and the hope for a future better than the past.[5] Swift is poised intellectually and emotionally between these two visions – the one rooted in the aristocratic order of the pastoral landscape, the other generated by the democratic chaos of the market-place.

As a psychological defence against the cultural revolution of the late seventeenth century, some writers developed with new urgency the concept of "The Republic of Letters," which had emerged from Renaissance humanism.[6] This self-styled élite, affecting an aristocratic disdain of commerce, defined themselves in contrast to writers without pretensions to Art, Eternity, or a sophisticated audience. Indeed, the term "Grub Street" became more and more prominent after first appearing in the mid-seventeenth century, and "hack," defined as a writer for hire, was another coinage of the period that reflected the growing anxiety of the self-styled "Republic of Letters" about the relation of writing to the market forces that increasingly controlled the production of print.[7]

Those in the "Republic of Letters" saw themselves as writing and reading works worth keeping; in other words, worth binding. They concerned themselves with *books* (defined usually as having more than 100 pages), the most important of which were in folio form, designed to be passed on for generations. By their bulk, their claims to timelessness, and their presumption of an élite audience, these books fostered the fiction of an aristocracy of learning. The books of the self-styled "Republic of Letters" were a minuscule part of the trade in print that was dominated by publications of a few pages, most designed for a short-term use. New research on the distribution and readership of these broadsides and small books indicates that they were consumed in all parts of England and by all classes – that they

---

[3]   See Jürgen Habermas, *The Structural Transformation of the Public Sphere: An Inquiry into a Category of Bourgeois Society* (1962), trans. Thomas Burger and Frederick Lawrence (Cambridge, MA, 1982), p. 20.

[4]   (New York, 1986), p. 361.

[5]   See J. Paul Hunter, *Before Novels: The Cultural Contexts of Eighteenth-Century English Fiction* (New York and London, 1990), pp. 138–39.

[6]   See Elizabeth L. Eisenstein, *The Printing Press as an Agent of Change: Communications and Cultural Transformations in Early-Modern Europe*, 2 vols (Cambridge, 1979), I, 137n287.

[7]   See Elisabeth L. Eisenstein, *Grub Street Abroad: Aspects of the French Cosmopolitan Press from the Age of Louis XIV to the French Revolution* (Oxford, 1992), pp. 133-34.

were not merely "popular" literature for provincials and quasi-literates.[8] Single-sheet broadsides carried the latest news, often in ballad form, but these were increasingly supplemented by cheap, short publications that fall into three, somewhat overlapping, categories: almanacs, pamphlets, and chapbooks.[9] Chapbooks connoted the "timeless" world[10] of myth and archetype manifest in chivalric romances, folktales, fables, and jests. Pamphlets, on the other hand, signified small books that dealt with topical or practical issues – juicy scandals, political intrigue, bizarre occurrences, horrible crimes, useful instruction, clever hoaxes, "true" confessions, humorous stories, deathbed scenes, new discoveries, intriguing proposals, miraculous cures.

In 1715, Myles Davies, in *Icon Libellorum: or, A Critical History of Pamphlets*, described the pervasiveness of pamphlets at all levels of society:

> In *Pamphlets*, Merchants may read their profit and loss, Shopkeepers their Bills of Parcels, Countrymen their Seasons of Husbandry, Sailors their Longitude, Soldiers their Camps and Enemies; thence School-boys may improve their Lessons, Scholars their Studies, Ministers their Sermons, and Zealots their Devisions. *Pamphlets* furnisht Beau's with their Airs, Coquets with their Charms: Pamphlets are as Modish Ornaments to Gentlewomen's Toylets as to Gentlemen's Pockets: Pamphlets carry reputation of Wit and Learning to all that make them their companions: The Poor find their account in Stall-keeping, and in hawking them: The Rich find in them their Shortest Way to the Secrets of Church and State.[11]

Because of their claims to purveying the "newest" and the "latest," pamphlets by their nature are subversive of the *status quo*. Unwelcome changes or oppositional discourse was blamed on the emergence of "pamphlets." In 1703, for instance, Bernard Mandeville published a satire entitled "The Pamphleteers," in which he complained about the smearing of King William's reputation – "So far from Gratitude, that, to our shame, / They [the pamphleteers] dare in open Streets lampoon his Name,"[12] and an anonymous author, writing in 1711, attacked pamphleteers as "*Kidnappers* of the Press [that] make a Livelihood of Watching the Motions and Postures of the Publick, and catch them as they come, to Clap them aboard."[13] Whether the "Republic of Letters" liked it or not, national discourse on everything from politics to poultices was shaped by the hundreds of thousands of cheap publications that were never meant to be bound, the products of what this self-styled élite disdainfully referred to as "Grub Street." As Frank Ellis notes, by the beginning of the eighteenth century, "the world's great age of publicity, propaganda, and projection of public image had clearly begun."[14]

In the print market-place, Fame less and less depended on the judgement of a few, but rather on the recognition of the many, not only in London, but in the distant shires of the

---

[8]  See Margaret Spufford, *Small Books and Pleasant Histories: Popular Fiction and its Readership in Seventeenth-Century England* (Athens, GA, 1982), pp. 45–82; see also Tessa Watt, *Cheap Print and Popular Piety, 1550–1640* (Cambridge, 1991), pp. 3–5.

[9]  See Watt, *Cheap Print*, p. 264.

[10]  See Watt, *Cheap Print*, p. 268.

[11]  Quoted in Leslie Shepard, *The History of Street Literature* (Newton Abbot, Devon, 1973), p. 25.

[12]  (London, 1703), p. 6. The satire is attributed to Mandeville.

[13]  *The Way to Bring the World to Rights: or, Honesty is the Best Policy* (London, 1711), p. 4.

[14]  See "Background," Jonathan Swift, *A Discourse of the Contests and Dissentions Between the Nobles and the Commons in Athens and Rome*, ed. Frank H. Ellis (Oxford, 1967), p. 3.

realm. The most famous names were those connected with the timeless world of the chap-books: Dick Whittington, Long Meg of Westminster, King Arthur, Robin Hood, and Aesop. These figures were inextricably woven into the cultural fabric, so well known that they were "part of the consciousness of the learned or educated as well as of the uneducated; read or seen or talked about by so many people that we can say they were taken for granted as part of the environment."[15] No names in contemporary society were so well known as those of the chap-book characters. A provocative or useful broadside, pamphlet or almanac, distributed in market stalls or by "flying stationers," could make a modern author's name "part of the environment." In the late seventeenth century, for instance, the names of polemicists like Daniel Defoe or the sensationally vituperative almanac maker John Partridge were known in corners of England that had never heard of John Dryden, yet Dryden had the respect of the high and mighty, the traditional arbiters of national culture. What was a young aspiring writer to do? In the past, Fame had been awarded to poets (not prose writers) who developed universal themes in classical genres under the aegis of royal or aristocratic patronage for a learned audience. But now it was unclear whether Fame emanated from above or below, from discerning approval or broad popularity. Swift hedged his bets with his first two publications – the "Ode to the Athenian Society" and *Contests and Dissensions* – by treating topical issues in classical contexts or genres, and *The Battle of the Books* follows this pattern. Both its form and content epitomize the conflict produced in Swift's mind between his understanding of the transient trade of the print market-place and his yearning for something transcendent.

As Joseph M. Levine points out, the debate about the relative merits of the Ancients and the Moderns had bubbled quietly since the medieval period but erupted into a full boil at the end of the seventeenth century, particularly in France. In England, the precipitating event was Sir William Temple's "Essay upon the Ancient and Modern Learning" (1690), in which he espoused the view that no Modern accomplishments could ever rival the monuments of the Ancient world. Temple's essay provoked lengthy responses from two classical scholars, William Wotton and Richard Bentley, who pointed out factual errors in Temple's argument, particularly his assertions about the authorship of the *Epistles of Phalaris* and *Aesop's Fables*.[16] As a gentleman, Temple did not deign to defend himself, especially since his embrace of the Ancients derived not from historical knowledge but from a sentimental longing for a time when hierarchies were unchallenged and educated élites, such as himself, prevailed. Swift took up Temple's thesis, yet not without ambivalence, for Swift was on the outside looking in at the world of privilege. Between the honoured Ancients, whose advocates in England – Sir William Temple and the future Earl of Orrery (Charles Boyle) – were aristocrats, and the demonized Moderns, there was no clear place for Swift to stand. Perhaps this is one reason why the *Battle* dissolves into asterisks and ends with a note, "*Desunt caetera.*"[17]

---

[15] This is Ronald Paulson's definition of phenomena in "popular culture;" see his *Popular and Polite Art in the Age of Hogarth and Fielding* (Notre Dame, IN, 1979), p. x.

[16] See *The Battle of the Books: History and Literature in the Augustan Age* (Ithaca and London, 1991), pp. 1–7. See also Martin Kämper, *Sir William Temples Essays "Upon Ancient and Modern Learning" und "Of Poetry": eine historisch-kritische Ausgabe mit Einleitung und Kommentar* (Frankfurt/M., 1995).

[17] See Jonathan Swift, *"The Battle of the Books": eine historisch-kritische Ausgabe mit literarhistorischer Einleitung und Kommentar*, ed. Hermann Josef Real (Berlin und New York, 1978), p. 22.

While he may not have been able to accept the logical extension of Temple's argument, Swift uses the *Battle* to explore the nature of Fame in the print market-place. He raises again the question he posed in the "Ode to the Athenian Society" – how readers, now typically removed from authors in time and space, will know whether a name on a title-page is "he, or you, or I;"[18] whether an author's work is a "thing" – a commodity with a certain label on it – or the utterance of a living person. In *The Battle of the Books*, the tension between the author-as-speaker (ancient oral culture) and author-as-title-page label (modern print culture) is highlighted by Swift's contradictory strategies. On the one hand, Swift admonishes the reader to remember that his *Battle* is a bloodless abstraction, "So, when *Virgil* is mentioned, we are not to understand the Person of a famous Poet, call'd by that Name, but only certain Sheets of Paper, bound up in Leather, containing in Print the Works of the said Poet, and so of the rest."[19] Yet by anthropomorphizing the texts as soldiers, Swift reinvests them with life. The blurred boundaries between authors and books, people and commodities, are also accentuated, for instance, when Criticism, personified as a monstrous female, transforms herself "into an *Octavo* Compass: her Body grew white, and arid, and split in Pieces with Driness; the thick turned into Pastboard, and the thin into Paper ... and that which before was a Cover of Skin, did still continue so."[20] In the famous engraving that accompanied the text of the 1710 edition, books and soldiers/authors fill the space with no indication of relation, literally in a state of suspension. As Swift discovered for himself with *Contests and Dissensions*, texts do not need authors at all. In such a world, traditional ideas of Fame are problematic.

In each of the three works published in the 1704 volume – *The Battle of the Books*, *A Discourse Concerning the Mechanical Operation of the Spirit*, and *A Tale of a Tub* – Swift revisits a scene that is obviously traumatic – the rapid disappearance of title-pages posted on street corners to advertise new works. Within hours or days, one array of title-pages is replaced by a newer one. In the past, the supplanting of authors by more recent ones proceeded more slowly. For example, Scotus and Aristotle "both concerted together to seize *Plato* by main Force, and turn him out from his antient Station among the *Divines*, where he had peaceably dwelt near Eight Hundred Years. The Attempt succeeded, and the two Usurpers have reigned ever since in his stead."[21] Now, though, constant broils and revolutions are promoted by "a new Species of controversial Books ... instinct with a most malignant Spirit,"[22] and something as obvious (to those who hold that view) as the superiority of the Ancients becomes trivialized in the babel of the "Grub Street" press.[23] As Swift's narrator in *The Battle of the Books* reports, the contretemps between Temple and his attackers is the latest battle to flood the market with pamphlets "known to the World under several Names; As, *Disputes, Arguments, Rejoynders, Brief Considerations, Answers, Replys, Remarks, Reflections, Objections, Confutations*," whose title-pages remain in the streets "for a *very few Days*."[24] In the Modern Age, crowds of pamphlet-writers compete for momentary influence

18  See *Poems*, p. 51, l. 168.
19  *The Battle of the Books*, ed. Real, p. 1.
20  *The Battle of the Books*, ed. Real, p. 14.
21  *The Battle of the Books*, ed. Real, pp. 5–6.
22  *The Battle of the Books*, ed. Real, p. 6.
23  See Sharon Achinstein, "The Politics of Babel in the English Revolution," *Pamphlet Wars: Prose in the English Revolution* (London, 1992), pp. 14–44.
24  *The Battle of the Books*, ed. Real, p. 5 (emphasis added).

in the public sphere of print. They constitute the bulk of the Modern army in *The Battle of the Books*. Swift's narrator describes the "infinite Swarms of *Calones*, [as] a disorderly Rout … All without *Coats* to cover them," to which Swift adds a note: "*These are Pamphlets, which are not bound or cover'd.*"[25] (Perhaps to put his publication in the category of book, rather than non-book, Swift published *The Battle of the Books*, *A Tale of a Tub*, and *A Discourse Concerning the Mechanical Operation of the Spirit* together as a substantial unit.) Although the Ancients win the battle on Friday night in St James's Library, it is clear that the Moderns will win the war: numbers and demographics are on their side.

*The Battle of the Books* epitomizes Swift's existential stalemate as an author. By definition, he cannot be an Ancient. Being an honorary Ancient, like Temple, consigns one to cheer-leading a defunct team, a futile exercise in nostalgia. Being a Modern puts him among company he has been taught to despise as lowbrow mercenaries, but it is difficult to see what else he can be. And in the Modern Age, no work persists long in public consciousness. *The Battle*-historian reports that most "*Books of Controversy*" last but a short time before the next wave of print washes them from the coffee-houses and the street corners. A very few – "the chiefest and largest" – are temporarily preserved in libraries.[26] But becoming part of the library collection does not promise that the memory of an author will live – only that it will be briefly prolonged. For, according to the narrator, a library is a graveyard of literary ambition – "it is with Libraries as with other Cemetaries" that the spirit [of the author] remains with the book a short time, "till *Dust* or *Worms* have seized upon it; which to some may happen in a few Days, but to others, later."[27] The library, a symbol of cultural memory, is the last preserve of a few authors and their works, but even there, decay and succession make fame illusory. The *Battle* presents a vision horrific to the aspiring writer of a world where all texts – both Ancient and Modern – and the authors who created them, "vanish[] or dissolve[]."[28]

Swift's use of St James's Library as setting is highly significant. Although Wotton accused Swift of plagiarizing *The Battle of the Books* "out of a *French* Book, entituled, *Combat des Livres*,"[29] neither of the two likeliest possibilities, François de Callières' *Histoire Poëtique de la Guerre nouvellement déclarée entre les Anciens et les Modernes* (1688) or Antoine Furetière's *Nouvelle allégorique ou Histoire des derniers Troubles arrivés au Royaume d'Éloquence* (1658) uses the library setting. Swift's battle takes place in St James's Library because Richard Bentley, who had incurred the wrath of the honorary Ancients by attacking Sir William Temple, was head librarian, and so it was natural to beard the lion in his den. But more than that, Bentley's conception of libraries and his role as librarian represented an unsettling vision of the future. In 1697, Bentley had published *A Proposal for Building a Royal Library, and Establishing it by Act of Parliament*, which made clear his ambitions to create a grand national library open to the public. This idea was first promoted in England by John Evelyn, who translated Gabriel Naudé's *Instructions Concerning Erecting of a Library* (1627; trans. 1661), and dedicated it to Edward, Earl of Clarendon, for his promotion and encouragement of the Royal Society. Naudé's faith in the liberating effects of ever-

---

[25]  *The Battle of the Books*, ed. Real, p. 12.
[26]  *The Battle of the Books*, ed. Real, p. 5.
[27]  *The Battle of the Books*, ed. Real, p. 5.
[28]  *The Battle of the Books*, ed. Real, p. 5.
[29]  See *The Battle of the Books*, ed. Real, p. lxiv.

increasing knowledge fit into the Royal Society's agenda. (Bentley was a member of the Royal Society, and a friend of Evelyn's.) Bentley's concept of a national library was guided by the taxonomic impulses and democratic principles of the Royal Society, both at odds with the hierarchies the honorary Ancients admired. Not until 1753, when an Act of Parliament established the British Museum, was Bentley's proposal fully enacted.

Many of the ideas on library organization attributed to Bentley in *The Battle of the Books* are directly derived from Naudé. Rather than a shrine to prevailing ideologies, Naudé conceived of the library as a place where "whoever had occasion for it, should have free accesse"[30] to the whole range of opinions on an issue. For instance, he welcomed the works of both the Church Fathers and the heretics; both Aristotle and the "more then thirty or fourty Authors" who have written against him; both the classics and street literature.[31] Naudé's suggestion that contemporary ephemera should be collected was a radical one, but he reasoned that future scholars would want details of contemporary controversies.[32] Indeed, such items as "*Libels, Placarts, Theses, Fragments, Proofs*, and the like" should not be despised, but sought out for the library; by dismissing them as "mean baubles, and pieces of no consideration, we happen to lose a world of rare collections, and such as are sometimes the most curious pieces of the whole Library."[33] Rather than shelving materials chronologically or by size and format (both accepted methods), Naudé makes the revolutionary proposal that works should be shelved by subject, no matter when they were written or whether they are octavo pamphlets or folio volumes, for in an "infinity of little [modern] Books ... there is more profit and contentment" than in books of greater bulk and antiquity.[34] In general, Naudé disparages any deference to the Ancients. There is ample evidence, he claims, that "the wits are stronger, more polite, and abstracted than ever formerly they were ... From hence we may infer, that it would be a fault unpardonable in one who professes to store a Library, not to place in it ... *Clavius, Maurolicus* and *Vietta* after *Euclide* and *Archimedes*; *Montagne* ... next to *Seneca* and *Plutarch* ... *Ariosto, Tasso, du Bartas*, next to *Homer* and *Virgil*."[35] Naudé's shelving procedures put Ancients and Moderns cheek to jowl.

Bentley's application of Naudé's ideas seems to be the cause of the "Battle of the Books" in St James's Library. In accordance with Naudé's directives, Bentley included in the collections topical works, refugees of various "paper wars," in this case the debates on the Ancients *vs* the Moderns. *The Battle*-narrator ruefully predicted that when the "new Species of controversial Books" were "admitted into the publick Libraries ... they would create Broyls."[36] In addition, Bentley, again following Naudé, ignored the hierarchical ranking of the books and organized them by subject, resulting in strange shelf mates – "*Des-Cartes* [was] next to *Aristotle*; Poor *Plato* had got between *Hobbes* and the *Seven Wise Masters*, and *Virgil* was hemm'd in with *Dryden* on one side, and *Withers* on the other." The battle ensued because the Ancients could not force the Moderns, especially librarian Bentley, to

---

[30] See *Instructions Concerning Erecting of a Library* ... By Gabriel Naudeus, P. *And now Interpreted by Jo. Evelyn, Esquire* (London, 1661), p. 91.

[31] See Naudé, *Instructions*, p. 28.

[32] See Naudé, *Instructions*, pp. 30–31.

[33] Naudé, *Instructions*, p. 57.

[34] See Naudé, *Instructions*, p. 43.

[35] Naudé, *Instructions*, pp. 41–42.

[36] *The Battle of the Books*, ed. Real, p. 6.

concede that "Priority was due to them, from long Possession, and in regard of their Prudence, Antiquity, and above all, their great Merits."[37]

Aside from his espousal of Naudé's ideas and his unmannerly correction of Sir William Temple's "facts," Bentley epitomized other Modern errors that the honorary Ancients thought pernicious. His *Proposal for Building a Royal Library* would strike them as a bid to increase the power of the "money-men" and the scientific "projectors," neither of whom had a proper respect for the English caste system. Most of the items in Bentley's *Proposal* were projects for financing the library and enhancing its influence. Bentley argued, for example, that the library superstructure should be improved to attract international scholars, whose foreign currency would stimulate the national economy and more than make up for the investments required.[38] Bentley's materialism would also have been evident in his bid to make the library an institutional home for the Royal Society. To the honorary Ancients, the Royal Society and "Grub Street" were both epitomes of anti-humanistic (that is, anti-hierarchical) thinking. In Swift's *Battle*, the patron deity of the Moderns, the monstrous goddess Criticism, inspires the assault against the "Priority" of the Ancients and, for aid and comfort, particularly blesses "her Seminaries of *Gresham* and *Covent-Garden*,"[39] metonymies for new, relatively egalitarian, centres of discourse – the Royal Society and the coffee-houses.[40] Bentley's proposal to increase funding for the library to expand it to 200,000 volumes and to enhance its national and international status would be seen by Temple and the allies of the Ancients as a form of cultural imperialism that would raise Bentley's private stock and the general welfare of a class that did not know its place – the traders and entrepreneurs who would make England a "nation of shop-keepers" and whose tastes did not run to Greek and Latin poetry. No doubt, the honorary Ancients would not be surprised to learn that Karl Marx did his research in the British Library.

The terms of Swift's *Battle* are echoed in the apocalyptic rhetoric of our current "Battle of the Books," in which Alan Bloom and E. D. Hirsch represent the Ancients, and Henry Louis Gates, Jr, and Gayatri Spivak, the Moderns. At stake for the combatants is the survival of a civilization (as epitomized in the literary canon) that assures their dominance. Today, as in the early eighteenth century, the academic debate may be moot, because cultural discourse is only marginally controlled by the educated élite. Rather, the construction of issues and celebrities occurs in broadly available media that shapes, and is shaped by, the sensibilities of the many. As the current "canon wars" became a staple of talk shows and weekly magazines, Alan Bloom himself was made famous by the cultural democracy he deplored. In a similar fashion, the victory in Swift's *Battle of the Books* would not be won in the library, but in the "town." It was the opinion of "the Town"[41] that Temple's character had been besmirched, thus prompting defences by Swift and others. Their strategy was to smear Bentley to the town, making him "the Jest and Sting of ... many thousand Periods, the Common Chat of Coffee-houses and Taverns."[42] Yet in truth, general interest in the debate may have been

---

[37] *The Battle of the Books*, ed. Real, p. 7.
[38] See Richard Bentley, *A Proposal for Building a Royal Library, and Establishing it by Act of Parliament* (London, 1697), p. 2.
[39] *The Battle of the Books*, ed. Real, p. 14.
[40] On coffee-houses, see Habermas, *The Structural Transformation of the Public Sphere*, p. 33.
[41] *The Battle of the Books*, ed. Real, p. 1.
[42] See *An Answer to a late Book written against ... Dr. Bentley* (London, 1699), sig. A2v–A3, quoted in Levine, *The Battle of the Books*, p. 72.

exaggerated by the principals, for the judgement of Dunton's *Works of the Learned*, a prototype of *Reader's Digest*, was that the controversy was "a dry and insipid Business", "a meer Trifle," for "it signifies but little" who wrote the Phalaris epistles.[43]

Swift's unstable irony and his humorous detachment oscillate the *Battle* between epic and mock-epic, making its genre uncertain. In fact, it could be read as a gothic fiction that aestheticizes deeply repressed fears, the nightmares of the aspiring author, that is, that most works are dead on arrival and that those that manage to enter the sanctuary of the library find that death awaits them shortly. In the *Battle*, "Fame" is a displaced person – she "much frequented, and had a large Apartment formerly assigned her in the *Regal Library*" – all in past tense.[44] Swift obviously fears that "modern Fame" is an oxymoron.

One figure, playing a central role in *The Battle of the Books* exemplifies textual endurance: Aesop.[45] Aesop enters the narrative to draw the moral of the fable of the spider and the bee, an act that precipitates the battle. Jayne Elizabeth Lewis argues that "Aesop enjoyed a celebrity perhaps unrivalled by any other literary figure of the day, living or dead,"[46] and Annabel Patterson asserts that Aesop "had become an institution"[47] in the late seventeenth century. Then and now, Aesop is a household word, "part of the environment," a "universal literary figure ... alive today as he was in Caxton's day."[48] In the 1993–94 *Books in Print*, twenty-seven texts were listed under Aesop-as-author, and eleven under Aesop-as-subject. Then and now, Aesop is the province of scholars and beginning readers, of the "Republic of Letters" and of "Grub Street." In the Restoration, for example, Aesop and the fables attributed to him were the subjects not only of learned essays by gentlemen like Temple and Wotton, but of chap-books as well.[49] Aesop was not only a name, however, but a legendary character whose life was renarrated and elaborated.[50] In short, Aesop was famous.

Swift seems to have sought the kind of fame Aesop had – a fame made more elusive by the crowded competition of texts and authors for the short attention span of a diverse audience. Although Swift's accomplishment as a writer is clear, we need to appreciate a neglected aspect of his genius: his uncannily accurate analysis of the mechanisms that create fame in the Modern Age. Indeed, Braudy urges us "to investigate the process by which fame becomes a matter of premeditation, a result of media management as much as of achievement, as well as how the great of the past behaved in such a way as to project larger-than-life images of themselves that would last longer than any specific action."[51] In *Self-Crowned Laureates*, Richard Helgerson analyses how Spenser, Jonson, and Milton each self-consciously worked to construct themselves as "laureates" – a nationally recognized voice – by differ-

---

[43] Quoted in Levine, *The Battle of the Books*, p. 83.

[44] See *The Battle of the Books*, ed. Real, p. 12.

[45] I am much indebted to Jayne Elizabeth Lewis for the recognition of Aesop's significance.

[46] "Swift's Aesop/Bentley's Aesop: The Modern Body and the Figures of Antiquity," *The Eighteenth Century*, 32 (1991), 106.

[47] *Fables of Power: Aesopian Writing and Political History* (Durham, NC, and London, 1991), p. 18.

[48] Edward Hodnett, *Aesop in England: The Transmission of Motifs in Seventeenth-Century Illustrations of Aesop's Fables* (Charlottesville, VA, 1979), p. 3.

[49] See William Coolidge Lane, ed., *Catalog of English and American Chapbooks and Broadside Ballads in Harvard College Library* (Cambridge, MA, 1905), p. 28.

[50] See Patterson, "Aesop's Life: Fathering the Fable," *Fables of Power*, pp. 13–43; and Lewis, "Swift's Aesop/Bentley's Aesop," pp. 105–8.

[51] *The Frenzy of Renown*, p. 15.

entiating themselves from the other voices of the past and present.[52] Swift, beginning his career when the old "literary system" was being revolutionized by the print market-place, had new, and perhaps more difficult, problems to solve.

That Swift succeeded in his desires to be remembered – not just as a name on a title-page but as a biographical presence – is evident. "Swiftian," like "Aesopian," has entered the language, often in lower case. Swift, like Aesop, is read by children and adults. Swift's life, like Aesop's, is grist for both the mills of "Grub Street" and the "Republic of Letters" – versions of Swift's life have appeared in jest-books carried by the chapmen and in scholarly biographies, in Sunday supplement magazines and literary journals, in melodramas and in medical treatises. When writing his definitive biography, Ehrenpreis had to struggle to clear away the "fables" and "legendary Swiftiana" that had accumulated around his subject.[53] With the hindsight of history, we know that Swift's anxieties as a young author were unfounded.

Swift shows a prophetic understanding of the dynamics of modern fame in *The Battle of the Books*. In that and his other works, Swift, like the author of the *Tale of a Tub*, has his finger on "the World's Pulse, and [his] own,"[54] information he used in pursuit of literary fame – a prize he won and retained for almost three hundred years. In *The Battle of the Books*, as Hermann J. Real remarks, Swift's writing brilliantly defends the Ancients, yet paradoxically clinches the case for the Moderns.[55] Real ends his introduction to *The Battle of the Books* by quoting a poem from James Sterling that will serve nicely for this conclusion as well:

> In spite of his learning, fine reasons, and style,
> – Would you think it? – he favours our cause all the while:
> We raise by his conquest our glory the higher,
> And from our defeat to a triumph aspire;
> Our great brother-modern, the boast of our days,
> Unconscious, has gain'd for our party the bays:
> St. James's old authors, so famed on each shelf,
> Are vanquish'd by what he has written himself.[56]

No doubt that Swift planned it this way.

---

[52] See *Self-Crowned Laureates: Spenser, Jonson, Milton, and the Literary System* (Berkeley, Los Angeles, London, 1983).

[53] See *Mr Swift*, p. ix.

[54] *Prose Works*, I, 135.

[55] See *The Battle of the Books*, ed. Real, p. lxxv.

[56] *The Battle of the Books*, ed. Real, p. lxxv.

Michael DePorte
*University of New Hampshire, Durham*

# Contemplating Collins: Freethinking in Swift

ABSTRACT. One of the striking things about Swift's parody of Anthony Collins's *Discourse on Freethinking* is how much of its language is drawn from Collins himself. Whole passages are lifted verbatim, though Swift is at pains to adapt them in ways that make Collins's witty, generally reasonable defence of freethinking look monumentally stupid. Swift is also at pains to underscore and embellish Collins's irreverent observations so that they are even more disturbing to belief than in the original. Swift's aim, no doubt, was to demonstrate how truly damaging Collins's *Discourse* was to Christian faith, to show what happens once one starts thinking "freely." But the effect of these elaborations is to exacerbate doubt. Swift's versions of Collins's impieties linger in mind more vividly than those of the *Discourse* itself. The *Abstract* thus has some of the same, disorientating ambiguity in its treatment of religious questions as *A Tale of a Tub*.

Swift's view of freethinkers is well known. He despised them as people who, under cover of disinterested inquiry, aimed "to overthrow those Tenets in Religion, which have been held inviolable almost in all Ages by every Sect that pretends to be Christian."[1] He ridiculed them as men who found belief in the Gospel "too difficult" for their meagre capacities, and who would have languished in obscurity had they not got the idea of attacking religion. "Who would ever have suspected *Asgill* for a Wit, or *Toland* for a Philosopher, if the inexhaustible Stock of Christianity had not been at hand to provide them with Materials? What other Subject through all Art or Nature could have produced *Tindal* for a profound Author, or furnished him with Readers?"[2]

So it is hardly surprising that when Anthony Collins published his exuberantly irreverent *Discourse on Freethinking*, Swift should take notice, especially since Collins had attacked one of Archbishop King's sermons only a few years before. "I came home at 7," he wrote to Stella in mid-January of 1713, "& began a little Whim wch just came into my Head, & will make a threepenny Pamphlet, it shall be finished and out in a Week, and if it succeds you shall know what it is, otherwise not."[3] To appreciate what Swift does in *Mr. Collins's Discourse of Free-Thinking, Put into Plain English, by way of Abstract for the Use of the Poor,*

---

[1]  *Prose Works*, II, 60.
[2]  *Prose Works*, II, 36. In *Jonathan Swift and the Millennium of Madness* (Leiden, New York, Köln, 1992), Kenneth Craven argues that Swift's preoccupation with freethinkers was such that he made Toland the principle object of satire in *A Tale of a Tub*; see Chapter 2.
[3]  *Prose Works*, XVI, 603–4.

it is useful to know something of Collins himself. He was certainly the most genteel of the "Tribe of *Free-Thinkers*" Swift scornfully catalogued in the *Examiner*[4] and elsewhere, a man to whom things seem to have come easily. Born to wealth, educated at Eton and Cambridge, in his twenties the trusted friend of Locke, and already, Locke said, possessed of "an estate in the Country, a Library in Town, Freinds every where."[5] Collins wrote often to thank Locke for sharing his thoughts with him and to express his concern with discovering truth, particularly in matters of religion. Locke responded that loving truth for its own sake was "the principal part of humane perfection in this world and the seed plot of all other vertues," and that were he just "seting out in the world," he would consider it a "great happyness" to have a companion like Collins, with whom he might seek truth "in earnest," from whom he "might receive it undisguisd," and to whom he might "communicate what [he] thought true freely." Now that he was nearing the end of his life, Locke said, he felt he could "see openings to truth, and direct paths leading to it wherein a little industry and application would setle ones mind with satisfaction" – even in matters of religion – "and leave noe darkeness or doubt even to the most scrupulous." But it was for younger people like Collins to carry on the work, and Locke urged him to do so.[6]

Collins needed no urging. He had a nose for direct paths in matters of religion, and took off down them with a vengeance. When the *Discourse of Free-Thinking* was published, there was an enormous hue and cry. Bentley savaged his scholarship. Berkeley mocked him in the *Guardian*. Benjamin Ibbot devoted the Boyle Lectures of 1713 and 1714 to taking his arguments apart. Steele proposed that he be "denied the common Benefits of Air and Water."[7] There was good reason for their distress. Collins's *Discourse* is full of ideas that became the staples of later polemics against organized religion, notably those of Voltaire, who took the work quite seriously, and who had copies of it and three other of Collins's tracts in his library.[8] Years later, Temple, in *A Portrait of the Artist*, would hail Collins as the "first man in Europe" to preach freedom of thought.[9]

The *Discourse* develops from a compelling premise: if God requires us to know certain truths as necessary to our salvation, then clearly we have a right, indeed an obligation, to discover those truths. Which is better, Collins asks, to accept without examination whatever opinion is endorsed by authorities of the country in which one happens to live, or to study those crucial issues for oneself and make the best judgement of them possible? Collins reminds readers that Christ was considered a dangerous freethinker by the orthodox of his day – "all the Priests upon earth were Enemys to [him] and his Gospel." Whoever thinks ser-

---

[4]   See *Prose Works*, III, 55.

[5]   *The Correspondence of John Locke*, ed. E. S. de Beer, VIII (Oxford, 1989), 189 (7 February 1704).

[6]   See *Correspondence of Locke*, VIII, 97–98 (29 October 1703).

[7]   *The Guardian*, ed. John Calhoun Stephens (Lexington, KY, 1982), p. 49 (14 March 1713). Robert Phiddian has identified no less than 20 attacks on Collins in 1713. See "The Reaction to Collins's *A Discourse of Free-Thinking* 'Not Politicks'?" *Swift Studies*, 4 (1989), 69–70. For another account of the response to Collins, see James O'Higgins, SJ, *Anthony Collins: The Man and his Works* (The Hague, 1970), pp. 78–79.

[8]   For Collins's influence on Voltaire, see Norman L. Torrey, *Voltaire and the English Deists* (New Haven, 1930), pp. 25–58. For a discussion of Collins's contribution to the development of atheism, see David Berman, *A History of Atheism in Britain* (London and New York, 1990).

[9]   James Joyce, *A Portrait of the Artist as a Young Man* (New York, 1964), p. 197.

iously about this should hesitate before subordinating his judgement to that of any priests. The history of theological controversy within the Anglican Church alone should make one think twice about the whole idea of religious authority. As for the objection often raised by the orthodox, that the *"Bulk of Mankind"* lacks the *"Capacity to think justly about any Speculations,"* Collins counters that it is absurd to think God would require people to believe something without giving them the means to know it. If most people lack the capacity to distinguish between truth and falsehood, they cannot be held responsible for believing one thing rather than another. It cannot really matter what they believe.[10]

As for concerns that *Free-Thinking* will lead to a clamorous proliferation of doctrines and consequent social chaos, Collins asks readers to recall the harmony in which Pythagoreans, Epicureans, Stoics, Platonists, Skeptics, and Cynics all lived together in ancient Greece and Rome, though differing from one another in their views of the gods, the immortality of the soul, and the freedom of the will. Anticipating Gibbon's nostalgia for an easy-going, tolerant pre-Christian world in which religions were regarded by ordinary people as equally true; by philosophers as equally false; and by magistrates as equally useful, Collins writes that such happy coexistence was possible because the "mild and peaceable Principle of allowing one another to *think freely*, and to have different Opinions" was universally accepted. If, like Christians in subsequent times, the ancients had "condemn'd one another to Fire and Faggot, Imprisonment and Fines in this World, and Damnation in the next," and stirred up the "Passions of the ignorant part of Mankind in their several Parties; then Confusion, Disorder, and *every evil Work* had follow'd, as it does at this day among those who allow no Liberty of Opinion." The way to assure that ideas do not disrupt the harmony of society is to allow greater freedom of expression, not less. Collins notes that the Turks have been far more tolerant of Christians than Christians have been of other religions, that they permitted Christians to live among them "(upon the terms of paying a small Tribute) tho those Christians esteem their Prophet an Impostor, and would infallibly extirpate with Fire and Sword their present Protectors, if the Empire was in their hands."[11]

Reading Collins's *Discourse* after reading Swift's parody of it makes clear that Swift is not kidding a bit when he speaks of using Collins's *"very Words"* and *"only adding some few Explanations"* of his own.[12] Whole passages are lifted verbatim; in fact the greater part of Swift's *Abstract* is lifted verbatim or in paraphrase. One might almost say Swift thought Collins's views so absurd that merely to extract them, to stuff them "back down his own throat," as Clive Probyn put it, would be satire enough – *almost* say this, because Collins is selectively quoted, wickedly paraphrased, and strangely amplified.[13]

---

[10] *A Discourse of Free-Thinking, Occasion'd by the Rise and Growth of a Sect Call'd Free-Thinkers* (London, 1713), pp. 99–100.

[11] See Collins, *Discourse*, pp. 101–3.

[12] *Prose Works*, IV, 28.

[13] "'Haranguing upon Texts': Swift and the Idea of the Book," *Proceedings of The First Münster Symposium on Jonathan Swift*, eds Hermann J. Real and Heinz J. Vienken (München, 1985), p. 190. Many of those who touch on *Mr. Collins's Discourse* fail to note how closely Swift follows Collins's language. Daniel Eilon, for example, speaks of Swift translating Collins's "obscurantist jargon … into plain English," when the language of Swift's parody is mostly Collins's own. See *Factions' Fictions* (Newark, London, Toronto, 1991), p. 120. Until Probyn's essay, no one had much to say about Swift's parody of Collins. Harold Williams refers to it, in a footnote, as one of Swift's most "successful essays in the art of irony" (*Prose Works*, XVI, 603n33). John Bullitt calls it "brilliant" and discusses

Swift's most obvious tack is to make Collins's defence of freethinking look stunningly dumb, taking care, as he says in his preface to the *Abstract*, to obliterate that "*shew of Logick*" in the original which may have frightened away "Well-willers to Infidelity."[14] Swift reduces Collins's insistence on the right to think freely to a demented, unbeguiling slogan:

> Whoever cannot *think freely*, may let it alone if he pleases, by virtue of his Right to *think freely*; that is to say, if such a Man *freely thinks* that he cannot *think freely*, of which every Man is a sufficient Judge, why then he need not *think freely*, unless he *thinks* fit.[15]

Swift ignores what Collins says about toleration in the ancient world, and pounces on his remark about the relative tolerance of the Turks:

> There *Christians* and *Jews* are tolerated, and live at ease, if they can hold their Tongues and *think freely*, provided they never set foot within the *Moschs*, nor write against *Mahomet*: A few Plunderings now and then by their *Janisaries* are all they have to fear.[16]

And he everywhere attributes to Collins a nonsensical dogmatism of which the *Discourse* provides no real instance: "It is the indispensable Duty of a *Free Thinker*, to endeavour *forcing* all the World to think as he does, and by that means make them *Free Thinkers* too."[17]

Collins is not only a more interesting and plausible writer than one would surmise from Swift's *Abstract*; he is a more ironical one as well. Just before his death in 1729, he wrote a defence of ridicule and irony in which, among other writers, he defended Swift, though not in a manner likely to gratify the Dean. The occasion for this tract was a call from Nathanael Marshall, the Canon of Windsor, for a moratorium on levity in writing about religious matters. Collins replied that he thought "the Opinions and Practices of Men in all Matters, and especially in Matters of Religion ... so absurd and ridiculous that it is impossible for them not to be the Subjects of Ridicule." And he wondered how any High Churchman could object to ironic treatments of religious subjects when the Church had received such "Advantages ... from the *Berkenheads*, the *Heylins*, the *Ryves's*, the *Needhams*, the *Lestranges*, the *Nalsons*, the *Lesleys*, the *Oldesworths* ... the *Eachards*, the *Tom Browns*, and *Swifts*." Collins may well have learned from Swift the power of a nice, unflattering list. Later, focusing on Swift himself, he asked whether the Church "would be willing to have the reverend Author of the *Tale of a Tub*, one of the greatest *Droles* that ever appear'd upon the Stage of the World, punish'd for that or any other of his *drolling* Works."[18]

Swift saw to it that Collins's wit was either lost in translation to the *Abstract* or turned back upon him. Witness his treatment of the remarks on missionaries in the *Discourse*, in-

---

Swift's use of the "refutative enthymeme" (*Jonathan Swift and the Anatomy of Satire* [Cambridge, MA, 1953], pp. 97–102). Irvin Ehrenpreis, on the other hand, finds the mockery too simplistic "to hold one's interest" or deserve much comment (see *Dr Swift*, p. 588). Since Probyn's article, another piece, by happy coincidence, winner of the Center's first Rodino Prize, has appeared on Swift's parody of Collins: Judith C. Mueller's "The Ethics of Reading in Swift's *Abstract* on Freethinking," *Studies in English Literature*, 31 (1991), 483–98. Both Probyn and Mueller take a penetrating look at the way Collins's attack on priestly authority raised disturbing issues for Swift regarding the interpretation of texts – texts in general, but most importantly, the Bible.

14  *Prose Works*, IV, 27–28.
15  *Prose Works*, IV, 38.
16  *Prose Works*, IV, 39.
17  *Prose Works*, IV, 36.
18  See *A Discourse Concerning Ridicule and Irony in Writing* (London, 1729), pp. 19, 26–27, 39.

cluding Collins' suggestion that resolute churchmen like Swift and Atterbury should be sent out to preach the Gospel in remote, uncomfortable corners of the world:

> Here is a Society in *London* for propagating *Free-thinking* throughout the World, encouraged and supported by the Queen and many others. You say perhaps, it is for propagating the Gospel. Do you think the Missionaries we send, will tell the Heathens that they must not *think freely*? No surely; why then, 'tis manifest those Missionaries must be *Free-thinkers*, and make the Heathens so too. But why should not the King of *Siam*, whose Religion is Heathenism and Idolatry, send over a parcel of his Priests to convert us to *his Church*, as well as we send Missionaries there? Both Projects are exactly of a Piece, and equally reasonable.[19]

Swift's burlesque has undeniable satiric force. But the remarks he mocks have a force and wit of their own.

Elaborating on a point Toland had made in *Christianity not Mysterious*, Collins observes that Church missionaries tacitly endorse freethinking because they encourage prospective converts to think freely about *their* "Notions of God and Religion," beliefs "they have receiv'd from their Ancestors, or which are *establish'd by Law* among them." Otherwise, they could never be open to the truths of Christianity. "Can it be suppos'd," he asks, "that our *Missionaries* would begin with telling 'em, that they ought not to *think freely* of their own, or our Religion?" And once they have, "by the means of *Free-Thinking*," embraced Christianity, can it be supposed the missionaries would tell them they ought to think freely no more? "This were to proceed very inconsistently in the Work of Conversion, while no other Arms but Reason and Evidence were made use of to convert."[20] Nor, Collins continues innocently, can we think that those who urge the Siamese, say, to take an unbiased look at their sacred doctrines would be so unreasonable as to deny a request from the King of Siam to send missionaries to England. After all, the Church of England could, and should, counter by sending those who would make the best possible case for its *"Doctrine and Discipline"* – hence the proposal to ship out parsons like Swift and Atterbury. Surely, it would be of enormous benefit to both countries, Collins concludes slyly, to have their most zealous priests busy elsewhere.[21]

Swift burlesques the analogy Collins had made between *Free-Thinking* and *Free-Seeing* even more brilliantly than he does his reflections on missionaries:

> Why may not I be deny'd the liberty of *Free-seeing*, as well as *Free-thinking*? Yet no body pretends that the first is unlawful, for a Cat may look on a King; though you be near-sighted, or have weak or soar Eyes, or are blind, you may be a *Free-seer*; you ought to see for your self, and not trust to a Guide to chuse the Colour of your Stockings, or save you from falling into a Ditch.[22]

---

19  *Prose Works*, IV, 30–31.
20  Collins, *Discourse*, pp. 41–42. Toland stressed the importance of rational inquiry in the gaining of converts, and used the example of Siam: "Suppose a *Siamese* Talapoin should tell a *Christian* Preacher that *Sommonocodom* forbad the Goodness of his Religion to be tri'd by the Light of Reason; how could the *Christian* confute him, if he likewise should maintain that certain Points of Christianity were above Reason? The Question would not be then, whether *Mysteries* might be allow'd in the true Religion, but who had more Right to institute them, *Christ* or *Sommonocodom?*" (*Christianity not Mysterious: or, A Treatise Showing that there is nothing in the Gospel Contrary to Reason, nor Above it* [London, 1696], p. 142).
21  See Collins, *Discourse*, pp. 41–43.
22  *Prose Works*, IV, 29.

But again, the passage in the *Discourse* has its own sting. Suppose, Collins says, "that certain Men have a fancy in their heads, that it is absolutely necessary either to the Peace of Society or some other great purpose, that all Men should have the same Belief with relation to certain Objects of the Eyes; and in order to obtain that end, will make all Men under their power subscribe to the same *Confession* of *Eye-sight Faith*." Suppose further, he continues, they insist the various articles of *Eye-sight Faith* are "*above,* but *not contrary to Eye-sight,*" that they point to "ten thousand Mistakes" we make in using our eyes, argue that "trusting to *carnal Eye-sight*" is an alarming thing, and insist that we should "rely on the Authority of those Men who have Pensions and Salarys on purpose to study those things." As for the few who dared "use their own Eyes, no Punishments would be too bad for them." They would be "represented sometimes as Madmen, at other times as subtle cunning Fellows who acted by Confederacy, and had secret underhand Pensions from the Lord knows who, and who were assisted by the Devil." Those who would restrict freethinking are no different than those who would argue that "I should be deter'd from using my Eyes, for fear I should mistake in using them; and ... walk abroad with my Eyes shut, because of the possibility of falling if I should walk abroad with my Eyes open."[23]

Understandably, Swift would be eager to take the edge off Collins' sarcasm in a passage like this, with its strong echoes of the *Tale*: Peter's decree that whatever the bread *looks* like to his brothers, they'll be damned forever if they do not believe it mutton; Jack's credo that "*the Eyes of the Understanding see best, when those of the Senses are out of the way.*"[24] Swift would be eager to mute these echoes not least because in his preface to the parody he had already reminded readers how in the past freethinking writers used "*artful Disguises, by which a Jury could only find them guilty of abusing Heathenism or Popery*"[25] – the very charge Wotton had levelled against the *Tale* eight years before.[26] Swift had good reason to discourage comparisons given that the narrator of the *Tale* is, if anything, a more extravagant "freethinker" than Collins.[27] Bound to no fixed doctrine, constrained by no internal principle of consistency, always ready to pursue an idea to the limits of metaphor, the narrator of the *Tale* is a brilliant projection of that young Swift who once told his cousin Thomas he was never miserable so long as his "thoughts were in a Ferment," and told him another time that he could write nothing "easy to be understood thô it were but in praise of an old Shoo."[28] Especially, one might add, when he did not wish to be easily understood.

---

23  Collins, *Discourse*, pp. 15, 18, 26–27.

24  Jonathan Swift, *A Tale of a Tub*, eds A. C. Guthkelch and D. Nichol Smith, 2nd ed. (Oxford, 1958), pp. 118 and 193.

25  *Prose Works*, IV, 27.

26  Under the pretence of attacking "the Ridiculous Inventions of Popery," Wotton wrote, "our *Tale-teller* strikes at the very Root ... and shows at the bottom his contemptible Opinion of every Thing which is called Christianity" ("Wotton's Observations," *A Tale of a Tub*, eds Guthkelch and Smith, pp. 321–22). Roger Lund makes the important point that since no one in the period "openly confessed to his heterodoxy ... such tendencies had to be detected and ferreted out" ("Strange Complicities: Atheism and Conspiracy in *A Tale of a Tub*," *Eighteenth-Century Life*, 13, no 3 [1989], 38).

27  Margaret C. Jacob writes that when divines and university men met over dinner to rail at freethinking publications, the most frequent targets of their indignation were Toland, Tindal, Collins, Asgil, and the author of *A Tale of a Tub*. See *The Newtonians and the English Revolution, 1689–1720* (Ithaca, NY, 1976), pp. 207–8.

28  *Correspondence*, I, 13, 10.

For while Swift detested freethinkers, he always defended free thought as such. "You may force men, by interest or punishment, to say or swear they believe, and to act as if they believed: You can go no further."[29] He regarded the execution of Thomas More with particular horror. More had been condemned not for treasonous words or actions, but for private opinions he had artfully concealed. Only a monster like Henry VIII would kill a man for what he *thought*.[30] Swift's defence of free thought, including his own, is entirely premised on secrecy: "I am not answerable to God for the doubts that arise in my own breast, since they are the consequence of that reason which he hath planted in me."[31] What people *thought* was their own business so long as they did not communicate subversive ideas to the public, or, one is tempted to add, so long as they did not communicate those ideas directly. "All we want," he confided to Stella, is a "little wealth, And much health, And a life by stealth."[32] He was horrified by a proposal put forward in Parliament during the Tory ministry to regulate the press by requiring that an "Author's Name and Place of Abode ... be set to every printed Book, Pamphlet or Paper." Had such a law passed, Swift wrote, "there would have been an End in all likelihood of any valuable Production ... either in Wit or Learning."[33] He told Vanessa he was glad his writing puzzled her, that it cost him "a great many thoughts" to make his letters difficult, and that he wished her letters were as difficult as his, "for then they would be of no consequence if they were dropt by careless messengers."[34]

Few writers have been so possessed by an awareness of "things which must not be expressed." Of course, like those "things" in "The Lady's Dressing Room," or the word "Clap" Swift half smudged out in a letter to Stella because he did not care to write it "plain," all sorts of ideas find a way to expression in his writing.[35] In later years, Pope teased Swift about the effectiveness of his protective cover: "Your method of concealing your self puts me in mind of the bird I have read of in India, who hides his head in a hole, while all his feathers and tail stick out."[36] Many peculiar feathers do indeed protrude from the *Tale*, some of which hint at possibilities as alarming to orthodoxy as anything in Collins.[37] The story of the coats would be a straightforward, if somewhat risky, Anglican parable of Church history, had Swift not complicated it by suggesting that all coats, plain, adorned, or ragged, also belong to a system of belief which regards everything in the universe as an article of clothing, a garb for one ugly nakedness or another, that can be put on and slipped off as occasion demands. The description of religious innovators as mad would be untroubling,

---

29  *Prose Works*, IX, 261.
30  This is perhaps why Swift urged Thomas Beach to soften a reference to James II's misrule in a poem entitled *Eugenio* which Beach had sent him for corrections: "*James* he was a weak bigoted Papist, desirous like all Kings of absolute power, but not properly a tyrant" (*Correspondence*, IV, 321).
31  *Prose Works*, IX, 262.
32  *Prose Works*, XV, 303.
33  *Prose Works*, VII, 105–6.
34  *Correspondence*, II, 353. Vanessa wrote to him soon after to say she thought "no humane creature" capable of guessing his thoughts because "never any one liveing" thought like him (*Correspondence*, II, 364).
35  *Prose Works*, XVI, 519.
36  *Correspondence*, IV, 217–18.
37  I have discussed the question of Swift's personal religious views in "The Road to St Patrick's: Swift and the Problem of Belief," *Swift Studies*, 8 (1993), 5–17.

had Swift explicitly exempted the innovations of Christianity, but he did not. We may say that he obviously had in mind religions other than Christianity, religions introduced without the sanction of Divine Revelation. We can point out that the observations about religion and madness come from a former inmate of Bedlam and that we should consider the source. Yet for all we say, the assertion that the propagators of new religions are crazy is left unqualified, except by the ambiguous statement that without madness, "Mankind would unhappily be reduced to the same Belief in Things Invisible."[38] *Which* same belief we are not told. Whatever Swift's intentions may have been, despite the disclaimers of his later "Apology," the *Tale* does invite conjectures unfriendly to Christian belief, considering that the very term, "New Testament," declared a break from the then received "Pattern of Human Learning."

Voltaire liked the *Tale* for the same reason many churchmen hated it, and Collins evidently found in the *Tale* hints he could exploit to his own ends, as he does with his account of "*Eye-sight Faith*." Like Swift, Collins loathed zealots. "*Zeal* to impose Speculations," he says, "has carry'd Men to a pitch of Wickedness, which otherwise *Eye had not seen, nor Ear heard, nor had enter'd into the Heart of Man to conceive.*"[39] But the zealots Collins had in mind are those of established religions, those with institutional power to impose their speculations. He further appropriated the rhetoric of the *Tale* by saying that such people deny "*self-evident Truths*" and suffer from a "distemper'd State of Mind," which leads them to fall under the spell of their own "disorder'd Fancys" or those of others.[40] He, too, sees a problem in the vast number of pretenders to inspiration who in all ages have sought to introduce "new Notions of the Deity, new Doctrines, new Commands, new Ceremonys, and new Modes of Worship." How, he asks, are we to "distinguish between the true Messenger from Heaven and the Impostor?"[41] This is no trivial dilemma, but unlike Swift, Collins sees it as a dilemma with a ready solution. All people need to do is freely consider the evidence for and against each claimant and make a reasoned judgement. And far from implying that the radical origins of Christianity might pose any kind of intellectual dilemma, Collins insists that those origins confirm the value of freethinking and the need to distrust orthodoxy:

> THE Design of the *Gospel* was, by preaching, to set all Men upon *Free-Thinking*, that they might think themselves out of those Notions of God and Religion which were every where *establish'd by Law*, and receive an *unknown God* and an *unknown Religion* on the Evidence the *Apostles* ... produced to convince them.[42]

For Collins, the original newness of Christianity is the most attractive thing about it. He finds in the ministry of St Paul support for his conviction that a true religion will gain converts through rational persuasion. Paul "went frequently into the Synagogues of the *Jews*, and *reason'd* with them; which was not only putting the *Jews* upon *Free-Thinking* on matters of Religion, but taking (according to the present Notions of *Christians*) a very extraordinary step to put them upon *Free-Thinking*." Collins wishes the Church had remained true to its roots and continued to support theological innovations. Paul's preaching, he observes wryly, set a splendid example which, to its shame, the Church of England shows

---

[38]  *A Tale of a Tub*, eds Guthkelch and Smith, p. 169.
[39]  Collins, *Discourse*, p. 112.
[40]  Collins, *Discourse*, pp. 3–4.
[41]  Collins, *Discourse*, p. 40.
[42]  Collins, *Discourse*, p. 44.

no inclination to follow: "For should WILLIAM PENN the *Quaker*, or other religious Person differing from the *Establish'd Church*, come to *St. Paul's* during the time of *Divine Service* to *reason* with the *Court of Aldermen, Preacher*, and *Singing-Men* ... [he] would be treated as a *Madman* and *Fanatick*."[43]

No wonder Swift so often lumped Dissenters and freethinkers together. Both set individual judgement against the Established Church, and both had the annoying habit of invoking the Apostles by way of justification: Dissenters reminding the Church that the Apostles, like themselves, had been humble men, despised and oppressed by priests in power; freethinkers, noting that the Apostles, too, had been thought dangerous radicals in their time.[44] In fact, Collins says, he can think of no man of "Sense and Virtue" who has not given "some proofs of his *Free-Thinking*," nor can he name a single *"Enemy to Free-Thinking*, however dignify'd or distinguish'd, who has not been either Crack-brain'd and Enthusiastical, or guilty of the most Diabolical Vices."[45]

There is a breezy playfulness in Collins's *Discourse* as he runs through his improbable roll-call of freethinkers – Solomon and Socrates, Spenser and Hooker, Bishop Tillotson and Sir William Temple – quotes one Anglican Churchman against another; proposes the exchange of missionaries with Siam; points out resemblances between Christian and pagan doctrines; describes bizarre Catholic rituals on the Continent; and calls High Churchmen enthusiasts. This playfulness made Collins a shiftier target than Wotton, Partridge, or Tindal, and probably annoyed Swift more than anything else about the *Discourse* – not least by suggesting to him how little idea Collins had of what he was playing with. In the "Digression concerning Madness," Swift asks, and leaves unanswered, a powerful question: how can we know the difference between a mad religious vision and authentic inspiration? On the one hand, we need a common faith; on the other, all propagators of faith are doubtful. On the one hand, we accept Christianity as the true religion; on the other, there is no clear rational basis for thinking so. Swift shows reason breaking down, unable to resolve these contradictions. Collins confronts the question of distinguishing delusion from inspiration and answers blandly, weigh the evidence. What, precisely, constitutes "evidence" in spiritual matters, the *Discourse* never makes clear, though from Collins's tongue-in-cheek references to the Bible – which he describes as "a Collection of Tracts given us at divers times by God" – the evidence of Scripture would not seem to count for a great deal.[46] In conversation, Collins is reputed to have said that he regarded St Paul as a man of sense and a gentleman, and that, had Paul claimed in his letters to have performed miracles himself, Collins would have believed him.[47] Had Swift known of this story, it would hardly have increased his estimation of Collins' seriousness. In one respect, Swift's charge that as a freethinker Collins wanted everyone to think like him has a point. For all its appeals to individual judgement, the *Discourse* is less open-ended than the *Tale*. The *Tale* provokes continuing reflection on hard quandaries – on how we should judge revolutionary ideas, on whether common acceptance of an idea makes

[43]  Collins, *Discourse*, pp. 44–45.
[44]  In the *Tale*, Swift ridicules the Dissenters' identification with the persecution of early Christians by describing Jack soliciting street-corner beatings so he can represent himself to his followers as a martyr for the cause; see *A Tale of a Tub*, eds Guthkelch and Smith, pp. 197–98.
[45]  Collins, *Discourse*, pp. 177–78.
[46]  Collins, *Discourse*, p. 10.
[47]  See *Dictionary of National Biography, s.v.*

it valid, or whether delusion is essential to happiness. The ironies of the *Discourse* are essentially simplifying. They encourage one to dismiss the doctrines of Christianity rather than think about them, to share the author's cockiness rather than examine one's own assumptions.

Collins seems to assume a world in which ideas do not have the kind of consequence they have for Swift. He contemplates liberty of expression, and thinks happily of ancient Rome. Swift contemplates such liberty and thinks of the English Civil War. Thoughts, Swift wrote, are the seeds of action.[48] Coming upon a passage in Burnet's *History of His Own Time* (1724–34) which dismissed the Rye House plot as mere talk, he jotted irritably in the margin, "All plots begin with talk."[49] It was a matter of pride to Swift, *as a writer*, to affirm the power of words. "I have found out one secret," he told Temple's nephew, Lord Palmerston, during an angry exchange of letters, "that although you call me a great wit, you do not think me so, otherwise you would have been too cautious to have writ me such a letter."[50]

Collins's appeal for free expression rests on two cheerful suppositions. The first appears early in the *Discourse*, when he draws a glib analogy between religion and the arts and sciences, and suggests that freethinking will lead to better and better religions: "As in *manual Arts* we do only by *free* Trial, Comparison, and Experience of every thing, come to know what is best and perfect in each Art; so in the *Sciences*, Perfection is only to be attain'd by *Free-Thinking*."[51] Painting would never have reached the level it has in Italy if artists had been forbidden to paint living creatures. Astronomy would not have progressed if the "Impositions of Priests" had continued. Freedom of thought and expression are, Collins assures us, "the only way of arriving at perfection" in any science, including "the sublimest of all Sciences, *Theology*."[52] The second supposition, flowing naturally from this analogy, is that God is a reasonable being in human terms, that He would not make certain truths essential for our salvation without giving us the means to figure them out on our own, and that we can therefore have confidence that whatever conclusions we reach through the exercise of our reason will meet with His approval.

It is hard to say which of these suppositions Swift, that fierce student of the book of Job, would find more offensive. What would happen to the doctrine of eternal rewards and punishments, that "great Principle for Conscience to work upon,"[53] as he called it, if the Church were to offer her tenets up to improvements by Collins and his friends? Once the examination of tenets began, would it not end, as Swift suggests in the *Argument against Abolishing Christianity*, with ordinary people concluding that if some doctrines are doubtful, then they may "safely whore and drink on, and defy the Parson?"[54] Collins is not worried. Loss of belief should not matter much one way or the other, he casually observes. Most people only seek pleasure in the moment anyway, and "are very little mov'd *even* by their Belief of future Happiness and Misery to become *virtuous*."[55] The spread of freethinking

---

48  *Prose Works*, IV, 49.
49  *Prose Works*, V, 280.
50  *Correspondence*, III, 126.
51  Collins, *Discourse*, p. 6.
52  Collins, *Discourse*, pp. 8, 12.
53  *Prose Works*, IX, 156.
54  *Prose Works*, II, 38.
55  Collins, *Discourse*, p. 122. In the last paragraph of *Christianity not Mysterious*, Toland acknowledges the possibility that loss of faith in certain articles of belief might affect every-

should, he contends, improve morality, because the "great Diligence and Application of Mind" required in freethinking would by "Habit expel all those vicious Dispositions and Passions" which normally affect people.[56] The image here is obviously of a gentleman with time and inclination to spend long hours in his study, someone rather like Collins himself. For Collins was no loose-living libertine. In fact, he was such a model of propriety that a year after his death the *Universal Spectator* published a eulogy which makes him sound like a paragon of the very virtues Swift admired:

> He had an opulent Fortune, descended to him from his Ancestors ... He lived on his own Estate in the Country, where his Tenants paid him moderate Rents, which he never enhanced on their making any Improvements; he always oblig'd his Family to a constant attendance on Publick Worship; as he was himself a Man of the strictest Morality, for he never suffer'd any Body about him who was deficient in that Point; he exercised a universal Charity to all Sorts of People, without any Regard either to Sect or Party; being in the Commission of the Peace, he administred Justice with such Impartiality and Incorruptness, that the most distant Part of the County flock'd to his Decisions; but the chief Use he made of his Authority was in accommodating Differences.[57]

Were England populated by freethinkers of Collins' sort, for whom ideas seem to have been largely a recreation, Swift might have grudgingly agreed that no very terrible thing would result from universal freedom of expression. But nothing could be farther from the state of the world as Swift saw it. In that world, where people were in dead earnest about their ideas and passions, eager to turn them to account, Collins's facetious reflections were sure to spawn freethinkers of a different stripe altogether. However harmless Collins himself may have been, Swift could not but regard his ideas as profoundly threatening.

This is why Swift not only parodies Collins so as to make most of his reasoning seem more foolish and inept than it actually was; he also underscores Collins's irreverences so that they are more disturbing to belief than in the original. Collins writes that the Bonzes in China call Fo-he "*God and Saviour of the World*" and say that he was "*born to teach the way of Salvation, and to give satisfaction for all Mens Sins.*"[58] Swift quotes this and adds, "Which you see is directly the same with what our *Priests* pretend of *Christ*."[59] Collins writes that the "*Talapoins* of *Siam* have *a Book of Scripture* written by SOMMONOCO-DOM, who, [they] say, was *born of a Virgin*, and was the *God expected by the Universe*."[60] Swift quotes, and adds, "just as our *Priests* tell us, that *Jesus Christ* was born of the *Virgin Mary*, and was the *Messiah* so long expected."[61] Collins writes that Socrates "disbeliev'd the

---

day morality: "Some good Men may be apt to say, that supposing my Opinion never so true, it may notwithstanding occasion much harm; because when People find themselves impos'd upon in any part of *Religion*, they are ready to call the whole in question." But Toland insists that his "Design is nothing the less good, if ill-dispos'd Persons abuse it, as they frequently do *Learning, Reason, Scripture*, and the best things in the World" (pp. 175–76).

56  Collins, *Discourse*, p. 121.
57  *Universal Spectator, and Weekly Journal*, no 98 (22 August 1730), quoted by Edward A. Bloom and Lillian D. Bloom in their introduction to Anthony Collins, *A Discourse Concerning Ridicule and Irony in Writing, in a Letter to the Reverend Dr. Nathanael Marshall* (London, 1729), Augustan Reprint Society, no 142 (1970).
58  Collins, *Discourse*, p. 52.
59  *Prose Works*, IV, 32.
60  Collins, *Discourse*, pp. 52–53.
61  *Prose Works*, IV, 32.

*Gods* of his Country, and the common Creeds about them, and *declar'd his Dislike*, when he heard Men attribute *Repentance, Anger*, and other *Passions* to the Gods, and talk … of the *Gods getting Women with Child*, and such-like fabulous and blasphemous Storys."[62] Swift adds, "I pick out these Particulars, because they are the very same with what the Priests have in their Bibles, where *Repentance* and *Anger* are attributed to God, where it is said, there was *War in Heaven*; and that the *Virgin* Mary *was with Child by the Holy Ghost*, whom the Priests call God; all fabulous and blasphemous Stories."[63] Collins writes that "VARRO, the most learned of all the *Romans*, speaking of their Theology, said, *That it contain'd many Fables below the Dignity and Nature of Immortal Beings; such for instance, as Gods begotten and proceeding from other Gods Heads, Legs, Thighs, and Blood.*"[64] Swift omits "*Heads, Legs, Thighs, and Blood*," and fastens on "begotten and proceeding": "These two Words I desire you will particularly remark, because they are the very Terms made use of by our Priests in their Doctrine of the *Trinity*."[65]

In embellishing Collins's impieties, Swift was doing one of the things he did best – develop unpleasant ramifications of an idea. When Walpole threatened to make the Irish swallow Wood's halfpence in fire balls, Swift took fierce delight in suggesting what it would take to execute that threat. Each inhabitant would have to swallow 17 balls of wildfire, and the government would need to recruit 50,000 "*Operators*" to administer the dose, "allowing one *Operator* to every Thirty; which, considering the *Squeamishness* of some Stomachs, and the *Peevishness* of *Young Children*, is but reasonable."[66] Even in personal correspondence to a cousin on sensitive family matters, Swift was compelled to work out all the distasteful contingencies:

Madam.
I have been considering the account you gave me of your eldest daughter's privately carrying her self out of your house and taking all her cloaths with her … I have been assured that there is a man in the case, and that she hath been enticed by some Servant of yours to run into the arms of some beggarly rascal, who would pass for a Gentleman of fortune. Although such an action in a daughter whom you have used so well can deserve no pardon, yet I would have you leave her without excuse. Send to her to come home. If she refuse send to her a second and third time, and if she still refuseth; Let her know, in plain terms, that you will never have the least correspondence with her, and when she is ruined, as will certainly be the case, that you will never see her, nor give or leave her or her children (if she shall have any) a morsel of bread. Let her know, You have given her fair warning, and if she will run into destruction with her eyes open, against common sense, and the opinion of all rational people, she hath none to blame but her self; And that she must not expect to move your compassion some years hence with the cryes of half a dozen children at your door for want of bread. Let this and whatever you think proper, be writ to her in your own hand and let your letter be given her before witnesses, and keep a copy of it to produce when there is occasion; And show the Copy you keep, to any Acquaintance who may be willing to see it. And let whoever pleaseth, see this Letter of mine as the best advice I can give you. For you are to suppose that you never had such a daughter, and that her children will have no more title to your charity, than the bratts and bastards of any other common beggar. This is all I think necessary to say upon so disagreeable a Subject.[67]

[62]  Collins, *Discourse*, p. 123.
[63]  *Prose Works*, IV, 41–42.
[64]  Collins, *Discourse*, p. 134.
[65]  *Prose Works*, IV, 43.
[66]  *Prose Works*, X, 68.
[67]  *Correspondence*, IV, 178–79.

Swift's elaborations on the *Discourse* are not calculated to make it seem more ridiculous, but to seem more dangerous. Bentley had assailed Collins by catching him up on linguistic errors, sneering at his imperfect knowledge of ancient languages, much as he had earlier sneered at Temple and Boyle. He had not, however, really invalidated Collins's basic arguments. Swift's tack is to discredit the arguments by showing the consequences of taking them seriously.[68] By spelling out how Collins's forays in comparative religion compromise the central doctrines of the Church, Swift shows what happens once one starts thinking "freely," how such thoughts cut to the very heart of Christianity.

Five days after he first wrote to Stella about *Mr. Collins's Discourse*, Swift told her he had given it to the printer, and five days after that, had it advertised in *The Examiner*. So far as we know, he never spoke of the piece again. The satire was not included in the Swift-Pope *Miscellanies* of 1727–1732, and though Charles Ford cited it in the list of pamphlets and papers he had available for use when the Faulkner edition was in the planning stages,[69] it was not included in those volumes either, or reprinted at all until 1776. Why did Swift not want it among his acknowledged works? Because it "didn't take"? Because he did not think it good enough? Given the slightness of some pieces he *did* authorize for inclusion, other reasons seem more probable. Perhaps he felt there was too *much* Collins in the *Abstract*. On reflection, Swift may have decided that there were things in this hastily written piece he did not wish associated with his name – any more than he wished to be publicly identified with the *Tale*. He would later advise young clergymen to avoid preaching against freethinkers because in the process they risked stirring up doubts that would never otherwise have occurred to their parishioners.

Swift is likely to have recognized that his satire of Collins cut more ways than one. No doubt, his aim had been to demonstrate for presumably church-going readers how truly damaging Collins's *Discourse* was to Christian faith, and, in consequence, how necessary an Established Church and trained clergy were for the protection of that faith. But the effect of his elaborations was more to exacerbate than to allay doubt. Ehrenpreis suggests that the parody of Collins falls far short of Swift's other great satires because Swift dared not "risk the subtleties" of the *Tale* "for fear of sounding blasphemous himself."[70] I would argue that while the *Abstract* may lack the subtleties of the *Tale* it has much of the same, disorientating ambiguity. Swift does make the assurances of freethinking seem absurd. Yet by heightening Collins's most troubling assertions – that other religions have saviours for whom they make claims similar to those made for Christ, that important elements of Christian doctrine have antecedents in paganism – Swift makes them linger in mind more vividly than they do in the *Discourse* itself. As in the *Tale*, he invalidates one point of view, only to raise questions about the other, and in so doing converts the stable ironies of Collins's tract into ironies that, like those of the *Tale*, unsettle and complicate our view of Christianity.

---

[68] In his sermon *On the Trinity*, Swift argues that we should believe because the consequences of disbelief are unthinkable: "Men should consider, that raising Difficulties concerning the Mysteries in Religion, cannot make them more wise, learned, or virtuous; better Neighbours, or Friends, or more serviceable to their Country; but, whatever they pretend, will destroy their inward Peace of Mind, by perpetual Doubts and Fears arising in their Breasts" (*Prose Works*, IX, 166–67).

[69] See *Correspondence*, IV, 203–4.

[70] *Dr Swift*, p. 588.

D. W. Hayton

*The Queen's University of Belfast*

# The High Church Party in the Irish Convocation 1703–1713[1]

ABSTRACT. The full dimensions of the crisis which overtook the Church of Ireland in the age of Swift can only be grasped if we can understand the motives and ambitions of the "High Churchmen" who constituted the majority of the clergy, and who apparently rejected programmes of ecclesiastical reform, and initiatives towards popular evangelism, in favour of the sterile sloganeering of party politics. Hitherto, the history of the Church in this period has been written from the viewpoint of would-be reformers – progressive bishops and lay philanthropists; largely, it would seem, because of the greater availability of their private papers. But the unusually well documented history of the Convocation of the Church of Ireland during its "Indian summer" in the reign of Queen Anne provides a unique opportunity to study the personnel and activities of the conservative majority. Although some of the most prominent and vocal of Convocation's members were exiled Englishmen, a close examination reveals that the High Church party was no exotic import, but included many clerics who had been born and/or educated in Ireland, and who were animated by some distinctively Irish issues. In part, the factionalism of Convocation can be interpreted as a natural function of such secular political forces as patronage, clanship, and partisan animosity. Where the two sides were divided on principle, the issues at stake had little to do with matters of theology, liturgy, or church organisation; nor was it a question of conflicting attitudes towards church reform and evangelical strategies. Instead, the differences arose from the more intense involvement of the High Churchmen in lay politics, which was also a propensity to see the broader picture, to set their own local problems in a religious and political context that encompassed all three kingdoms of the British Isles.

Traditionally, historical writing on the Church of Ireland in the eighteenth century has fixed the reader's attention on the many problems, material, cultural, and intellectual, with which churchmen were beset: their lack of resources, in terms of men, money, and infrastructure;

---

[1]   An important essay by S. J. Connolly, "Reformers and Highflyers: The Post-Revolution Church," in Alan Ford, James McGuire, and Kenneth Milne, eds, *As By Law Established: The Church of Ireland since the Reformation* (Dublin, 1995), pp. 152–65, appeared after the original version of this paper had been written and goes some way towards answering the problems I have raised. However, I draw encouragement from Professor Connolly's confession (p. 160) that, despite his efforts, "the internal politics … of Church and Convocation remain obscure." I should like to thank Professor Connolly, and Dr T. C. Barnard, for commenting on this paper, and the following individuals and institutions for permission to consult, and to quote from, documents in their possession: His Grace, the Archbishop of Armagh; the Earl of Midleton; the Governing Body, Christ Church, Oxford; the Director, Public Record Office of Northern Ireland; and the Board of Trinity College, Dublin.

the corrosive effects of patronage, in undermining the spiritual commitment of parish priests; the hostility of the Catholic community towards the Established Church, and the continuing mutual incomprehension of settler and native, which defeated any attempts at conversion. Consequently, the kind of clergymen who have attracted the attention of historians and biographers have been would-be problem-*solvers*: "reforming" bishops like William King of Dublin, Peter Browne of Cork, and William Nicolson, the English antiquarian translated from Carlisle to Derry in 1718.[2] Little has been written about the mainstream of the Anglican clergy in Ireland, conservative "High Churchmen" conventionally represented in the literature as lacking the exalted ambitions of their "reforming" brethren, as complacent or even mildly corrupt, and in general concerned not so much to extend their reach as to keep what already lay within their grasp.

This generalization holds true despite the recent transformation which has been effected in the historiography of the eighteenth-century Church of Ireland, by authors offering a more balanced picture of its strengths and weaknesses; most radically perhaps by S. J. Connolly, in a far-reaching analysis of the structural role of the Established Church in a country which he sees as having much in common with other states of the European "ancien régime"; and more obliquely by T. C. Barnard, in a series of penetrating essays on Protestant mentalities, on the movement in Ireland for the reformation of manners, and on various educational and proselytizing initiatives.[3] This new research, celebrating successes as much as it exposes failings, has rescued many pious and diligent clerics from the undeserved censure of posterity. Not all the reputations which have been salvaged belong to reformers, by any means. But it is still "progressive" or "improving" clergymen who hold the limelight, as men responding proactively rather than reactively to the Church's problems of ministry and mission.

A ready explanation for this historiographical imbalance may be found in the bias of the surviving documentation. That we know so much about the ideas and achievements of "reformers" in the Church is owing to the remarkable riches contained in two major clerical archives: the comprehensive out-letter books and collected in-letters of Archbishop King, who provided determined leadership for the cause of ecclesiastical reform in general and was accounted by his contemporaries as the chief of the "Low Church" party in Convocation;[4]

---

[2]   See, for example, J. C. Beckett, "William King's Administration of the Diocese of Derry, 1691–1703," *Irish Historical Studies*, 4 (1944–45), 164–80; F. G. James, *North Country Bishop: A Biography of William Nicolson* (New Haven, CT, 1956); Clyve Jones and Geoffrey Holmes, eds, *The London Diaries of William Nicolson, Bishop of Carlisle 1702–1718* (Oxford, 1985), pp. 3–61; R. Wyse Jackson, *Peter Browne, Bishop and Provost* (Dublin, 1963); A. R. Winnett, *Peter Browne: Provost, Bishop, Metaphysician* (London, 1974). For bibliographical information, see in general S. J. Connolly, "The Church of Ireland: A Critical Bibliography ... 1690–1800," *Irish Historical Studies*, 28 (1992–93), 362–69.

[3]   See S. J. Connolly, *Religion, Law and Power: The Making of Protestant Ireland, 1660–1760* (Oxford, 1992), especially Chapter 5; S. J. Connolly, "Reformers and High-Flyers;" T. C. Barnard, "Reforming Irish Manners: The Religious Societies in Dublin during the 1690s," *Historical Journal*, 35 (1992), 805–38; T. C. Barnard, "Protestants and the Irish Language, c. 1675–1725," *Journal of Ecclesiastical History*, 44 (1993), 243–72; T. C. Barnard, "Improving Clergymen, 1660–1760," Ford, McGuire, and Milne, eds, *As By Law Established*, pp. 136–51. See also Mark Gilmore, "Anthony Dopping and the Church of Ireland," unpublished M.A. thesis, Queen's University, Belfast, 1988.

[4]   King's out-letter books are T[rinity] C[ollege] D[ublin], MSS 750/1–8 (originals), 2531–7 (transcripts); the in-letters are MSS 1995–2008. Significant extracts have been printed in

and the private papers of William Wake, George I's Archbishop of Canterbury, who maintained a regular correspondence with many episcopal colleagues in Ireland, invariably those of a "Low Church" or Whiggish disposition.[5] On the "High Church" or Tory side, the only personal collection of any substance belongs to the Veseys, Archbishop John of Tuam and his son Sir Thomas, Bishop of Killaloe and then Ossory, but these papers are a comparatively recent discovery, yet to make a wide acquaintance among scholars.[6] To describe the "High Churchmen" as a "silent majority" would doubtless have seemed absurd to contemporaries, since in pursuit of their factional ends in ecclesiastical and secular politics they were not only vociferous but positively shrill. None the less, they remain for the most part an undocumented majority. Besides the lack of private papers there is relatively little printed evidence of their ideas, at least in comparison with their "Low Church" opponents, who tended to publish more extensively, whether it be controversial or devotional tracts, or set-piece sermons. It would be true to say that the "High Churchmen" as a group threw their energies into party politics rather more than pious contemplation or theological controversy; and only when the Tory Duke of Ormond was Lord Lieutenant, in 1703–7 and 1710–13, were they given many opportunities to preach the great public sermons (on state occasions, commemorations and official fasts) which customarily found their way to the press.

It is because of the scarcity of other evidence that the relatively well documented activities of the Convocation of the Church of Ireland, which met alongside Parliament from early 1704 until 1713, must possess a peculiar interest. For here was a body which represented the generality of clerical opinion, consisting of an Upper House of bishops, and a Lower House containing the dean and archdeacon of each diocese, and proctors elected by cathedral chapters and parochial clergy. Surviving journals and minute-books record proceedings in both houses;[7] and in 1711, the Convocation as a whole drew up a *Representation of the Present State of Religion … in Ireland*, in which the manifold difficulties facing the Church were anatomized.[8] To supplement these official records, there are some private accounts of de-

---

H[istorical] M[anuscripts] C[ommission], *2nd Report*, Appendix, pp. 231–56; and in Sir Charles Simeon King, ed., *A Great Archbishop of Dublin, William King, D.D.* (London, 1906), pp. 57–267.

[5]   Wake's papers are at Christ Church, Oxford. See in particular Volume XII (unfoliated). There are also two volumes of letters in Dublin City Library, Gilbert collection, MSS 28–29.

[6]   The bulk of this collection is to be found in Lord De Vesci's MSS, formerly divided between Abbeyleix, Co. Laois, and Damer House, Roscrea, Co. Tipperary, but recently acquired by the N[ational] L[ibrary of] I[reland]. A catalogue (compiled prior to the deposit at the National Library) can be found at P[ublic] R[ecord] O[ffice of] N[orthern] I[reland], T3738, to which reference is made in the citations below. A smaller quantity of Vesey material survives in the Sarsfield-Vesey MSS in the National Archives, Dublin. The correspondence of Arthur Charlett, master of University College, Oxford (Bodleian Library, MSS Ballard 8, 36) also contains a significant number of letters from Irish "High Churchmen."

[7]   See PRO NI, Armagh diocesan registry papers, DIO 4/10/3/2–3, journals of the Upper House, 1704–11; TCD, MS 556, journals of the Upper House 1707; 668/1, list of members of Lower House, and committee minutes 1704; 668/2, minutes of proceedings in Lower House 1704–12; 668/3, acts of the Lower House, 1704. There is another copy of the journals of the Lower House in the Public Library, Armagh; and a printed list of the members elected in 1703 in Sir James Ware, *The Antiquities and History of Ireland* , 2 vols (London, 1705), I, 163–64.

[8]   See *A Representation of the Present State of Religion, with Regard to Infidelity, Heresy,*

bates, compiled for anxious government officials and other interested parties (such as absentee Irish bishops or the masters of Oxford colleges). We thus have a unique record of the views of the clerical estate, as expressed in a public context, instead of the private opinions of a handful of individuals, albeit influential individuals, like Archbishop King.

Ironically, the first demands for the recall of Convocation, after an interval of some forty years, had come from the very cohort of "reforming" bishops – especially King and Archbishop Narcissus Marsh of Armagh – who, as leaders of the "Low Church" or Whiggish minority, were to expend much time and trouble in seeking to frustrate the factional designs of the majority.[9] These "reformers" had seen in Convocation a potential instrument to develop and put into practice a detailed programme for the reconstruction and reinvigoration of the Church. They hoped that abuses like pluralism would be extinguished; incumbents be obliged not merely to reside in their parishes and preach to their congregations but fulfil their other responsibility of catechizing the young; and that a start might be made, by means of a revived and improved system of ecclesiastical courts, to combat the general decline in public morality and religious observance which seemed to many to threaten the very existence of the Protestant establishment.[10] It was largely owing to pressure from Marsh and King, assisted by the newly appointed Tory viceroy, Ormond, that Queen Anne was prevailed upon to issue the writs for calling an Irish Convocation together with an Irish Parliament in the autumn of 1703.[11]

But just as the campaign for the recall of Convocation came within sight of success, it seemed to be hijacked into a rather different direction. Several of the bishops who now lent their weight to the call, William Moreton of Kildare, Edward Smyth of Down and Connor, and Thomas Lindsay of Killaloe, were men of strongly Tory sympathies. Lindsay in particular had a different agenda from the constructive reform envisaged by Marsh and King. He brought the Irish episcopate into close contact with Francis Atterbury and other high-flyers in England, to whom the situation offered obvious political opportunities: in the first place to use Irish precedents to further their own juridical ambitions for the Convocation of Canterbury, and in the long run to secure a public platform in Ireland for the expression of grievances and prejudices which they assumed would echo their own.[12] Atterbury, who has

---

*Impiety, and Popery: Drawn up and Agreed to by Both Houses of Convocation in Ireland, Pursuant to Her Majesty's Command in Her Royal Licence* (Dublin, 1712).

[9] The ideals and activities of the reforming bishops have been covered in some depth; see W. Alison Phillips, ed., *History of the Church of Ireland from the Earliest Times to the Present Day*, 3 vols (Oxford, 1933), III, 162–68, 181–84; Beckett, "William King's Administration of the Diocese of Derry;" J. C. Beckett, "The Government and the Church of Ireland under William III and Anne," *Irish Historical Studies*, 2 (1940–41), reprinted in J. C. Beckett, *Confrontations: Studies in Irish History* (London, 1972), pp. 87–110; Barnard, "Reforming Irish Manners;" Barnard, "Protestants and the Irish Language;" and most recently, Connolly, "Reformers and Highflyers."

[10] See Beckett, "The Government and the Church of Ireland," pp. 98–100.

[11] See *Calendar of State Papers, Domestic, 1703–4*, pp. 49–51, 155; J. Nichols, ed., *The Epistolary Correspondence of the Right Reverend Francis Atterbury, D.D., Lord Bishop of Rochester*, 4 vols (London, 1783–87), especially III, 120–22; TCD, MS 668/3, copies of Edward Southwell to Archbishop King, 4 July 1703, Archbishop Marsh *et al.* to Ormond, 10 August 1703; Beckett, "The Government and the Church of Ireland," pp. 100–1.

[12] See Nichols, ed., *Epistolary Correspondence*, III, 104–6, 110–11, 122, 129–31. For Lindsay's Toryism, see B[ritish] L[ibrary], Add. MS 47087, fol. 57, "Character of the Primate and Earl of Anglesea" by Sir John Perceval; for Moreton's, HMC, *Ormonde MSS*, n.s. VIII, 179–80, 206–7; Christ Church, Wake MSS, XXIII, no 161, Maurice Wheeler to Wake, 28

been aptly described as "the stormy petrel of the High Church movement,"[13] quickly added his considerable energy and skill to the task of lobbying ministers, while at the same time cultivating his contacts in Ireland to influence clerical opinion there. He found a willing agent among the clerical rank and file in the person of the newly appointed archdeacon of Cashel, William Perceval, like Atterbury himself a product of that citadel of Oxonian Toryism, Christ Church.[14] Fired with enthusiasm, the lower clergy took up the struggle and made their own representations. Although government ministers naturally began to counsel caution in the face of this outburst, they had been effectively overtaken by events. The suggestion from Dublin Castle that the Crown call elections but indefinitely postpone an actual meeting of Convocation was not a practical possibility, the expectations created by the issue of the writs being such as to generate an unstoppable political momentum.[15]

When the Convocation did meet, in January 1704, the worst fears of "moderate men" were soon realized. Looking back on events a decade afterwards, Archbishop King recalled how

> When we met I ... frequently admonished my brethren both of the upper and Lower House to be very quiet and modest ... and this prevailed for some time, but not for long, for the present lord Primate [Thomas Lindsay, promoted to Armagh in 1714], the late Bishop of Raphoe Dr [John] Pooley, and the late Archbishop of Tuam [John Vesey] among the bishops, and Mr [William] Perceval, Mr [Francis] Higgins, and Mr [John] Dogherty got the management of the clergy and Convocation into their hands ... and, being pretty violent in their tempers, and entirely in with and guided by Dr Atterbury and his party in England, they run us into many inconveniencies.[16]

At first, factional violence and obstructionism seem to have been centred on the Upper House. King, Marsh, and their friends found themselves opposed by a phalanx of Tory bishops: besides Lindsay, Pooley, and Archbishop Vesey, these included Thomas Smyth of Limerick and an old client of the Ormond family, John Hartstonge of Ossory. To the reformers' embarrassment (and quite unlike the situation in England, where predominantly Whiggish bishops were at odds with the Toryism of the lower clergy), it was episcopal squabbling rather than partisanship in the Lower House which to begin with frustrated the passage of business.[17] By contrast, the lower clergy had begun promisingly, by choosing a moderate man for their prolocutor, Dean Samuel Synge of Kildare, and by appointing "standing committees" on such subjects as "the inspection of canons," and "the reformation of manners and promoting public works of piety and charity," as well as for "grievances," "rights and privileges" and the inspection of objectionable books. What is more, they agreed

September 1706; Bodleian, MS Ballard 36, fol. 96, William Perceval to [Arthur Charlett], 1 December 1715; and for Smyth's, HMC, *Ormonde MSS*, n.s. VIII, 85–86; [Henry Joy], *Historical Collections Relative to the Town of Belfast* (Belfast, 1817), pp. 85–88; and Christ Church, Wake MSS, XIII, Archbishop Lindsay to [Wake], 29 March 1716.

13   G. V. Bennett, "Conflict in the Church," Geoffrey Holmes, ed., *Britain after the Glorious Revolution, 1689–1714* (London, 1969), p. 165.

14   See Bodleian, MS Eng. letters c. 28, fol. 34, Perceval to Henry Dodwell, 19 October 1697; MS Ballard 36, fol. 22, Perceval to Arthur Charlett, 10 December 1701; PRO NI, D906/62, Archbishop William Palliser to Perceval, 22 August 1702.

15   See TCD, MS 668/3, address of lower clergy to archbishops and bishops, 10 August 1703; *Calendar of State Papers, Domestic, 1703–4*, pp. 155, 190, 210.

16   Christ Church, Wake MSS, XII, King to Wake, 12 September 1717.

17   See TCD, MS 750/3/1, p. 151, Archbishop King to Bishop St George Ashe of Clogher, 28 April 1705.

on positive resolutions, calling for the consolidation of thinly populated or poorly resourced parishes, and for improvements in the collection of the parish rate, the functioning of the ecclesiastical courts, and the rate of popular attendance at Sunday worship.[18] It may even be that at the very outset supporters of the "reforming" or "Low Church" bishops enjoyed a working majority. In the first session, William Perceval was twice selected by the Lower House to preach public sermons, but so, too, was a prominent "Low Churchman," Ralph Lambert, and when Primate Marsh's chaplain, William Tisdall, was accused of publicly denouncing, by his master's order, Bishops Hartstonge, Lindsay, and Thomas Smyth as "the incendiaries of the Upper House," he was vindicated by his colleagues.[19]

This petty dispute, over what Tisdall had, or had not, said, and at whose bidding, indicated the morass into which the business of Convocation was to fall. Inevitably, the members of the Lower House were diverted from the discussion of constructive measures for the benefit of the Church into the more exciting but ultimately futile manifestations of factional strife: allegations of libel; witch-hunts after authors and printers; protests, addresses and counter-addresses; delegations sent from one house to the other, to Dublin Castle, even to Whitehall. There were disputes between the two houses of Convocation, and with the Irish Parliament, over privileges and jurisdiction;[20] quarrels over the wording of loyal addresses, such as occurred in 1705 when high-flyers in both houses followed the pattern established by Tories in counties and boroughs across England and sought to equate the naval actions of the English Tory admiral, Sir George Rooke, with the victories of the Duke of Marlborough; and vindictive personal attacks of the kind levelled at Marsh in 1707 when members of the Lower House took exception to the parliamentary bill establishing his library as a public institution.[21] "'Tis an uncomfortable thing," Archbishop King wrote, "that all assemblies of men come to some conclusion and agreement, only clergymen: that all that have controversies can write with temper and humanity, only they treat one another with passion and bitterness."[22]

The influence which party politics had come to exert over Convocation's proceedings was vividly illustrated by the disastrous events of the session of 1709. "High Churchmen" had been on tenterhooks ever since the appointment the previous autumn of a Whig Lord Lieutenant; and not only a Whig but a notorious rake, with a reputation for anticlerical irreverence, and an avowed friend to the cause of Protestant Dissenters. Lord Wharton seemed

---

[18] See TCD, MS 750/3/1, p. 68, King to Samuel Synge, 16 January 1704[/5]; MS 2002/1141, Synge to King, 22 February 1704[/5]; MS 668/1, fols 1, 4, 13–15, 19, 27–28, 35, 43; MS 668/2, 4 March 1704; Phillips, ed., *History of the Church of Ireland*, III, 178–79.

[19] See TCD, MS 668/2, 4, 17, 24, 28 February 1704; MS 668/3, 26 February 1704.

[20] TCD, MS 668/2, 8, 12, 17, 23–24 February 1704, 22 February, 5, 10, 13–15, 19–21 March 1705; PRO NI, DIO 4/10/3/2, pp. 261–62, 432; Phillips, ed., *History of the Church of Ireland*, III, 184.

[21] See PRO NI, DIO 4/10/3/2, pp. 164, 173; BL, Add. MS 32096, fols 67–69; Bodleian, MS St Edmund Hall 9, pp. 138–43, William Perceval to Henry Dodwell, 26 February 1704/5; MS Ballard 36, fols 27–34, Perceval to Arthur Charlett, 1 March 1704/5; MS Ballard, fol. 43, William Perceval to Arthur Charlett, 18 December 1707; MS Ballard, fol. 45, "A short account of the proceedings in the Lower House of Convocation in relation to my lord primate's library bill;" MS Eng. misc. 23, fols 166–67, Marsh to Thomas Smith, 13 December 1707; Richard Mant, *History of the Church of Ireland from the Revolution to the Union* (London, 1840), pp. 115–17.

[22] Quoted in Mant, *History of the Church of Ireland*, p. 179.

to embody all that the high-flyers feared and detested, and when he chose as one of his chaplains a leading Irish "Low Churchman," Ralph Lambert, proctor for the chapter of Down, he gave opposition in Convocation an obvious target. For Lambert had recently trodden on "High Church" sensitivities when he had joined in what was essentially an English controversy over the constitution of the Convocation of Canterbury.[23] In its long drawn-out conflict with the "Low Church" establishment, Atterbury's party had been seeking to deny the claim of the bishops to be able to adjourn sittings of the Lower House. William Perceval and another notorious Irish "High Churchman," Francis Higgins, had provided an account of practice in Dublin to bear out Atterbury's claims, which Lambert had then contradicted in an anonymous but widely acknowledged letter included in a Whig pamphlet, *Partiality Detected*. When Perceval and his allies formed a committee of the Lower House of the Irish Convocation to investigate the pamphlet, Wharton acted to protect his chaplain. Under viceregal pressure, the committee chairman, Peter Browne, provost of Trinity, postponed the report, only to find himself forced in due course to give way, and moreover to reveal the extent of the Lord Lieutenant's personal intervention. An attempt by "High Churchmen" to censure Browne was defeated by what one observer described as "the Archbishop of Dublin's and my Lord Lieutenant's party," but the matter was not laid to rest and thirteen proctors, led by William Perceval, entered their protest. Wharton now poured petrol on the flames by preparing to prosecute the protesters. As rumours spread, enraged "High Churchmen" who had hitherto stayed away from Dublin raced to the capital intent on confrontation. The bishops ignored an official request to adjourn and in turn registered their own protest. At this point, the viceroy could do nothing but prorogue Convocation. It did not meet again during his term in office.

So politicized had ecclesiastical politics become that not even in the very much more favourable circumstances of 1711, with a Tory ministry in England and the Duke of Ormond once again installed as viceroy, were the members of Convocation able to achieve anything very substantial for the advancement of the Church. Instead, in that session the energies of "High Churchmen" were channelled into the composition of their *Representation*, a comprehensive denunciation of speculative theology, skeptical freethinking, aggressive Presbyterianism, moral dereliction, and the perennial danger of "popery," in that order.[24] Two years later came the nadir: a short-lived and fruitless session to accompany the brief and bitter Parliament of 1713, with Convocation acting as nothing more than an auxiliary arm of the Tory party, passing resolutions in direct contradiction to the votes of the Whig majority in the Irish House of Commons.[25] Naturally enough, when the Whigs came to power

---

[23] For what follows, see PRO NI, DIO 4/10/3/3, pp. 65–71, 81–83, 96–97; BL, Add. MS 61634, fols 106–13, "A Narrative of some late Proceedings in the Lower House of Convocation in Dublin," 1709; Winnett, *Peter Browne*, pp. 37–47; L. A. Dralle, "Kingdom in Reversion: The Irish Viceroyalty of the Earl of Wharton, 1708–10," *Huntington Library Quarterly*, 15 (1951–52), 412–14; D. W. Hayton, "Ireland and the English Ministers, 1707–16," unpublished D. Phil. thesis, Oxford University, 1975, pp. 162–65.

[24] See PRO NI, DIO 4/10/3/3, pp. 96–97, 106–8, 113–16, 155–57, 204, 222–39, 241–51, 257–58, 271–73, 276; *A Representation of the Present State of Religion*.

[25] See *Journals of the House of Lords of the Kingdom of Ireland*, 8 vols (Dublin, 1779–1800), II, 441–42; D. Hayton, ed., "An Irish Parliamentary Diary from the Reign of Queen Anne," *Analecta Hibernica*, 30 (1982), 138; TCD, MS 2536, pp. 222–23, 228, Archbishop King to Bishop Nicolson, 24 March 1714[/5], and to Archbishop Wake, 26 March 1715; MS 2004/1728, Bishop John Stearne to Archbishop King, 21 September 1715.

after the Hanoverian Succession, Convocation (like its equivalent in England) was no longer permitted to sit. Time and again, the obsession with party-political posturing and personal vendettas had prevented the discussion of constructive proposals. In a decade of existence, Convocation's only practical achievements had been a few additional canons agreed at the same time as the *Representation* in 1711, relating to the routine working of the ecclesiastical courts, and some new forms of prayer to be used by the clergy when visiting prisoners.[26]

With only a few divisions, and no division lists, it is impossible to arrive at an accurate calculation of the relative strength of the developing parties in Convocation, but some general observations may be attempted. In the Upper House, the substantial Tory presence seems if anything to have strengthened over the years, despite (or even perhaps because of) the considerable persuasive powers of Archbishop King, whose commitment to the cause of the Whig party in Parliament was often stridently proclaimed. An assessment of party strengths in the House of Lords in 1713 listed only three bishops on the opposition, that is to say, the Whig, benches (King and his cronies, St George Ashe of Clogher and John Stearne of Dromore), and no less than seventeen on the government, or Tory, side (Archbishops Palliser of Cashel and Vesey of Tuam, and the Bishops of Clonfert, Cloyne, Cork, Derry, Down, Elphin, Ferns, Kildare, Killala, Killaloe, Limerick, Meath, Ossory, Raphoe, and Waterford).[27] As far as the Lower House was concerned, there was a sharp movement in the balance of opinion towards the "High Church" position after the very early experiences of the first session, in which the influence of the "reforming" bishops was detectable. In 1705, the high-flyers' demand for the inclusion of Sir George Rooke's name in their loyal address released a surge of Tory emotion, and, according to William Perceval, the question was passed "by so great a majority, that the other party were ashamed to divide with us."[28] Similarly in 1707, "High Churchmen" carried their point against Marsh's Library Bill even though their arguments were tainted by personal spite. When Wharton arrived as viceroy, Whig fortunes temporarily improved: the scholarly "Low Churchman" John Stearne, a protégé of Archbishop King, was elected prolocutor in place of the deceased Dean Synge, possibly as a compromise candidate, and Perceval and his dozen followers were left in a minority on the question of censuring Provost Browne.[29] But the change of scene was an illusion: what had really happened was that dejected "High Churchmen" had not bothered to attend the early meetings of the Lower House in what they felt was a useless exercise. The Lord Lieutenant's high-handedness breathed new life into the party, so that Perceval was soon able to report "a very full house, and on a division about proceeding anew against [Lam-

[26] See P[ublic] R[ecord] O[ffice, London], SP 63/368/2, SP 67/17, fols 11–131, printed in L. Stoddart, ed., *Constitutions and Canons Ecclesiastical, Treated upon by the Archbishops and Bishops, and the Rest of the Clergy of Ireland* (Dublin, 1864), pp. 60–64.

[27] See BL, Add. MS 61640, fols 29–30, analytical list of the membership of the Irish House of Lords [1714/5]. See also Add. MS 61637A, marked printed list of the Parliament of 1713; and the Lords division lists of 24 August 1709 on the Popery Bill (BL, Add. MS 34777, fol. 68; Walter Graham, ed., *The Letters of Joseph Addison* [Oxford, 1941], p. 183), and 16 December 1715 on the Mountgarrett peerage case (Surrey RO, Guildford, Midleton MSS 1248/3, fol. 283, Lord Brodrick to Thomas Brodrick, 18 December 1715).

[28] Bodleian, MS St Edmund Hall 9, pp. 138–43, Perceval to Henry Dodwell, 26 February 1704/5.

[29] See BL, Add. MS 47025, fols 123–24, Sir John Perceval to Philip Perceval, 30 June 1709; PRO NI, DIO 4/10/3/3, pp. 1–3; Christ Church, Wake MSS, XII, Archbishop King to Wake, 8 May 1716, Bishop John Evans to [Wake], 21 January [1718].

bert's] letter we carried by 72 against 9."[30] In 1713, when Perceval was borne to the prolocutor's chair unchallenged, there was no questioning the "High Church" ascendancy.[31]

As to how it had become so entrenched, after what seems in retrospect to have been an unpromising beginning for the high-flyers, two possible lines of explanation suggest themselves. One obvious approach would be to look at the changes in the personnel of the Lower House (through deaths, promotions, and the ensuing appointments and by-elections), and the conversion of individual proctors from one side to another. There is certainly evidence of a modest turn-over in membership, but except for the new elections in 1713 this would be insufficient to account for the establishment of such a clear "High Church" majority by the later stages of the session of 1709. We can also observe shifts in the standpoint of particular individuals. William Tisdall, for instance, who had been a thorn in Perceval's side in 1704/5, had effectively "crossed the floor" of the Lower House by 1709, when he published the first of his vigorous pamphlet attacks on the Presbyterians of Ulster, *A Sample of Trew-Blue Presbyterian Loyalty*. Clearly, the attractions of Primate Marsh's continued patronage were becoming outweighed by growing anxiety at the power of Presbyterian interests in Tisdall's own parish of Belfast.[32] Peter Browne was another who changed sides, in his case more than once. Originally something of a "reformer," he had aligned himself by early 1709 with those who condemned Lambert's letter about the bishops' right of adjournment, but then allowed himself to be talked round by Wharton and Archbishop King, for which forbearance he was duly rewarded with preferment to the bishopric of Cork. At last, having put on lawn sleeves, he altered his political alignment once more, and mutated into a strong Tory with scruples about subscribing the loyal association to King George I.[33] Examples like this are interesting, but there are nowhere near enough of them to explain group behaviour in the Lower House. Nor do they necessarily indicate that any of the individuals concerned had experienced a fundamental shift in outlook or allegiance; that they had altered their views, or been bought off. Tisdall and Browne may not have foregone their former principles, so much as altered the balance of emphasis they placed on some issues as opposed to others. For Tisdall, the threat from Presbyterianism came to take precedence; for Browne, the material needs of the Church and the spiritual needs of society had to be set

---

[30]  PRO NI, DIO 4/10/3/3, pp. 53–54; HMC, *Egmont MSS*, II, 238; Bodleian, MS Ballard 36, fols 55–56, William Perceval to Arthur Charlett, 3 September 1709.

[31]  See TCD, MS 2004/1728, Bishop John Stearne to Archbishop King, 27 September 1715.

[32]  Bodleian, MS St Edmund Hall 9, pp. 95–110, 138–43, Perceval to Henry Dodwell, 2 September 1704, 26 February 1704/5; [Joy], *Historical Collections*, pp. 84–85; William Tisdall, *A Sample of True-Blew Presbyterian Loyalty, in All Changes and Turns of Government* (Dublin, 1709); William Tisdall, *The Conduct of the Dissenters in Ireland, with Respect Both to Church and State* (Dublin, 1712); William Tisdall, *A Seasonable Enquiry into that Most Dangerous Political Principle of the Kirk in Power* (Dublin, 1713); William Tisdall, *The Nature and Tendency of Popular Phrases in General* (Dublin, 1714); William Tisdall, *The Case of the Sacramental Test, Stated and Argued* (Dublin, 1715). The tensions, and occasional conflicts, between Church and Presbytery in Belfast are covered most comprehensively in Jean H. Agnew, "The Merchant Community of Belfast, 1660–1707," unpublished Ph.D. thesis, Queen's University, Belfast, 1994.

[33]  Besides the biographies cited in n. 2, see Bodleian, MS Ballard 8, fol. 68, Thomas Lindsay to [Arthur Charlett], 20 March 1694/5; MS Ballard 36, fol. 55, William Perceval to [same], 3 September 1709; HMC, *Portland MSS*, V, 113; TCD, MS 2536, p. 263, Archbishop King to Bishop Stearne, 3 May 1715; BL, Add. MS 61640, fols 78–79, Enoch Sterne to Lord Sunderland, 21 January 1715/6; and Mant, *History of the Church of Ireland*, pp. 193–95.

against the integrity of divinely ordained political obligations. This is a roundabout way of coming to the second line of explanation: that what was happening between 1703/4 and, say, 1709, might not have been a wholesale change of personnel or of heart among members of the Lower House but a shift in the focus of debate. In other words, that when wider issues were raised than ecclesiastical reform, relating to the role of the Church in society, and in the political system, the majority of clergy in the Church of Ireland naturally gravitated to a position best characterized as "High Church" or Tory.

We thus arrive at the central question of this paper, namely how best to characterize the opposing parties or positions, within the Convocation and indeed in the Church at large. The best place to start would seem to be in England, for the participants in the factional strife in the Irish Convocation tended to adopt the terminology of English clerical politics in order to describe themselves and their opponents. Lindsay, William Perceval and their friends were "Atterburians" or "High Churchmen;" Archbishop King and his adherents the "Low Church party." The classic account of the divisions within the Church of England in this period remains that of the late G. V. Bennett, as developed in his magisterial biographies of Bishops White Kennett and Atterbury.[34] In contrast to previous writers, who had traced a "High Church" tradition in Anglicanism back to the liturgical and ecclesiastical reaction under Archbishop Laud,[35] Bennett rooted his interpretation firmly in social, economic, and above all political, realities. He saw it as his task to "penetrate beneath the slogans of 'High' and 'Low' Church, to discover what was the nature of the great Anglican crisis after 1688."[36] He was quick to dispose of the assumption that these fundamental differences between clergymen were matters of theological belief, nor was he much impressed by those who stressed the High Church party's commitment to restoring the independence of the Church from lay control and the dignity of the clerical estate, in contrast to the supposed Erastianism of their Low Church opponents, though he recognized that such ideas, and high-flying political theories of divine hereditary right, passive obedience, and non-resistance, were a frequent accompaniment to the central message of High Church polemic. But Bennett located the real origin of High Church reaction in the desperate crisis which gripped the Church of England after the Glorious Revolution, and in particular the passage, in 1689, of a statutory religious toleration for Protestant Dissenters.

---

[34] See G. V. Bennett, *White Kennett, 1660–1728: Bishop of Peterborough* (London, 1957); see also Bennett's *The Tory Crisis in Church and State, 1688–1730: The Career of Francis Atterbury, Bishop of Rochester* (Oxford, 1975); "Conflict in the Church," Holmes, ed., *Britain after the Glorious Revolution*; and "The Convocation of 1710: An Anglican Attempt at Counter-Revolution," in G. J. Cuming and Derek Baker, eds, *Councils and Assemblies: Studies in Church History*, VII (Cambridge, 1971), pp. 311–19.

[35] See, in particular, George Every, *The High Church Party, 1688–1718* (London, 1956). On the English "Laudian" tradition, see F. M. G. Higham, *Catholic and Reformed: A Study of the Anglican Church, 1559–1662* (London, 1962); and more recently, Peter Lake, "The Laudian Style: Order, Uniformity and the Pursuit of the Beauty of Holiness in the 1630s," Kenneth Fincham, ed., *The Early Stuart Church, 1603–1642* (London, 1993), pp. 161–85. The lack of continuity between Laudianism and the "High Church" party of the 1690s and 1700s is emphasized in John Spurr, *The Restoration Church of England, 1646–1689* (New Haven, 1991), p. 380.

[36] Bennett, "Conflict in the Church," p. 155. For a different interpretation of one aspect of the "High Church" movement, concentrating on constitutional and ecclesiological differences, see Mark Goldie, "The Nonjurors, Episcopacy, and the Origins of the Convocation Controversy," Eveline Cruickshanks, ed., *Ideology and Conspiracy: Aspects of Jacobitism, 1689–1759* (Edinburgh, 1982), pp. 15–35.

In the minds of loyal English churchmen, the disastrous chain of events in James II's reign, and its unhappy aftermath, had shattered that promising alliance of mitre and crown which in the 1670s and 1680s had succeeded in imposing a remarkable uniformity of worship.[37] Under the leadership of Archbishop William Sancroft, and backed up by the determined efforts of lay magistrates, the Church had succeeded in suppressing many manifestations of religious Dissent and had pushed the numbers of Easter communicants to stratospheric heights. But with King James's Declaration of Indulgence, and the subsequent passage of the Toleration Act, this policy of enforced uniformity had been abandoned. Dissenting meeting-houses multiplied; attendance at parish churches dropped; there was a renewed resistance to the collection of tithe. Clergymen everywhere were forced to come to terms with sparser congregations and shrinking incomes. Finally, the expiry of the press Licensing Act in 1695 released a spate of free-thinking literature to challenge not only Anglican orthodoxy but the basic tenets of the Christian faith.[38] Moreover, for high-flying parsons, painful recollection of the constitutional trauma of the Glorious Revolution was aggravated by the sight of their Whig enemies in power: men who not only protected and promoted the cause of Protestant Dissent but who also were notorious in Tory propaganda as men of doubtful moral probity and, what was worse, openly scornful of the Established Church and its clergy. Denunciations of "priestcraft" by English Whig writers such as the M.P. Sir Robert Howard tarred the party as a whole with anti-clericalism.[39] Thus, whatever the personal merits possessed by bishops of the character of John Tillotson and Thomas Tenison of Canterbury, the open alliance of many on the English episcopal bench with Whig politicians in Parliament enraged the lower clergy and turned them towards other spokesmen, fiery clerical tribunes such as Atterbury, who could articulate popular discontents, and, as they saw it, more properly represent their interests.

To adopt Bennett's analysis, and transpose it directly into the Irish situation, has certain superficial attractions. After all, several of the most prominent of the "High Churchmen" in Ireland were themselves Englishmen, who, having been educated at English universities (usually Oxford), and begun their careers in England, had arrived in Ireland comparatively recently. William Perceval, the student of Christ Church drafted into Cashel cathedral, would be one glaring example; and he was not the only newcomer to disturb the political waters in Ireland. Two of the most formidable spokesmen for the "High Church" party among the bishops, Thomas Lindsay, and Charles Hickman, hailed from the same college. One of Francis Atterbury's most frequent correspondents, Lindsay had come to Dublin in

---

[37] The picture drawn by Bennett may be filled out by R. A. Beddard, "The Restoration Church," J. R. Jones, ed., *The Restored Monarchy, 1660–1688* (London, 1979), pp. 155–75; Anthony Fletcher, "The Enforcement of the Conventicle Acts, 1664–1679," W. J. Sheils, ed., *Persecution and Toleration: Studies in Church History*, XXI (Oxford, 1984), pp. 235–46; and Spurr, *Restoration Church of England*, Chapter 2.

[38] See M. C. Jacob, *The Newtonians and the English Revolution, 1689–1720* (Hassocks, 1976); John Redwood, *Reason, Ridicule and Religion: The Age of Enlightenment in England, 1660–1750* (London, 1976); J. A. I. Champion, *The Pillars of Priestcraft Shaken: The Church of England and Its Enemies, 1660–1730* (Cambridge, 1992).

[39] See Sir Robert Howard, *The History of Religion* (London, 1694). See also Mark Goldie, "Priestcraft and the Birth of Whiggism," Nicholas Phillipson and Quentin Skinner, eds, *Political Discourse in Early Modern Britain* (Cambridge, 1993), pp. 209–31; Champion, *The Pillars of Priestcraft Shaken*, Chapter 6.

1694 as a chaplain to Lord Capell, and been advanced by his patron to the see of Killaloe.[40] Hickman was an even more recent recruit, his presence bestowed on the Irish episcopate by the High Tory viceroy, Lord Rochester, whose chaplain he had been during Rochester's brief sojourn in Dublin in 1701, and who eventually found for him, in 1703, the exceptionally lucrative see of Derry. In return, according to one hostile commentator, Hickman helped sow "the seeds of Toryism" among the clergy of his diocese.[41]

However, despite the impact made by these three individuals, and the extensive contacts between Irish churchmen in general and their English counterparts, it would be misleading to follow some contemporary critics in representing the "High Church" movement in Ireland simply as an exotic infection brought into the country by English immigrants. For one thing, a great many of the "High Church" party in Ireland, especially in the Lower House of Convocation, were native-born Irishmen, educated at Trinity College, Dublin: men like the firebrand Francis Higgins, the "Irish Sacheverell," who hailed from Limerick, where his brother was a Tory alderman active in the politics of the municipal corporation;[42] John Dogherty, precentor of the cathedral of Cashel, whose intemperate partisanship was also condemned by Archbishop King;[43] Archdeacon Benjamin Neale of Ferns, who, according to one source, was satirized alongside Perceval and Higgins as a member of an extreme Tory dining club at the Swan Tavern in Dublin in 1705;[44] John Travers, one of the most vocal of a skein of high-flying canons of Christ Church, Dublin, and chosen to preach in 1713 on a notable occasion for the "High Church" party, the consecration (by Archbishop Palliser) of Sir Thomas Vesey as Lindsay's successor at Killaloe;[45] and John Hinton, the Archdeacon of Ossory (born in England but the son of the master of the Kilkenny school), who in 1713

[40]  In retrospect, the first Lord Egmont was to explain Lindsay's early association with such a strong Whig as Lord Capell by asserting that Lindsay had "set out in the world a Whig, then turned High Churchman and at last died a Jacobite" (BL, Add. MS 47025, fol. 118).
[41]  Bodleian, MS Ballard 36, fols 15, 19, William Perceval to Arthur Charlett, 7, 10 November 1701; Nichols, ed., *Epistolary Correspondence*, IV, 359, 374; Christ Church, Wake MSS, XII, Isaac Manley to [Wake], 1 March 1717/8.
[42]  Higgins has an entry in *DNB*. Details of his career are given in Bodleian, MS North a. 3, fols 237–38, memorial of Higgins for preferment [1712?]. His brother the alderman is noticed in T. C. Barnard, "Athlone, 1685; Limerick, 1710: Religious Riots or Charivaris," *Studia Hibernica*, 27 (1993), 73.
[43]  See Christ Church, Wake MSS, XII, King to Wake, 12 September 1717.
[44]  *The Swan Tripe-Club: A Satyr on the High-Flyers, in the Year 1705* (London, 1710); J. Barrett, *An Essay on the Earlier Part of the Life of Swift* (London, 1805), pp. 107–23; F. E. Ball, *Swift's Verse* (London, 1929), p. 59; Harold Williams, ed., *The Poems of Jonathan Swift*, 2nd ed., 3 vols (Oxford, 1958), III, 1077–78.
[45]  TCD, MS 2003/1465, John Stearne to [Archbishop King], 14 July 1713. For Travers' High Churchmanship, see also BL, Add. MS 47025, fols 123–24, Sir John Perceval to Philip Perceval, 30 June 1709; and John Travers, *A Sermon Preach'd at Christ-Church in Dublin, before His Grace James Duke of Ormonde, Lord Lieutenant of Ireland: On Monday the Fifth of November, 1711* (Dublin, 1711). I am obliged to Professor Robert Eccleshall for this last reference. The generally "High Church" or "Tory" complexion of the Christ Church canons is noted in TCD, MS 2536, pp. 19–20, Archbishop King to Bishop Charles Crowe, 14 August 1714. In 1705, they had filled two vacancies in the chapter by electing John Francis and Francis Higgins: see TCD, MS 2002/1169, John Stearne to King, 14 July 1705; HMC, *Ormonde MSS*, n.s. VIII, 206–7.

was tipped, together with Higgins, for promotion to a deanery.[46] Nor, for our purposes, was there much difference between such indigenous Irishmen and those Englishmen, like Archbishop Vesey, Bishops Hartstonge, Moreton, or Pooley, and Dean John Francis of Leighlin, who had been resident in Ireland for many years and had come to identify themselves with their adopted country and the distinct interests of its own Established Church.[47]

Even for imported exotics like Perceval or Bishop Hickman (and we know that Perceval came very rapidly to think of himself as belonging to a different Protestant community than the one he had left behind), the peculiar history and circumstances of the Church of Ireland would have modified the ideological preconceptions of English High Churchmanship. In matters of doctrine and liturgy, Irish Protestantism had always tended towards consensus at the "lower" end of the scale. The "Caroline" tradition of sacramentalism and elaborate ceremonial was much thinner than in England and thus even less important as a source of division.[48] There was clearly some potential for conflict if "Low Churchmen" could be represented as slipping too far in the direction of the practices of Presbyterians or Independents, but ultimately consensus would reassert itself. In the autumn of 1714, rumour-mongers tried to stir up animosity towards the new Whig bishop of Raphoe, Edward Synge, with tales of alleged neo-Puritan tendencies. "They say he spoke slightly of the ring in marriage, cross in baptism, surplice, and kneeling at the sacrament," reported an outgoing Tory judge, Sir Richard Cox. But when the relevant sermon appeared in print, Cox was forced to admit that not only was the story a fabrication, but that Synge's exposition had in fact been "very good."[49]

Political and social realities also dictated the necessity of a more consensual approach to those sensitive questions of constitutional principle over which churchmen elsewhere so frequently, and so disastrously, stumbled. While high-flying clergymen in England could afford the exercise of conscience involved in refusing the oaths to William and Mary, the luxury of denouncing "Revolution principles" from the pulpit, and even the occasional fit of Jacobitism, their Irish counterparts had every reason to move with circumspection. The history of the Reformation in Ireland, its dependence on English conquest, and, more recently, the providential intervention of William III to deliver the Protestant interest from what was seen as imminent destruction, were a powerful inhibition on the excesses of divine-right monarchism. Thus the Revolution exposed only a handful of nonjurors in the Church of Ireland, of whom the most prominent, Charles Leslie, went on to pursue his career in England.[50] Although the increasing bitterness of party strife in Queen Anne's reign eventually

[46]  National Library of Ireland, MS 13242/9 (Lismore MSS), John Waite to Richard Musgrave and Thomas Baker, 9 January 1713/4. Hinton, like William Tisdall, seems to have begun his career as a chaplain to Archbishop Marsh (Bodleian, MS Smith 52, p. 59, Marsh to Thomas Smith, 25 May 1697).

[47]  For Francis, see Surrey RO, Guildford, Midleton MSS, 1248/2, Alan to Thomas Brodrick, [October 1705]; BL, Add. MS 47025, fols 123–24, Sir John to Philip Perceval, 30 June 1709; Christ Church, Wake MSS, XII, Archbishop King to Wake, 11 March 1717[/8], Bishop Evans to Wake, 14 March [1718].

[48]  See F. R. Bolton, *The Caroline Tradition of the Church of Ireland* (London, 1958).

[49]  BL, Add. MS 38157, fols 133–34, Cox to Edward Southwell, 9, 12 October 1714.

[50]  See James I. McGuire, "The Church of Ireland and the 'Glorious Revolution' of 1688," Art Cosgrove and Donal McCartney, eds, *Studies in Irish History* (Dublin, 1979), pp. 137–49.

provoked some Irish clergymen into indiscretions that their opponents interpreted as proving disloyalty to the Revolution settlement, it is hard to find concrete evidence of Jacobitism, or a conscious disapproval of the events of 1688–91. If we look closely at what Irish "Jacobites" are supposed to have said, their extremism almost invariably takes the form of extravagant denunciations of their enemies as would-be republicans and regicides.[51] Tories in Ireland certainly subscribed in droves to the martyrology of Charles I, but even the most vehement invective against the King's "murderers" was careful to distinguish between the events of the Civil War and the more recent "happy Revolution," and to skate around the difficult question of what had actually occurred in 1688.[52] A personal regard for the nonjuror Henry Dodwell did not prevent Archbishop Palliser from disagreeing with Dodwell's constitutional and ecclesiastical purism,[53] while William Perceval, another friend and correspondent, after defending Dodwell's *Paraenesis* from censure in Convocation, concluded his report to the author in the following terms:

> For the little share I have had in this controversy I have been severely aspersed and brand-ed a Jacobite, which is a title I am not fond of, and which you well know I have no ways deserved. But it is the way with the low, moderate, lukewarm churchmen to cast any char-acter that they think most odious upon those who espouse better principles than them-selves. I freely own to you (whom I know to be otherwise) that I am none of the well wishers to the Prince of Wales, but on the other hand am heartily for maintaining the succession [as] it now stands limited and established by law, and this I hope I may be without abandoning my church principles.[54]

But undoubtedly, the most significant difference which obtained in the Church of Ireland was its numerical inferiority. In the south of Ireland, with the exceptions of Dublin, Cork, and some of the larger port towns, members of the Established Church constituted a small minority of the total population. Even in Ulster, where Protestants were more heavily con-centrated, Churchmen were often outnumbered by Scottish Presbyterians.[55] In these circum-stances, the clergy would approach their duties with at best a pragmatism, and at worst a resignation, born of low expectations. If Bennett is right, and English parsons harked back to a departed "golden age" of Sancroftian authoritarianism, which many of them could remember, this was not the kind of nostalgia their Irish counterparts could share, at least so far as the Church of Ireland itself was concerned, for the simple reason that such high standards of church attendance had never been achieved, or could ever be achieved, in Ire-

51  See, for example, Francis Higgins in 1707, Bodleian, MS Ballard 7, fol. 7, George Smal-ridge to Arthur Charlett, 1 March 1706/7; see also fol. 9, Higgins's printed justification [1707]); and the diocesan clergy of Cloyne four years later (E. Curtis, J. C. Beckett, and J. B. Leslie, eds, "Address of the Bishop and Clergy of Cloyne to the Queen, 1711," *Jour-nal of the Cork Historical and Archaeological Society*, 46 [1941], 138–42).
52  See Dillon Ashe, *A Sermon Preach'd before the Honourable House of Commons, at St An-drew's Church, Dublin, January the 31st, 1703/4* (Dublin, 1704), a rare example of a pub-lished commemorative sermon on this quintessentially Tory occasion from a Tory or "High Church" point of view. (Again, I owe this reference to Professor Eccleshall.) See also Barnard, "Improving Clergymen," p. 145.
53  Bodleian, MS Eng. letters c. 28, fol. 34, Palliser to Dodwell, 19 October 1697.
54  Bodleian, MS St Edmund Hall 9, p. 110, Perceval to Dodwell, 2 September 1704. See also MS Ballard 36, fols 37–38, Perceval to Arthur Charlett, 15 January 1705/6; and for a more formal denial of charges of Jacobitism, by the Upper House of Convocation, PRO NI, DIO 4/1/10/3/2, pp. 288–89.
55  See Connolly, *Religion, Law and Power*, pp. 144–49, 159–62.

land. Admittedly, the Lower House of Convocation, in one of its very earliest meetings in 1704, did resolve to ask the Lord Lieutenant to proclaim the strict execution of the laws against those who failed to attend a Sunday service, and to press the bishops to charge churchwardens with presenting the offenders.[56] But in this case the perceived enemy was not error and schism so much as irreligion and indifference. The population were to be coerced into observing the requirements of the Sabbath – even in a Nonconformist meeting or a Catholic mass-house – rather than coerced into their parish church as such. It was another aspect of that general concern with Protestant backsliding which informed contemporary campaigns for the reformation of manners, and the foundation of charity schools.

That there were some attempts at the coercion of non-Anglicans into the Established Church cannot be denied. What we have to be clear about is their extent, and whether churchmen differed seriously about their justification and utility. The first point to be made is that where legal duress was resorted to at a local level the victims were always Protestant Dissenters: Quakers, Huguenot refugees, and above all the Ulster Presbyterians.[57] The incidence of prosecutions, however, depended very much on the vigour with which the clergy and magistrates on the spot, and even more the diocesan authorities, pursued a coercive policy. Some bishops – Edward Smyth would be one example – were active while others did little, and not even at the zenith of Tory reaction, in 1711–14, was there anything approaching a consistent or co-ordinated campaign.[58] Certainly, Convocation did not follow up its first call for action. But can we see a difference in attitude between types of clergymen rather than individuals? In his pioneering study of Archbishop King's early episcopal career in Derry, J. C. Beckett argued that King favoured a strategy of "persuasion rather than compulsion" in his dealings with local Presbyterians.[59] There would be an obvious contrast with the more vigorous approach adopted by the "High Churchman" Smyth in Down and Connor. More recently, this roseate picture of King as a liberal reformer has been dissolved by S. J. Connolly, who has highlighted not only the opposition given by King and his cronies to the repeal of the "Test clause" of 1704, and even to the modest concessions contained in the 1719 Toleration Bill, but the apparent determination shown by King in Derry to impose moral discipline by legal means.[60] At close quarters, it becomes difficult to distinguish "Low" from "High Churchmen" on this issue. And in any case, one would have to proceed with particular care in dealing with clerical policy towards Protestant Dissent, because of the complicating cross-currents of party politics. It was in the nature of Whiggism, and King was certainly "a state Whig,"[61] to advocate "unanimity" among Protestants against the greater threat of a Catholic universal monarchy, just as it was in the nature of Toryism to focus attention on the primacy of the danger posed to the establishment in church and state by "the old leaven" of Presbyterian "republicans."

It is still possible that the distinction between "High" and "Low" Churchmen, as advocates of contrasting policies of coercion and persuasion, might work in another context, if applied to evangelism among Catholics rather than Protestant Dissenters, and there is some

---

[56] See TCD, MS 668/1, fol. 28; MS 668/2, 4 March 1704.
[57] Connolly, *Religion, Law and Power*, pp. 174–75.
[58] See Marsh's Library, Dublin, MS Z.3.1.1, no xxiii, deposition of James Bell [?1717].
[59] Beckett, "William King's Administration of the Diocese of Derry," pp. 171–72.
[60] See Connolly, *Religion, Law and Power*, pp. 174–75.
[61] King, *A Great Archbishop*, p. 275.

evidence which would support this view. The opposition by High Churchmen in both houses of Convocation in 1711 to the project advanced by John Richardson, the rector of Belturbet in Co. Cavan, for the publication and distribution of Irish-language translations of the New Testament, Book of Common Prayer and Church catechism, has been taken to demonstrate a party difference over the issue of proselytism, "in which Tories looked to a restoration of the church's legal monopolies and coercive authority, while missionary efforts tended to be associated with Whiggery."[62] The first objection to this generalization would be that Tories and "High Churchmen" were not unanimous in disliking Richardson's scheme. Lord Anglesey, "the darling of the Church party," and Edward Wetenhall, the "High Church" Bishop of Kilmore, were among its backers.[63] And even allowing for the fact that it was William Perceval who led the opposition in the Lower House, and the "High Church" majority among the bishops who finally rejected the proposal, it would not be true to say that they had acted out of any disregard for proselytism as such.[64] What was happening was a conflict, not over whether to coerce or persuade, but over the respective merits of different means of persuasion. On the one side were the enthusiasts for preaching and teaching in Irish; on the other those who advocated the establishment of charity schools to teach the natives through the English language.[65] There were no hard and fast party distinctions here, either. Some "High Churchmen," like Lindsay, or Bishop Vigors of Ferns, were apathetic towards vernacular translations and charity schools alike, while others, notably Archbishop Vesey, and even Perceval himself, were keen supporters of popular education through the medium of English. Among the "Low Church" party, Archbishop King promoted the use of the Irish language but was strongly suspicious of the charity school movement, as of all private intrusions on ecclesiastical preserves, while Bishop Nathaniel Foy of Waterford and Edward Synge preached for subscriptions to schools, and in Foy's case founded one himself.[66] The determining factor, as far as Convocation's vote was concerned, was probably a personal one. Richardson enjoyed the public patronage of Archbishop King, which in the febrile political atmosphere of 1711 was reason enough for "High Churchmen" to throw out his project.[67]

---

62  Connolly, *Religion, Law and Power*, pp. 299–301. There appears to be some qualification of this view in the account given of coercive ecclesiastical policies in Connolly, "Reformers and Highflyers," pp. 161–64. On Richardson and his schemes, see also Barnard, "Protestants and the Irish Language," pp. 254–60.

63  See King, *A Great Archbishop*, pp. 296–98. For Anglesey's politics, see BL, Add. MS 47087, fol. 57, "Character of the Primate and Earl of Anglesea" by Sir John Perceval, and D. Hayton, "The Crisis in Ireland and the Disintegration of Queen Anne's Last Ministry," *Irish Historical Studies*, 22 (1980–81), 193–215, especially p. 200; for Wetenhall's, Cambridge University Library, Add. MS 1, fol. 84, James Bonnell to John Strype, 10 November 1690.

64  See HMC, *Portland MSS*, V, 105–6; Bodleian, MS Ballard 36, fols 82–83, Perceval to Arthur Charlett, 14 May 1713; PRO NI, DIO 4/1/10/3/3, pp. 215–17, 253–54.

65  See Barnard, "Protestants and the Irish Language," pp. 261–63; D. Hayton, "Did Protestantism Fail in Early Eighteenth-Century Ireland? Charity Schools and the Enterprise of Religious and Social Reformation, c. 1690–1730," Ford, McGuire, and Milne, eds, *As By Law Established*, pp. 173–74.

66  See Bodleian, MS Ballard 36, fols 82–83; Barnard, "Protestants and the Irish Language," pp. 252, 256, 258; Hayton, "Did Protestantism Fail?" pp. 168–69, 171, 178–79, 270n29; King, *A Great Archbishop*, pp. 294–95 .

67  See Bodleian, MS Ballard 36, fols 76–77, William Perceval to Arthur Charlett, 12 May 1712; Hayton, "Did Protestantism Fail?" pp. 173–74.

Similarly negative answers await if we look beyond the question of proselytism to wider issues of ecclesiastical policy. The presumption that "High Churchmen" longed for a separation of Church from state, while their opponents limply acquiesced in subordination to the secular power, an idea which would find little encouragement in Bennett's analysis of the divisions within the Church of England, has been dismissed by S. J. Connolly, who has suggested that there was a consensus in favour of the supposed "High Church" demand for clerical independence. In fact, "Low Churchmen" like Archbishop King were as determined as their opponents to establish Convocation's rights as against those of the Irish Parliament (even to the extent of separate taxation of the clergy), and to recover impropriate advowsons, tithes, and glebe.[68] By the same token, we should be wary of accepting at face value the criticisms advanced by "reformers" against their adversaries, as if to imply that the "High Church" party as a whole did not share a commitment to build up the material resources of the Church and improve the standard of pastoral provision. King derided his fellow archbishop, Palliser of Cashel, as a chronic absentee, while John Vesey of Tuam was held up as a prime exponent of nepotism, and dismissed by his successor, Edward Synge, as a man who had done little by way of reconstruction during his long tenure of the see.[69] These snap judgements are at best one-sided. Palliser's surviving correspondence reveals a character of refinement and dedication, with a serious interest in theological exposition, while the charge of absenteeism against him was forcefully denied by his friends.[70] As for Vesey, the intensity of his personal piety was never in doubt: he gave his patronage to the Irish societies for the reformation of manners, and took a keen interest in the foundation of charity schools.[71] A case could indeed be made for ranking him among the more prominent ecclesiastical "re-

---

[68] Connolly, *Religion, Law and Power*, pp. 173–74, a point developed in "Reformers and Highflyers," p. 161. There is further supporting evidence in Bodleian, MS Eng. letters c. 29, fol. 33, St George Ashe to Henry Dodwell, 30 April 1703; Christ Church, Wake MSS, XII, Archbishop King to Wake, 12 September 1717.

[69] Bodleian, MS Ballard 36, fol. 87, Perceval to Arthur Charlett, 27 August 1713; Cambridge University Library, Add. MS 1, fol. 89, James Bonnell to John Strype, 13 February 1691 [/2]; Christ Church, Wake MSS, XII, Synge to Wake, 27 September 1717. See also Phillips, ed., *History of the Church of Ireland*, III, 182.

[70] King, *A Great Archbishop*, p. 85; TCD, MS 750/3, pp. 105–9, King to Palliser, 30 April 1707. William Perceval pointed out that Palliser's absence in England in 1713 had been for an acceptable purpose, namely to oversee the education of his only son, while his accuser, Archbishop King, had himself been over in England at the same time in order to buy horses; see Bodleian, MS Ballard 36, fol. 87, Perceval to Arthur Charlett, 27 August 1713. Some clearer examples of prolonged episcopal absenteeism on the part of "High Churchmen" can be documented. John Hartstonge was given leave of absence by the Crown for periods amounting to nearly four years between 1706 and 1713; Charles Hickman, leave for two and a half years in all between 1704 and 1713; and William Moreton, continuous leave for eighteen months from the summer of 1706; see Royal Irish Academy, MS 3.A.54, pp. 135, 139–41, 146, 154–58. But on the other side we should note that King's crony St George Ashe, Bishop of Clogher, spent a year in England from June 1712, and went over again for the first half of 1714; see Royal Irish Academy, MS 3.A.54, pp. 155, 167. A fellow Whig bishop, the Welshman John Evans of Meath, who clearly disliked Ashe, later declared him unfit for promotion as one who "would not reside, and [would] prefer none but his own kindred;" see Christ Church, Wake MSS, XII, Evans to [Wake], 18 January [?1718].

[71] *An Account of the Societies for the Reformation of Manners, in England and Ireland*, 3rd ed. (London, 1700), list of subscribers; Hayton, "Did Protestantism Fail?" pp. 178–79. See also TCD, MS 2002/1128, Vesey to Archbishop King, 11 January 1704[/5], expressing a vision for the regeneration of the Church by means of the remitted first-fruits and tenths.

formers," together with other "High Churchmen" like Edward Smyth and Edward Wetenhall, who in the 1690s laboured alongside Marsh and King on the episcopal bench;[72] and
Peter Browne, who as provost of Trinity actively promoted "moral reformation" from the
pulpit.[73] It is also worth noting in this context that Vesey's arch-critic, the priggish Edward
Synge, before gravitating into the orbit of Archbishop King and becoming a "Low Churchman," had appeared in Convocation as a vocal member of the "High Church" faction.[74]

There was one way in which the movement for ecclesiastical reform might have aggravated
divisions within the Church, in spite of its essentially non-partisan character, for the programme adopted by some of the more vigorous-minded bishops did intrude quite significantly upon the lives of country parsons, compelling them to exertions they may not have
considered reasonable or appropriate, and sharpening their general sense of grievance. As
Beckett and others have shown, King and his like-minded colleagues were expending much
of their energy in seeking to force their diocesan clergy to harder work and higher standards.
Visitations highlighted non-residence, and, by obliging incumbents to maintain parish
schools (as the law declared), meant to deprive absentees of the opportunity of employing
their putative schoolmasters as, in practice, low-paid curates.[75] Nothing could have been
more finely calculated to arouse the resentment of parsons struggling on inadequate endow-
ments, and although other reforming schemes aimed at improving the economic position of
the clergy, through uniting parishes or increasing the allotment of glebe, the interference of
an overbearing bishop (and the incurably quarrelsome King was the very model of an overbearing bishop) would rarely be welcome. There are significant examples of "High Churchmen" at odds with their bishop over questions of privilege or discipline, as the entire chapter
of Christ Church were united in resisting what they regarded as the unjustified assertions of
authority made by King as Archbishop of Dublin.[76] We can find others, too, whose finances

---

[72] See John Ainsworth, ed., *The Inchiquin Manuscripts* (Dublin, 1961), p. 754; PRO NI, Fos-
ter-Massereene MSS, D562/23, John Campbell to Lord Massereene, 6 June 1701; Cambridge University Library, Add. MS 1, fols 84, 117–18, James Bonnell to John Strype, 10
November 1690, 6 May 1695; Edward Wetenhall, *Be Ye Also Ready: A Method and Order
of Practice* (London, 1694); and the same author's *The Frequency of the Lord's Supper:
Stated and Proved from Holy Scripture* (London, 1703); Phillips, ed., *History of the Church
of Ireland*, III, 173–74, 182; Barnard, "Reforming Irish Manners," p. 809.

[73] See Peter Browne, *A Sermon Preached at St Bride's Church, Dublin, April 17 1698* (Dublin,
1698). See also Browne's *A Sermon Preach'd at the Parish Church of St Andrew's, in Dublin,
on Sunday, the 15th April 1716, for the Benefit of the Charity School for Boys in that Parish*
[?1716]; Jackson, *Peter Browne*, pp. 8–11.

[74] See Christ Church, Wake MSS, XVII, fol. 148, Synge to William Wake, 20 August 1703;
Bodleian, MS Ballard 36, fol. 76, William Perceval to Arthur Charlett, 12 May 1712.
Perceval claimed that Synge had deserted his "old friends" in 1709 because he saw in
Whiggism "the high road to preferment" (MS Ballard 36, fol. 97, to Charlett, 26 April
1711). Archbishop King was recommending him for the vacant deanery of Down as early
as February of that year (TCD, MS 2531, pp. 61–62, King to Edward Southwell, 16 February 1708[/9]).

[75] King, *A Great Archbishop*, p. 106; *The Charge Given by Narcissus, Lord Archbishop of Dublin, to the Clergy of the Province of Leinster, at His Primary Visitation, Anno Dom. 1694*
(Dublin, 1694); HMC, *Ormonde MSS*, n.s. VIII, 190.

[76] Bodleian, MS Ballard 36, fols 34, 128–29, William Perceval to Arthur Charlett [October
1703], state of the Bishop of Kildare's case; *Calendar of State Papers, Domestic*, 1703–4, p.
38; TCD, MS 2002/1188, Lady Dun to Archbishop King, 10 January 1705[/6]; HMC,
*Ormonde MSS*, n.s. VIII, 91, 105, 110, 113–14, 179–80, 206–7; King, *A Great Archbishop*, pp.
108, 210, 245–47; Mant, *History of the Church of Ireland*, pp. 168–73.

were embarrassingly straitened, despite their possession of a multiplicity of cures – Francis Higgins, John Francis, and Benjamin Neale are among the more obvious[77] – and who could not be expected to welcome the demand that they relinquish any of their preferments or perform the impossible task of attending to all responsibilities in person.[78] But however strong it might have been in individual cases, resentment at the imposition of more exacting conditions of employment in a time of economic hardship was not the determining factor in the creation of the "High Church" party. There was no widespread and conscious resistance to episcopal reform; indeed, the Lower House of Convocation voluntarily adopted some of its elements, producing proposals to oblige the performance of pastoral duties, and to revive the parochial school system, though with an accompanying request that diocesan officials treat the clergy "tenderly" in extracting fees.[79] Doubtless the poverty of the lower clergy was a factor in raising political consciousness, but it was at best only a catalyst.

If the two parties within the Church were not seriously divided on questions of doctrine, liturgical practice, the relationship of church and state, evangelical strategies, or the campaign for ecclesiastical reform, the question arises as to what separated them. A case might be made, along Namierite lines, for the simple effects of personality and patronage. William Perceval frequently described his opponents in the Lower House of Convocation as the followers, even the "dependants" of Archbishops Marsh and King. In explaining the behaviour of William Tisdall, for example, who occupied the position of *bête noire* in Perceval's accounts of debates in the first two sessions, it was sufficient for him to allude to Tisdall's position as Marsh's chaplain. Later, after the Archbishop of Dublin had taken over leadership of the "Low Church" cause, the defenders of Ralph Lambert in 1709 were described as "my Lord Lieutenant's and the Archbishop of Dublin's party."[80] The outline of King's clerical affinity may easily be traced through his own voluminous correspondence, not only with fellow bishops like St George Ashe of Clogher and John Stearne of Dromore (the prolocutor in 1709), but with many of the lower clergy, whom he repeatedly recommended for preferment to the incoming Whig ministry in 1714: men like Edward Synge, Theophilus Bolton, Andrew Hamilton, George Story, and Charles Whittingham.[81] Without a similar personal archive on the "High Church" side, one can only speculate on the existence of alternative networks of patronage. But the clustering of activists in particular dioceses is certainly suggestive: the nest of "High Churchmen" at Christ Church, where for a time the Tory Bishop Moreton of Kildare was Dean; John Hinton and Francis Higgins in Ossory under Hartstonge's episcopate; John Francis and Benjamin Neale together in Leighlin. As the most senior of the Tory bishops, John Vesey seems to have enjoyed a far-flung

---

77  TCD, MS 2002/1100, Higgins to Archbishop King, 9 July 1704; Bodleian, MS North a. 3, fols 237–38, memorial of Higgins for preferment [1712?]; King, *A Great Archbishop*, pp. 208–9; PRO NI, D906/80a, William Perceval to his sister, 31 July 1733. For another detailed example of the fragility of clerical incomes in this period, see PRO NI, DIO4/5/3/67, memorial by Robert Mossom on the deanery of Ossory.

78  Higgins was charged by the Dublin diocesan authorities in 1714 with failure to attend his parish duties at Balrothery, in what may well have been an exemplary proceeding; see TCD, MS 2536, p. 20, King to Bishop Charles Crowe, 14 August 1714.

79  See TCD, MS 668/3, 4 March 1704.

80  See BL, Add. MS 47025, fol. 126, William Perceval to Sir John Perceval, 7 July 1709.

81  See TCD, MS 2536, fols 82–85, Archbishop King to Archbishop Tenison, 30 September 1714; Christ Church, Wake MSS, XII, King to Wake, 8 May 1716, Bishop Evans to Wake, 1 February [1717].

clientage beyond his own province of Tuam, where his "cousin" Fielding Shaw was registrar, and one of Perceval's dozen supporters in the protest of 1709, Theodore Maurice or Morice, was archdeacon;[82] and one is also inclined to suspect, from the presence of William Perceval, John Dogherty, and others of a similar kidney in the cathedral chapter of Cashel, that the relatively undocumented obscurity suffered by Archbishop Palliser cloaks a figure of much greater influence than historians have hitherto realized.[83]

Important as personal relationships may have been in cementing political groupings among the clergy, the divisions in Convocation cannot have been simply a matter of rivalries between different episcopal "connections," so deep were the passions expressed in debate, so violent the animosities. In this respect, there are analogies to be drawn with the situation in England, even though the religious history of the two kingdoms is sufficiently divergent to preclude a direct parallel. We must return to Bennett's explanation of the conflicts between "High Church" and "Low" in England, as originating in different responses to a "crisis" in the affairs of the Church after the Glorious Revolution. The clergy of the Church of Ireland were equally convinced of the existence of a "crisis" in their own affairs. As in England, the Established Church seemed beset by perils. There was a general belief that public morals, especially among the Protestant community, had declined to such a pitch as to provoke a Providential judgement; hence the emphasis on reforming manners and providing a moral education for the children of the Protestant poor.[84] There was fear of the spread of freethinking: the brief return to Ireland of the gadfly publicist John Toland in 1697 had provoked a flurry of public denunciations of his pseudo-Deist philosophizing; and not long afterwards a conflict had broken out in Irish Presbyterian circles over the doctrine of the Trinity, which had resulted in the imprisonment of the Arian Thomas Emlyn.[85] But above all, the clergy were conscious of the threat still posed by their traditional enemies. This was where the predicament of the Church of Ireland differed most sharply from that of the Church of England, and where the sense of "crisis" in Ireland was focused. On the one hand, there were the vast numbers of Roman Catholics, politically defeated but remaining loyal to their religious faith despite the imposition of the "penal laws," and fortified by the dream of a Jacobite invasion underwritten by the military power of France. On the other,

---

[82] For Shaw, see De Vesci MSS T3738/G/5, p. 30; T3738/G/10A, letters from Shaw to John Vesey, 1702–16. For Maurice, see National Archives, Dublin, Sarsfield-Vesey MSS, Corr./ 53, John to [Agmondisham Vesey], 8 August 1703; BL, Add. MS 47025, fols 123–24, Sir John to Philip Perceval, 30 June 1709.

[83] One might add to this number the Dean of Cashel, Henry Price, and the proctors for the clergy of the diocese, Anthony Irby and Richard Leake, all absentees who left their proxies with William Perceval; see TCD, MS 668/2 (unfol.). It is worth noting, however, that Perceval, while undoubtedly obliged for his preferments to his "relation" Archbishop Palliser (Bodleian, MS Eng. letters c. 28, fol. 34, Palliser to Henry Dodwell, 19 October 1697; PRO NI, D906/58, Palliser to Perceval, 8 February 1700), was also a long-standing friend of the Veseys (De Vesci MSS, T3738/J/3A (DH), letters from Perceval to Sir Thomas Vesey, 1697–1720).

[84] See Barnard, "Reforming Irish Manners," pp. 805–8, 835–37; Hayton, "Did Protestantism Fail?" pp. 168–75.

[85] See Connolly, *Religion, Law and Power*, p. 175; J. G. Simms, "John Toland (1670–1722), a Donegal Heretic," reprinted in D. Hayton and G. O'Brien, eds, *War and Politics in Ireland, 1649–1730* (London, 1986), pp. 36–38; Peter Brooke, *Ulster Presbyterianism: The Historical Perspective, 1610–1970*, 2nd ed. (Belfast, 1994), pp. 72–73. See also PRO NI DIO4/ 1/10/3/3, p. 228; *Representation of the Present State of Religion*, pp. 3–7.

and in some respects even more ominous, was the rapidly increasing strength of Protestant Dissent, especially in Ulster, where the Scottish Presbyterian presence had been powerfully reinforced following large-scale immigration from Scotland in the "lean years" of the 1690s. The establishment of the General Synod of Ulster had given institutional expression to the new confidence felt by Ulster Presbyterians. In the eyes of Anglican critics, they seemed to be setting themselves up as a rival establishment, their ministers marrying and burying parishioners, and their sessions, presbyteries and Synod usurping the disciplinary function of the church courts. Finally came a series of well-publicized incidents in which new Presbyterian congregations were established in "frontier" areas on the border of the province of Ulster and beyond, at Drogheda and Belturbet. Many clergymen were convinced of a co-ordinated campaign to subvert the position of the Church and establish a Presbyterian government in its stead.[86]

In secular politics, it was the relative importance accorded by each party to the threats posed by Catholics and Presbyterians which formed the basis of the division between Whigs and Tories in Ireland. Indeed, some Tories went further than their party's customary dismissal of "no popery" as an empty shibboleth, a distraction from the real business of combating the aspirations of the General Synod, and, presumably on the basis that "my enemy's enemy is my friend," took a sufficiently charitable view of Irish Catholics to oppose the strengthening of the penal laws, and to welcome electoral support from crypto-Catholic *conversos*.[87] Undoubtedly, this tendency to indulge in extravagant posturing rubbed off on some clerical politicians. "High Church" rant occasionally declared that a papist was preferable to a Presbyterian; as one proctor in the Lower House of Convocation put it in 1705,

> if he must be under a necessity of ranking himself with one or the other of them two parties [Presbyterians or Catholics] he had much rather side with the latter than with the former, for that they were Christians tho' bad ones, whereas the others were such a medley of men, such a mixture of ill principles, such a herd – that he wanted words bad enough to describe them with.[88]

Occasionally, too, discretion was abandoned by Tory clerics who openly consorted with recently converted Catholics, as in 1711 when a former priest, Dominic Langton, was taken up by Francis Higgins and Bishop Hartstonge as a (barely credible) witness to some fantastic tales of Whig conspiracy.[89]

These were extreme cases, however. It would be profoundly misleading to suggest that "High Churchmen" were indifferent to the progress of the Reformation, or for that matter that "Low Churchmen" were unconcerned by Protestant schism. In general, the "softness" of secular Tories on the Catholic question was not matched by their clerical counterparts, for whom proselytism was still a major concern. Nor were Whiggish clergymen apathetic

---

[86]  See Hayton, "Ireland and the English Ministers," Chapter 5; Connolly, *Religion, Law and Power*, pp. 159–71.

[87]  See Hayton, "Ireland and the English Ministers," pp. 132–34.

[88]  Bodleian, MS St Edmund Hall 9, pp. 140–42, William Perceval to Henry Dodwell, 26 February 1704/5.

[89]  See Abel Boyer, *The Political State of Great Britain*, 60 vols (London, 1711–40), II, 346–66; HMC, *Portland MSS*, V, 20; Williams, ed., *Correspondence*, I, 199–200, 250, 264, 270; Christ Church, Wake MSS, XII, "J. H." to Wake, 12 October 1711. In 1709, Thomas Lindsay observed that he thought parliamentary opposition to Catholic voting rights "was levelled at the Church;" Ainsworth, ed., *The Inchiquin Manuscripts*, p. 99.

about the problem of Dissent, as King had shown when at Derry.[90] It is certainly true that "High Churchmen" developed a fixation with the problem posed by the growth in Presbyterianism in Ulster, but again one must be careful in emphasizing this obvious point. His own struggles with the minister and congregation in Belfast duly turned William Tisdall into a Tory, but a close exposure to the activities of the General Synod did not invariably make a high-flyer, and against the "High Churchmen" who held sees in Ulster (Edward Smyth in Down and Connor, John Pooley in Raphoe) or lesser dignities (the 1709 protest was signed by the Dean of Armagh, Peter Drelincourt, the Dean of Down, John Leslie, and two proctors from the province),[91] one might set the Bishops of Clogher (Ashe) and Dromore (Stearne), the Deans of Derry (John Bolton), Down (Ralph Lambert), and Connor (George Story), and the Archdeacons of Armagh (William Hamilton) and Raphoe (Andrew Hamilton), all of whom belonged at various stages to the opposing party.

Where a clear difference is visible between "High" and "Low Church" is in the context in which each side placed the local difficulties with which they, and the Church as a whole, were confronted. The distinguishing mark of the "High Churchman" in this period was his more intense involvement in secular politics, as evinced in the determination with which the cause of Sir George Rooke was argued in the session of 1705, or the campaign against the viceregal management of Lord Wharton was waged in 1709. This might be thought of as a narrowing of vision, yet in one sense it represents the very opposite; a willingness to see the mission of "High Churchmen" in Ireland as part of a broader crusade, across all of Queen Anne's dominions, against the forces of irreligion, Whiggism, and Presbytery. The terms in which Convocation framed its *Representation* in 1711 did not reflect the peculiar difficulties faced by the Church of Ireland so much as the general concerns of Tories in all three kingdoms. "Infidelity," "heresy," and "impiety" were given a higher priority than the advances of Ulster Presbyterianism, or the persistence of popery, and concern was expressed over the growth in "occasional conformity" by Protestant Dissenters, even though this was a phenomenon of English rather than Irish politics.[92] Making the identification explicit, a sermon preached before the Duke of Ormond by Canon John Travers in 1711, on the anniversary of the Gunpowder Plot, recalled the "remarkable deliverances of our church," in the singular, "and nations," in the plural, and cited, as proof "that the church is countenanced and encouraged; that religion, and the good of souls, and the glory of God, are taken care of and promoted, to the discouragement of heresy, schism, and irreligion," the building of the Fifty New Churches in London, "the great metropolis."[93]

It is also as a manifestation of a sense of common purpose that one can account for the remarkable attention paid by so many Irish "High Churchmen" to cultivating the good opinion of English Tory politicians, as they sought to acquire patronage through professing devotion to a unitary party cause. The most aggressive tuft-hunter was undoubtedly Francis

---

[90]  See Beckett, "William King's Administration of the Diocese of Derry," pp. 171–76.

[91]  See BL, Add. MS 47025, fols 123–24, Sir John to Philip Perceval, 30 June 1709.

[92]  See PRO NI, DIO4/1/10/3/3, pp. 228–39, 241–51, 257–58; *Representation of the Present State of Religion*, pp. 3–9, 18. I have discussed the question of "occasional conformity" in "Exclusion, Conformity, and Parliamentary Representation: The Impact of the Sacramental Test on Irish Dissenting Politics," Kevin Herlihy, ed., *The Politics of Irish Dissent, 1650–1800* (Dublin, 1997), pp. 64–65, 70–71.

[93]  John Travers, *A Sermon Preach'd at Christ-Church*, pp. 19–20.

Higgins, whose foray into England in 1707, distinguished by a much-publicized disputation with Archbishop Tenison, and an exceedingly intemperate, Whig-bashing sermon in London, for which he was almost prosecuted, resulted in the attraction of a flock of influential admirers, who in 1713/4 tried Lord Treasurer Oxford's patience with demands for an Irish bishopric for their hero.[94] Lindsay and Perceval, too, could boast similar racks of well-placed patrons; Mossom Wye, proctor for the chapter of Raphoe, attached himself to Secretary of State Dartmouth; Sir Thomas Vesey applied to Anglesey and Speaker Hanmer; and John Francis, himself a transplanted Englishman, nurtured friendships with a string of Lancashire and Cheshire squires, who were willing to advocate his claims to promotion.[95]

The "High Churchmen" were thus primarily political operators, which in the event proved their undoing, as they were stranded by the permanent triumph of Whiggism after the Hanoverian Succession. Those who had already attained the heights of the episcopal bench found themselves ignored by Government, particularly Thomas Lindsay, who had been advanced to Armagh in 1714 on the death of Narcissus Marsh, and spent the decade of his primacy in political isolation. The minor players remained camped in the foothills of preferment: Francis Higgins, in his "little vicarage" near Dublin, apologizing to English correspondents for the "coarseness" of the only writing paper he could obtain "in our village;" William Perceval, soldiering on as Dean of Emly, and lamenting, perhaps a trifle archly, of his humdrum existence "in a little refined country parsonage, where I hear what passes, and can only grieve at the affliction of Joseph."[96] Such an attitude of mute resignation only reemphasizes the essentially political nature of the "High Church" movement. For the Church of Ireland did not sail into safer waters after 1714. The danger of a Presbyterian coup may have become far less credible, with the demographic changeover to a net emigration from the Ulster Scot community, and the growing preoccupation of the General Synod with the Subscription Controversy, but in its place arose greater fears of the progress of heterodoxy and rationalism, even within the Irish episcopate itself, and of the avowed anticlericalism of many Whig parliamentarians. At the same time, the complacency which had characterized some early eighteenth-century attitudes towards Catholics was dispelled in the 1720s and 1730s by a growing realization that the penal laws had failed to extirpate popery from the island. Moreover, the Church itself was no better equipped to meet the challenge than it had been in 1703, despite the efforts of the episcopal improvers. This rather different "crisis" in the affairs of the Church of Ireland failed to produce a Tory renaissance. Instead, the most important responses came from Whiggish bishops, like Edward Synge and Theophilus

[94] See Bodleian, MS Ballard 7, fol. 7, George Smalridge to Arthur Charlett, 1 March 1706/7; see fol. 9 for Higgins's printed justification, [1707]; TCD, MS 2002/1249, [Francis Annesley] to Archbishop King, [?January 1707]; MS 2002/1282 a, "Notes of Mr Higgins' Conference with Abp. Cant. 1707;" Charles Leslie, *A Postscript to Mr Higgins' Sermon, Very Necessary for the Better Understanding It* (Dublin, 1707); HMC, *Ormonde MSS*, n.s. VIII, 30, 333–34; *Portland MSS*, V, 11–12; X, 383.

[95] See BL, Add. MS 47025, fols 123–24, Sir John to Philip Perceval, 30 June 1709; PRO, SP 54/4/3, Wye to Lord Dartmouth, 13 January 1710[/1]; De Vesci MSS, T3738/G/6 (DH), Anglesey to Archbishop Vesey, 1713; T3738/J/9, Hanmer to same, 8/19 May 1712, 11 May 1713; King, *A Great Archbishop*, pp. 208–9.

[96] Hereford and Worcester Record Office, St Helen's, Worcester, Pakington MSS, Ref. b 705:349, B.A. 4657/(v), fol. 6, Higgins to Sir John Pakington, 29 September 1719; Bodleian, MS Ballard 36, fols 102–3, Perceval to Arthur Charlett, 18 April 1717.

Bolton, who had cut their political teeth in Archbishop King's "Low Church" party, while the remnants of the high-flying tradition remained for the most part silent in their rustication. Of course, Irish clergymen did not cease to be politically aware, and many continued to involve themselves in elections, Parliament, and government long after 1714. But in order to flourish in Hanoverian Ireland, it was necessary to sing a very different tune to the tantivy chorus "High Churchmen" had been accustomed to bellow.

Carole Fabricant
*University of California, Riverside*

# The Voice of God and the Actions of Men: Swift among the Evangelicals

ABSTRACT. While much has been written about Swift's opposition to the Dissenters, his rejection of central aspects of Church-of-Ireland ideology and polemics has been largely ignored. A comparison between Swift's sermons (and related writings) and contemporary Anglican sermons delivered at Christ Church and St Werburgh's reveals the extent to which Swift's outlook challenged the providentialist, evangelical, virulently anti-Catholic strains that helped to nourish the "colonial nationalism" – and the colonialist apologetics – of the Protestant ruling class in Ireland. Such a comparison enables us to understand the progressive as well as conservative aspects of Swift's position as Church-of-Ireland cleric, and indirectly invites us to rethink some of the implications of his critical stance toward the Dissenters.

Swift has traditionally been characterized as a staunch Anglican whose lifelong polemical endeavours were devoted to promoting the interests of the Church and to lamenting the latter's declining power in the face of challenges from Whigs, Dissenters, and freethinkers opposed to the Test Act.[1] Curiously, a recent Marxist study of Swift intended to counteract traditional interpretations essentially echoes this view by presenting the Anglican Church as an "ideological state apparatus," and Swift as spokesman for its hegemonic interests.[2] Overlooked by these critics was Swift's ambivalent relationship to the Established Church, and his resistance to major strains of its combined religious and political agenda: that peculiar blend of messianic zeal, capitalist fervour, and anti-Catholic diatribe, allied to some form of British chauvinism and/or colonial nationalism, which constituted a dominant ideological strain of the Church of Ireland throughout Swift's tenure as Dean of St Patrick's. If Swift saw fit to invest a significant amount of his energies in responding to the writings of freethinkers, deists, and Presbyterians, he simultaneously felt moved to respond critically to much of what he heard proclaimed from Anglican pulpits, in Ireland in particular. While his oppositional stance can no doubt be explained in part by his hostility to the Hanoverian and

---

[1]  See, for example, Louis A. Landa, *Swift and the Church of Ireland* (Oxford, 1954); Basil Hall, "'An Inverted Hypocrite': Swift the Churchman," *The World of Jonathan Swift: Essays for the Tercentenary*, ed. Brian Vickers (Oxford, 1968), pp. 38–68; and J. C. Beckett, "Swift as an Ecclesiastical Statesman," *Fair Liberty Was All His Cry: A Tercentenary Tribute to Jonathan Swift*, ed. A. Norman Jeffares (London, 1967), pp. 146–65.

[2]  See Warren Montag, *The Unthinkable Swift: The Spontaneous Philosophy of a Church of England Man* (London and New York, 1994), chapter 1 and *passim.*

Walpolean establishment, it was rooted in ideological differences that cannot simply be reduced to labels such as "Whig," "Tory," or "Jacobite."[3]

Swift's targets included sermons preached in nearby Christ Church and St Werburgh's, the centres of royal Anglican worship in Dublin, and bastions of Church-of-Ireland orthodoxy. These were sermons often delivered for particular occasions decreed by Parliament as official holy days: for example, November 5, October 23, January 31, the anniversaries, respectively, of the discovery of the Gunpowder Plot, of the Irish Rebellion of 1641, and of the execution of King Charles I. Starting with a specific scriptural passage, the sermon-giver, with varying degrees of dispatch, moved on to an extended reflection on the historical significance of the events commemorated by the anniversary and on the lessons to be derived from them for the present. Among other things, what Swift discovered from these sermons was that Dissenters were not the only ones to fuse religious and political zeal in ways that offended his sensibilities and fanned the flames of his distaste for cant.

We might consider, in this context, the sermon preached by Nicholas, Bishop of Rapho, at Christ Church on November 5, 1721, commemorating the discovery of the Gunpowder Plot. Using as his text a passage from St James's Epistle, "The Wisdom that is from above is first Pure, then Peaceable, Gentle and easy to be Intreated, full of Mercy, and good Fruits, without Partiality, and without Hypocrisy," the sermonizer seems at first to be laying the groundwork for a general contemplation of the distinction between heavenly wisdom and the wisdom of this world, between a striving for purity and an accommodation to earthly vice.[4] Indeed, that is the way Swift applies this same scriptural passage in *his* sermon, *Upon the Excellency of Christianity*, which invokes the ideal of heavenly wisdom to argue the superiority of Christianity in general to pagan religions and philosophy. The Bishop of Rapho's sermon, however, quickly moves from a consideration of heavenly wisdom to a scathing attack not only on the specific Catholic conspirators involved in the Gunpowder Plot, but on Catholicism in general, insisting "it was a mistaken and furious Zeal for Propagating the Errors of the Church of *Rome*," actively "supported by the Authority of the See of *Rome*," that produced yet one more in a long line of papist conspiracies designed to overturn the Protestant nation, the memory of which horrid act causes the sermonizer to lament "How far the Church of *Rome* has fallen from this Heavenly Wisdom, described in the [biblical] text" (pp. 7, 9).

Although the initial warning against "any Society of Men ... [who] shall disturb the Peace of Kingdoms, and overthrow their Government" (pp. 5–6) would seem to be far more applicable to the Puritans of the previous century, the latter are never mentioned in the sermon. Instead, its admonitory remarks are reserved solely for the Catholics, here figured implicitly, as they are described explicitly in other sermons, as a leopard that will never change its spots: "For the *Popish Religion*, so pernicious to both [our Church and our Country] heretofore, continues still the same ... nor does it appear that [the Catholics'] fiery Zeal for the Extirpation of our Religion is at all abated, or become more gentle, or tractable than it was before" (pp. 11–12).

---

3    For a recent study that argues for the Jacobite tendencies in Swift's writings, see Ian Higgins, *Swift's Politics: A Study in Disaffection* (Cambridge, 1994).
4    Nicholas, Lord Bishop of Rapho, *A Sermon Preached in Christ's-Church, Dublin, on Sunday, November 5th, 1721* (Dublin, 1721), pp. 3–5. Hereafter cited in the text.

But if the papists have forfeited any possibility of a connection with heavenly wisdom, the Bishop of Rapho's audience can take comfort in the knowledge that they at least, as members of the Irish Protestant nation, have ready access to such wisdom, as well as to all other blessings from on high. For at the centre of this sermon, as of so many written during this period, is a ringing testimonial to providence: not merely to a general providence that affirms a divine order in the universe and promises the creation of good out of evil, but to a particular or special providence – in this case, God's personal protection of English and Irish Protestants, his intervention in human history to ensure their safety and survival. Thus the Gunpowder Plot was foiled only "when it pleased God in his great Mercy to overrule the Counsels of these wicked Men, and to make a dark Hint in a Letter writ by one of the Conspirators, the means of disclosing their Secret Purposes, [and] defeating their pernicious Designs ... thereby giving us an Occasion on this Day to bless his Name for so great a Deliverance" (p. 10). This blessed event, the sermon makes clear, was but one of a series of such divine redemptions; for "God has ... by many signal Acts of his Divine Providence often rescued us from the brink of Destruction" (p. 22), another more recent example being the appearance of William of Orange, who was specifically sent by God as "the instrument of so great Deliverance," in order to "fulfil the Wishes of an injured People" (p. 15). The sermon assures us that, as faithful and dutiful Protestants, "we need not be afraid while God is on our side" (p. 20).

The ultimate proof of divine favour was the assumed analogy between British Protestants and the Israelites, God's Chosen People. Thus, in another sermon commemorating the discovery of the Gunpowder Plot, in this instance by Edward, Bishop of Ferns and Leighlin in 1737, the passage from 1 Samuel, "Only fear the Lord, and serve him in Truth, with all your Heart: For consider how great Things he hath done for you," is immediately related to contemporary circumstances: "It is easy to see, how properly these Words may be apply'd, to the present Occasion. The People of these Nations [Britain and Ireland], as well as *Israel*, have receiv'd many great Deliverances from God."[5] Confident in the belief that he is speaking as one of God's chosen people, the Bishop assures his congregation: "It is therefore fit and proper to say, that *God hath done great things for us*, and our Fore-fathers" (p. 4). A half-century earlier, Spinoza had observed that he who loves God cannot expect to have God love him in return,[6] but the world of eighteenth-century Protestant preachings ensured against the anxieties of such unrequited love. For the Bishops of Rapho and Ferns and their High-Church brethren, the Protestants of Ireland could love God with unwavering devotion, in the soothing knowledge that the feeling was mutual, that they were well-loved in return – indeed, that they were the very apple of God's eye, the nation God repeatedly sided with in its encounters with the enemy.

Confronted by a body of self-centred and self-aggrandizing beliefs that in other contexts he associated with a variety of his satiric butts, Swift, as Dean of St Patrick's, found himself having to perform dual, indeed opposing, roles, one hegemonic, the other counter-hegemonic: the first, devoted to preaching the faith, exhorting obedience to God's law, and offering spiritual consolation to those of his parishioners suffering material deprivation; the

---

5   Edward, Lord Bishop of Ferns and Leighlin, *A Sermon Preach'd in Christ-Church, Dublin, on Saturday, November 5, 1737* (Dublin, 1737), p. 3. Hereafter cited in the text.
6   See *Ethics and Treatise on the Correction of the Intellect*, trans. Andrew Boyle; rev. G. H. R. Parkinson (London, 1993), p. 205.

second, devoted to refuting various official positions taken by the Church and undermining the network of myths invoked by church leaders – many of them Englishmen sent over to fill vacant Irish bishopricks – for the purpose of promoting the part-colonialist, part-nationalist ideology of the Protestant Ascendancy. By the same token, St Patrick's Cathedral during Swift's deanship played a similarly bifurcated role, standing as a bastion of Anglican dominance, but also serving as a sanctuary for an oppressed minority by virtue of the fact that French Protestant refugees in Dublin were allowed to use one of its chapels as a place of worship,[7] and also periodically transformed by Swift into a site of resistance against English policies: for example, during the Drapier's agitations against Wood's Halfpence, which were explicitly supported by the Dean from the pulpit, and as part of Swift's opposition a decade later to the lowering of the gold standard in Ireland, when the Dean hung a black flag from the steeple of St Patrick's Cathedral and ordered its bells to be rung as if in mourning.[8]

While the sermons delivered in neighbouring churches regularly called upon their listeners to pledge their undivided allegiance to the English monarchy – typical is the Bishop of Ferns's exhortation "to continue, as we have hitherto been, steady and zealous in our Duty and Affection to His Majesty and His Royal House" (p. 23) – Swift showed a readiness to use his pulpit to call for open resistance to royal policy, as in his sermon, *Doing Good*, written "On the Occasion of WOOD'S PROJECT," where he urged his congregation to be patriotic but hastened to explain: "By the love of our country, I do not mean loyalty to our King, for that is a duty of another nature; and a man may be very loyal, in the common sense of the word, without one grain of public-good at his heart."[9] Swift at times viewed his pastoral duties in an explicitly adversarial role *vis-à-vis* the Crown. Thus, when King George I, soon after ascending the throne, issued a directive prohibiting the delivery of sermons that meddled in affairs of state in order to ensure "preserving the peace and quiet of the state," Swift defiantly noted to a correspondent: "I saw in a print that the K[ing] has taken care to limit the clergy what they shall preach; and that has given me an inclination to preach what is forbid."[10]

That this was not simply an idle boast is evident from the delivery shortly thereafter of his sermon, *On False Witness*, which, despite its nod to orthodoxy by counselling obedience to a reigning king, devotes most of its content to an attack on the arrogance of power – referred to as "the prevailing Side," who may say whatever they please "with Security; and generally do it in the most provoking Words they can invent," while those out of favour are subjected to constant surveillance and accusations by false witnesses and paid informers (IX, 183–84). Although it advises the members of the congregation "to have nothing at all to do with that which is commonly called Politicks" (IX, 185–86), the sermon is itself highly political, deliberately snubbing its nose at the newly issued royal decree by presenting to all intents and purposes a sweeping indictment of a government that operates through cor-

---

[7]  See *Correspondence*, II, 411 and n1.

[8]  This incident is commemorated in Swift's (?) ballad, "PATRICK astore, what news upon the town?" (*The Poems of Jonathan Swift*, ed. Harold Williams, 2nd ed., 3 vols [Oxford, 1958], III, 840). The relevant lines are the following: "And Patrick's bell she was ringing all in muffles; / She was ringing very sorry, her tongue tied up with rag; / Lorsha! and out of her shteeple there was hung a black flag" (ll. 7–9).

[9]  *Prose Works*, IX, 233. All subsequent references to Swift's prose are hereafter cited in the text.

[10]  *Correspondence*, II, 155 and n2.

ruption and fraud, whose judiciary is incapable of protecting innocence because its members "are often prejudiced to Causes, Parties, and Persons" (IX, 185). Swift's observation, in his sermon *Doing Good*, that "perhaps it may be thought by some, that this way of discoursing is not so proper from the pulpit" (IX, 235), and his coyly ironic comment at the end of it, "And this, I am sure, cannot be called meddling in affairs of state" (IX, 240), further reflect his calculated defiance of royal decree.

In response to the virulent strain of anti-Catholicism permeating Church-of-Ireland sermons, expressed through their insistence upon the continuing threat posed by Irish papists, Swift repeatedly emphasized the powerlessness of the country's Catholics, their habitual obedience to authority, and their loyalty to the English Crown rather than to Rome. In his *Letter ... Concerning the Sacramental Test*, he labels as "nothing but Misrepresentation and Mistake" the contention that "the *Popish* Interest is here so formidable; that all Hands should be joined to keep it under," assuring his English reader that "on the contrary, we look upon [Irish Papists] to be altogether as inconsiderable as the Women and Children" and "out of all Capacity of doing any Mischief" (II, 120). Playing upon, and subverting, the common characterization of Catholicism as a savage beast ready to rend apart the Protestant Church, Swift describes it as "a *Lyon* at [our] Foot, bound fast with three or four Chains, his Teeth drawn out, and his Claws pared to the Quick" (II, 122). He echoes the same message from the pulpit, assuring his congregation, in his sermon *On Brotherly Love*, that the Catholics have been "put out of all visible Possibility of hurting us" (IX, 172). Swift's statement that the number of papists "is always magnified in Proportion to the Zeal, or Politicks, of the Speaker and Writer," and his scornful repudiation of "those Reports of an Invasion [by the Pretender] ... formed and spread by the Race of small Politicians, in order to do a seasonable Jobb" (XII, 258; 272) make it clear that, for Swift, the overblown claims of the Catholic threat in Ireland were the result, not of naive fears or innocent miscalculation, but of a very deliberate campaign aimed at furthering a specific political agenda.

Nowhere was this alleged threat insisted upon with greater urgency than in the sermons preached on the anniversary of the Irish Rebellion of 1641, an event that was subsequently transformed into one of the centre-pieces of Protestant historical mythology, functioning as a vivid symbol of Catholic treachery and deceit.[11] In his highly influential history of the uprising, written five years afterward, Sir John Temple, arguing that the rebellion could ultimately be traced to the machinations of the pope, related its events through provocatively graphic and inflammatory descriptions – for example, of "Husbands cut to pieces in the presence of their Wives, [and] their Childrens brains dashed out before their faces" – and excoriated the Ulster rebels for committing "those horrid massacres, and execrable murders, as would make any Christian ear to tingle at the sad commemoration of them."[12] Thus an initially localized revolt by a group of Irish Catholic gentry, which (according to the most credible estimates) resulted in the death of between 2,000 and 4,000 Ulster settlers, became transformed, in Anglican pulpits and history books alike, into a brutal slaughter of up to

---

[11] For a useful narrative of the events of this uprising, see R. F. Foster, *Modern Ireland, 1600–1972* (New York, 1989), pp. 85–90. A discussion of sermons written for the occasion may be found in T. C. Barnard, "The Uses of 23 October 1641 and Irish Protestant Celebrations," *English Historical Review*, 106 (1991), 889–920.

[12] Sir John Temple, *The Irish Rebellion* (London, 1646), pp. 40; 90. The Dublin edition of 1724 was in Swift's library; see Harold Williams, *Dean Swift's Library: With a Facsimile of the Original Sale Catalogue* (Cambridge, 1932), item 542.

150,000 Protestants, perpetrated by scheming papists under the direction of Rome.[13] The Parliamentary Act formally commemorating October 23 as "an Anniversary Thanksgiving" throughout Ireland characterized the Rebellion as "a Conspiracy so generally inhumane, barbarous, and cruel, as the like was never before heard of in any Age or Kingdom; and if it had taken effect, in that fulness which was intended by the Conspirators, it had occasioned the utter ruine of this whole Kingdom, and the Government thereof." The Act mandated that "every Minister shall give warning to his Parishioners" at morning prayer the day before the anniversary and that "after Morning Prayer, or Preaching, upon every 3rd and 20th day of October, [the Ministers] read publickly, distinctly and plainly, this present Act."[14]

In the sermon he preached on 23 October 1731 to commemorate the anniversary of the Irish Rebellion, Edward, Bishop of Clonfert, praises Temple as "an Author of great Credit" and quotes generously from his *History*.[15] The sermon invokes a text from Genesis as a parallel to the historical event being memorialized:

> *Simeon and Levi are Brethren: Instruments of Cruelty are their Habitations. O my Soul, come not thou into their Secret: Unto their Assembly, mine Honour be not thou united: For in their Anger they slew a Man, and in their Self-will they digged down a Wall. Curs'd be their Anger, for it was fierce, and their Wrath, for it was Cruel: I will divide them in Jacob, and scatter them in Israel.*

The story tells of the seduction of Jacob's daughter, Dinah, by Sechem son of Hamor, who then petitions to marry her on any terms deemed satisfactory by her father, and the subsequent betrayal of the agreement by Jacob's sons Simeon and Levi, who treacherously slay all the males of Shalem and lay their town waste to avenge their sister's honour. The final words are Jacob's deathbed curse in response to his sons' act of cruel deceit. Swift used this same biblical text – indeed, more than once – with a very different application to modern history, as we shall see. For the Bishop of Clonfert, however, there is an "exact Resemblance" between the Genesis story and the events of the Irish Rebellion: another instance in which a group of well-intentioned and trusting souls, in this case the Protestant settlers, are seduced into embracing peaceful coexistence with a devious foe and then treacherously slaughtered when caught off guard.

The bulk of the sermon is devoted to an at times vitriolic attack not only on the papist rebels of 1641, accused of putting into effect designs that were "astonishingly barbarous and wicked" (p. 8), but also more generally on the proven untrustworthiness of the Irish Catholics, who produced "one continued Scene of Treachery and Rebellion" from the reign of Queen Elizabeth onward on the strength of having "imbib'd all the false and bloody Principles of [the *Romish* Superstition]" (pp. 6, 10), and who have dedicated themselves to the destruction of the Protestant religion: For "had the Success been equal to the Cruelty of [the Irish rebels'] Intentions, the very Name and Memory of a *Protestant* had been rooted out of the Land" (p. 11). Two and one-half centuries later, the sermons of the Reverend Ian Paisley continue to decry the supposed atrocities of 1641, "when Rome sought to exter-

---

[13] W. E. H. Lecky put the number of fatalities at 4,000. Foster suggests the lower figure of 2,000 (see *Modern Ireland*, p. 85).

[14] This Parliamentary Act is quoted in its entirety by Sir Edmund Borlase in his *History of the Execrable Irish Rebellion* (London, 1680), pp. 323–25.

[15] Edward, Lord Bishop of Clonfert, *A Sermon Preach'd at Christ-Church, Dublin, on Saturday, the 23d of October, 1731* (Dublin, 1731), pp. 18–19. Hereafter cited in the text.

minate the Protestant planters of this province," and to pay tribute to Irish Protestants (represented by the members of Paisley's own Free Presbyterian Church) as a Chosen People whom God has personally assured, "Fear not, little flock, it is the Father's good pleasure to give you the kingdom."[16]

Not only did Swift refrain from following the example of his church peers (and superiors) by commemorating the anniversary of the Irish Rebellion in a sermon, he took several opportunities to express his disagreement with the official version of the insurrection, and even wrote a tract presenting the events from the viewpoint of a Catholic *persona*. Countering the commonly held Protestant view of the instigators of the uprising having inflicted widespread destruction on the kingdom, making it – in the words of Archbishop William King – "a Heap of Rubbish, and a Slaughter-House,"[17] Swift argued that the havoc wreaked in 1641 paled in comparison with "the ravages and ruin executed on both sides" during the Williamite Wars in Ireland, which constituted a particularly bloody chapter in "the contention of the British empire" that "[left] the kingdom a desert, which, in some sort, it still continues" (XII, 132). Here, in one forceful paragraph, Swift in effect distances himself from the two major linchpins of Protestant mythology in eighteenth-century Ireland: the execration heaped on the Catholic treachery of 1641, and the glorification of the heroic deliverance from an attempted papist takeover in 1688–89. Repeatedly, Swift extenuated Catholic responsibility for the bloody events of 1641, declaring that it was the *Puritans* who "were the principal Cause of the *Irish Rebellion* and *Massacre*" (XII, 257) – a position he boldly reiterated from the pulpit, in direct opposition to what was regularly preached in neighbouring Anglican churches: "The Irish rebellion was wholly owing to that wicked English parliament. For the leaders in the Irish Popish massacre would never have dared to stir a finger, if they had not been encouraged by that rebellious spirit in the English House of Commons" (IX, 223).

In his tract, *Reasons Humbly Offered to the Parliament of Ireland, for Repealing the Sacramental Test, in Favour of the Catholicks* (1733), Swift presents an account of the Irish Rebellion from the viewpoint of a Catholic apologist determined to set the historical record straight by separating myth from fact. Although on the most obvious level an ironic piece aimed at demonstrating that repeal of the Sacramental Test for Dissenters would necessarily have to be applied to Catholics as well, this tract embodies perspectives whose merits Swift seriously argued in others of his writings. The tract's speaker, offering an interpretation of the events in question similar to that put forward by contemporary Catholic historians such as Hugh Reily in their attempts to counteract the highly sectarian accounts of Temple and Company,[18] contextualizes the 1641 Uprising by observing that English Catholic settlers "were often forced to rise in their own Defence, against new Colonies from *England*, who

---

[16] Ed Moloney and Andy Pollak, *Paisley* (Dublin, 1986), pp. 127; 259. See also in this connection Anthony D. Buckley, "The Chosen Few: Biblical Texts in the Symbolism of an Ulster Secret Society," *The Irish Review*, 2 (1987), 31–40.

[17] William King, *The State of the Protestants of Ireland under the Late King James's Government* (London, 1691), p. 57.

[18] See Hugh Reily, *Ireland's Case Briefly Stated* (1695). For a fuller discussion of the attempts by Reily and other seventeenth- and eighteenth-century Irish Catholic historians to refute biased Protestant historical accounts, see my essay "Jonathan Swift as Irish Historian," *Walking Naboth's Vineyard: New Studies of Swift*, eds Christopher Fox and Brenda Tooley (Notre Dame, IN, 1995), pp. 40–72.

treated them like mere native *Irish*, with innumerable Oppressions; depriving them of their Lands, and driving them by Force of Arms into the most Desolate Parts of the Kingdom" (XII, 285). The speaker repeatedly affirms the basic loyalty of the Catholics to established government and to the English Crown, insisting that they "had no Design to change the Government; they never attempted to fight against, to imprison, to betray, to sell, to bring to a Tryal, or to murder their King" (XII, 288). A similar argument recurs throughout Swift's non-ironic tracts, in which, for example, he examines the course of action pursued by Catholics during the late 1680s and concludes that "it cannot be asserted, that [they] had the least Design to depose or murder their King, much less to abolish kingly Government" (XII, 257).

Swift's only extant sermon written to commemorate one of the official Anglican anniversary holy days is his sermon *Upon the Martyrdom of K. Charles I*, where (not surprisingly) we find some of his most forceful and eloquent attacks on the disastrous consequences of religious schism for the tranquillity of the state. One might assume that, in the light of its officially designated occasion, Swift's sermon was fundamentally similar in subject matter to other contemporary sermons written for the same purpose (even if, perhaps, a little more strident in tone). Such is far from the case, however, as a brief comparison with the sermon preached on the anniversary of Charles's "martyrdom" in 1723, by Francis, Bishop of Down and Connor, readily demonstrates. Taking as his biblical text a passage from Psalm 133, "Behold how good and pleasant it is for Brethren to dwell together in Unity," the sermon-giver briefly laments the tragic consequences of schisms in the past only to stress the need for overcoming them in the present, with a view to achieving national unity in the future. Not that the author of the sermon is arguing for the erasure of all religious distinctions, since the vision of unity he propounds is no less sectarian on one level than it is ecumenical on another: "There never was a Schism that lasted always; and therefore surely there may be some way or other of putting an End to this by making our island a Protestant Nation."[19] The conception of national unity put forward here is as much dependent on the absolute distinction between Protestant and Catholic as it is on the blurring of the distinction between Anglican and Presbyterian. And indeed, while the sermon calls for a show of tolerance for "all Papists that will shew themselves safe Neighbours and good Subjects" (p. 18), it devotes much of its energies to attacking Irish Catholics, whom it makes a point of distinguishing from foreign papists; for whereas the latter tend to be peaceable and loyal to the rulers of their respective countries, the Irish ones "run after Priests that have been fed out of the Pope's baskets" and "join not only with the Pope, but foreign Princes also if they be Popish" (p. 13).

Passages such as these serve to point up the rather astonishing fact that sermons commemorating the martyrdom of Charles I tended to be attacks not on the Puritans who were the direct cause of Charles's death, but on both English and Irish Catholics of the recent past. Reading over some of these sermons, indeed, one is apt to wonder whether their authors were somehow under the impression that Cromwell had been a papist. Through the techniques of temporal conflation and a kind of montage effect, the beheading of the King was transformed into but one small piece of a larger historical tapestry whose pattern revealed a very different struggle, against a far more treacherous foe; in the words of the

---

[19]  Francis, Lord Bishop of Down and Connor, *A Sermon Preach'd in Christ-Church, Dublin, on the 30th of January, 1723* (Dublin, 1723), p. 18. Hereafter cited in the text.

Bishop of Down, presenting an overview of English history, "Our Protestant and just Prince must be murdered; a Massacre must be made, and a Popish *Pretender* be brought from *Rome* to settle Us in our Protestant Religion and *English* Liberties" (p. 9).

Swift, in undertaking to commemorate Charles's martyrdom by writing a sermon of his own, makes it clear that he viewed his text as a polemical response to what was usually preached on the occasion: "Of late times, indeed, and I speak it with grief of heart, we have heard even sermons of a strange nature … Pray God we may never more hear such doctrine from the pulpit" (IX, 226–27). In opposition to "such doctrine," which he obviously found repugnant, Swift eschews the Catholic-bashing so common in contemporary sermons on the occasion, and instead focuses his criticism on those directly responsible for the overthrow of both king and monarchy. A major thrust of his sermon is to challenge the enthusiastic embrace of Protestant unity underlying the period's other commemorations of this event; hence its assertion, "Neither will the bare name of Protestants set [the Dissenting sects] right. For, surely, Christ requires more from us than a profession of hating Popery, which a Turk or an Atheist may do as well as a Protestant" (IX, 228). In constructing his sermon, Swift uses as his biblical text the same passage from Genesis used by the Bishop of Clonfert for his sermon commemorating the anniversary of the Irish Rebellion. The latter text, we may recall, proclaims an "exact Resemblance" between the events described in the Bible and what happened in the Ulster plantation in 1641, applying the abominable behaviour of Simeon and Levi to the perfidious actions of the rebellious Catholic gentry. That Swift deemed the analogy to be, on the contrary, between Jacob's vindictive sons and the Puritans during the English Civil War serves to underscore a point attested to in various ways throughout his writings: that is to say, that no text, sacred or otherwise, is fixed in meaning, free from temporal mutability or the variability of subjective interpretations.

Swift applies the broken wall alluded to in the scriptural passage both metaphorically, to signify the general chaos and social disintegration caused by the Puritans, and literally, to represent "the destroying or defacing [of] such vast numbers of God's houses" throughout the English countryside (IX, 224). This biblical passage clearly had a special appeal for Swift. It appears again, for example, as the conclusion to his tract, *The Presbyterians Plea of Merit … Impartially Examined*, where, interestingly, its application is extended to include elements of Swift's own church. Expressing concern over a report that certain Dissenters were claiming to have found patrons among the Anglican clergy, Swift laments, "What *secret* Reasons those Patrons may have given for such a Return of brotherly Love, I shall not inquire: *"For, O my Soul come thou not into their* Secret, *unto their* Assembly *mine Honour be not thou united. For in their Anger they slew a Man, and in their Self-will they digged down a Wall"* (XII, 279). The imagery, if not the precise context, of this same biblical passage plays an important role in Swift's *Preface to the Bishop of Sarum's Introduction to the Third Volume of the History of the Reformation*. Responding to Bishop Burnet's ominous warnings about the dangers of *"Popish Iniquity … working among us"* to create *"a great Breach,"* Swift declares:

> He *thanks God, there are many among us who stand in the Breach*: I believe they may; it is a *Breach* of their own making, and they design to come forward, and storm and plunder, if they be not driven back. *They make themselves a Wall for their Church and Country …* Let us examine this Metaphor: The *Wall of our Church and Country* is built of those, who love the Constitution in both. Our domestic Enemies undermine some Parts of the *Wall*, and place themselves in the *Breach*; and then they cry, *We are the Wall*. We do not like such Patch-Work; they build with untempered Mortar; nor can they ever cement with us,

till they get better Materials and better Workmen: God keep us from having our *Breaches*
made up with such Rubbish ... Who assigned them that Post [of standing upon the Watch-
tower], to give us false Intelligence, to alarm us with false Dangers, and send us to defend
one Gate, while their Accomplices are breaking in at another? (IV, 80; 81–82)

It is not difficult to understand the rhetorical appeal of the metaphor central to the Genesis
passage and informing the language of both Burnet's *Introduction* and Swift's rebuttal. A
wall marks the boundary between insider and outsider; it separates the builder from the
leveller, the friend guarding the gate from the enemy eager to tear it down. Depending
upon its location and the angle from which it is viewed, a wall can signify either unity or
division, a protected space or an area under siege. In the context of Irish affairs, it came to
function as a means of defining religious and national identity, as a way of characterizing
the nation's worldly and divine mission. That Swift's adaptation of this metaphor differed so
significantly from his fellow clerics' usage suggests (among other things) a fundamental
disagreement between their respective conceptions of Irish community and nationhood.

Perhaps the most telling aspect of Swift's ongoing polemical struggles to rebut various
pulpit orthodoxies was his repeated undermining of the providentialist ideology informing
them. Where his colleagues proclaimed Ireland's unique status and destiny as a nation favoured by God, Swift countered that Ireland was unique only in its wretchedness and degree
of deprivation. In his *Maxims Controlled in Ireland*, he identifies what he terms "the singular
fate of Ireland," not with miraculous deliverances from above, but with a series of political
and economic disasters here on earth that have metaphorically transformed Ireland into "a
nation where each of the inhabitants ha[s] but one eye, one leg, and one hand" (XII, 136;
131). Instead of identifying the Irish with the Israelites, God's Chosen People, Swift associated them variously throughout his writings with Laplanders, Hottentots, American Indians, and Africans: alien races, suffering oppression and exploitation without the promise
of divine favour, whose only hope lay with "solutions" worthy of a "Modest Proposer": "If
we had the African custom or privilege, of selling our useless bodies for slaves to foreigners,
it would be the most useful branch of our trade" (XII, 135).

While Swift, as we know, forcefully defended the Established Church on a number of
occasions, the grounds of his defence were invariably pragmatic and empirical, hence based
neither on theological doctrine nor on the assertion of a divine destiny unique to Protestantism. Again and again, what Swift emphasized as the strongest argument for the Established Church was not the validity of its spiritual claims but its role of preserving peace and
stability in society:

I leave it among *Divines* to dilate upon the Danger of *Schism*, as a Spiritual Evil; but I
would consider it only as a Temporal one. And I think it clear, that any great Separation
from the established Worship, although to a new one that is more pure and perfect, may
be an Occasion of endangering the publick Peace ... For this Reason, *Plato* lays it down
as a Maxim, that *Men ought to worship the Gods, according to the Laws of the Country*. (II,
11–12)

Along with Swift's eschewal of the ideals of spiritual perfection and purity, his invocation
here of Plato's authority, suggesting that even pre- or non-Christian religions can fulfil the
primary purpose of a national system of worship, anticipates his somewhat relativistic arguments in support of the Sacramental Test decades later, where he presents himself as "one
who is altogether indifferent to any particular System of Christianity" as long as the system
in question is deemed the most appropriate one for the country in which it predominates
(XII, 243); where, after noting that Holland, Geneva, and the Swiss Cantons are all repub-

lics established by the Reformed Church, he explains, "I do not say this in Diminution, or Disgrace to Commonwealths; wherein, I confess, I have much altered many Opinions under which I was educated" (XII, 278); and where he concedes that when a national religion grows corrupt or widely unpopular "it ought to be changed; provided the Work might be done without Blood or Confusion" – though characteristically, he warns of the inevitability that "some other Establishment must succeed, although for the worse" (XII, 244).

A major consequence of Swift's eminently pragmatic and commonsensical stance on matters of religion, with its avoidance of all strictly theological, fundamentalist, and mystical appeals, was the ongoing critique he levelled against what we might call Protestant semiotics, the elaborate sign system according to which worldly conditions and events were understood to be integral parts of a divine code, to be deciphered – and brandished as proof of their own authority – by the spokesmen for God's elect. Works such as *The Bickerstaff Papers*, *A Famous Prediction of Merlin, the British Wizard* (1709), and *An Examination of Certain Abuses, Corruptions, and Enormities in the City of Dublin* (1732) satirize the arrogant presumption and self-delusion informing such an outlook. In the latter piece (see XII, 217–32), the speaker's patently absurd decodings of Dublin signs and street cries mock the paranoid search for political conspiracies which Swift frequently protested against (and on various occasions himself fell victim to) even as they comment sarcastically on a larger hermeneutic that insists upon the inextricable connection between mundane phenomena and deeper, more mysterious – or more miraculous – designs. Consistent with this demystifying outlook was Swift's view of William of Orange. Instead of elevating William to the status of divine saviour and deeming him a direct instrument of God's providence, Swift tended to portray him in a decidedly more down-to-earth light, as a man with certain abilities who happened to be in the right place at the right time: "Our deliverance [from the reign of James II] was owing to the valour and conduct of the late King [William]; and, therefore, we ought to remember him with gratitude, but not mingled with blasphemy or idolatry. It was happy that his interests and ours were the same" (IX, 224).

In a similar vein, Swift rejected the inevitable tendency of the "special providentialists" to see power and riches as proof of divine favour, as outward signs of inner election. His writings are filled with scathing portraits of those, like the Duke of Marlborough, whose affluence and worldly success, to the extent that they signified anything beyond themselves, were tokens of overweening ambition, greed, and deceit. Making this point in no uncertain terms from the pulpit, Swift declared to his congregation, "Power, Wealth, and the like outward Advantages, are so far from being the Marks of God's approving or preferring those on whom they are bestowed, that, on the contrary, he is pleased to suffer them to be almost engrossed by those who have least Title to his Favour" (IX, 144). He urged his parishioners to consider "how few among the Rich have procured their Wealth by just Measures; how many owe their Fortunes to the Sins of their Parents, how many more to their own?" (IX, 194). In these and related ways, Swift's sermons dealing with the economic divisions in society challenge the constellation of views we have come to identify as the Protestant Ethic, with its rationalization of capitalist accumulation and its denigration of poverty as a moral failing.

We have only to compare Swift's sermons *On Mutual Subjection* and *On the Poor Man's Contentment* with, for example, the sermon preached at St Anne's in January 1723/4 by Timothy, Bishop of Kilmore and Ardagh, to appreciate the depth of Swift's challenge, however conventionally couched. Readily acknowledging "a great Inequality in the Distribution of the Things of this World," since "Abundance and Wealth are but in a few Hands; [while by] far the greatest Part of Mankind, have nothing but what they get by their own Labour," the Bishop immediately proceeds to justify this inequality on the grounds that such social and economic division is necessary "so [that] they who have the Wealth, and consequently the Power in their Hands, may be able to restrain the unruly Passions of the Multitude."[20] Seeing the division of the world into rich and poor as God's method of "bestow[ing] Rewards and Punishments in this Life," the Bishop of Kilmore celebrates industrious labour while assailing poverty as "just Punishment for [idle men] being useless Burthens to their [*sic*] Country they live in" (p. 7). He exhorts his listeners to appreciate "the Wisdom of God's Providence in this unequal Distribution of the Things of this World" (p. 7).

For his part, Swift, too, offers consolations to the poor and suggestions of ways in which they can and should accommodate themselves to the existing socio-economic structures, but he does not rationalize the latter as a direct expression of God's will, nor does he claim that those at the bottom of the hierarchy are inherently inferior to those at the top, hence subject by natural law – or providential design – to the latter's authority. On the contrary, Swift wryly observes that "Princes are born with no more Advantages of Strength or Wisdom than other Men; and, by an unhappy Education, are usually more defective in both than thousands of their Subjects," and he sarcastically exposes "the Compliment of Course, when our Betters are pleased to tell us they are our humble Servants, but understand us to be their Slaves" (IX, 142–43; 141). Moreover, he argues that "the Poor are generally more necessary Members of the Commonwealth than the Rich" (IX, 143), reminding his congregation that Jesus himself turned his back on worldly riches and status because he "was pleased to chuse his Lot among Men of the lower Condition," and urging his listeners to follow a course of sober living so "that they may obtain that glorious Reward promised in the Gospel to the Poor, I mean, the Kingdom of Heaven" (IX, 198). Rather than celebrating economic inequality as a direct sign of God's will, in the manner of the Bishop of Kilmore, Swift – tacitly invoking *Acts* 4:32 – posits the ideal of mutual subjection as a means of "bring[ing] us back as it were to that early State of the Gospel when Christians had all things in common" (IX, 147).

Two and one-half centuries later, these same Gospel passages and similar constructions of them would be used to articulate far more revolutionary proposals for addressing the disparities of worldly distribution and for combatting the oppression of the poor. We know, of course, that Swift was not interested in developing *any* kind of systematic theology, liberation or otherwise; and even if he *had* been so inclined, his basically orthodox religious views coupled with his position in the Church of Ireland would almost certainly have militated against the production of any very radical body of belief. Nevertheless, Swift's attacks on that form of Christian semiology which allowed even the most corrupt aspects of the capitalist and colonialist systems to be sanctified as expressions of God's will – we need only recall his scathing exposure, at the conclusion of *Gulliver's Travels*, of the brutal exploits of an "execrable Crew of Butchers," whose wanton murders and depredations become, as it were, mystically transmuted into "a new Dominion acquired with a Title by *Divine Right*" (XI, 294) – suggest that he would have been able to appreciate Gustavo Gutiérrez's point

---

[20] Timothy, Lord Bishop of Kilmore and Ardagh, *A Sermon Preach'd in the Parish Church of St. Anne, Dublin, January, the 19th, 1723–24* (Dublin, 1723–24), p. 6. Hereafter cited in the text.

that "the denunciation of injustice implies the rejection of the use of Christianity to legitimize the established order."[21]

Let me close by making explicit what I see to be the larger implications of my argument. Contrary to views of Swift as a reactionary extremist within the Anglican Church, one whose Tory affiliations and Jacobite leanings made him assume a basically repressive and backward-looking role in it, my discussion points to the progressive as well as conservative aspects of Swift's position as Church-of-Ireland clergyman. His role in this regard – no less than in other areas – needs therefore to be understood dialectically, as fulfilling the functions of both an organic and a traditional intellectual:[22] one whose endeavours anticipated (among other things) major ideological realignments in the later eighteenth century, serving as inspiration for subsequent Irishmen intent upon redefining the relationship between Catholic and Protestant, between England and Ireland.

By the same token, we need to reassess the common view of Swift's religious position as anachronistic and retrograde – as a paranoid reaction to a set of uniquely pre-Restoration phenomena no longer relevant to his own time. As this essay has indicated, the mind-set Swift was attacking by no means disappeared with the end of the Interregnum, remaining on the contrary a potent force within the ideological matrix of eighteenth-century British, and especially Irish, affairs, and extending well beyond the parameters of Dissenting thought. Considering Swift's writings on these politico-theological issues, what I am struck by most of all is not their surface Ludditism but their remarkable prescience: the ways in which they identify potential dangers and raise disturbing questions not only immediately pertinent to their own time, but also of direct relevance to the present.

One such question has to do with the problem of tolerating intolerance, of allowing the exploitation of a pluralistic ideal by those whose design is ultimately to destroy pluralism – indeed, to suppress all beliefs but their own. Inevitably, Swift posed this problem in terms of extended toleration of Presbyterians, who, as he projected, "will be ready enough to insinuate themselves into any Government: But, if they mean to be honest and upright, they will and must endeavour by all Means, which they shall think lawful, to introduce and establish their own Scheme of Religion, as nearest approaching to the Word of GOD ... Wishing with St. *Paul, That the whole Kingdom were as they are.* But, what Assurance will they please to give, that when their Sect shall become the National Established Worship, they will treat Us DISSENTERS as we have treated them[?]" (XII, 276). Regardless of how we judge Swift's assessment of the Dissenters, we can surely appreciate the fact that he is raising a significant problem here, one that deserved to be taken seriously in his own time precisely because it needs to be taken seriously at *any* time, as even a cursory consideration of twentieth-century history makes clear.

---

21  Gustavo Gutiérrez, *A Theology of Liberation: History, Politics, and Salvation*, ed. and trans. Sister Caridad Inda and John Eagleson (Maryknoll, NY, 1973), p. 115. In contrast to the associations I (obviously very loosely) suggest here, Patrick Reilly argues a kinship between Swift's views and those of recent "Latin American conservatives, surveying with frightened disgust the upsurge of 'liberation' theologies" (*Jonathan Swift, the Brave Desponder* [Manchester, 1982], p. 2).

22  Edward W. Said discusses Swift in terms of Gramsci's conception of the intellectual in "Swift as Intellectual," *The World, the Text, and the Critic* (Cambridge, MA, 1983), pp. 82–83.

The other, obviously related problem Swift foregrounds is the predicament of how to deal with fanatics who claim to have a direct pipeline to God, whose beliefs are therefore by definition immune to rational inquiry, pragmatic negotiation, and criticism by mere mortals. These include the religious enthusiasts who, according to Swift's sarcastic characterization, "must *obey God rather than Man*, must *cry aloud and spare not*; must *lift up their Voice like a Trumpet*" (XII, 244). Those guilty of such delusions, like the Puritans, "must needs overturn heaven and earth, violate all the laws of God and man, make their country a field of blood, to propagate whatever wild or wicked opinions came into their heads, declaring all their absurdities and blasphemies to proceed from the Holy Ghost" (IX, 227). Here again, I would argue, Swift is not simply revealing a fixation with the past, but demonstrating a sensitivity to the political dilemmas of his own age while anticipating a problem that would reappear, at times quite menacingly, in future ages.

Which brings us to our own age, and its not dissimilar engagements with the forces of fanaticism and violence that Swift continually inveighed against. When we are confronted – as we were in Dallas, Texas, in 1992 – with the spectacle of a national political convention presenting itself as an evangelical revival meeting, with keynote speakers declaring religious war against their opponents and in effect claiming God's support for their party; when we hear of Paisley putting himself forward as a man "whom God has commissioned, whom God has called, whom God has sent to be a prophet to his generation;"[23] and when we read that a fundamentalist Christian who shot an abortion-clinic doctor in Wichita, Kansas, justified her actions by comparing herself to Jesus at the time of her sentencing, it is surely a highly salutary experience to reread the words Swift puts into the mouth of Jove in his poem, *The Day of Judgement*:

> "Offending Race of Human Kind,
> By Nature, Reason, Learning, blind;
> You who thro' Frailty step'd aside,
> And you who never fell – *thro' Pride*;
> You who in different Sects have shamm'd,
> And come to see each other damn'd;
> (So some Folks told you, but they knew
> No more of Jove's Designs than you)."[24]

---

[23] Cited in Moloney and Pollak, *Paisley*, p. 440.
[24] *Poems*, ed. Williams, II, 579, ll. 11–18.

# III. *Gulliver's Travels*

Michael Treadwell
*Trent University, Peterborough, Ontario*

# Observations on the Printing of Motte's Octavo Editions of *Gulliver's Travels*[1]

ABSTRACT. In the two hundred and seventy years since *Gulliver's Travels* was first published, little or no attention has been paid to its printing. Most scholars who have referred to
the matter have assumed that the work was printed by its first publisher, Benjamin Motte, and
even those few (Hubbard, Teerink and Scouten, Ehrenpreis) who have recognized that the
truth was more complex, and that more than one printing house was involved, have never
attempted to identify the particular printers employed. Examination of the details of the printing of Motte's four octavo editions, particularly the evidence of the use of press figures and of
a wide variety of printers' ornaments, suggests that the first edition of *Gulliver's Travels*
(1726 A) was the work of five different printing houses and enables us to identify them as
those of Say, Woodfall, Bettenham, Pearson, and Ilive. The second edition (1726 AA) employed a sixth printer (Aris) in addition to the original five, but for the third (1726 B) the
number was reduced to three (Bettenham, Woodfall, Bowyer), and for the fourth (1727 8°) to
two (Bowyer, Palmer). The desire to avoid delay, and a concern that no one but the publisher
himself have any overall sense of a potentially explosive work prior to publication, were the
probable motives for the spreading of the first edition among so many printing houses.

On 16 November 1925, Harold Williams read before the Bibliographical Society a paper on
"The Motte Editions of *Gulliver's Travels*," in which he attempted to describe and to differentiate the editions of *Gulliver* which Swift's London publisher had issued between 1726
and 1731. In that paper, subsequently published in *The Library*, Williams noted what he
took to be the irony that "a great work of English literature had to wait for an American
Doctor of Geology adequately to investigate the bibliography of its early editions," and to
acknowledge that "Dr. Lucius L. Hubbard, of the University of Michigan, by a line for line
and word for word comparison of the early editions, [had] brought to light typographical
and bibliographical secrets which had previously passed unnoticed. The reader of this paper,"
Williams continued, somewhat plaintively, "had covered independently much of the ground
traversed by Dr. Hubbard in his admirable *Contributions towards a Bibliography of Gulliver's Travels* (1922) before, by meeting with that book, his task was lightened."[2]

---

[1]   I had originally hoped to deal with all of the early Motte editions, but was forced to omit
    the 1727 duodecimo in order to keep this paper within even distant sight of the thirty-
    minute length proposed. The other omissions catalogued in n. 12, below, stem from the
    same time constraint.
[2]   *The Library*, 4th ser., 6 (1925), 233. Lest the coming analogy seem a subtle form of self-

Unfortunately, the author of this present paper must also begin by confessing that he, too, had independently covered much ground, and was indeed within three months of the date set for his paper's delivery, when he suddenly discovered that another scholar had recently traversed much the same ground and had presented his findings a year earlier to a conference at Otago University in Dunedin in a still unpublished paper on "The Printing of the Motte Editions of *Gulliver's Travels*."[3] As irony would have it, that other scholar was my friend and, alas, too-occasional correspondent Dr John Ross of Massey University, Palmerston North, New Zealand, who, with characteristic generosity, faxed me his draft paper the moment he learned of my interest in the same field. In that paper, Ross had two main aims. One was to explore "the modes of framing the text ... to manipulate contemporary reader-responses through a semiotic of typographical mimicry," and in this area our work did not overlap. Ross's other aim, however, was almost identical with mine, namely to revisit "the printing history [of *Gulliver*], employing ornament-study to identify the printers," and those who know Ross's monograph on *Charles Ackers' Ornament Usage*,[4] or his general expertise in ornament use among London printers of the 1720s and 1730s, will not be surprised to hear that he had succeeded very well. They will be more surprised to hear that, although I agree with the vast majority of Dr Ross's identifications, I am nevertheless going to propose a rival candidate for the printing of one important section of the first and second editions of *Gulliver*.

Because I had initially approached the problem of printer identification from a slightly different angle than Dr Ross, and because I had worked for a considerable time in a vast field in ignorance of his findings, I had inevitably accumulated evidence which was different from his even where it led to the same conclusions. For that reason, and also because my second aim was to explore the reasons for the very unusual pattern of printing evident in the earliest editions of *Gulliver's Travels* – something outside Ross's brief – I do not hesitate to offer here, with Dr Ross's blessing, a paper several of whose conclusions he has anticipated elsewhere.

Although it must appear at first glance a curious coincidence that two scholars have turned their attention to the question of who printed *Gulliver's Travels* at virtually the same time, it is surely far more curious that no one else has done so in the preceding two hundred and seventy years. There are, I believe, two different reasons for this lack of curiosity, and these were that the ignorant thought they already knew, and that the learned recognized that the problem was a far more complicated one than it seemed – or than they had time for at that moment. For the former group, the printer was obviously Benjamin Motte, "master printer of London," as Case styled him in 1945, presumably because authority in the form of the *Dictionary of National Biography* or Plomer's *Dictionary of ... Printers and Booksellers ... 1668–1725* described Motte in those terms. Thus Williams writes in 1952 of the manuscript

---

flattery, I hasten to add that I regard Hubbard's work as not merely prior to Williams's, but superior to it on almost every count, in spite of Williams's advantage of hindsight.

[3] I owe the discovery, as I owe so much more in the way of scholarly assistance, to Professor Don McKenzie. Dr Ross's paper was originally delivered in February 1993. I received the faxed copy from Ross on 4 March 1994 and delivered the present paper in Münster on 1 June 1994. The quotations which follow are from Ross's faxed draft, not from the revised version of his paper eventually published as "The Framing and Printing of the Motte Editions of *Gulliver's Travels*," *Bibliographical Society of Australia and New Zealand Bulletin*, 20, no 1 (1996), 5–19.

[4] *Charles Ackers' Ornament Usage*, Oxford Bibliographical Society Occasional Publication, no 21 (1990).

"from which ... Motte printed the first edition in London," Jenkins in 1968 of "the first edition, printed in London by Benjamin Motte," and an anonymous reviewer in *The Scriblerian* even as late as 1981 of "Swift's claim that the printer, Benjamin Motte, 'mangled' the text of the first edition."[5] Unfortunately, as I pointed out at The First Münster Symposium in 1984, both the *DNB* and Plomer conflate the careers of the distinguished master printer Benjamin Motte, Sr, who died in 1710, and of his son and namesake who, though raised and trained in the family printing house in Aldersgate Street, had given it up in 1723 or 1724 to devote himself to bookselling and publishing in partnership with the Tooke family in their long-established shop at the Middle Temple Gate in Fleet Street. "Because Benjamin Motte began as a printer," I wrote in 1984, "it is often assumed that he printed as well as published *Gulliver's Travels*, but this is almost certainly not the case."[6]

So much for the ignorant. The learned have been more cautious, beginning with Lucius Hubbard himself, on whose meticulous work all subsequent bibliographical investigation of *Gulliver's Travels* has been based, and who, while endlessly calling attention to changes in ornaments or type faces or paper stock or the dimensions of the printed page of the Motte editions, only rarely hazards an inference such as "that the first and third units [of Volume I of 1726 AA] were not only set, but actually printed in a different establishment, or in different establishments, from the second."[7] In this exemplary caution about naming names, Hubbard was followed by Teerink and Scouten, who wrote of the first edition that "judging from the ornaments, type, and page numbers, the four Parts were printed in four different printing-houses."[8] They in turn were followed by Ehrenpreis, who, in pronouncing that "Motte gave each of the four parts [of the first edition] to a different printer," was the first to clearly and correctly imply that Motte was not himself one of those printers.[9] Significantly then, none of those who knew enough to recognize the complexity of the printing history of the Motte editions of *Gulliver's Travels* felt tempted to venture a guess as to who Motte's various printers might have been.

Not, at least, where the first edition was concerned. However, on 14 October 1951, Herbert Davis used the occasion of a joint meeting of the Bibliographical Society and the Oxford Bibliographical Society to cite the testimony of the Bowyer Paper Stock Ledger as proof that Bowyer had been the printer of Part IV of Motte's 1726 B edition and of "Part I ... and all the preliminaries, including the two extra leaves inserted in some copies before sheet A" of the 1727 octavo edition.[10] Davis was thus the first to claim any part of the early editions of *Gulliver's Travels* for a particular printer, but unfortunately the claim was in-

---

[5]　Arthur E. Case, *Four Essays on "Gulliver's Travels"* (Princeton, NJ, 1945), p. 1; Harold Williams, *The Text of "Gulliver's Travels"* (Cambridge, 1952), p. 2; Clauston Jenkins, "The Ford Changes and the Text of *Gulliver's Travels*," *PBSA*, 62 (1968), 1; anonymous review of F. P. Lock, "The Text of *Gulliver's Travels*," *Scriblerian*, 15 (1982), 19. After hearing the present paper, Professor Alan Downie confessed that he was the anonymous reviewer involved.

[6]　"Benjamin Motte, Andrew Tooke and *Gulliver's Travels*," *Proceedings of The First Münster Symposium on Jonathan Swift*, eds Hermann J. Real and Heinz J. Vienken (München, 1985), p. 293n26.

[7]　*Contributions towards a Bibliography of Gulliver's Travels* (Chicago, 1922), pp. 29–30.

[8]　Herman Teerink, *A Bibliography of the Writings of Jonathan Swift*, 2nd ed., rev. Arthur H. Scouten (Philadelphia, 1963), p. 196.

[9]　See *Dean Swift*, p. 497.

[10]　"Bowyer's Paper Stock Ledger," *The Library*, 5th ser., 6 (1951), 82–83.

1727(8°) Part III, I3ʳ                                    1727(8°) Part IV, E6ʳ

Figure 1

correct, or rather incomplete, and at The Second Münster Symposium in 1989, in the course of a general discussion of the 1727 octavo, I took the opportunity to correct it, noting that "Davis's own figures on paper used, to say nothing of the ornaments and type, reveal that Bowyer in fact printed the entire first volume," adding for the record that the second volume of the 1727 octavo edition "was also the product of a single printing house, namely that of Samuel Palmer whose monogram SP printer's device appears in Part III and whose punning palm tree ornament occurs in Part IV" (see Figure 1).[11]

This, to the best of my knowledge, was the extent of what had been revealed publicly about the printers of *Gulliver's Travels* when John Ross and I independently turned our minds to the problem. Ross's methods and conclusions will appear in his, I hope, soon-to-be-published paper, and I will say no more about them here. My own method of proceeding was to begin by looking at the basic bibliographical structure of the four Motte octavos, which I will refer to for reasons of tradition and convenience as 1726 A, 1726 AA, 1726 B, and 1727(8°). In Table 1, I provide in tabular form the standard Teerink-Scouten collation for each edition together with two classes of additions. The first of these consists of the observations of Hubbard (H.) or Williams (W.) concerning similarities or differences in type face, printing from standing type, or other features which might suggest either the work of a single printer or, conversely, a sudden change of printer. The second addition is of the press figures, which are found consistently in all or part of nine of the sixteen parts of the four octavo editions.[12] The reader will recall that a press figure is, in Gaskell's phrase, "an arabic figure or other symbol [set] at the bottom of a page of the forme" just before it was to be worked off in some London printing houses of this period, probably "to enable the master to identify the pressmen's work so that he could penalize individuals in cases of bad

---

11  "The Text of *Gulliver's Travels*, Again," a paper delivered at The Second Münster Symposium on Jonathan Swift in May 1989, and subsequently published in *Swift Studies*, 10 (1995), 62–79; quotation on p. 69. Dr Ross did not know of this paper or of my conclusions about the 1727 octavo, but by 1991 had available the implicit correction to Davis in Keith Maslen and John Lancaster, eds, *The Bowyer Ledgers* (London and New York, 1991), **1261** and **1302**. Moreover, because these two ornaments later passed from Palmer to Ackers, Ross will have recognized them, and Palmer's share in the 1727 octavo, at a glance.

12  The Teerink-Scouten numbers for these four editions are: 1726 A-289, 1726 AA-290, 1726 B-291, and 1727(8°)-293. The collations in Table 1 assume that all gatherings are of eight leaves except where otherwise specified and omit all cancels, all the engraved portraits, maps, and plans, and also the verses inserted into Volume I of 1727(8°). Press figures for full gatherings are given in the order: outer forme/inner forme.

Table 1: Teerink-Scouten collations for the Motte octavos with press figures from McMaster University copies B 10, 747-8(A); B 8,678-9(AA); B 8,671-2(B); B 15,957-8(1727). Observations on type by Hubbard (H.) and Williams (W.) follow at the top of p. 162.

| 1726 A | 1726 AA | 1726 B | 1727 (8°) |
|---|---|---|---|
| A | A | A: 2/2 | A: 1/1 |
| B | B | B: 3/3 | B: /6 |
| C | C | C: 4/4 | C: 8/1 |
| D | D | D: 1/1 | D: 8/3 |
| E | E | E: 4/4 | E: 3/3 |
| F | F | F: 4/1.. | F: 1/1 |
| G | G | G: 1/1 | G: 3/3 |
| H | H | H: -3/4 | H: 3/3 |
| I | I | I: 1/4 | I: 8/8 |
| K | K | K: 1/1 | K: 8/8 |
| $L^2$ | | | |
| $[\pi]^3:4$ | $[\pi]^3$ | $L^3$: 2 | $[L]$:1/1 |
| B: 1/2 | B: 4/4 | M: 4/4 | M: 6/6 |
| C: 2/3 | C: 2/2 | N: 3/3 | N: 6/3 |
| D: 3/3 | D: 3/3 | O: 4/2 | O: 3/6 |
| E: 1/2 | E: 4/2 | P: 2/4 | P: 3/ |
| F: 2/1 | F: 3/4 | Q: 2/4 | Q: 6/6 |
| G: 4/ | G | R: 3/2 | R: 8/8 |
| H: 3/2 | H | S: 1/1 | S: 8/6 |
| I: 3/3 | I | T: 4/ | T: 8/8 |
| K: 4/3 | K | U: 3/4 | U: 8/8 |
| L: 2/2 | L | X: 1/2 | $X^4$: 1 |
| $M^2$ | $M^2$ : 4 | $Y^1$ | $Y^1$ |
| $A^3$ | $A^3$ | $A^3$ | $A^4$ |
| B | B | B | B |
| C | C | C | C: /1 |
| D | D | D | D |
| E | E | E | E: 3/ |
| F | F | F | F |
| G | G | G | G: /4 |
| H | H | H | H: 1/ |
| I | I | I | I: /5 |
| K | K | K | K: /3 |
| $L^4$ | $L^5$ | $L^5$ | $L^4$: 3 |
| $M^2$ | | | $M^2$ |
| $A^4$ | $A^4$ | M: 8/1 | $A^4$ |
| B | B | N: 6/6 | B |
| C | C | O: 3/1 | C |
| D | D | P: 3/6 | D: /1 |
| E | E | Q: 8/1 | E: 1/ |
| F | F | R: 3/6 | F: 5/3 |
| G | G | S: 3/8 | G |
| H | H | T: 6/1 | H: /5 |
| I | I | U: 3/8 | I: 5/ |
| K | K | X: 1/6 | K: /5 |
| L | L | Y: 6/3 | L |
| M | M | Z: 1/8 | M: 5/ |
| N | N | Aa: 3,3/6 | N |
| $O^4$ | $O^4$ | | $O^4$ |

1726 A: "The text of Vol. I is printed uniformly from the same font; that of Vol. II is also uniform throughout, but ... larger" (H. p. 27).

1726 AA: "Vol. I ... is separable into four units ... [I: A–D; I: E–K & II: π–F; II: G–L; II M]" (H. p. 29). In Vol. II, Part III, "in the body of the text ... the same font ... as in the first edition seems to have been used throughout" (H. p. 32). "In Part III ... F1 a–F6 a, there seem to be no differences between the two editions" (W. p. 248). "I and K ... are identical with those of the first edition" (H. p. 32). In Part IV, "signature I ... occurs in two entirely different settings" and "in signature N [recte N and O] ... the same settings were used both in the first and second edition" (H. p. 34).

1726 B: "The first three Parts are printed in uniform type, the fourth in larger type" (H. p. 21).

1727 (8°): "The two volumes are printed from type of different fonts" (H. p. 37).

workmanship,"[13] but possibly also to enable him to keep track of pressmen's productivity. The most recent figures known to me suggest that at the time of *Gulliver*'s publication just under half of all volumes printed in the British Isles contained press figures, though a more useful figure for our purposes – and one which does not, to the best of my knowledge, exist – would be the proportion of printing houses employing press figures. This was presumably smaller than the percentage of figured works since logic suggests that larger printing houses were more likely than smaller ones to require press figures in order to keep track of their pressmen or production.[14]

The first thing to notice about Table 1 is the reassuring way in which both Hubbard's observations and the press figures confirm what we already know from our one piece of external evidence, namely that a single printer, William Bowyer, printed all of Part IV of 1726 B and all of Volume I of 1727 (8°), and no other part of these four editions. In the first place, Hubbard observed that the fourth part of 1726 B was set in a larger type than the first three parts, and that the two volumes of 1727 (8°) were printed from different founts of type. In the second, we can see at a glance that, with the exception of two sheets figured in one forme only and one where a forgetful pressman has figured one forme twice, all the full sheets printed in Bowyer's shop are figured systematically in both formes, and always with the figures 1, 3, 6, or 8, a combination of figures which occurs in no other Motte edition. Moreover, although the evidence for it was internal rather than external, our other previous attribution of Volume II of 1727 (8°) to a single printer, Samuel Palmer, seems also to be supported both by Hubbard's observation on the type and by the pattern of the press figures which, although they occur only randomly, occur with a particular pattern of randomness which is unique to this particular volume.

The rest of what is revealed in Table 1 is considerably less reassuring since it suggests repeated contradictions between the evidence of the typography as described by Hubbard and that of the press figures. Specifically, in Volume I of 1726 A which Hubbard describes as "printed uniformly from the same font" (p. 27), the evidence of the press figures clearly suggests different printers for Parts I and II. In 1726 B, which Hubbard describes as having

---

[13] Philip Gaskell, *A New Introduction to Bibliography* (Oxford, 1974 [1972]), p. 133.

[14] These most recent figures are those of Daria Fedewytsch-Dickson, "A New Century of Press Figures," *Bibliographical Society of Australia and New Zealand Bulletin*, 17, no 2 (1993), 85–86, who, however, gives no indication where in the British Isles her sample volumes were printed, nor what proportion of each volume contains press figures.

"the first three Parts ... printed in uniform type, the fourth in larger type" (p. 21), the evidence of the press figures implies a different printer for Part III than for the first two parts. And, most complicated of all, in Volume I of 1726 AA where Hubbard had detected "four units, to-wit: pages 1–52, Part I [A–D]; page 53, Part I to p. 80, Part II, inclusive [E–K, [π]³ 2B–2F]; pages 81–160 [2G–2L], and 161–164 [M²], Part II" (p. 29), the evidence of the press figures, while providing further evidence for the divisions between the second and third, and third and fourth units (though not for that between the first and second), strongly suggests that Hubbard's second unit is in fact made up of sheets from two different printing houses.

The problem with the evidence from press figures is, of course, that while the *use* of press figures, and in particular of a certain pattern of press figures, may provide a clue to a particular printer's involvement in a work,[15] the *absence* of press figures in a city where the majority of printing houses were still not employing them proves nothing at all. And what is true of press figures is also true of evidence based on particular founts of type such as Hubbard employed. That is to say, while a sudden, otherwise inexplicable change in fount from one sheet to the next should always raise suspicions of a possible change of printer, the continued use of a single fount in a city where seventy-five printing houses were being supplied by only three or four type foundries proves nothing in itself.[16] Accordingly, where the evidence from press figures or from type is absent, inconclusive, or downright contradictory, we have inevitably to fall back on what is still the most distinctive feature of any eighteenth-century printer's output, namely his ornament use. Moreover, it is worth remembering that, unlike Hubbard's or Williams's, our aim is not merely to differentiate the work of the various printers employed in the Motte editions, but also to identify the printers themselves. And no London printer of this period that I know of has ever been identified on the basis of his types or of his use of press figures alone.

The possible pitfalls in the use of ornament evidence for printer identification are well known. They are, first, that although the vast majority of ornaments were carved in wood and thus unique (though not always appearing so at first glance; see Figure 2),[17] they might

---

15   I am here acutely aware of the cautions of D. F. McKenzie in "Printers of the Mind: Some Notes on Bibliographical Theories and Printing-House Practices," *Studies in Bibliography*, 22 (1969), 49–53.

16   The numbers of London typefounders is set out in Michael Treadwell, "Some Notes on London Typefounding, 1620–1720," an unpublished paper delivered at the international conference on typefounding in Oxford in July 1982. A particular *combination* of founts, particularly when enough different founts are involved, may, of course, be unique, but identifying an individual printer by such means is almost impossibly difficult.

17   Figure 2 provides illustrations of five different ornaments of similar design all in use in London around the time of the printing of *Gulliver's Travels*, one of which occurs in Part IV of the 1726 A first edition of *Gulliver* itself. That numbered 91 is labelled according to the information given in Ross's *Charles Ackers' Ornament Usage*, p. 46. However, Ross now informs me that ornament 91 was used by Palmer, and his then partner John Huggonson, in 1731–32 only, and that it was the ornament which I have illustrated from Joseph Mitchell's *Lugubres Cantus* (1719) which was used by Palmer from 1718 to 1732 (personal communication of 4 July 1994).
   The existence of reversed copies suggests that an existing ornament was used to transfer the design onto the woodblock from which a new ornament was to be cut. (Using this reversed second ornament to transfer the design to a third would, of course, mean that the third faced the same way as the first.) This method of transfer would explain both the great similarities and the many small differences in such ornaments, differences which can be-

Joseph Mitchell, *Lugubres Cantus*, for McEuen in Edinburgh and Cox, 1719

Ross, *Charles Ackers' Ornament Usage*, no 91 in use by Samuel Palmer, 1718–1732; ill. 1734; but see p. 163 n17.

Edmund Ludlow, *Memoirs Third and Last Part*, 2nd ed., for Mears, Clay, Hooke, and Woodward, 1720

*The Gentleman's Recreation*, 6th ed., for N. C. and sold by Wilcox, Sackfield, Batley, and Chetwood, 1721

1726 A, Part IV, C 8$^v$, McM. U. B 10,748

Figure 2

have been loaned by one printer to another; and second, that there seem to have existed a small number of ornaments which were mass-produced by casting and which may therefore have belonged to more than one printer. Both these possibilities make it dangerous to attribute any work to a particular printer on the evidence of a single ornament. Neither, however, seriously threatens attributions based upon the appearance in a work of a wide range of ornaments known to have been used by a particular printer in a number of his acknowledged works over the period in question. And this, as we shall see, is the case with the Motte editions of *Gulliver* which contain a wide variety of ornaments of every kind.

Let us begin once again on solid ground. Because of the survival of the Bowyer ledgers, we have long had good evidence for the works, and even parts of works, printed by the Bowyer house over many years. From that evidence, Keith Maslen was able to compile his monograph on *The Bowyer Ornament Stock*, in which he lists the 238 ornaments or series of ornaments known to have been used by the Bowyers between 1705 and 1778. Part IV of 1726B, printed by Bowyer, contains seven headpieces used a total of thirteen times, nine tailpieces used ten times, and a single factotum used once; and Volume I of 1727(8°), also printed by Bowyer, contains eleven headpieces used twenty times, fourteen tailpieces used once each, seven initials used eleven times, and four factotums used six times. The total, allowing for re-use between the two editions, is twelve different headpieces, eighteen tailpieces, seven initials, and four factotums, every single one of which is known independently to be part of the Bowyer ornament stock.[18] Even without the direct evidence of the ledgers, therefore, we should have no hesitation in attributing the printing of these sections to William Bowyer.

Volume II of 1727(8°) which we have attributed to Samuel Palmer is a less simple case only because we have, to date, no published list of Palmer's complete ornament stock. We do, however, have John Ross's monograph on the ornament usage of Charles Ackers, who began to print late in 1727 and at least 62 of whose ornaments came down to him from Palmer, whose apprentice he had been. Since Ross takes care to specify which of Ackers's ornaments had been in use by Palmer and at which dates, the reproductions he provides allow us to confirm that Volume II of 1727(8°) contains at least one Palmer headpiece and six Palmer tailpieces, two of the latter being the SP monogram device and the palm tree ornament referred to above.[19]

---

come almost imperceptible when the quality of the paper or inking or presswork in a particular edition or individual impression is poor.

David Pearson, in a fascinating paper on "English Centrepiece Bookbindings, 1560–1640," *The Library*, 6th ser., 16 (1994), 1–17, calls attention to a similar phenomenon among bookbinders' metal tools by illustrating (p. 11) no fewer than eight *almost* identical centrepiece tools in use between c. 1560 and c. 1615.

[18] K. I. D. Maslen, *The Bowyer Ornament Stock*, Oxford Bibliographical Society Occasional Publication, no 8 (1973). The ornaments occurring in Part IV of 1726B are headpieces 43, 53, 72, 76, 77, 79, 82; tailpieces 149, 154, 158, 162, 167, 168, 169, 177, 178; and factotum 208. Those in Volume I of 1727(8°) are headpieces 33, 45, 53, 62, 64, 71, 72, 76, 77, 79, 81; tailpieces 146, 151, 158, 162, 164, 168, 172, 174, 175, 176, 177, 178, 179, 185; initials 187 A(2), B, H, M, T(1), W and 189 T(2); and factotums 208, 209, 211, 212.

[19] See Ross, *Charles Ackers' Ornament Usage*, pp. 8, 56. The headpiece is Ackers 22 and the tailpieces are Ackers 85, 87, 90 (the SP monogram), 99, 102 (the palm tree ornament), and 111. The other ornaments in Volume II are also Palmer's; they simply seem not to have passed to Ackers.

Unfortunately, there are only five printers of this period whose ornament stocks have been catalogued and published, the other three besides Ackers and Bowyer being Samuel Richardson, Henry Woodfall, and John Wright.[20] John Wright as the one-time foreman and eventual successor to Swift's former printer John Barber seems a likely candidate for some part in the Motte editions, but his ornaments are nowhere to be found,[21] and neither are those of Richardson. Henry Woodfall, however, turns out on the evidence of his ornaments to have played almost as large a part in the overall printing as Bowyer and, perhaps more important, to be the first printer we can identify as having contributed to the printing of the 1726 A first edition. In that edition, every single ornament in sheets B to L of Part I is Woodfall's, and all but one of those sheets contain at least one and generally two or more of his ornaments, the exception being sheet H which contains no ornaments, but which, given the recurrence of a damaged upper case I in the running titles of sheets G, H, and I, may safely be assigned to Woodfall as well.[22] Sheet A, on the other hand, contains five ornaments, none of which are Woodfall's, and which must therefore belong to another printer.

In the 1726 AA second edition, every single ornament in sheets E to K of Part I is again Woodfall's, and each of those sheets also carries at least two of Woodfall's ornaments except sheet I which has no ornaments.[23] Sheets A to D, however, contain among them nine different ornaments, none of which are Woodfall's, and which must once more be the work of another printer. Woodfall's ornaments also appear nowhere in sheets [π] and B to F of Part II, a fact which supports what we had already guessed from the evidence of the press figures: namely that although Hubbard was right in suspecting a change in printer between sheets D and E of Part I, his supposed second "unit" was not the product of one printer, but of two.

Finally, in the 1726 B third edition every single ornament in Part III is Woodfall's, with every sheet in that part containing at least two with the exception of sheets C and K which have no ornaments.[24]

We have now identified the printers of just under half of the sheets of the four Motte octavo editions, but we have also exhausted all the external evidence, like the Bowyer ledgers, and all the modern scholarly aids in the form of ornament collections. What remains is the ornaments themselves, but now instead of merely looking them up in reference sources, we must first study the patterns of their recurrence in the editions with which we are concerned, so as to determine which sheets of which editions were the work of particular

---

[20] William M. Sale, Jr, *Samuel Richardson: Master Printer* (Ithaca, NY, 1950), pp. 251–316, but Keith Maslen is engaged on a revision; Richard J. Goulden, *The Ornament Stock of Henry Woodfall, 1719–1747*, The Bibliographical Society Occasional Papers, no 3 (1988); J. McLaverty, *Pope's Printer, John Wright: A Preliminary Study*, Oxford Bibliographical Society Occasional Publication, no 11 (1977).

[21] Wright's precise whereabouts between the time Barber seems to have left off printing, around 1724, and his moving into his own premises in St Peter's Hill, in 1728, remain a mystery. See McLaverty, *Pope's Printer*, p. 2.

[22] The ornaments by sheet and as numbered by Goulden are B-35, 380M(2); C-109, 236, 335; D-43, 339; E-242; F-44, 101, 231, 332, 334; G-44, 331; I-43, 334; K-44, 217, 334; L-238.

[23] The ornaments by sheet and as numbered by Goulden are E-44, 231, 334; F-109, 236, 331; G-36, 339; H-109, 331; K-109, 217, 228, 331.

[24] The ornaments by sheet and as numbered by Goulden are A-21, 340; B-35, 43, 217, 339, 347; C-109, 141, 228, 335, 375 A(2); D-109, 141, 228, 335, 375 A(2); E-127, 331; F-109, 220, 334; G-44, 340; H-19, 225, 340, 354; I-43, 127, 227, 230, 339, 375 T(2); L-225, 334.

printing houses. Only then can we begin the search for these recurring groups of ornaments in other printing of the period in an attempt to identify the printers to whom they belonged.

In identifying the first and largest group of such recurring ornaments, we have one remaining clue in the form of the press figures 1, 2, 3, and 4 which occur in Part II of 1726 A, Part II of 1726 AA (excepting sheets G to L), and Parts I and II of 1726 B. These press figures once again represent a significant pattern since the sheets on which they appear also turn out to be united by a variety of patterns of recurring ornaments. Of the various types of ornament involved, I have chosen the factotums to illustrate the interrelatedness of the sections involved, first, because they are used more frequently than any other type of ornament; second, because they are so widely distributed throughout these sections; third, because a number of them exhibit damage which renders them unmistakable; and fourth, because factotums were cheap and therefore unlikely to require borrowing.

By my count, there are fifteen different factotums used a total of thirty times in the four sections involved, which I will abbreviate here to AII, AAII, BI, and BII. Of the fifteen, five appear only once (one in AII, three in BI, one in BII), two more twice, but only within their own section (one on sheets D and I in AII, one on sheets N and T in BII), and one twice, but in two sections of the same edition (on sheet F in BI and U in BII). For the remaining seven, however, the cross-usage is very clear with one appearing six times (on sheets F, H, and K in AII, F in AAII, and Q and S in BII), one three times (on sheet B in AII, and A and G in BI), and five twice each (on sheet F in AII and Q in BII; on sheet B in AAII and E in BI; on sheet C in AAII and O in BII; on sheet D in AAII and K in BI; and on sheet F in AAII and C in BI). Put another way, each of sheets B, F, H, K of AII, B, C, D, F of AAII, and A, C, E, G, K, O, Q, S of BI and BII contains at least one factotum which occurs again in at least one other of these sheets *but from another edition*. And this is merely the evidence of the factotums; other types of ornaments provide further evidence which identify these press-figured sections in the first volumes of 1726 A, 1726 AA, and 1726 B as the work of one printer.[25]

Having identified these particular sections as the work of a single printer, one searches for that printer by first identifying in the Eighteenth-Century Short Title Catalogue all the items printed in London in 1726 whose printers are identified,[26] and then by examining as many of the items of each individual printer as can be found, printer by printer. Happily, Bettenham comes early in the alphabet, and the Bodleian Library holds four of the five works to which Bettenham put his name in 1726.[27] All four offer an almost identical pattern of

---

[25]  For example, the same tailpiece appears on K5ʳ in Part II of 1726 A and Q1ᵛ in Part II of 1726 B, and the same headpiece on B1ʳ in Part II of 1726 AA and A7ʳ in Part I of 1726 B.

[26]  I am extremely grateful to Philip M. Oldfield of the Thomas Fisher Rare Book Library, University of Toronto, for his expert help in searching ESTC on my behalf. Printers are identified when works are described as "printed by" them either in the imprint or colophon, or when they include ornaments which carry the printer's name. However, given the frequency of shared printing, each such work must be examined with great care to ensure that it does not contain sheets printed by another printer or printers than the one named in the imprint. See, for example, the Latin Bible and Chandler's *Vindication* mentioned in nn. 27 and 41, below.

[27]  The four, all dated 1726, are Francis Atterbury, *Sermons and Discourses on Several Subjects*, 2 vols; William Lowth, *Directions for the Profitable Reading of the Holy Scriptures*, 3rd ed.; Samuel Parker, *De rebus sui temporis commentariorum libri quatuor*; and an edition in 4 volumes of the Latin Bible, *Biblia Sacra ex Sebastiani Castellionis interpretatione*, of which, however, Bettenham seems to have printed volume 1 and part of volume 4 only.

press figures with that we see in the sections of *Gulliver* we are concerned with, and among them they contain a wide range of ornaments found in those same sections, one containing a trio of similarly damaged factotums which occur repeatedly in what I have been calling sections AII, AAII, and BII,[28] and another having on its title-page the ornament which serves as tailpiece at the end of BI.[29]

Not all the rest was so easy, but as the reader will see from Table 2, a revised version of Table 1 showing the work of those printers already identified, the rest is also far smaller than when we began. In seeking to attribute these remaining sections to particular printers, our first step is again to discover, on the basis of recurrent ornament use (though now without the help of press figures), which sections constitute units that are the product of a single printing house. The first of these units, as it turns out, is that comprising sheet A of Part I of 1726 A and sheets A to D of Part I of 1726 AA. Four of the five ornaments which appear in sheet A of 1726 A reappear in the corresponding sheet of 1726 AA, while another ornament which first appears in sheet A of 1726 AA also occurs in sheet C of that same edition, thus adding support to Hubbard's judgement, made on the basis of typographical evidence, that these first four sheets of 1726 AA are the work of a single printer.

The second and largest unit to derive from a single printing house is that made up of Part IV of both 1726 A and 1726 AA. Something of this we might also have suspected from Hubbard's observations of printing from standing type in sheets N and O of 1726 AA,[30] and it is richly confirmed from the evidence of ornament use. Of the eighteen different ornaments used in Part IV of 1726 A, fifteen recur in Part IV of 1726 AA. And if we omit the half-sheets A and O and sheets G and N, which contain no ornaments in either edition, all but one of the sheets in both the A and the AA editions contain at least one ornament which occurs somewhere in the other edition.[31]

There is, however, a wrinkle in the neat pattern linking the two Part IVs, and this is that a particular headpiece, which occurs once in Part IV of 1726 A and twice in Part IV of 1726 AA, also appears in sheet L of Part III of 1726 A although neither it nor any of the other ornaments in Part IV appear anywhere else in Part III.[32] And when we look closely at the printing of sheet L and the surrounding sheets of Part III, we notice two things. First, that immediately below the headpiece in question, both the roman and italic type used for the chapter heading of Chapter XI are distinctly smaller than that used for the preceding chapter headings of Part III.[33] Second, that from the beginning of sheet L and continuing to

[28]  Lowth, *Directions* has on B3$^r$ and D9$^r$ the factotum which appears on D6$^r$ and I5$^v$ of AII; on B5$^v$ and E10$^v$ the factotum which appears on F7$^v$ of AII and Q7$^v$ of BII; and on E2$^v$ the factotum which appears on F2$^r$, H3$^r$, and K5$^v$ of AII, F7$^v$ of AAII, and Q2$^r$ and S3$^r$ of BII.

[29]  Parker, *De rebus sui temporis* has on its title-page and again on O7$^r$ the tailpiece which appears on K8$^v$ of BI.

[30]  Hubbard writes of "marred letters on pages 183 to 197, show[ing] that signature N is the same in both [of the first two] editions" (p. 36); however, since signature N ends with p. 192, he presumably means signatures N *and* O.

[31]  The exception is sheet L of Part IV of 1726 A, but that sheet contains an ornament also present in sheet H of 1726 A, a sheet which contains a second ornament which does occur in the other edition.

[32]  The headpiece concerned appears at C1$^v$ of Part IV of both 1726 A and 1726 AA, at H1$^v$ of Part IV of 1726 AA, and at L2$^r$ of Part III of 1726 A.

[33]  The exception is Chapter I of Part III whose chapter heading is also set in smaller type than that used in the headings of Chapters II–X.

Table 2: Teerink-Scouten collations for the Motte octavos with press figures from McMaster University copies B 10,747-8(A); B 8,678-9(AA); B 8,671-2(B); B 15,957-8(1727).

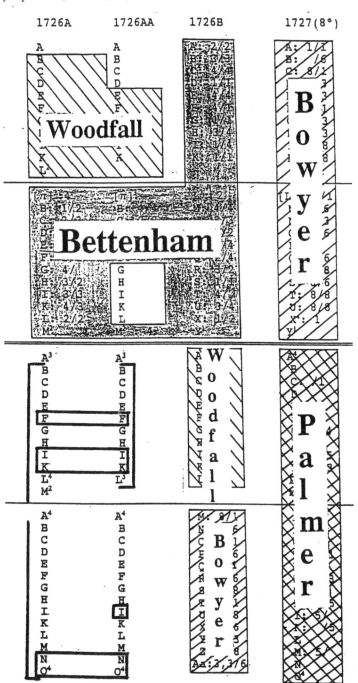

the end of sheet M, that is to the end of Part III, there has been a change in the type used for the running titles particularly noticeable in the U in LAPUTA and in the ampersand following. Sheets L⁴ and M² of Part III of 1726 A are thus almost certainly the work of a different printer from that responsible for the rest of Part III, and are presumably the work of the same printer who printed Part IV in both the 1726 A and AA editions.

The third major unit to originate in a single printing house is that comprising sheets B to K of Part III of 1726 A, and F to K of Part III of 1726 AA. That sheets B to K of Part III of 1726 A constitute a single unit can be seen in the recurrence of a tailpiece in sheets B, F, and I, one factotum in B, E, and H, and another in D, G, and I. As for sheets F to K of 1726 AA, Table 1 already notes Hubbard's and Williams's observations that part of sheet F and all of sheets I and K were printed from the standing type of 1726 A, while G and H also contain ornaments from the first edition. Unlike I, sheet K contains no ornaments which link it to the earlier sheets, but an examination of its other typographical features shows clearly that the change occurs between K and L, and that K is the work of the printer of I and the preceding sheets in Part III, rather than of the printer of L and M.

The fourth and final unit of printing in the Motte octavos to originate in a single printing house, bizarre though it may appear, is that made up of sheets G to L of Part II and B to E and L of Part III, all in the 1726 AA edition. Again, the ornament evidence is overwhelming with one headpiece appearing in sheet H of Part II and sheets B and E of Part III, a second headpiece in sheet K of Part II and sheets D and L of Part III, a factotum in sheet K of Part II and sheets B, D, and L of Part III, and a tailpiece in sheets D and L of Part III. Sheet L, as the most isolated, is certainly the most suspect of this group, but examination shows that each of the three ornaments it contains appears at least once, and in one case three times, in the other sheets of this unit.[34]

Table 3, a further revised version of Tables 1 and 2, shows the four numbered units I have distinguished, and there being no overlap in ornament use among these four units, it seems safe to assume, for the moment at least, that they represent the work of four different printing houses.[35] Of these, the easiest to identify is the fourth, since the presence, at the beginning of Part III of the 1726 AA edition, of a headpiece containing a book open to pages headed by the letters S and A (see Figure 3) is a strong hint of the involvement of Samuel Aris, and other books bearing his imprint in 1725 or 1726 offer ample confirmation that he was indeed the printer concerned.[36]

---

[34] The factotum at L2ʳ also appears at K5ᵛ of Part II, and B1ʳ and D5ᵛ of Part III; the headpiece at L2ʳ also appears at K5ᵛ of Part II and D5ᵛ of Part III; and the tailpiece at L5ᵛ also appears at D8ʳ of Part III, all of these in 1726 AA.

[35] Readers may note that sheet A3 of Part III of 1726 A is not assigned to any unit, though it is normally assumed to be part of 3. Ross, for example, places it there, but in the absence of press figures or ornaments beyond mass-produced printers' flowers, and in the face of typographical evidence which seems to me ambiguous, I have preferred to leave it unassigned.

[36] Gabriel Daniel, *The History of France*, 5 vols (1726) is assigned to Aris by ESTC on the strength of an ornament bearing his name in volume 3, a volume which also contains at F8ʳ the tailpiece which appears at I5ʳ of Part II of 1726 AA. Other evidence comes from Eliza Haywood, *Secret Histories, Novels, and Poems*, 2nd ed., 4 vols (1725), volumes 2 and 3 of which appear to have been printed by Aris. Volume 3 contains at N8ᵛ the same tailpiece referred to above and at F9ᵛ another tailpiece which appears at D8ʳ and L5ᵛ of Part III of 1726 AA.

Table 3: Teerink-Scouten collations for the Motte octavos with press figures from McMaster University copies B 10,747-8(A); B 8,678-9(AA); B 8,671-2(B); B 15,957-8(1727).

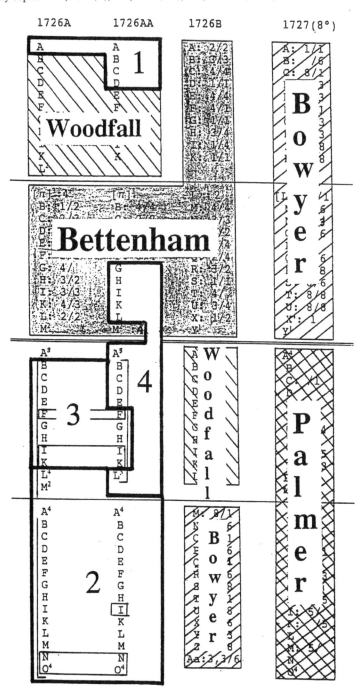

# TRAVELS.

## PART III.

### *A* VOYAGE *to* LAPUTA, BAL-

1726 AA Part III, B1$^r$, McM. U. B 8,679

Figure 3

For the other three, there are no such clues, but a concentration on printers with a known personal, professional, or even geographical connection with Motte eventually produced results. One was Edward Say, who had served his apprenticeship first with the widow Motte and then presumably with Benjamin himself,[37] and whose ornaments show that he was responsible for unit 1, namely sheet A of Part I of 1726 A and sheets A to D of Part I of 1726 AA.[38] The second was William Pearson, who had lived for many years not far from the Mottes in Aldersgate Street and who had within the two previous years printed de Moivre's *Annuities upon Lives* and an edition of Euclid, both works with which Motte was involved.[39]

---

[37] Edward Say was apprenticed to Benjamin Motte, Sr, 27 September 1710, but when Motte died three months later was apparently rebound to his widow Anne 5 March 1711. Benjamin Jr, who was only 16 at his father's death, was freed by patrimony 7 February 1715, and if he helped run the business thereafter (he bound an apprentice in June 1715), he will have overseen the work of Say, who was not freed until September 1719. See D. F. McKenzie, *Stationers' Company Apprentices, 1701–1800* (Oxford, 1978), nos 5630, 5622, 5626, and 5638.

[38] Daniel Bellamy, *The Young Ladies Miscellany* (London: Printed by E. Say, 1726) is in fact a reissue of the sheets of the 1723 edition, but that earlier edition was also printed by Say and contains a number of ornaments found in unit 1: a headpiece on B3$^r$ (and elsewhere) which is found at A3$^r$ of Part I of 1726 A and A2$^v$ of Part I of 1726 AA; a tailpiece on F4$^r$ which is found on the Part I title-pages of both 1726 A and AA; an initial T on H2$^r$ which is found at A3$^r$ of Part I of 1726 A and A2$^v$ of Part I of 1726 AA, etc.

[39] The de Moivre was advertised in the *Monthly Catalogue* of January 1725 (p. 8) as sold by F. Fayram and B. Motte, though the imprint added Pearson himself as a third seller. The Euclid was advertised in the *Monthly Catalogue* of September 1726 (p. 98) as sold by Fayram, Motte, and R. and J. Bonwicke. When a work was published or distributed by a group of booksellers, we normally have no way of determining who made the choice of, or carried on the negotiations with, the printer, though Motte's printing experience would have made him the logical person for such a role.

Pearson's ornaments are those which occur throughout sheets B to K of Part III of 1726A and F to K of Part III of 1726AA.[40] Finally, there was J. Ilive, who had been for twenty-five years a near neighbour of the Mottes in Aldersgate Street and whose ornaments, or so I believe, appear throughout sheets L and M of Part III of 1726A and all of Part IV of both 1726A and AA.[41]

The reader will have noticed my qualification where J. Ilive is concerned. It is in deference to John Ross whose conclusions about printers differ from mine at this one point only, and who believes that this unit was printed not by Ilive but by Edward Say, who then went on, as Ross and I both agree, to print the preliminaries to the whole work. Reprints follow their own logic, but in first editions the preliminaries are normally printed last, and in a work printed sequentially would have followed the concluding sheets of the text proper. *Gulliver's Travels* was not, of course, printed sequentially, and yet there is a plausibility in the printer of Part IV going on to print the prelims. However, the ornament evidence cited above has convinced me that this was not what happened in this particular case. If I am right, it means that the greatest part of Swift's greatest work was first printed under the direction of a woman, Jane Ilive having succeeded to the family printing house on her husband's death in December 1724.[42]

I come finally to the question of why *Gulliver's Travels* was printed in the way it was, for if Keith Maslen has taught us to regard shared printing as commonplace in the early eighteenth century, he has still not taught us to regard five or six different printers for successive editions of a single work as anything but highly exceptional.[43] The usual reason for shared printing was speed, not so much in the sense of a desire to set records as in the desire to avoid the myriad delays which were the inevitable result of the relatively casual methods of work in the pre-industrial world. Since Motte had originally committed himself to seeing

---

[40]  Tom D'Urfey's *Wit and Mirth: or, Pills to Purge Melancholy*, 4th ed., 6 vols (1720–21) contains a variety of ornaments later found in *Gulliver*. Volume 2, for example, contains all four tailpieces which appear in Pearson's unit 3: (1) on A3ᵛ, D4ʳ, G9ᵛ, and K8ʳ the headpiece which appears on D8ʳ of Part III of 1726A; (2) on B9ᵛ, L7ʳ, M12ᵛ, and O4ʳ that on I7ᵛ of Part III of 1726A and AA; (3) on D9ʳ, F6ʳ, and I12ᵛ, that on H4ʳ of Part III of 1726A and AA; (4) on F9ʳ that on B7ᵛ of Part III of 1726A and F8ʳ and I3ʳ of Part III of 1726A and AA.

[41]  Timothy Greated, *An Essay on Friendship* (London: Printed by J. Ilive, 1726) contains at B1ʳ the headpiece which appears at B1ʳ of Part IV of both 1726A and AA, and at π2ᵛ the tailpiece which appears at E6ʳ of Part IV of both 1726A and AA. Moreover, four of the five ornaments found in Greated's *Essay*, including the two just mentioned, are also found in Samuel Chandler, *A Vindication of the Christian Religion* (London: Printed for Samuel Chandler, 1725). Although *A Vindication* had more than one printer (sheets B to E appear to be printed by Samuel Palmer), those sheets apparently printed by Ilive contain a further nine ornaments which also appear in sheets L and M of Part III of 1726A and Part IV of 1726A and AA.

[42]  See Michael Treadwell, "London Printers and Printing Houses in 1705," *Publishing History*, 7 (1980), 24. The Ilives' son Jacob, also a printer, was freed by service to his father on 2 August 1726, but it appears that the J. Ilive at the head of the business was still Jane at this time; Salem Pearse, *The Second Part of the Coelestial Diary*, an almanac printed annually for the Stationers' Company by the Ilives, carries Jane's full name from the number for 1726 (printed in the autumn of 1725) until that for 1733, with Jacob's name first appearing on the edition for 1734.

[43]  K. I. D. Maslen, "Shared Printing and the Bibliographer: New Evidence from the Bowyer Press," *Studies in the Eighteenth Century*, IV, eds R. F. Brissenden and J. C. Eade (Canberra, 1979), pp. 193–206.

the work published within a month of receiving the copy – a commitment which he was not able to keep – this may have been part of his motive, though the reply he received from Swift merely requested that the work be "published by Christmas at furthest," a deadline which Motte anticipated by almost two months.[44] A second reason for shared printing was what we might broadly call security. The Stationers' Company, for example, regularly assigned the printing of the three sheets required for the majority of the almanacs in its monopoly to separate printers. The aim was to prevent any one printer from pirating such a saleable property by simply running off for his own profit a few more copies than he had been commissioned to produce.

I am not, of course, suggesting that Motte was nervous about the potential pirating by his own printer of an unknown and still unpublished work, any more than that he was rushing to meet some vague, self-imposed deadline. And yet I do believe that Motte was, in a sense, influenced by both of these motives for shared printing, namely by his sense that this was not a work to dawdle over until rumours about its contents began to circulate, and by his calculation that such rumours were less likely to circulate if no one beyond the publisher had any very clear idea what it was all about. Motte was convinced enough of *Gulliver*'s likely popular appeal to agree to publish it, and under his own name. He was, however, nervous enough about its possible reception in some quarters that he was prepared to take liberties with its text, and I strongly suspect that he also hoped to avoid the circulation of any pre-publication rumours about, let alone copies of, the work which might have tempted a nervous Ministry to interfere *before* publication. Once it had been produced in the theatre, Walpole had no recourse but to encore *The Beggar's Opera*; *Polly* he took care to see was never staged.

It might, of course, be argued that assigning each part of *Gulliver* to a different printer – essentially Motte's proceeding with the first edition – achieved less in the way of obfuscation than assigning even less comprehensible fragments to even more printers. But if Motte was perhaps anxious to avoid attention, he was certainly anxious to avoid chaos; and if complete secrecy had been a real priority with him, he would certainly have opted for much slower production at a single printing house upon whose discretion he could count, followed by publication through a trade publisher. Five printers seem, therefore, to be as many as it was really practicable to employ.

We cannot, of course, know that the five printers chosen were Motte's first choices, but we may observe that they represent a wide geographic spread: Woodfall, just to the west of Motte by Temple Bar, Bettenham to the north in St John's Lane, Pearson and Ilive farther east again in different stretches of Aldersgate Street Without, and Edward Say in the northeast corner of the city in Bishopsgate Street Without.[45] Say, it is worth noting, was as far

---

[44] For an account of the correspondence between Sympson/Swift and Motte regarding the timing of *Gulliver*'s publication, see Treadwell, "Benjamin Motte, Andrew Tooke and *Gulliver's Travels*," p. 297. *Gulliver* was published on 28 October 1726.

[45] General addresses for all five in 1723 are given in the Negus list referred to in n. 47, below. More detailed locations may be determined for Ilive, Pearson, and Say from the Land Tax returns for 1726 for the 2nd and 4th precincts of the ward of Aldersgate Without (Ilive and Pearson), and the 4th precinct of the ward of Bishopsgate Without (Say), Guildhall Library, MS 11,316/81. A more detailed location for Woodfall may be determined in the Rate Books of the parish of St Clement Danes, Royal Ward, in the Westminster Public Library.

from Motte geographically as any printer in London, yet possibly the closest to him in terms of personal relations. Perhaps, it is not a coincidence then that it was Say who was also the printer of the preliminaries, including the contents, the one printer who knew what all the parts were and how they fit together – though of course even he may not have seen all of them.

About the choice of particular printers I have, with one exception, nothing to say. All except Say were extremely experienced, and all were Motte's seniors. Although Bettenham and Woodfall had each been established as master printers for only six or seven years, both were about forty and had spent twenty-five years in the trade since beginning their apprenticeships in 1700 and 1701 respectively. Pearson and the widow Ilive were even more experienced, being in their late fifties and at the head of printing houses which had been in continuous operation since before the turn of the century. And in case one were tempted to see Jane Ilive as perhaps less experienced than the others, it is well to remember that she was the daughter as well as the wife of a master printer and had spent her entire life in the printing house.[46] However, although alike in their experience, Motte's printers were surprisingly diverse in their politics, at least in the judgement of the would-be press spy Samuel Negus, who in the notorious list which he submitted to the Secretary of State in 1723 described two (Pearson and Woodfall) as "well-affected to His Majesty," two more (Ilive and Say) as "High-Flyers," and Bettenham as one of the "Nonjurors." The only one of Negus's "political" categories from which Motte did not choose a printer was the "Roman Catholicks."[47]

The one case in which one can detect a possible motive behind the selection of a particular printer is the choice of Pearson to print Part III. Pearson's speciality within the London trade was printed (as opposed to engraved) music, and with that went an expertise in the setting of lined tables and mathematical diagrams of all sorts. The printing mentioned above that Pearson had done for Motte just prior to *Gulliver* was of this latter sort. The point is not that it will have tickled Motte's sense of humour to assign the bizarre doings of the music- and mathematics-obsessed Laputians to one of London's foremost printers of both. Rather we may suspect that when he recalled the passage beginning "let *A B* represent a Line drawn cross the Dominions of *Balnibarbi*, let the Line *c d* represent the Loadstone" and so on, Motte instinctively thought of Pearson, whether or not he had at that point decided (or been instructed) to add a diagram. In the event, both that diagram and the illustration of the Grand Academy's word frame which also occurs in Part III, the only part of the *Travels* to have such diagrams, were engraved rather than set in type. Perhaps in the

---

[46]  For Say, see n. 37, above; for Woodfall, see Goulden, *The Ornament Stock of Henry Woodfall*, pp. iii–xi; for Jane Ilive, daughter of the printer Thomas James and his extraordinary wife, Eleanor, and Pearson, see Treadwell, "London Printers and Printing Houses in 1705," pp. 24–25, 33–34. James Bettenham was from 1700 to 1707 the apprentice of the elder William Bowyer, whose step-daughter he eventually married. He presumably set up for himself about the time he bound the first of his many apprentices in February 1720. See McKenzie, *Stationers' Company Apprentices*, nos 989, 782.

[47]  For an account of the Negus list and its dating, as well as a copy of the list itself, see Michael Treadwell, "Lists of Master Printers: The Size of the London Printing Trade, 1637–1723," *Aspects of Printing from 1600*, eds Robin Myers and Michael Harris (Oxford, 1987), pp. 153–55, 165–66. The Ilive in the Negus list is, of course, Jane's husband Thomas, who was still alive at that time.

long run, Pearson's role as expert was merely to convince Motte that the typesetting could not be done.

Aside from the decision to divide the printing of *Gulliver* in five in the first place, the one major anomaly in the way the division was done was the assignment of sheets L and M of Part III to the printer of Part IV, particularly when the break between K and L occurs in the middle of a sentence rather than at some natural pause in the narrative. Perhaps Pearson's section was proceeding more slowly than expected and Ilive's more quickly.

This anomaly was eliminated in the 1726 AA second edition, but a number of others appeared in its place. To begin with, and in sharp contrast to what was to happen from this point on, the number of printers actually increased with the addition of a sixth. This was Samuel Aris of Creed Lane, another "well-affected" printer of the generation of Bettenham and Woodfall, whose assigned part involved a bizarre assortment including five sheets or part-sheets previously printed by each of Bettenham and Pearson, and eleven pages (now reduced to ten) previously the work of Jane Ilive. Since these three printers were all still engaged in the printing of the second edition, this is, at the very least, peculiar although the assigning of sheet L of Part III to the printer (or at least one of the printers) of that part rather than to the printer of Part IV did remove an existing anomaly. But if to one of the printers of Part III, why not to the printer of the immediately preceding sheets? We cannot, of course, be sure, but the fact that part of sheet F and all of sheets I and K were printed from standing type may imply that Pearson had agreed, not to participate in a full reprinting, but merely to work off the requisite numbers of those sheets he had previously printed, the type for which had not yet been distributed. If so, he may either have mistakenly believed that the type for G and H was still standing and only later discovered his mistake, or agreed to their reprinting to fill out a run of sheets between those for which the type *was* still standing. This may explain why Pearson printed only five sheets of Part III of 1726 AA, and why he only began at sheet F. It is not, however, the real explanation for his *not* printing sheet L. The reason for that is not simply that he had no type standing for a sheet he had not printed in the 1726 A edition, but that although L follows K in the alphabet, in the printing house L may well have come together with A as part of a single printed sheet, subsequently divided.[48]

With Bettenham, the case is somewhat different, for although he had to reset all his sheets for the second edition anyway, he, too, printed only half as many sheets in AA as in A. There are a dozen *possible* explanations for why Aris was suddenly assigned five of the sheets Bettenham had previously printed, but no one seems *probable*. However, the fact that Bettenham continued to print the four pages of M in what appears to be the midst of Aris's run is again less peculiar than it looks. First, there is evidence that some of M may have been printed from standing type, but more important still M, like sheet L in Part III, is most likely to have originally been part of the same sheet as the preliminaries, $[\pi]^3$.

The one other change in the printing of the second edition for which I will venture an explanation is the increase in Say's share from one sheet to four. A glance at the generous spacing of the opening pages of the first edition evidently convinced Motte that the printer could achieve compression sufficient to eliminate the need for the final four-page quarter

---

[48] The resolution of this and many other questions about the details of the printing of *Gulliver* awaits the study of a far larger number of copies than was practicable in the time available for the present study.

sheet ($L^2$) in Part I. My guess is that Motte allowed Say four sheets on the rough principle that saving an average of one page per sheet would achieve the desired reduction. In fact, Say was able to achieve the full four-page saving in the A gathering alone, thus leaving, if I am correct, no visible clue to the motive for the original reassignment of sheets.

After the first two editions which Hubbard has described as showing in parts "abundant evidence of haste," the third or B edition "contains scarcely a dozen errors of spelling ... mostly of minor importance" and shows signs that it "has been carefully edited."[49] Carefully printed, we might rather say, noting that the number of printers has been reduced to three, two of whom are assigned an entire part and the third an entire volume. And this trend is continued in the fourth edition which, with its conventional allotment of one printer per volume, simply underlines in retrospect how extraordinary the printing arrangements for the first two editions of *Gulliver* really were.

Moreover, the only new printers involved were, as we noted at the outset, William Bowyer, perhaps the most senior and respected printer in London, and Samuel Palmer. Palmer was Motte's exact contemporary and had served his apprenticeship in the Motte family printing house. He was also, however, the most ambitious young printer of his generation, the projector of a history of printing, and the printer chosen to supervise the royal hobby press at St James's in 1731.[50] His collaboration with Bowyer on the 1727 octavo *Gulliver*, though certainly fortuitous, thus seems a curious case of overkill for an edition which, at least for the London trade, had largely settled into the category of a routine reprint.

---

[49] Hubbard, *Contributions*, pp. 22, 21.
[50] See J. C. Ross, "A Progress Report upon a Study of Samuel Palmer: A London Printer as Icarus," *An Index of Civilisation: Studies of Printing and Publishing History in honour of Keith Maslen*, eds R. Harvey, W. Kirsop, and B. J. McMullin (Clayton, Victoria, 1993), pp. 111–28.

J. A. Downie
*Goldsmiths' College, University of London*

# Swift and the Making of the English Novel

ABSTRACT. Although *Gulliver's Travels* was included in various anthologies of "novels" which appeared in the later eighteenth and early nineteenth centuries, Swift is usually omitted not only from accounts of "the rise of the novel," but from studies of eighteenth-century popular fiction. His exclusion from consideration by modern critics appears therefore to be a retrospective judgement, based largely on his classification as a satirist rather than a novelist – a classification which also excludes *Gulliver's Travels* from consideration as popular literature. Much of the confusion appears to be generated by ante-dating the emergence of the novel as a stable genre so that this takes place in the first, rather than in the second half of the eighteenth century. As Bakhtin points out, the period of the novel's creative ascendancy is preceded by a period in which are published "parodies that are the precursors, 'companions' to the novel, in their own way studies for it." For these reasons, accounts of the making of the English novel must also take into account the contribution of Swift.

Rereading John J. Richetti's seminal study, *Popular Fiction before Richardson: Narrative Patterns, 1700–1739*, in its recently reissued paperback version, one is struck by a certain paradox: how much has now been written on the "non-canonical" texts which, all those years ago, Professor Richetti virtually apologized for mentioning at all – tales of rogues and whores, travellers, pirates, and pilgrims, as well as the multifarious prose fictions of Delarivier Manley, Eliza Haywood, Penelope Aubin, Jane Barker, and Elizabeth Rowe; and yet how little criticism of these texts appears to have developed in the past twenty years other than in the application of fashionable critical terminology.[1]

Although he acknowledges, in his "Introduction: Twenty Years On," that the works of early-eighteenth-century popular fiction which he treats are now viewed very differently, what is most striking about rereading Richetti is the sanity of most of his conclusions. There is one curious authorial decision, however. Professor Richetti's book is about *popular* fiction. "It is one of the more appalling and therefore interesting facts of literary history," he writes at one point, "that the three most popular works of fiction before *Pamela* were *Gulliver's Travels*, *Robinson Crusoe*, and Mrs. Haywood's first novel, *Love in Excess: or, The Fatal*

---

[1] There are of course notable exceptions, like Percy G. Adams, *Travel Literature and the Evolution of the Novel* (Lexington, KY, 1983); Jane Spencer, *The Rise of the Woman Novelist from Aphra Behn to Jane Austen* (Oxford, 1986); Lincoln B. Faller, *Turned to Account[:] The Forms and Functions of Criminal Biography in Late Seventeenth- and Early Eighteenth-Century England* (Cambridge, 1987); and J. Paul Hunter, *Before Novels: The Cultural Contexts of Eighteenth-Century English Fiction* (New York and London, 1990). (This list does not pretend to be comprehensive.)

*Enquiry* (1719)."[2] Two quibbles can be made immediately about this statement: first, it takes no account of Bunyan's *Pilgrim's Progress*, which almost certainly was *the* most popular work of fiction before *Pamela*; second, without hard figures, one wonders if *Love in Excess* really was more popular than, say, Delarivier Manley's *New Atalantis*. Of more significance to my argument, however, is this question: why does *Gulliver's Travels* not figure more prominently in Richetti's account of *popular* fiction before Richardson?

To be fair, Professor Richetti begins his chapter on "Travellers, Pirates, and Pilgrims" – a chapter which includes extended reference to *Robinson Crusoe* – by commenting on "one of the ironies of literary history," the fact that "the most durable survivor from the mass of travel literature that flooded Europe during the seventeenth and eighteenth centuries was meant to satirize the genre." Richetti goes on to argue that *Gulliver's Travels* "is in spirit an attack upon the ethos that produced the travel book and caused its enormous vogue."[3] Given Swift's fondness for travel books,[4] this must be debatable. Certainly, as I shall emphasize in due course, *Gulliver* parodies travel literature, but that, in itself, does not mean that it is primarily an attack "upon the ethos that produced it." What Richetti's argument does not explain, however, is his decision effectively to exclude the most popular fiction of all, *Gulliver's Travels*, from his discussion of early-eighteenth-century "popular" fiction.

Perhaps it has something to do with the context in which *Popular Fiction before Richardson* was written. As Professor Richetti explains in his new Introduction, his work should be seen partly as a reaction to *The Rise of the Novel* (1957), which excluded from consideration not only *Gulliver's Travels*, but all prose fiction written prior to 1740 other than that written by Defoe. Ian Watt's decision has been enormously influential on the way in which the early English novel has subsequently been approached. As Deborah Baker Wyrick has recently pointed out, since the publication of *The Rise of the Novel*, "it has been difficult to place *Gulliver's Travels* within a university course in the early English novel."[5] Most critics have simply endorsed Watt's judgement. Despite the plethora of books on the early novel which has appeared in the past few years, only Michael McKeon's devotes space to *Gulliver's Travels*.[6] (Watt of course does not even mention the book by name.)

This is all the more curious when one considers late-eighteenth- and early-nineteenth-century reactions to *Gulliver's Travels*. Swift's satire, after all, was included in various anthologies of the works of novelists which appeared in magazines in that period. Richard C. Taylor has recently drawn attention as "a barometer of late eighteenth-century taste" to James Harrison's *The Novelist's Magazine*, which published twenty-three volumes of novels from 1779 onwards.[7] All the "canonical" writers are represented: Defoe, Swift, Richardson,

---

2   *Popular Fiction before Richardson: Narrative Patterns, 1700–1739* (Oxford, 1992), p. 179.
3   Richetti, *Popular Fiction*, p. 60. See also Adams, *Travel Literature*, p. 143.
4   Swift wrote to Esther Vanhomrigh from Loughall on 13 July 1722: "I doubt the bad weathr has hinderd you much from the Diversions of your Country house; and put you upon thinking in your Chamber. The use I have made of it was to read I know not how many diverting Books of History and Travells" (*Correspondence*, II, 429–30).
5   See her "*Gulliver's Travels* and the Early English Novel," *Critical Approaches to Teaching Swift*, ed. Peter J. Schakel (New York, 1992), p. 133.
6   See *The Origins of the English Novel, 1600–1740* (Baltimore and London, 1987), pp. 338–56.
7   See "James Harrison, *The Novelist's Magazine*, and the Early Canonizing of the English Novel," *Studies in English Literature*, 33 (1993), 638.

Fielding, Smollett, Johnson, Sterne, Goldsmith, as well as Cervantes, Fénelon, Le Sage, Marivaux, and Voltaire. More interestingly, Harrison also included female novelists like Eliza Haywood (though not *Love in Excess*), Sarah Fielding, Charlotte Lennox, and Frances Sheridan.

Over forty years later, as Taylor also points out, *Gulliver's Travels* was still being classified as a novel. It was included in Volume IX of *Ballantyne's Novelist's Magazine*, alongside Richard Cumberland's *Henry*, and three novels by Robert Bage, *Mount Henneth*, *Barham Downs*, and *James Wallace*. Clearly, it cannot have been any *similarity* between Swift's narrative and the writings of Bage and Cumberland which led to it being included in the same volume. *Gulliver's Travels* simply appeared in 1824 in a magazine devoted to the work of novelists, alongside such "canonical" eighteenth-century novelists as Richardson, Fielding, and Smollett. Two other interesting observations can be made about the list of works included in *Ballantyne's Novelist's Magazine*: first, no women writers are included other than Clara Reeve and Ann Radcliffe; second, and of at least equal interest to my purpose, two of the five "great" "canonical" "novelists" of the eighteenth century are missing, Defoe and Sterne.

P. N. Furbank and W. R. Owens have recently told the story of the construction of Defoe-the-novelist.[8] Until Francis Noble reissued *Roxana* in 1775 with "Published by Mr Daniel De Foe" on the title-page, only *Robinson Crusoe* and *Colonel Jack* of what we now call the "novels" had been attributed to Defoe. In addition to *Roxana*, Noble published the following as Defoe's in the years after 1775: *Memoirs of a Cavalier*; *Moll Flanders*; *Captain Singleton*; *A Journal of the Plague Year*, and *A New Voyage Round the World*. Previously, not only had these been anonymous publications; they had been regarded as genuine accounts. In other words, they were supposed to be factual. (In that sense, one should call some of them pseudonymous rather than anonymous.)

What I find especially curious about all this is the way in which, patently influenced by the thesis put forward in *The Rise of the Novel*, critics like John Bender have insisted that Defoe's narratives appeared in "the period when the novel was becoming a recognizable mode of writing."[9] Undoubtedly, works called "novels" were being published in the 1720s. The Preface to *Moll Flanders* begins by complaining that because "the World is so taken up of late with Novels and Romances ... it will be hard for a private History to be taken for Genuine."[10] What is less clear is whether contemporaries were prepared to make a clear-cut distinction between "the novel" and other forms of prose fiction, particularly the romance. In referring to "Novels and Romances," is Defoe trying to distinguish between the two? Or is he tacitly acknowledging that generic confusion exists in the 1720s? Defoe is, after all, at least ostensibly trying to pass *Moll Flanders* off as fact, not fiction. He could even be making use of that figure of speech, the hendiadys, "in which a single complex idea is expressed by two words connected by a conjunction" (*OED*). Perhaps, in other words, Defoe joins

---

[8] See P. N. Furbank and W. R. Owens, "Defoe and Francis Noble," *Eighteenth-Century Fiction*, 4 (1992), 301–13. See also their *Defoe De-Attributions: A Critique of J. R. Moore's "Checklist"* (London and Rio Grande, 1994), pp. xvii–xx.

[9] See his *Imagining the Penitentiary: Fiction and the Architecture of Mind in Eighteenth-Century England* (Chicago and London, 1987), p. 74.

[10] *The Fortunes and Misfortunes of the Famous Moll Flanders*, ed. G. A. Starr (Oxford, 1971), p. 1.

"novel" and "romance" together not because contemporary readers knew how to distinguish between the two, but because he is aware that early-eighteenth-century readers were no longer certain how to classify works of prose fiction.

One of Richard C. Taylor's most interesting observations on the list of works included in *The Novelist's Magazine* sixty years after the first appearance of Defoe's narratives is that "the discrete generic distinctions that marginalized the 'romance' and other 'sub-categories' in the 'history of the novel' was a retrospective judgment."[11] J. Paul Hunter has written that "no single word or phrase distinguishes the novel from romance or from anything else, and to settle for 'realism' or 'individualism' or 'character' as the defining characteristic diminishes the very idea of the novel and trivializes the conception of a literary species,"[12] while Mikhail Bakhtin insists that the "utter inadequacy of literary theory is exposed when it is forced to deal with the novel."[13]

Surely they are right. In 1692, in the Preface to *Incognita: or, Love and Duty Reconcil'd,* Congreve pointed out the distinction between novel and romance in terms which have been echoed by critics down the years:

> *Romances are generally composed of the constant Loves and invincible Courages of Hero's, Heroins, Kings and Queens, Mortals of the first Rank, and so forth; where lofty Language, miraculous Contingencies, and impossible Performances, elevate and surprize the Reader into a giddy delight ... Novels are of a more familiar nature; Come near us, and represent to us Intrigues in practice, delight us with Accidents and odd Events, but not such as are wholly unusual or unpresidented.*[14]

And yet in 1785, almost 100 years later, Clara Reeve in *The Progress of Romance* was forced to explain: "The word *Novel* in all Languages signifies something new. It was first used to distinguish these works from Romance, though they have lately been confounded together and are frequently mistaken for each other." "The Novel is a picture of real life and manners and of the times in which it is written," she went on. "The Romance, in lofty and elevated language, describes what never happened nor is likely to happen."[15]

The descriptions of the characteristics of the novel offered by Congreve and Reeve as they attempt to distinguish it from the romance are of course remarkably similar to Ian Watt's account of "formal realism." Is it not curious, then, that Watt should argue that the rise of the novel starts with three writers who insisted that they were *not* writing novels or romances? Indeed, of the five "great" eighteenth-century English novelists, only Smollett acknowledged that he was writing a novel.[16] Notoriously, Defoe, Richardson, Fielding, and Sterne all implied that, whatever it was that they were doing, they were not writing novels

---

[11]  Taylor, "James Harrison, *The Novelist's Magazine*," p. 638.

[12]  Hunter, *Before Novels*, pp. 22–23.

[13]  *The Dialogic Imagination: Four Essays*, ed. Michael Holquist, trans. Caryl Emerson and Michael Holquist (Austin, TX, 1981), p. 8.

[14]  *Incognita: or, Love and Duty Reconcil'd. A Novel* (London, 1692), Preface.

[15]  *The Progress of Romance, through Times, Countries, and Manners*, 2 vols (New York, 1970 [Colchester, 1785]), I, 110–11. Clive T. Probyn makes the same point in his *English Fiction of the Eighteenth Century, 1700–1789* (London, 1987), pp. 1–3.

[16]  Smollett's Dedication to *The Adventures of Ferdinand Count Fathom* (1753) begins: "A novel is a large diffused picture, comprehending the characters of life, disposed in different groupes, and exhibited in various attitudes, for the purposes of an uniform plan, and general occurrence, to which every individual figure is subservient."

and, further, that, whatever it was that they were doing, it was not the same as what any of the others was doing, or anyone else for that matter.

Pondering this problem in relation to Sterne-the-novelist, Melvyn New points out:

> In all his writings, including his letters, Sterne never refers to Defoe or Richardson or Fielding, yet because we teach him after these authors, we are compelled to draw not merely a relationship, but a teleological one – that is, since Sterne comes after them in chronology, and since we are tracing the "development" of the novel, Sterne *must* be doing something better, more modern, than they ever accomplished.[17]

Defoe, Richardson, Fielding, and Sterne all tend to figure in accounts of the development of the English novel. Yet Swift, the author of the most popular prose fiction published in the early eighteenth century, does not. What makes it all stranger still is that Sterne insisted that there was indeed a relationship between his writing and Swift's. As Professor New puts it, "Swift was the *only* English author in the preceding generation that Sterne consistently referred to as his model and his own delight."

Michael McKeon's account of the origins of the English novel is the only one to include a chapter on Swift alongside chapters on Defoe, Richardson, and Fielding. McKeon is aware that some critics might baulk at the idea. "The notoriously discontinuous quality of Gulliver's character throughout much of his travels has frequently been cited to confirm the status of *Gulliver's Travels* as a 'satire' rather than a 'novel,'" he writes. "But the retrospective standards by which we judge what is 'novelistic' are of problematic relevance to the generically uncertain narratives that are native to the period of the novel's gradual stabilization."[18]

I shall return to a couple of aspects of Professor McKeon's remarks in due course. What is immediately striking is how his approach to the prose fiction of the 1720s appears to be diametrically opposed to, say, John Bender's. For Professor Bender, this is the period in which "the novel was becoming a recognizable mode of writing;" for McKeon, this, "the period of the novel's gradual stabilization," throws up "generically uncertain narratives" like *Gulliver's Travels*. Relying on Bakhtin's idea of "novelization," Bender is prepared to argue that, in *The Beggar's Opera*, "Gay used essentially novelistic techniques of realism and generic contradiction," and yet, following Watt perhaps, he virtually ignores Swift, and totally ignores *Gulliver's Travels*.[19]

Bender, then, joins Watt and Richetti in electing to eschew detailed discussion of Swift's writings even though their studies focus on early-eighteenth-century prose fiction. As their approaches more or less span the range of current critical opinion, I should like briefly to suggest why they wish to exclude Swift from their accounts, and although I hope to show how the reasons are interlinked, I shall deal with each in turn.

As everybody knows, in searching for the distinguishing characteristic of the novel, Ian Watt described "formal realism" as its "lowest common denominator." The classic formulation of the term is as follows:

> Formal realism, in fact, is the narrative embodiment of a premise that Defoe and Richardson accepted very literally, but which is implicit in the novel form in general: the premise, or primary convention, that the novel is a full and authentic report of human experience, and

---

[17] See his "Swift as Ogre, Richardson as Dolt: Rescuing Sterne from the Eighteenth Century," *The Shandean*, 3 (1991), 51.

[18] McKeon, *The Origins of the English Novel*, p. 341.

[19] Bender, *Imagining the Penitentiary*, pp. 74, 89.

is therefore under an obligation to satisfy its reader with such details of the story as the individuality of the actors concerned, the particulars of the times and places of their actions, details which are presented through a more largely referential use of language than is common in other literary forms.[20]

> I HAD been for some Hours extremely pressed by the Necessities of Nature; which was no Wonder, it being almost two Days since I had last disburthened myself. I was under great Difficulties between Urgency and Shame. The best Expedient I could think on, was to creep into my House, which I accordingly did; and shutting the Gate after me, I went as far as the Length of my Chain would suffer; and discharged my Body of that uneasy Load. But this was the only Time I was ever guilty of so uncleanly an Action; for which I cannot but hope the candid Reader will give some Allowance, after he hath maturely and impartially considered my Case, and the Distress I was in. From this Time my constant Practice was, as soon as I rose, to perform that Business in open Air, at the full Extent of my Chain; and due Care was taken every Morning before Company came, that the offensive Matter should be carried off in Wheel-barrows, by two Servants appointed for that Purpose. I would not have dwelt so long upon a Circumstance, that perhaps at first Sight may appear not very momentous; if I had not thought it necessary to justify my Character in Point of Cleanliness to the World; which I am told, some of my Maligners have been pleased, upon this and other Occasions, to call in Question.
> WHEN this Adventure was at an End, I came back out of my House, having Occasion for fresh Air.[21]

How many "particulars of the times and places of [the characters'] actions" does the reader want? "Enough, or too much!" The first edition of *Gulliver's Travels* begins with Richard Sympson's account, addressed to "the Reader," of his "Cousin" Lemuel Gulliver's book:

> The Style is very plain and simple; and the only Fault I find is, that the Author, after the Manner of Travellers, is a little too circumstantial. There is an Air of Truth apparent through the whole; and indeed the Author was so distinguished for his Veracity, that it became a Sort of Proverb among his Neighbours at *Redriff*, when any one affirmed a Thing, to say, it was as true as if Mr. *Gulliver* had spoke it.

And of course Sympson's preface ends by assuring the reader that, should he wish "for any further Particulars relating to the Author," he "will receive Satisfaction from the first Pages of the Book."[22] And, in a manner of speaking, he does.

It would be difficult to deny that *Gulliver's Travels* offers the sort of "circumstantial view of life" which Watt defines as "formal realism" – "a set of narrative procedures which are so commonly found together in the novel, and so rarely in other literary genres, that they may be regarded as typical of the form itself."[23] I am not suggesting it is new to draw attention to the realism of the style of *Gulliver's Travels*. On the contrary, it is virtually a critical commonplace. As long ago as 1929, Ernest A. Baker noted it in the chapter on Swift in his *History of the English Novel*.[24] Why, then, if formal realism is indeed "the lowest common denominator" of the novel, should *Gulliver's Travels* be excluded from any account of its development?

Obviously, Swift's giants and pigmies cause problems, let alone flying islands and spirits, Struldbruggs, Yahoos and Houyhnhnms. However, if Watt's formulation of formal realism

---

[20]  *The Rise of the Novel: Studies in Defoe, Richardson, and Fielding* (London, 1957), p. 32.
[21]  *Prose Works*, XI, 29–30 (I, ii, 2–3).
[22]  *Prose Works*, XI, 9–10.
[23]  Watt, *The Rise of the Novel*, p. 32.
[24]  See *The History of the English Novel, III: The Later Romances and the Establishment of Realism* (London, 1929), pp. 238–41.

cannot deal with the disjunction in *Gulliver's Travels* between style and subject-matter, then its usefulness as the distinguishing characteristic of the novel is open to question. Swift's style is avowedly "very plain and simple" and, allowing a certain leeway for the "notoriously discontinuous quality of Gulliver's character," the imagined world of *Gulliver's Travels* has an inner consistency. In other words, *Gulliver's Travels* is realistic *despite Swift's talking horses.*

Richetti's reasons for limiting his discussion of *Gulliver's Travels* are implied in the single paragraph he devotes to it. Although Swift's book was immensely popular, it was not "popular" literature. Instead, it "was meant to satirize the genre" of the travel book. It is curious that despite the writings of, say, Fielding, Smollett, Sterne, and Jane Austen – all of whom they are happy to call novelists – critics have difficulties dealing with the relationship between satire and the novel. Is it sufficient to argue that Swift should be excluded from accounts of the novel's development simply because he was a satirist? Northrop Frye drew attention to the problem in the same year in which *The Rise of the Novel* first appeared:

> Is *Gulliver's Travels* a novel? Here most would demur, including the Dewey decimal system, which puts it under "Satire and Humor." But surely everyone would call it fiction, and if it is fiction, a distinction appears between fiction as a genus and the novel as a species of that genus ... It must then be another form of fiction.[25]

Frye finally ends up including *Gulliver's Travels*, along with other "awkward" satirical fictions, in the special category of Menippean satire.[26]

In one sense, I have no objection to this. Richetti was of course writing before Bakhtin's influence on theories of the novel began to be felt. "Parodic stylizations of canonized genres and styles occupy an essential place in the novel," Bakhtin writes. "In the era of the novel's creative ascendency – and even more so in the periods of preparation preceding this era – literature was flooded with parodies and travesties of all the high genres (parodies precisely of genres, and not of individual authors or schools) – parodies that are the precursors, 'companions' to the novel, in their own way studies for it." Thus, while it might be reasonably argued that the travel book is scarcely a "canonized genre," if one follows Bakhtin, parody, on its own, is no reason for insisting that *Gulliver's Travels* should be excluded from consideration of the development of the novel. Indeed, Bakhtin subsequently refers to the manner in which the novel's "struggle against conventionality" is continued, "after his own special fashion, in Swift."[27] Unlike Frye's, Bakhtin's own championing of the concept of Menippean satire does not end up excluding *Gulliver's Travels* from consideration as a "companion" to the novel, rather the reverse.

G. S. Rousseau has recently returned to what he calls "the satirical tradition in prose narrative":

> Satire did not, of course, *lead* to the early eighteenth-century novel in any prescriptive or formal sense, but shaped it in so many ways that the overlaps of the two forms – satire and novel – have always been worthy of study, despite the frustrations involved in trying to arrive at neat conclusions about reciprocity or coherent theories about influence. A more secure approach reasons that satiric narrative enriched the early British novel.[28]

---

25  *Anatomy of Criticism: Four Essays* (Princeton, NJ, 1957), p. 303.

26  See *Anatomy of Criticism*, pp. 308–9.

27  Bakhtin, *The Dialogic Imagination*, pp. 6, 162, 164.

28  "From Swift to Smollett: The Satirical Tradition in Prose Narrative," *The Columbia History of the British Novel*, ed. John Richetti (New York, 1994), p. 128.

This is well put. Although the question of influence is always a thorny one, it is perfectly possible to demonstrate that Swift *informed* the prose narratives of writers like Fielding and Sterne. After all, they said as much. On the other hand, if we were to exclude from consideration all the early novels which could also be reasonably described as satiric narratives, then we would be forced to remove Fielding, Smollett, Sterne, and Austen (at the very least) from accounts of the development of the English novel.

Bender relies heavily on Bakhtin's concept of novelization in *Imagining the Penitentiary*, to such an extent that works of Gay and Hogarth are viewed as novelistic discourses. Curiously, Bender cites the same section from *The Dialogic Imagination* to which I have been referring to support *his* argument. "In an era when the novel reigns supreme," Bakhtin asserts, "almost all the remaining genres are to a greater or lesser extent 'novelized.'" There is, however, a significant difference between the chronology offered by Bakhtin and by Bender. For Bakhtin, it is not the earlier, but the *later* eighteenth century in which the novel "reigns supreme." This accommodates *Gulliver's Travels* perfectly, since Bakhtin argues that it is the period preceding "the era of the novel's creative ascendency" that we should look for a flood of "precursors" of the novel.[29]

Interestingly, Bender, like Watt, wishes to pre-date the predominance of the novel as a literary genre by about half a century, moving it back into the years in which Defoe was writing long prose narratives – the decade which also saw the publication of *Gulliver's Travels*. I am reminded of Foucault's sneering account of "We 'Other Victorians'": "By placing the advent of the age of repression in the seventeenth century, after hundreds of years of open spaces and free expression, one *adjusts* it to coincide with the development of capitalism: it becomes an integral part of the bourgeois order."[30] Having decided in advance that the novel rose in the *early* eighteenth century, one adjusts the timing of certain economic and social developments, bringing them forward by half a century or so, as it were, so that they seem to coincide with the publication of key works by Defoe, Richardson, and Fielding.

Thus Watt posits the emergence of capitalism, the rise of the middle class, and the growth of the reading public as crucial for the rise of the novel, even though there is precious little evidence that any of these took place in the *early* eighteenth century. Bender's thesis about the rise of the novel and the rise of the penitentiary is equally tendentious, it seems to me. For their theses to work, both critics *require* the rise of the novel in the earlier, rather than the later eighteenth century: "A very wholsome and comfortable Doctrine, and to which we have but one Objection, namely, That it is not true."[31] It was only really after mid-century – after Defoe, Richardson, and Fielding – that contemporaries appear to have begun to mean the same thing when they refer to "the novel." "By the middle of the eighteenth century," Michael McKeon argues, "the stabilizing of terminology – the increasing acceptance of 'the novel' as a canonic term, so that contemporaries can 'speak of it *as such*' – signals the stability of the conceptual category and of the class of literary products that it encloses."[32] This of course ushers in the era in which, according to Bakhtin, "the novel becomes the dominant

---

[29]  Bakhtin, *The Dialogic Imagination*, pp. 5–6.
[30]  Michel Foucault, *The History of Sexuality, I: An Introduction*, trans. Robert Hurley (Harmondsworth, Middlesex, 1981), p. 5.
[31]  Henry Fielding, *The History of Tom Jones: A Foundling*, eds Martin C. Battestin and Fredson Bowers, 2 vols (Oxford, 1974), II, 783.
[32]  McKeon, *The Origins of the English Novel*, p. 19.

genre," and I think that McKeon is, if anything, a trifle early. "At midcentury, the new form – innovative, rebellious, surprising, and full of novelty but not yet named 'the novel' – was still searching for a clear identity, terminology, and definition," Paul Hunter argues, "it took almost another half century for a name and a lasting description to stick."[33] It required this to happen for Jane Austen to be able to make her famous defence of novels in *Northanger Abbey*.

What I am particularly uneasy about as far as *The Rise of the Novel* is concerned are the evolutionary overtones which accompany Watt's thesis. Hunter comes uncomfortably close to this when he writes about the new form "searching for a clear identity, terminology, and definition." What we must not forget, above all, is that "the novel" is a construct, not a natural phenomenon. To paraphrase Clifford Geertz, the type of prose fiction called "the novel" is a fiction in another sense: it is "'something made,' 'something fashioned'– the original meaning of *fictiō*."[34] It was made by human beings – by writers, readers, publishers, and critics. Indeed, publishers and critics may have more to do with it than writers. Canon formation appears to have begun in the late eighteenth century with entrepreneurs like Francis Noble and James Harrison. *Ballantyne's Novelist's Library* was particularly influential in this respect. But the decision to exclude Swift and *Gulliver's Travels* from accounts of the making of the early English novel was taken by twentieth-century critics like Ian Watt. It was, I think, a decision based on false premises. In the absence of any convincing way to distinguish the early novel from the romance, or from the "companions" to the novel of which Bakhtin writes, any account of the making of the English novel has also to take into account the contribution of Jonathan Swift.

---

[33]  Hunter, *Before Novels*, p. 22.
[34]  See his *The Interpretation of Cultures: Selected Essays* (New York, 1973), p. 15.

Patrick Reilly
*University of Glasgow*

# Humbling Narcissus: Mirrors in *Gulliver's Travels*

ABSTRACT. Swift's chief source of bewildered outrage was not so much the vile behaviour of the human animal as the fact that men could commit their depravities while continuing to hold the most exalted opinion of themselves. The major, recurring objective in all of Swift's work was to expose and attack human pride, compelling Narcissus to find in the mirror his real, repulsive visage rather than the flattering image of his delusion. In the *Tale*, the narrator refers to satire as "a sort of glass" in which the beholder contrives to see everyone's face but his own. The argument being advanced here is that Swift employs mirror-imagery in the *Travels*, most notably in Books Two and Four, to make inescapable to men the loathsomeness of their moral and physical selves, in the hope of eradicating forever that pride which was, for Swift, the intolerable and unforgivable offence, the sin against the Holy Ghost for which there is no absolution.

"To justify the ways of God to men": so Milton loftily announced his grand design and pursued it, not only in *Paradise Lost*, but in each of the major works of his career. An equally insistent intent can be discerned in the major works of Swift, a programme to humble Narcissus, to scotch the self-infatuation that is man's besetting sin. Both in his own voice and in the ventriloquist utterances of his *personae*, we find the same reiterated complaint: "I never wonder to see Men wicked, but I often wonder to see them not ashamed."[1] A dearth of shame is, for Swift, the cardinal fault; not so much what men do as the self-congratulation with which they do it – this is the real outrage. Men look in the mirror and are, inexplicably, pleased with themselves. Each of us is Narcissus, strangely besotted with the image in the glass. Swift's chief aim is to unnerve Narcissus, inducing disgust where there had previously been enchantment.

Hence the bargain proposed at the close of the *Travels*: keep your vices but renounce your pride:

> My Reconcilement to the *Yahoo*-kind in general might not be so difficult, if they would be content with those Vices and Follies only which Nature hath entitled them to ... But, when I behold a Lump of Deformity, and Diseases both in Body and Mind, smitten with *Pride*, it immediately breaks all the Measures of my Patience: neither shall I be ever able to comprehend how such an Animal and such a Vice could tally together.[2]

Webster's Bosola is similarly baffled:

---

[1]  *Prose Works*, IV, 251.
[2]  *Prose Works*, XI, 296 (IV, xii, 13).

What thing is in this outward form of man
To be belov'd? ...
Man stands amaz'd to see his deformity,
In any other creature but himself.[3]

Gulliver and Bosola alike express their bewildered outrage at the unaccountable union of
vileness and pride: how can a creature so depraved be simultaneously so smug?

Swift's self-imposed task was to bring the culprit to a proper sense of his true condition,
and he knew just how difficult this would be. Narcissus sees only what he wants to see:
"Satyr is a sort of *Glass*, wherein Beholders do generally discover every body's Face but their
Own; which is the chief Reason for that kind of Reception it meets in the World, and that
so very few are offended with it."[4] Swift, intent on offence, accepts the challenge of presenting a glass that will frustrate evasion, compelling the beholder to see himself as he sorrily is
rather than as he narcissistically would have himself be. It will be a glass akin to that before
which Hamlet detains his mother:

Come, come, and sit you down, you shall not budge.
You go not till I set you up a glass
Where you may see the inmost part of you,[5]

or to that toward which O'Brien steers Winston in *Nineteen Eighty-Four* in order to demor-
alize him with the spectacle of his own ruin. Swift's mirror will be equally unforgiving.

There is no mirror-imagery in Books One and Three of the *Travels*. Gulliver is not under
the microscope in Lilliput – his little hosts are; it is only in Brobdingnag that Gulliver retro-
spectively learns that the Lilliputians were as sickened by the sight and smell of him as he
now is by the sight and smell of the giants[6] – Gulliver, as giant, is cheerfully unaware of
giving offence. In Lilliput, his faults are those of the *naïf* or the slow-witted, blundering
giant of fairy-tale, so easily outmanoeuvred by his little opponents who run rings round him.
Gulliver *cannot* look at himself in Lilliput – there is no mirror in which he could possibly do
so. It is precisely because he has no mirror in Lilliput and has, in consequence, lost touch
with his true image that Gulliver exposes himself to our loudest ridicule when he hotly
repudiates the absurd charge of having committed adultery with the Treasurer's wife. The
comedy results from hearing Gulliver idiotically defend himself against an impossible alle-
gation: how can a Man Mountain commit adultery with a six-inch woman even if he wished
to do so? Gulliver is a sexually displaced person in Lilliput. His massive member may be an
object of wonder and admiration to the soldiery marching between his bestrid legs and,
despite strict orders to the contrary, mischievously glancing upwards, but big is useless –
except as an instrument for dousing fires in the royal appartments. In his mind's eye, however, Gulliver has become a Lilliputian, and there is no mirror available to recall him to
himself – hence the ludicrously inappropriate protestations of sexual innocence. Similarly, in
Book Three, Gulliver is the observer rather than the observed, forever remarking others,
never contemplating himself.

---

[3]  John Webster, *The Duchess of Malfi*, ed. Elizabeth M. Brennan, 3rd ed. (London and
     New York, 1993), II, i, 48–49, 53–54 (p. 33).
[4]  *Prose Works*, I, 140.
[5]  *Hamlet*, ed. Harold Jenkins (London and New York, 1982), III, iv, 17–19 (p. 319).
[6]  See *Prose Works*, XI, 91–92 (II, i, 11–12).

In Brobdingnag, by contrast, mirror-imagery is an essential component in the strategy of humiliation pursued by Swift. Gulliver becomes a prime target of the satire as a repulsive little animal, forced by the contemptuous treatment of his captors to recognize himself as such. From the moment the first giant gingerly takes hold of the "small dangerous Animal" he finds in the field,[7] we are launched into a series of unflattering comparisons and associations with moles, rats, frogs, flies, wasps, and monkeys.[8] Gulliver's plight is visually rendered, as when the spiteful dwarf wedges him to the waist in a marrow-bone, thereby making him "a very ridiculous Figure."[9] Sight is all-important in Book Two, with Gulliver being constantly ridiculed not simply for the absurd spectacle he presents, but still more for the foolish posturings in which he indulges. The strutting manikin deserves the derision he attracts; he is a prime example of those whom Swift as satirist made his special prey:

> He spared a hump or crooked nose,
> Whose owners set not up for beaux.
> True genuine dullness moved his pity,
> Unless it offered to be witty.[10]

Gulliver is targeted by Swift, not for being small in stature, but small in mind.

Only once in Book Two does Gulliver succeed in looking into the mirror and smiling at himself, when he and the Giant Queen find amusement in the ridiculous contrast between their reflected forms.[11] Had he consistently possessed this redemptive sense of humour, he might have spared himself a deal of derision throughout his Brobdingnagian experience. But, although ridiculous to others, Gulliver is seldom so to himself. He is always showing off to the giants, always standing on his dignity, defensively reminding the reader that the King of Great Britain, similarly circumstanced, would have had to endure the same humiliations. He continues, embarrassments notwithstanding, to think well of himself; Brobdingnag does not humble Narcissus.

What Brobdingnag consummately does is show the world as ugly, reveal reality as hideous beneath the specious allure of its surface appearance. Gulliver, his senses of sight and smell excruciatingly enhanced by his physical diminution, is exposed to a series of revolting revelations – of giant wens and cancers, of the nauseatingly magnified breast, mottled and pimpled, of the Brobdingnagian wet-nurse, of a decapitated head bouncing thunderously while blood jets upwards like the fountains at Versailles, of lice rooting like pigs in people's clothes, of the "very nauseous Sight" of the Giant Queen (reckoned a somewhat fastidious and "picky" diner among her own folk) devouring her food like an earth-remover.[12] To heighten the disgust, the lynx-eyed Gulliver can plainly see what is so happily denied to the giants – the flies' excrement smeared on the food which the diners are so enjoyably, because unwittingly, cramming into their mouths.[13] It is a strikingly visual exemplification of a key Swiftian theme: the antithesis between cheerful nescience and loathsome knowledge.

---

7  *Prose Works*, XI, 87 (II, i, 6).
8  See *Prose Works*, XI, 117 (II, v, 4); 93 (II, i, 14); 95 (II, ii, 1); 139 (II, viii, 1); 109 (II, iii, 13); 109–10 (II, iii, 14); 121–22 (II, v, 12).
9  *Prose Works*, XI, 108 (II, iii, 12).
10  *Poems*, p. 497, ll. 471–74.
11  See *Prose Works*, XI, 107 (II, iii, 10).
12  See *Prose Works*, XI, 106 (II, iii, 8).
13  See *Prose Works*, XI, 109 (II, iii, 13).

A whole tradition of romantic love-poetry comes to grief in the bedrooms of the Brobdingnagian maids of honour when their brutal impudicity accords Gulliver a privilege for which Brobdingnagian males pine: a full-frontal amplitude of naked female flesh such as even Rubens never risked. Far from being a tempting sight, however, it provokes instead emotions of "Horror and Disgust."[14] These are, interestingly, the identical emotions provoked in Winston Smith as he surveys his own rotting carcass in the mirror, but Gulliver, unlike Winston, is looking at another, recoiling from the world, not the self – *that* recoil still lies in the future.

What Gulliver sees (or fails to see) has long occupied the attention of the critics. Pat Rogers congratulates W. B. Carnochan on being the first to note the symbolic importance of Gulliver's glasses, but then rebukes him for getting it wrong.[15] For Carnochan, Gulliver is the myopic hero whose lack of understanding is symbolized by the weakness of his eyesight.[16] Rogers retorts that the glasses represent visual over-development, hypertrophy of the sight – they are the badge of Gulliver's intrusive, prying nature, his fatal tendency to see too much. Precisely this over-intent scrutiny of what is better left unexamined is the cause of Gulliver's misfortunes; his insatiable desire to *see* the world brings only pain and revulsion.[17] Some may find it a strange view of the *Travels* that its hero would have done better to close his eyes and stay the happy jingoist he was before he went voyaging. But, waiving this larger question, it seems difficult to make the voyage to Brobdingnag serve the thesis of Gulliver as foolish meddler suffering a deservedly nauseating retribution. The gratuitous visit to witness the decapitation apart, Gulliver sees what he cannot avoid seeing – it is not a choice but a fate. The horrors of Europe, in large part avoidable back home, cannot be overlooked when magnified to Brobdingnagian proportions; only blindness could have saved him. Gulliver, held captive by the giantesses and humiliatingly made to serve their prurient antics, is hardly a Peeping Tom getting his come-uppance. He lives and suffers amid gigantic filth, and this would have been the case even had he been the least observant and curious of men.

It is not, of course, that Brobdingnag is different from Britain – Brobdingnag is Britain, enlarged to a point where the horrors customarily concealed or overlooked cannot be avoided. The mirror no longer misleads – we join Gulliver in seeing the world as it truly is. Brobdingnag is a magnifying glass helping us to see Europe aright. It functions as a teaching aid in a moral lesson: the fair breasts of our English beauties, which so arouse and attract us, are every bit as revolting could we but see them in the proper glass. Brobdingnag is such a glass, compelling us to see, magnified, the abominations which we otherwise miss. The glass of everyday life deludes us into seeing the world as fair, woman as beautiful, man as noble; the glass of Brobdingnag shows a very different reflection, and there can be little doubt as to which, for Swift, is the true reflector, which the distorter.

Gulliver not only fails to make the obvious application to Europe; he resists the mirror when it reflects upon himself, or what he continues to cherish. The Giant King's searching questions, following Gulliver's account of affairs back home, function as a kind of mirror,

---

[14] *Prose Works*, XI, 119 (II, v, 7).
[15] See Pat Rogers, "Gulliver's Glasses," *The Art of Jonathan Swift*, ed. Clive T. Probyn (London, 1978), p. 183.
[16] See W. B. Carnochan, *Lemuel Gulliver's Mirror for Man* (Berkeley and Los Angeles, 1968), p. 135.
[17] See Rogers, "Gulliver's Glasses," p. 187.

showing the sordid truth behind the panegyric and propaganda – and this despite Gulliver's admission that he strove to "hide the Frailties and Deformities of my Political Mother, and place her Virtues and Beauties in the most advantageous Light."[18] Gulliver abjectly fails to "sell" Europe to the Giant King, but the very fact that he tries to do so shows how completely he has missed the connection between the physical offensiveness of the maids of honour and the cultural squalor of his "political mother," as well as the nexus between the lice of Brobdingnag and his host's strikingly visual condemnation of European man: "the most pernicious Race of little odious Vermin that Nature ever suffered to crawl upon the Surface of the Earth."[19]

For Gulliver, Brobdingnag remains primarily a mere physical matter of enlarged bodies and magnified ugliness. Returned to normalcy, he views the rescuing sailors as "the most contemptible little Creatures I had ever beheld"[20] (a physical, not a moral judgement), and looks at his countrymen as though they were pygmies, "for such I took them to be, after having so long accustomed mine Eyes to the monstrous Objects I had left"[21] – clearly, this is no more than a tribute to the tyranny of habit.

One physical scale of being has simply been exchanged for another, with little gain in moral insight. Gulliver seems now to have either forgotten or suppressed the salutary, self-deprecatory amusement he once shared with the Giant Queen at the absurd contrast in the mirror. He now tells us that while in Brobdingnag he "could never endure to look in a Glass" because the unflattering contrast between himself and his giant companions "gave me so despicable a Conceit of my self."[22] Narcissus devotes himself to the glass only for as long as it shows him what he wants to see. The lesson is plain: avoid mirrors in Brobdingnag if you would really remain Narcissus.

Book Two ends with Swift's partial victory over Narcissus (total triumph must wait for the close of Book Four) in forcing the self-lover to shun the unflattering mirror. But, Gulliver's resistance notwithstanding, Brobdingnag does establish a link between size and shortcomings: "I winked at my own Littleness, as People do at their own Faults."[23] It is the same talent for evasion that men display when they look into the glass of satire and see somebody else's face. In the last book of the *Travels*, Swift presents a glass that compels men to see their own faces.

Houyhnhnmland teaches Gulliver to know himself, to look in the mirror and confess his own corruption; not just the world is vile – the self is, too. It is the more remarkable that this confession is extorted from a man who begins the voyage as one of humanity's most ardent lovers. From the outset, the problem of Gulliver's identity is paramount. There is a Father Brown story by G. K. Chesterton in which two celebrities in turn look unknowingly into a darkened mirror and fail to recognize their own reflections. Only the modest, unassuming priest succeeds in recognizing himself, and the lesson is obvious: it is the vain, for-ever contemplating themselves who are more at risk of going astray.[24]

---

18  *Prose Works*, XI, 133 (II, vii, 1).
19  *Prose Works*, XI, 132 (II, vi, 18).
20  *Prose Works*, XI, 147 (II, viii, 13).
21  *Prose Works*, XI, 143 (II, viii, 8).
22  *Prose Works*, XI, 147 (II, viii, 13).
23  *Prose Works*, XI, 148 (II, viii, 13).
24  See "The Man in the Passage," *The Father Brown Stories* (London, 1955 [1929]), pp. 207–20.

Soon after arriving in Houyhnhnmland, Gulliver is the object of a visual inspection by Yahoo and Houyhnhnm in quick succession. The Yahoo, Gulliver complacently tells us, "stared as at an Object he had never seen before,"[25] but, with hindsight, we may just as plausibly conclude that what really confounded the Yahoo was the sight of a stranger so similar to himself. That Gulliver, for his part, looks at the Yahoo and fails to see himself simply indicates that he has grown too accustomed to the more flattering image of himself presented in the mirror of Western humanism – the mirror that so gratifyingly assures him that he is the fairest of all. At the onset of his Houyhnhnm adventure, Gulliver finds himself in the same case as Chesterton's self-ignorant celebrities. His detailed description of the newly encountered Yahoos shows him blissfully unaware of any resemblance to himself.[26] Narcissus looks at the Yahoo and sees a creature completely other; the voyage will concern itself with teaching Narcissus to see true.

The horse likewise looks in Gulliver's face "with manifest Tokens of Wonder;"[27] but when the horses talk together, the recurring word that Gulliver hears them use is Yahoo, although he has no idea as to what it means[28] – it is ironic that the first word he speaks in Houyhnhnmland should be an unwitting reference to himself. Back at the Master's house, the mare has no difficulty, Gulliver's clothes notwithstanding, in identifying the stranger – one look is enough to pronounce him Yahoo.[29] Everyone sees the resemblance except himself – exactly as we might expect, given Swift's definition of satire as the glass in which we evade identification.

But even Gulliver, placed alongside the Yahoo in the yard, cannot deny the resemblance.[30] Only the accident of his clothes prevents complete exposure. Naked, he could not escape detection; clothes are his transient refuge. The horses spot the exact congruence of head, hands, and face – those parts that are uncovered and undisguised. Clothes alone – what Lear on the heath spurns as "lendings" – supply a temporary reprieve.

Mirror-imagery intensifies as the voyage heads for its climax. The Houyhnhnm master, having listened to Gulliver's account of Europe, denounces the perversion of reason in man as a mere subaltern to vice – "as the Reflection from a troubled Stream returns the Image of an ill-shapen Body, not only *larger*, but more *distorted*."[31] The allusion signals the increasing importance of water in the novel's economy. Gulliver uses the little brook to wash off the stink of the Yahoo child[32] – a Pilate-like attempt to repudiate kinship – but it is, ironically, in the river that, at last and irrefutably, Gulliver's Yahoo identity is established by the sexual test, when the lovesick female is overwhelmed with desire by the sight of the newcomer's naked body.[33] We desire only what is ours – Gulliver is decidedly no alien. It is an exact reversal of the situation with the Lilliputian lady – Gulliver has at last come sexually home, has found his true mate in this Yahoo Lolita.

25  *Prose Works*, XI, 224 (IV, i, 4).
26  See *Prose Works*, XI, 223–24 (IV, i, 4).
27  *Prose Works*, XI, 224 (IV, i, 5).
28  See *Prose Works*, XI, 226 (IV, i, 9).
29  See *Prose Works*, XI, 229 (IV, ii, 4).
30  See *Prose Works*, XI, 229–30 (IV, ii, 4).
31  *Prose Works*, XI, 248 (IV, v, 8).
32  See *Prose Works*, XI, 266 (IV, viii, 2).
33  See *Prose Works*, XI, 266–67 (IV, viii, 6).

Finally, in that decisive moment toward which the whole book moves, Gulliver looks in the pool (Houyhnhnmland's mirror) and sees staring back the face of the Yahoo. Recognition is at last inescapable: "I turned away my Face in Horror and detestation of my self."[34] The situation is far worse than in Book Two where he averted his gaze so as not to see his own pettiness. Narcissus has become Winston Smith, radically disenchanted, appalled at his true self, gagging at his own corruption. Confronting the bleak certitude of his abandonment, Gulliver becomes the unwitting progenitor of a gallery of moral castaways in the fiction of the twentieth century, from Conrad's Kurtz to Golding's schoolboys. The moment of appalled self-discovery, this dark epiphany, has become almost a trademark of modern literature, and Gulliver, catastrophically encountering himself, is its pioneer.[35]

Again, as in Book Two, sight is the key faculty. It is the sight of his wife and children that fills Gulliver with hatred and disgust[36] – it is the looking that he loathes. Defending his method of writing the *Travels*, Gulliver declares that he has rejected ornament in favour of truth: "I would *strictly adhere to Truth*."[37] It is in line with his new anti-Narcissus choice – no more misleading mirrors or flattering glasses; Narcissus has been reformed.

It seems pointless to talk about a Narcissus who turns away in loathing from his own reflection, since this is precisely what Narcissus did not do.[38] Narcissus in the myth loved himself to the very end, and that self-destructive end was the direct consequence of his inability to break the fetters of self-love. A self-disgusted Narcissus is no Narcissus at all, yet this is surely Gulliver's condition at the close.

Christopher Fox cites in evidence of his Gulliver-Narcissus thesis the story of the young nobleman in the *Memoirs of Scriblerus* diagnosed as being hopelessly in love with himself. The prognosis is pessimistic. If his self-infatuation is not cured, there is every chance that he will "run to the next pond to get rid of himself, the Fate of most violent Self-lovers."[39] Self-love leading to drowning – the allusion to Narcissus, the greatest self-lover of them all, could not be clearer. From Ovid's story of Narcissus to Milton's account of Eve's coming to consciousness in Book Four of *Paradise Lost*, there is a close connection between self-love and water, and so there is an understandable temptation to class Gulliver with these two self-infatuates when we find him, too, looking into a pool. Yet the situation could not be more different. Eve, first becoming aware, hears a sound and follows this to a pool of water, "a liquid plain."[40] She lies down to look into this and is both startled and pleased to see what is, in fact, her own reflection. She would have remained entranced with the delightful image but for God's voice warning her that this is self-infatuation and summoning her to leave the pool and come to "where no shadow stays / Thy coming"[41] – it is Adam, no mere reflection, who awaits her. She obeys reluctantly and, even after seeing Adam, still prefers "that smooth

---

[34] *Prose Works*, XI, 278 (IV, x, 4).

[35] See my *The Literature of Guilt: From "Gulliver" to Golding* (Houndmills and London, 1988), pp. 15–45.

[36] See *Prose Works*, XI, 289 (IV, xi, 17).

[37] *Prose Works*, XI, 292 (IV, xii, 3).

[38] See Christopher Fox, "The Myth of Narcissus in Swift's 'Travels,'" *Eighteenth-Century Studies*, 20 (1986), 27.

[39] Fox, "The Myth of Narcissus," p. 21.

[40] *Paradise Lost*, ed. Alastair Fowler (London and New York, 1971 [1968]), IV, l. 455. All quotations are from this edition.

[41] *Paradise Lost*, IV, ll. 470–71.

watery image,"[42] the reflection in the pool, as more enticing and more beautiful. She turns back toward the pool and is only persuaded to stop by Adam's pursuit and pleadings – only then does she recognize that this is indeed the better choice. This turning away from self to other is an essential stage in the maturation of Eve as mother of mankind; it was Narcissa who preferred to look into the water and dwell, not with Adam, but with her own lovely face.

Gulliver does not look into the pool to contemplate his own beauty. He does not belong in the same company as Narcissus or newly-created Eve or the wicked queen in Snow White – it is to mortify, not to flatter the self, that he consults *his* mirror. He is the antithesis of the young nobleman in Scriblerus who exhibits all the traits of the Narcissus syndrome as listed by Ovid's commentators: *dura superbia*, hostility to others, an aversion to women.[43] The young nobleman dislikes other people because he loves himself. Gulliver, by contrast, loves other people: his wife and children, his native land and fellow-citizens, the whole of mankind. Well into his sojourn in Houyhnhnmland, as he himself tells us, "there were few greater Lovers of Mankind, at that time, than myself."[44] Only after he stops loving himself, ceases to be Narcissus, does he become a hater of his kind. The young nobleman, like Narcissus, is cut off from the world through extravagant self-love; this is assuredly not Gulliver's complaint at the tale's close.

The apparent similarities with Narcissus mask irresolvable differences. In the *Metamorphoses*, Echo sees Narcissus and, inflamed with love, races up to embrace him, only to be repulsed.[45] Again, it is tempting to find here a rehearsal of Gulliver's rejection of the young  love-struck Yahoo female. But the two rebuffs have little in common, the first the product of conceit and self-love, the second of horror and self-loathing. Narcissus knows he is his only lover; Gulliver, appalled, knows that the female Yahoo is his proper mate. It is the same self-disgust that causes him later to lose consciousness when his wife attempts to kiss him, for he believes now that he is a Yahoo who has copulated with a she-Yahoo to produce young Yahoos. Rather than Narcissus, this identifies Gulliver as brother to Winston Smith, set free by the Thought Police but horrified at the very thought of sex with Julia – he could as soon levitate as take her to bed.[46] Such a turning away from sex as we see in Gulliver and Winston may superficially resemble the conduct of Narcissus; closer inspection reveals them as worlds apart.

"Every man is naturally a Narcissus." Fox quotes Glanvill, adding that Swift would surely have agreed.[47] What we must remark is that *Gulliver's Travels* is an exercise in disillusion, an education in disenchantment, with its erstwhile Narcissistic hero taught to see himself in a completely different light by the end of the text. "To love a man, it's necessary that he should be hidden, for as soon as he shows his face, love is gone."[48] Ivan Karamazov is referring to the impossibility of loving one's neighbours. Long before Dostoyevsky, Swift knew

---

[42]  *Paradise Lost*, IV, l. 480.
[43]  See Fox, "The Myth of Narcissus," pp. 22, 23.
[44]  *Prose Works*, XI, 230 (IV, ii, 5).
[45]  See *The Metamorphoses of Ovid*, trans. Mary M. Innes (Harmondsworth, Middlesex, 1961), p. 91.
[46]  See *Nineteen Eighty-Four* (Harmondsworth, Middlesex, 1987), p. 321.
[47]  Fox, "The Myth of Narcissus," p. 32.
[48]  *The Brothers Karamazov*, trans. David Magarshack (Harmondsworth, Middlesex, 1966), p. 276.

that this is equally applicable to love of self. In the *Travels*, Gulliver "shows his face," and the result is as Ivan predicts: love, including self-love, is gone.

Hence the crucial difference between the conclusions of Books Two and Four. Far from avoiding mirrors, Gulliver now regularly has recourse to them as an antidote to pride: "to behold my Figure often in a Glass, and thus if possible habituate my self by Time to tolerate the Sight of a human Creature."[49] How can you look and go on loving? After such knowledge, there is no forgiveness. It was not in such a spirit that Narcissus leaned longingly over the pool to see the beloved reflection in the water. This erstwhile Narcissus now holds a very different valuation of himself and his species. He uses the mirror as a medieval saint might wear a hairshirt or as a self-flagellant wield a whip – as a discipline, a self-mortification. The man who would be a horse looks in the glass to find the lineaments of his Yahoo nature and to forsake forever the dream of Houyhnhnm perfection. He looks to find the confirmation of guilt, not the sycophancy of compliment. It is the triumphant culmination of Swift's satiric art, his overcoming of man's apparently invincible penchant for looking in the mirror and loving what he sees – now Gulliver looks to remind himself of the filth that cannot be transcended.

And so it is consummately appropriate that a text so concerned with mirrors, reflections, perspectives, all that has to do with optics, should end with the word "sight." As always, Swift, using Gulliver as mouthpiece, is attacking pride – in Swift's eyes, there is nothing else to attack. Gulliver simply will not tolerate pride: "Therefore I here intreat those who have any Tincture of this absurd Vice, that they will not presume to appear in my Sight."[50] The greatness of this unrivallable text is underscored in the matchless artistry of its final word.

---

[49] *Prose Works*, XI, 295 (IV, xii, 10).
[50] *Prose Works*, XI, 296 (IV, xii, 13).

Christopher Fox
*University of Notre Dame, Indiana*

# Swift and the Spectacle of Human Science

ABSTRACT. Using as its starting point the examination of Gulliver by the Brobdingnagian virtuosi, this paper explores the wider implications of this scene for the emergence of human science in eighteenth-century Europe. Interesting here in Gulliver's story is the movement from the spectacle of the side-show to the spectacle of science, and the complications Swift's satire suggests for the "birth of the observer."

In Part II of *Gulliver's Travels* (The Voyage to Brobdingnag), we find the sailor and nominal hero, Lemuel Gulliver, stranded in a land populated by immense giants, and eventually brought to their king. Educated in natural philosophy and "particularly Mathematicks," the giant king (Gulliver notes) "observed my Shape exactly," and seeing "me walk erect, before I began to speak, conceived I might be a piece of Clock-work ... contrived by some ingenious Artist." But after Gulliver speaks in a "regular and rational" way, the King is astonished. He asks Gulliver several questions (which receive "rational Answers, no otherwise defective than by a Foreign Accent") and then calls in the scholars. After the scholars "had a while examined my Shape with much Nicety," Gulliver tells us, they

> were of different Opinions concerning me. They all agreed that I could not be produced according to the regular Laws of Nature; because I was not framed with a Capacity of preserving my Life, either by Swiftness, or climbing of Trees, or digging Holes in the Earth. They observed by my Teeth, which they viewed with great Exactness, that I was a carnivorous Animal; yet ... they could not imagine how I should be able to support my self ... which they offered by many learned Arguments to evince that I could not possibly do. One of them seemed to think that I might be an Embrio, or abortive Birth. But this Opinion was rejected by the other two, who observed my Limbs to be perfect and finished; and that I had lived several Years, as it was manifested from my Beard; the Stumps whereof they plainly discovered through a Magnifying-Glass. They would not allow me to be a Dwarf, because my Littleness was beyond all Degrees of Comparison; for the Queen's favourite Dwarf, the smallest ever known in that Kingdom, was near thirty Foot high.

Finally, after much debate, the scholars declare him to be a "*Lusus Naturae*," a freak of nature.[1]

In Swift's satire, this scene and the events surrounding it evoke all kinds of eighteenth-century questions about what it means to turn a human creature (or a creature resembling a

---

[1] See *Prose Works*, XI, 103–4 (II, iii, 5–6). On the general notion of *lusus naturae*, see Paula Findlen, "Jokes of Nature and Jokes of Knowledge: The Playfulness of Scientific Discourse in Early Modern Europe," *Renaissance Quarterly*, 43 (1990), 292–331.

human) into an object of science. How does this creature stand, walk, talk, think, eat, survive? Where does he fit into a known order of nature, a *scala naturae?* How does he compare to other known creatures? Is he subject to natural law? If not, how is this creature to be categorized? How did he get to be this way: by design or by accident? Portraying Gulliver as a little speaking animal also brings up a question raised by Locke's example of the "rational parrot" in *An Essay Concerning Human Understanding.*[2] To what extent is language a constituent of human identity? This would be explored throughout the eighteenth century by such figures as Vico, Rousseau, Monboddo, and Smith. The larger question of language itself propels numerous eighteenth-century attempts to construct a "science of man."

The scene in Swift also suggests ways in which the language of science – and of human science – penetrates the language of literature. The word "Clock-work," for example, in the question of how Gulliver moves, immediately evokes those "automatical men" and mechanical toys that had fascinated Descartes,[3] as well as subsequent debates over human motility and iatromechanical medicine satirized elsewhere by Swift and his friends, John Arbuthnot and Alexander Pope, in their *Memoirs of the Extraordinary Life, Works, and Discoveries of Martinus Scriblerus* (1741). There, we learn about a "great Virtuoso at Nuremberg" who has been employed "to make a sort of an Hydraulic Engine, in which a chemical liquor resembling Blood, is driven through elastic chanels resembling arteries and veins, by the force of an Embolus like the heart, and wrought by a pneumatic Machine of the nature of the lungs, with ropes and pullies, like the nerves, tendons and muscles: And we are persuaded that this our artificial Man will not only walk, and speak, and perform most of the outward actions of the animal life, but (being wound up once a week) will perhaps reason as well as most of your Country Parsons."[4]

The question of whether Gulliver is an "Embrio, or abortive Birth" similarly evokes scientific talk about teratology and embryology (though perhaps a more famous literary preformationist figure would be Laurence Sterne's "little gentleman," Tristram Shandy's *homunculus*).[5] Embryology had occupied such scientists as William Harvey and Marcello Mal-

---

2    2nd ed. (London, 1694), II, xxvii. For Locke's parrot who "spoke, and asked, and answered common Questions like a reasonable Creature," see II, xxvii, § 8 of *An Essay Concerning Human Understanding*, ed. Peter H. Nidditch (Oxford, 1975), pp. 332–33. Lokke found this example in Sir William Temple's *Memoirs*, transcribed by young Jonathan Swift for press. On the larger discussion of human identity, see Christopher Fox, *Locke and the Scriblerians: Identity and Consciousness in Early Eighteenth-Century Britain* (Berkeley, Los Angeles, London, 1988).

3    Descartes speaks of those "clocks, artificial fountains, mills and similar machines which, though made entirely of man, lack not the power to move, of themselves, in various ways;" later, of the water in the king's gardens that "is able of itself to move diverse machines and even to make them play certain instruments or pronounce certain words." See René Descartes, *Treatise of Man*, trans. T. S. Hall (Cambridge, MA, 1972), pp. 4, 21. For eighteenth-century discussion on this point, see especially John W. Yolton, "The Automatical Man," *Thinking Matter: Materialism in Eighteenth-Century Britain* (Minneapolis, MN, 1983), pp. 29–48. Elsewhere, Douglas Patey has called attention to possible connections of this passage to physico-theology in "Swift's Satire on 'Science' and the Structure of *Gulliver's Travels*," *English Literary History*, 58 (1991), 809–33, especially p. 828.

4    Jonathan Swift, John Arbuthnot, Alexander Pope, *et al., Memoirs of the Extraordinary Life, Works, and Discoveries of Martinus Scriblerus*, ed. Charles Kerby-Miller (New York and Oxford, 1988 [1950]), p. 141. The Nuremberg virtuoso may be a reference to the medical authority, Friedrich Hoffman (1660–1742).

5    See Laurence Sterne, *The Life and Opinions of Tristram Shandy, Gentleman*, ed. Graham Petrie (Harmondsworth, Middlesex, 1986 [1967]), p. 36.

pighi in the seventeenth century; in the eighteenth it would be vigorously pursued by Need-ham, Spallanzani, Bonnet, and Albrecht von Haller, among others.[6] Johann Friedrich Blu-menbach, for instance, would rely on the study to deflate the belief that the Ethiopian's depressed nose comes from the mother's method of carrying the child. That this results from nature and not art is shown, he says, by "the two Ethiopian foetuses preserved in the Royal Museum."[7] From the Renaissance on, teratology or "the study of monstrous living forms"[8] had increasingly interested such medicos as Fortunio Liceti, whose *Of Monsters* (1616) would be translated and updated by a French physician in 1708. In the *New Organon*, Fran-cis Bacon had called for the need to collect natural histories of "all monsters and prodigious births of nature;" by the eighteenth century, such investigations had become part of the normal study of anatomy and embryology, and viewed as the "key to understanding more regular phenomena."[9] The *Philosophical Transactions* of the Royal Society are filled with reports of anomalies like the Norfolk pigmy, John Coan, scrupulously weighed and measured by William Arderon on 3 April 1750.[10] Such pursuits did not escape satirists of the time. In *Tom Jones* (1749), Henry Fielding would complain that natural philosophy knows "nothing of Nature, except her monsters and imperfections" (XIII, v). In search of "the Curiosities of Nature," Swift's fictional scholar, Dr Martinus Scriblerus, becomes obsessed with and mar-ries a set of beautiful Siamese twins, described as "a Master-piece ... for none but a Philo-sopher."[11]

Not unlike those fantastic others who populated the pages of classical natural history and Renaissance cosmography[12] or the margins of maps, Gulliver fits no known Brobdingnagian category. It is as a sport of nature, a *homo monstrosus*, that he first attracts the court's attention. Before he is scrutinized by the scientists, Gulliver was discovered and exhibited by an enterprising farmer turned monster-monger. Being "carried about" and "exposed for

6   On embryology, see especially Shirley A. Roe, *Matter, Life, and Generation: Eighteenth-Century Embryology and the Haller-Wolff Debate* (Cambridge, MA, 1984); and Jacques Ro-ger, *Les sciences de la vie dans la pensée française du XVIIIᵉ siècle*, 2nd ed. (Paris, 1971).

7   "On the Natural Varieties of Mankind (1775)," *The Anthropological Treatises of Johann Friedrich Blumenbach*, trans. Thomas Bendyshe (London, 1865), p. 123.

8   See Annemarie de Waal Malefijt, "Homo Monstrosus," *Scientific American*, 219 (1968), 112–18, especially p. 118. Ambroise Paré's work on the subject was titled *Des monstres et prodigies* (1573). The secondary literature on literary monsters has grown of late. See, for instance, Rudolf Wittkower, "Marvels of the East: A Study in the History of Monsters," *Journal of the Warburg and Courtauld Institutes*, 5 (1992), 159–97. There is also a good deal of valuable material, both primary and secondary, in Dirk F. Paßmann, *"Full of Improbable Lies": "Gulliver's Travels" und die Reiseliteratur vor 1726* (Frankfurt/M., 1987). See espe-cially the fine book by Dennis Todd, *Imagining Monsters: Miscreations of the Self in Eight-eenth-Century England* (Chicago, 1995).

9   See Francis Bacon, *New Organon*, 3 vols (London, 1620), II, 29; see also Katharine Park and Lorraine J. Daston, "Unnatural Conceptions: The Study of Monsters in Sixteenth- and Seventeenth-Century France and England," *Past and Present*, 92 (1981), 20–54, espe-cially pp. 23, 25.

10  At 16 years of age, Coan stood 36 inches and weighed 27½ pounds. See David Erskine Baker, *"Extract of Letter from Mr.* William Arderon, F.R.S. *to Mr.* Henry Baker, F.R.S. *containing an Account of a* Dwarf; *together with a Comparison of his Dimensions with those of a Child under four Years old,"* *Philosophical Transactions*, 46 (1749–50), 467–70.

11  *Memoirs of Martinus Scriblerus*, ed. Kerby-Miller, pp. 144, 149.

12  See Margaret T. Hodgen, *Early Anthropology in the Sixteenth and Seventeenth Centuries* (Philadelphia, PA, 1964), pp. 127–28.

Money as a publick Spectacle" ruined Gulliver's health. In a few short weeks, the numerous performances (he says) nearly reduced him "to a Skeleton."[13] Having Gulliver transported in a box – much the way the German "Dwarf of the World" was in eighteenth-century London – plays off the popular rage for human oddities.[14] In Swift's century, argues one historian, the "taste for Monsters became a disease."[15] Whether or not this is true, the eighteenth century was certainly a time when man made a spectacle of himself. In early eighteenth-century London alone, along with the Dwarf of the World who arrived by request "in a little box," one could see the Painted Prince, in whom "the whole Mystery of Painting or Staining upon Human Bodies seem[s] to be comprised in one stately piece;" or, for more limited engagements during the weeks of Bartholomew Fair, that "Admirable Work of Nature, A Woman having Three Breasts; and each of them affording Milk at one time, or differently ... as they are made use of."[16]

Interesting here in Gulliver's story is the movement from the spectacle of the side-show to the spectacle of science – a pattern often repeated by actual eighteenth-century figures, such as the Norfolk pigmy, discovered on display in Norwich, or Hopkin Hopkins, the thirty-one-inch fifteen-year-old found on exhibition near Bristol in 1751 and reported in the *Philosophical Transactions* to be "*wonderful in the sight of all beholders.*"[17] A later and more dramatic case was that of the Irishman Charles Byrne, who suffered from acromegaly, or uncontrollable growth. After arriving in London in April 1782, he was advertised as the

> *Irish Giant.* To be seen this, and every day this week, in his large elegant room, at the cane shop, next door to late Cox's Museum, Spring Gardens. Mr. Byrne, the surprising Irish Giant, who is allowed to be the tallest man in the world; only 21 years of age. His stay will not be long in London, as he proposes shortly to visit the Continent ... Hours of admittance every day, Sundays excepted, from 11 till 3; and from 5 till 8, at half-a-crown each person.[18]

Despite Byrne's precautions to avoid such a fate, on his untimely death the hungry surgeons (so a report ran) "surrounded his house just as Greenland harpooners would an enormous whale."[19] Ironically, Byrne's performing days in London were not over. He reappears in a nineteenth-century catalogue of the Hunterian Museum, as

---

[13] See *Prose Works*, XI, 97, 96 (II, ii, 2); 101 (II, iii, 1). For Swift's connection with such shows, see especially Aline Mackenzie Taylor, "Sights and Monsters and Gulliver's 'Voyage to Brobdingnag,'" *Tulane Studies in English*, 7 (1957), 29–82; also Dennis Todd, "The Hairy Maid at the Harpsichord: Some Speculations on the Meaning of 'Gulliver's Travels,'" *Texas Studies in Literature and Language*, 34 (1992), 239–83.

[14] Another famous midget, John Wormberg, drowned in such a box in 1695. See Taylor, "Sights and Monsters," p. 58. For a more recent exploration of the eighteenth-century fascination with "monsters," see Barbara Maria Stafford, *Body Criticism: Imagining the Unseen in Enlightenment Art and Medicine* (Cambridge, MA, 1991), especially p. 38.

[15] Henry Morley, *Memoirs of Bartholomew Fair* (London, 1874), p. 246. See also Michael V. DePorte, *Nightmares and Hobbyhorses* (San Marino, CA, 1974), pp. 3–12.

[16] See Morley, *Memoirs*, pp. 251, 249, 255.

[17] See "*Extract of a Letter from* John Browning, Esq; of Barton-Hill near Bristol, *to* Mr. Henry Baker, F.R.S. concerning a Dwarf," *Philosophical Transactions*, 47 (1751–52), 278–81. The same volume of the *Philosophical Transactions* contains "An Account of a double Child, communicated to the Right Honourable the Lord Willoughby, of Parham, F.R.S. by Thomas Percival, Esquire." See pp. 360–62.

[18] Jessie Dobson, *John Hunter* (Edinburgh and London, 1969), p. 263.

[19] See Colin Clair, *Human Curiosities* (London, 1968), p. 32.

No. 1. The skeleton of Charles Byrne or O'Brian ... 'the famous Irish Giant, whose death is said to have been precipitated by excessive drinking. In August 1780 he measured eight feet.' This skeleton measures eight feet in height.[20]

Gulliver's complaint about being reduced to a skeleton was close to truth for some eighteenth-century "monsters."

Gulliver in Brobdingnag is not only strange because of his size; he also speaks with a "Foreign Accent"[21] and comes from parts unknown. This suggests a related point about the eighteenth-century presentation of human spectacles. Freaks and exotics often shared the same stage. At Bartholomew Fair, for example, one could see "A Prodigious Monster ... a Man with one Head and two distinct Bodies, both masculine," and "with him his Brother, who is a Priest of the Mahometan Religion."[22] The "discoveries that have been made by European navigators upon distant oceans and along distant coasts," Schiller would later say, "afford us a spectacle as instructive as it is entertaining."[23] Many exotics, from North American Indians to South Sea islanders, literally entertained audiences of the time.

William Dampier would bring the islander, Jeoly, from the southern Philippines to England in 1691. With his body painted in ornamental fashion "all down the breasts," on "his thighs," and in "several broad rings, or bracelets round his arms and legs," Jeoly would be shown in various side-shows before he died of smallpox at Oxford.[24] Years later, in the summer of 1762, three Cherokee chiefs from the Carolina-Tennessee mountains would be shipped to London by the Indian fighters, Henry Timberlake and Thomas Sumter, and subsequently shown in a pub that advertised "*Walk in, Gentlemen, see 'em alive!*" The *London Chronicle* lamented the Cherokees' reception at Vauxhall, asking

> What ... can apologize for people running in such shoals to all public places, at the hazard of health, life, or disappointment, to see the savage chiefs that are come among us? ... These poor creatures make no more than theatrical figures, and can be seen with no satisfaction from the pressure of a throng: why then are people mad in their avidity to behold them? ... to read in the papers, how these poor wild hunters were surrounded by as [many] wild gazers on them at Vauxhall, and that three hundred eager crouders were made happy by shaking hands with them ... I should like to read a letter (if they could write one) on that subject, to their friends at home, in order to learn what they think of the mad savages of Great Britain.[25]

The stage metaphor implied in these examples is not new, of course. The connection between theatre and display of the body had roots in the elaborate ritual attending medieval and Renaissance dissections, which seem to have been understood as a form of performance or entertainment. This element was heightened by the virtuosity of Vesalius[26] and, later, by

[20] *Synopsis of the Arrangement of the Preparations in the Museum of the Royal College of Surgeons of England* (London, 1845), p. 17.

[21] *Prose Works*, XI, 103 (II, iii, 5).

[22] Morley, *Memoirs*, p. 254.

[23] Friedrich v. Schiller, quoted in J. S. Slotkin, ed., *Readings in Early Anthropology* (Chicago, 1965), p. 384.

[24] See P. J. Marshall and Glyndwr Williams, *The Great Map of Mankind: Perceptions of New Worlds in the Age of Enlightenment* (Cambridge, MA, 1982), pp. 38–39.

[25] Richard D. Altick, *The Shows of London* (Cambridge, MA, and London, 1978), p. 47.

[26] "In the 1530s and 1540s," writes Luke Wilson, "Vesalius began a trend in which the anatomist seems to have become a central performer on the stage of the theater." The "dissection was understood as an entertainment or performance, an enactment whose significance went beyond the medical and forensic contexts from which it had evolved." See

such developments as the construction of the spectacular anatomy theatre at Leiden (1591)[27] and the appearance of various *Kunstkammern*, or cabinets of curiosities, like that in the Great Chamber at Delft. Here, the Surgeons' Guild displayed such marvels as "a baby's body preserved in alcohol," "hermaphrodites, bearded women, strange tumours and diseases," along with the skeleton of a murderer who served as a mannikin for American Indian feather work.[28] In Oxford in the seventeenth century, there was also an exhibit of anatomical specimens on the first floor of the south side of the Bodleian.[29]

Much of this carried over into the eighteenth century, including the interest in the drama of public dissection, still vivid in William Hogarth's "The Reward of Cruelty," exposing executed Tom Nero's fate under the knife at Surgeons' Hall. But there were also significant shifts of emphasis. Among these was the appearance of new exhibits that put more attention on the human place in nature, and on what Buffon came to call "the natural history of man."[30] The great seventeenth-century "collectors," said Blumenbach, had "embraced the history of all the three animal kingdoms; everything in fact, with the single and solitary exception of the natural history of man." It has been left to the eighteenth century to learn "that man also is a natural product."[31] That "MAN" is, as Adam Ferguson states, "an animal in the full extent of that designation"[32] was dramatically demonstrated by the growing inclusion of human artifacts and remains in various natural-history collections, the best known of which perhaps were those of Blumenbach and Camper on the Continent, and Brookes and Hunter in Britain. Like the British Museum (founded 1753) and the later Louvre (1793),[33] such collections were stocked by colonial expansion and the great voyages of dis-

---

"William Harvey's *Prelectiones*: The Performance of the Body in the Renaissance Theater of Anatomy," *Representations*, 17 (1987), 62–95, especially p. 69.

[27] On the extraordinary *Kabinet van Anatomie en Rariteiten* at Leiden, see Arthur MacGregor, "Collectors and Collections of Rarities in the Sixteenth and Seventeenth Centuries," *Tradescant's Rarities: Essays on the Foundation of the Ashmolean Museum 1683, with a Catalogue of the Surviving Early Collections*, ed. A. MacGregor (Oxford, 1983), pp. 78–79.

[28] See William Schupbach, "Some Cabinets of Curiosities in European Academic Institutions," *The Origins of Museums: The Cabinet of Curiosities in Sixteenth- and Seventeenth-Century Europe*, eds Oliver Impey and Arthur MacGregor (Oxford, 1985), pp. 172–73. In England, of course, one would also find John Woodward's famous cabinet of curiosities, which all Continental travellers made an effort to see; see Andreas Selling, *Deutsche Gelehrtenreisen nach England, 1660–1714* (Frankfurt/M., 1990), pp. 184–96, and Joseph Levine's *Dr Woodward's Shield: History, Science, and Satire in Augustan England* (Berkeley, CA, 1977).

[29] See Hodgen, *Early Anthropology*, pp. 114–15. Swift seems to have had an interest in anatomy. His library contained a copy of Nathaniel Highmore's *Corporis humani disquisitio anatomica* (The Hague, 1651). See William LeFanu, *A Catalogue of Books belonging to Dr Jonathan Swift, Dean of St Patrick's, Dublin, Aug. 19. 1715* (Cambridge, 1988), p. 20. I thank Dr Hermann Real for bringing this to my attention.

[30] See "The Natural History of Man," *Natural History, General and Particular, by the Count de Buffon*, trans. William Smellie, 20 vols (London, 1812), III, 95–446. For a recent excellent exposition of the term, see P. B. Wood, "The Natural History of Man in the Scottish Enlightenment," *History of Science*, 28 (1990), 89–123.

[31] See Blumenbach, "Contributions to Natural History, Part I," *The Anthropological Treatises*, pp. 299, 298.

[32] See *An Essay on the History of Civil Society* (Edinburgh, 1767), p. 69.

[33] Amy Boesky argues more strongly for a real continuity between the earlier wonder cabinets and eighteenth-century museums. See her "'Outlandish Fruits': Commissioning Nature for the Museum of Man," *English Literary History*, 58 (1991), 305–30, especially p. 307.

covery, especially into the eighteenth century's "new world," the Pacific.[34] With the improved navigational equipment of such instrument-makers as John Hadley (who died in 1744) and Jesse Ramsden (who died in 1800),[35] explorers visited and revisited exotic lands, returning with riches and rarities and "ever-increasing numbers of ethnographic specimens." As one recent commentator notes, "in the eighteenth century the *Kunstkammer*" in a sense "exploded so that instead of a collection including one or two amber bottles," a whole room would be filled with them.[36]

The collecting of human remains also picked up considerably in the latter part of the century, especially in the wake of the voyages of Captain James Cook (1768–1779). According to Georges Cuvier at the end of the century, however, this important work still lagged behind. In a memoir prepared for the Baudin Australian expedition (1800–1804), Cuvier would call for a search for savage skeletons. Every opportunity should be taken, he said, to bring the bones home. Once obtained, through (or by observing) battles with native peoples or by visiting "the places where the dead are deposited," preparing specimens for a trip to Europe would be easy. "To boil the bones in a solution of caustic potash and rid them of their flesh is a matter of several hours." It would also be advisable to save some heads with flesh intact. One had only to dip them in a solution of corrosive sublimate, and hang them out to dry.[37] Such head hunting had gone on for some time. In a collection he liked to call his "Golgotha,"[38] Blumenbach displayed in the late eighteenth century "the head of a Carib chief, who died at St. Vincent eight years ago, and whose bones, at the request of [Sir Joseph] Banks, were dug up there" during a voyage of Cook. In a prefatory letter to the third edition of *On the Natural Varieties of Mankind* (1795), Blumenbach would tell Banks: "For many years past you have spared neither pains nor expense to enrich my collection of the skulls of different nations with those specimens I was so anxious above all to obtain."[39]

One wonders about the natives' response to such activities. A gauge might be the reaction of Eskimos who came from Labrador to London in the 1770s. Rattled by the sight of skeletons in Dr John Hunter's Museum, one asked: "Are these the bones of Esquimaux whom Mr. Hunter has killed and eaten? ... Are we to be killed? Will he eat us, and put our bones there?"[40] Though such fears were laid to rest, they were in some sense justified. Blumenbach would later speak of those "wonderfully worn teeth in two Esquimaux skulls which have lately come to me," and list, among his ethnological rarities, "Ettuiack, an Esquimaux magician; brought to London in 1773 from the coast of Labrador."[41]

[34]  See especially Alan Frost, "The Pacific Ocean: The Eighteenth Century's New World," *Studies on Voltaire and the Eighteenth Century*, 152 (1976), 779–822.
[35]  See J. C. Beaglehole, "Eighteenth-Century Science and Voyages of Discovery," *New Zealand Journal of History*, 3 (1969), 107–23, especially p. 115.
[36]  See J. C. H. King, "North American Ethnography in the Collection of Sir Hans Sloane," *The Origins of Museums*, eds Impey and MacGregor, p. 236.
[37]  See George W. Stocking, *Race, Culture, and Evolution: Essays in the History of Anthropology* (New York, 1968), p. 30.
[38]  See Karl Marx, "Life of Blumenbach," *The Anthropological Treatises of Johann Friedrich Blumenbach*, p. 8: "Blumenbach used to call it his 'Golgotha,' and though they do not often go to a place of skulls, still the curious and inquisitive of both sexes came there to wonder and reflect."
[39]  See *The Anthropological Treatises*, pp. 162, 149.
[40]  See Altick, *Shows of London*, p. 48.
[41]  See "On the Natural Varieties of Mankind (1795)," *The Anthropological Treatises*, pp. 245, 161.

For the European scientists, such collecting was, of course, a prerequisite for systematic comparison and classification. An eighteenth-century Englishman would speak admiringly of Hunter's heads, which were

> placed upon a table in a regular series, first shewing the human skull, with its varieties, in the European, the Asiatic, the American, the African; then proceeding to the skull of a monkey, and so on to that of a dog; in order to demonstrate the gradation both in the skulls, and in the upper and lower jaws. On viewing this range, the steps were so exceedingly gradual and regular that it could not be said that the first differed from the second more than the second from the third, and so on to the end.[42]

Before John Hunter's museum, William Blizard would say in 1823, such collections had been simple "Gazing Stocks, for Admiration." After, another would add, the natural-history exhibit was no longer "a mere cabinet of rarities" but "a systematic and illuminated record of the operations and products of life."[43]

This does not downplay the performative aspect of such displays. John Hunter began his collection in the 1770s in his Jermyn Street residence and, when it outgrew his house, moved the exhibit to 28 Leicester Square. Shown periodically to visiting scientists and distinguished guests, the exhibit would end up on permanent view in the Royal College of Surgeons, where it would attract a reported 32,208 visitors between 1800 and 1833.[44] Blumenbach, whose own collection of skulls in his estimate surpassed those of Petrus Camper (the father of the facial angle) and of John Hunter, spoke of the spectacular force of human rarities. A "most beautiful skull of a Georgian female" seems to have been a prized possession. Fair even in death, this "beautiful typical head of a young Georgian female," Blumenbach said, "always of itself attracts every eye, however little observant."[45] Along with these exhibits, smaller ones proliferated, like that of Charles White of Manchester, the author of *An Account of the Regular Gradation in Man* (1799). "Mr. White's museum," said Thomas De Quincey, "furnished attractions to an unusually large variety of tastes." De Quincey, who visited White's exhibits as a child, would later regret that "nothing except the *humanities* of the collection" survived – one a skeleton, the other a modern mummy, of a former patient of White's who reportedly left him £25,000. She did so on the condition that he would embalm her "as perfectly as the resources in that art of London and Paris could accomplish" and that, annually in front of witnesses, he would lift the veil from her face. "The lady," said De Quincey, "was placed in a common English clock-case, having the usual glass face; but a veil of white velvet obscured from all profane eyes the silent features behind. The clock I had myself seen, when a child, and had gazed upon it with inexpressible awe."[46]

When Volney called in the 1790s for the establishment of a museum that would truly

---

[42] Charles White, *An Account of the Regular Graduation in Man, and in Different Animals and Vegetables, and from the Former to the Latter* (London, 1799), p. 41.

[43] See William Blizard, *The Hunterian Oration* (London, 1823), pp. 13–14; and Thomas Chevalier, *The Hunterian Oration Delivered before the Royal College of Surgeons* (London, 1823), p. 34. See also L. S. Jacyna, "Images of John Hunter in the Nineteenth Century," *History of Science*, 21 (1983), 85–108, especially p. 93.

[44] See Altick, *Shows of London*, p. 28; and George Quist, *John Hunter, 1728–1793* (London, 1981), p. 72.

[45] See *The Anthropological Treatises*, pp. 155, 237, 300.

[46] See *The Collected Writings of Thomas De Quincey*, ed. David Masson, 14 vols (London, 1896–97), I, 387–88.

represent the "science of man,"[47] his suggestion had been prepared for by a series of eighteenth-century exhibits. The involvement of the spectator connects these eighteenth-century productions with the larger "practice of public display" which has been found to mark natural philosophy of the time.[48]

Other spectacles were available to more exclusive audiences. Among these were the live specimens shown in "the laboratory of polite society"[49] or to more specialized individuals and groups, such as the Society for the Observation of Man. The first category would include the parade of feral children who marched in and out of attention – Wild Peter of Hanover, sent to Dr John Arbuthnot for study, the Wild Girl of Champagne, the Wild Boy of Aveyron entrusted to Dr Itard, and others.[50] This group would also take in the long line of exotics – Bougainville's Ahutoru, Furneaux's Omai, Banks's Tupaia – brought back for European view. When Banks left Tahiti with his very own Tahitian, the plan was to keep him as a curiosity, the way (said Banks) "some of my neighbors do lions and tygers," though "at greater expense than he will probably ever put me to."[51] When Duke Frederick built an oriental village (with gardens and pagodas) in Germany, he planned a grander display, to be completed by the insertion of live Chinese. When none could be found, he settled a group of Africans there instead, to study "their customs and anatomy." Most died, at least one committing suicide. The anatomist Samuel Thomas von Soemmerring dissected several and wrote a basic book on African physique.[52] In France, L.-F. Jauffret's Society for the Observation of Man (founded in late 1799) had better luck locating an actual Chinese, when the Cantonese Tchong-A-Sam was taken off an English ship and brought to Paris. Tchong-A-Sam was examined by Cuvier to ascertain race and nationality. His skull was measured to Blumenbach's classifications. His face was sketched for J.-J. Virey's *Histoire naturelle*. His reactions were monitored as he was handed various objects and instructed to put on (what were believed to be) Chinese clothes. He was studied intensely by the director of the Institute for the Deaf-Mute. Tchong-A-Sam also managed to escape.[53]

---

47  See Constantin François Volney, *A New Translation of Volney's Ruins*, 2 vols (New York and London, 1979 [1802]), I, 171–72.

48  See Simon Schaffer, "Natural Philosophy and Public Spectacle in the Eighteenth Century," *History of Science*, 21 (1983), 1–43, especially p. 1.

49  See Roy Porter, *The Enlightenment* (Atlantic Highlands, NJ, 1990), p. 18.

50  For connections between the "wild child" and the history of human science in the eighteenth century, see especially David E. Leary, "Nature, Art, and Imitation: The Wild Boy of Aveyron as a Pivotal Case in the History of Psychology," *Studies in Eighteenth-Century Culture*, 13 (1984), 155–72. See also Roger Shattuck, *The Forbidden Experiment: The Story of the Wild Boy of Aveyron* (New York, 1980), and Harlan Lane, *The Wild Boy of Aveyron* (Cambridge, MA, 1976). On Wild Peter of Hanover, seen by Swift in April 1726, see Maximillian E. Novak, "The Wild Man Comes to Tea," *The Wild Man Within: An Image in Western Thought from the Renaissance to Romanticism*, eds Edward Dudley and Maximillian E. Novak (Pittsburgh, 1972), pp. 183–221. On the Wild Girl of Champagne, see the fascinating study by Julia Douthwaite, "Rewriting the Savage: The Extraordinary Fictions of the 'Wild Girl of Champagne,'" *Eighteenth-Century Studies*, 28 (1994–95), 163–92.

51  See Sir Joseph Banks, *The Endeavour Journal of Joseph Banks, 1768–1771* (Sydney, 1962), pp. 312–13.

52  See Londa Schiebinger, "The Anatomy of Difference: Race and Sex in Eighteenth-Century Science," *Eighteenth-Century Studies*, 23 (1990), 387–405, especially p. 387.

53  On Tchong-A-Sam, see Sergio Moravia, *La scienza dell'uomo nel settecento* (Bari, 1970), pp. 112–17. For other comments, see also George W. Stocking, Jr, "French Anthropology in 1800," *Isis*, 55 (1964), 134–50, especially p. 134.

If Tchong-A-Sam's experience highlights the eighteenth-century interest in human spectacle, it also returns us to our originating scene in Swift, and points to some larger issues. Not the least of these pertains to the "birth of the observer." The Brobdingnagians, we recall, do not simply look at Gulliver; they stare at him.[54] Even after being removed from the public eye, Gulliver is "observed" by the King, then handed over to the scholars who "examined" his shape "with much Nicety," "observed" his teeth (which are "viewed with great Exactness"), "observed" his limbs, and finally put him under "a Magnifying-Glass."[55] The operative verb here is obvious. Gulliver is under the gaze.

But it is not that simple, for Gulliver is gazing back. In his minute view of such objects as Brobdingnagian breasts, Gulliver indeed becomes a kind of human microscope, detailing the coarseness and dark patches of skin in graphic ways that parody descriptions in works such as Hooke's *Micrographia* and the *Philosophical Transactions*.[56] Like any scientifically literate sailor, Gulliver also manages to return from Brobdingnag with his own "Collection of Rarities" (mostly anatomical).[57] And he later publishes an account of the Brobdingnagian land and people as part of his larger book subtitled *Travels into Several Remote Nations of the World*. (As one scholar quips, "No fellow of the Royal Society could do more."[58]) Gulliver celebrates modern ways of knowing – including the modern love of quantification – and criticizes the Brobdingnagians for "not having hitherto reduced *Politicks* into a *Science*, as the more acute Wits of *Europe* have done."[59] Along with being observed, Gulliver, then, is also an observer, in a self-consciously scientific sense.[60]

---

[54] On this point, see John F. Sena, "*Gulliver's Travels* and the Genre of the Illustrated Book," *The Genres of "Gulliver's Travels,"* ed. Frederik N. Smith (Newark, London, Toronto, 1990), pp. 109-10.

[55] See *Prose Works*, XI, 103–4 (II, iii, 5–6).

[56] See Frederik N. Smith, "Scientific Discourse: *Gulliver's Travels* and *The Philosophical Transactions*," *The Genres of "Gulliver's Travels,"* ed. Smith, pp. 139–62, especially pp. 141–42.

[57] See *Prose Works*, XI, 146 (II, viii, 10). Still helpful here are the chapters on "The Traveller and The Scientific Approach," in R. W. Frantz, *The English Traveller and the Movement of Ideas, 1660–1732* (New York, 1968 [1934]), pp. 15–71.

[58] See David Oakleaf, "*Trompe l'Oeil*: Gulliver and the Distortions of the Observing Eye," *University of Toronto Quarterly*, 53 (1983–84), 166–80, especially p. 166.

[59] *Prose Works*, XI, 135 (II, vii, 5). Gulliver's emphasis on "first-hand experience" and "the production of knowledge acquired in a rigorously empirical way" points to a distinctly "modern" sensibility, parodied by Swift. On such attributes of the enlightened traveller, see the introduction to *The Enlightenment and its Shadows*, eds Peter Hulme and Ludmilla Jordanova (London and New York, 1990), p. 12. The ancients guess, the moderns count, argued Samuel Johnson. Like another Swift figure, the modest proposer, Gulliver likes to count. For a recent exploration of eighteenth-century social science in the light of the new stress on quantification, see Karin Johannisson, "Society in Numbers: The Debate over Quantification in 18th-Century Political Economy," *The Quantifying Spirit in the 18th Century*, eds Tore Frängsmyr, J. L. Heilbron, and Robin E. Rider (Berkeley and Los Angeles, 1990), pp. 343–61. Johannisson reminds us (p. 344n) that the word "statistics" was used for the first time in England in the 1770s. See also Peter Buck, "People Who Counted: Political Arithmetic in the Eighteenth Century," *Isis*, 73 (1982), 28–45.

[60] The word "observation" (in various forms) occurs 140 times in *Gulliver's Travels*. On this point, see Pat Rogers, "Gulliver's Glasses," *The Art of Jonathan Swift*, ed. Clive T. Probyn (London, 1978), pp. 179–88, especially p. 184.

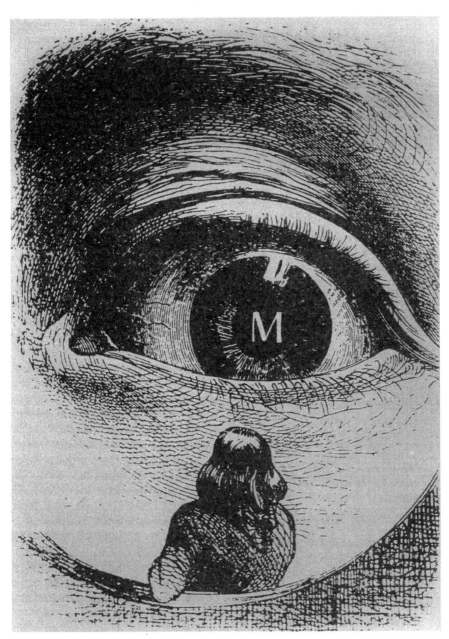

Figure 1: Grandville (Jean Ignace Isidore Gérard), for *Gulliver's Travels* (1838).
Courtesy of the University of Notre Dame Library

The complications of this relation are captured nicely in a nineteenth-century illustration by J. J. Grandville[61] which shows Gulliver observing and simultaneously being observed by a great Brobdingnagian eye. In this illustration (Figure 1), both spectators are so close that it is hard to see how either can get a clear view of the other. Gulliver's position, resting an elbow on a rounded ledge, makes him almost appear to be *inside* the giant eye. Gulliver cannot remove himself from what he sees. Though what he sees – that sharp "M" in the gigantic lens – appears to be clear and distinct, what it means is far from clear and distinct. What we have here is the illusion of clarity, the fiction of some objective truth. The "loss of the detached spectator 'out there'"[62] has been a recent theme in the history of the human sciences (especially since Foucault's analysis in *The Order of Things*), as has the question of how one "can be both an object in the world and a subject constituting that world."[63] In Swift's satire, we find a similar questioning of the very possibility of a detached point of view.

The Brobdingnagians' view of Gulliver raises other issues, among these, questions about the uses of comparison. Comparison, of course, is central to *Gulliver's Travels*. As Samuel Johnson would comment, one only had to imagine the big people and the little people, and the rest of Swift's work would follow.[64] Yet, it is the failure to find such grounds that frustrates the Brobdingnagian scientists. Gulliver's littleness is "beyond all Degrees of Comparison."[65] Establishing clear criteria for comparison was a key question in human science. "Not until the late seventeenth and early eighteenth centuries," we learn, for instance, "did comparison become, instead of an ... accessory to anatomy, the primary aim of the science."[66] The comparison of humans with other primates in such works as Edward Tyson's *Anatomie of a Pygmie* (1699) and Petrus Camper's *Account of the Organs of Speech in the Orang-Outang* (1779)[67] was increasingly matched by comparisons *within* the human group itself – between different races, cultures, and sexes.

The last is suggested by the title alone of Moreau's 1750 work, *A Medical Question: Whether apart from Genitalia There is a Difference between the Sexes?* (1750). Moreau and others sparked a movement in the second half of the century to establish comparative differences between men and women that go well beyond their respective modes of reproduction.[68] Sexual difference also played a part in eighteenth-century discussions of cultural dif-

---

[61]   The illustrations of J. J. Grandville (1838) are discussed by David S. Lenfest, "Grandville's Gulliver," *Satire Newsletter*, 10 (1972–73), 12–24, and by Sena (see n. 54).

[62]   The language is from Gillian Beer's "Science and Literature," *Companion to the History of Modern Science*, eds R. C. Olby *et al.* (New York and London, 1990), p. 785.

[63]   See Gary Gutting, *Michel Foucault's Archeology of Scientific Reason* (Cambridge, 1989), p. 212.

[64]   See James Boswell, *Life of Johnson*, ed. George Birkbeck Hill, rev. L. F. Powell, 6 vols (Oxford, 1971 [1934–50]), II, 319.

[65]   *Prose Works*, XI, 104 (II, iii, 6).

[66]   William Coleman, *Georges Cuvier, Zoologist: A Study in the History of Evolution Theory* (Cambridge, MA, 1964), p. 61.

[67]   See Robert Wokler, "Tyson and Buffon on the Orang-Utan," *Studies on Voltaire and the Eighteenth Century*, 155 (1976), 2301–19.

[68]   See Londa Schiebinger, "Skeletons in the Closet: The First Illustrations of the Female Skeleton in Eighteenth-Century Anatomy," *The Making of the Modern Body: Sexuality and Society in the Nineteenth Century*, eds Catherine Gallagher and Thomas Laqueur (Berkeley and Los Angeles, 1987), pp. 42–82, especially p. 51. See also Schiebinger's *The Mind Has No Sex? Women in the Origins of Modern Science* (Cambridge, MA, 1989), and Thomas

ference, if we judge by such writings as J. F. Lafitau's *Customs of the American Indians* (1724), with its comments on gynocracy and the occupations of Iroquois women,[69] or Francis Moore's *Travels into the Inland Parts of Africa* (1736), with its account of an evening encounter with a *"Mumbo Jumbo."* This figure, "a kind of cunning Mystery" among "the *Mundigoes"* is, Moore says,

> dressed in a long Coat made of the Bark of Trees, with a Tuff of fine Straw on the Top of it, and when the Person wears it, it is about eight or nine Foot high. This is a Thing invented by the Men to keep their Wives in awe, who are so ignorant (or at least are obliged to pretend to be so) as to take it for a Wild Man; and indeed no one but what knows it, would take it to be a Man, by reason of the dismall Noise it makes, and which but few of the Natives can manage. It never comes abroad but in the Night-time, which makes it have the better Effect. Whenever the Men have Dispute with the Women, this *Mumbo Jumbo* is sent for to determine it; which is, I may say, always in Favor of the Men.[70]

Cross-cultural comparison was also important to various attempts to construct stadial theories of progress[71] and conjectural histories of man. In "the beginning all the World was *America,"* said Locke.[72] Eighteenth-century Europeans believed that travelling in space also meant travelling in time; the Others they encountered were earlier versions of themselves. It is in the Indians' "present condition, that we are to behold, as in a mirrour, the features of our own progenitors," claimed Adam Ferguson.[73] We "possess at this time very great advantages towards the knowledge of human nature," wrote Edmund Burke, for "now the map of mankind is unrolled at once; and there is no state of gradation of barbarism, and no mode of refinement which we do not have at the same instant under our view."[74]

It was understandable, then, to identify North American Indians with earlier peoples in the Bible or with the German tribes in Tacitus. It was also a measure of how far Europeans had come, especially in an age that coined the term "civilization" and embraced the idea of progress. This raises a related question. To what extent did cultural hegemony and nationalism shape various human sciences – anthropology, for example, inventing a "past" by which the progress of present European civilization might be judged?[75] In any case, defining the

---

Laqueur, *Making Sex: Body and Gender from the Greeks to Freud* (Cambridge, MA, 1990), especially pp. 149–92. Elsewhere, Sylvana Tomaselli has discussed the emergence in the later eighteenth century of a "science of woman" to parallel the new science of man. See "Reflections on the History of the Science of Woman," *History of Science*, 29 (1991), 185–205.

[69] See Joseph François Lafitau, *Customs of the American Indians, Compared with the Customs of Primitive Times*, trans. William H. Fenton and Elizabeth L. Moore, 2 vols (Toronto, 1974), I, 71–74; II, 47–97.

[70] Francis Moore, *Travels into the Inland Parts of Africa: Containing a Description of the Several Nations for the Space of Six Hundred Miles up the River Gambia ... To which is added, Capt. Stibb's Voyage up the Gambia in the Year 1723, to Make Discoveries* (London, 1736), p. 116; see also p. 122.

[71] For the most popular of these views, the "four stages theory" of progress from hunting, pasturage, agriculture, to commerce, see especially Ronald L. Meek, *Social Science and the Ignoble Savage* (Cambridge and New York, 1976).

[72] John Locke, "The Second Treatise of Government," *Two Treatises of Government*, ed. Peter Laslett (Cambridge and New York, 1964 [1960]), §49, p. 319.

[73] See *An Essay on the History of Civil Society*, p. 122.

[74] Burke, quoted in Marshall and Williams, *The Great Map of Mankind*, p. 93.

[75] The earliest known use of the word "civilization" was c. 1756. See Jean Starobinski, "Le mot civilization," *Temps de la réflexion*, 4 (1983), 13–51; Anthony Pagden, "The 'Defence

uses of comparison is an issue that cuts across many eighteenth-century concerns. Important here, in closing, is the extent to which an early work, like *Gulliver*, in envisioning human science, enters into a critique.

of Civilization' in Eighteenth-Century Social Theory," *History of the Human Sciences*, 1 (1988), 33–45; and Lucien Febvre, "Civilization: Evolution of a Word and a Group of Ideas," *A New Kind of History*, ed. Peter Burke (New York, 1973), pp. 217–57. On the attempt to invent the present by constructing a place called "the past," see Johannes Fabian, *Time and the Other: How Anthropology Makes its Object* (New York, 1983). I thank my colleague, Kathleen Biddick, for bringing Fabian to my attention. See her consideration of the same question in "Decolonizing the English Past: Readings in Medieval Archeology and History," *Journal of British Studies*, 32 (1993), 1–23, especially pp. 3–4.

# IV. Poetry of the 1720s and 1730s

Peter J. Schakel
*Hope College, Holland, Michigan*

# What Success It Met: The Reception of *Cadenus and Vanessa*

ABSTRACT. This paper re-examines *Cadenus and Vanessa* through reading and reception, particularly how it was read and received by Esther Vanhomrigh. The reading of *Cadenus and Vanessa* – like all reading – has always occurred contextually: within the context of Swift's life (biographically) or the context of other works by Swift (sometimes *Gulliver's Travels*, sometimes other poems), and judgements about it have varied widely. Assessing the poem would be aided by knowledge of when and how Esther Vanhomrigh read and received it. The correspondence suggests that Esther did not see the poem until 1719, and that she received it then as a complimentary poem demonstrating Swift's affection for her. References to reading in the poem and in the correspondence create a humorous, contradictory situation in which Esther was, and was not, Vanessa. The result is a playful, ambiguous, inconclusive, and – for many readers – delightful poem.

It has widely been held that Jonathan Swift wrote *Cadenus and Vanessa* not for publication, but for Esther Vanhomrigh's eyes alone. Harold Williams called the poem private and temporary, "written for Vanessa, and not intended for publication."[1] Others before and after him have agreed: W. E. H. Lecky wrote "it was never intended to see the light, and was sent to Vanessa for herself alone;"[2] Richard Rodino posited that "*Cadenus and Vanessa* was written only for Swift and Esther Vanhomrigh."[3] Despite that supposition, Esther has not been taken seriously into account as a reader of the poem. Studies almost without exception have been text-oriented, not reader-oriented.[4] In this paper, I want to start with reading. Approaching *Cadenus and Vanessa* with reading as a problematic issue, and through the poem's reception, opens it up in ways that formalistic approaches have not been able to.

---

[1]  Harold Williams, ed., *The Poems of Jonathan Swift*, 2nd ed., 3 vols (Oxford, 1958), II, 684. All quotations of *Cadenus and Vanessa* are from this edition, II, 686–714.

[2]  "Biographical Introduction," *The Prose Works of Jonathan Swift*, ed. Temple Scott (London, 1897), I, lii.

[3]  "The Private Sense of *Cadenus and Vanessa*," *Concerning Poetry*, 11 (1978), 41.

[4]  K. Richard Wade, in "Of 'Weighty Arguments' and 'Rational Delight': Swift's Comical Strategy in *Cadenus and Vanessa*," *Swift Studies*, 9 (1994), 65–76, raises the issue of reading and reception (pp. 73–74), but his text-oriented approach does not permit him to deal with those issues fully.

To approach the poem through reading is invited and justified by the fact that reading is a central activity within the poem. The world the poem projects is a bookish world.[5] Early in the poem, we find Venus consulting her books – "The *Lovers Fleta's, Bractons, Cokes*" – and a bit later slamming those "Law-books on the Shelf" (ll. 107, 140). She then creates the perfect child, Vanessa, a woman for whom "Scholars wou'd forsake their Books" (l. 234). Cadenus, having "Eyes with Reading almost blind," had spoiled his fashionable airs through "Time, and Books, and State Affairs" (ll. 527, 544). And Venus, near the end, disillusioned and wanting to escape this world and fly back to heaven, tells the lawyers to be quick, "Nor spend their Time to shew their Reading; / She'd have a summary Proceeding" (ll. 848–49).

Vanessa herself is characterized as a great reader. When Vanessa, in her bloom, leaves her cloistered life and enters the world, she knows well "from the Books she read / What dangerous Paths young Virgins tread" (ll. 310–11). When the glittering dames come early to her room to "see the Girl in Deshabille," they find "The Room with Volumes litter'd round / *Vanessa* held *Montaigne*, and read, / Whilst Mrs. *Susan* comb'd her Head" (ll. 367, 371–73). Cadenus protects her from Cupid's arrows by "placing still some Book betwixt" (l. 480). The poem mentions the "secret Joy" he took, "To see the Virgin mind her Book" (ll. 552, 551). It is high praise of her that "She noted all she ever read" (l. 756).

And it is books that ultimately prove her undoing: Vanessa, "Searching in Books for Wisdom's Aid, / Was, in the very Search, betray'd" (ll. 490–91). She called for Cadenus's "Poetick Works," "And while the Book was in her Hand," Cupid shot a dart of such prodigious strength "It pierc'd the feeble Volume thro', / And deep transfix'd her Bosom too" (ll. 512, 514, 518–19). It is fitting, then, that, in love with Cadenus, Vanessa talks of him as a book: "one short Volume" which comprised "All that was witty, learn'd, and wise"; "*Cadenus* answers every End, / The Book, the Author, and the Friend" (ll. 696, 697, 704–5). Thus, it is appropriate that the ambiguous passage on "what Success *Vanessa* met" ends with this image: whether "They temper Love and Books together" must "never to Mankind be told" (ll. 818, 825, 826).

Reading, in the poem, extends metaphorically beyond written texts. As the roles of Cadenus and Vanessa are reversed and she becomes his tutor in matters of the heart, she recognizes that he lacks capacity to reach the science she designs to teach:

> Wherein his Genius was below
> The Skill of ev'ry common Beau;
> Who, tho' he cannot spell, is wise
> Enough to read a Lady's Eyes;
> And will each accidental Glance
> Interpret for a kind Advance. (ll. 812–17)

The lines suggest that the beaux may be misreading, misinterpreting an authoritative text (an "accidental Glance" as "a kind Advance"). But they are doing what reading always involves to some extent. Norman Holland claims that as we read we inevitably shape texts to conform to our individual identity patterns. In the process of reading, the text must pass through our unconscious defences, expectations, fantasies, and transformations, which shape

---

[5]   For a quite different approach to the motifs of bookishness and textuality in the poem, see Thomas E. Maresca, "Men Imagining Women Imagining Men: Swift's *Cadenus and Vanessa*," *Studies in Eighteenth-Century Culture*, 24, eds Carla H. Hay and Syndy M. Conger (Baltimore and London, 1995), 243–57.

the work in our own image.[6] In *Cadenus and Vanessa*, everything said about ladies undermines our confidence that their "accidental Glance[s]" are stable authoritative texts. We are left with uncertainty. Are the beaux misreading? Or are they participating in a process in which meaning is shaped from a subjective text? (An "accidental Glance" may have been intended as, or through mutual interaction turn out to be, a "kind Advance.")

Upon reflection, this "bookish" poem appears to be full of "misreadings" which are in fact Holland-style "readings." Vanessa begins to "read" Cadenus in terms of the love which forms her identity:

> *Cadenus* now no more appears
> Declin'd in Health, advanc'd in Years.
> She fancies Musick in his Tongue,
> Nor further looks, but thinks him young. (ll. 528–31)

Her love becomes a lens which shapes her reading of everything:

> Thro' this she made all Objects pass,
> Which gave a Tincture o'er the Mass:

And:

> as Philosophers, who find
> Some fav'rite System to their Mind,
> In ev'ry Point to make it fit,
> Will force all Nature to submit. (ll. 718–19; 722–25)

But it is not just Vanessa, and not just Vanessa in love. Venus needs to believe that men and women love each other on pure and lofty grounds, on the basis of merit and worth, not irrationality. Since her identity is based on the irresistible power of love, she blinds her eyes to contrary evidence and carries out her "Project" (her visionary scheme) involving Vanessa. Similarly, the fops and dames impose on Vanessa the standards and values which define themselves, thus find her wanting, and conclude " – That Lady is the dullest Soul –" (l. 359).

Most significantly, Cadenus does the same. As he attempts to understand Vanessa, he is confined by the past baggage of his scholarly life and his role as her tutor: "Time, and Books, and State Affairs / Had spoil'd his fashionable Airs; / He now cou'd praise, esteem, approve, / But understood not what was Love" (ll. 544–47). Thus, he sees only what will fit his identity pattern: "That innocent Delight he took / To see the Virgin mind her Book, / Was but the Master's secret Joy / In School to hear the finest Boy" (ll. 550–53).

The poem, thus, suggests the difficulty with reading which the poem itself presents, particularly the difficulty with determining the context in which to read it. Reception theory reminds us that no reading is independent, autonomous, and complete.[7] All readers read contextually, placing works in relation to other works and to previous readings of the same work. They attempt to construe a poem in ways that make coherent sense. Readers come with horizons of expectations which are applied (and must be modified) as they engage with

---

[6]   See "UNITY IDENTITY TEXT SELF," *PMLA*, 90 (1975), 813–22.

[7]   The approach in this paper adapts rather freely the ideas of Hans Robert Jauss, *Toward an Aesthetic of Reception*, trans. Timothy Bahti (Minneapolis, 1982). For an application to Swift, see Richard H. Rodino, "'Splendide Mendax': Authors, Characters, and Readers in *Gulliver's Travels*," *PMLA*, 106 (1991), 1054–70, slightly revised in *Reading Swift: Papers from The Second Münster Symposium on Jonathan Swift*, eds Richard H. Rodino and Hermann J. Real, with the assistance of Helgard Stöver-Leidig (München, 1993), pp. 167–84.

a text. Readers inevitably are selective as they bring previously known works to bear in reading and as they give emphasis to details and features of the work at hand. Readers shape a text to fit their needs and identities, listening for what they want to hear and unconsciously blocking out what they do not want to.

But this text resists and subverts our usual efforts to create coherence, stability, and relevance. Readers in a variety of contexts and a variety of personal situations have produced a wide range of assessments of *Cadenus and Vanessa*, which in turn become additional contexts for reading the poem. Text and context have led readers to turn the poem into what they want it to be, or call it a failure, or go from it frustrated and disappointed.

Readers of the poem, throughout its history, have read it in the context of Swift's life. Even as it circulated in manuscript in the early 1720s and after its publication in 1726, it (naturally) raised speculations about the nature of the relationship between Swift and Esther and was used "to calumniate the Dean's character"[8] – or Esther Vanhomrigh's. Orrery spent two pages attacking "Vanessa" as excessively vain, fond of dress, romantic, ambitious, haughty, disdainful[9] – but it is clear that he meant those adjectives to apply to Esther. As Delany, in reply, defended Vanessa and Cadenus, he was in fact defending Esther and Swift.[10] Readers in the nineteenth and twentieth centuries continued to read in a biographical context. Scott argued for the "evident truthfulness [of] the whole story."[11] Stephen Gwynn asserted explicitly that Swift's "method is so literal that the outline of the relation may be taken as authentic in essentials."[12] Leslie Stephen concluded it "impossible to believe that Swift would have done anything so unmeaning, so futile, as to write an account of the matter which was not strictly true."[13] Irvin Ehrenpreis said it "must reflect Swift's real attitude."[14]

Regarding the poem as autobiographical renders it stable and manageable: although the ending and precise point are inconclusive, they are inconclusive for biographical reasons. One can defend Swift through Cadenus, or chastise him – but at least one knows what he was up to: he was using a poem to clarify, comment on, and perhaps change a real-life situation. But it ultimately leaves questions. Deane Swift, in reply to Orrery, asserted that it

---

[8]  Thomas Sheridan, *The Life of the Rev. Dr. Jonathan Swift* (London, 1784), p. 333.

[9]  John Boyle, fifth Earl of Cork and Orrery, *Remarks on the Life and Writings of Dr. Jonathan Swift* (London, 1752), pp. 107–8.

[10]  See Patrick Delany, *Observations upon Lord Orrery's Remarks* (London, 1754), pp. 111–24.

[11]  Walter Scott, "Memoirs of Jonathan Swift," *The Works of Jonathan Swift*, 19 vols (Edinburgh, 1814), I, 237–38, echoed by Lecky, "Biographical Introduction," *Prose Works*, ed. Temple Scott, I, lii–liii. John Aikin similarly treats Swift as synonymous with Cadenus, Esther with Vanessa: "The melancholy truth was, that after uniting himself secretly with another woman, he continued to visit Vanessa, and she retained her hopes of softening his obduracy, till a final explanation broke her heart" (*Letters to a Young Lady, on a Course of English Poetry* [Boston, 1806], p. 56). See also Nathan Drake, *Essays, Biographical, Critical, and Historical* (London, 1805), III, 151.

[12]  *The Life and Friendships of Dean Swift* (London, 1933), p. 164.

[13]  *Swift* (New York, 1882), p. 127.

[14]  *Dr Swift*, p. 647. David Nokes discusses the biographical "Vanessa" and the Vanessa in the poem interchangeably and describes the poem as "an attempt to reassert control, to put back a conventional frame on their relationship" (*Jonathan Swift, A Hypocrite Reversed: A Critical Biography* [Oxford, 1985], p. 164).

is frequently the case that works are "partly *real*, and partly *fictitious*."[15] Readers make selective decisions about which details to consider "real" and which "fictitious," and that leaves uncertainty about what "real attitudes" the poem reflects.

Instead of, or in addition to, a biographical context, other readers have placed the poem in the context of Swift's prose works, or the works of his contemporaries; but here, too, selectivity inevitably enters in. Which works, and which details in those works? Initially, such readings followed the trail blazed by Ricardo Quintana, George Sherburn, and Louis Landa as they rescued Swift from the vilifications of Thackeray and found clarity and stability in a moral rigorism grounded in "perennial Reason and achieved through restraint and discipline."[16] Reason and the Houyhnhnms were posited as ideals (even if unattainable ones) in the *Travels*, while passion and the Yahoos were seen as a threat to order and civilized values. In that context, Peter Ohlin compared *Cadenus and Vanessa* to such works as the *Letter to a Young Lady on her Marriage*, *Gulliver's Travels*, and passages from sermons and maxims, and found that *Cadenus and Vanessa*, like *Gulliver's Travels*, "presents the problems of a man of mixed reason and passion who is trying to live rationally, but is surprised by uncontrolled passion and has to defend himself strongly."[17] And James L. Tyne, SJ, from within a similar context, concluded that "Vanessa, like the Houyhnhnms, represents a super-human ideal that is not realizable in the actual world."[18]

Other readings consider *Cadenus and Vanessa* in the context of a different *Gulliver's Travels*, the *Travels* of Edward Stone, Kathleen Williams, or Samuel H. Monk, who viewed the Houyhnhnms as placed in unresolvable tension with the Yahoos, both equally undesirable and equally the brunt of comic and satiric attack.[19] Thus, Gareth Jones stressed the comic aspects of *Cadenus and Vanessa*, the way it constantly employs paradox and irony to undermine rational, logical abstractions as they are confronted with "the chaotic world of sense and passion."[20] And A. B. England argued that, as the "unresolved oppositions of *Gulliver's Travels* simply *have* to be held in a state of tension,"[21] so, too, unruly forces in *Cadenus and Vanessa* disrupt its formal and rhetorical structurings and leave the poem in an unresolved

---

[15]  Deane Swift, *An Essay upon the Life, Writings, and Character of Dr. Jonathan Swift* (London, 1755), p. 243. Among the fictitious details is Vanessa's request, in line 512, to see Cadenus's "Poetick Works." There was no edition of Swift's "Poetick Works." Pat Rogers, reading biographically, suggests that Vanessa was referring to the 1711 *Miscellanies*, "though it is more than half prose, is scarcely a 'feeble volume' (running to 416 pages), and contains distinctly few tender lines to inspire the passions" (*Poems*, p. 662).

[16]  Ricardo Quintana, *Swift: An Introduction* (London, New York, Toronto, 1955), p. 32.

[17]  "'Cadenus and Vanessa': Reason and Passion," *Studies in English Literature*, 4 (1964), 495–96.

[18]  "Vanessa and the Houyhnhnms: A Reading of 'Cadenus and Vanessa,'" *Studies in English Literature*, 11 (1971), 518.

[19]  See Stone, "Swift and the Horses: Misanthropy or Comedy?" *Modern Language Quarterly*, 10 (1949), 367–76; Williams, "Gulliver's Voyage to the Houyhnhnms," *Journal of English Literary History*, 18 (1951), 275–86, and "*Animal Rationis Capax*: A Study of Certain Aspects of Swift's Imagery," *English Literary History*, 21 (1954), 193–207; Monk, "The Pride of Lemuel Gulliver," *Sewanee Review*, 63 (1955), 48–71.

[20]  "Swift's *Cadenus and Vanessa*: A Question of 'Positives,'" *Essays in Criticism*, 20 (1970), 435.

[21]  "World Without Order: Some Thoughts on the Poetry of Swift," *Essays in Criticism*, 16 (1966), 32.

tension, with the conclusion that "human nature is not amenable to the type of ordering arrangement" that Cadenus relies on to keep his world under control.[22]

*Cadenus and Vanessa* can also be read in the context of other poems by Swift – but again, which poems, and which details in them? A. B. England's *Energy and Order* stressed ways in which *Cadenus and Vanessa* departs from certain orderly forms of discourse that have traditionally been associated with "Augustan" literature. But books by Louise K. Barnett, John Irwin Fischer, and me, reading *Cadenus and Vanessa* in the context of other poems, or other characteristics of the same poems, accepted and assessed the kind of orderly forms England finds subverted.[23] And it can be read in the context of poems by Swift's contemporaries, as Ellen Pollak juxtaposed it with Pope's *The Rape of the Lock* and "Epistle to a Lady" and found that Swift avoided the "entrapment in the rigid mythic structures on which the *Rape* and 'To a Lady' both depend," and plumbed the "insufficiencies of reason" in Cadenus while affirming the heroic, redemptive power of Vanessa's love.[24]

Thus, the reception of *Cadenus and Vanessa* presents a history of widely divergent views and assessments. It has been described, on the one hand, as "a poem, which is built on the finest model; supported with infinite humour, wit, and gaiety; embellished with ideas the most lovely and delicate; beautifully adorned with variety of the most attractive images; and conducted throughout the whole with such perfect regularity, that beyond all other pieces, whether of DR. SWIFT, or any Poet that ever writ in *English*, it appears calculated to abide the severest examination of criticks" and, on the other, as "fractured and contradictory," "consequently a failure."[25] Perhaps, through its "control, complexity, and comprehensiveness," it becomes "a serious statement on love, self-understanding, and human nature," or perhaps it is an elaborately gallant fiction which is "vitiated by a kind of bad faith," "a repellent poem, at once self-castigating and archly defensive."[26]

For the most part, analyses of the poem have not given attention to its readers or the reading process, most notably not to the response of its first reader, presumably Esther Vanhomrigh.[27] Part of the uniqueness of this poem is that it was written for one particular reader

---

[22] *Energy and Order in the Poetry of Swift* (Lewisburg, London, Toronto, 1980), p. 175.

[23] See Barnett, *Swift's Poetic Worlds* (Newark, London, Toronto, 1981), pp. 106–11; Fischer, *On Swift's Poetry* (Gainesville, FL, 1978), pp. 110–20; Schakel, *The Poetry of Jonathan Swift: Allusion and the Development of a Poetic Style* (Madison, WI, 1978), pp. 82–96.

[24] *The Poetics of Sexual Myth: Gender and Ideology in the Verse of Swift and Pope* (Chicago and London, 1985), pp. 134, 156, 148. For another appreciation of *Cadenus and Vanessa* from a feminist perspective, see Margaret Anne Doody, "Swift among the Women," *The Yearbook of English Studies*, 18 (1988), 68–82.

[25] Deane Swift, *An Essay upon the Life, Writings, and Character*, pp. 240–41, quoted without citation by W. H. Dilworth, *The Life of Dr. Jonathan Swift* (Dublin, 1758), pp. 85–86; Fischer, *On Swift's Poetry*, pp. 111, 110. F. Elrington Ball calls it "the longest and perhaps the best metrical piece" Swift wrote (*Swift's Verse: An Essay* [London, 1929], p. 134). Its artistry is praised highly by Oliver Goldsmith, *Collected Works*, ed. Arthur Friedman, 5 vols (Oxford, 1966), V, 329, and Maurice Johnson, *The Sin of Wit: Jonathan Swift as a Poet* (Syracuse, NY, 1950), p. 43.

[26] Schakel, *The Poetry of Jonathan Swift*, pp. 83, 96; Claude Rawson, "Rage and Raillery and Swift: The Case of *Cadenus and Vanessa*," *Interfaces: Image, Texte, Langage*, 4 (1993), 21; see also the same author's Introduction to *Jonathan Swift: A Collection of Critical Essays*, ed. Claude Rawson (Englewood Cliffs, NJ, 1995), p. 2.

[27] At least two essays include passages reminiscent of the "strategies in the text" variety of reader-response developed in Stanley Fish's *Surprised by Sin* (London, 1967). Gareth Jones asserts that Swift's purpose in the conclusion of *Cadenus and Vanessa* is "not to thwart

(as well as, perhaps, for a general readership). Some of the difficulties in reception of the poem – its place in relation to other poems, the expectations it raised or needed to satisfy – may be a result of failure to take that initial reader into account as a reader, and to make her reception of the poem a part of its history. How did Esther Vanhomrigh read the poem? When did she read it? Where did she read it?

When and where she read it depend in part on when and where it was written, of course, and these are disputed issues. Swift himself claimed, after manuscript copies of *Cadenus and Vanessa* began circulating, that he wrote it in 1712, in Windsor (even dated the copy), and that he had never seen it since and could not remember what was in it.[28] This creates problems. It is perplexing that Swift could remember precise details *about* the poem, though he forgot what was *in* the poem. Also, he would not have called himself Cadenus in 1712 – he did not become Dean until 1713. Since Swift was always unreliable about dates, and since it was greatly to his advantage, in the 1720s, to put the poem as far in the past as possible, most scholars are skeptical about this statement. A more likely possibility is that he drafted part (or all) of it during another stay in Windsor, in the autumn of 1713. This dating falls after he was installed as Dean of St Patrick's, and just shortly after the occurrence of the events it describes.

The usual assumption has been that Swift showed the poem to Esther immediately after he wrote it, or even as he worked on it, in 1712 or 1713. As J. A. Downie put it, "One can imagine him showing his verses to Vanessa as they flowed from his pen, as Sidney perhaps showed *Astrophil and Stella* to Penelope Devereux."[29] It is a pleasing thought, but there are no objective data to support it – no contemporary mention of the poem, no indications of how Esther received it or reacted to it. References to the poem appear only later, beginning in 1720. Until then, the names "Cadenus" and "Vanessa" are not found in their correspondence; afterward they are used often. The first reference to "Vanessa" in a letter is July, 1720: "I reckon by this time the Groves and Fields and purling Streams have made Vanessa Romantick."[30] Swift first refers to himself as "Cad" a week later;[31] from then on, "Cad" occurs repeatedly in letters by both Swift and Esther.

About that time, Swift included in a letter 22 lines of verse very much in the *Cadenus and Vanessa* vein:

> Nymph, would you learn the onely Art
> To keep a worthy Lover's heart
> First, to adorn your Person well,
> In utmost Cleanlyness excell.

---

and confuse, but to compel us, by tempting us ever and again to rest thankful in the easy certainties of judgment, and then subverting those certainties, not merely to contemplate but to live the difficulties of our predicament" ("Swift's *Cadenus and Vanessa*," p. 436; see also p. 439). And Ellen Pollak asserts that the poem's lack of resolution "throws the full burden of responsibility for lurid curiosity and unsavory conclusions on the reader ... [Swift's] studied evasion provokes a sin of imagination, demanding of the reader that very indiscretion which the poet has nimbly managed to avoid" (*The Poetics of Sexual Myth*, pp. 130–31).

[28]  See *Correspondence*, III, 130.

[29]  *Jonathan Swift, Political Writer* (London, Boston, Henley, 1984), p. 173.

[30]  *Correspondence*, II, 350. In several other cases, he uses a dash instead of writing out "Vanessa." His usual names for her were "Hessy," "Miss Hessy," "Mishessy," "Skinage," or "Misheskinage."

[31]  See *Correspondence*, II, 353.

It goes on to praise Virtue, Honour, Sense, and Wit, says that a Nymph who possesses such will never be abandoned, and concludes,

> But – here Vanessa cannot err,
> Nor are these Rules applyd to Her:
> For who could such a Nymph forsake
> Except a Blockhead or a Rake.[32]

They have very much the feel of lines for which he could not find a place in *Cadenus and Vanessa*.

All of this has led some scholars to argue for a later date of composition – or revision – around 1719. Joseph Horrell contended, in the notes to his edition of Swift's verse, that the poem was written in late 1719 or early 1720.[33] Pat Rogers, in reply, says that Horrell's arguments "seem to me of some force, but not quite sufficient to overset the conventional dating."[34] Easier to accept is Sir Henry Craik's case that, although most of it was written in 1712, the poem was revised and completed and given to Esther in 1719.[35]

If Esther did see the poem in 1712 or 1713, we have no indication of how she read and responded to it. But the tone and wording of the letters between Swift and Esther in 1719 and 1720 suggest a good deal about her reception of the poem then. First in this group is the letter Swift wrote to Esther, in French, on 12 May 1719. It is not a passionate love letter, but it is an expression of deep admiration and affection, including such statements as "do you think it possible not to esteem you above the rest of human kind? What beasts in petticoats are the most excellent of those [ladies], whom I see dispersed throughout the world, in comparison of you." Also,

> It is no merit, nor any proof of my good taste, to find out in you all that nature has bestowed on a mortal; that is to say, *honour, virtue*, good sense, wit, sweetness, agreeableness, and firmness of soul: *but by concealing yourself as you do, the world knows you not, and you lose the eulogy of millions*.[36]

On 8 August 1720, Esther wrote to Swift, "We have had a vast deal of thunder and lightning where do you think I wished to be then" and "is my dateing my letters wrong the only signe of my being in love."[37] Swift replied with a letter full of memories of special times they had together:

---

[32]  *Correspondence*, II, 350.

[33]  See *Collected Poems of Jonathan Swift*, 2 vols (London, 1958), I, 388–90.

[34]  *Poems*, p. 658.

[35]  See *The Life of Jonathan Swift*, 2nd ed., 2 vols (London and New York, 1894), II, 28–29. Williams concludes that the poem was written in 1713 but adds, "It is probable that 'Cadenus and Vanessa' was later revised, and perhaps extended, possibly more than once" (*Poems*, II, 684–85). Williams also calls attention to the "Aynho transcript" of part of the poem. The transcript is currently in the possession of the Cotterell-Dormer family, Rousham Park; a photocopy is in the Williams Collection at the Cambridge University Library. The transcript, headed "Windsor. August 1st 1712," includes the title "Cadenus & Vanessa" and the first 303 lines, with only incidental variations from the text of Roberts's first edition. The handwriting clearly is not Vanessa's, and in August 1712, there was no basis for the "Cadenus" in the title. This copy appears to be either a copy of part of one of the manuscripts which began to circulate after Esther's death in June 1723, or a transcript of the poem published three years later, in either case dated so as to conform with Swift's account of the composition of the poem.

[36]  *Correspondence*, II, 325–26; trans. Sheridan, *Life*, p. 349.

[37]  *Correspondence*, II, 354.

What would you give to have the History of Cad– and – – – exactly written through all its
steps from the beginning to this time. I believe it would do well in Verse, and be as long
as the other [presumably, *Cadenus and Vanessa*]. I hope it will be done. It ought to be an
exact Chronicle of 12 Years; from the Time of spilling the Coffee to drinking of Coffee,
from Dunstable to Dublin with every single passage since. There would be the ... Chaptr
of long walks. The Berkshire Surprise. fifty Chapters of little Times: The Chaptr of Chelsea:
[etc.].[38]

In his previous letter, Swift had instructed Esther to substitute strokes (or dashes) for terms
of affection: "A Stroak thus – – signifies every thing that may be said to Cad – at the beginning or Conclusion." Such strokes clutter both their letters from then on. Esther's next
letter but one opens, "–, –, – Cad. is it possible that you will come and see me ... I would
give the world to see you here." Two months later, Swift wrote, "I have the same Respect
esteem and Kindness for you I ever professed to have and shall ever preserve, because you
will always merit the utmost that can be given you;" the letter ends with five strokes. Vanessa
replied, after six strokes, "nor is the love I beare you only seated in my soul for there is not
a single atome of my frame that is not blended with it."[39]

In these letters, clustered around the only references we have to *Cadenus and Vanessa*,
nothing points toward the conclusions some critics have drawn by attempting to determine
Swift's intent in writing the poem – that it was an effort to "discourage the green girl's
romantic yearnings," or to "cool or end" their relationship.[40] On the contrary, the letters on
both sides not only express but foster a deep and continuing affection. They supply an important context for speculating about how Esther presumably read *Cadenus and Vanessa*,
and that points in a direction quite different from cooling or ending the relationship.

How would she read the poem? If Norman Holland is correct, she would shape the poem
to fit her identity, listening for what she wanted to hear and unconsciously blocking out
what she did not want to. She would drink in the complimentary passages; she would hear
the expressions of affection as a love which might, still, sometime, take on a tinge of passion
toward her. She would fashion from it a coherent, consistent reading which gratified her
wishes and minimized her fears. The evidence of the letters suggests she did read the poem
just that way, as a love poem, as an expression of Swift's deep feeling for her.

Even as she fashioned a stable, assuring meaning, however, that reading would be destabil-
ized by the poem's emphasis on reading in its characterization of Vanessa. As Esther read
the account of Vanessa as a great reader and scholar, she would surely recall references to
reading in letters to herself from Swift – or could she block those out, too, in order to make
the text say what she wanted it to say? On 18 December 1711, Swift wrote a letter to
Esther's cousin, Anne Long, which he sent to Esther and directed her to read before de-
livering it to Mrs Long. In it is a description of Esther, intended of course for Esther's eyes:

> I think there is not a better Girl Upon Earth. I have a mighty Friendship for her: she had
> good Principles, and I have corrected all her Faults; *but I cannot persuade her to read*, tho
> she has an Understanding, Memory and Tast, that would bear great Improvement: but she
> is incorrigibly idle and Lazy: thinks the world made for nothing but perpetual Pleasure;
> and the Deity she most adores is Morpheu[s].[41]

---

[38] *Correspondence*, II, 356.
[39] *Correspondence*, II, 353, 357, 360, 361, 363.
[40] Tyne, "Vanessa and the Houyhnhnms," p. 518; Rodino, "The Private Sense of *Cadenus and Vanessa*," p. 41.
[41] *Correspondence*, I, 278; emphasis added.

Eight months later, Swift encouraged Esther to go out walking with her sister Moll, "and do not sit moping at home, You that can neither work *nor read* nor play, nor care for company."[42] In 1720, he told her (now living in Dublin) that he never read her letters to him "without wondring how a Brat *who cannot read*, can possibly write so well."[43] Between poem and letters, there is paradox and inconsistency, but playful, humorous paradox and inconsistency. As Esther read the poem, she must have projected herself into the text, identified with Vanessa and the expressions of praise and love which came through so clearly; yet the references in the letters simultaneously subverted her identification with Vanessa. She was, and was not, Vanessa. That is but one of the poem's many paradoxes, like Cadenus's *passionate* defence of *reason* and Vanessa's *reasonable* defence of *passion*. The poem is ambiguous, self-contradictory, and open-ended. Esther was left with nothing stable and objective to hold onto except a powerful sense of Cadenus's affection for Vanessa – but even its expressions in the poem were confusing and contradictory, impossible for Esther to pin down securely and apply to herself confidently.

Where does that leave us? With a work that is (and is not) a love poem, that is (and is not) biographical, that develops persuasive themes and ordering devices, but also subverts them. If we can accept the poem for what it is, we will find a playful, humorous, inconclusive poem celebrating "a genuine love affair in verse."[44] As readers we may crave more, may even try to make it more, as various critics, myself included, have tried to do in the past. But in the end, I now believe, we have to be satisfied, as Esther had to be, with very little that is objective and solid to hold onto.

This interpretation of *Cadenus and Vanessa*, like the others summarized above, grows out of a context – one in which studies of Swift have paid increasing attention to the "typical Swiftian evasion of textual certainty."[45] It, too, is selective and partial. It joins the others in becoming part of the reception history of the poem, and by extension part of the poem itself, each shaping (sometimes by reaction) the responses of subsequent readers. What it may perhaps contribute to the ongoing conversation is a reinforcement of the understanding that this poem does not conform to what we are accustomed to in much verse of the eighteenth century, does not fit our usual horizon of expectations, does not offer the kind of stable, tightly knit text formalist critics delight in. Perhaps, in the end, we should try to see *that* as the beauty of this poem, and simply accept and enjoy it in all its baffling uniqueness, ambiguity, and playfulness.

---

[42]  *Correspondence*, I, 308; emphasis added.

[43]  *Correspondence*, II, 335–36; emphasis added.

[44]  Downie, *Jonathan Swift, Political Writer*, p. 173.

[45]  Pollak, *The Poetics of Sexual Myth*, p. 131. For post-structuralist studies of Swift, see especially Clive T. Probyn, "'Haranguing upon Texts': Swift and the Idea of the Book," *Proceedings of The First Münster Symposium on Jonathan Swift*, eds Hermann J. Real and Heinz J. Vienken (München, 1985), pp. 187–97, and "Swift and Typographic Man: Foul Papers, Modern Criticism, and Irish Dissenters," *Reading Swift: Papers from The Second Münster Symposium on Jonathan Swift*, eds Rodino and Real, pp. 25–43. See also pp. 14–15 in the Introduction to *Critical Approaches to Teaching Swift*, ed. Peter J. Schakel (New York, 1992).

Clive T. Probyn
*Monash University, Clayton, Victoria*

# Jonathan Swift at the Sign of the Drapier

ABSTRACT. Much remains unclear about Swift's relationship with what has been called the Dublin Grub Street. This essay is concerned with the fabrication and evolution of Swift's image as M.B., Drapier. Largely through an analysis of contemporary signs traced in newspapers and broadsides, and to a lesser extent in Dublin street processions, it seeks to situate Swift's defence of Irish weavers in the wider writing context of the time and show how, in his *Examination of Certain Abuses, Corruptions, and Enormities in the City of Dublin* (1732), Swift took a keen interest in Dublin's semiotic system.

"The truth is," Swift once remarked, "that the woollen manufacture of this kingdom sate always nearest my heart."[1] His efforts to promote Irish industry in the second decade of the eighteenth century continue to be celebrated in the final decade of the twentieth. Only the medium of that celebration has changed. Thus, in 1993, Liam O'Flynn recorded on compact disc an orchestrated version of Swift's "An Excellent New Song on a Seditious Pamphlet: To the Tune of Packington's Pound," a poem which defiantly (though sardonically) celebrates the symbiotic relationship between "a Printer [Edward Waters] and Dean" [Swift himself] in the production of the latter's *Proposal for the Universal Use of Irish Manufacture*.[2] This was in 1720, and of course the best was yet to come, in the *persona* of M.B. Drapier, the counterfeit image used by Swift in his contest with England over true and false currency, colonial dependency, and the arrogance of English imperialism. "M.B.," the drapier, existed only within the symbolic, material world of print. This paper is concerned with the transformations of that material image within the sign-system of Swift's Dublin, and, to a lesser extent, with aspects of the sign system itself.

---

[1] "Observations Occasioned by Reading a Paper, Entitled, The Case of the Woollen Manufacturers of Dublin, &c. (1733)," *Prose Works*, XIII, 90.

[2] Liam O'Flynn, "The Dean's Pamphlet," *Out to An Other side*, Tara CD 3031, Tara Records (Dublin, 1993). The accompanying note includes the following: "The dexterity of the lyrics necessitated Rita [Connolly], who found them, in taking her verses at a slower tempo than the instrumental which follows." Swift's poem is here re-set to the tune of "Tatter Jack Walsh."

# I

When Thomas Sheridan first proposed the public celebration of Swift's birthday in *The Intelligencer*, no 18 (26–30 November 1728), he presented to his Irish audience a thoroughly familiar object, an already disseminated Swift, an allegorical figure in the public sphere.[3] Sheridan's proposal makes no mention of Swift by name, referring only to the "DRAPIER," whose fictive birthday was the actual birthday of his creator, 30 November, St Andrew's Day. Sheridan's proposal was adopted and decoded, and for many years thereafter the Dublin newspapers faithfully record the weaving of "Swift" into the ceremonial and symbolic texture of Dublin's processional calendar. Here is a typical entry, immediately preceding an advertisement for the "just published" *Gulliver's Travels*, from *The Dublin Intelligence, or Weekly Gazette*, Tuesday, 29 November 1726:

> Wednesday last being kept as the Anniversary of the Birth Day of the Reverend Dr. Jon. Swift, Dean of St. Patrick's; the same was Usher'd in with Ringing of Bell's [*sic*], and unusual Demonstrations of Joy and Gladness for his Reverence's Health, were observed in most parts of the City, at Night there were some Bonfires and other Illuminations on the same Occasion.

Whatever the term "unusual" might mean here, it was, like the Freedom of the City of Cork granted to him in 1737, a recognition of the extraordinary symbolic and civic status accorded to Jonathan Swift the private individual.[4] The mythologized Drapier, Swift's allegorical simulacrum, was transacted as public property, and passed on into Irish history, though not quite in the way Swift envisaged. In a typical example of Swift's ability to speak proleptically, from beyond the material circumstances of his own writing and of his own death, his 1729 poem "Drapier's Hill" savours the transformation of the Drapier, originally a political and economic signifier, into a relationship with Nature and Writing:

> when a Nation long enslav'd,
> Forgets by whom it once was sav'd;
> When none the DRAPIER's Praise shall sing;
> His Signs aloft no longer swing;
> [No Drapier's head in ev'ry street,
> Where honest Clubs were us'd to meet.]
> His Medals and his Prints forgotten,
> And all his Handkerchiefs are rotten;
> His famous LETTERS made waste Paper;
> This Hill may keep the Name of DRAPIER:
> In Spight of Envy flourish still,
> And DRAPIER's vye with COOPER's Hill.[5] (ll. 11–20)

Swift regarded his involuntary inscription within history as no cause for celebration. His

---

[3]  Jonathan Swift and Thomas Sheridan, *The Intelligencer*, ed. James Woolley (Oxford, 1992), pp. 197–203. Sheridan's secondary purpose was to raise money to relieve the distress of Sarah Harding, the widow of the printer of the *Drapier's Letters*.

[4]  See *Correspondence*, V, 67 (Swift to the Corporation of Cork, 15 August 1737). In returning their box, Swift complained that without an inscription the gesture was not only inappropriate but also meaningless, since there were no "Motives assigned in the Instrument of his Freedom."

[5]  *The Poems of Jonathan Swift*, ed. Harold Williams, 2nd ed., 3 vols (Oxford, 1958), III, 874–75. If only for their informative value, I include in parentheses the two MS lines added in the Acheson copy and recorded by Williams. Drapier's Hill, of course, was never built.

birthday (unlike Stella's) was an occasion for reading the Book of Job and for cursing the day whereon he was born.[6] Dubliners nevertheless annexed his anniversary celebration to those of a highly select group which included William III, George II, Queen Caroline, Frederick Prince of Wales, the current Lord Lieutenant, and to the commemorative days set aside for certain mythical and historical persons and events such as St Cecilia, the 1641 rebellion, and the Gunpowder Plot. We should not forget that the marginalized Catholic majority observed an alternative political calendar: while the Anglo-Irish Protestant Ascendancy celebrated a Hanoverian monarch, the Catholics celebrated the birthday of the Pretender on St Stephen's Green in their own carnivalesque way.[7] Swift's close friends and allies celebrated in a variety of private and public ways.[8]

Swift's dissemination, his semiotic transformation into a Dublin event, proceeded quickly, and "Swift's Head" eventually joined "Homer's Head," "Virgil's Head," "Milton's Head," and "Newton's Head" as a bookseller's sign. The son of the printer of the *Drapier's Letters*, John Harding, baptized shortly after his father's death in 1725, was named John Draper Harding,[9] and George Faulkner proudly displayed Cunningham's bust of Swift outside his house on a bracket, before it was eventually presented in 1776 by Thomas Todd Faulkner to St Patrick's Cathedral, where it still stands over Swift's monument. Birthday poems for Swift became a minor genre,[10] and James Hamilton's *Dublin Daily Advertiser* for 7 January 1737 marked the commodification of Swift in its poetry competition on "the Reverend PATRIOT of IRELAND, J. SWIFT, D.D.," with a cash prize and a year's free subscription to five daily copies of the newspaper printed on Royal Paper. Taverns and coffee-houses adopted the "Drapier's Head" as their icon; Drapier's Clubs sprang up in 1724, and songs and poems survive which commemorate meetings at Taplin's club at the sign of the Drapier's Head in Truck Street, convened not only to express political solidarity with Swift, but also to acknowledge the power of the symbolic system which had produced the figure of M.B. Drapier in the first place:

> With brisk merry Lays,
> We'll sing to the praise
> Of that honest Patriot, the *Drapier*;
> Who all the World knows,
> Confounded our Foes,
> With nothing but Pen, Ink and Paper.[11]

---

[6] See *Correspondence*, V, 128 (Swift to Mrs Whiteway, 27 November 1738), referring to Job 3.3: "Let the day perish wherein I was born, and the night in which it was said, There is a man child conceived."

[7] See *Dublin Journal*, 13 June 1724.

[8] See Mrs Whiteway's letter to Swift, 29 November 1735: "I shall make a great entertainment to-morrow for my family, to celebrate the Drapier's birth-day, and drink his health" (*Correspondence*, IV, 443). In 1733, when news of the defeat of the Excise Bill in England came through, a "dozen young Men of the Liberty of St Patrick's joined together to have a Bonfire on the Steeple, and another before the Dean's House; where they gave a Barrel of Ale in Tubs to express their Joy, and the following Healths were drunk with great Solemnity, and at the close of each, A Health to that Worthy Patriot the DRAPIER, who saved our Nation from Ruin" (*Dublin Journal*, 17 April 1733).

[9] See Robert Munter, *The History of the Irish Newspaper, 1685-1760* (Cambridge, 1967), p. 150 n 1 (quoting the *Parish Records of St John the Evangelist*, Dublin, for 28 June 1728).

[10] For three examples, see *Select Poetical Works of the late William Dunkin, D.D.*, 2 vols (Dublin, 1769–70), II, 357–70. Dunkin routinely associates "M.B." with Marcus Brutus.

[11] *Fraud Detected: or, The Hibernian Patriot. Containing All the Drapier's Letters to the People*

Faulkner's *Dublin Journal* (Saturday, 1 May 1725) solicited subscriptions for an edition of the *Drapier's Letters*, poems and songs, the subscriptions to be taken in under Taplin's sign of the Drapier, a strange semiotic migration from the figural to the material and back again.

The streets of Dublin during Swift's time were regularly turned over to anniversary processions, civic ceremonies, marches, guild pageants, and not infrequently such events became a theatre of organized cultural nationalism. We are no longer familiar with such occasions either as transformations of workplace skills into celebrations of history and genealogy, or as assertions of economic presence, and so the semiotic richness of such occasions now has the power to astonish us. On 8 August 1728, on the day appointed for riding the franchises of the city, and also to celebrate the proclamation day of the late George II, the *Dublin Intelligence* described several guild "Societies" each processing behind its respective emblem: bricklayers and masons marched "with King Solomon's Figure at their Front, and the Famous Temple of Jerusalem finely adorn'd in Miniature, carried before them;" the woolcombers' company of journeymen went by with the "Image or Appearance of Bishop BLAZE [St Blasius, Bishop of Sebaste, patron of wool-combers], on Horseback before them, the first Improver of their Occupation;" the chimney sweeps (archly described as "the Fraternity of Diabolists") apparently needed no "Ensigne of their Business, but in their Faces;" the company of cutlers and stainers, having chosen a typographer for their Master, were planning to walk behind "an Engine Call'd a PRINTING PRESS, which is to be work'd at in the Eyes of the World, and Discover some Secrets never yet heard of, from a Carriage Drawn by Six Horses; The Weavers are to have Looms, and the Taylors ADAM and EVE, to show the Antiquity of their Profession." The key figure among the draymen and brewer's servants evidently had no understanding of the purely symbolic function of his role: described as a "Natural Bacchus," he had to be carried to his bed senseless.

The printing press, we should notice, was a most prominent feature of this semiotic pageantry, exhibiting a wondrously new stage in its still mysterious technological progress (the reference is probably to the recently introduced technique of stereotyping, first mentioned in a report in Richard Dickson's *The Old Dublin Intelligence* for 6 October 1730), and it continues as a symbol of secular, political, and nationalistic enfranchisement. The poem printed on this machine on this very day maps the process from a manuscript to a print culture and sees Ireland as a particular beneficiary of a European technological enlightenment:

> The gen'rous Art, unable to withstand
> The Errors of the tedious Copyist's Hand,
> Unfaithful to its Trust, had almost dy'd,
> Till the fam'd Press the failing Pen supply'd:
> Scarcely sufficient to preserve its Name
> From *Tyrant's Malice* and the *Bigot's Flame*;
> Nor yet secure through mouldring Years to dwell,
> 'Midst Moths and Cobwebs in a Monkish Cell;
> Till what the great *Phoenician* had begun,
> Was finish'd by Germania's Godlike Son,

---

of Ireland, on *Wood's Coinage, &c.* (Dublin: George Faulkner, 1725). Swift presented a copy to the Bodleian, and inscribed it as follows: "Humbly presented/to the Bodleyan Library/in Oxford/ by M.B. Drapier" (cited in *The Drapier's Letters to the People of Ireland against Receiving Wood's Halfpence*, ed. Herbert Davis [Oxford, 1935], p. xc).

Learning revives, nor fears again t'expire,
Midst *Papal Ignorance* and *Gothic Fire*;
Let glad HIBERNIA Hail the Noble Art,
That mends the Mind, and cultivates the Heart!
New tune the Harp, with Permanence secure,
And charm inspiring Muses to thy Lure
The RARE MACHINE let all her Sons revere
Nor doubt an *Elzivir* and *Stephens* here;
While latest Times *Newton*, entire, shall boast,
Nor mourn an *Addison*, like *Livy*, lost![12]

There is no mention of Swift in this 1728 poem, but print was his natural medium, and the Dublin scene was the undisputed territory of his mastery. Apart from the obvious indecorum, there would be little point in carnivalizing Swift since he was already incarnated as the principle of opposition. Far away in London, however, the idea seemed not at all preposterous. In 1732, Swift's friend Alderman John Barber, soon (29 September 1732) to be Lord Mayor of London and a key figure in the print culture of his day, actually proposed a similar procession for the Lord Mayor's Day of 1733: "a raree-show (or pageant) as of old ... Mr. Pope and I were thinking to have a large machine carried through the city, with a printing-press, author, publishers, hawkers, devils, etc., and a satirical poem printed and thrown from the press to the mob, in public view, but not to give offence; but your absence spoils that design."[13] Swift, of course, would always be "absent" from such material pageantry.

In a world of transformation, Swift stayed the same, a creation of the press, transcendently the Drapier but always the Dean. The only surviving contemporary illustration of M.B. Drapier I know is manifestly not a portrait of a dealer in cloth and cloth goods, but a cartouche-like, three-quarter portrait of a bewigged and gowned cleric writing with a quill pen (Figure 1). It is Faulkner's title-page illustration to *A Proposal for Giving Badges to the Beggars in all the Parishes of Dublin* (1737), and it is perhaps the only surviving image we have of the unknown number of such signs which appeared all over Dublin after the Drapier's triumph in 1725.[14] For its purpose and occasion, this is an unusually and even

[12] [Constantia Grierson?], "A poem on the Art of Printing, Which was wrought at the PRINTING MACHINE carry'd before the Corporarion [*sic*] of Stationers, Cutlers and Painters, on Thursday the 8th of this Instant August 1728, the Day appointed for riding the Franchises of this City" (BL C. 121. g. 8. no 169). There are in fact two poems under this title, and I quote from the more elaborate second poem entitled "Verses added to the former by another hand," claimed by James Sterling in his *Works*, 1734; see further Bryan Coleborne, "Jonathan Swift and the Dunces of Dublin," diss., National University of Ireland (1982), pp. 302, 334. See also the same author's "The Dublin Grub Street: The Documentary Evidence in the Case of John Browne," *Swift Studies*, 2 (1987), 12–24, and A. C. Elias, Jr, "A Manuscript Book of Constantia Grierson's," *Swift Studies*, 2 (1987), 33–35. The early history of stereotyping is "uncertain"; for an account, see B. J. McMullin, "Joseph Athias and the early history of stereotyping," *Quaerendo*, 23, no 3 (1993), 184–207.

[13] *Correspondence*, IV, 62 (John Barber to Swift, 24 August 1732). For Swift's reply, see IV, 71 (11 September 1732).

[14] *Prose Works*, XIII, 129–40. I examined the Gilbert Collection (Dublin) copy of Faulkner's octavo (11.3 × 17 cm.), in which Hibernia's harp and Britannia's Union Jack are clearly shown, and the British Library copy of the 1737 London quarto printed for T. Cooper (18.5 × 23.27 cm.), which omits portrait, head- and tail-pieces. For a discussion of Dublin shop-signs, see Thomas Wall's study of Catholic printers in Dublin at this time, *The Sign of Doctor Hay's Head* (Dublin, 1958).

# A
# PROPOSAL
### FOR GIVING
# BADGES
### TO THE
# BEGGARS
### IN ALL THE
## Parifhes of *DUBLIN*.

By the Dean of St. PATRICK's.

*M. B. Drapier*

*DUBLIN*:
Printed by GEORGE FAULKNER, Bookfeller, in
*Effex-Street*, oppofite to the Bridge,
M DCC XXX VII.

Figure 1: Title-page of Faulkner's 1737 Dublin octavo

A

# PROPOSAL

FOR GIVING

# BADGES, &c.

I T hath been a general Complaint, that the Poor-Houfe, efpecially fince the new Conftitution by Act of Parliament, hath been of no Benefit to this City, for the Eafe of which it was wholly intended. I had the Honour to be a Member of it many Years before it was new modelled by the Legiflature; not from any perfonal Regard, but meerly as

A 2 one

Figure 2: Head-piece of Faulkner's 1737 Dublin octavo

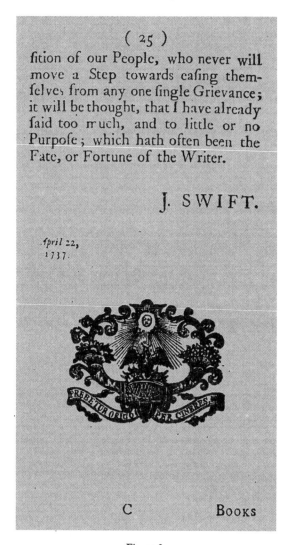

Figure 3

ironically decorative pamphlet. Part of its aesthetic purpose is undoubtedly to celebrate Swift's earlier writing as M.B. Drapier, since the head-piece on A2 has been re-used from an earlier text, that is, copies of the second issue of the fourth volume of Faulkner's 1735 edition of the *Works* (which contains the *Drapier's Letters*).[15] There are thus two images of

---

[15] *The Drapier's Letters to the People of Ireland against Receiving Wood's Halfpence*, p. xciii. Davis points out that the head-piece illustrates the content of *Tom Punsibi's Dream* (see pp. 298–302). See also Ehrenpreis, *Dean Swift*, p. 208, on the Drapier's address and voice. For a dozen locations for Drapier signs, see Davis (1935), p. 382 n 1. In his 1935 and 1941 editions of the *Drapier's Letters*, Davis used different states of the title-page illustration, that is, Vertue's allegorical portrait of Swift as the Drapier seated between two female

the Drapier in *A Proposal*, the title-page image of a writing cleric and the political allegory of the same figure turning away from Britannia on his left in order to alleviate the miseries of Hibernia on his right, under the emblematic message, "DETUR INDIGENTI" (Figure 2). The text is closed with a further allegorical emblem (Figure 3) which might suggest that the Drapier, like Phoebus, draws the phoenix of Ireland from the flames of its own destruction.[16]

The mimetic specificity of the first two portraits is designed not to conceal Swift behind the image of a tradesman but to depict the Drapier as an ecclesiastical statesman. The political point, therefore, is not to merge Swift with his *persona* in some kind of symbolic gesture but to preserve their separate identities, to allegorize Swift by *flaunting* both the gap and the identity between the middle-class tradesman of St Francis' Street, and the Dean of St Patrick's. Just as the markedly Christian "voice" of the Drapier contrasts with the voice of Gulliver, so Swift's signature at the end of the *Proposal* contrasts with the authorial gamesmanship of his major satires.[17] The pamphlet is thus prefaced with a graphic likeness of the absent Dean as public man in the frame of an authentic image of the fictive Drapier, and the text is authenticated with a printed image of Swift's absent signature.

The business of the pamphlet is explicitly semiotic: it proposes that beggars be compelled to wear metal signs declaring not their poverty (which would have been obvious enough), but their parish of origin. The analogy with another of Swift's signed pamphlets, the *Proposal for Correcting, Improving, and Ascertaining the English Tongue* (1712) is striking: in both cases the inconvenient tendency of the human being and the linguistic signifier to a wandering life is to be fixed by stabilizing the sign. Those who originate in Dublin parishes are the proper responsibility of the metropolis; those who are from elsewhere are not. Again, the issue is not one of authentic as opposed to inauthentic beggary, nor with the substance to which it refers, nor even to beggary, but essentially with the efficacy of the sign system as such.

---

figures (residually based on Hibernia and Britannia?), signed "Vertu[e]" only in Davis 1935. The Monash copies of 1735, 1738 and 1742 are the same as Davis 1935. But what did Davis use for the 1941 *Prose Works*, X, facing p. 1? (An examination might begin with the enlargement and elaboration of the Irish harp in the bottom right-hand corner, which obliterates the original signature.)

[16] This may or may not have been originally intended as a "portrait" of Swift as Phoebus. It is re-used elsewhere to ornament other Irish texts by Swift in Faulkner's various editions. Was the sign of the Drapier already beginning to fade from the public memory in 1736? One stanza of "The Devil upon Two Sticks: or, A Hue and Cry after the Drapier's Club." Written by the Clerk of the Parish" (Dublin, 1736) describes a variant of Faulkner's Drapier, though still a writer: "The Sign, if you must know it, was / The witty WOLLEN [*sic*] DRAPIER, / With wreath of Lawrel on his Head, / In hand a piece of Paper." See further Bryan Coleborne, "Jonathan Swift and the Voices of Irish Protest against Wood's Halfpence," *Monash Swift Papers*, 1, eds Clive Probyn and Bryan Coleborne (1988), p. 79.

[17] The distinction I adopt is explained at length in Paul de Man, *Blindness and Insight: Essays in the Rhetoric of Contemporary Criticism* (New York, 1971), particularly on pp. 187–89. Wordsworth and Swift have their proleptic capacities in common, I believe (compare my comment above on "Drapier's Hill" with de Man's comment on p. 225).

## II

Swift was very interested in the economy of signs in contemporary Dublin. It was already rich and complex before he inserted the Drapier into it, although once inserted the Drapier materialized in an unusually wide range of print and non-print locations – on swinging shop-signs, signposts, medals, and handkerchiefs from 1724 until at least 1729. But before looking at Swift's own published essay on the modern city's commercial semiology, we should remind ourselves that signs always demand interpretation, and no signs can ever be either autonomous or transparent, least of all those which we transact in what passes for "ordinary life." Here is one example. Scanning the pages of the *Dublin Weekly Journal* for 4 June 1737, the eye and the mind cannot fail to be arrested by this astonishing item of news:

> On Saturday last one Jakes a Butchers [*sic*] in Truck-street, hanged himself in a Cellar between two Lambs that he had just killed and dressed; the Place was so low that he was found in a kneeling Posture.

The fact that a butcher who spends his time slaughtering animals should one day slaughter himself is already saturated in ironic potentialities and permeated with symbolic doublings and pre-texts. Did the newswriter perceive any relationship between the lambs, the symbols of sacrificial innocence, and the act of suicide? Was the kneeling posture only the consequence of a low ceiling, itself the consequence of poverty? Why did Jakes dress the lambs before hanging himself between them? Was this small and unframed text meant to be seen as a fragment of the larger and grander narrative of Christian typology?

In the pages of James Carson's *Dublin Weekly Journal* on one single day, Saturday, 15 October 1726, there are examples among the advertisements of classical or iconic signs, which signify exactly and precisely – thus, John Exshaw sells lace and "Edging of the newest and most fashionable Patterns of every Kind ... at the Sign of the Laced Hood in Golden Lane." Thomas Gold, card maker, similarly, is "naturally" to be found at the sign of the Knave of Clubs. In another example, Anne Exhee, "living at the Sign of the Coat and Britches in Patrick's Close, Dublin, continues to sell all sorts of Cloaths, Druggets, German Sarges, and Sagathees ... at very reasonable Rates." In each of these examples, and in countless more, the sign behaves as de Saussure says it does: the signifier and the signified (the latter being an inanimate object) are inextricably attached to each other. But in other examples, those in which the human (naming) agent is involved, the signifier is split from its signified, and becomes a link in an endless chain of signifiers. Gaps and slippages now open up which generate disjointedness at the least, and downright meaninglessness at times. Thus, on the same page of the *Dublin Weekly Journal* (15 October 1726), there is the following example of signs floating completely free of their original signified: "Martha Saise, who formerly liv'd at the Sign of the Royal Garter in Crane Lane ... [has] now removed to the Sign of the Drapers Head on Temple-Bar, where Persons of Quality and others may be furnished with Servants and Nurses, as formerly." Where, we might ask, is the semiological sense in this? The Drapier's head now signifies a location for a domestic employment agency, where once it was an index to a purveyor of woollen goods. And one final example, in which the sign's original referential function has now turned into the marker of an individual's wandering life: "At the Spread Eagle on the Blind Key, opposite Smoke Alley, at the Shop in which Mr. Holland formerly liv'd, are sold all sorts of Sooty colour'd Hair, and Trimmings for Wigs, with good weaving Silk, at reasonable Rates, By John Roe." In this example, the concrete particulars that once validated iconic signs have become purely symbolic sedimentary layers in an increasingly complex system of topographical codes: they only make a pattern in the individual biography of John Roe. A new trajectory of signification is built on the ruins of the old, and only the already initiated can decipher the intended relationship.

Swift's own semiotic transformation into a figure of Irish resistance is mirrored in his appearance as M.B. Drapier as "the Darling of the populace; His Image and Superscription on a great many Sign-Posts in this City and other great Towns," in the words of Bishop Nicolson.[18] Such a shop-sign dating from before the *Drapier's Letters* would have been an index of trade, and may have included a bolt of cloth, or an item of clothing, for example. But a shop-sign described as "the Drapier's Head" in 1729 (with or without a portrait) would now be inescapably plural, doubled, ironic, an allegory of reading and writing, for it would signify as an icon of trade, an image of a fictitious writer, a literary image of Swift perhaps, a graphic likeness of the Dean of St Patrick's, and also a sign of Irish economic resistance. In one printed advertisement from *The Old Dublin Intelligence*, Tuesday, 2 December 1729, the proprietor promises to give "all possible Encouragement, for the Consumption of the Manufactures of this Kingdom," and the typography signals a special effort to sell "*Irish Broad Cloaths.*" In this example, the sign of the Drapier is textualized not only by Swiftian energies, but also by more pragmatic considerations, since mobs had been roaming the streets of Dublin stripping foreign clothes off their wearers' backs. The sign expresses its political filiation in the language of commerce and also, one might suspect, as a form of insurance against damage.

In the spring of 1732, Swift published his own analysis of the modern city's commercial semiology under the title *An Examination of Certain Abuses, Corruptions, and Enormities in the City of Dublin.*[19] The pamphlet is a kind of semiotic witch-hunt, using the voice of a blustering, politically paranoid Whig apologist bent on flushing out Tory plots against the Administration: it transmits Swift's memories of the Atterbury trial and the Layer Plot of 1722, alluded to in the poem "Upon the Horrid Plot discovered by Harlequin the B[ishop] of R[ochester]'s French Dog" (1722), and in Chapter six of the Voyage to Laputa (1726). Here were two moments in modern politics when the signifier was so completely detached from the signified that "a Close-stool [may] signify a Privy-Council; a Flock of Geese, a Senate; a lame Dog, an Invader; the Plague, a standing Army; a Buzard, a Minister; the Gout, a High Priest; a Gibbet, a Secretary of State; a Chamber pot, a Committee of Grandees," and so on.[20] As Swift's narrator walks along the streets of Dublin, he notices, among other examples, apparently innocent shop signs such as the spread eagle, the cock, or the swan, and each is deciphered as a coded message of dissent and subversion. Thus, the superscript "G.R. II" on signs bearing the King's head signifies not, as the naive reader might think, "George the Second," but a dangerous supplement, George King the Second, the usurper of the authentic and natural king (the Pretender) who is by implied right in first place as the true and authentic King. Another example from Swift's excursion into what he calls "the rules of *Hieroglyph*" is the sign of the punch bowl, where the action of squeezing an orange in order to make punch is interpreted as a covert Jacobite insult against the memory of the Protestant William of Orange. Swift may perhaps be arguing that one of the

---

[18]  Bishop Nicolson to Archbishop Wake (*Wake MSS*, ccxlvii), quoted by Davis, *Prose Works*, X, xxx-xxxi.

[19]  *Prose Works*, XII, 215–32.

[20]  *Prose Works*, XI, 191 (III, vi, 12).

consequences of the collapse of the Tory Government in 1713 is that language which once signified consensually has now been deconstructed by the paranoid suspicion of perverse, insecure, undereducated, factional and Whiggish misreaders. But for Swift the ironist (and what is Swift other than an ironist?) it could also be argued that the sign always covers a rupture, and always contains the potentiality of its own contradiction and substitution.

The play of the signifier in a satirical fantasy is one thing; doing the same thing in the real world of eighteenth-century Dublin, where the relationship between the signifier and the signified was in some cases rigidly policed, is something else. In an example from *The Dublin Intelligence* for 2 August 1726, there is a report of a man called Bennett who set up a public house in the rules of the Fleet under the sign of the Bishop's Head, with the announcement *"I marry at reasonable Rates"* inscribed beneath it. Like the drunken Bacchus noted above, Bennett invited potential clients to see substance where there was only a sign, and he was accordingly committed to Newgate for his hermeneutical transgression. For a Swiftian example, in addition to the *Proposal for Correcting, Improving, and Ascertaining the English Tongue*, we need look no further than the zeal with which the Dean asserted his own prerogatives and dignity both as a private citizen and as a public functionary charged with certain symbolic responsibilities. Writing to the newspapers could serve him as an effective equivalent of a sentence to Newgate. For both the high and the low his most effective weapon was print. On 21 October 1735, he wrote to Bathurst:

> If a tradesman cheats me, I put him immediately into a newspaper, with the bare matter of fact, which the rogues are grown so afraid of, that they are often ready to fall on their knees for pardon.
> I began this scheme with a long record upon a large peice [*sic*] of black marble in my own Cathedral, on the north side of the Altar, whereon I put a Latin inscription which I took care to have published in 7 London news papers. The granddaughter of the old Duke of Schomberg w^d not send me 50^ll to make him a Monument over his burying-place; upon which I ordered the whole story to be engraved, and you must have seen the writing several years ago to the scandall of the family; particularly because his present M[ajesty] said, G— d— D^r S. whose design was to make him quarrell with the K. of Prussia. Thus I endeavour to do justice in my station, and give no offence.[21]

If our lives are always already organized at the level of the sentence, as Paul Ricœur has told us, then how much more potent ("scandalous") are those sentences when chiselled in marble for all to see, for they go on telling the story of the neglect of a great man by his family to the last syllable of recorded time. This is what John Browne, the owner of an iron works in County Mayo and the target of Swift's attack in the third Drapier's letter, discovered:

> The cause for which you undertook my ruin, was the Cause of my Country: it was a good Cause and you shall ever find me of that side, you have carryed it and I know you will noe longer be My Enemy; But alas S^r as long as your Works subsist, where ever they be read, even unto the end of time must I be branded as a Villain? tis a hard Sentence and yet unless the Spear of Achilles, the same instrument which gave the wound administers the remedy it must be soe.[22]

---

21   *Correspondence*, IV, 409–10. A report of this incident, complete with Swift's Latin inscription and an English translation also appeared in the *Dublin Weekly Journal* for 17 April 1731. For a further example, relating to the attempted removal of the Duke of Ormonde's scutcheon from the cathedral after the Duke's "expatriation," see "The Streets of Dublin," *Irish Quarterly Review*, 3, no 7 (June 1853), 583. See also n. 4 above.

22   *Correspondence*, III, 282–83 (John Browne to Swift, 4 April 1728). Swift's attack on Browne will be found in the earlier editions of the Drapier's third *Letter*. After this letter, Swift deleted the attack for Faulkner's 1735 *Works* (see *Prose Works*, X, xv, and 210–11). On his part, Browne erected a monument in honour of Swift.

Browne was forgiven by Swift, and if only because he recognized the profoundly ambiguous power of Swift's writing to administer both a cure and a poison, Browne deserves our forgiveness, too. The power of Swift's textual *pharmakon*, a weaving and at the same time an unravelling, provided in the *Drapier's Letters* the cloth for a distinctly Irish resistance and the textual stripping bare of the English Government's policy. The *Drapier's Letters*, long after the episode which prompted them, go on spelling out the perfidy in a line of fixed, unmovable print.

The sign of the Drapier was thus always a compound, doubled sign. Weaving is, after all, an ancient metaphor for writing, and Lucien Dällenbach has reminded us that the loom is "the image par excellence of the textual machine."[23] A drapier once wove cloth; then the drapier sold the textile manufactured by the weaver; the writer always weaves a text from inherited fabric. Swift's cathedral was surrounded by the poor dwellings of the weavers, who idolized him. The Drapier thus depended on the weavers in a double sense, as suppliers of material and as subjects for his own trade of writing. With his extraordinary gift for turning language inside out, for showing the constructedness of all narrative, and for showing the material source of his Irish writing in the negativities of poverty, knavery, and foolishness, Swift wrote to Charles Ford in 1721 about the print world of Dublin:

> We abound in Papers as well as you, and I have observed it to be one of the Consequences of wretched Times, and it seems naturall enough, that when People are reduced to Rags they should turn them to the onely Use that Rags are proper for.[24]

---

[23] Lucien Dällenbach, *The Mirror in the Text*, trans. Jeremy Whateley, with Emma Hughes (Cambridge, 1989), pp. 97–98 (first published as *Le récit spéculaire* [Paris, 1977]). Robert Ashton's "Congratulatory POEM to the Reverend DAEN [*sic*] Swift" (BL, Poems C. 121. g. 8, no 64) includes the line: "Swift both in Name, in Shuttle and in Pen," and from the same source (no 10), there is Swift's "An EPILOGUE, To be spoke at the THEATRE-ROYAL This present Saturday being *April* the 1st. [1720] In the Behalf of the Distressed *WEAVERS:*"

> Perhaps you wonder whence this Friendship Springs,
> Between the *Weavers* and us Play-House Kings.
> But Wit and Weaving had the same beginning,
> *Pallas* first taugh[t] us Poetry and Spinning;
> And next Observe how this Alliance fits,
> For *Weavers* now are just as poor as Wits;
> Their Brother Quill-Men Workers for the Stage,
> For sorry *Stuff*, can get a Crown a Page. (ll. 35–42)

The point here, of course, is that Latin *textus*, "text," is derived from *texere*, "to weave."

[24] *Correspondence*, II, 380–81.

Phillip Harth
*University of Wisconsin, Madison*

# Friendship and Politics: Swift's Relations with Pope in the Early 1730s

ABSTRACT. The letters that Swift and Pope exchanged during the five or six years following the appearance of *The Dunciad* in 1728 show a gradual but significant change taking place in the relations between the two friends. The bond that had developed between them earlier, in which they had come to adopt a somewhat exaggerated view of themselves as authors sharing a fund of common interests, tastes, and attitudes, began to weaken as Swift grew increasingly absorbed in Irish politics: a subject that was alien to Pope's own concerns, sympathies, and political goals. Yet their letters also reveal that while Swift and Pope were forced to recognize their diverging attitudes, they did so without openly admitting to each other their extent, or allowing them to affect their cherished friendship.

Six months after the *Dunciad Variorum* appeared in 1729, Pope wrote to Swift: "It was my principal aim in the entire work to perpetuate the friendship between us, and to shew that the friends or the enemies of one were the friends or enemies of the other."[1] Read as a factual statement of Pope's purpose in writing the *Dunciad*, this is a preposterous claim as well as an egregious piece of flattery. Read, however, as Swift presumably did read it, as a testimonial to the special relationship they had enjoyed in the years 1726 to 1728 and the respects in which, for themselves, at least, the *Dunciad* had come to memorialize that period of intimacy, Pope's remark would have seemed entirely appropriate. For it was during this very period of the *Dunciad*'s inception, composition, and original publication that Swift had spent two springs and summers in England, most of the time living with Pope at Twickenham – a far longer and more continuous intimacy than they were ever to enjoy at any other period of their lives – and that, under Pope's instigation, they had jointly planned, sponsored, and published the first two volumes of their *Miscellanies*, another venture intended, according to Pope, to perpetuate the unique relationship between the two friends as authors sharing a fund of common interests, tastes, and attitudes. "I am prodigiously pleas'd with this joint-volume," Pope wrote to Swift in 1727 when the earliest of them had been printed but still awaited publication, "in which methinks we look like friends, side by side, serious and merry by turns, conversing interchangeably, and walking down hand in hand to posterity."[2] It was this same cohesiveness between the two friends, expressed particularly in their ven-

---

[1] *Correspondence*, III, 351 (9 October 1729).
[2] *Correspondence*, III, 201 (17 February 1727).

tures into satire, that Pope was proclaiming in his assertion two years later "that the friends or the enemies of one were the friends or enemies of the other."

Swift and Pope had never, of course, shared such perfect unanimity as Pope was given to celebrating, and they would both be far less interesting writers if they had. Their sympathies and aversions, as well as the causes these led them to embrace were in some cases noticeably different, and their recognition of these differences at certain periods of their long friendship is expressed in letters and even poems where they engage in a process of self-definition, sometimes delineating their own norms and attitudes by contrasting them with those of their opposite number. I have discussed elsewhere one such intermittent sparring match in which Swift and Pope treated each other as amiable foils at the time Swift was at work revising *Gulliver's Travels* in the autumn of 1725.[3] What I intend to talk about here is a more prolonged interchange between the two friends in which they were forced gradually to recognize an increasing divergence of sympathies, interests, and goals, but without openly admitting to each other its extent or allowing it to affect their friendship. This process had already begun, in fact, by the time the *Dunciad Variorum* appeared, and the exaggeration of Pope's insistence on their perfect unanimity soon afterwards suggests that he was characteristically denying cracks in this picture which were becoming all too visible.

We can begin with a letter Swift sent to Pope in June 1728. The passage is a familiar one, but it will bear closer examination. Swift is responding to a letter, now lost, in which Pope had called him a patriot:

> I do profess without affectation, that your kind opinion of me as a Patriot (since you call it so) is what I do not deserve; because what I do is owing to perfect rage and resentment, and the mortifying sight of slavery, folly, and baseness about me, among which I am forced to live. And I will take my oath that you have more Virtue in an hour, than I in seven years; for you despise the follies, and hate the vices of mankind, without the least ill effect on your temper; and with regard to particular men, you are inclined always rather to think the better, whereas with me it is always directly contrary. I hope however, this is not in you from a superior principle of virtue, but from your situation, which hath made all parties and interests indifferent to you.[4]

Swift defines himself here by drawing a series of polarities between himself and Pope that at first sight appear to yield all the moral advantage to his friend: his rage and resentment at the slavery, folly, and baseness about him set over against Pope's equanimity of temper; his scorn for individuals as opposed to Pope's charity toward particular men; and his willingness to equate Pope's calm detachment with virtue, his own emotional involvement with its absence. But in reality, Swift is not confessing his moral inferiority to his friend so much as he is defining himself in response not just to Pope's latest letter, but to a theme that had been growing increasingly prominent in his friend's letters over the past five years, and to which Swift had reacted with irritation on more than one occasion earlier. From about the time that Bolingbroke had returned from exile in 1723 and settled near Twickenham, Pope's letters had been celebrating with growing insistence the virtues of retirement, indifference to the world, and calmness of temper, and applying them to himself and his new neighbour. Swift responds here by accepting Pope's familiar equation of virtue with equanimity, but showing that it is their different situations – Ireland and England respectively – and the

---

[3]    See "Swift's Self-Image as a Satirist," *Proceedings of The First Münster Symposium on Jonathan Swift*, eds Hermann J. Real and Heinz J. Vienken (München, 1985), pp. 113–21.

[4]    *Correspondence*, III, 289 (1 June 1728).

radically dissimilar conditions of the two friends that accounts for their moral disparity. On those grounds, Swift stands excused for his intemperate outbursts, while Pope's greater virtue proves to be an accidental attribute he owes entirely to his circumstances rather than to his principles.

When Pope replied with a light-hearted letter completely ignoring his friend's moving words,[5] Swift waited more than a year before trying again. "I am very sensible," he writes to Pope in August 1729 at about the time he would have been at work on *A Modest Proposal*, published two months later, "that in a former letter I talked very weakly of my own affairs, and of my imperfect wishes and desires." Nevertheless, he stubbornly returns to the subject, this time specifying in greater detail than before the appalling condition of Ireland:

> As to this country, there have been three terrible years dearth of corn, and every place strowed with beggars, but dearths are common in better climates, and our evils here lie much deeper. Imagine a nation the two-thirds of whose revenues are spent out of it, and who are not permitted to trade with the other third, and where the pride of the women will not suffer them to wear their own manufactures even where they excel what come from abroad. This is the true state of Ireland in a very few words. These evils operate more every day, and the kingdom is absolutely undone, as I have been telling it often in print these ten years past.[6]

As if increasingly conscious of the drawbacks of his friend's cherished indifference, Swift continues: "What I have said requires your forgiveness; but I had a mind for once to let you know the state of our affairs, and my reason for being more moved than perhaps becomes a Clergyman, and a piece of a philosopher." When this drew nothing but a perfunctory sentence of personal sympathy from Pope, Swift insistently returned to the sufferings of Ireland in his next letter, only to have Pope at last observe impatiently, "Your continual deplorings of Ireland, make me wish, you were here long enough to forget those scenes that so afflict you," that is to say, to acquire some much-needed indifference, like Pope himself.[7] Then, after bantering Swift as an incorrigible patriot, the very epithet his friend had sharply disclaimed already, he turns to his own affairs.

A few months later, in early 1730, Swift's *Libel on Dr Delany, and a Certain Great Lord* was published in Dublin and London. It is Swift's response to his friend Delany's *Epistle to Lord Carteret*, in which Delany had openly sought a better clerical living from the Lord Lieutenant as a token of the easy familiarity that he, as well, he emphasized, as his friend Swift, enjoyed with Carteret. Swift's vehement rejoinder, as Robert W. Uphaus showed some years ago, was motivated by his anger at Delany's innocently implicating him in this plea for patronage based on reciprocal favours.[8] In the early part of his poem, Swift reproves Delany's misplaced ambition by detailing the disappointments and indignities suffered by other poets, including Swift's friend Gay, who had sought preferment from princes or ministers. In contrast to these, Swift praises Pope for his independence:

---

5   See *Correspondence*, III, 290–91 (28 June 1728).
6   *Correspondence*, III, 340–41 (11 August 1729).
7   *Correspondence*, III, 363 (28 November 1729). For the letters preceding this one, see *Correspondence*, III, 351–52 (Pope to Swift, 9 October 1729), and III, 355–56 (Swift to Pope, 31 October 1729).
8   See his "Swift's 'Whole Character': The Delany Poems and 'Verses on the Death of Dr. Swift,'" *Modern Language Quarterly*, 34 (1973), 406–16.

> Hail! happy Pope, whose generous mind,
> Detesting all the statesman kind!
> Contemning courts, at courts unseen,
> Refused the visits of a queen;
> A soul with every virtue fraught
> By sages, priests, or poets taught:
>
> His heart too great, though fortune little,
> To lick a rascal statesman's spittle;
> Appealing to the nation's taste,
> Above the reach of want is placed:
> By Homer dead was taught to thrive,
> Which Homer never could alive:
> And, sits aloft on Pindus' head,
> Despising slaves that cringe for bread.[9]

Once again, as in the letter we examined earlier, Swift generously compliments his friend and praises him particularly for his virtue. And as before, he equates virtue with independence and equanimity, while polarizing Pope with others. But this time Pope is contrasted not with Swift – with whose own attitudes toward courts and ministers Swift freely associates him on this occasion – but with their mutual friend Gay in particular. And as we might expect, knowing Swift's warm feelings for the latter, the contrast is only apparently to Gay's disadvantage. For while Pope is more independent than the others, and therefore the most virtuous of all, Swift is at pains to remind us that there is a solid economic base supporting Pope's virtue. It is the profits from his translation of Homer that have secured Pope's independence, a luxury that Gay cannot afford because he lacks a steady income and must therefore seek patronage out of financial necessity. Hence once again Pope's virtue is shown to be really due to his circumstances and a peculiarly fortunate situation that has placed him "above the reach of want" where he can despise the "slaves that cringe for bread." And by the same token, the clerical living Delany already enjoys deprives him of any excuse for compromising his own independence as he has tried to do.

As is well known, no sooner had Pope read Swift's poem than he wrote in agitation to his friend Fortescue: "I've had another Vexation, from the sight of a paper of verses said to be Dr Swift's, which has done more by praising me than all the Libels could by abusing me, Seriously troubled me: As indeed one indiscreet Friend can at any time hurt a man more than a hundred silly Enemies. I can hardly bring myself to think it His, or that it is possible his Head should be so giddy."[10] Students of Swift and Pope have widely misunderstood the latter's complaint, obscuring the true significance of Swift's poem to his friend. Almost invariably it is said that at a time when Pope was hoping, with Fortescue's aid, to reach some kind of accommodation with the Government, he was greatly embarrassed by the two or three lines claiming that he had avoided the Court and refused a visit from the Queen while scorning to make any overtures to a rascal statesman – Walpole. Pope may very well have regretted Swift's inclusion of these two or three lines and deplored their unfortunate timing, but this is hardly enough to explain the deeply pained reaction he expressed to Fortescue, suggesting some far graver cause.

---

[9] *Poems*, p. 406, ll. 71–76, 81–88.
[10] *The Correspondence of Alexander Pope*, ed. George Sherburn, 5 vols (Oxford, 1956), III, 91 (20 February 1730).

What has been overlooked about this passage extolling Pope is that he himself was actually pleased with it. We would not expect him to repeat to Swift the reaction he had disclosed to Fortescue, but his comments about them to Swift far exceed the polite expression of thanks that was called for. In no fewer than five letters to Swift over the next three years, Pope keeps expressing his gratitude to his friend for these lines "flattering his virtue," as he modestly described their significance to him at first.[11] But as time passed and he kept returning to the verses, Pope began to speak more directly; they were "the best panegyrick on myself, that either my own times or any other could have afforded, or will ever afford to me," and the reason, as he disclosed shortly afterwards, was that in these lines "I am immortal for my Morality: I never took any praise so kindly," he adds, "and yet I think I deserve that praise better than I do any other."[12]

The confusion seems to arise from critics' assuming that Pope's complaint to Fortescue (that Swift's poem "has done more by praising me than all the Libels could by abusing me") is an objection against the compliments themselves rather than against the poem in which they appear. In reality, Pope is distressed because Swift has innocently implicated him in his poem by the lines in which he associates Pope's attitudes with his own and proceeds to praise him for them. Thus, just as Delany's *Epistle to Lord Carteret* had unintentionally implicated his friend Swift to the latter's disgust, Swift's poem in answer to this has thoughtlessly served his own friend Pope much the same turn. This, not the praise itself, is what Pope deplores as Swift's indiscretion.

I shall consider in a moment the reasons Pope would have had for wishing so eagerly to dissociate himself from the attitudes expressed in Swift's poem, the first of a series of such verses his friend would publish over the next few years. But the embarrassments *A Libel on Dr Delany* would cause Pope had not yet ended. They came to a head, as they were bound to do, when the two friends began sorting through their existing verse and prose early in 1732 in preparation for the long-delayed final volume of their *Miscellanies*, entrusted like the earlier three volumes to Pope's silent editorship but carrying the public imprimatur of both the friends. In June 1732, Swift wrote to Pope offering him for the new volume a selection of verse and prose that had appeared since their previous one.[13] The list included, not surprisingly, *A Libel on Dr Delany*, which Swift would later describe to Motte as "the best thing I writt as I think."[14] Pope's earlier objections to being associated with this poem through Swift's compliments must have been compounded many times over by the prospect of including it now in the *Miscellanies*, where, as co-sponsor of the volume, he must join Swift in publicly implicating himself in the poem's political sentiments. When the volume appeared in October 1732, *A Libel on Dr Delany* was not to be found there. In exercising his authority as editor and deliberately excluding Swift's poem from their *Miscellanies*, Pope was forced into a position well beyond that of expressing his dissatisfaction privately to Fortescue two years earlier. He was distancing himself unmistakably from Swift now in the

---

[11] See *Correspondence*, III, 378 (4 March 1730) and III, 386 (9 April 1730).

[12] *Correspondence*, IV, 116 (16 February 1733) and IV, 148 (20 April 1733). See also *Correspondence*, IV, 158 (28 May 1733), where Pope declares: "My Poetry I abandon to the criticks, my Morals I commit to the testimony of those who know me: and therefore I was more pleas'd with [my praise in] your Libel [on Dr Delany], than with any Verses I ever received."

[13] See *Correspondence*, IV, 31 (12 June 1732).

[14] *Correspondence*, IV, 83 (4 November 1732).

matter of a recent poem that his friend particularly valued, and doing so by rejecting it from a publishing venture that had been originally conceived as a public testimonial to their on-going affinity with one another as writers.

Pope delayed explaining to Swift why he had omitted *A Libel on Dr Delany* until February 1733. The letter in which he did so shows him engaging in a charade of elaborate denial, refusing to admit to his friend that their paths had already diverged some distance since they first planned the *Miscellanies* in 1726, and reminding him of the words with which they had publicly launched the series as a way of insisting that nothing had in fact changed in the course of seven years. Pope appeals to the preface to the first volume of the *Miscellanies*, published over both their signatures and dated at Twickenham, 27 May 1727, at a time when Swift had been staying with Pope there. That preface, almost certainly written by Pope alone to serve his own ends of reserving the *Dunciad* for separate publication later, had declared: "We are obliged to confess, that this whole Collection, in a manner, consists of what we not only thought unlikely to reach the future, but unworthy even of the *present* Age; not our Studies, but our Follies; not our Works, but our Idlenesses."[15] Now, six years later, Pope loosely quoted those words of the 1727 preface to Swift, insisted that the publication of their follies and their idlenesses was also "the whole end of the last Vol. of Miscellanies, without which our former declaration in that preface … would have been discredited," and concluded that their mutual honour obliged them, though "it went indeed to my heart," to omit from this collection of "trifling *Jeux d'Esprit*" so important a work of Swift's as *A Libel on Dr Delany*, since "I meant principally to oblige a separation of what you writ seriously from what you writ carelessly; and thought my own weeds might pass for a sort of wild flowers, when bundled up with them."[16]

The significance of this letter is not that it illustrates the kind of duplicity Pope was capable of practising on occasion, but that it shows how important it was to him to distance himself from Swift's poem on the one hand, to exonerate himself to his friend on the other, and to seek out a justification, however far-fetched and even absurd, that would allow him to deny any rift in their cherished literary alliance.

But two months later, in April 1733, Pope did write to Swift a well-known letter in which he appeared at last to concede the existence of important differences between them in the satiric directions each was already embarked upon. He begins by referring to the verse portraits in his *Epistles* to Burlington and Bathurst, already published, and announcing that he will continue in this vein, neither "sparing Vice and Folly" nor "betraying the cause of Truth and Virtue." He continues: "I have not the courage however to be such a Satyrist as you, but I would be as much, or more, a Philosopher. You call your satires, Libels; I would

---

[15] *The Prose Works of Alexander Pope, II: The Major Works, 1725–1744*, ed. Rosemary Cowler (Oxford, 1986), p. 92.

[16] *Correspondence*, IV, 115–16 (16 February 1733). Sherburn adds a misleading note to this passage in his edition (*Correspondence of Pope*, III, 347) that obscures Pope's strategy of pretending that the terms in the Preface of 1727 were binding on all subsequent volumes of the *Miscellanies*. Williams incorporates Sherburn's note in his own edition at this point, thus perpetuating the confusion. Pope's appeal to "our former declaration in that preface" refers not to the "Book-seller's Advertisement" prefixed to the 1732 volume, as Sherburn and Williams believe, but to the following statement in the Preface of 1727: "We declare, that this Collection contains every Piece, which in the idlest Humour we have written" (*Prose Works of Pope*, II, ed. Cowler, p. 92).

rather call my satires, Epistles: They will consist more of morality than wit, and grow graver, which you will call duller."[17]

Pope's series of polarities between himself and Swift, along with his willingness to grant Swift a virtue – courage – that he professes to lack himself, reminds us at first sight of Swift's similar tactics in his letter to Pope of June 1728. But not for long. For although neither Sherburn nor Williams seems to have noticed as much, Pope is almost certainly echoing deliberately, if not actually parodying here, the close of the first of his *Imitations of Horace*, the dialogue with Fortescue. This had been published only two months earlier, in February 1733, when Pope had immediately sent off a copy to Swift, who, for his part, had already read and admired Pope's new poem a full month before Pope began the letter I am now considering.[18] In that letter, Pope tells his friend Swift that while "you call your satires, Libels; I would rather call my satires, Epistles," and warns him that "they will consist more of morality than wit, and grow graver, which you will call duller." At the close of his recent poem, he responds to his friend Fortescue, who had warned him of the laws against libels and satires, by exclaiming:

> *Libels* and *Satires*! lawless Things indeed!
> But grave *Epistles*, bringing Vice to light,
> Such as a *King* might read, a *Bishop* write,
> Such as Sir *Robert* would approve –

and Fortescue replies that in that case Pope can proceed to write in safety. But of course we are not meant to take seriously Pope's mock resolution to avoid offending the powerful in his future poetry. And when we go on to recall that the entire latter half of this poem is meant to display Pope's heroic courage in rejecting Fortescue's cautions and insisting that, "arm'd for *Virtue* when I point the Pen," he will "Brand the bold Front of shameless, guilty Men,"[19] we realize that Pope's disclaimer of courage in his letter to Swift is no more than a feigned concession. Lastly we notice, on closer examination, that Pope has not really conceded any important difference between them as satirists when he implies to Swift that with greater courage he would write just such satires as his friend has now taken to writing in *A Libel on Dr Delany*.

And so Pope's letters offer us an enigma, and in order to understand what had come to divide the two friends as satirists, we must turn to the poems themselves. Pope certainly makes no secret in his poetry of the conditions that inspire his satires and epistles of the 1730s: "Ask you what Provocation I have had? / The strong Antipathy of Good to Bad."[20] When he descends from such generalities to mention particulars, Pope deplores a wide range of evils that include corruption and depravity of manners, the debasement of taste, the neglect of literature, an obsession with money, and the pervasive presence, in Westminster and London, the country's twin capitals of government and finance, of bribery, embezzlement, vote-selling, and other crimes that are not just condoned but actively encouraged and

---

[17] *Correspondence*, IV, 147 (20 April 1733).

[18] See *Correspondence*, IV, 116 (16 February 1733); IV, 124 (22 March 1733); IV, 134 (30 March 1733).

[19] "Imitations of Horace: Sat. II, i," *Imitations of Horace, with An Epistle to Dr Arbuthnot and The Epilogue to the Satires*, ed. John Butt, 2nd ed. (London and New Haven, 1953), pp. 21, ll. 150–53; 15, ll. 105–6.

[20] *Imitations of Horace*, ed. Butt, p. 324, ll. 197–98.

exemplified by the Court of George II and the Ministry of Walpole, who must therefore bear ultimate responsibility for this continual erosion of the old country values. On these very terms, Pope's poems of the 1730s, at least until the disillusionment of the end of the decade, are Opposition satires. If the principal cause of the nation's moral decline is a particular Court and a specific Ministry, then there is always hope that the trend can be reversed by the replacement of that Ministry with incorruptible statesmen and the eventual succession to the throne of a worthy heir. That is why, in his satires, Pope is careful both to excoriate corrupt courtiers and venal City men, and also to single out and praise a virtuous brotherhood of like-minded friends: "Chiefs, out of War, and Statesmen, out of Place,"[21] who supply not only the moral norms for his satire but a reserve force of public servants ready at hand to replace those who do not deserve to rule, and to begin the work of cultural and ethical reconstruction within the existing social and political order that can yet save the nation.

"If these be of all crimes the worst; / What land was ever half so cursed?"[22] Swift asked in 1726, referring to England and to just such crimes of bribery and malfeasance as fill Pope's poems of the following decade. But in the interval, Swift had come increasingly to recognize that there were greater crimes than these, and that there was another land more cursed. The appalling condition of Ireland could have been mitigated to some degree, he continued to believe, if the Irish themselves had not stubbornly refused to adopt any of the remedies he had at last tired of proposing. But it was England that was responsible for enslaving the Irish and for creating the conditions that had led to nationwide unemployment, beggary, starvation, and the desperate state of affairs in which "the kingdom is absolutely undone." On any conceivable scale, crimes that produce human suffering must be ranked worse than bribery, vote-selling, and the debasement of taste, and they deserve far harsher language. If the chief perpetrators of both sets of crime were the same – the English Court, Walpole and his minions – there was one important difference, as Swift had come to recognize. No change of kings, no alteration of the ministry would significantly improve the condition of Ireland. As long as she remained a subordinate and dependent kingdom, subject to a British crown, ministry, and parliament in whose sole interest every viceroy and other resident official must continue to act, it mattered little who was in power at Westminster. That is why Swift's major political poems beginning with the publication of *A Libel on Dr Delany* in 1730, continuing with *An Epistle to a Lady* and *On Poetry: a Rhapsody*, issued within a month of each other in 1733, proceeding to *The Legion Club* of 1736, and reaching their climax in Faulkner's Dublin edition of *Verses on the Death of Dr Swift* in 1739 are not Opposition poems in any sense of the word but radically subversive satires which declare in the very first of this series, *A Libel on Dr Delany*, that every Irish viceroy, never mind his identity, "comes to tie our chains on faster, / And show us, England is our master,"[23] and which denounce not this king or that minister but express their hatred for all kings and ministers of state, vituperate them as devils, monsters, and strutting, chattering vermin, expose the suffragan Parliament in Dublin as a madhouse filled with gibbering sycophants, and implicitly reject the constitutional system itself responsible for Ireland's enslavement.[24]

---

[21] *Imitations of Horace*, ed. Butt, p. 17, l. 126.

[22] "On Reading Dr Young's Satires," ll. 47–48, *Poems*, p. 318.

[23] *Poems*, p. 407, ll. 125–26.

[24] I mention, in the order of their publication, only those subversive poems by Swift that

Pope set about deliberately putting a distance between himself and Swift's major political poems beginning with *A Libel on Dr Delany* not just because he remained unmoved by Ireland's plight, which he did, or was bored by what he preferred to call "Hibernian Politicks," which he was, or showed himself less willing than Swift to jeopardize his safety, which also proved to be the case.[25] Pope's political beliefs remained from start to finish as conservative as those of most of his friends in the Opposition, beginning with his mentor Bolingbroke. From such a perspective, how could he be expected to react with anything but surprise and puzzlement at such alarming political sentiments – not just their intemperate language – as he found expressed with increasing frequency in Swift's later political poems, or to bring himself easily to believe that his friend's "Head should be so giddy?"

Pope does, we recall, praise Swift unreservedly as an Irish patriot in several of his poems: in the *Dunciad Variorum* as the author of the *Drapier's Letters* (1724–25) that did "thy griev'd Country's copper chains unbind,"[26] and in his *Epistle to Augustus* as the penman of the Irish tracts of the early 1720s.[27] And we need to remember also that when Pope was editing, or advising William King to edit, *Verses on the Death of Dr Swift* for its London publication in 1739, three of the lines he transferred into the poem from the *Life and Genuine Character of Dr Swift* were again a reminder of the debt Ireland owed to the Drapier.[28] But these works of Swift's were past history: they belonged to the previous reign, they could fit easily into Pope's own version of the Irish Patriot, and the *Drapier's Letters* in particular emerge in Pope's telling as a notable example of Opposition pamphleteering, the dangerous sentiments of the Fourth Letter ignored. That series of letters had successfully challenged a specific policy of Walpole's in Ireland, forcing him at last to withdraw Wood's Patent, and to suffer acute embarrassment and chagrin in doing so. As such, it could be viewed in retrospect as an earlier analogue to Walpole's defeat over the Excise Bill in 1733, both of them becoming hallowed examples for the future of what a determined Opposition could achieve against a hated minister. No wonder Pope grew so fond of invoking the *Drapier's Letters*. But we also need to remember that the three lines on the Drapier inserted into the London printing of *Verses on the Death of Dr Swift* in 1739 were replacing no fewer than sixty-four others on Ireland, many of them as defiant and subversive as any Swift ever wrote, jettisoned from the poem without his authorization and on Pope's advice.[29] Once again, as with his omission of *A Libel on Dr Delany* from the *Miscellanies* seven years before, Pope was censoring his friend's outrageous political outbursts, but pretending to act from other motives:

---

were issued in his or Pope's lifetime. In order of composition, *Verses on the Death of Dr Swift*, written in 1731, follows *A Libel on Dr Delany*, while *The Legion Club* comes last. *Directions for a Birthday Song*, written in 1729 but not published until 1765, is the earliest of this series.

[25] See *The Dunciad*, ed. James Sutherland, 3rd ed. (London and New Haven, 1965 [1963]), III, ll. 327–28: "Hibernian Politicks, O Swift, thy doom, / And Pope's, translating three whole years with Broome" (pp. 190–91), where both pursuits are reduced to the same level of comic discomfiture.

[26] *The Dunciad*, ed. Sutherland, I, l. 22 (p. 62); see also p. 271, l. 24.

[27] See *Imitations of Horace*, ed. Butt, pp. 213–15.

[28] See "The Life and Genuine Character of Dr Swift," ll. 95–97, *Poems*, p. 482; and *Verses on the Death of Doctor Swift* (London: Bathurst, 1739), ll. 291–93 (p. 14).

[29] See *Verses on the Death of Dr. Swift* (Dublin: Faulkner, 1739), ll. 345–54; 395–434; 443–54; 483–84.

in this case to abbreviate an aesthetically uneven poem and to protect Swift from charges of vanity.[30]

Toward the end of his biography, Irvin Ehrenpreis observed of Swift and Pope: "Their friendship had something in it of the self-consciousness of a famous acting team whose stage association has started a myth of mutual affection – a myth not without value to its subjects."[31] The theatrical image for the long relationship expressed in their letters is an excellent one, for since at least as early as 1730 Swift had known of Pope's intention of preserving and publishing their correspondence at a later date.[32] Thereafter, both men were obliged to act out their partnership on a stage that was now their only meeting place, but was also a forum where no word or gesture must be allowed seriously to affect their relations and to disappoint a public who would in the course of time be invited to witness two friends "walking down hand in hand to posterity."

[30] See *Correspondence of Pope*, ed. Sherburn, IV, 130 (25 September 1738).
[31] *Dean Swift*, p. 883.
[32] See *Correspondence*, III, 386 (9 April 1730).

A. C. Elias, Jr

*Philadelphia*

# *Senatus Consultum*: Revising Verse in Swift's Dublin Circle, 1729–1735

ABSTRACT. Comparing early with revised texts by members of Swift's Dublin circle who collected and published their poems in the early 1730s – Mary Barber, Constantia Grierson, and Matthew Pilkington – reveals patterns of revision very similar to those found in Samuel Fairbrother's 1732 and George Faulkner's 1735 collected editions of Swift's own poetry. All show signs of revision by ear, rather than eye alone; of attention to minor questions of prosody and logic, of a sort easily settled by debate; and a certain convergence of individual style and tone. With hardly any exceptions, all lack the kind of major, creative reworkings possible for an author working alone in his study. All correspond to what we would expect from group editing sessions of the kind which Pilkington's wife describes in her *Memoirs*, for readying the Barber poems for publication. To the extent that the Faulkner and Fairbrother editions of Swift reflect group editing work – whatever the degree of Swift's personal approval and participation – future editors may wish to tread more carefully in dealing with them.

Near the end of her life, in her last volume of *Memoirs*, Laetitia Pilkington turned her attention back to the good old days in Dublin, before her divorce and exile, when she and her husband Matthew enjoyed an easy footing in the circle of Jonathan Swift and his friend Patrick Delany, the celebrated preacher, wit, and Old Testament scholar. What glowed in Mrs Pilkington's memory were the friendships which she and her husband developed. "I believe there never was any Set of people so happy in sincere and uninterrupted Friendship," she wrote, "as the Dean, Doctor Delany, Mr. Pilkington, and myself; nor can I reflect, at this Hour, on any thing with more Pleasure, than those happy Moments we have enjoyed!" Specifically, she instances an odd kind of party which Delany hosted ("frequently," she said) where the chief entertainment, besides eating and drinking, was editing another friend's poetry. This was the Dublin woollen-draper's wife, Mary Barber, whose much-delayed *Poems on Several Occasions* – including a number by her friend Constantia Grierson and her son Constantine Barber – finally appeared in the late spring of 1735. Some copies, Mrs Pilkington adds fourteen years later, "I fancy might [still], at this day, be seen in the Cheesemongers, Chandlers, Pastry-cooks, and Second-hand Booksellers Shops." But "dull as they were," she continues, Mrs Barber's poems,

> certainly would have been much worse, but that Doctor Delany frequently held what he called a *Senatus Consultum*, to correct these undigested Materials; at which were present sometimes the Dean (in the Chair) but always Mrs. Grierson, Mr. Pilkington, the Doctor, and myself.[1]

---

[1]  Laetitia Pilkington, *Memoirs*, ed. A. C. Elias, Jr (Athens, GA, and London, 1997), I, 283.

We may quibble with Mrs Pilkington's Latin usage – *Senatus consultum* more commonly means a decree rather than a meeting of the Roman senate – but there is good reason to credit the substance of her story. In the commendatory letter to Lord Orrery which Mrs Barber prints at the beginning of her volume, Swift acknowledges that he has "read most of her Poems" and praises her for being "ready to take Advice, and submit to have her Verses corrected, by those who are generally allow'd to be the best Judges" – including, we may infer, himself (pp. vi–vii). In her own preface, which follows, Mrs Barber similarly acknowledges "the Goodness of some Men of Genius, who with great Condescension undertook to correct what I had written" (p. xxiii).

Two other members of Delany's circle had collected editions of their poems published about this time, also by subscription, making exactly the same claim – that the poems had been reviewed and corrected by the author's judicious friends, sometimes including the great Dr Swift. So far as I know, the kinds of revisions made in them have never been studied, much less compared – for Mrs Barber's and the second collection, probably because the authors were small fry, beneath our dignity as serious literary scholars. For the third collection, more central to Swift studies, we could not know until recently just what changes had been made. In the first two cases, the claims about Swift's input have usually been ignored because, once again, the authors were small fry, ambitious and therefore likely to exaggerate their connections with Swift. In the third case, because Swift's own verse is at stake, we have usually downplayed the claim of others' input and assumed that all, or almost all, improvements came from Swift. It is time to take a closer look all around.

Chronologically, the first of the projects belonged to Mrs Pilkington's husband Matthew, who brought out his own collected poems under the same title as Mary Barber's, *Poems on Several Occasions*, a few months after Mrs Barber first travelled to England in 1730 to try the cure at Tunbridge Wells and seek subscribers for her own collection. Not only has "the admired Doctor *Swift* ... condescended to peruse the following Poems" and "honour'd them with his Corrections and Remarks," we read in the preface, but Matthew has also been "as careful as possible, in engaging my judicious Acquaintance to point out to me those Faults, which an Author is very ill qualify'd to distinguish in his own Performances" (pp. v–vi). The second such collection was the four-volume edition of Swift's *Works* – including the collected poems in Volume II – which George Faulkner published in Dublin just a few months before the Barber *Poems* appeared in 1735. Noting how few of his writings the Dean openly acknowledged (which leaves Swift the "supposed Author" of the works now being published), Faulkner claims the advantage of "consulting the supposed Author's Friends, who were pleased to correct many gross Errors" in the earlier scattered printings and "strike out some very injudicious Interpolations" here and there. Moreover, Faulkner says or is made to say in his preface, the "supposed Author" himself "was prevailed on to suffer some Friends to review and correct the Sheets after they were printed; and sometimes he condescended, as we have heard, to give them his own Opinion" (I, preface, p. 3).

---

The passage occurs in her final instalment, *The Third and Last Volume of the Memoirs* (London, 1754), which she wrote during 1749–50. For the date of composition, see I, xxii–xxiv, xxvii. Subsequent references to the *Memoirs* will be noted in the text by the initials LP with volume and page numbers. For other short references used in the text, consult the Appendix.

If we accept Mary Barber's claims for her text, as witnessed by the *senatus* anecdote, what do we make of Matthew Pilkington's? On the title-page of the expanded London edition of his *Poems*, in 1731, Matthew had even added the phrase "Revised by the Reverend Dr. SWIFT" after his own by-line. Had Swift really helped him? One good test is the birthday ode printed in his *Poems* volume with a half-title linking it to the official Dublin Castle celebration for George II's birthday on October 30. This was the authorized ode sung on October 30, 1729, as we find in Dickson's *Old Dublin Intelligence* for November 1 of that year. At least since the time of Harold Williams, scholars have recognized its affinity to Swift's rollicking *Directions for a Birth-Day Song*, which instructs a would-be royal ode-writer how to proceed. Swift dates the *Directions* the same day in manuscript, October 30, 1729. But the ode had also been performed at the Castle the year before, as we find by a broadside discovered at Trinity College, Dublin, by James Woolley. According to the title, the ode was "To be performed at the Castle of Dublin, On the 30th of October ... By the special Command of their Excellencies the Lords Justices," who were presiding that year in the absence of the viceroy, Lord Carteret. Comparing the 1728 text with the 1729 text (as printed in Dickson's newspaper), and the 1729 text with Matthew's collected *Poems* text of 1730, reveals that the ode received extensive revision *before* its second performance in October 1729, when Lord Carteret was back at Dublin Castle to preside over the festivities. The revisions strike me as eminently Swiftian in quality, especially in the shortening of the long blood-soaked section praising the King's military prowess ("Your Hero now another Mars is," Swift advises, "Makes mighty Armies turn their Arses" [ll. 29–30]). In Matthew's original text, the Muse quickly turns aside from the King's peacetime activities to view him in "a nobler Light":

> See! see! He *burns* amidst the thickest Throng!
> Slaughter wastes at his Command
> And Thousands sink beneath his Hand;
> Death and all its ghastly Train
> Rave along the purpl'd Plain;
> Glory flies before, to charm,
> And Conquest waits upon his Arm.
>   Thro' the thick-embattl'd Lines
> In horrid Pomp Destruction shines. (pp. 4–5)

In the 1729 text – carried into the collected *Poems* volume of 1730 and its London reprint of 1731 – Matthew tones down the first three lines (no more bloody-minded *burning* for George), drops the next six altogether (no more raving Death with charming glory in his train), and removes the claim that George's military prowess (of questionable use in peacetime) gives the "nobler Light" in which we should view him. Instead, acknowledging Carteret's presence at the Castle that year, Matthew extends and emphasizes the section praising George's peacetime activities. Now he asserts that "To bless, is nobler than command." Even more Swiftian – we remember Swift's success advising Carteret about Irish church appointments – Matthew now hints that George might receive even higher praise if he made more appointments by merit:

> That *Learning*, *Virtue*, *Wisdom* gain
> Distinguish'd Honours in his Reign,
>   Let CARTERET's Worth high-rais'd proclaim,
> If *Wisdom* yet may higher soar,
> If *Merit* be rewarded more,
>   Yet greater Glories shall exalt his Name. (MP, p. 183)

The satire in Swift's *Directions* grows more out of Matthew's original ode of 1728 than the text we thought we knew, the revised version of 1729 and 1730, which softens the worst absurdities and exaggerations of the original. For "your Encomiums to be strong," Swift had ironically advised, they "Must be apply'd directly wrong" (ll. 117–18). In the original, George's unlovely but beloved queen is termed blooming and "beauteous;" in the revision, she is charming because "gracious." In the original, she is "Worthy over *Kings* to reign" – awkward because most people thought she *did* reign over George – but the revision makes her "Worthy over *Hearts* to reign," as George himself would cheerfully have agreed. Swift had advised his poet against making comparisons with "some obscure inferior fellow, / Like Julius, or the Youth of Pella" (ll. 141–42). In Matthew's original, George as military figure is indeed compared favourably to Julius Caesar. In the revision, the comparison is instead with "Brunswick," his own late father, whom he disliked anyway.

In a similar vein, new information now forces us to reconsider the verse revisions made in George Faulkner's 1735 edition of Swift. Because of Swift's known co-operation with Faulkner – and because Faulkner's poetry volume incorporates most of the autograph corrections which we know Swift made in his set of the Swift-Pope *Miscellanies* – most of us had assumed that the revisions in Faulkner's edition represented Swift's work almost exclusively. John Irwin Fischer's recent findings challenge that assumption. For the poems which had appeared in the "Last" volume of the *Miscellanies* (1727), Fischer discovered that Faulkner's copy-text was an obscure and unheralded Dublin reprint, or reprint of a reprint, put out sometime in 1732 by Samuel Fairbrother. This is the same Fairbrother who was soon to pirate Faulkner in turn, earning him the nickname "Foulbrother" from Swift and his friends.[2] In the 1732 Fairbrother edition, which otherwise reprints Fairbrother's accurate 1728 reprint of the 1727 London original, it now appears that virtually all of Swift's autograph corrigenda which made it into Faulkner are already present. For this large group of poems, in other words, the textual revisions which authenticate Faulkner's edition – which best prove Swift's personal role in correcting it – did *not* enter print with Faulkner after all, but with the piratical Whig Fairbrother, whose work Faulkner then followed for his own "authorized" edition. True, it is conceivable that some spy or interloper gained access to Swift's annotated set of the London *Miscellanies*, copied out most of his revisions, and hotfooted them over to Fairbrother's shop in Skinner Row. But if so, how do we account for the other revisions in Fairbrother's edition? By a rough preliminary count – excluding stanzas restored from early separate editions, couplets deleted to spare people's feelings, and the authenticating revisions from Swift's copy of the *Miscellanies* – I find 47 substantive changes made in poems printed in the 1732 Fairbrother edition. This is almost exactly the same number as first enter in Faulkner's edition three years later. Nor is there anything in these Fairbrother revisions which seems stylistically any less "Swiftian," if so questionable a term may be used. Arguing for Swift's active role in preparing the Faulkner *Works* of 1735, Sir Harold Williams in his 1950 Sandars Lectures pointed out a remodelled couplet in the *Description of a City Shower* which, he suggests, could not have come "from any hand but Swift's." In the 1727 London text, apropos the needy poet's plight in the shower, we are asked to imagine,

---

[2]   See John Irwin Fischer and James Woolley, "The Swift Poems Project: An Edition and an Electronic Archive," unpublished paper, delivered at *The Third Münster Symposium on Jonathan Swift*, 30 May 1994.

> His only Coat, where Dust confus'd with Rain
> Roughen the Nap, and leave a mingled Stain.

Even apart from subject-verb agreement – "dust *with* rain," properly speaking, takes a singular, not plural verb – there is something not quite logical here. In the cognitive sense of the word, how can dust be *confused* with rain, a very different article? And once the two mingle into something which can stain a coat, how can the stain itself properly be called *mingled*? In Faulkner's 1735 text, Williams finds the problem neatly sorted out:

> Sole Coat, where Dust *cemented* by the Rain
> *Erects* the Nap, and leaves a *cloudy* Stain.

Here Williams asks the rhetorical question, "Surely this, pictorially, in versification, and, it may be added, in grammar, is an author's improvement?"[3] Improvement it may be, but it first enters *not* with Faulkner in 1735, nor with Swift's autograph annotations in the Rothschild set, but with the unheralded Fairbrother edition of 1732 (p. 31). Similarly in *Apollo to the Dean*, it is the Fairbrother edition which first deletes an inadvertently awkward couplet, which might have been misconstrued, in which Swift's Stella, Esther Johnson, "can swear to the Parson, whom oft she has seen / At Night between Cavan's-street and College-Green" (Fairbrother, p. 174). What was Stella doing, malicious readers might have wondered, so often out in the Dublin streets by night, especially in a part of town (St Kevin's Street) where Swift's deanery was located? And who but that lady's devoted friend Swift would have cared enough about her reputation, four years after her death, to bother taking the couplet out?

If the Fairbrother revisions are "authorial," we should be asking ourselves exactly what we mean by that term. Swift's ties to Faulkner are well documented, but we have no evidence of anything similar between Swift and Fairbrother. Could there have been middlemen involved, some judicious friend or friends of the author's like those claimed in the Faulkner preface, or even a *senatus* group (with or without Swift) of the kind described by Mrs Pilkington? And what of the poem revisions which *do* enter with the Faulkner edition of 1735? How do they compare with the Fairbrother? How do both sets of revisions compare with those in Mary Barber's volume, corrected by the Delany-Swift *senatus*, and those in Matthew Pilkington's volume, reviewed by Swift and (he claims) by others? Is there a common sensibility, and if so, whose is it?

Although sometimes rough and ready, there is a way of gauging the revisions here. For Matthew Pilkington, besides the early printings of his birthday *Ode*, we have four early poems printed together in 1725, the year he married Laetitia and five years before his collected *Poems on Several Occasions* came out. For Constantia Grierson, represented in the Barber *Poems on Several Occasions*, we have the author's autograph fair copies of three poems there, as well as of several others never published. For Mary Barber, thanks to the Boys-Mizener card index at Kansas, we can trace the original versions of six poems which she composed at Tunbridge Wells in 1730 and contributed anonymously to that year's spa miscellany, *Tunbrigialia*, nearly five years before they reappear in her collected *Poems*. For another 13 of her poems there, early texts occur variously in separate Foxon printings between 1725 and 1728, in a scattering of other English miscellanies, in a Dublin newspaper

---

[3]   *The Text of "Gulliver's Travels"*, The Sandars Lectures in Bibliography, 1950 (Cambridge, 1952), p. 82.

and a London monthly, as well as in a couple of early manuscripts, most notably an Irish poetry miscellany now at the Brotherton Library, Leeds. When two or more early texts of a poem survive, they resemble each other closely enough, in a great majority of cases, to assure us that our later editors must have worked from something very similar.

For all three of our lesser poets, when we compare their early with their late-collected texts, there is clearly a coming together in ways which, if not self-evidently Swiftian, are at least consistent with what we find in the Fairbrother and Faulkner volumes. For instance, we know that Swift disapproved of rhyming triplets; indeed, the Faulkner volume adds a footnote to that effect (II, 42). Not surprisingly, the few triplets in the early Barber and Pilkington texts all come out, leaving both volumes completely clear of them except in one poem, a last-minute addition of Mrs Barber's probably written too late to send back to Dublin for revising (MB, p. 273, commenting on news of November 1734).

So, too, with certain contractions, forms like *can't, haven't, shan't, didn't, couldn't, isn't,* and other such "abominable curtailings and quaint modernisms," which Swift attacked in *Polite Conversation* and later denounced to Pope.[4] Useful in verse, to keep within the metre, they suit an informal style – and none of our poets attempts the full formality of elegy or epic, at least serious elegy or epic. Even so, we find a few contractions expanded in both the 1732 Fairbrother and 1735 Faulkner editions of Swift, perhaps most noticeably in his verse monologue *Apollo to the Dean*, whose doggerel metre can handle the extra syllables produced when "I've" is expanded to "I have" and "they're" to "they are" (Fairbrother, p. 173; Faulkner, II, 183). A certain number of contractions are similarly winnowed out of Mary Barber, who characteristically writes the most informally of our group. "Can't fail of" gives way to "Must have," "won't ease us of our pains" is altered to "refuse to ease our Pains" (MB, pp. 11, 70). With Constantia Grierson, there seem to be fewer contractions to revise, comparing the three poems printed with Mrs Barber's to their autograph originals, but a check of her other manuscript poetry reveals a good many. Possibly the three poems later printed had already received some attention before she copied them down. Only with Matthew Pilkington – in style the least informal of our three poets, and the only one with a university education – do I find practically no contractions either in his early known texts or the others collected in his *Poems* volume.

In lesser accidentals, there is a similar convergence or coming together in our different poets' work – and not because there were universally accepted standards then, or because the different volumes came from the same publisher and press-correctors. In fact, there was considerable diversity in the printing arrangements, even apart from the rivals Fairbrother and Faulkner in Dublin. Matthew Pilkington's London edition, which adds a section of poems not present in his earlier Dublin volume, was printed by and for William Bowyer; Mary Barber's collection was also printed in London, but by Samuel Richardson for herself and Charles Rivington. The only shared history comes with Pilkington's original Dublin edition, which George Faulkner printed for him, and Faulkner's own edition of Swift published five years later. At first glance, in all these cases, the finished product looks pretty much the same, with almost all the nouns routinely capitalized and the emphases denoted by italics. For Constantia Grierson and Matthew Pilkington this went against the grain, if we may judge by her autograph poems and his earlier printings. Indeed, in the collected poems

---

[4] *Prose Works*, IV, 113, and *Correspondence*, V, 58–59.

of the two Scriblerians closest to Swift, Gay's collected *Poems* of 1720 and Pope's collected *Works* volumes of 1717 and 1735, all common nouns are lower case as is standard today. As a further test, I searched sample passages of all five Barber, Pilkington, and Swift volumes for the incidence of certain usages which I thought might be diagnostic, ranging from lower-case nouns and emphases by italics or by initial capitals, to colons, semicolons, and the spelling of such forms as *though* and *could*.[5] Faulkner has sometimes been accused of exaggerating Swift's old-fashioned usages, but interestingly enough, the strongest divergence in my sampling came in the two volumes printed by Faulkner, the Pilkington *Poems* and the Swift poetry volume. In my Pilkington samples, the verb forms *could, would,* and *should* are consistently spelled with an apostrophe in place of the *l*. With *though, although* and *through*, an apostrophe consistently replaces the final *ugh*. In the Swift *Works*, apart from a few apostrophe'd *could/would* forms still surviving in *Cadenus and Vanessa*, the samples show the full spelling throughout. With *though/although* it is the full spelling more often than not. Similarly, when I checked the incidence of heavy pointing – especially colons and semicolons, which we associate with Swift in his late, Faulkner-associated years – it is Faulkner's Pilkington volume which scores the lowest. The highest incidence occurs not in Faulkner's Swift volume alone, but at least equally in the Barber quarto produced in London by Richardson and Rivington. The pattern holds true for Mrs Grierson's poems in the volume, although her autograph originals show that, left to herself, she hardly used any punctuation at all beyond the occasional comma.[6] Whatever the idiosyncrasies of the poet, whatever the identity of the printing house, we see a marked tendency towards convergence.

With little things like accidentals, it would be foolish to force patterns of evidence too far. Before we proceed to substantive changes, though, we might consider for a moment the phenomenon of convergence among writers. The shared values of one's culture surely play a central part in the creative act, but before the advent of the modern publisher's editor, how are we to account for a trio or quartet of writers, all friends, whose revised work grows more rather than less like each others'? Did they become more conventional as they grew in age and wisdom, or at least more apt to agree in their style? Today, the closest equivalent to Patrick Delany's *senatus* is probably the writers' group. One author I know – a good writer at that, despite her Ph.D. in English – gave me some insight about them. "I've noticed that writers' groups *do* tend to influence members' styles," she told me. "We want to please the

---

[5]   For Mary Barber, MB pp. 7–19, 54–76, 173–94, and 270–83; for her son Constantine, MB pp. 246–55; for Constantia Grierson, MB pp. xlv–xlviii, 87–89, 138–39, 155, 218–21, 243–45 and all finished verse in her MS volume; for Matthew Pilkington, MP pp. 3–25, 52–66, 135–50, 153–77, and all the verse added in the 1731 London edition, pp. 133–51; for Swift, Faulkner II, 53–63, 21–38, 125–36, 159–63, 185–88, and the same texts in Fairbrother, pp. 1–7, 25–30, 55–60, 92–99, 137–44. Categories checked: common nouns in lower case; emphasis by initial capital; emphasis by italics; whole phrases in italics; head- and footnotes; contractions; spelling of *its* [of it]; triplets present; *hath* and other -*eth* verb forms; semicolons (frequency per ten lines); colons (frequency per ten lines); spelling of *could/would* forms; spelling of *though, although,* and *through*.

[6]   For frequency of semicolons, expressed in batting-average fashion, the sample Barber texts in MB measure .170, .102, .232, .240, .230, for her son Constantine in the same .229, and for Constantia Grierson in the same .367 and .318. Compare Swift in Faulkner at .219, .225, .148, .173, and .143; and Matthew Pilkington in MP .100, .063, .000, .056, and .044, and in his 1731 London additions, .121. For colons, the Barber texts in MB work out to .068, .031, .080, .123, .182, for her son Constantine in the same .136, and for Mrs. Grierson in the same .136. Compare Swift in Faulkner at .157, .167, .099, .115, and .066; and Matthew in MP .058, .031, .045, .075, and .036, and the 1731 additions, .058.

audience we know will hear our work and so we write to them – never mind what we might have thought truth in our study."[7]

Her words struck an echo as I looked through substantive changes in the Barber and Pilkington volumes. Certainly some of our poets' chief idiosyncrasies – even charming ones, as we might count them today – seem to fade between the early texts and the later versions collected in the two *Poems* volumes. For Mary Barber, the woollen-draper's wife, the informal can sometimes cross the line into the colloquial, betraying her tradesman origins. These passages are often touched up in the 1735 *Poems on Several Occasions*. In its original 1728 version, for instance, her "True Tale" begins in rough-and-ready fashion,

> A Mother, who vast Pleasure finds
> In *forming of* her Childrens Minds,
> *In midst of whom*, with *great* Delight,
> She passes many a Winter's Night …
> (*A Tale*, p. 3, my emphases)

As revised for her *Poems* volume, her accents become more genteel. "In forming of her Children's Minds" changes to

> In *modelling* her Childrens Minds,
> With whom, in *exquisite* Delight,
> She passes many a Winter Night …
> (MB, p. 7, my emphases)

Elsewhere in the poem "Says she," slangy when used for the past tense, becomes more properly "said she;" "Her favourite Boy" becomes "Her fav'rite Son" (MB, pp. 7, 9, 10). With the better-educated Matthew Pilkington, by contrast, there are no such slips to correct. Instead, some of the purpler poetic clichés which appear in his early texts are toned down for the collected *Poems*. Metaphorical "gaping Wounds" become "op'ning Wounds." Where first "Love distress'd Resistless sways the heart," "ev'ry kind Emotion" sways it later (MP, pp. 8, 75). With the small core of revised Constantia Grierson texts, I find no specific rhetorical usages singled out for correction, but there is a perceptible moderating of the overall emotional temperature. An idealist who wore her heart on her sleeve, Mrs Grierson was apt to gush. In her manuscript text, for instance, she describes the traditional role of poets as "The Praise of Godlike Kings & Virtuous Love" – "godlike" being one of her favourite adjectives – while the version which appears in the Barber volume reads a bit more soberly, as "The Praise of *Heroes* and of virtuous Love." Her admired friend Mary Barber, in the manuscript, "by her Lays has renderd thousands blest," but in print that lady only takes pleasure in helping others, "raise[s] her Joys, by making others blest" (MB, pp. xlv, xlvii).

Slang, clichés, and gushing make up only a small proportion of the idiosyncrasies levelled out of the Pilkington and Barber volumes. Allowing for some difference in frequency – unlike Barber's and Pilkington's, Swift's verse had previously been collected and edited at least once before – the great bulk of the changes are of exactly the kind which were made in Swift's verse, both for the Fairbrother and the Faulkner editions. They are corrections in the root sense of the word, fixings-up of potentially mixed metaphors, of slightly skewed logic, debatable grammar, or unintended implications. This is precisely the sort of thing

---

[7]   Laura B. Kennelly, personal communication, 2 February 1994, quoted by permission.

which a writer has difficulty recognizing without outsiders' help. We have already seen it in Swift's couplet in *A Description of a City Shower*, where originally we found "dust confused with rain" when the verb *confuse* could imply unintended similarities between dust and rain – and where the mingling in the "mingled stain" on the coat more properly appertains to the causal agent, muddy water, than to the stain itself. I am not sure that we really have better poetry in the corrected version, where the stain is now *cloudy* and the dust is *cemented* by the rain. By logical standards, though, it is much easier to justify. So, too, with our other three authors. With them as well as with Swift, I find very few revisions – good, bad, or indifferent – which cannot be logically argued and justified among friends. In Mrs Barber's original *True Tale*, for instance, her son "the Author seiz'd" to read him. Properly speaking, one does not seize authors but books. In the *Poems* volume, the boy accordingly "the Volume seiz'd." "*Inexpressive* woe" in the original *Widow Gordon's Petition* – that is, woe which cannot be expressed, in one of the two different meanings of the word then current – changes to the less ambiguous "unutterable Woe" in the collected *Poems* (MB, pp. 10, 3). With Mrs Grierson, similarly, her tragic heroine in the prologue to *Theodosius* supposes herself and her predicament transferred for a moment to the eighteenth century, "*preserv'd* ... to the present Age." If taken literally, this would leave her 1,300 years old. The version in the Barber *Poems* corrects this to "*reserv'd* ... to the present Age" (MB, p. 245). In one of his Mira poems, Matthew Pilkington originally imagines his beloved retiring alone with a sad book, "To breathe those *Thoughts*, which Solitude inspires." Properly speaking, we breathe vocal expressions of mental or emotional states rather than those states themselves. In his collected *Poems*, accordingly, Mira retires "To breathe those *Sighs*, which Solitude inspires" (MP, p. 74). Mixed metaphors are untangled, grammar shored up, and unintentionally ambiguous comparisons straightened out, as when Mrs Grierson's tragic heroine in the prologue likens the depth of her love to the Viceroy and Vicereine's – as famed a pair "As ever blessd the world or *trod the stage*," which Lords Lieutenant were hardly likely to do (MB, p. 244). In similar fashion, Matthew Pilkington speaks of "*greedy* Ears *devouring*" such-and-such (MP, p. 18), which in reality would have left him with a mastoid infection or other complications from foreign articles lodged in the auditory canal. In both instances, the phrasing is changed to something more logical but less memorable.

The same kind of reasoning – careful, literal-minded, at times even plodding or unpoetic – stands behind most of the substantive changes in both the Fairbrother and Faulkner editions of Swift. "'Tis an old Maxim in the Schools," we originally read in *Cadenus and Vanessa*, "That *Vanity*'s the Food of Fools" (ll. 758–59). But in this context, Vanessa providing food for Cadenus, vanity is not something which an outsider can provide, only cater to. In the Fairbrother edition, the line is accordingly changed to "*Flattery*'s the Food of Fools," which any good caterer could supply (Fairbrother, p. 20). Similarly in *Baucis and Philemon*, the chair turning into a pulpit is first depicted crawling like a snail "*along* the Wall." Given the usual position of pulpits, raised above the nave floor, this is not quite correct. Through Fairbrother the phrase remains unaltered, but in the 1735 Faulkner edition it is changed to read "*half up* the Wall" (II, 25). Whether in Fairbrother or Faulkner, grammar is paid its full due. Though clear enough, a phrase in *The South Sea* about the ocean's being covered with gold evidently proved too elliptical: "Look round about, how thick it lies!" That we should see how thick, once we have looked, is implicit but not stated. The Faulkner edition corrects the problem, if it is one, by making the line read "Look round, *and see* how thick it lies" (II, 152). Similarly, there is a change in the first line of *Pro-*

*metheus*, from "*When first* the 'Squire and Tinker, Wood" to "*As, when* the 'Squire and Tinker, Wood" – in this case, a change first introduced in Fairbrother's edition (pp. 126–27), not Faulkner's. The change makes no sense until we recognize that the poem's first ten lines form an elaborate simile to be applied in the section following, beginning "*So, to confound this hated Coin ...*" Strictly speaking, this application, beginning with *So*, requires the preceding simile to begin with *As*.

Taken in the aggregate, changes like these look like group work, the sort of revisions which someone may suggest when he reads or hears a poem, without wasting others' time on too much pondering or experimenting, and which can then be briefly discussed and settled by those present. One thing for which we look in vain, in the Swift volumes as well as the others, are creative reworkings – the sort of revisions which an author will make when alone in his study, free to play with his poems, to experiment in places he is not quite satisfied with, and to spend whatever time he feels like spending on the problem. After several false starts, a better trope occurs to him for a couplet, changing the literal meaning but enhancing the effect he had been aiming at. The beginning or ending of a poem strikes him as weak; he throws it out, writes another, and then fiddles with the section leading up to or away from it. Another example comes to mind, so he writes it up and inserts it. Except for one of Mary Barber's Tunbridge pieces, which doubles in length for the collected *Poems* volume (pp. 144–45), and except for the ending of Constantia Grierson's congratulatory poem to Mrs Barber, containing an incomprehensible patch which really needs rewriting, I find no such reworkings in any of the four collected volumes which we are dealing with. The revisions keep strictly within the bounds of what is already there. With Swift, at least, the Fairbrother and Faulkner revisions are sometimes so logical and pedestrian that some of the original grace is lost. In *The Humble Petition of Frances Harris*, for instance, Swift originally has that lady explaining how she safeguards her money which, because her trunk has a bad lock, "I *keep* in my Pocket, ty'd about my Middle, next my Smock" (S-P, p. 57). Now the premise of the poem is that she has unaccountably lost her money, which means that there is nothing left to keep. With unimpeachable logic, therefore, the Fairbrother text corrects this to money which "I *kept* in my Pocket" (p. 50). In the process, though, Frances Harris is made to sound almost level-headed, not the amusingly thoughtless flibbertigibbet depicted elsewhere in the poem. A similar change occurs in the epitaph from the *Elegy on Mr Demar*, with its jokes about that miser's "other Self," his surviving money. The Faulkner edition changes the punch line from "Will think his *better Half* alive" to "Will think his *better Self* alive" (p. 139). Logically this makes sense, in that Demar has just been defined (twice) as a man with two selves, not two halves. Even so, the phrase "better *Half*" is not likely to confuse us. Without it, we lose the wit of the implicit pun on a beloved spouse, one's "better half" who survives. Instead, there is nothing but heavy-handedness and repetition of the obvious.

If many of the substantive changes in our poets look like committee work, others make me suspect that they grew out of listening to the verse, not just looking at it on the page. Whether a modern-day editing session consists of two people or twelve, we would need a xerox machine to make sure that everyone present has a written text to follow with the eye. In Swift's day – except for previously printed works of which one happened to have sufficient copies on hand – such luxury was impossible. Someone would have read the text aloud while the others listened, and hearing the verse, picked up problems which the eye alone might have missed. Constantia Grierson's poem to Mary Barber, for instance, opens clearly enough,

Long have the Heroes deed, the Lover's flame
Been every Muse's, every Poet's Theme.

Until it is read aloud, there seems nothing amiss here – and not much to prefer in the revised version from the Barber *Poems* volume: "Long has the Warrior's, and the Lover's Fire, / Employ'd the Poet, and ingross'd the Lyre" (MB, p. xlv). The difference, it turns out, is that the same rhyme scheme, now "Name/Flame," recurs only two couplets later in the original – a fact which eluded me when I silently transcribed and proofed the poem, and then twice collated it (in silence) against the printed version. To catch unwanted repetitions, there is nothing like actually hearing the text. In Mrs Barber's poem for her son putting on breeches, for instance, the words "keep," "tight," and "scales" all repeat within a couple of lines, to no good effect, in the text originally printed. In the collected edition, synonyms now substitute for one or the other element in each pair (MB, pp. 13, 14, 15). So, too, with Swift – though he is less subject to such blunders – we find stop-press corrections in Faulkner to weed out one of two *but*'s occurring within three lines and one of two *then*'s repeated in two (II, 407, 411). Similar oversights are corrected in Fairbrother: "Earth" repeated within two lines, "plain" within five, "Wars" within four (pp. 3, 70, 142). In Matthew Pilkington, by contrast, there are few outright repetitions in the early texts. Over-reliance on adjectives can give much the same effect, however, as in "Let Scalding Sorrows fill my Red'ning Eyes." In the collected *Poems* volume, the adjectives are pared and the line changed to "Let ceaseless Sorrows overflow my Eyes" (MP, p. 127).

All our different collected *Poems* volumes – Matthew Pilkington's, the two of Swift's, and, to a lesser extent, Mrs Barber's – show other signs of attention to the way the verse should sound. A pun, a *double entendre*, a witty sally can be spoiled without proper emphasis. "To Statesmen would you give a wipe," Swift had advised about this time in *On Poetry: A Rapsody*,

You print it in *Italick Type*.
When Letters are in vulgar Shapes,
'Tis ten to one the Wit escapes,
But when in *Capitals* expresst,
The dullest Reader smoaks the Jest. (ll. 95–100)

As befits collected *Works*, presenting one's acknowledged verse to a broad readership, all of our volumes have been scored for clear and easy out-loud reading, with the desired emphases indicated by the use of italics. In Mrs Barber, who had used italics in her earliest printings, the emphases are reworked for the collected *Poems*, with some new ones added and a few old ones taken away. For Matthew Pilkington, who had seldom used italic emphases in his early printings, the collected *Poems* introduce them in systematic fashion. The Faulkner edition of Swift goes about adding emphases fairly systematically, by my count adding 40 such italicizations to the poems reprinted from Fairbrother, while the Fairbrother edition paid a more sporadic attention, adding 14 to poems reprinted from the previous Fairbrother edition. I had thought it a particularly Swiftian ploy to italicize cant phrases or conscious literary borrowings, like the lawyer pleading before Venus in *Cadenus and Vanessa*, "Which Crimes aforesaid (*with her Leave*) / Were (*as he humbly did conceive*)" (ll. 15–16), or the ironic paraphrase of *Ecclesiastes* 11:1 in *The South Sea*, "*Upon the Water cast thy bread* ..." All are italicized in the Fairbrother edition (pp. 1, 114). This practice is absent from the Pilkington *Poems* but, to my surprise, I found it in Mary Barber, both in her collected volume and in some of her early printings. Nor are all the Swift italicizations, even in Faulkner, necessarily attributable to the Dean. In his Horatian address to Harley, for instance, Harley notices a parson in the street (Swift) who is browsing at an old-book stall, "Cheap'ning old Authors on a Stall." This is how the line ought to read, without special emphases. Unfortunately, someone had the bright idea of making a bow to Swift as champion of the Ancients against the Moderns, not that Ancients and Moderns have anything to do with the story at hand. Accordingly, in Faulkner, Harley now encounters his parson, "Cheap'ning *old* Authors on a Stall" (II, 101, original emphasis) – a pointless refinement which detracts from the thrust and humour of the poem. Taken on their merits, quite apart from Faulkner's preface, it is hard to believe that Swift alone could have originated all the revisions in the Faulkner and Fairbrother editions.

With this in mind, it is time to return to Patrick Delany's *senatus*. It or something very similar would account for the kind of work we have seen going on in the Pilkington, Barber, and Swift volumes. Although they hardly provide proof positive, they suggest that there had been some sort of group effort, reading the poems aloud and adopting minor corrections – mainly small logical adjustments which may be argued pro and con but which fall short of an author's creative reworking. To a considerable degree – all four editions add explanatory footnotes here and there – they also cater to a middling sort of reader, whose needs (including the need for explanatory notes) we know Swift espoused in letters to Pope about this time.[8] Like Swift himself, Mary Barber, Constantia Grierson, and Matthew Pilkington had for the most part written about particular incidents, private or public, when they were still fresh in mind. Like Swift, they had almost always published their efforts (if they published at all) anonymously. To assemble these occasional poems years later, for an openly acknowledged collection to be printed by subscription, introduced a new and different set of circumstances – circumstances to which the original poet, without outside help, might well have had trouble adapting his verse. If for no other reason, a group of outside readers should have been useful.

If the revisions we have traced represent a group effort, was it always the same group? Did Patrick Delany's *senatus* convene over the Pilkington volume and the two Swift editions as it did over Mary Barber's collection? Even with Mrs Barber's, was the group's membership always the same? Almost certainly the answer is no. As an authenticating detail, Mrs Pilkington quotes part of a verse letter which Delany sent out as an invitation for a *senatus* meeting, on "one Day that he had appointed for this Purpose." The invitation itself mentions "a long winding Walk," which suggests Delany's suburban villa at Delville. Pretty clearly, the occasion could not have been the open house which he held every week in town at his Stafford Street lodgings, where he entertained a regular group of friends sometimes termed his "Club" or the "Dublin Thursday society."[9] As members of the *senatus*, Mrs Pilkington lists her husband, herself, Delany, Mrs Grierson, and sometimes Swift, but the verse invitation which she quotes adds an unexpected figure, her own mother Elizabeth Van Lewen. Elsewhere in her narrative, Mrs Van Lewen figures not as a judge of poetry but as someone who tried to keep young Laetitia away from it, lest she spoil her eyes (LP, I, 13). The reference suggests that the Delany *senatus* was more variable in its composition, and very likely more informal in its arrangements, than Mrs Pilkington implies. So, too, does her

8   See *Correspondence*, IV, 104, 134–35.
9   See *Correspondence*, IV, 339, 172, 271, 199, 135–36, and *The Autobiography and Correspondence of Mary Granville, Mrs. Delany*, ed. Lady Llanover (London, 1861–62), I, 396–97.

later reference to Swift, *not* Delany, "summoning a *Senatus Consultum*, as he called those few Friends whom he peculiarly regarded," in this case to adjudicate the case of a murdered hen (LP, I, 310). Whose pet phrase was it anyway, Delany's or Swift's? She cannot have it both ways. Then, too, her personal animosities may distort the picture. We look in vain for Thomas Sheridan, perhaps Swift's closest literary friend in Ireland. By the late 1740s, when Mrs Pilkington wrote, she was feuding bitterly with Sheridan's son Tom and claiming that Swift only entertained the father "more as a Buffoon, than a Friend or Companion" (I, 328). By the late 1740s, she was also feuding with her ex-husband Matthew, to whose volume of poems she alludes only once in passing – and rather bitterly at that (I, 299&n). We would not expect her to describe a *senatus* convened over his work.

Of the group or groups which may have met to read Swift's poems, for Fairbrother's edition and/or for Faulkner's, we know if possible even less. Almost certainly, the cast did not include Mrs Pilkington. She would have boasted about her role if she had one, as she boasts of giving Swift the idea for putting *Polite Conversation* into dialogue form (I, 309). At one point, she describes a kind of editing session with Swift, but it has no apparent connection with Faulkner and involved only Swift and herself. To pass time one Sunday afternoon, the Dean made her read aloud to him one of his unpublished prose pieces (I, 29). Seventeen years after Swift's death, looking back on the evolution of his edition, Faulkner himself claimed something similar. Before publication of the *Works*, Swift had made Faulkner attend every morning and read aloud to him,

> that the Sounds might strike the Ear, as well as the Sense the Understanding, and [he] had always two Men Servants present for this Purpose; and when he had any Doubt, he would ask them the Meaning of what they heard? Which, if they did not comprehend, he would alter and amend, until they understood it perfectly well ...[10]

At this late date, Faulkner says nothing about "the supposed Author's Friends" whom he originally claimed had corrected the texts and then proofread the 1735 volumes. After all, he is puffing the authenticity and exclusivity of his editions of Swift, still in print and now grown to 11 volumes. What should strike us here is the emphasis on reading aloud, and on fitting texts to a broad readership. Whichever friends may have been involved in the early 1730s, we have reason to believe they would have worked with Swift's active backing, whether or not he were present for each session.

Group editing and reading by ear may have been central factors, but we should bear in mind that some of the editorial work must have been done solo, in the study. A group of people listening to a poem will not pick up variations in spelling and capitalization, for instance. If our three lesser authors show convergence in accidentals – and if we cannot attribute it to the variety of printers and publishers employed – then someone must have worked through the texts in stock editorial fashion at some point before or after the group sessions. This kind of attention is especially apparent in Faulkner's edition of Swift. Originally, in the 1727 Swift-Pope *Miscellanies*, someone had helpfully added datelines (for instance, "Written *Anno* 1713") at the head of a few poems, mainly *Cadenus and Vanessa* and the yearly birthday poems to Stella. In the 1732 Fairbrother edition, the first such dateline is helpfully expanded ("Written at *Windsor, Anno* 1713"), while two others are added

---

[10]  Faulkner, "To the Reader," *The Works of Dr. J. Swift, D.S.P.D. In Eleven Volumes* (Dublin: by George Faulkner, 1763), I, iv. This edition is Teerink-Scouten, *Bibliography*, p. 38 (46); Faulkner dates his preface October 1762.

before poems referring to political events long past (pp. 1, 38, 61). In Faulkner, however, this scattershot approach gives way to blanket coverage, probably because Faulkner had decided to print Swift's poems in chronological order. Dates were now needed across the board. Except for one inadvertent omission, which Faulkner appends to a later volume, every poem still without a dateline duly receives one. Whether Swift or a deputy who could quiz him about the poems' dates, someone had methodically gone through all the texts to supply them. For Faulkner, Fairbrother, and the Barber and Pilkington volumes, the overall pattern of substantive revision clearly points to group editing. With any *individual* revision, however, there is always a chance that it originated in the more traditional way, before or after the group had done its work.

Where are we left with our poets? Today we set great stock by a writer's individual style, his distinctively personal voice which no one else can duplicate. In Swift's Dublin, this does not seem to have been the case. We have seen how editing toned down the individual voices of Mary Barber, Constantia Grierson, and Matthew Pilkington, and left them sounding much more alike than they originally did. True, they were lesser figures. Would they or even Swift have dared to revise his immortal friend Pope, for instance? Almost certainly the answer was yes. In a surviving letter about the *Epistle to Bathurst*, Swift complained to Pope that "the obscurity of several passages by our ignorance in facts and persons ... make[s] us lose abundance of the Satyr" in Dublin. "Had the printer given me notice," he continues, he would personally have filled in the blanks for the Irish edition and "writ explanatory notes."[11] In the Fairbrother edition a few months earlier – it reprints the Swift-Pope *Miscellanies*, we remember – I also collated the Pope and other texts alongside Swift's. Generally, they have received much less editorial attention, but they do not escape unscathed. A certain number of blanks are filled, several explanatory notes materialize, and for one poem, originally entitled "Song by a Person of Quality" ("I said to my Heart, between Sleeping and Waking"), the Fairbrother edition openly supplies the attribution, "By The Earl of Peterborough" (Fairbrother, p. 101). These are all original changes, not duplicated in the London editions. Even Pope's poetic texts are here and there tinkered with. In the satiric fragment on Addison, for instance, there is a nice, logical-looking change in the famous lines, "View him with scornful, yet with fearful eyes, / And hate for Arts that caus'd himself to rise." The Fairbrother text changes "hate for Arts" to read "hate those Arts, that caus'd himself to rise" (p. 85). After all, the verb "hate" properly requires a direct object – even though, in the process, the sense of the verse has been changed and much of its force dissipated.

How do we apply these findings to Swift, to the problem of editing his poems and other works? Where do we find the texts which come closest to his intentions? Thanks to Harold Williams and Herbert Davis earlier in this century, Faulkner's editions have assumed an often pre-eminent position. John Irwin Fischer's discovery about the 1732 Fairbrother edition will inevitably weaken this a bit. Even if we accept Fairbrother as a secretly authorized precursor of Faulkner – a logical inference, considering the kinds of revisions in both – there is still a problem. In both Swift editions, there are enough signs of group editorial activity, and enough resemblance to the changes made in the group-edited Barber *Poems*, to weaken the claim that they give us the full and final expression of Swift's literary genius. Does this mean, then, that we should automatically turn to the original first editions of each work –

---

[11] *Correspondence*, IV, 104 (January 1732/3).

almost always anonymous and, in practice, all too often hasty little affairs printed by who knows whom under uncertain circumstances? From his many letters on the subject, if from nothing else, there is no reason to doubt Swift's active co-operation in, and approval of, George Faulkner's four-volume *Works*. Whether or not Swift personally originated all the textual changes, they passed his muster collectively if not individually.

Should we stick with Faulkner, then, and winnow out all individual revisions which strike us as un-Swiftian? A number of Swift scholars, some very good, maintain that they can always identify the Dean by his style. Once I thought I might someday join their number, but now I am less hopeful. The phenomenon of convergence in the Barber, Grierson, and Pilkington poems – indeed, the phenomenon of mutual influence in writers' groups – has an important corollary, the tendency of the lesser-known, somewhat less gifted writers in a group to follow their leader. In the early and mid-1730s, there were a number of authors in Dublin – fairly good authors at that – who were writing in a recognizably Swiftian style. Matthew Pilkington took great pride that some of his things could pass for Swift's, including his own modest proposal, *An Infallible Scheme to Pay the Publick Debt*, reprinted in London with the by-line "By D——n S——T." If anyone doubts Patrick Delany's ability to write good Swiftian verse, let him read the *Epistle to Carteret* or try to disentangle Delany's contributions from Swift's in their verse riddles. Indeed, as James Woolley has argued, we should probably strip Swift of *An Apology to the Lady Carteret* and attribute it to Delany instead. Swift's crony Thomas Sheridan was no slouch, as we know from his and Swift's *Intelligencer*, and the young Trinity scholar William Dunkin, who translated Swift's *Carberiæ Rupes* for Faulkner, could write comic Swiftian tetrameters with the best of them, if we may judge from his posthumously collected poems. Even a Scotsman and a Whig, the limping journalist James Arbuckle, could turn out verse like *Momus Mistaken*, which we might take for Swift's if Faulkner had not assigned it to Arbuckle, and the slanderous *Panegyric on Dean Swift*, which we *did* take for Swift's until Aubrey Williams and James Woolley disabused us.[12] Like Pilkington, Dunkin, and Arbuckle before us, we are also tempted to assume that Swift actually had a characteristic style – usually an amalgam of the individual Swift poems and prose pieces which each one of us happens to like best. In fact, as we know or ought to know, Swift was a master mimic, a protean presence who could and did assume a bewildering variety of styles and guises, from the sober businessman in the *Modest Proposal* to some malignant Whig not too different from Arbuckle, imitating and slandering Swift in the *Life and Genuine Character*. Picking and choosing among a text's readings by style alone is bound to be a risky business.

Where this leaves the poor editor, I am not sure. As we well know, the exact choice of phrasing in a poem – even the pointing and italicizing – can have a profound if subtle effect

---

[12] See further in Swift, *Correspondence*, V, 254 (Pilkington on his *Infallible Scheme*); Faulkner's note on *Momus Mistaken* in Swift's *Works*, XVII (Dublin: by George Faulkner, 1768), iii; James Woolley, "The Canon of Swift's Poems: The Case of 'An Apology to the Lady Carteret,'" *Reading Swift: Papers from The Second Münster Symposium on Jonathan Swift*, eds Richard H. Rodino and Hermann J. Real, with Helgard Stöver-Leidig (München, 1993), pp. 245–64; and Aubrey L. Williams, "'A vile Encomium': That 'Panegyric on the Reverend D–n S–t'" and James Woolley, "Arbuckle's 'Panegyric' and Swift's Scrub Libel: The Documentary Evidence," both in John Irwin Fischer and Donald C. Mell, Jr, eds, *Contemporary Studies of Swift's Poetry* (Newark, London, Toronto, 1981), pp. 178–209.

on the reader's experience of it. For the responsible modern editor, I sense a certain amount of agonizing ahead. There is something in Patrick Delany's rhyming invitation to his little group of editors which should also give us pause. He promises them food and drink, cracks jokes, and very strongly leaves the impression that he and they will have fun, not agonize, in their deliberations. He seems to consider poetry something to be enjoyed in company, not just studied. This is a view which, despite Pope's *Dunciad* and the Romantics to come, would permit us to take pleasure in light verse, poems about recent events (even minor or personal happenings), and when they are reasonably apt, the poetic effusions of people unlikely ever to be enshrined as great or significant writers. Without sacrificing our scholarly standards with Swift and his circle, is there some way that we can appropriately respond to the invitation which reached Matthew Pilkington, here addressed as Tom Thumb? "Mighty Thomas, a solemn *Senatus* I call," Delany writes,

> To consult for Sapphira [*Mrs Barber*], so come one and all:
> Quit Books, and quit Business, your Cure and your Care,
> For a long winding Walk, and a short Bill of Fare.
> I've Mutton for you, Sir; and as for the Ladies,
> As Friend Virgil has it, I've *Aliud Mercedes*;
> For Letty, one Filbert, whereon to regale,
> And a Peach for pale Constance, to make a full Meal;
> And for your cruel Part [*Mrs Van Lewen's*], who take Pleasure in Blood
> I have that of the Grape, which is ten times as good:
> Flow Wit to her Honour, flow Wine to her Health,
> High rais'd be her Worth, above Titles or Wealth.
>
> (LP, I, 283)

# Appendix: Texts Collated

Mary Barber (and son Constantine)

Mary Barber, *Poems on Several Occasions*. London: for C. Rivington, "1734." (Referred to as MB.) This is the subscribers' quarto edition issued sometime between March and early June 1735. ESTC t042622, Teerink- Scouten, *Bibliography*, p. 362 (747); copies consulted: Penn fEC75.B2334.734p (Teerink), own (2). See also William M. Sale, Jr, *Samuel Richardson: Master Printer* (Ithaca, NY, 1950), no 135.

–, *Poems on Several Occasions*. London: for C. Rivington, 1735. Octavo edition announced as "just printed off" and "will be speedily published," in the *Daily Journal* (London), 4 June 1735, in the earliest advertisement I have traced announcing delivery of the quarto subscribers' edition. Same ornaments as in MB, often in same places. Excluded from discussion because the text is essentially the same as in MB; corrections minimal. ESTC t042623; copy consulted: own. See also Sale, *Samuel Richardson: Master Printer*, no 165.

[–,] *Apollo's Edict*. [Dublin, 1725?]. ESTC t189605, Foxon B75; copy consulted: Trinity College, Dublin, P.gg.9/16. Collated against the very similar version in Jonathan Smedley, supposed ed., *Gulliveriana: or, A Fourth Volume of Miscellanies* (London: for J. Roberts, 1728), pp. 50–54 (Case 351, Teerink-Scouten, *Bibliography*, pp. 12–13 (32); copy consulted: Penn EC7.SM324.728g), and against MB, pp. 105-10.

[–,] *The Prodigy: or, The Silent Woman. In a Letter from a Lady in Town to a Friend in the Country*. Dublin, printed by E. S., [1726?]. ESTC n039835, Foxon B76; copy consulted: T.C.D. Press A.7.4/63. Collated against MB, pp. 22–27.

[–,] *A Tale being an Addition to Mr. Gay's Fables*. Dublin: by S. Powell for George Ewing, 1728. ESTC n013607, Foxon B77; copy consulted: National Library of Ireland JP.6266. Collated against MB, pp. 7–12.

[–,] *To His Excellency the Lord Carteret, occasion'd by seeing a Poem intituled, The Birth of Manly Virtue*. Dublin: by S. Harding, 1725. ESTC t005242, Foxon B78; copy consulted: British Library C.121.g.8/71. Collated against MB, pp. 136–37.

[–,] *The Widows Address To the Rt: Hon. the Lady Carteret*. By M. B. Dublin: by C. C., 1725. ESTC t005241, Foxon B80; copy consulted: B.L. C.121.g.8/72. Collated against MB, pp. 1–3. Omits the second half of the poem printed in MB, for which see the Brotherton MS.

[–,] ["Written in the Conclusion of a Letter to Mr. Tickell, entreating him to recommend the Widow Gordon's Petition"], here untitled and unattributed, printed in *The Dublin Weekly Journal*, 19 March 1725/6. Collated against MB, p. 6.

Constantine Barber, *To the Right Honourable the Lady Elizabeth Boyle, daughter to the Right Honourable John Earl of Orrery, on her birth-day, May the 7th, 1733*. Dublin: by George Faulkner, 173[3]. ESTC t215879, Foxon B67; copy consulted: Royal Irish Academy, Haliday Pamphl. 110/2. Near-identical text printed in Faulkner's *Dublin Journal*, 19/22 May 1733, correcting version printed in issue of 15/19 May. Also reprinted (from the uncorrected *Dublin Journal* text) in the *London Magazine* for May 1733, II, 260. Collated against MB, pp. 250–51.

*A Collection of Epigrams. To which is Prefix'd, A Critical Dissertation on this Species of Poetry*. [Vol. I.] London: for J. Walthoe, 1727. ESTC t000041; Case 341 (1) (a); copy consulted: Princeton Ex.PN6280.C6.1727, copy 1. Collated "On the Death of the late Earl of Mount-Cassel, who dyed in his Tenth Year," no 40, against MB, p. 143.

[Matthew Concanen, ed.,] *The Flower-Piece: A Collection of Miscellany Poems*. London: for J. Walthoe and H. Walthoe, 1731. ESTC t102877, Case 367; copy consulted: Princeton Ex.3598.352. Collated "Spoken by a little Boy at his first putting on Breeches," pp. 228–30, against MB, pp. 13–16.

–, ed., *Miscellaneous Poems, Original and Translated, By Several Hands*. London: for J. Peele, 1724. Case 332; copy consulted: own. Collated "Stella and Flavia," p. 234, against versions in James Ralph, ed., *Miscellaneous Poems, by Several Hands* (London: by C. Ackers for W. Meadows *et al.*, 1729), p. 168 (Case 354; copy consulted: Library Company of Philadelphia), in Faulkner's *Dublin Journal* 18/22 March 1728/9, in the Brotherton MS below, and in MB, pp. 126–27. MB text closest to Concanen's.

*Tunbrigialia: or, Tunbridge Miscellanies, for the Year 1730.* London: for T. B. and sold by the booksellers, 1730. ESTC t135335, Case 364; copy consulted: Princeton Ex.PN6110.P7T86. 1719. Collated "Occasion'd by seeing two Subscribers wanting to fill up a Raffle for Addison's Works," p. 10, against MB, p. 46; "Upon seeing Lady Betty Germain do a generous humane Action at Tunbridge-Wells," p. 14, against MB, pp. 116–17; "To Dr. Lynch, on his Excellent Sermon preach'd at Tunbridge-Wells Aug. 23, 1730," p. 4, against MB, p. 141; "An Epigram on the same Occasion," p. 5, against MB, p. 142; "An Apology for the Clergy, who were at Tunbridge-Wells when the Minister read Prayers," pp. 16–17, against MB, pp. 144–45; and "Written upon the Rocks at Tunbridge," p. 11, against MB, pp. 147–48.

Irish poetical miscellany in two or more hands, main portion datable by internal references and state of texts to c. 1725–1732, Brotherton Library, University of Leeds, MS Lt.9. Provenance: Sotheby's (London), 13 May 1963, lot 238. Collated "An Hymn to Sleep," p. 3, against MB, p. 70; "Written in A Leaf of A Bible left yᵉ Author by his Godmother," p. 5, against MB, p. 82; "To the Honᵇˡᵉ Miss Carteret," pp. 35–36 (full text of the poem, earliest version seen) against Foxon B80 above (*The Widows Address*, curtailed text) and against MB, pp. 1–5; "Stella and Flavia," p. 43, against the Concanen *Miscellaneous Poems* and other texts cited above and against MB, pp. 216–17; "The Prodigy," pp. 44–46, against Foxon B76 above (text very close) and against MB, pp. 22–27.

Strafford Papers, British Library, Add. MS 31,152, f. 58. Early transcript of "To the Right Honᵇˡᵉ the Earle of Orrery" ("Tho' the muse had deny'd me so often before"). Near-identical text printed in the *London Magazine* for July 1733, II, 363. Collated against MB, pp. 171–72.


## Constantia Grierson

Mary Barber, *Poems on Several Occasions*, 4to, "1734," as above. (Referred to as MB.) Six poems by Mrs Grierson included in the volume.

Constantia Grierson, autograph volume of her poems (fair copies), c. 1731, in a private collection; see A. C. Elias, Jr, in *Swift Studies*, 2 (1987), 33–56. Includes "To Saphira on the Respect her Works in England" (*sic*), ff. 30–34, collated against MB, pp. xlv–xlviii; "The Speech of Cupid upon seeing himself painted on a Fan by the Hon. Miss Carteret," ff. 2–5, collated against MB, pp. 218–21; and the "Prologue to *Theodosius* design'd to be spoken by Athenaïs written when the Lord & Lady Carteret were in Dublin," ff. 15–17, collated against MB, pp. 243–45.

[–,] *The Goddess Envy to Doctor D—l—y.* Dublin: printed [by George Grierson], 1730. ESTC t163030, Foxon G205; copy consulted: T.C.D. P.pp.10/18. Collated against Mrs Grierson's MS, ff. 8–9. Excluded from the discussion because not collected in MB. Anonymously defends Delany against Swift's and others' jesting attacks this year; doubtful that either man was consulted about revisions.


## Matthew Pilkington

Matthew Pilkington, *Poems on Several Occasions*. Dublin: by George Faulkner, 1730. (Referred to as MP.) ESTC t123124, Teerink-Scouten, *Bibliography*, p. 346 (702); copy consulted: own. This is Pilkington's original subscription edition with printed subscribers' list.

–, *Poems on Several Occasions ... To which is added, the Plague of Wealth ... With several Poems not in the Dublin Edition ... Revised by the Reverend Dr. Swift.* London: for T. Woodward, Charles Davis, and W. Bowyer, 1731. ESTC t134719, Teerink-Scouten, *Bibliography*, p. 346 (703); copy consulted: own. See Keith Maslen and John Lancaster, *The Bowyer Ledgers* (London and New York, 1991), no 1647. Apart from the additional pieces, the text is essentially the same as in MP; corrections minimal.

–, *An Ode, To be performed at the Castle of Dublin, On the 30th of October, being the Birthday Of his most Excellent and Sacred Majesty King George II.* Dublin: by S. Powell, for George Ewing, 1728. ESTC t185858, first noted by James Woolley in his review of Foxon, *MP*, 75 (1977), 69. Copy consulted: T.C.D., P.hh.22/32. Collated against the text of the 1729 Ode as printed in *Dickson's Old Dublin Intelligence*, 1 November 1729, and against MP, pp. 180–89.

[–,] *The Progress of Musick in Ireland, A Poem. Together with A Pastoral Elegy on the Death of a Lady's Canary-Bird. And a Poem on Mr. Pope's Works, Written to the same Lady.* The Second Edition Revis'd and Corrected by the Author. Dublin: by Pressick Rider and Thomas Harbin, 1725. ESTC t179003, Foxon P282; copy consulted: N.L.I., P.1848. Collated "The Progress of Musick in Ireland In a Letter to a Young Lady," pp. 1–9, against MP, pp. 3–25; "A Hymn to Sleep," p. 10, against the versions in Ralph's *Miscellaneous Poems by Several Hands* of 1729 (cited above under Mrs Barber), p. 201, and in MP, pp. 26–27 (text much closer to Pilkington's 1725 version); "To a Young Lady With the Works of Mr. Alexander Pope," pp. 11–13, against MP, pp. 71–77; and "A Pastoral Elegy on the Death of a Lady's Canary-Bird," pp. 15–20, against MP, pp. 125–34. Publishers' advertisement in the *Dublin Weekly Journal*, 19 June 1725, warns against the previous edition that year which "was printed against the Author's Knowledge or Consent, it being very incorrect."

## Jonathan Swift

Jonathan Swift, *The Works of J.S., D.D., D.S.P.D.*, 4 volumes in 8vo, poems in *Volume II. Containing the Author's Poetical Works*. Dublin: by and for George Faulkner, 1735. (Referred to as Faulkner.) Teerink-Scouten, *Bibliography*, pp. 26–28 (41 [2]); copy: own. For the poems in question, further revised and set up from Fairbrother below.

Jonathan Swift and Alexander Pope, *Miscellanies in Prose and Verse. The Second Volume. To which are added Several Poems, and other Curious Tracts not in any former Impression.* "The Third Edition." Dublin: by and for Sam. Fairbrother, 1732. (Referred to as Fairbrother.) Teerink-Scouten, *Bibliography*, p. 22 (33 [2b]); copy: Cambridge University Library, Hib.7.732.26, film courtesy of John Irwin Fischer. For the poems in question, revised and set up from Fairbrother's 1728 printing below.

–, *Miscellanies in Prose and Verse. The Second Volume. To which is added, A Poem written on the North-Window of the Deanary-House of St. Patrick's, Dublin.* "The Second Edition." Dublin: by and for Sam. Fairbrother, 1728. Teerink-Scouten, *Bibliography*, p. 21 (33 [1b]); copy: own. Except for its add-on texts, the poems here represent an exceptionally close and faithful reprint of the London edition S-P below.

–, *Miscellanies. The Last Volume* [Vol. III]. London: for B. Motte, 1727. (Referred to as S-P.) Teerink-Scouten, *Bibliography*, p. 8 (25 [3a]); copy: own. Collected and edited by Pope with Swift's full co-operation; some of Swift's poems presented here had previously been collected and edited for Swift's *Miscellanies* of 1711.

Jonathan Swift, autograph corrections in his own set of the London Swift-Pope *Miscellanies*, including the "Last" volume, now at Trinity College, Cambridge (Rothschild no 1422), as recorded in the apparatus of *The Poems of Jonathan Swift*, ed. Harold Williams, 2nd ed. (Oxford, 1958) and checked against an independent transcription made by John Irwin Fischer.

Peter Wagner

*Universität Koblenz-Landau*

# Of Painted and Graven Images: On the Function of Pictures in Swift's Writings

ABSTRACT. In a close reading of illustrations and allusions to paintings in two Swiftian texts – *Gulliver's Travels* and "Strephon and Chloe" – this article ignores "the intention of the author" while providing a fresh, post-structuralist, view of the ekphrastic potential of Swift's writings. After detailed scrutiny, "false" images (portraits of Captain Gulliver) and real paintings (rococo art) prove to be visual rhetoric that is in turn framed by, and subjected to, the Swiftian verbal discourse. While the various "portraits" of Gulliver already deconstruct the idea that there is truth in visual representations, the allusions to paintings in "Strephon and Chloe" obviously try to arrest meaning for the satirical purpose. The article maintains that this captation occurs at the cost of the ambiguity of visual art, which is denied its essential indeterminacy.

Inspired and indeed encouraged by what the late Richard H. Rodino termed the "tiny dribs and drabs" of post-structuralist analyses that have appeared in Swift studies since 1980, I now intend to go the whole hog and do away with Swift – or rather the author concept of a "Jonathan Swift" which, as Ann Cline Kelly has shown, continues to be a central, pivotal, construct in almost every study of Swiftian texts.[1] Simultaneously, I want to demonstrate in two very brief case studies of Swift's prose and poetry what one can do without him/it. To my knowledge, Richard H. Rodino was the first Swift scholar to pluck up his courage, in 1987, to tell the busy Swift industry what had been amiss with its productions.[2] This lack, which has been a hallmark not only of Swift studies, could be described as the resistance to, if not downright rejection of, post-structuralist theory.[3] It is only over the past five years or

---

[1]  See Richard H. Rodino, "'Splendide Mendax': Authors, Characters, and Readers in *Gulliver's Travels*," *Reading Swift: Papers from The Second Münster Symposium on Jonathan Swift*, eds Richard H. Rodino and Hermann J. Real (München, 1993), p. 169, where Rodino quotes articles by Grant Holly, Louise K. Barnett, and Terry J. Castle; see also Ann Cline Kelly, "The Birth of 'Swift,'" *Reading Swift*, pp. 13–23.

[2]  See Rodino's review of *Proceedings of The First Münster Symposium on Jonathan Swift* in *Scriblerian*, 20 (1987), 66–67.

[3]  In this context, see Brean Hammond's apposite critique of Continental European research in reader-reception theory ("founded" as it were by Iser in the 1960s). Responding to Lothar Černy's critique of Iser's view of irony in Fielding's fiction, Hammond argues convincingly that both critics present "intentionalist accounts" which, from a more radical (reader's) point of view, are far from a true metacommentary. See Hammond's article, "'Mind the Gap': A Comment on Lothar Černy," *Connotations: A Journal for Critical Debate*, 3, no 1 (1993), 72–78 (quotation from p. 78).

so that feminists and deconstructionists have made inroads into the field, a phenomenon that has not really found much acclaim.[4] Judging from my personal experience at national and international meetings, there seems to exist a tremendous if unacknowledged fear in traditional quarters that post-structuralism in general, and deconstruction in particular, might destroy the halo of the great and genial writer that has been successfully established and carefully maintained around the Dean.

In this article, I want to do what I suspect Richard H. Rodino would have done, had he lived, and what Clive Probyn almost did in his recent, insightful essay on the "textuality" of Swift's satire, an essay that takes us to the very threshold of a room most of us have tried or managed to avoid. I feel that both Rodino and Probyn have done a power of good to Swift studies by outlining the fascinating intertextual nature of the Swiftian discourse. Both critics have proved beyond doubt that Swift's texts may be studied with great profit as palimpsests and networks, as writing that infallibly consigns the pre-figured texts to a *mise en abîme*, that is, a dramatization and foregrounding of the treacherous ways words defer meaning from one text to another.

But, we might ask with the little lady in the TV commercial, where is the beef? For both Rodino and Probyn still operate with the author concept. A genuine post-structuralist reading, however, would proceed entirely without the author. Thus I would contend that Swift is not a deconstructionist (be it *avant ou après la lettre*) but rather a conservative if brilliant parodist. Hence, both Swift and his texts still await a reading that does not see the author (intention) in control of the sense that is being made.[5] Indeed, I will be arguing with the support of Roland Barthes and Michel Foucault[6] that it is our very obsessive search for, or listening to, the voice of the almighty author (that immortal remnant of the Romantic notion of a god-like genius[7]) which has prevented other – and perhaps more important – (inter)-

---

4    See, for instance, the outstanding studies by Laura Brown, "Reading Race and Gender:
     Jonathan Swift," *Eighteenth-Century Studies*, 23 (1990), 425–43; and Carol Houlihan Flynn,
     *The Body in Swift and Defoe* (Cambridge, 1990).

5    Although he provides a penetrating reading of the intertextual networks in Swift's works,
     Clive T. Probyn significantly still has resort to the author concept. It is precisely because
     Probyn gets in Swift (the author) through the back door that he ultimately deprives the
     reader/critic of the essential task of deconstructing Swift's ambiguous texts. "The twen-
     tieth-century reader in the deconstructionist academy," Probyn argues, "is robbed of his
     active hermeneutic role and given a tertiary function as witness and by-stander." See Pro-
     byn, "Swift and Typographic Man: Foul Papers, Modern Criticism, and Irish Dissenters,"
     *Reading Swift*, eds Rodino and Real, p. 38. However, a deconstructive approach as I
     propagate it in this paper will inquire into the gaps and cracks which the Swiftian texts
     ignore or patch over. My reading relies not on the genial author or the meaning that is
     hidden somewhere in his text, but rather on the reader making sense while rejecting the
     idea of establishing hermeneutic hierarchies of fixed meaning and signification.

6    See the famous if still misunderstood essays on the "death of the author" by Barthes, "La
     mort de l'auteur," *Manteia*, 5 (1968), 12–17; and Foucault, ["Qu'est-ce qu'un auteur?" first
     published in 1969] "What is an Author," trans. D. F. Bouchard and S. Simon, *Contem-
     porary Literary Criticism*, 3rd ed., eds Robert C. Davis and Ronald Schleifer (New York,
     1994), pp. 341–54.

7    On the creation of the idea of the authorial genius in the eighteenth century, and the need
     of the Victorian age of this notion, see John Hope Mason, "Thinking about Genius in the
     Eighteenth Century," *Eighteenth-Century Aesthetics and the Reconstruction of Art*, ed. Paul
     Mattick, Jr (Cambridge, 1993), pp. 210–40.

textual voices to reach our ears and minds, including especially those voices that "wrote" the author in a manner of speaking.[8]

In what follows I will try to show that a post-structuralist approach working without the author concept[9] can be beneficial and profitable, precisely because this approach abandons a chimera: the artificial, unreliable, construct of "Swift" the genial author. What expects our attention is the prefigured rhetoric, both verbal and visual, which Swift the author has either misrepresented or partly, sometimes even completely, silenced while imposing his own rhetoric upon texts and images which need our critical help. My subject is the function of pictures as rhetoric in two Swiftian texts: in Part I, the frontispieces in several early editions of *Gulliver's Travels*; and, in Part II, painted images as visual rhetoric in "Strephon and Chloe." My authority is not Swift, but the host of texts and images called up by allusions in Swift's texts. It will be obvious that in such an approach I cannot respect traditional disciplinary boundaries (English Literature; Art History; Rhetoric): I will be crossing borders to demonstrate that images can be as rhetorical as texts and that, more often than not, images and texts form an undissolvable unity (iconotexts is my favourite term in this case) with a common denominator: the verbal/visual sign as rhetoric.[10]

---

[8]  In this context, I would like to pay homage to the critical work of Claude Rawson on eighteenth-century fiction, including some pieces on Swift. From the very beginning of his critical career, Rawson has outlined the extent to which Swift's texts draw on earlier models, both ideologically and structurally. Although he does not belong to any post-structuralist school (at least not to my knowledge), Rawson has always tried to place and understand Swift's writings in what might be termed an intertextual network encompassing pretexts and contexts. See especially his latest edited collection, *Jonathan Swift: A Collection of Critical Essays* (Englewood Cliffs, NJ, 1995).

[9]  This also includes "author intention," which continues to be a highly embattled issue in literary theory. For a recent discussion, see the essays by E. D. Hirsch, Jr, "Transhistorical Intentions and the Persistence of Allegory" (pp. 549–67); John R. Searle, "Literary Theory and Its Discontents" (pp. 637–67); Steven Knapp and Walter Benn Michaels, "Reply to John Searle" (pp. 669–75); and John R. Searle's "last word," "Structure and Intention in Language: A Reply to Knapp and Michaels" (pp. 677–81); all in *New Literary History: A Journal of Theory and Interpretation*, 25 (1994). This issue of the journal pits the intentionalists (Hirsch and Knapp/Michaels), who hold that textual meaning depends on speaker/author intention, against Searle (best known for his research in speech act theory), who argues that "speaker meaning" is different from textual meaning. Searle argues quite convincingly, except in the passages where he attacks Derrida's views on/of language and the production of meaning (pp. 657–65) : here, dislike and downright polemics (expressed in attacks *ad hominem* instead of arguments) lead him into confusing linguistics and philosophy, and epistemology and ontology – the very charge he makes against Derrida (p. 662). In view of Searle's vehement attacks on deconstructionist approaches as propagated by Derrida, it is a solace to read that Searle, too, rejects the idea that it is the author's intention which determines how the text is interpreted (see p. 655).

[10]  For detailed discussions of the critical and hermeneutical implications for research in iconotexts (word-image constructs), see my introduction in Peter Wagner, ed., *Icons – Texts – Iconotexts: Essays on Ekphrasis and Intermediality* (Berlin and New York, 1996), pp. 1–40; and the close readings of eighteenth-century prints in my *Reading Iconotexts: From Swift to the French Revolution* (London, 1995).

# I

Picking up some threads I had to leave dangling while discussing the portraits of Captain Gulliver on two other occasions,[11] I want to reconsider the engraved portraits in *Gulliver's Travels*. The Swiftian text exposes them as iconotextual rhetoric, as sophistic and sophisticated ways of misrepresenting reality. In my earlier readings, I stressed the intertextual and intermedial play of these iconotexts, and more precisely the way they subvert the conventions of visual representation. From a deconstructive viewpoint, they can also be read with the Derridean concepts of dissemination and différance: in addition to intertextual

Figure 1: "Captain Lemuel Gulliver"; frontispiece of the first issue of Motte's edition of 1726. Engraving, first state, by John Sturt and Robert Sheppard

---

[11]  See my article, "Swift's Great Palimpsest: Intertextuality and Travel Literature in *Gulliver's Travels*," *Dispositio: American Journal of Comparative and Cultural Studies*, 17, nos 42–43 (1992), 107–32 (especially pp. 112–20); and the chapter on "Captain Gulliver and the Pictures" in my *Reading Iconotexts*, pp. 37–74. I draw especially on the latter.

Figure 2: "Captain Lemuel Gulliver"; frontispiece of a later issue of Motte's
edition of 1726. Engraving, second state

aspects, they imply polysemy, indeterminacy, and the construction of meaning and authority
through a "signature," that is to say, the creation of the illusion of a presence by referring
to absent authorities.[12] In the case of the differing engraved portraits of Captain Gulliver
(Figures 1–3), which appeared in editions published in 1726 and 1735, I am not arguing,

---

[12] For a case study of dissemination in art and art history, see Mieke Bal's splendid essay,
"Light in Painting: Dis-Seminating Art History," *Deconstruction and the Visual Arts: Art,
Media, Architecture*, eds Peter Brunette and David Wills (Cambridge, 1994), pp. 49–64.
Written in the wake of Bal's equally penetrating feminist and deconstructionist analysis of
Rembrandt (see *Reading "Rembrandt": Beyond the Word-Image Opposition* [Cambridge,
1991]), this is a wonderfully challenging collection of articles that takes deconstruction
into the field of writing about art (in the double sense of the term), and includes an interview with Derrida (pp. 9–33) in which he argues that "the most effective deconstruction is
that which is not limited to discursive texts" (p. 14).

Figure 3: "Captain Lemuel Gulliver"; frontispiece of the third volume
of Faulkner's edition of Swift's *Works*, 1735. Engraving

like Clive Probyn, that Swift or the Swiftian texts (or, in this instance, iconotexts[13]) perform
the deconstructive work, but rather that it must be done by the reader or critic. I have
already shown in detail how the engravings engage in an intertextual, parodic play with
visual representation as yet another code of signification which, like verbal language or body
language, should not be trusted precisely because it is rhetoric and hence as deceitful as
cosmetics or painting. But a deconstructive reading, which is always a close reading, will
refuse to accept the rhetoric and argument of the engravings that expose silent, untenable

---

[13]  Mieke Bal argues that "images are also texts precisely in that they constitute a network of
discursive practices, albeit visually shaped" ("Light in Painting," p. 52 n 8). I prefer the
term visual rhetoric in this case. For a detailed discussion of visual poetics, the problem of
ekphrasis, and the way texts and images may be studied together (and not as allegedly
separate and different codes), see my introduction in *Icons – Texts – Iconotexts*, pp. 1–40.

Figure 4: Portrait of Captain John Smith, from his *A Description of New England*, 1616.
Engraving by Robert Clerke, after (?) Simon van de Passe

assumptions, such as the confusion of signifier and signified, and the existence of an ultimate truth or master code. To be sure, the different portraits of Gulliver engage intertextually and generically with a great variety of verbal and visual pre-texts that include the frontispiece in Defoe's *Robinson Crusoe* (and the text of course), illustrations in travel literature, and even the verbal portraits of the heroes in More's *Utopia* and Rabelais's *Pantagruel*.

But in order to understand the paradoxical process of meaning-making in the Swiftian fictional engravings, a process that constantly defers signification to other (absent) signifiers, I propose to take a brief look at similar iconotexts of another illustrious captain, a real one, who was also quite capable of lying, thus confirming the bad reputation of ships' captains (which is, of course, one of the points of the elaborate title of *Gulliver's Travels*). I am referring to the travel reports of John Smith, the "Admiral of New England." Like Gulliver, John Smith makes visual appearances (in engraved portraits) in the front matter and even

Figure 5: A map of John Smith's *The Generall Historie of Virginia, New-England, and the Summer Isles*, 1624. Engraving by Robert Clerke, after (?) Simon van de Passe

within the text of two of his books. It is telling, I believe, that the first portrait (Figure 4) forms part of a map in *A Description of New England* (1616). The confluence of scientific mapping and painterly portraiture is nothing else but an attempt to persuade the reader of the semblance of the real in the mimetic. It is an act of simulation that promises what Derrida terms "la vérité en peinture" precisely by referring the observer to other images, codes, and texts, quite apart from the fact that it tells us something about the relation between mapping (in the Renaissance), perception, representation, and believing. Smith's various exploits and adventures are iconically represented (another act of dissemination and différance) in four miniature scenes in the corners outside the frame, and again in the verses below the illustration(s). In the map cum portrait that was used again (Figure 5) for Smith's *Generall Historie of Virginia, New-England, and the Summer Isles* (1624), we find a person with slightly different features. As Ishmael says in Chapter I of *Moby-Dick*, after a typically inconclusive ekphrasis of a verbally created landscape, "surely all this is not without meaning."[14] In his *Generall Historie*, however, Smith is deliberately shown as a rather small man as he takes Indian chiefs prisoners; and quite a different man, it seems, appears in the plate of illustrations intended for *The True Travels, Adventures, and Observations of Captain John Smith* (1630). Representation, whether it is done in words or in images, is always a re-presentation of something that has been. It is, in deconstructive terms, the attempt to produce the illusion of reality by making us believe that what we see is the signified, not the signifier.

## II

Once upon a time but not so very long ago, when I was still a virginal scholar uncorrupted by feminism, deconstruction,[15] and other recent shocking developments, I cast an hermeneutical look at Swift's "drawing room poems," reading them in terms of the Dean's Platonic iconoclasm as attacks on the male, voyeuristic gaze that casts the female body into an idealized object, into an idol.[16] I now want to return to one particular poem, "Strephon and Chloe" (1734),[17] for a brief exploration of the *mise en abîme* in this satire of what might be called visual rhetoric, that is, the alleged misrepresentation of reality in painting.

"Strephon and Chloe," we remember, dramatizes the corruption of a man's perception (of the female body) by verbal and visual art. This corruption, the poem argues, is due to the exaggerated representation of women in the pastoral scenes of poetry and painting, depicting as they do goddesses, nymphs, and other heavenly bodies. Unlike the other "drawing room poems," which show the consequences of such a "wrong" perception in males who become mad or dejected or both when confronted with the physicality of femininity,[18] "Stre-

---

14  See Herman Melville, *Moby-Dick: or, The Whale*, eds Harrison Hayford, Hershel Parker, and G. Thomas Tanselle (Evanston and Chicago, 1988), p. 5.

15  On the way deconstruction can "ruin" one's ability to appreciate traditional scholarship, see Peter Brunette and Jacques Derrida in *Deconstruction and the Visual Arts*, eds Brunette and Wills, pp. 30–31.

16  See my article on "Swift and the Female Idol: The Dean as Iconoclast," *Anglia*, 110 (1992), 347–67.

17  See *Poems*, pp. 455–63.

18  See the poems entitled "The Lady's Dressing Room," "A Beautiful Young Nymph Going to Bed," and "Cassinus and Peter." To these may be added the thematically related "The Progress of Beauty."

phon and Chloe" presents a hero who eventually adopts a new view of the female body. The poem argues that this view is realistic and correct because it controls passion by insisting on "sense and wit," cementing the whole with "decency" (ll. 307–8). It is this unacceptable moral of the poem – it is unacceptable precisely because it literally writes sexuality out of the picture by eliminating the otherness of women – which feminist critics have lambasted with good cause.[19] This is a subject worth exploring, beyond the recent studies of Flynn and Crow (who are still very much concerned with the author as perpetrator): what needs more attention is the re-presentation of the female body in the textual misrepresentation and subordination as we encounter it in Swift's poems. Their recourse to the feminine serves to authenticate discourses, but does so by occulting "femininity" in the process. Although this is not my subject here, I should like to point out that a deconstructive analysis of the way "Strephon and Chloe" appropriates and misreads verbal pre-texts, to give just one example, must resist the Platonic, moral rhetoric of the poem in order to unveil another metamorphosis of sorts, that is, its construction of a sexless, and hence harmless, female body. Such an analysis would have to begin with the title, which contains implicit allusions to the male shepherds in Sidney's *Arcadia* and the female goddesses of pastoral poetry.[20] From the title, which is an important threshold or access to the main text,[21] one could move on to the exploration of the texts that are alluded to in lines 50–66 and 100–10, where Strephon appears in the role of the male reader as characters from Ovid's *Metamorphoses* open the sluice gates for a wave of pre-texts and, ultimately, dissemination and différance.

My concern, however, is with the visual pre-texts in this poem, although I must admit that many allusions in "Strephon and Chloe" are *iconotextual*: they refer to texts *and* images, a fact that augments their polyvalence and multifunctional role. We shall see that a number of references open up the signifying process by alluding not to one text or a series of texts, but rather to a certain kind of rhetoric shared by poetry and art. Like most Swiftian literary products, "Strephon and Chloe" is a highly intertextual piece, studded as it is with allusions. These are always the first links in a fascinating chain of différance that takes us from Swift's poem to, say, a mythological scene in (a) painting, on to the verbal representations behind it, and from there to the vast horizons of intertextuality and orality. In what follows I should like to outline how différance and misrepresentation work on the iconotextual level, and more precisely on the level of allusions to painting(s).

In "Strephon and Chloe," Chloe's celestial body – as seen by the distorted gaze of her lover – is the female body as represented in poetry and painting from the beginning of the Renaissance to the early eighteenth century. This means that the borrowed metaphors and images in the poem fit both verbal and visual art. Chloe's physical shape is described as "milk-white," "ivory dry," and "soft as wax" (ll. 25–26). Since these allusions are to the goddesses and nymphs in literature, mythology, and pastoral painting, the body is one "with

---

[19] See Penelope Wilson, "Feminism and the Augustans: Some Readings and Problems," *Critical Quarterly*, 28 (1986), 80–92 (especially pp. 87–88); Flynn, *The Body in Swift and Defoe*, Chapter 4; Ruth Salvaggio, *Enlightened Absence: Neoclassical Configurations of the Feminine* (Urbana and Chicago, 1988), p. 93; and Nora Crow Jaffe, "Swift and the 'agreeable young Lady, but extremely lean,'" *Contemporary Studies of Swift's Poetry*, eds John Irwin Fischer and Donald C. Mell, Jr (Newark, London, Toronto, 1981), pp. 149–58.

[20] Strephon and Klaius are shepherds in *Arcadia*; and Chloe is of course a common name of "nymphs" in numerous pastoral lyrics.

[21] See Gérard Genette's analysis of its function in literary works, in *Seuils* (Paris, 1987).

constitution cold and snowy" (l. 152). These comparisons are so iconic that one can hardly overlook the implication of plastic art and painting. Lines 47–66 and 97–108 (through Strephon's role as reader/listener in the latter: see ll. 101 and 105–6) engage with representations of mythological characters, partly staging the age-old paragone of text and image and all the misrepresentations that struggle implies:[22]

> *Imprimis*, at the temple porch
> Stood Hymen with a flaming torch.
> The smiling Cyprian goddess brings
> Her infant loves with purple wings;
> And pigeons billing, sparrows treading,
> Fair emblems of a fruitful wedding.
> The muses next in order follow,
> Conducted by their squire, Apollo:
> Then Mercury with silver tongue,
> And Hebe, goddess ever young.
> Behold the bridegroom and his bride,
> Walk hand in hand, and side by side;
> She by the tender Graces dressed,
> But, he by Mars, in scarlet vest.
> The nymph was covered with her *flammeum*,
> And Phoebus sung the epithalamium.
> And, last to make the matter sure,
> Dame Juno brought a priest demure.
> Luna was absent on pretence
> Her time was not till nine months hence. (ll. 47–66)

> And goddesses have now and then
> Come down to visit mortal men:
> To visit and to court them too:
> A certain goddess, God knows who,
> (As in a book he heard it read)
> Took Colonel Peleus to her bed.
> But, what if he should lose his life
> By venturing *on* his heavenly wife?
> For, Strephon could remember well,
> That, once he heard a schoolboy tell,
> How Semele of mortal race,
> By thunder died in Jove's embrace. (ll. 97–108).[23]

The characters mentioned in these two passages had been represented many times in poetry and art – hence the allusions are to both media. To provide just two examples, the seduction of Thetis and Semele, which is hinted at in lines 100–8, evokes Books XI (221–65: the conception of Achilles) and III (253–315) of Ovid's *Metamorphoses*, and the painterly and graphic treatments of the episodes. Again, what needs to be pointed out is that there is no origin, no ultimate source that can be marked and fixed in this case, but rather an endless series of texts and images ranging from Italian erotic prints of the Renaissance and Cornelisz van Haarlem's painting, *The Marriage of Thetis and Peleus*, to frescoes and decorated vases from the fifth century B.C.[24]

---

[22] For a detailed discussion of the paragone, see James A. W. Heffernan, *Museum of Words: The Poetics of Ekphrasis from Homer to Ashbery* (Chicago and London, 1993); and the introduction in *Icons – Texts – Iconotexts*, ed. Wagner, pp. 1–40.

[23] *Poems*, pp. 456, 457.

[24] Van Haarlem's painting and a scene from a vase are reproduced in black and white in *Lexikon der antiken Mythen und Gestalten* (München, 1983), *s.v.* "Thetis".

The most obvious allusion to painting as a rhetorical art, an art the Swiftian texts frequently liken to cosmetics and rhetoric, occurs in lines 193–202, where Strephon literally discovers the physical, naturalistic aspect of his goddess. As Strephon "filled the reeking vase" and "let fly a rouser in her face," the iconoclastic text tries to destroy the representations of idealistic female bodies by facing them with the scatological obscenity of the human body:

> The little Cupids hovering round,
> (As pictures prove) with garlands crowned,
> Abashed at what they saw and heard,
> Flew off, nor ever more appeared.
>
> Adieu to ravishing delights,
> High raptures, and romantic flights;
> To goddesses so heavenly sweet,
> Expiring shepherds at their feet;
> To silver meads, and shady bowers,
> Dressed up with amaranthine flowers. (ll. 193–202)[25]

It is precisely because the allusions in this section are not to specific images ("As pictures prove" does not say which pictures, but simply that the statement is made by or in pictures, that is to say, graphic and painted images) that art as such is concerned, and more particularly the depiction of women in that art, with their various accoutrements including cupids. In two short lines, the Swiftian text recalls the entire heritage of European (and especially Italian and French) pastoral and erotic art. But in appropriating this visual art, Swift's text functions both ekphrastically and iconoclastically, for it claims that *all* such representations (the genre of pastoral and erotic scenes) because they are based on illusion produced by paint/cosmetic, are false and dangerous. It is this strategy of the text and its consequences which a deconstructive reading must resist in order to bring to light the polyphonic and polysemic discourse and the dissemination that are really at work in the art maligned by Swift's poem.

Even if we select only a few examples from the welter of genres to which the poem alludes (pictures showing "sweet goddesses" accompanied by cupids with garlands; and female nudes in Arcadian landscapes), we recognize immediately how the poetic text attempts to arrest and silence the ambiguous rhetoric of these paintings.[26] To a certain extent, art history, down to our day and age, has done a similarly thorough iconoclastic job in its critical ekphrases of canvases lumped together because they allegedly share such themes as "the lady at her toilette" or "the female nude reclined on a bed."[27] Chronologically, these paintings

---

[25] *Poems*, p. 460.

[26] Paradoxically, this attempt to limit and arrest (dangerous) meaning is one of the principal functions of ekphrasis. In its widest sense now used, the term implies "the verbal representation of visual representation" (Heffernan, *Museum of Words*, p. 3). Images are silent; they need language (titles, commentaries, art-historical criticism) to express what they mean. But as Foucault wrote several decades ago, what they mean never resides in language and cannot be fully expressed in language. See Michel Foucault, *Les mots et les choses: une archéologie des sciences humaines* (Paris, 1966), p. 25. See also my discussion of this eternal dilemma in criticism concerned with verbal and visual rhetoric, in *Reading Iconotexts*.

[27] See, for instance, the articles by Elise Goodman-Soellner, "Boucher's *Madame de Pompadour at Her Toilette*," *Simiolus*, 17 (1987), 41–58; and "Poetic Interpretations of the 'Lady at her Toilette' Theme in Sixteenth-Century Painting," *The Sixteenth-Century Journal*, 14

Figure 6: William Hogarth, *Marriage à-la-Mode*, 1745. Engraving, Plate 1

and prints encompass the works of Titian and Bellini, the Carrachi brothers, Guido Reni, Domenichino, Nicolas Poussin, and Rubens,[28] as well as Swift's contemporaries, Watteau and Boucher. Teeming with cupids hovering around female "heavenly bodies" as objects of adoration and desire, their works were often reproduced in engravings and consequently very well known in England. We only need to look at Hogarth's prints (with the caveat in mind that Hogarth's graphic art is not realistic but as partisan and rhetorical as Swift's verse[29]) to

---

(1983), 426–42. I do not deny the value of these very informative studies. Thus Goodman-Soellner discusses the partly misogynist critique of idealized women in French art and verse. In the first article, she notes that, paradoxically, the iconography of many pictures extolled the beauty of women, but that they also contained verses (sometimes within the frame) against female artifice and "maquillage" as a sign of hypocrisy, illusion, and corruption.

However, the disadvantage of such thematic analyses is that they cannot give pride of place to the rhetorical statement of each individual work. I am arguing that it is the difference between the various works that we need to analyse, precisely because that difference produces dissemination and différance.

[28] On Rubens, see especially Elise Goodman, *Rubens: The Garden of Love as "Conversatie à la mode"* (Amsterdam and Philadelphia, 1992).

[29] It is in this respect only that I see a parallel of the arts, not a correspondence (which assumes that essentially different sign systems of different media, poetry and painting, ex-

Figure 7: William Hogarth, *Marriage à-la-Mode*, 1745. Engraving, Plate 4

find proof of the popularity of that art. Like the Swiftian texts, the Hogarthian engravings allude to Old Master paintings in what has been described as an iconoclastic attempt to break and remake,[30] although a post-structuralist view (which Paulson would never accept[31]) will disclose further interesting dimensions, including the manner in which Hogarth's graphic art misrepresents the artistic discourse of the past even while appropriating it. Thus the walls and the ceiling of the room shown in Plate 1 of *Marriage-à-la-Mode* (1745), for instance, are decorated with works by Titian, Reni, Caravaggio, Domenichino, and others (Figure 6).[32] While these paintings within a print are predominantly religious, Plate 4 of the

---

press the same "messages" – something I find impossible to accept); see Donna G. Fricke, "Swift, Hogarth, and the Sister Arts," *Eighteenth-Century Life*, 2 (1975), 29–33, which still operates with this untenable assumption.

[30] See Ronald Paulson, *Breaking and Remaking: Aesthetic Practice in England, 1700–1820* (New Brunswick and London, 1989).

[31] See my critique of Paulson's author-orientated approach (which explains as Hogarth's "intention" what is essentially Paulson's opinion), in "How to (Mis)Read Hogarth, or Ekphrasis Galore," *1650–1850: Ideas, Aesthetics, and Inquiries in the Early Modern Period*, 2 (1994), 99–135; and in the review of his *Hogarth*, 3 vols (Cambridge, 1991–93), in vol. 3 (1995) of the same journal.

[32] For discussions of this art-historical sub-text, see Frederick Antal, *Hogarth and His Place in European Art* (London, 1962); and Robert L. S. Cowley, *Marriage à-la-Mode: A Review of Hogarth's Narrative Art* (Manchester, 1983), pp. 27–55.

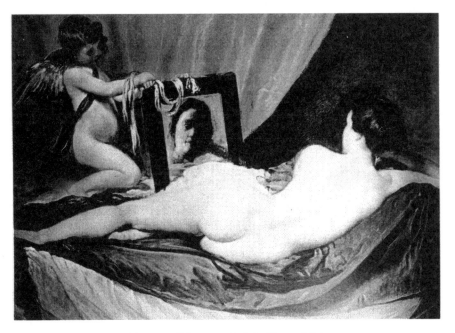

Figure 8: Velazquez, *Rokeby Venus*, 1651

same series also contains an erotic example, Correggio's *Jupiter and Io* (Figure 7).[33] Similarly, the fiction of the first half of the eighteenth century frequently alludes to erotic paintings. In the late 1740s, to provide just one example, John Cleland has his narrator, the simple country girl Fanny Hill, remark on "the touch and colouring" of Guido Reni's painted erotica.[34]

Had I space enough and time, I might provide a detailed tracing of the displacements and appropriations of signs and codes in a series of pictures showing Venus and Cupid, or Venus at her toilette, both favourite and popular subjects throughout the sixteenth and seventeenth centuries, and even more so in Swift's time. A study of such works would need to include, in chronological order, Bellini's *The Lady at her Toilette* (1515); Titian's *Young Woman at her Toilette* (c. 1515); Annibale Carrachi's fresco, *The Triumph of Bacchus and Ariadne* (1595–1605); Domenichino's *Diana* (1617); Rubens's *Nymphs, Satyrs, and Dogs*; Poussin's *Diana and Endymion* (c. 1631) and *Apollo and Daphne*; and Watteau's various "fêtes galantes." One could go all the way to Boucher's *Rinaldo and Armida* (1734), which was painted when Swift published his poem.

Deconstructing the misrepresentations of such paintings in "Strephon and Chloe," one

---

[33]  Hogarth also plays with the observer's knowledge of painted erotica, inviting him/her to guess what is hidden behind the partially drawn curtain in front of a painting on the wall of the dining-room in plate 2 of *Marriage à-la-Mode*.

[34]  See John Cleland, *Fanny Hill or Memoirs of a Woman of Pleasure*, ed. Peter Wagner (Harmondsworth, Middlesex, 1985), p. 68 (see also n. 18).

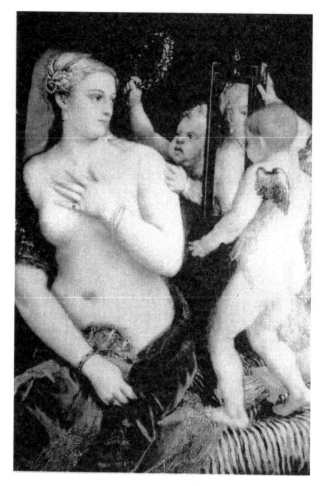

Figure 9: Titian, *Venus with a Mirror*, 1555

needs to consider not only what Derrida calls the "mutism" of a painted or plastic work of art (the fact that, as Foucault pointed out long ago, it cannot speak itself and needs words to express meaning[35]: a title, a commentary, or an ekphrastic poem) but also the fact that each painting is itself an iconotext drawing on both verbal and visual sources to express its message.

Moving back in time from Velazquez's *Rokeby Venus* (1651), I will outline this process of what has been termed the "textual re-cycling" of others' texts (and, I want to add, im-

---

[35]  See Derrida's remarks on the mutism in art (as compared to, say, taciturnity, which is the "silence of something that can speak") in his interview with Peter Brunette and David Wills, *Deconstruction and the Visual Arts*, pp. 12–13. Foucault discussed the problems involved in the way art works depend on language in order to convey meaning (always the first step of a misunderstanding) in his famous analysis of Velazquez's *Las meninas*, in *Les mots et les choses*, quoted above (see Chapter 1, especially p. 25).

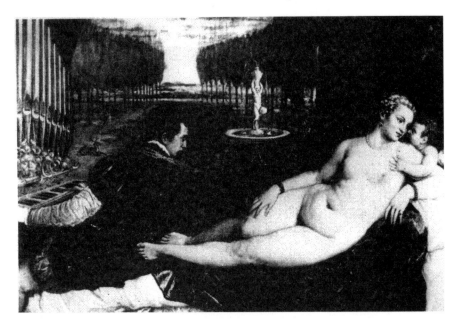

Figure 10: Titian, *Venus with Cupid and Organ Player*, c. 1545

ages)[36] with a few selected examples from a potentially endless line of pictures, a line that does not allow the fixation of meaning because it always relies on the "traces" of verbal and visual discourse. Art-historical commentaries tell us that Velazquez painted from a living model but that the canvas is also based on a Renaissance engraving.[37] But these are merely two pre-figured texts (a body and a print); a look at the painting (Figure 9) evokes additional pre-texts which the picture needs in order to keep up its pretence of signification: for instance, stories about Venus; tales involving Amor (the cupid facing her); and the representations in word and image of Vanitas (texts about Narcissus, for example). Semiotically, the mirror is as important a signifier as the naked female body (which alludes to the code of rear-view representations – a *déjà vu* effect) or the cupid. Indeed, the conjunction of woman and mirror is a highly charged, iconotextual signifier – among other topics, it refers to the essence of femininity in representation: the narcissistic woman as demonized criminal or deified muse. It also thematizes a male fascination with an uncanny (the German, Freudian "unheimlich") figure, a site of self-sufficiency and indifference that is as threatening for man as death.[38] Focusing exclusively on visual antecedents (to which the Velazquez alludes),

---

[36]  See Probyn, "Swift and Typographic Man," p. 34.
[37]  See D. M. Field, *The Nude in* Art (London, 1981), p. 84.
[38]  On these fascinating issues of the representation of the female body, see Elisabeth Bronfen, *Over Her Dead Body: Death, Femininity, and the Aesthetic* (Manchester, 1992). Although Bronfen is mainly concerned with Victorian and nineteenth-century representations of the (dead or dying or sleeping) female body, an age apparently marked by a decidedly antifeminist necrophilia, her fascinating insights may be applied to eighteenth-century representations, too.

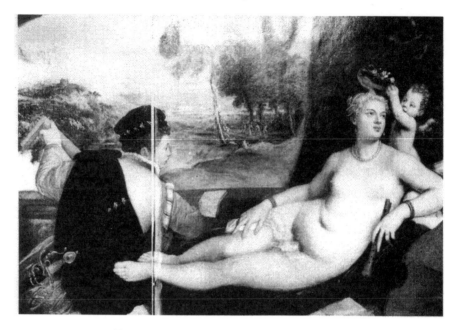

Figure 11: Titian, *Venus with Lutanist*, c. 1560–62

we will encounter similar, but semantically different, images by Titian – for instance, his *Venus with a Mirror* (1555; Figure 9) – in which bashfulness and pride, narcissism and love, the critique of self-love and the celebration of beauty do not unite to form a complete whole, as art history would have it. Rather, what one encounters in such visual representations is a *point de capiton*, Lacan's term for the kind of fixing or captation that occurs in the act of representation.[39] From a deconstructive angle, I see signifiers in opposition, codes at war, and, ultimately, no clarification of meaning but its suspension in references to other signifiers.[40] Like Hillis Miller, I believe that this warfare within images, usually denied by an art history in search of logocentric meaning, needs more of our attention.[41] In Titian's *Venus with Cupid and Organ Player* (c. 1560; Figure 10), it is not only Venus who is different – the whole female body now serves a new purpose (or rhetoric). Here, it is less a polyvalent code representing vanity and beauty than an embodiment of Arcadian topography. The woman's body (without the paratextual title we would have difficulties reading her as Venus[42]) be-

---

[39]  Quoted by Bronfen, *Over Her Dead Body*, p. 46.

[40]  It may be compared to a speech act in which someone uses the expression or tag "You know" in order to make meaning by referring to a "déjà lu/vu" and while assuming that the listener will produce such meaning.

[41]  See Miller's insightful study, *Illustration* (London, 1992), in which he focuses on the codes that are at war within an image.

[42]  In fact, Elise Goodman, in her monograph *Rubens*, plate 5, gives the title of the painting, now in the Museo del Prado (Madrid), as *The Lady and the Organist*, a title that suppresses the textual and visual connotations of Venus. For a detailed iconographic study of the painting and the related works, see Volker Herzner, "Tizians Venus mit dem Orgelspieler," *Begegnungen: Festschrift für Peter Anselm Riedl* (Heidelberg, 1993), pp. 80–108.

Figure 12: Titian, *Venus of Urbino*, c. 1538

comes an area as inviting for the (male, voyeuristic) gaze as the landscape beside it. The body is in fact landscape to be appreciated,[43] but perhaps also to be invaded and appropriated.[44] There is also an interesting note of melancholy, another code that again seems to provide meaning but only defers it by urging us to consider other, contemporary or older, representations of this kind, for example, Titian's *Venus with Lutanist* (c. 1560–62; Figure 11); *Venus of Urbino* (c. 1538; Figure 12), and Giorgione's *Sleeping Venus* (c. 1505–10; Figure 13).

A similar series of displacements and suspensions is at work in the erotic canvases showing pastoral and Arcadian gardens of love, which are the very target of attack in Swift's poem (identified as expiring shepherds, silver meads, and shady bowers [ll. 200–1]). We may begin our search and comparison, in Swift's time, with Watteau's celebrated *Embarkation for Cythera* (Figure 14) which, among many other topics, gives expression to the idea of aristocratic pleasure even while, perhaps, voicing a critique of that pleasure in an essential void

---

[43] See especially Chapter 7 (*Garden of Love:* Relating the Lady to the Landscape) in Goodman, *Rubens*, pp. 57–63.

[44] There is now an extensive critical literature on the function of the male gaze in reading pictures and texts. See especially Norman Bryson, *Vision and Painting: The Logic of the Gaze* (New Haven, 1983); Norman Bryson, eds *et al.*, *Visual Theory: Painting and Interpretation* (Cambridge, 1991), and the chapter on "Still Life and 'Feminine' Space" in Bryson, *Looking at the Overlooked: Four Essays on Still Life Painting* (London, 1990).

Figure 13: Giorgione, *Sleeping Venus*, c. 1505–10

symbolized by the cupids forming an empty circle at the left.[45] It is against this expression of (useless, amoral) erotic love that Swift's text strongly militates. But Watteau's canvas dramatizes so many things, including a "fête galante," that – at least from a deconstructive angle – a definite hierarchy of meaning becomes as impossible as the answer to the question whether the lovers are coming or going. Once again, we need titles or an ekphrasis, a text that is, to solve a painterly riddle and to provide meaning and critical happiness.[46]

One of Watteau's visual pre-texts is Rubens's *The Garden of Love* (1633; Figure 15).[47]

---

[45] Catherine Cusset has provided a splendid and intelligent interpretation of the contradictions establishing meaning in this canvas; see her article "Watteau: The Aesthetics of Pleasure," *Icons – Texts – Iconotexts*, pp. 121–35.

[46] The different titles of the two versions of the painting (in the Louvre and in Berlin) are worth considering as paratexts. The version in the Louvre, delivered to the Académie Royale in 1717, was given a title in the protocol: *Le pèlerinage à l'isle de Cithère* (1717). The Secretary then barred the title, replacing it with "une feste galante" [*sic*]. The French title is ambiguous, for it can be understood as both the pilgrimage *to* or *at* the island of Cythera. See Jutta Held's German monograph on the versions of the painting: *Antoine Watteau: Einschiffung nach Kythera* (Frankfurt, 1994 [1985]) where she notes (p. 12) that the first version (Louvre) bore the above title; but on p. 82 that title has miraculously changed into *L'embarquement pour l'île de Cythère*, which implies a clarification of meaning – and, ultimately, of the painting itself. This is just one case that foregrounds the semantic, ekphrastic, function of titles – the way they create, support or destroy meaning.

[47] Again, we notice how the title of the picture may influence our reading. In her detailed iconographic study of Rubens's painting, Goodman tells us that *The Garden of Love* is the popular title, but that it "should be more properly termed *Conversatie à la mode*" (Goodman, *Rubens*, Preface, p. ix).

Figure 14: Antoine Watteau, *Embarkation for Cythera* (Berlin version)

This picture also employs cupids in a rather playful manner. Like Watteau, Rubens defers meaning by way of reference to other locations where such gardens can allegedly and ultimately signify. In the Watteau, the allusions are to bucolic, Arcadian landscapes of Renaissance poetry and painting; in the Rubens, they are to Italian and Roman architecture and, at the left, to "natural" scenery (which observers would again recognize as a *déjà vu* and a *déjà lu*). The human bodies in the Rubens canvas conflate French and Dutch/Flemish models, clad in seventeenth-century clothes and in conjunction with mythological figures: Juno, for instance (goddess of marriage and femininity), or the three Graces, in the centre. All these signifiers can be read as iconotextual allusions to texts and images that had appeared before.[48] Like Watteau's picture, Rubens's painting cannot do without pre-texts: it only promises signification; what it really tells the observer is to look elsewhere for meaning. For instance, in François Clouet's *The Bath of Diana* (1555–58), which is also a palimpsest (Figure 16), Clouet, too, includes a contemporary figure in the background, a modern Actaeon, who may suffer the same fate as his mythological brother devoured at right. The meaning we make of this painting thus depends once again on how we decode the welter of allusions, including a story that was highly cherished by Renaissance artists and writers – Diana surprised by Actaeon. Not surprisingly, this is also a sub-text and a pre-text in Swift's drawing room poems.[49] The Arcadian paradise in *The Bath of Diana* is another example of différance, constituting presence by alluding to many absences: the well-known texts of

---

[48] Goodman's comprehensive study, *Rubens*, explores a great deal of the verbal and pictorial context of the painting (the version in the Prado); see especially pp. 1–22; and 65–72.

[49] I have discussed the importance of the myth for the poems in "Swift and the Female Idol," pp. 360–67.

Figure 15: Rubens, *The Garden of Love*, 1633

Figure 16: François Clouet, *The Bath of Diana*, 1555–58

Figure 17: Sandro Botticelli, *Spring*, c. 1475–86

Ovid, the Bible, and such canvases as Sandro Botticelli's *The Birth of Venus* or *Spring*. In Botticelli's *Spring* (1475–86; Figure 17), for instance, we can still find the "traces" that extend from this painting in the fifteenth century to their parodic destruction in Swift's poem: the cupid above, the dancing Graces as goddesses, the metamorphosis of a nymph, at right (Chloris, pursued by Zephir, turns into Flora), and a Venus Humanitas in the centre. This figure in turn points back (through such codes as gestures, attitude, facial expression, and colouring) to medieval religious art (representations of madonnas) as well as Roman frescoes and bas-reliefs.[50]

With this very brief outline of différance in the intermedial networks stretching from "Strephon and Chloe" to Botticelli and beyond, I am not arguing the case of iconological influence studies in the manner of Panofsky,[51] for this approach, which is still very popular in art history, implies that we can ultimately make meaning with the help of visual antecedents. My point is, rather, that neither pictures nor texts can engender a stable, fixed meaning by themselves since they always rely on traces of pre-figured representations. To borrow a Derridean title, I maintain that there is no "truth" in painting but only the illusion of such a truth nourished by allusions in the picture and essentially upheld by art-historical discourse, the most influential and paradoxical version of ekphrasis. It is my contention that Swift's "Strephon and Chloe" imposes limited and definite meaning upon paintings that, once we subject them to a close reading, prove to contain signifiers referring to other signifiers. As

---

[50] For interesting visual and thematic comparisons of Botticelli's Venuses with early Roman "models," see Peter Webb, *The Erotic Arts* (London, 1983), pp. 107–10.

[51] See Erwin Panofsky, *Meaning in the Visual Arts* (Gloucester, MA, 1957 [1955]).

we have seen, representation works over a constantly receding, ungraspable signified. Mean-ing-making occurs only in this process of what Derrida terms dissemination and différance, a highly paradoxical phenomenon which the Swiftian text must deny and ignore, precisely because it wants to arrest meaning somewhere. Supported by critical author-oriented read-ings, this captation occurs at the cost of visual art, which is denied its essential indeter-minacy. "Strephon and Chloe," then, is a classical case of both Derridean erasure (the ab-sence of a presence allegedly constituted by an allusion) and Bloomian misprision, of the establishment of meaning in a new text that deliberately misreads older texts or voices in order to be heard and read alone.[52]

Deconstruction can be extremely helpful in this case, for it will teach us to resist the invitation of the Swiftian text to accept its use and view of visual art. We must resist this invitation, not because it urges us to adopt its moral, Platonic condemnation of Baroque and Rococo erotic art as false and misleading (for this view is rather close to late twentieth-century readings of this art), but because the poem misrepresents, levels, and denies the individual rhetorical statement of each single image. These pictures may share common themes; but this does not mean that their rhetoric is also the same in each case. Creating the impression that they can engender meaning, they always have to suspend what they claim to be saying. A deconstructive approach will reject the unifying misprision of highly compli-cated visual images, a misreading "Strephon and Chloe" needs to establish the alleged value of its own message.

I hope to have shown that there is life after the death of the author. Looking at "Strephon and Chloe" without the author – from a feminist or deconstructive perspective – at long last allows us to hear (and, in the case of art, to see) the fascinating and contradictory voices of what might be termed a visual prologue and polylogue which the Swiftian text (and perhaps Swift himself) suppresses for reasons that are both strategic and rhetorical.[53] If deconstruc-tion ignores the author (it does not really kill him) as a patriarchic, god-like figure, it is because it intends to boost what so far has only been a murmur: those voices which the author-father-figure would never allow us, the children-readers, to hear. But children, if they want to become adults, must, at some point in their lives, be able to cope without their fathers.

---

[52]  Harold Bloom explains his concept in *A Map of Misreading* (New York, 1975).

[53]  Some of these voices have, of course, been explored by humanist critics. One thinks, for instance, of the work of Claude Rawson who has directed our attention to the fact that Swift draws on anterior rhetorical models. Exploring the "zeitgeist" of Swift's age, Donna G. Fricke has argued that "Swift is not so peculiarly unique as some critics make him out to be" ("Swift, Hogarth, and the Sister Arts," p. 31). I would contend, however, that Swift, or rather his texts, are unique in the particular way they appropriate and misrep-resent verbal and visual rhetoric, even if this misprision takes place within satirical frame-works he shared with some of his contemporaries.

# V. Sources and Impacts

J. T. Parnell
*Goldsmiths' College, University of London*

# Swift and Lucian

ABSTRACT. Specific local parallels and correspondences between the satires of Swift and Lucian have long been noted; however, the identification of borrowed motifs has tended to obscure more substantial areas of congruence. Bakhtin's insight that while a genre "lives in the present [it] always remembers its past" enables a productive reinvestigation of the relationship between Swift and Lucian. The nature of Lucian's generic legacy to later satirists like Swift should not be conceived in purely formal terms, but in the light of the particular historical development of Menippean satire in the sixteenth and seventeenth centuries. By reconstructing in general terms the "Lucian" inherited in the late seventeenth century, we gain an important understanding of the ideological saturation of Swift's chosen satiric forms. A developed sense of Swift's "debt" to Lucian casts significant light upon some complex and troubling features of the Dean's characteristically skeptical satiric rhetoric.

In Charles Jervas's memorable portrait of Swift, now hanging in London's National Portrait Gallery, the then prebendary of St Patrick's and notorious author of a "dangerous treatise writ against the spleen"[1] is figured gazing to his left during a break from composition. On the desk behind him lie a nameless open book and three volumes inscribed with the names of "Esop," Horace, and Lucian. Aesop's presence is apt in the light of his role as defender of the Ancients in the *Battle of the Books*, and the volume of Horace reminds the viewer – lest there be any doubt – of affiliations between Swift and the "sportive" and "good-natured"[2] Roman satirist. But of the three writers chosen as a short-hand means of evoking Swift's literary genealogy, it is, perhaps, Lucian whom Swift's contemporaries would have seen as the most significant of his classical precursors.

That Jervas's placement of Lucian's works as a tutelary presence behind Swift's quill is far from arbitrary is borne out by Henry Fielding's several comments on the relationship between the ancient and modern satirists. In his obituary in *The True Patriot* of 5 November 1745, Fielding describes Swift as a possessor of the "Talents of a Lucian, a Rabelais, and a Cervantes."[3] Six years later in *Amelia*, Fielding has Captain Booth argue that the one writer Swift "studied above all others"[4] was Lucian. And in the *Covent-Garden Journal* of 30 June

---

1    "The Author upon Himself," *Poems*, p. 164, l. 48.
2    The epithets are applied to Horace in E. Chambers, *Cyclopaedia: or, An Universal Dictionary of Arts and Sciences*, 5th ed., 2 vols (London, 1741–43), *s.v.* "Satyr, Satyra, or Satira."
3    Printed in Kathleen Williams, ed., *Swift: The Critical Heritage* (London, 1970), p. 109.
4    *Amelia*, Book VIII, Chapter V, printed in Williams, ed., *Swift: The Critical Heritage*, p. 110.

1752, in an advertisement for his planned translation of Lucian, he ranks only Swift as "worthy" to be described as an "Imitator" of the satirist of Samosata. The kinship between the two is stated forcefully:

> To say Truth, I can find no better Way of giving the English Reader an Idea of the Greek Author, than by telling him, that to translate Lucian well into English, is to give us another Swift in our own Language.[5]

Although at least one early reader of *Gulliver's Travels* had identified a Lucianic influence, Fielding appears to be unique in stressing a relationship which transcends the mere "borrowing" of literary motifs.[6] To be sure, Fielding's grouping of Swift with Lucian, Rabelais, and Cervantes is to some extent an eighteenth-century commonplace.[7] In an age when a somewhat anxious defence of satire was frequently performed by an obligatory reference to classical practice, invocations of Lucian as a satirist in prose might be dismissed as little more than nervous tics. Yet Fielding's real familiarity with Lucian suggests that in this instance the linking of the satirists is a critical judgement rather than just a convention.

For a variety of reasons, our own century has not found Fielding's assessment of the Swift/Lucian linkage of particular interest, and in recent years an increased critical suspicion of traditional "influence studies" has meant that the nexus has been largely unexplored. While it has been customary for critics to cite Lucian's name in discussions of *Gulliver*, William A. Eddy's 1923 monograph remains the most substantial treatment of Lucian in relation to Swift.[8] Indeed, *"Gulliver's Travels": A Critical Study* for all of its painstaking identification of actual and possible "sources" might be seen to offer the last word in such approaches to the Swift canon. In the end, the truism that Gulliver is not *Utopia*, the *True History* nor *A Voyage to the Moon* must force us out of the archives and back to Swift's texts. That said, there are good reasons for following up Fielding's insight in a slightly different spirit. Direct parallels and correspondences between the two satirists are clearly significant, yet Fielding's characterization of the Dean of St Patrick's as an English Lucian is suggestive of more substantial areas of congruence.

Even so, the very effort to investigate Swift's relationship with Lucian may now seem a pointless one. In the introduction to her essay "Deconstructing *Gulliver's Travels*," Louise K. Barnett urges that we forego the positivist dream of "recreating ourselves as earlier readers" and concentrate instead upon reading eighteenth-century texts "from the vantage point of today."[9] The argument is by no means unique to post-structuralist criticism, but it has been given a sharper edge in the last twenty years as the old literary-critical certainties have

---

[5]    Printed in Williams, ed., *Swift: The Critical Heritage*, pp. 110–11. See also Henry Fielding, *Amelia*, ed. Martin C. Battestin (Oxford, 1983), pp. 324–25 and nn.

[6]    For an early recognition of a relationship between *Gulliver* and the *True History*, see Abbé Desfontaines, "Preface du Traducteur," *Voyages de Gulliver* (1727), I, v–xxviii; printed in Williams, ed., *Swift: The Critical Heritage*, p. 80. See also *The British Magazine*, 2 (1761), 300–1. Among other things, the anonymous essayist suggests that Swift "appears to have taken [Lucian] as his model" (I owe this reference to Hermann Real).

[7]    See *Tristram Shandy: The Notes*, eds Melvyn New, Richard R. Davies, and W. G. Day, The Florida Edition of the Works of Laurence Sterne (Gainesville, FL, 1984), III, 234.

[8]    See *"Gulliver's Travels": A Critical Study* (Gloucester, MA, 1963 [1923]).

[9]    "Deconstructing *Gulliver's Travels*: Modern Readers and the Problematic of Genre," *The Genres of "Gulliver's Travels*," ed. Frederik N. Smith (Newark, London, Toronto, 1990), pp. 230–31.

come in for some much-needed reassessment. While much of the theorizing has encouraged a productive critical self-consciousness, it has also become settled, at one extreme, into an orthodoxy whereby all texts from the past are miraculously metamorphosed into postmodernist artefacts. Radically skeptical about the possibility of understanding the past, Barnett is surprisingly confident about assessing the "temper of our own age" which we are told uniformly "prefers other theoretical bases."[10] Not only does Barnett uncritically celebrate the postmodern as a cultural dominant, but her reading of Gulliver winnows the text down to the reductive binary of "life/death."[11] In so doing, she elides what Edward W. Said has called the "worldliness"[12] of the text and is in danger of reviving the kind of essentialism which Derridean deconstruction seeks to collapse.

The debate engendered by the essays in *The Genres of "Gulliver's Travels"* is a fruitful one, yet it is noteworthy that in dismissing certain generic categories the contributors ignore the work of Mikhail Bakhtin – a critic who has done so much to enhance our understanding of prose forms which are often inadequately served by traditional criticism. Bakhtin's approach to generic traditions is both flexible and complex, and yet he insists upon the importance of knowing "the possible sources of a given author, the literary and generic atmosphere in which his creative work was realized."[13] For Bakhtin, "the more complete and concrete our knowledge of an artist's *generic contacts*, the deeper can we penetrate the peculiar features of his generic form and the more correctly can we understand the interrelationship, within it, of tradition and innovation."[14] With such a focus on *generic* influence, it is possible to pursue a productive investigation of Swift's links with Lucian – an investigation which may enable us to understand better some features of the troubling and problematic rhetoric of Swift's satires. Bakhtin's emphasis upon investigating genres *in* history makes possible an escape from the impasse encountered by the kind of genre criticism which views form as somehow inhabiting a Platonic realm of types.

To be sure, establishing precise generic links between Swift and Lucian is no simple matter. One of the problems in assessing Lucian's general influence in the West is that most writers after Erasmus come to Lucian through a complex of "tangled traditions."[15] Swift's familiarity with a collection of diverse, and to varying degrees Lucianic, Menippean satires makes it difficult to isolate an unmixed or unmediated relationship with Lucian. Unlike the Renaissance humanists, Swift's literary and generic milieu included not only Lucian at first hand but also *The Praise of Folly, Utopia,* Burton's *Anatomy* and, perhaps more importantly, the "French Lucian['s]"[16] *Gargantua and Pantagruel.* Without wishing to efface the individuality of these texts or to suggest that literary genres necessarily carry their own versions of DNA, I would like to pursue Bakhtin's insight that while a genre "lives in the present [it] always remembers its past."[17]

---

[10] "Deconstructing *Gulliver's Travels*," p. 231.
[11] "Deconstructing *Gulliver's Travels*," p. 237.
[12] See *The World, the Text, and the Critic* (Cambridge, MA, 1983), pp. 31–53.
[13] *Problems of Dostoevsky's Poetics*, trans. C. Emerson (Manchester, 1984), p. 157.
[14] *Problems of Dostoevsky's Poetics*, p. 157.
[15] Christopher Robinson, *Lucian and his Influence in Europe* (London, 1979), p. 135.
[16] The phrase is Burton's and is quoted by Philip H. Holland in "Robert Burton's 'Anatomy of Melancholy' and Menippean Satire," diss., University of London, 1979, p. 121.
[17] *Problems of Dostoevsky's Poetics*, p. 106.

It is possible to isolate Lucianic devices in the *Tale* and *Gulliver*, but such an activity becomes fruitful only when we have some grasp of the complex literary and cultural contexts which would have informed Swift's contact with such devices. In his discussion of the formative role of Menippean satire in the creation of Dostoevsky's polyphonic novels, Bakhtin identifies two channels of influence: the one direct and related to the author's conscious generic contacts, and the other indirect and described paradoxically as the "objective memory"[18] of the genre itself. Distinctions between direct and indirect "influence" are not easily made, nor can they be easily separated. Nevertheless, Bakhtin's formulation points us in two useful directions. Firstly, we are reminded that devices and conventions can elude authorial control or intention and have a discursive life of their own. And secondly, that generic conventions do not simply present an author with a set of hermetically sealed literary options. Indeed, what is striking about the absorption and transformation of Lucianic forms in Europe from the Renaissance into the eighteenth century is the extent to which a coherent *tradition* can be identified. Correspondences between Renaissance and "Augustan" uses of, and reactions to, Lucian offer a most powerful indication of the continuing resonance of a generic memory which includes, but also transcends, individual influence.

This is not to suggest that Lucian's impact in Europe was somehow predetermined by hidden generic codes, but rather to argue that generic conventions and the historical specificity of their employment can never be usefully separated. Swift's "Lucian" was not the pristine "Lucian" of the second century A.D., but a "Lucian" saturated with the ideological baggage accrued during the two-hundred years of his dissemination in Europe. The post-Restoration Lucian had already been re-read by the humanists during the Reformation crisis so as to harness his destructive rhetoric in the service of embattled Christian belief. And while Lucian's influence was not solely confined to defenders of orthodoxy, Swift's contact with the Christianized Lucianic satires of Erasmus, More, Rabelais, and Burton would inevitably have informed his reading of the Syrian satirist.

To make sense of the relationship between Swift and Lucian, then, we need to reconstruct in general terms the "Lucian" inherited by the late seventeenth century. The history of the classical satirist's fortunes from the Renaissance into the eighteenth century can tell us much about both the conscious development of a modern Menippean tradition *and* the tangible presence of the "objective" generic memory of Lucianic forms. The importance of More's and Erasmus's translation of some of the canon into Latin is generally agreed, but critics have placed less stress on the arenas in which the humanists made use of the formal and rhetorical techniques which they had learnt from Lucian. Erasmus, in particular, appropriated devices and strategies from the satires and employed them in battles with the Protestant reformers over pressing intellectual and theological issues.[19] It was Erasmus who was largely responsible for the revival and circulation of Menippean satire during the Renaissance, and who in the *Praise of Folly* "'Lucianized' the paradoxical encomium" so as to create the first modern menippea.[20] In stimulating "menippean 'neo-classicism,'"[21] Erasmus showed the many satirists who followed him what potent rhetorical weapons a modern rendering of

---

[18] *Problems of Dostoevsky's Poetics*, p. 121.
[19] See, in particular, Eugene P. Kirk, *Menippean Satire: An Annotated Catalogue of Texts and Criticism* (New York and London, 1980), pp. xxi–xxii.
[20] Kirk, *Menippean Satire*, p. xxii.
[21] Kirk, *Menippean Satire*, p. xxi.

Lucianic forms could afford. Lucian's central preoccupation with false belief and false learning ensured that both his themes and forms were readily adaptable to post-Reformation debates.

If eighteenth-century satirists inherited a clear sense of the polemical uses of Lucianic satire, they were also the inheritors of a less welcome legacy. Partly as a result of the skeptical and destructive tendencies of Lucian's own satires and partly because of the nature of the controversies in which the humanists employed Lucianic forms, Menippean satire after the Renaissance was to carry with it a reputation which it never quite lost. When Luther condemned Erasmus as a skeptic and as more guilty than the heathen Lucian in laughing at religion, or when Gabriel Harvey denounced Robert Greene as "a contemner of God and man, a desperate Lucianist,"[22] they were drawing upon something more than empty rhetoric. Overcharged as they are, such accusations prefigure similar charges levelled in the eighteenth century at the serio-comic satires of Rabelais, Swift, and Sterne. This is not, I think, simply a matter of a clash between comic and grave world-views, nor finger-pointing at closet atheists, but rather a response to an ambivalence and relativizing impulse which is deeply inscribed within Lucianic satire. For opponents of the ideological positions advocated by Menippean satirists like Erasmus, epithets such as "Lucianist" or "skeptic" *may* have been simply reductive rather than a matter of conviction. But if we consider the *effects* of Lucian's satires or the bewilderingly skeptical rhetoric of the *Praise of Folly* instead of the humanists' protestations of moral ends (however sincere), we can clearly identify the basis for the accusations.

Furthermore, the manner in which More and Erasmus argued for the didactic and moral uses of Lucian anticipates similar "apologies" for satire after the Restoration. And in both cases, a somewhat uncomfortable defensiveness bespeaks a degree of anxiety that the monsters released on the opposition might just come back to devour their masters.[23] For our present purposes, it is important to stress that Lucian's reputation as a dangerous skeptic tended to haunt his translators and imitators from the outset. The tenacity of such an unwelcome ghost is further suggested by the fact that, in spite of Lucian's status as an approved author during much of the eighteenth century, by the nineteenth century he was once again condemned as an "irresponsible nihilist."[24]

While serendipity played a part in the Renaissance revival of Lucian, after Erasmus and More Lucianic Menippean satires were to be deployed during the cultural crises of the seventeenth century with a conscious awareness of their destructive potential.[25] However, it is not until after the Restoration that interest focuses again on Lucian himself. A clear index of such interest is the first English "translation" of the complete works. In 1684, while Swift was at Trinity, Ferrand Spence published his version of the works – albeit rendered into English from D'Ablancourt's French translation of 1634.[26] As well as Spence's Lucian and

---

[22] Quoted in *The Complete Works of St. Thomas More*, III, pt i, ed. Craig R. Thompson (New Haven and London, 1978 [1974]), xxivn3.

[23] For a discussion of More's and Erasmus's defence of Lucianic satire, see *The Complete Works of St. Thomas More*, III, pt i, xlii–xliv.

[24] R. Bracht Branham, *Unruly Eloquence: Lucian and the Comedy of Traditions* (Cambridge, MA, and London, 1989), p. 212.

[25] See Kirk, *Menippean Satire*, p. xxix.

[26] See Hardin Craig, "Dryden's Lucian," *Classical Philology*, 16 (1921), 144.

an abundance of imitative dialogues, there are eight different editions of selections from the works published between 1663 and 1702. And it is, of course, in the last years of the seventeenth century that the collaborative "Dryden Lucian" was prepared for publication.[27]

Why the late seventeenth century turned to Lucian with such interest will remain a matter of speculation. Yet while neither the Renaissance nor the eighteenth century appear to have concerned themselves overmuch with the historical context of Lucian's writings, they do seem to have been acutely aware of the topical urgency of his satires. Bakhtin argues that the classical *menippea*, of which many of Lucian's satires offer the fullest extant examples, were formed "in an epoch of intense struggle among numerous and heterogeneous religious and philosophical schools and movements."[28] And it is surely more than chance that the two great periods of the satirist's popularity in England coincide with comparable ideological struggles in the sixteenth and seventeenth centuries. Hardin Craig suggests that in "times of stress [Lucian was] used as a fulcrum to upset hierarchies,"[29] and indeed that the "Dryden Lucian" of 1711 was significantly motivated by the deist leanings of some of the translators. While Craig's evidence is not entirely convincing, that the likes of Charles Blount and Charles Gildon should be interested in Lucian indicates a perception of the unsettling rhetorical potential of the satires.

The possibly subversive intentions of some of the translators of the "Dryden Lucian" notwithstanding, the "Life" of Lucian and the Epistle Dedicatory which preface the edition are redolent of a more pious desire to rehabilitate the satirist's tarnished image. In the "Life," Dryden follows Spence in defending Lucian against charges of atheism, homosexuality, and threatening Christianity itself. He also explicitly constructs the Syrian's character in terms which reflect his own favoured skepticism. For Dryden, Lucian's satires

> [give] us an Idea of the Age in which he liv'd; for if that had been devout, or ignorant, his scoffing Humour wou'd either have been restrain'd, or had not pass'd unpunish'd: all knowing Ages being naturally *Sceptic* and not at all bigotted; which, if I am not much deceiv'd, is the proper Character of our own.[30]

Elsewhere in the "Life," Dryden argues that Lucian is an "Enemy to nothing but to Vice, and Folly"[31] and a positive aid to Christianity in his satire on "false" heathen gods. In this passage, however, Dryden pinpoints an aspect of Lucianic satire which appears to have made it particularly congenial to satirists after the Restoration. In fact, Dryden celebrates the very skepticism which Luther and others had seen as Lucian's most dangerous legacy.

The matter, manner, and range of Lucian's satires make it difficult to extract an informing world-view which is amenable to neat labelling. Nevertheless, Lucian's writings do share a profound skepticism about scientific and philosophical enquiry with the codified philosophical skepticism of his contemporary Sextus Empiricus.[32] Of course, Dryden's concern is not with the history of ideas, but rather with a Lucian made for the needs of an England for whom the Civil Wars were still a sensitive memory and the ramifications of the Glorious

---

[27] See Craig, "Dryden's Lucian," pp. 148–63.
[28] *Problems of Dostoevsky's Poetics*, p. 119.
[29] "Dryden's Lucian," p. 142.
[30] *The Works of Lucian: Translated from the Greek by Several Eminent Hands* (London, 1711), pp. 27–28.
[31] *The Works of Lucian*, p. 35.
[32] See Branham, *Unruly Eloquence*, pp. 15–16.

Revolution were yet to work themselves out. More particularly, an England in which the
factions and sub-factions of Protestants and Catholics, High-Church and Low-Church,
Trinitarians and Socinians, Deists and theists were consistently felt to threaten the fabric of
Church and State. Dryden did not, any more than his contemporaries, embrace a full-blown
Pyrrhonism, but rather discovered in a mitigated Christian skepticism both a position and a
rhetoric which enabled a defence of a belief system which was threatened by fragmentation
and dissolution.[33] Without wishing simply to endorse Dryden's monolithic construction of
his age as "naturally *Sceptic*," I think the perception is an illuminating one for understanding
something of Lucian's appeal to Swift. That Dryden should have penned his "Life" while
Swift was composing the greater part of the *Tale* is much more than a coincidence. The *Tale*
not only manifests Lucianic influence, but its bewildering rhetoric aimed at "*gross Corruptions in Religion and Learning*"[34] ultimately recommends Anglican fideism rather than the
minefield of rational debate. The skilful combination, in the *Praise of Folly*, of the skeptical
tendencies of Lucianic satire with some of the arguments of classical skepticism opened a
particularly fruitful path for later satirists who, like Swift, were keen to defend Christian
dogma. This is not the place to further the debate about the character of Swift's skepticism,
but it is worth pointing out that the Lucian revival of the late seventeenth century runs, just
as it had in the Renaissance, alongside an increased willingness to embrace a tactical skepticism in battles with enemies of religious orthodoxy. And it is, perhaps, an index of some
desperation that Dryden and Swift, like Erasmus before them, were prepared to employ such
double-edged weapons in defence of their own positions.

Throughout Dryden's "Life," one senses the interplay between a conventional apology
for a "heathen" author with a dubious reputation and a more serious desire to present Lucian as a writer qualified to answer contemporary needs. Nevertheless, the fact that Lucianic
forms *were* deployed in theological and philosophical controversies in the seventeenth century gives substance to the claims that Lucian's blend of "Raillery and Reason" made him an
ideal model for satiric defences of "Orthodox Divinity."[35] The point is borne out in the
Epistle Dedicatory, inscribed to Henry Duke of Beaufort, as the anonymous author makes
explicit some of the implications of Dryden's argument:

> [Lucian's] Wit and happy Address were never question'd; and his Satires on the Luxury
> and Hypocrisie of his Contemporaries, are Lessons of use in our Times; and will therefore
> justly recommend him to Your Grace, whose Zeal for the CHURCH OF ENGLAND, and
> against its Hypocritical Enemies, render you so deare to All that are Friends to our Con-
> stitution in Church and State.[36]

The conventions of the caressing dedication notwithstanding, the broad tenor of the claims
can be taken at face value in the light of the extent to which "Augustan" satirists took
seriously their role as ideological guardians.

Although it has been argued that it "is practically certain that Swift ... knew the *Dryden
Lucian*,"[37] we only have evidence that he owned a Greek/Latin edition of the works and

---

[33] See Louis I. Bredvold, *The Intellectual Milieu of John Dryden: Studies in Some Aspects of
Seventeenth-Century Thought* (Ann Arbor, 1943).

[34] *Prose Works*, I, 1.

[35] *The Works of Lucian*, pp. 44–45.

[36] *The Works of Lucian*, p. 5.

[37] Eddy, *"Gulliver's Travels": A Critical Study*, p. 53.

D'Ablancourt's translation, which he purchased for Stella.[38] However, Swift's awareness of the "Dryden Lucian" is not the issue here. Dryden's "Life" and the dedication give us an important sense of late seventeenth-century attitudes towards Lucian and offer an indication of the climate within which Swift would have come to the satirist. Most commentators have stressed Swift's advantageous position in coming to Lucian at a point when his influence on modern versions of the satirical dialogue, the fantastic voyage, and the dialogue of the dead was already established.[39] That the tradition itself had become associated with a conservative defence of hard-pressed ideologies has been ignored in discussions of Swift and Lucian. Yet the extent to which the humanists and later apologists like Spence and Dryden were willing to re-read Lucian in order to draw the sting from his relativizing rhetoric is telling. Questions about whether the "Augustan" satirists actually believed in the efficacy of satire as a didactic mode will necessarily remain unresolved.[40] Nevertheless, there can be little doubt that in the complex of concerns which may have led Swift to develop his own Lucianic satiric forms, a keen sense of the adaptability of Lucian's motifs and devices to his own ideological needs was not insignificant.

In claiming that Lucian's influence on Swift is best understood as a generic one, I have deliberately conflated Lucianic and Menippean satire. The reason for doing so is that from the moment More and Erasmus translated Lucian his principal influence was upon the modern development of this genre. Even so, such an approach raises once again the vexed question of the generic status of Swift's narrative satires. Claude Rawson's insight that readers of *Gulliver* experience a "teasing fluctuation, or bewildering uncertainty, of *genre*"[41] is one which is borne out by the still ongoing debate. Yet, in an otherwise tentative collection of essays, two of the contributors to *The Genres of "Gulliver's Travels"* dismiss the Menippean genre with surprising confidence. Louise K. Barnett claims that the genre was "revived more or less to accommodate"[42] Swift. And Maximillian E. Novak cites with approval Christine Brooke Rose's question of where we placed Rabelais and Swift "before the term 'Menippean satire' was rediscovered," and then concludes that it is a "meaningless category."[43] Caveats about the reductive tendencies of rigid generic taxonomies accepted, it remains rather perverse to reject a category before any attempt has been made to understand it. Recent work on Menippean satire has done much to highlight the importance of a genre which hitherto we have known little about. But even without such work, the notion that the label has been invented, or revived, to accommodate unclassifiable prose forms flies in the face of the evidence.

---

[38] See Hermann J. Real and Heinz J. Vienken, "A Catalogue of an Exhibition of Imprints from Swift's Library," *Proceedings of The First Münster Symposium on Jonathan Swift*, eds Hermann J. Real and Heinz J. Vienken (München, 1985), pp. 371–72.

[39] See Robinson, *Lucian and his Influence*, pp. 68, 137; Benjamin Boyce, "News from Hell: Satiric Communications with the Nether World in English Writings of the Seventeenth and Eighteenth Centuries," *PMLA*, 58 (1943), 402–37, and Frederick M. Keener, *English Dialogues of the Dead* (New York and London, 1973).

[40] For a full discussion of eighteenth-century debates about the nature of satire, see P. K. Elkin, *The Augustan Defence of Satire* (Oxford, 1973).

[41] *Gulliver and the Gentle Reader: Studies in Swift and our Time* (London and Boston, 1973), p. 5.

[42] "Deconstructing *Gulliver's Travels*," p. 232.

[43] "*Gulliver's Travels* and the Picaresque Voyage: Some Reflections on the Hazards of Genre Criticism," *The Genres of "Gulliver's Travels*," ed. Smith, p. 25.

Not only can we find discussions of Menippean satire in such well-known sources as Da-
cier, Rapin, and Dryden, but also in Chambers's *Cyclopaedia*, which offers a suggestive account of the genre. Chambers describes "*Varronian* or *Menippean*" satire as the "third kind"
of Roman satire and includes "Petronius's Satyricon, Lucian's Dialogues [and] the Golden
ass of Apuleius" as "so many *satyrs* in the Varronian taste."[44] Of more interest for our
present purposes are the modern satires which are listed by Chambers as examples of the
genre:

> To the same head may also be refered [*sic*] the Catholicon of Spain, the Moriae Encomium
> of Erasmus, the Don Quixot of Cervantes ... the Tale of a Tub by Dr. S[wift]. &c.

That Swift made use of the *Catholicon* and the *Praise of Folly* is well known,[45] but the
inclusion of the *Tale* in such a list offers a powerful reminder that the genre of Menippean
satire is far from being a convenient twentieth-century construct. To be sure, *Gulliver* is not
included by Chambers, but given that the list makes no attempt to be exhaustive, this need
not surprise us. Furthermore, the discussion of the genre in a reference book such as the
*Cyclopaedia* suggests a much wider familiarity with Menippean satire than we might expect.
And if we turn to more recondite sources, we find further evidence that the genre was
sufficiently established for Swift to have been fully aware of it. The preface to Swift's annotated copy of the *Satyre Menippée* contains what one critic has called the "first modern
formulation of Menippean satire as a modern as well as an ancient genre"[46] and quite explicitly links Lucian and Rabelais as Menippean satirists.

Merely labelling Swift's satires is a pointless task. The generic category is only useful to
the extent to which it enables a fuller understanding of the texts themselves. While "Menippean satire" can meaningfully describe both ancient and modern satires, for our purposes it
is more important to pay attention to a particular grouping of texts which represent a
significant branch of the tradition. If we concentrate upon the genre's historical development into Swift's lifetime, we are not left simply with a list of shared generic conventions
but with a real sense of the ideological saturation of the form which Swift inherited. Bakhtin
has dubbed the ancient *menippea* the "'journalistic' genre of antiquity,"[47] and it is precisely
the topical engagement of Menippean satires which makes it dangerous to homogenize all
mutations of the form without regard to their historical specificity. Indeed, one of the key
problems with Bakhtin's treatment of the genre is an uncritical celebration of the joyful
relativity of the *menippea*, which is only made possible by his indifference to the polemical
uses to which the form was put after the Reformation. In Erasmus, Rabelais, Burton, and
Swift, Lucianic forms retain their ability to destabilize all systems, but they do so in the
service of dogmatic world-views which are keen to efface their own dogmatism. It is, however, the very tensions between dogmatic ends and the anarchic and exuberant energies released by such works as the *Praise of Folly*, *Gargantua and Pantagruel*, the *Anatomy of Melancholy*, the *Tale* and *Gulliver* which make them such fascinating texts.

---

[44] *Cyclopaedia*, *s.v.* "Satyr, Satyra, or Satira."
[45] See William LeFanu, *A Catalogue of Books belonging to Dr Jonathan Swift, Dean of St
Patrick's, Dublin, Aug. 19. 1715* (Cambridge, 1988), pp. 17, 28; see also Ronald Paulson,
*Theme and Structure in Swift's "Tale of a Tub"* (New Haven, 1960), pp. 79–80.
[46] Holland, "Robert Burton's 'Anatomy of Melancholy,'" p. 100.
[47] *Problems of Dostoevsky's Poetics*, p. 118.

It is commonplace in Swift criticism to account for some of the most bewildering effects of Swift's satires in terms of a radical skepticism which is often seen to be an unconscious symptom of the Dean's darkest thoughts. Consequently, we have grown familiar with a schizophrenic "Swift." At once we have the public Church of England man and the private individual so racked with doubts that he was too honest to prevent some of the poison from seeping out of the closet and infecting the world itself. To some extent, we might explain this particular construction of "Swift" in terms of our own reluctance to accept that someone so manifestly intelligent could entertain beliefs which we now regard as archaic or even faintly absurd. Yet there is clearly more to it than this. One of the few continuities linking Swift's eighteenth- and twentieth-century readers is the perception that the satiric "stick" employed by Swift with such dexterity was simply "so long"[48] that it battered everything in sight rather than just its selected targets. Patrick Reilly's comment on the phenomenon neatly sums up a widely held view:

> Using Swift's official status to dictate meaning to [*Gulliver*] is like brandishing the crucifix to scare away other readings as though they were vampires, for the text itself justifies us no further than seeing the world as a place of filth and folly, where you pay for truth by forfeiting happiness.[49]

In fact, Reilly identifies two of the key approaches which have characterized modern readings of *Gulliver*: contextual readings which attempt to delimit semantic horizons and textual readings which are content to focus on what another reader calls "the endless flickering uncertainties of local effect."[50] Without denying the validity of either approach, we can, perhaps, better understand the apparent disjunction between the rhetoric of *Gulliver* and what we know of Swift's world-view if we turn away from the Dean's psyche and look instead at the generic tradition within which he developed his own narrative satires.

The real parallels between readers' responses to the Lucianic satires of Erasmus, Rabelais, Burton, and Swift make it more difficult to account for the disturbing rhetoric of the *Tale* or *Gulliver* in the light of the Dean's troubled personality. Voltaire may have had his own reasons for claiming that Rabelais and Swift "hurled more taunts against Christianity than Molière did against medecine,"[51] but the echo of Luther's reaction to Erasmus is telling. If we turn to a modern critical response to Burton, a similar pattern can be discerned. In his discussion of the *Anatomy*, Stanley E. Fish describes Burton's satiric rhetoric in terms which might equally apply to the *Tale* or *Gulliver*:

> The strategy of inclusion, which collapses speaker, reader, and a thousand or more "authorities" into a single category of unreliability, extends also to every aspect of what we usually think of as "objective reality"... The base of irresponsibility is widened to include everyone ... every *thing*, every structure, every institution, every profession, every nation, every concept.[52]

---

[48]  Voltaire, "Letter XXII (1734)," printed in Williams, ed., *Swift: The Critical Heritage*, p. 74.

[49]  *Jonathan Swift: The Brave Desponder* (Manchester, 1982), p. 223. For a stimulating discussion of the beliefs which might lie behind Swift's orthodox statements, see Michael DePorte, "The Road to St Patrick's: Swift and the Problem of Belief," *Swift Studies*, 8 (1993), 5–17.

[50]  Rawson, *Gulliver and the Gentle Reader*, p. 17.

[51]  "Letter V," printed in Williams, ed., *Swift: The Critical Heritage*, p. 75.

[52]  *Self-Consuming Artifacts: The Experience of Seventeenth-Century Literature* (Berkeley, Los Angeles, London, 1972), p. 314.

Indeed, Fish's discussion of the *Anatomy* as a self-consuming artefact might describe at almost every turn the unsettling effects of Swift's, or for that matter, Lucian's satires.

Most critics of Lucian have noted the radically relativizing tendency of his satires which, in many ways, distinguishes him from verse satirists such as Horace and Juvenal. Ronald Paulson, for example, argues that Lucian destroys illusions by confronting them with the "real," while never allowing the reader to believe in that "reality" as a good in itself. For Paulson, Lucian is "the rhetorician first, the moralist second."[53] And for F. Anne Payne, Lucian differs from traditional "prescriptive" satirists in attacking or parodying "the concept of the norm itself."[54] Such accounts share with many critical responses to Swift and Burton an attempt to grapple with the problem of a satiric discourse which appears to make no concessions to a normative centre. The felt absence of the centre is not exclusive to reactions to Lucian, but it is the overriding issue which informs responses to his satires from the Renaissance to the present day. To be sure, the feeling that Lucian undercuts *all* stabilizing norms may in some part result from an ignorance of the cultural and historical contexts within which he wrote.[55] Nevertheless, the Menippean satirists of the Renaissance and eighteenth century read Lucian as a satirist of "*Mankind in general,*"[56] and as such were prepared to plunder his satires for their most devastating effects without, perhaps, a full awareness of the more subversive energies such rhetoric might release.

Fielding's comments on the kinship between Swift and Lucian are forthright, yet so general as to suggest a perception of affiliations which are sufficiently clear to render further elaboration redundant. However, it is worth rehearsing the more obvious parallels in order to see how particular generic conventions might account for some of the most characteristically vexing effects of Swift's satiric strategies. The *general* similarities between *Gulliver* and the *True History* and the cluster of Lucianic motifs in Part III are clear, the flying island and Gulliver's dialogues with the dead in Glubbdubdrib offering instances of direct borrowing from Lucian's parody. But critics have also stressed Swift's more general "conceptual" debt to Lucian.[57] For Robinson, this debt is wide-ranging but finds its clearest expression in a shared distrust of scientific and philosophical enquiry, and in the radical use of perspective as a means of interrogating habitual perceptions. In this respect, the use of the fantastic voyage as device in *Gulliver* can be meaningfully compared to Lucian's practice in *Icaromenippus* and *Menippus* as well as the *True History*. Indeed, defamiliarization of this kind is one of the most potent weapons in Lucian's and Swift's satiric armouries.

Reading *Gulliver* alongside the *True History*, *Icaromenippus*, *Philosophies for Sale*, or *Nigrinus* one is so struck by the manner in which Swift has developed and expanded Lucianic devices that it is easy to ignore the extent to which both satirists rely upon a common fund of motifs and techniques. Of course, the increased development of narrative and representational elements as well as the typically Swiftian interweaving of political and metaphysical levels in *Gulliver* are not to be found in Lucian. Even so, formal and thematic affinities between the satirists are striking.

---

[53]  *The Fictions of Satire* (Baltimore, 1967), p. 40.
[54]  *Chaucer and Menippean Satire* (Madison, WI, 1981), p. 39.
[55]  For a discussion of Lucian's contexts, see C. P. Jones, *Culture and Society in Lucian* (Cambridge, MA, and London, 1986).
[56]  *The Works of Lucian*, p. 304.
[57]  See Robinson, *Lucian and his Influence*, p. 138.

Paulson suggests that Lucian's satiric devices coalesce in the technique of travesty, the reduction of "romance, ritual, and religion to the concrete particularity of a group of petty, squabbling people."[58] Just so, but the observation is further illuminated by Bakhtin's point that the focus of Menippean satire is not upon the individual's relation to the world but rather on "the progress of an idea in the world."[59] Thus the reader of Menippean satire constantly meets "the stripped-down *pro et contra* of life's ultimate questions."[60] For Bakhtin, *Philosophies for Sale* is most typical in this respect, and Swift's satires clearly follow Lucian's lead here. Swift's technique of "stripping-down," or reducing, life-threatening debates between Protestants, Catholics, and Dissenters to the absurd particularity of Big-Endians and Little-Endians, or squabbles over the dress code, is massively effective on one level. Yet just as Lucian's embodiment of grand philosophies in less than grand philosophers serves to smash the authority of the big idea itself, so Swift's tactic runs the risk of reducing *all* belief to absurdity. Similarly, although Part IV of *Gulliver* can be read as an orthodox Anglican's intervention in the urgent debate about the role of reason in human affairs, the embodiment of the pro and contra in the Houyhnhnms and Yahoos casts shadows which threaten to throw the whole debate off-centre.

Paulson's discussion of the quest motif in Lucian is also applicable, with some modifications, to Swift:

> Aristophanes focused on the solution; Lucian focuses on the quest and on the witnesses and their testimony. He is interested in the separate encounters, knowing that there is no solution but only the people who offer false solutions.[61]

A comparable treatment of the quest is a Lucianic legacy which is felt in Rabelais and Burton as well as Swift. When, after seven-hundred pages of anatomizing, Burton concludes with the reductively simple "Be not solitary, be not idle,"[62] he recalls Bacbuc's bathetic solution to Panurge's quest. And the spectacle of Gulliver in earnest dialogue with his horses comically inverts the notion that "By Travel, generous Souls enlarge the Mind."[63] Certainly in Rabelais, Burton, and Swift, and perhaps in Lucian, it is the reader who is meant to learn a lesson about human pride. But even so, the sense that all human quests will fail to discover the grail promotes a sense of vertigo which we might more easily associate with postmodernity than with the eighteenth century.

For Bakhtin, the presence of "inserted genres"[64] is an important characteristic of Menippean satire, and other critics have fruitfully developed the idea of the form's hybrid generic status. Holland argues that Menippean satires have "no single characteristic literary form of [their] own, only a relation of parody or distance – of dialogue – to other forms."[65] While this might seem hopelessly vague as a description of a literary form, its value becomes clearer

---

[58]   *The Fictions of Satire*, p. 37.
[59]   *Problems of Dostoevsky's Poetics*, p. 115.
[60]   *Problems of Dostoevsky's Poetics*, p. 116.
[61]   *The Fictions of Satire*, p. 32.
[62]   *The Anatomy of Melancholy*, ed. Holbrook Jackson, 3 vols (London and New York, 1961 [1932]), III, 432 (Part III, Section iv).
[63]   "The Words of the King of Brobdingnag," line 11, in *Gulliver's Travels* (London, 1731), p. vi.
[64]   *Problems of Dostoevsky's Poetics*, p. 118.
[65]   "Robert Burton's 'Anatomy of Melancholy,'" p. 370.

when we move from the general to the particular. Lucian's *True History* is not only in parodic dialogue with the Homeric epic but also with the discourse of historians such as Herodotus, Thucydides, and Tacitus. Likewise, many of Lucian's dialogues engage in an implicit parodic relationship with the Platonic philosophical dialogue. And in Burton's *Anatomy*, we are constantly reminded of the presence of a host form, the Ramist medical treatise.[66] Similarly, *Gulliver* inhabits the genre of travel narrative and contains hybridized traces of other forms. Thus Novak is right when he suggests that *Gulliver*

> is at once a pure (if tongue in cheek) imaginary voyage, written, as Swift has Richard Sympson say, for the benefit of seamen; a journey to utopia and dystopia; a spiritual autobiography; a picaresque narrative; and a parody of all of these forms.[67]

However, Novak misses the point in insisting that this places the text outside of the Menippean category. The novel, too, is a hybrid form, but its dialogic energies generally lack the satiric function of such genre-mixing in Menippean satire. And, all caveats accepted, the novel's commitment to a degree of verisimilitude makes this kind of genre-mixing inappropriate. In her discussion of this feature of Menippean satire, Payne argues that local parody and mongrel generic origins keep before the reader "multiple views of the universe."[68] By denying the reader the comforts of stable generic conventions, Menippean satirists also deny him or her the security of easily graspable positions, to the extent that all positions tend to become Protean.

Clearly, Swift's strategy owes much to Lucian and his post-Renaissance imitators, but it is difficult to see how ends and means can be reconciled here. Comedy, reader entrapment, and a calculated general assault upon the reader's unexamined prejudices all play a part in Swift's tactic, but it is hard to escape the conclusion that the satirist also sets in motion a freeplay of discourses which militates against his didactic intentions. This is not a matter of accusing Swift of an artistic "failure" but rather to suggest that many of the generic conventions which Swift appropriated and absorbed from the Lucianic tradition are not merely destructive of "false" belief but relativize the notion of epistemological or ontological certainty of any kind. To be sure, the norms *are* identifiable: the good sense of the wise paternalistic King of Brobdingnag, the glimpses of utopia in Lilliput and, perhaps, Houyhnhnmland, not to mention the context of orthodox Anglican belief within which Swift might have hoped his readers would place his satire on the corruptions of human nature. Yet the critical history of *Gulliver*, from first reactions to the present day, amply testifies to a satiric discourse in which such norms are so consistently jumbled with a plethora of exuberant images and energies that they escape the attention of all but the already converted reader. A similar pattern can be discerned with many of the other Menippean and Lucianic elements which Swift deploys. The use of the lower body as a levelling device is ambivalent at best and, at worst, works against the civil ideal which Swift seeks to recommend. The radical play with perspective that informs *Gulliver* and which is central to *Icaromenippus* and *Menippus* is enormously effective in defamiliarizing the complacent patriotism of the True-Born Englishman but inevitably transcends such local satiric demands.

---

[66] See "Robert Burton's 'Anatomy of Melancholy,'" p. 145.
[67] Novak, "*Gulliver's Travels* and the Picaresque Voyage," p. 30.
[68] Payne, *Chaucer and Menippean Satire*, p. 14.

Much has been made recently in post-structuralist criticism generally, and in Bahktin's work in particular, of the tendency of dialogic and plural texts to offer a liberating discursive alternative to the more common experience of the reification of ideologies as dogma. Such an approach informs Terry Eagleton's view on the positive effects of Swift's strategies in *Gulliver*:

> There is no way for the reader to "totalize" [the] contradictions which the text so adroitly springs upon him or her; he or she is merely caught in their dialectical interplay, rendered as eccentric to himself as the lunatic Gulliver, unable to turn to the refuge of an assuring authorial voice.[69]

Yet if we simply accept such a reading without attempting to understand why Swift should anticipate what Terry Eagleton goes on to describe as "a discourse concerned with Derrida [which] circles to the name of Brecht,"[70] then we might as well forget Swift and go straight to work with Derrida. It is surely more productive to attempt to understand the complex of forces which enabled Swift's enduringly interesting satires. Lucian and the Menippean tradition which he stimulated cannot, of course, offer the key to what is perhaps one of the central tensions in Swift's works. But the fascinating traces of the generic memory of Lucianic forms in *Gulliver* and the *Tale* are worthy of a fuller investigation.

---

[69] *Walter Benjamin or towards a Revolutionary Criticism* (London, 1981), pp. 18–19.
[70] *Walter Benjamin*, p. 19.

Brean S. Hammond
*University of Wales, Aberystwyth*

# "Low and un-Gentleman-like Reflections":
# Swift and Pope

ABSTRACT. This essay offers a conspectus of recent approaches to Swift and Pope, arguing that the major biographies of the two writers published in the 1980s represent the high-water mark of liberal-humanist readings. They appeared when there was already a backlash to this way of reading led by materialist and feminist critics. Those readers, however, tend to make their points by raising Swift's stock at the expense of Pope's, which I see as tactically dangerous for eighteenth-century studies and, in the case of Ellen Pollak's influential approach wherein Pope plays modernist to Swift's postmodernist, of doubtful validity. I discuss briefly with reference to Swift's *Mr. Collins's Discourse of Free-Thinking* the reasons why the "Swift the postmodernist/deconstructor" reading is not soundly based.

Laetitia Pilkington furnishes me with my title. She recalls in her *Memoirs* that Swift showed her a letter from Pope which was "fill'd with low and un-Gentleman-like Reflections both on Mr. *Gay* and the two noble Persons who honoured him with their Patronage after his Disappointment at Court."[1] Pope receives only occasional mention in the *Memoirs*, but always dishonourable: he is shown to be an envious, two-faced, sneaking fellow. Pope is jealous of Gay's success with *The Beggar's Opera*: "The Dean very frankly own'd he did not think Mr. *Pope* was so candid to the Merits of other Writers, as he ought to be."[2] Pope's compliment to Swift in *The Dunciad* is pronounced cold and forced by comparison with the warm, sincere generosity of Swift's lines "Hail! happy Pope, whose generous mind" in his *A Libel on Dr Delany* – lines which Pope came to regard as a considerable embarrassment. Later in the *Memoirs*, Mrs Pilkington tells us that Swift had given her husband a letter of introduction to Pope, who invited him to stay at Twickenham for a fortnight on the strength of it. Pilkington writes back to his wife enthusing over the warmth of his welcome, which letter Mrs Pilkington naively shows to Swift:

> The Dean ... told me, he had, by the same Pacquet, receiv'd a Letter from Mr. *Pope*, which, with somewhat of a stern Brow, he put into my Hand, and walk'd out into the Garden.

In his letter to Swift, Pope calls Pilkington a "forward, shallow, conceited Fellow" and tells Swift that he was sick of Pilkington's impertinence before the end of the third day:

---

[1] *Memoirs of Laetitia Pilkington*, ed. A. C. Elias, Jr, 2 vols (Athens and London, 1997), I, 34.

[2] Pilkington, *Memoirs*, ed. Elias, I, 34.

By the Time I had read it thro', the Dean return'd, and ask'd me what I thought of it? I told him, I was sure Mr. *Pilkington* did not deserve the character Mr. *Pope* had given of him; and that he was highly ungenerous to caress and abuse him at the same Time. Upon this the Dean lost all Patience, and flew into such a Rage, that he quite terrify'd me; he ask'd me, Why did I not swear that my Husband was six Foot high? and, Did I think myself a better Judge than Mr. *Pope*? or, Did I presume to give him the Lie? – and a thousand other Extravagancies. As I durst not venture to speak a Word more, my Heart swell'd so that I burst into Tears, which, he attributing to Pride and Resentment, made him, if possible, ten Times more angry, and I am not sure he would not have beat me; but that, fortunately for me, a Gentleman came to visit him.[3]

Mrs Pilkington often finds Swift's conduct eccentric and unfathomable (on other occasions, according to the *Memoirs*, Swift actually *did* beat her) but she is certain that, in contrast to Pope's, it proceeds from *excessive* principle rather than from lack of it. Her anecdotes remind us that contemporaries did not always regard Swift and Pope as inseparable Siamese twins – the Castor and Pollux of Tory satire – as has been a prominent tendency amongst more recent readers. Characterizations of the friendship like the very engaging one given in Pope's description of the *Miscellanies* project are difficult to resist: "Methinks we look like friends, side by side, serious and merry by turns, conversing interchangeably, and walking down hand in hand to posterity;"[4] and on the basis of their many celebrations of it in the letters, one can see why Pope's most recent biographer invokes the friendship as "the deepest and most sustaining" of Pope's lifetime.[5] Currently, however, scholars are more aware of the *distance* separating the two writers than of their proximity.

For many scholars working on Swift and Pope in the seventies and early eighties, the pressing imperative was to relate their lives and *oeuvres* to the political circumstances of the period. Charismatic accounts of the two writers presented them as sharing an ideology of nostalgic conservatism, formed from elements both of aristocratic privilege and of the middling-status progressivism that opposed it. Whereas an aristocratic ideology puts emphasis on landowning and the code of honour, and considers personal merit and virtue to be a consequence of social rank, the progressive ideology measures individual worth by enterprise, intelligence, survival instinct and, increasingly, by the amassing of wealth. The great satirists of the early century – the Scriblerians and, more controversially, the young Samuel Johnson and Henry Fielding – formed their ideology as a conservative backlash to this mercantile upstartism. They were contemptuous of money circulation, especially invisible money, and of accumulation of capital, despised financiers but tolerated honest tradesmen, and hated rapacious land stewards and other dishonest racketeers. The residual aristocratic élitism of their standpoint emerges most clearly in their distrust of the effects of the "open élite" on cultural standards. Their most celebrated literary works are, in J. Paul Hunter's terms, "an exposure of the cast of mind and set of values that ultimately produced novels."[6] Works like *A Tale of a Tub* and *The Dunciad* are opposed both to the professionalization of the arts and of scholarship, and to its popularization. My own earlier work contributed in some small measure to the enunciation of this complex of ideas, attitudes, and beliefs by emphasizing the importance of the Scriblerus Club as a matrix for satirical projects that would imply

---

3   Pilkington, *Memoirs*, ed. Elias, I, 53.
4   *Correspondence*, III, 201.
5   Felicity Rosslyn, *Alexander Pope: A Literary Life* (Basingstoke and London, 1990), p. 83.
6   J. Paul Hunter, *Before Novels: The Cultural Contexts of Eighteenth-Century English Fiction* (New York and London, 1990), p. 108.

them as absent norms, by dwelling on the period during which Pope and Swift were together in Twickenham as an *annus mirabilis* of creativity, and by foregrounding the part played by Bolingbroke and the *Craftsman* in the conversion of this ideology into a political persuasion in the 1730s (the "Country" party).[7]

There are, I think, three main respects in which this analysis is no longer adequate. And in all three respects, a better analysis is liable to throw Swift and Pope into starker contrast as representatives of different tendencies within the Augustan hegemony. In the first place, the political universe that it assumes is too simplistic. It is, so to speak, a Newtonian universe, in which every Tory has an equal and opposite Whig, whereas the universe created by recent historical research and critical commentary is an Einsteinian one. Political phenomena in this relativistic dimension depend on the state of motion of the observer. Secondly, the "gloomy Tory satirists" account of Pope and Swift is Anglocentric and metropolitan, overestimating the extent to which Swift's vital concerns remained those of the English political scene. Thirdly, the Popes and Swifts of the seventies and early eighties were bound together by the liberal humanistic assumptions of the scholars who re-created them. The long-awaited publication of the majestic biographies by Ehrenpreis and Mack was the high-water mark of such assumptions. These were perceived by many to be inadequate as soon as they were triumphantly articulated, and the inadequacy was most clearly flagged up by feminists. All of these points require some amplification, so let me begin with the point about the political universe.

In the political macrocosm, the central question is how to describe the affiliations that existed after the death of Queen Anne and the Hanoverian Succession. In what form, if any, did the Tories survive? Until the mid-eighties, the answer that led the market was "in none." Divisions between Whig and Tory were progressively meaningless as the genuine issues separating them, deriving from the Revolution Settlement, faded into insignificance. For some, the binarism that began to matter was the Court/Country split, where the Court comprised the Whigs in office and their clients, and the Country comprised all those who, for one reason or another, wished to get them out of office. For others, this split called into question the definition of "party" in our period: the "Country" ideology that was a factor in orchestrating aspects of anti-Government campaigns could not be designated a "party" because it lacked the structure and organization that this implies. Peter D. G. Thomas speaks for many when he asserts:

> After the Hanoverian Succession there occurred the initial split and gradual disintegration of the dominant Whig party, and the eclipse of the Tories as serious contenders for office … The political battle was between administrations composed of Whigs against other Whigs ambitious to take their places, and the latter relied for much of their voting-strength on independent M.P.s, many of whom professed to be or were called Tory, and some of whom were Jacobites.[8]

The last decade has seen, however, a revival of faith in the real existence of a Tory party distinguished from the Whigs by the strength of its genuine commitment to Jacobite restoration and of its opposition to toleration. The Whigs themselves are not the unprincipled

7   See Brean S. Hammond, *Pope and Bolingbroke: A Study of Friendship and Influence* (Columbia, MO, 1984); and *Pope* (Brighton and New Jersey, 1986).

8   "Party Politics in Eighteenth-Century Britain," *British Journal for Eighteenth-Century Studies*, 10 (1987), 208.

oligarchic monolith they once appeared to be. Viscount Cobham's circle, the Cobham's Cubs who emerged in opposition to the Walpolean Whigs in the early 1730s, can be regarded as carrying on a tradition of Old Whig radicalism that gained real, if temporary, political meaning when it found a figure-head in Frederick, Prince of Wales, and coined potent watchwords like "liberty" and "patriotism."

Mapping the partisan affiliations of individual writers onto this expanding political universe is not an easy task. In this endeavour, Alan Downie has been most consistent in allowing his skeptical intelligence to play over the "shop labels" carelessly affixed to the writers of the period. His conclusion in *Jonathan Swift, Political Writer*, contrary to that of F. P. Lock who had argued that Swift was a mainstream Tory, was that we should take Swift at face value when he describes himself as "much inclined to be what they called a Whig in politics."[9] More recently, two young scholars out of the same stable have argued powerfully that Swift was not mainstream at all but radical: though to one, he is a radical Whig and to the other a radical Jacobite Tory. Daniel Eilon contends that the strength of Swift's belief in political consent coming from below, from the *people* rather than from their rulers, amounts to a belief in contract that is not merely Whig, but *radical* Whig, though he does recognize the authoritarianism that comes out in Swift's clerical stance, and in many of his actions and pronouncements. In Eilon's final analysis, Swift is "a Tory by temperament and a Whig by principle."[10] Ian Higgins does not accept this "split ticket" characterization. For him, it is not credible that Swift could be a Tory in matters religious and a Whig in matters political because religion occupies too much of the ground of politics in the period. Swift's hatred of Dissent, Higgins argues, is what shapes his politics: he is "a disaffected High Church Anglican extremist with Jacobite inclinations."[11] Many ideological positions that others have taken to be "Old Whig" or "Country" are argued by Higgins to be consistent with those taken by Jacobites. Pope's case is just as difficult. Here, Downie's argument that if we want to know what Pope's partisan allegiances were, we should attend to his explicit statements about them – and then we will discover that Pope was a Whig – seems touchingly naive, and a bad basis on which to arrive at *any* judgement about Pope.[12] Pope was a Roman Catholic monarchist who, if it was too dangerous post-Atterbury to speak out in favour of the monarch he really wanted, would make do with Frederick Prince of Wales provided he proved "every inch the king," that is, more convincingly a British monarch than King George. As Christine Gerrard's book on Whig Patriotism and its associated writings demonstrates, Pope's output in the 1730s cannot be confidently associated with *either* characteristically Tory *or* Whig forms of literary expression.[13] Pope's aversion to being labelled was deeply rooted in his personality, and there was in Pope an unusual degree of suggestibility and openness that is not present in Swift. For a brief period in the mid-1730s, to judge from the correspondence, Swift became morbidly sensitive to the extent of Pope's involvement

---

[9]  See J. A. Downie, *Jonathan Swift, Political Writer* (London, Boston, Henley, 1985 [1984]), pp. 82–84; F. P. Lock, *Swift's Tory Politics* (London, 1983), pp. 116–18.

[10]  *Factions' Fictions: Ideological Closure in Swift's Satire* (Newark, London, Toronto, 1991), p. 114.

[11]  *Swift's Politics: A Study in Disaffection* (Cambridge, 1994), p. i.

[12]  See J. A. Downie, "1688: Pope and the Rhetoric of Jacobitism," *Pope: New Contexts*, ed. David Fairer (Hemel Hempstead, 1990), pp. 13–14.

[13]  See *The Patriot Opposition to Walpole: Politics, Poetry, and National Myth, 1725–1742* (Oxford, 1994).

with the Patriots, because it made him aware of how far away he now was from metropolitan political life, and because it seemed that Pope had spring-cleaned his old friends and acquired a younger set.

Reference to the correspondence brings into focus the second broad area of dissatisfaction with earlier accounts of Swift and Pope – to wit, their Anglocentrism. Carole Fabricant's *Swift's Landscape* (1982) had already alerted us to the extent of Swift's commitment to specifically *Irish* issues before the third volume of Ehrenpreis was published; and, as Philip Harth put it, the "real revisionism" of the biography consists in the dispelling of the "'giant in chains'" mythology, "the bitter exile forced to drag out an infirm existence far from his friends and from his natural milieu."[14] Ehrenpreis alerts us to the likelihood that the single most influential individual in Swift's life was – certainly not Pope – but Archbishop King; that Swift in Ireland had a lively social circle and coterie of literary acquaintance; and that he was capable of appealing to a lower-class readership, indeed, of developing democratic sympathies that he could not conceivably have done if he had remained part of Pope's circle. Swift *needed* Ireland, if only to write a poem about it in which he refers to it as "this land of slaves, / Where all are fools, and all are knaves; / Where every knave and fool is bought, / Yet kindly sells himself for naught,"[15] and goes on to show that Irish politicians are too stupid even to demand the appropriate perquisites of betrayal. Although rumours of Swift's dying in Ireland "a poisoned rat in a hole"[16] were greatly exaggerated, unappetizing confections served up for his English friends, nevertheless his residence there ultimately entails that he does not have, *cannot* have, a complete coincidence of interests with a poet who actively contested the reins of power in a colonizing state. If poems like *Windsor Forest* and *The Rape of the Lock* are part of the "literature of mercantile capitalist apologia,"[17] it ought at least to be recognized that the epithet "mercantile" is a powerful *qualifier* of the noun "capitalism," not a natural extension of it. Mercantilism was a complex of theory and practice that encouraged a positive balance of trade by routing trade through certain governmentally sponsored restrictions. Merchants were encouraged to import raw materials rather than manufactured goods and to export manufactured goods rather than commodities. Mercantilist practice advocated embargos on luxury goods because in paying for these in specie, the importing nation was depleting its money supply, paying the wages of foreign workers and taking work away from domestic workers. Colonialism relates directly to mercantilism in that colonies can be made to supply cheap raw materials and then can be forced to accept expensive finished goods. All this Swift perceived with absolute clarity, so that there is actually a vast gulf separating Pope's infatuated inhalation of "all *Arabia* [breathing] from yonder Box," and statements like Swift's that "if the ladies [of Ireland], till better times, will not be content to go in their own country shifts, I wish they may go in rags."[18]

Yet at a deeper level still, the great biographies of the mid-eighties did more to *join* Pope and Swift than to put them asunder. Critical reception of the third volume of Ehrenpreis and of Mack's *Alexander Pope: A Life*[19] was not as rapturous as a lifetime spent in research

---

[14]  *Eighteenth-Century Studies*, 18 (1985), 406.

[15]  *Poems*, p. 330, ll. 1–4.

[16]  *Correspondence*, III, 383.

[17]  Laura Brown, "Reading Race and Gender: Jonathan Swift," *Eighteenth-Century Studies*, 23 (1990), 429.

[18]  *Prose Works*, XII, 127.

[19]  New Haven, New York, London, 1985.

would have entitled their authors to expect. Irish reception of Ehrenpreis's biography was hostile in the main. Denis Donoghue, Andrew Carpenter, and others resented the de-mythologizing aspects of Ehrenpreis. It seems the Irish actually *want* their Swift to have expired a driveller and a show! Or if not quite that, Denis Donoghue complained that Swift had been assimilated so closely to his age by the encyclopaedic knowledge of his Boswell that he was finally made to *coincide* with it.[20] Yet there should be a residue, what Carole Fabricant calls the "extreme, outrageous, and demonic side of Swift"[21] and what is called by Andrew Carpenter Swift's "mystery,"[22] the heart of which Ehrenpreis threatens to pluck out. When Martin Battestin's life of Fielding met with an even more severe fate in 1989,[23] one suspected that the kind of biography called by Julian Barnes in *Flaubert's Parrot* a "ten pound one," the kind that "stands, fat and worthy-burgherish on the shelf, boastful and sedate," giving you all the hypotheses as well as the facts, was a form of "master-narrative" discountenanced in our time.[24] Recent literary theory has done so much to decentre intentionalist accounts of authorship and unsettle organic accounts of the individual self that it is considered naive in some quarters to express wholehearted approval of a mere biography. But Ian Campbell Ross, in a review article on Ehrenpreis registers a perceptive objection not merely fashionable. The Swift that emerges from the biography is really an *accepted* Swift, even a very familiar Swift, by the time Ehrenpreis publishes. Ehrenpreis is really in dialogue with such as D. H. Lawrence and Middleton Murry, who took Swift to be a dangerous lunatic. By 1983, however, the Swift we knew was a benevolist, convinced of corrupt human nature and of the need to adhere to rigid Christian principles as a way of alleviating the misery that corruption brings in train.[25] And by 1983, many readers, feminists prominent among them, did not believe in this Swift and wanted a different one. This is presumably why David Nokes's *Jonathan Swift: A Hypocrite Revers'd*[26] could win a prize only a year later. If any biography ever lived up to its subtitle "critical," this one does: Nokes's biographical hypothesis is that Swift may have been a churchman, but he was no Christian, finding central elements of Christ's teaching unacceptable.

The point about the big biographies representing the *end* of something rather than the beginning – to wit, the end of the liberal-humanist consensus – is more clearly made with respect to Maynard Mack's biography of Pope published in 1985. Mack, too, wanted to "normalize" Pope, wanted to bring him within the bounds of acceptable conduct, and he, too, was combatting a view of Pope (in this case, a Victorian view) that was a straw man by the time he came to publish. Reviewer after reviewer singles out the central problem of Mack's biography as being his *advocacy* of Pope and, allied to that, the densely allusive style, replete with scores of unacknowledged literary quotations, in which he conducts it. James McLaverty's review presented as its main strength just those aspects of Mack to which others took exception:

---

[20] See "Clergyman and Clown," *TLS*, 10 February 1984, p. 143.
[21] *Scriblerian*, 17 (1985), 168.
[22] *Irish University Review*, 14 (1984), 280.
[23] Martin C. Battestin with Ruthe R. Battestin, *Henry Fielding: A Life* (London and New York, 1989).
[24] *Flaubert's Parrot* (London, 1992 [1984]), p. 47.
[25] See "'If we believe report': New Biographies of Jonathan Swift," *Hermathena*, 137 (1984), 34–39.
[26] Oxford, 1985.

This biography is ... a powerful expression of Professor Mack's humanism; it is permeated by his sense of the importance of the past to the present, of the limitations always to be found in human nature, and of the value of moderation, tolerance, kindliness, and friendship.[27]

Virtually the same point was made by Larry Lipking in a provocative review article,[28] except that for Lipking this is the *problem*, not its solution. Pope is the poet of allusion. His work revels in its awareness of living amongst a "club of wits" that perceives the continuity of human culture across widely separated times and places. The threnodic tone that connects Mack to his subject, giving Christopher Ricks his aperçu that "*Alexander Pope: A Life* is a worthy climax to Maynard Mack, a life" is also responsible for smudging the trail, for failing finally to distinguish Pope's life from the life of Pope's own creation in his art.[29] Mack is thrown back upon applying to Pope's life a moral calculus designed to assess whether Pope was more sinned against than sinning. Pope, in Mack's account, is a better writer than the dunces he attacked. He really *was*, as he said he was, trying to protect the cultural practice of writing from the depredations of the "shifty, needy and incompetent," and his enemies deserved all they got. This is to fail to recognize an ideological dimension that *mediates* the poet and his age. The biographer permits Pope to set the agenda, when he should be setting up a model of the "real" social, political, and economic conditions that existed in the period, to which the poet relates imaginatively, partially and in a way that cannot be disinterested.[30] In the provinces of gender relations and of the economic conditions governing authorship, it was particularly evident that Swift and Pope could not speak anything like the entire truth about their cultures. In a recent article, Ellen Pollak puts the point thus:

> Critics would have to look beyond the surface of Swift's positive and negative images of women to ways in which gender is implicated in the production of meaning both in Swift's writing and in eighteenth-century British culture as a whole.[31]

Swift's misogyny becomes a given, a fundamental condition of the production of intelligible meaning. The Marxist-feminist backlash of the mid- and late eighties was fuelled rather than headed off at the pass by the inadequacy of the theoretical models adopted by Ehrenpreis and Mack.

There are, however, some peculiarities in the nature of recent feminist reaction to Swift and Pope. There is an amusing passage in Robert Graves's *Good-Bye to All That*, where he reports an Oxford College tutor as having said to him:

> I understand, Mr. Graves, that the essays that you write for your English tutor are, shall I say, a trifle temperamental. It appears, indeed, that you prefer some authors to others.[32]

Feminist critics of our period also prefer some authors to others. In *The Poetics of Sexual Myth: Gender and Ideology in the Verse of Swift and Pope*, Ellen Pollak reached conclusions that are deeply counter-intuitive to those who come at Pope and Swift from a biographical

[27] *Notes and Queries*, 232 (1987), 89.

[28] See *American Scholar*, 56 (1987), 435–39.

[29] See *Encounter*, 66 (1986), 38.

[30] See Brean S. Hammond, "Rev. Maynard Mack, *Alexander Pope: A Life* (New Haven, 1985)," *Yearbook of English Studies*, 18 (1988), 311.

[31] "Swift among the Feminists: An Approach to Teaching," *College Literature*, 19 (1992), 116.

[32] *Good-Bye to All That* (London, 1929), p. 362.

point of view – in the process driving Swift and Pope as far apart as they have ever been in any critical account.[33] Pope becomes the gender-villain and Swift the gender-hero. While Pope accommodates himself comfortably to bourgeois sexual myths like that of "passive womanhood," Swift exposes the contradictions inherent in the myths and refuses to naturalize them. *Ideologiekritik* arrives at conclusions that are difficult to sanction on the basis of what we know about the lives of the two writers. As contemporaries never failed to remind Pope, he was a scandal to masculinity, yet Pollak tells us that Pope's poetry expresses canonical forms of sexism. Swift, whose entire life could be viewed as a flight from the responsibility of feeling for women, turns out to be a good guy who has written, in *Cadenus and Vanessa*, a great love poem. This can happen because, as Pollak puts it, Swift is better than Pope because worse, "and 'worse' is 'better' when value is mediated by the poetic imperatives of an alienating ideology."[34] I concur entirely with John Sitter's review of Pollak, who argues that what she has actually done is to reassign the qualities of savage indignation, unstable irony, and extremism that have always been recognized in Swift to a postmodernist conception of the authorial self:

> Pope's poetry looks for "balance" and "stability," Swift's for the point where "certainty dissolves." Pope's imposes "wholeness," Swift's "fractures" such impositions. Pope seeks to *re*center authorial presence, Swift to *de*center it. Pope's attempted fusion of new and classical modes is a "more accommodating response to 'modernism'" than Swift's rejection of "the idea of the modern subject altogether."[35]

To Pollak, Swift is valuable because he is a deconstructor *avant la lettre*. Swift, the apostle of the "post," the harbinger of cultural critiques that dispense with liberal-humanist emphasis on *evaluation*, is himself appropriated for a sweeping evaluative act that, like some eighteenth-century pantomimic special effect, transmutes Castor and Pollux into Punch and Judy.

Even if this characterization – the Postmodern Swift – is intended as no more than an illuminating analogy, it is seductive enough to be worth worrying over. Only by concentrating narrowly on representation of gender, and editing out all other aspects of Swift's religious and political writing, will the critic succeed in flying this kite at all. All major theorists of postmodern culture argue that postmodernism is a radical reaction against a certain conception of rationality that had its origin in "the Enlightenment." Scientific and instrumental forms of reason provided the major thinkers of the nineteenth century, Marx and Freud in particular, with tools for producing their highly influential views of the individual and of society – the "grand narratives," as these powerful explanatory systems are dubbed. Postmodernists apply principally to Nietzsche and to Heidegger for an alternative (divided, multiple, historically contingent) view of human subjectivity, of reality and of thought, that defines "truth" as the outcome of power-struggles and as a relativistic concept dependant on specific conceptual frameworks.[36] Many theorists of the postmodern claim that

---

[33] Chicago, 1985.
[34] *The Poetics of Sexual Myth*, p. 183.
[35] *Scriblerian*, 20 (1987), 61.
[36] Useful summaries are contained, for example, in Steven Best and Douglas Kellner, *Postmodern Theory: Critical Interrogations* (Houndmills, Basingstoke, London, 1991), Chapter 1, and Alex Callinicos, *Against Postmodernism: A Marxist Critique* (New York, 1990), Chapter 2.

the constellation of ideas and cultural products that they wish to delineate results from a
significant alteration in the nature of modernity which can be accounted for by reference to
technological change and/or developments in the global economy. If postmodernity is a
distinct epoch causally related to ruptures or radical changes in modernity, there is an obvious sense in which it would be anachronistic to situate Swift within it. More than that,
however, it fundamentally mistakes the nature of Swift's ideology. If postmodernism is,
whatever else it is, a critique of Enlightenment rationality, we can ask what Swift might
have contributed to such a project. Certainly, Swift did not have a high opinion of human
rationality: if a reader of *Gulliver's Travels* gleans nothing else, s/he will glean that. Yet
Swift's critique of human rationality was not a turning away from its played-out assurance:
it was an intense disgust that would have stopped "the Enlightenment project" in its tracks.
Swift's reaction to disappointment with human reason was not to retreat into the ludic ab-
stentions from political authority typical of postmodern theoreticians like Baudrillard and
Lyotard. On the contrary, he asserted a rigidly traditional authoritarianism in politics and
religion that interdicted the challenging of established orthodoxies. "Free thinking" of the
kind practised by the Deists in England, comparable in some respects to that of the *phi-
losophes* in France, was for Swift a potent enemy of social stability.

We can study Swift's set towards what might be considered an early English manifestation
of "the Enlightenment project" in his satirical attack on Anthony Collins's *A Discourse of
Free-Thinking, Occasion'd by the Rise and Growth of a Sect call'd Free-Thinkers*, published
in the same year (1713) under the title of *Mr. Collins's Discourse of Free-Thinking, Put into
Plain English, by way of Abstract, for the Use of the Poor*. Collins defines "free-thinking" as
"the Use of the Understanding, in endeavouring to find out the Meaning of any Proposition
whatsoever, in considering the nature of the Evidence for or against it, and in judging of it
according to the seeming Force or Weakness of the Evidence."[37] Employing a robustly ironic
prose style, Collins argues that it is absurd to rely on creeds or established authority in
arriving at religious belief. Swift's method of exposing the captious, clever-schoolboyish
limitation of Collins's thought, the reductiveness and harm in his granting free play to the
disembodied powers of logical reason, is to produce a brief abstract of Collins's *Discourse*.
Using almost entirely Collins's own words but reducing his argument to its bare bones, and
occasionally changing an emphasis or adding a few telling words of his own that devastat-
ingly tease out the unwanted consequences of Collins's logic, Swift's *Abstract* implies its
immaturity and perilousness. Here is an example:

| Collins[38] | Swift[39] |
|---|---|
| *It is objected, That to suppose Men have a right to think on all Subjects, is to engage them in Enquiries for which they are no ways quali-fy'd; the Bulk of Mankind really wanting a Capacity to think justly about any Speculations: and therefore 'tis absurd to assert that Men have a right to think freely, much more that it is their Duty to think freely.* To which I answer, | But to this it may be objected, that the Bulk of Mankind is as well qualified for *flying* as *thinking*, and if every Man thought it his Duty to *think freely*, and trouble his Neigh-bour with his Thoughts (which is an essential Part of *Free-thinking*,) it would make wild work in the World. I answer; whoever cannot *think freely*, may let it alone if he pleases, by virtue of his Right to *think freely*; |

---

[37] (London, 1713), p. 5.
[38] *Discourse*, pp. 99–100.
[39] *Prose Works*, IV, 38.

1. That to assert only a bare Right in any Man to do a thing, implies a Right in him to let it alone, if he thinks fit. And therefore no Man need engage himself in any Enquiries by virtue of his Right to *think freely*, unless he judges himself sufficiently qualify'd.

that is to say, if such a Man *freely thinks* that he cannot *think freely*, of which every Man is a sufficient Judge, why then he need not *think freely*, unless he *thinks* fit.

Swift begins by colouring Collins's concession that some men may not be capable of independent thought with the comparison to flight and with the positioning of the phrase "the Bulk of Mankind." The subtext of this irony is, of course, that we have an Established Church and its clergy *precisely because* the majority of people need to be told what to think and to believe, how to interpret Scripture, what customary and ritualistic practices to adopt, and so forth. Swift then introduces a thought, not in Collins, that is several times reiterated in his *oeuvre* and is of incalculable importance to him: what is the relationship between freedom of thought and freedom of expression? Swift is surely right to say that for such as Collins there is no distinction. For Swift, there was all the difference in the world.[40] In what follows, Swift hilariously exposes the muddle in Collins's logic that puts him in the position of saying that a man can freely think that he cannot think freely. Unerringly, Swift homes in on the breezy colloquialism that cheapens Collins' style – "let it alone;" and by hopping up and down on the italicized phrase "*think freely*" (six times repeated), Swift exposes it as a vacuous slogan. The passage ends with a brilliant pun on the common phrase to "think fit": Collins provides an excellent example of unfit thinking.

There is another point that should be made here, besides the point that Swift's quarrel with rationality is not configured in the same way as is postmodern anti-rationalism. It is perhaps most clearly made with respect to Swiftian irony. Undoubtedly, Swift was offended as much by Collins's way of making his points as he was by the points themselves. An aspect of Collins's deistical confidence in free-thinking was a belief in irony and ridicule as fit means of expression for conducting theological debate. Towards the end of his career, Collins tried to justify this in *A Discourse Concerning Ridicule and Irony in Writing* (1729), taking time to repine that writers like Swift himself appear to have used the same methods and got away with it (and accusing him of Jacobitism and unChristianity into the bargain):

> I question whether High-Church would be willing to have the reverend Author of the *Tale of a Tub*, one of the greatest *Droles* that ever appear'd upon the Stage of the World, punish'd for that or any other of his *drolling* Works.[41]

Although claims are often made for the depthlessness of Swiftian irony, this example shows that there is a normative dimension to it. It is, finally, quite clearly *grounded*. One can infer, in the last analysis, the position that Swift is recommending by negative example. Recent accounts of postmodernist culture have foregrounded the character of its irony as a salient identifying feature. Whereas modernist irony retains a normative dimension, postmodernism, according to Fredric Jameson, folds irony into pastiche:

---

40  On this, see the valuable paragraphs in Higgins, *Swift's Politics*, pp. 119–20.
41  Augustan Reprint Society, no 142, eds Edward A. Bloom and Lilian D. Bloom (Los Angeles, 1970 [1729]), p. 39.

a neutral practice of such mimicry, without any of parody's ulterior motives, amputated of the satiric impulse, devoid of laughter and of any conviction that alongside the abnormal tongue you have momentarily borrowed, some healthy linguistic normality still exists.[42]

On this analysis, Swift is a modernist rather than a postmodernist. And all of this suggests that the mapping of Pope and Swift onto the modernist/postmodernist grid exaggerates the stability of Pope's irony and the instability of Swift's.

Ellen Pollak's book was quite well received, partly because her method of contrasting Pope and Swift enabled her to salvage something out of the literature of a period whose ideology, nakedly expressed, is not altogether politically correct. Laura Brown's book on Pope attracted hysterical reviews because it *expressed* that ideology nakedly, considering Pope's poems to be "documents of the ideological structures of the period;" and these ideological structures are such as she cannot approve.[43] No matter that over and over again in Pope's poetry he takes exception to economic activities that grind the faces of the poor and that he, like the Hogarth who comes out of David Solkin's recent *Painting for Money*, repeatedly sees national economic success as having a trickling-down effect that would be of widespread benefit. Brown tends to use ideology as a kind of pulling rank over the men in wigs and stockings who thought they knew what they were doing, to paraphrase Felicity Rosslyn.[44] This element of political correctness continues to appear in Brown's work. Recently, she presents the problem that from the perspective of gender Swift is a bad guy, but from that of race, he is a good guy because anti-colonialist. Or, in her words,

> Swift's texts lend themselves equally well to a negative and a positive hermeneutic, and a critic concerned with the political aim of her readings of literary culture might well pause between the exposure of misogyny in the canon and the discovery of an early ally in the struggle against colonialism. Which to choose? What is a marxist/feminist to do?

What she might do, in answer to this plaintive question, is to accept that Swift himself was not a marxist/feminist and that there is only a difficulty if one's purpose in writing is to distinguish oneself from "most American Foucauldians, whose historical analyses emphasize the coercive strategies of structures of power to the exclusion of effective opposition."[45]

Margaret Anne Doody takes a different methodological approach, but her conclusion that "in any modern comparison of Swift and Pope in relation to their views on women Swift is likely to come off much better: that is, if the person making the comparison be a woman"[46] might be just as worrying, at least to the *Popeans* in this gathering. In a fascinating article, she shows how Swift's iambic tetrameter and interest in "that which is homely, unofficial, and truthful" enabled a succession of female poetic voices, including Laetitia Pilkington's. Doody's claim that Swift, rather than Pope, was the true role model for eighteenth-century women poets would be hard pressed to stand up to statistical analysis; but it is yet more convincing than her claim that "in his relations with women Swift (inside and outside his own poems) never shuts them up."[47] This remark moves me to remind you of how the story

---

[42] "Postmodernism, or The Cultural Logic of Late Capitalism," *New Left Review*, 146 (1984), p. 65.

[43] *Alexander Pope* (Oxford and New York, 1985), p. 3.

[44] See *Cambridge Quarterly*, 15 (1986), 166.

[45] "Reading Race and Gender: Jonathan Swift," p. 426.

[46] "Swift among the Women," *Yearbook of English Studies*, 18 (1988), 91.

[47] "Swift among the Women," pp. 79; 77.

with which I began my paper ends. Pilkington writes an abject letter to the Dean apologizing for her outburst and explaining her anxiety that Pope's poor opinion of her husband
might prejudice Swift's. She quotes Swift's reply to her:

> You must shake off the Leavings of your Sex. If you cannot keep a Secret and take a
> Chiding, you will quickly be out of my Sphere. Corrigible People are to be chid, those
> who are otherwise, may be very safe from any Lectures of mine: I should rather chuse to
> indulge them in their Follies, than attempt to set them right. I desire you may not inform
> your Husband of what has past.[48]

If this is not shutting women up, and coming between husband and wife to boot, I would
like to know what is. It is curious, in conclusion, that one of the greatest dangers to Pope's
reputation in our time should be the rising stock of his closest friend, Swift.[49]

---

[48] *Memoirs*, ed. Elias, I, 54.
[49] In an article entitled "Beyond Consensus: *The Rape of the Lock* and the Fate of Reading
Eighteenth-Century Literature," *New Orleans Review*, 15 (1988), 68–77, Robert Markley
has defended Brown and Pollak against the "old-line humanist criticism" of various an-
tagonistic reviewers, but he has not taken on the full force of what the future is likely to
be for Pope studies if feminist strictures are accepted.

Peter Sabor

*Université Laval, Québec*

# "St Jonathan" or "wild beast": Horace Walpole's Swift*

ABSTRACT. The several hundred references to Swift in the 48 volumes of Horace Walpole's correspondence, as well as in unpublished marginalia to his copies of Swift's printed letters and poems, show that despite his antipathy to Swift's politics, Walpole was fascinated by Swift's satirical technique, especially in *Gulliver's Travels* but also in *A Tale of a Tub* and other prose works. For Walpole, whose copious remarks on Swift were made over a period of fifty years, Swift was a thoroughly ambiguous figure. Swift's ability to tell lies solemnly, that great gift for the writer of fiction, was also, in Walpole's view, the disfiguring characteristic of Swift as a political commentator.

In her introduction to the Critical Heritage volume on Swift, Kathleen Williams takes a gloomy view of the eighteenth-century reception, which "cannot make a large book." "Much contemporary comment," she writes, "is not criticism at all, but deliberate misinterpretation, modulating into personal attack on the writer;" the "search for eighteenth-century Swift criticism is therefore a rather frustrating one."[1] Among her collection of early critics, Horace Walpole plays a distinctly minor role. He is represented only by a brief sequel to *Gulliver's Travels*, composed in 1771 but not published in his lifetime; his critical views on Swift are not portrayed at all.[2]

If critics, as Williams contends, must be disinterested and dispassionate, Walpole's views of Swift can be dismissed from the outset. A fervent defender of his father, the great Sir Robert, Walpole reacted violently to Swift's opposition to Sir Robert's government and his support of Bolingbroke, Oxford, and other Tory politicians. Walpole also became a close friend of Henrietta Howard, and was repelled by Swift's turning on her after his failure to

---

\*   For their assistance in commenting on and providing materials for this paper, I am indebted to my former colleague F. P. Lock and to Anna Malicka of the Lewis Walpole Library. I am also indebted to the Advisory Research Committee of Queen's University for financial support.

1   *Swift: The Critical Heritage*, ed. Kathleen Williams (London, 1970), pp. 1, 3.

2   In addition to the sequel, Williams prints a single letter, not by Walpole but by his correspondent Madame du Deffand, who found *Gulliver's Travels* disagreeable: "The conversation with the horses is the most forced, the most frigid, the most tedious thing that one can imagine." Williams does note that the "personal and literary differences of Swift and Walpole (1717–97) did not prevent *Gulliver's Travels* from appealing to Walpole's imagination." See *The Critical Heritage*, ed. Williams, pp. 191, 189.

find favour at court in 1727. Walpole's judgements of Swift are inevitably coloured by these personal factors, as he himself would have acknowledged. I hope, however, to show that what Williams sees as "deliberate misinterpretation" can constitute a valuable response, an example of what Harold Bloom terms "antithetical" criticism.[3]

Walpole is at best an unconventional, unmethodical, and highly tendentious literary critic. There are a few passing references to Swift in his catalogue of English royal and noble authors (1758), such as the remark that English prose was refined by Dryden and Roscommon, "flowed pure from Addison; was kept within severe bounds by Swift; was ennobled and harmonized by Bolinbroke [sic]."[4] There is also a mention of Swift in the entry on John Lord Somers, who "was at once the model of Addison, and the touchstone of Swift; the one wrote from him, the other for him." To the second edition of the Catalogue, Walpole added a lengthy note, deploring Swift's depiction of Somers in his newly published History of the Four Last Years of the Queen (1758). "Can one wonder," demands Walpole, "that lord Bolingbroke and Pope always tried to prevent Swift from exposing himself by publishing this wretched ignorant libel? And could it avoid falling, as it has, into immediate contempt and oblivion?"[5]

Walpole also turned at least briefly to Swift in his "Conversations with Lady Suffolk," written in the 1760s but first published only in 1924. In an entry for 15 May 1766, Walpole writes:

> I carried to Lady Suffolk the two new volumes of Swift's correspondence, in which are three letters from her. She told me the one in the second volume with algebraic directions was dictated to her by Arbuthnot. She told me Pope and Gay believed that Mrs Johnson was Swift's sister, & that that was the reason of his not cohabiting with Her.[6]

Both claims are intriguing. The letter with "algebraic directions" is one of 17 November 1726, in which Mrs Howard adroitly uses the height of the dwarf in Brobdingnag to calculate the measurements of silks for the Princess of Wales.[7] Its ingenuity and detailed knowledge of Gulliver's Travels make the attribution to Arbuthnot plausible. The report that Esther Johnson and Swift were siblings (both illegitimate children of Sir William Temple) was already current,[8] but Lady Suffolk, as reported by Walpole, gives the story additional force by asserting that it was accepted by Pope and Gay.

In general, however, it is not in formal writings that Walpole's views on Swift are to be found; to see him as a critic we must turn to his marginalia, to his correspondence, and even to his creative works. And the kind of Swift criticism found here is remarkable for its inconsistency. On the one hand, Walpole responded with intuitive sympathy to the wit and dex-

---

[3]  See The Anxiety of Influence: A Theory of Poetry (New York, 1973), p. 65.
[4]  Walpole, A Catalogue of the Royal and Noble Authors of England (1758), reprinted in The Works of Horatio Walpole, Earl of Orford, 5 vols (London, 1798), I, 518.
[5]  Walpole, Works, I, 430.
[6]  Reminiscences Written by Mr. Horace Walpole in 1788, ed. Paget Toynbee (Oxford, 1924), p. 144.
[7]  See Correspondence, III, 184–86. Walpole made a similar reference to a letter "in mathematical terms, dictated by Arbuthnot," in his unpublished "Book of Materials" for 1759 (p. 100), now at the Lewis Walpole Library. Sir Harold Williams notes this reference (pp. 184–85 n6), but not the one in the "Conversations with Lady Suffolk."
[8]  See, for example, John Boyle, Earl of Orrery, Remarks on the Life and Writings of Dr. Jonathan Swift (London, 1752), p. 15.

terity of Swift's imagination, especially as revealed in *Gulliver's Travels*. Conversely, when Walpole wrote on Swift's politics, as he did on numerous occasions, the prevailing tone was one of disgust. Walpole's personal involvement with issues central to Swift, moreover, gave him both strengths and weaknesses as a Swift critic. His insider's knowledge of Sir Robert Walpole's government and the role of Mrs Howard made him better equipped to understand Swift's letters than other eighteenth-century Swift critics – including John Hawkesworth, editor of the letters that Walpole read and annotated. But his insider's involvement also impelled him to make gross errors of interpretation: the "wild beast" that Walpole saw in Swift was at times a *bête noire* of his own fabrication.

Since the completion in 1983 of Wilmarth Lewis's magisterial forty-eight volume edition of Walpole's correspondence, the epistolary remarks of Walpole and his correspondents on Swift have been readily available.[9] Far less accessible are Walpole's marginal observations in his copies of Swift's works. In his catalogue of Walpole's library, Allen Hazen lists some 7,300 volumes owned by Walpole and indicates, where possible, the extent of Walpole's marginalia for each item.[10] Walpole himself repeatedly drew attention to his love of "writing notes in my books." There are annotations, as Wilmarth Lewis has observed, "in at least two-thirds of his books that have been recovered."[11] In addition to correcting errors, filling in blanks, and supplying discursive comments, Walpole used various symbols to express his responses: notably a large cross or an asterisk for passages of particular interest, and an exclamation mark to express scorn.[12] Several sets of Walpolean marginalia have been separately printed, including those on Pierre Bayle's *Dictionary*, on the works of Ovid (dating from Walpole's schooldays at Eton), on Chesterfield, Pope, Chatterton, Bubb Dodington, and William Mason, on Thomas Warton's edition of Milton, on Gray's *Odes*, and on Edward Young's satirical poem *Love of Fame*.[13] Walpole's marginal comments on Swift, how-

9   See *The Yale Edition of Horace Walpole's Correspondence*, eds W. S. Lewis *et al.*, 48 vols (New Haven, 1937–83). The index, with some 300,000 entries in all, occupies the last five volumes. There are about seventy entries for Swift, including one with twenty-five sub-entries for *Gulliver's Travels* and another with a dozen sub-entries for Swift's letters. For the presence of other major authors in Walpole's correspondence, see Peter Sabor, "Horace Walpole's *Correspondence*: 'A Mighty Maze but not without a Plan,'" *Eighteenth-Century Life*, 10, no 2 (1986), 105. Jeanne K. Welcher first drew attention to Walpole's writings on Swift in her pioneering article, "Horace Walpole and *Gulliver's Travels*," *Studies in Eighteenth-Century Culture*, 12 (1983), 45–57.
10  See Allen T. Hazen, *A Catalogue of Horace Walpole's Library*, with *Horace Walpole's Library*, by Wilmarth Sheldon Lewis, 3 vols (New Haven and London, 1969), I, liii.
11  See Hazen, *Catalogue*, I, lxii.
12  See Hazen, *Catalogue*, I, lxiii.
13  See "Horace Walpole's MS Notes on Bayle's Dictionary," *Philobiblon*, 1 (1861–62), 5–8, 27–32, 46; "Walpole's Ovid," *Philobiblon*, 1 (1861–62), 44; R. S. Turner, ed., *Horace Walpole's Marginal Notes, Written in Dr. Maty's Miscellaneaus Works and Memoirs of the Earl of Chesterfield* (Philobiblon Society Miscellanies, 11 [1867–68]); Sir William August Fraser, ed., *Notes on the Poems of Alexander Pope*, 2nd ed. (London, 1876); George Sherburn, "Walpole's Marginalia in *Additions to Pope* (1776)," *Huntington Library Quarterly*, 1 (1938), 473–87; E. H. W. Meyerstein, "Horace Walpole's Marginalia in Dean Milles's Edition of the Rowley Poems," *TLS*, 18 January 1923, p. 45; E. Beresford Chancellor, "Horace Walpole's Marginalia," *Literary Diversions* (New York, 1925), pp. 40–46; Paget Toynbee, ed., *Satirical Poems Published Anonymously by William Mason, with Notes by Horace Walpole* (Oxford, 1926); William Colgate, *Horace Walpole on Milton* (Toronto: privately printed, 1953); Lord Rothschild, "Odes by Mr. Gray," *The Rothschild Library: A Catalogue of the Collection of Eighteenth-Century Printed Books and Manuscripts Formed by Lord Rothschild*,

ever, which survive in the Lewis Walpole Library, have not hitherto been published or discussed.[14]

Walpole annotated Swift in a collected edition of fourteen royal-quarto volumes, edited by John Hawkesworth and published between 1755 and 1768. There are markings and notes by Walpole throughout the volumes, including identifications of persons in some of the poems, but the substantial comments are confined to Swift's correspondence.[15] Walpole also owned a set of the Swift-Pope *Miscellanies* (1727–32), and separate editions of *A Tale of a Tub* (1704), *A Short Character of the Earl of Wharton* (1710), *Some Remarks on the Barrier Treaty* (1712), *The Publick Spirit of the Whigs* (1714), *Directions to Servants* (1745), and the *History of the Four Last Years of the Queen* (1758), although only the last of these is known to have marginal annotations. In addition, Walpole's considerable Swift collection contained related works, such as Deane Swift's *Essay upon … Swift* (1755), and an English translation of a French continuation of *Gulliver's Travels*.[16]

In volume one of the *Works*, Walpole inserted an account of Swift by the father of an anonymous "Gentleman in Dublin," printed in the *Morning Chronicle* for 22 October 1782. This account, written by one who claimed to have known Swift for much of his life, is in general highly critical. Walpole might have been attracted in particular to its attack on Swift's politics, which are said to be "factious in the extreme. He never could forgive the Ministry who superceded his friends, because they were not equally inclined to gratify his unbounded ambition; hence arose his violent opposition to government, and all the rancorous effusions of a party spirit, by which he inflamed the spirits of the vulgar."[17] At the same time, the writer commended Swift's unbounded wit and his "natural propensity to humour." It is significant that Walpole thought enough of this characterization to preserve it in his copy of Swift's works. His own response to Swift was similarly divided and similarly acerbic, as his marginal remarks on Hawkesworth's edition reveal.

In a letter to Archbishop King of October 1711, for example, Swift declares: "I promise your grace that this shall be the last sally I will ever make to a court." Walpole notes tersely, "he did not keep this resolution in 1727," alluding to Swift's kissing the hand of George II three days after his accession to the throne in June of that year.[18] Walpole is also, however,

---

2 vols (Cambridge, 1954), I, 266–68; Antony Coleman, "Walpole's Annotations in a Copy of *Love of Fame, The Universal Passion*," *Notes and Queries*, 224 (1979), 551–54. All of these items are summarized in Peter Sabor, *Horace Walpole: A Reference Guide* (Boston, 1984). Further sets of Walpole annotations are printed as appendices to volumes of the *Yale Edition of Horace Walpole's Correspondence*.

14  The Lewis Walpole Library, Farmington, Connecticut, originally Wilmarth Lewis's collection and now part of Yale University Library, contains more than a thousand of the books in Walpole's library; see Lewis, *Horace Walpole's Library*, I, lxxxv n 24.

15  Hazen counts "about 30" markings and identifications by Walpole in the eight-volume *Works*, which includes some of Swift's correspondence. There are many more notations in the four-volume *Letters*. See *A Catalogue of Horace Walpole's Library*, III, 77.

16  Although most of these items are preserved in the Lewis Walpole Library, some have not been recovered, including Walpole's copy of *A Tale of a Tub* and Deane Swift's *Essay*. For the whereabouts of each item, see Hazen's *Catalogue*. See also Teerink-Scouten, *Bibliography*.

17  The source and date of the clipping are recorded in Walpole's hand.

18  Swift to Archbishop King, 1 October 1711, *The Works of Jonathan Swift*, ed. John Hawkesworth (London, 1755–65), VII, pt 2, 62; *Correspondence*, I, 263. Quotations from Swift's

capable of seeing Swift's politics in a more positive light. Thus beside Swift's remark in a letter to Archbishop King of March 1713 that "a free man ought not to confine his converse to any one party," Walpole writes: "He altered this opinion afterwards, when he was a free man; & yet it is just to say, that when his friends were in power, he was very kind to several Whigs who were men of parts."[19] Walpole substantiates this comment by citing Swift's letter to King of December 1716, in which Swift declares that "while I was near the late Ministry I was a common Advocate for those they called the Whigs, to a degree that a certain great Minister told me I had always a Whig in my sleeve."[20] In this case, Walpole sought out a cross-reference not to undermine Swift but to support his veracity.

Walpole's most extensive marginalia on the correspondence are on two letters from Bolingbroke to Swift of 1727. Bolingbroke's letter of May begins by celebrating the joys of friendship and retirement: "Would to God my whole life could be divided in the same manner; two thirds to friendship, one third to myself, and not a moment of it to the world." Understandably unimpressed by this specious claim, Walpole inscribed a large exclamation mark in the margin. Bolingbroke's letter continues with a reference to Sir Robert Walpole's employing "one of his spies" to report on the activities of Gay, a reference explained by an editorial note. Beneath this note, an indignant Horace Walpole, ever ready to defend his father's honour, provides his own account of political intrigues in mid-1727, shortly before and after the beginning of George II's reign:

> The probability is that Gay as well as Swift were disappointed by the Queen at least as much as by Sr R. W. Swift & his friends were such poor Politicians, or so ignorant of the true State of the Court, that they hoped to rise by the recommendation of the Mistress [Mrs Howard] to the Wife, the Princess of Wales. When they discovered that error, they fell into another; on the death of George 1st they concluded that the mistress wd have more power with the new King than the Wife; and at last their Junto determined that Mrs Howard should, to try her credit, insist on Lord Bathurst being created an Earl. This the Queen & Sr R. W. prevented, & Swift returned to Ireland, again full of disappointment & rage, tho he himself had condescended to be presented to Sr R. W. by Ld Peterborough before the death of George 1st.[21]

Walpole's analysis here is very close to that of modern commentators such as Alan Downie, who writes: "Swift's bitterness was largely unwarranted. He had been backing the wrong horse ... [Mrs Howard] had offered Swift the best advice in her power, and it proved unfounded. But Swift built it up in his own chagrin to a studied attempt to mislead." Irvin Ehrenpreis similarly observes that the Scriblerians "grossly overestimated Mrs Howard's influence on either Caroline or her spouse," and that Swift "felt mortified and charged the mood on Mrs Howard."[22]

Bolingbroke's letter to Swift of June 1727 also moved Walpole to comment. Bolingbroke is reflecting on the folly of political ambition:

letters annotated by Walpole are from the Hawkesworth edition; corresponding references to Sir Harold Williams's edition are also provided for convenience. For Swift's kissing George II's hand, see his letter to Thomas Sheridan, 24 June 1727, *Correspondence*, III, 218–19.

19 Swift to King, 28 March 1713, *Works*, VII, pt 2, 82; *Correspondence*, I, 339.
20 Swift to King, 22 December 1716, *Correspondence*, II, 236.
21 Bolingbroke to Swift, 18 May 1727, *Letters Written by the Late Jonathan Swift*, ed. Hawkesworth and Deane Swift (London, 1766–68), I, 357; *Correspondence*, III, 211.
22 See J. A. Downie, *Jonathan Swift, Political Writer* (London, Boston, Henley, 1985 [1984]), p. 290; and Ehrenpreis, *Dean Swift*, pp. 591, 593.

Good God! what is man? polished, civilized, learned man! A liberal education fits him for slavery; and the pains he has taken gives him the noble pretension of dangling away life in an ante-chamber, or of employing real talents to serve those, who have none.

Walpole responds acidly:

If their Intrigue had succeeded, tho these virtuous Philosophers stooped to make use of a King's Mistress to serve their ambition & interest, they wd have reverted to use the Court language they had held in the reign of Q. Anne; & who certainly had none of the talents of Queen Caroline. It is only surprising how Bolingbroke & Swift could have the impudence to write to one another in this style, when both were conscious of what they had been just aiming at – a return to Court.[23]

These remarks, doubtless written with posterity in mind but unknown to Walpole's contemporaries, are much harsher than the evaluation of Bolingbroke in Walpole's *Catalogue of Royal and Noble Authors*. Here, more circumspectly, Walpole describes Bolingbroke as "one of our best writers; though his attacks on all governments and all religion [neither of which views he cared directly to own] have necessarily involved his style in a want of perspicuity."[24] The "want of perspicuity" is a deftly feline phrase; Walpole is implying, in a suitably measured tone, that Bolingbroke lacked the courage to write plainly.

Some of Walpole's annotations on Swift are designed to throw light on the customs of earlier times. In a letter of September 1726, Gay writes to Swift about a coach accident in which Pope "was thrown into the river, with the glasses of the coach up, and was up to the knots of his perriwig in water." Walpole notes with surprise, "they must then have worn tye wigs even on the road."[25] And when Bolingbroke, in a letter of June 1727, refers to "the *Pall-mall*," Walpole underlined the definite article and wrote "not used now, 1782."[26]

Other annotations by Walpole are designed to correct editorial errors by Hawkesworth. Deane Swift, one of several later eighteenth-century Swift editors, condemned both the text and notes of Hawkesworth's edition, "the vilest that ever was yet published."[27] John Abbott, Hawkesworth's modern biographer and principal defender, finds many saving graces in the edition, but he, too, concedes that "few students of the Dean from his day to our own" are satisfied with Hawkesworth's performance.[28] Walpole's view of Hawkesworth's editing was closer to Deane Swift's than to Abbott's. One striking error in Hawkesworth is his misidentifying the recipient of Swift's letters to Archbishop King as Narcissus Marsh. Hawkesworth himself, however, provides a note to Swift's letter to King of December 1710 identifying the ailing primate named in that letter as Marsh; Walpole observes, "These letters therefore

---

[23]  Bolingbroke to Swift, 17 June 1727, *Letters*, I, 360; *Correspondence*, III, 216.

[24]  Walpole, *Works*, I, 448.

[25]  Gay to Swift, 16 September 1726, *Letters*, I, 341; *Correspondence*, III, 164.

[26]  Bolingbroke to Swift, 11 June 1727, *Letters*, II, 1; *Correspondence*, III, 213. The date of Walpole's annotation, as well as that of the newspaper clipping in volume one of the *Works*, shows that Walpole was rereading Swift's works and letters in 1782.

[27]  John Nichols, *Illustrations of the Literary History of the Eighteenth Century*, 8 vols (London, 1817–58), V, 376; cited in John Lawrence Abbott, *John Hawkesworth: Eighteenth-Century Man of Letters* (Madison, WI, 1982), p. 207n9. For Hawkesworth as editor of Swift, see also Pierre Danchin, "The Text of *Gulliver's Travels*," *Texas Studies in Literature and Language*, 2 (1960), 233–50, and Sir Harold Williams, "Deane Swift, Hawkesworth, and *The Journal to Stella*," *Essays on the Eighteenth Century, Presented to David Nichol Smith*, eds James Sutherland and F. P. Wilson (Oxford, 1945), pp. 33–48.

[28]  Abbott, *John Hawkesworth*, p. 56.

were to Dr King."[29] Elsewhere, Hawkesworth identifies Lady Catherine Hyde as "the present duchess of *Queensbury*." Walpole writes: "This is a mistake … The lady Catherine Hyde mentioned above was Aunt to the Dss of Queensbury, was Lady of the bedchamber to Q Anne & died unmarried in the reign of Geo. 2d."[30] Beside an erroneous mention of Lord Oxford, Walpole, the future Earl of Orford, not surprisingly comments: "I think it shd be *Orford*, Russel E. of Orford."[31] When Hawkesworth states that Mrs Howard was "created countess of *Suffolk*," Walpole responds bluntly: "a gross mistake; she became so by her Husband's succeeding to the title."[32]

Walpole also put his command of French to good use in correcting the text of some of the letters by Swift's French correspondents. Next to the garbled transcription of Lady Bolingbroke's letter to Swift of February 1727, Walpole twice writes "not sense," and makes numerous corrections in an attempt to make the text meaningful.[33] He likewise corrects errors in Hawkesworth's text of Voltaire's letter to Swift of June 1727. An editorial note to this letter claims that "*Swift*, at this time, was preparing to visit the lord *Bolingbroke* in *France*": Walpole responds tartly that "Ld Bol. was not then in France, as the Editor ought to have seen by the very next letter."[34]

At times, Walpole's annotation of Swift's letters furnishes information missing not only from Hawkesworth but from Sir Harold Williams' standard modern edition. In a letter of November 1726, one of many Gulliverian letters sent to Swift at that time, the Earl of Peterborough writes that he had "depended much upon a lady, who had a good ear, and a pliant tongue, in hopes she might have taught me to draw sounds out of consonants." Williams, drawing on F. Elrington Ball, suggests that the lady is the earl's wife, Anastasia Robinson; Walpole's annotation, however, provides the necessary supplemental information that she "had been a Singer in the Italian Operas."[35] Williams is silent when William Pulteney writes to Swift, in a letter of February 1731, that "Villain, traitor, seditious rascal, and such ingenious appellations, have frequently been bestowed on a couple of friends of yours." Walpole identifies the friends as Pulteney himself and Bolingbroke.[36]

The lack of annotation in these two instances could be merely a question of editorial policy: Williams's notes are generally sparse, whereas Walpole enjoys providing details. On at least two occasions, however, Walpole's superior knowledge of Swift's cultural milieu enabled him to explain passages that have defeated other editors. In August 1727, Mrs Howard wrote to Swift from court: "I likewise insist upon your taking no resolution to leave *England* till I see you; which must be here, for the most disagreeable reason in the

---

[29]  Swift to King, 30 December 1710, *Works*, VII, pt 2, 38; *Correspondence*, I, 200.

[30]  *Journal to Stella*, 20 February 1713, *Letters*, I, 154; *Prose Works*, XVI, 623.

[31]  Erasmus Lewis to Swift, 12 January 1717, *Letters*, I, 276; *Correspondence*, II, 246.

[32]  Swift to Mrs Howard, ?14 September 1727, *Letters*, II, 6; *Correspondence*, III, 238.

[33]  Lady Bolingbroke to Swift, February 1727, *Letters*, I, 354; *Correspondence*, III, 197–98.

[34]  Voltaire to Swift, *Letters*, I, 358; *Correspondence*, III, 214.

[35]  The Earl of Peterborough to Swift, 29 November 1726, *Letters*, I, 351; *Correspondence*, III, 191. The shortcomings of Williams's edition of Swift's correspondence, "obsolescent as soon as it was published," are noted by J. A. Downie, "Editor Extraordinaire," *The Scriblerian*, 13 (1980), 4. For more on Anastasia Robinson, see David Woolley, "An Alembicated Footnote to the King of Sicily's Watch, Including a New Letter from Alexander Pope," *Swift Studies*, 6 (1991), 10–29.

[36]  Pulteney to Swift, 9 February 1731, *Letters*, II, 41; *Correspondence*, III, 439.

world, and the most shocking: I dare not go to you." Williams has no explanation for her inability to leave her residence at St James's Palace.[37] Although the threats made by Charles Howard to abduct his estranged wife had been fully described by Lewis Melville in *Lady Suffolk and her Circle* (1924), neither Williams nor George Sherburn, in his edition of Pope's correspondence, understood what Walpole immediately grasped.[38] In a letter to Mrs Howard of October 1727, Pope commented on her "uneasy, tormenting, situation." Sherburn's erroneous note postulates that "Mr. Howard thought, all things considered, some honours or a place were his due."[39] Walpole's annotation to Mrs Howard's letter to Swift, however, succinctly describes her dilemma: "She did not dare to stir out of the palace, for fear of being seized by her Husband."

A similarly telling marginal comment by Walpole on Swift's correspondence is that on a letter from Bolingbroke of February 1727, which contains the remark: "satire on one side, and defamation on the other. Ah! *ou est Grillon?*" In his edition of Swift's correspondence, Ball claims that the "allusion is to the speech in which the King of Brobdingnag thanked Gulliver, whom he called Grildrig, or mannikin, for his exposition of the British Constitution." Williams follows Ball, but introduces two errors: writing "Gildrig" for Grildrig and implying that the King of Brobdingnag coined the name, rather than hearing it from Glumdalclitch. But Ball's explanation is in any case clearly wrong; why should Bolingbroke adopt the *persona* of the Brobdingnagian king, while addressing Swift in French? Walpole's gloss solves the problem: "The brave Crillon in his old age hearing a sermon on Christ's passion, started up in a rage & cried, ah! Crillon ou etais tu alors?"[40] Williams, like all previous Swift editors, failed to recognize the allusion to the famous French warrior Louis Balbis de Berton de Crillon (1543–1615). Bolingbroke, who married a Frenchwoman and spent twenty years of his life in France, expected Swift, who read widely in French himself, to appreciate references of this kind.[41] And Walpole, whose favourite writers were French, shared a cultural milieu with Swift and his circle that is alien to most modern anglophone scholars.

Walpole's Swift marginalia are not always, of course, as *à point* as his gloss on Crillon, and at times he errs as badly as Hawkesworth himself. In a letter to Archbishop King of August 1711, Swift states in cryptic fashion that Harley and Bolingbroke "vary a little about their notions of a certain general." Williams tentatively identifies the general as Marlborough, although it is possible that Swift was alluding to John Hill.[42] Walpole's suggestion

[37] Mrs Howard to Swift, 16 August 1727, *Letters*, II, 3; *Correspondence*, III, 231.

[38] See Lewis Melville, *Lady Suffolk and her Circle* (London, 1924), pp. 156–72. Walpole also writes about the life of Mrs Howard and her marital difficulties in his "Anecdotes of Lady Suffolk" (?1752), *Yale Edition*, XXXI, 419–22, and in *Reminiscences*, ed. Toynbee, pp. 58–69, 101–2.

[39] Pope to Mrs Howard, October 1727, *The Correspondence of Alexander Pope*, ed. George Sherburn, 5 vols (Oxford, 1956), II, 446.

[40] Bolingbroke to Swift, 17 February 1727, *Letters*, I, 355; *Correspondence*, III, 199; *The Correspondence of Jonathan Swift*, ed. F. Elrington Ball, 6 vols (London, 1910–14), III, 379n4.

[41] For Swift's knowledge of French, much inferior, of course, to that of Bolingbroke, see David Woolley, "Swift's Letter to Desfontaines, 1727: The Autograph First Draft," *Swift Studies*, 2 (1987), 107–13.

[42] Swift to King, 26 August 1711, *Works*, VII, pt 2, 67; *Correspondence*, I, 249. I owe the suggestion of John Hill, brother to Lady Masham and commander of the ill-fated Canadian expedition, to F. P. Lock.

of the Duke of Ormonde, however, is clearly wrong; in 1711 Swift would certainly not term the then Lord Lieutenant of Ireland a general.

In another instance, astonishingly, Walpole mistakes Lord Bathurst for Bolingbroke, filling in the latter's name for a letter from Lord B to Swift of June 1730. In this letter, Bathurst writes of the delights of rural retirement: "This dominion, which I prefer to any other, has taken up my time from morning to night." So eager is Walpole to convict the loathed Bolingbroke of hypocrisy that he contrives to misread Bathurst's thoroughly coarse and unliterary prose for Bolingbroke's polished cadences. A scornful marginal exclamation mark here, intended to indicate incredulity at Bolingbroke's boasting of the joys of retirement, is thus completely misplaced.[43] Walpole's personal involvement with the material at hand, which elsewhere gives him insights that modern editors lack, in this case does the opposite and makes his annotation otiose.

Walpole's letters provide copious further commentary on Swift, his correspondence, and his other writings, notably *Gulliver's Travels*. In a letter to George Montagu of June 1766, Walpole discusses the volumes of Swift's correspondence in Hawkesworth's edition that he has just acquired. Here, still more plainly than in his marginalia, Walpole's antipathy to Swift becomes apparent. The collection, he tells Montagu, is amusing "though abominable, for there are letters of twenty persons now alive;" Swift is "that brute, who hated everybody that he hoped would get him a mitre and did not."[44] In this letter, too, Walpole comments on both Vanessa and Stella. Alluding to Swift's letter to Vanessa of July 1722, Walpole claims that Swift "lay with her, notwithstanding his supposed incapacity, yet not doing much honour to that capacity, for he says he can drink coffee but once a week, and I think you will see very clearly what he means by coffee."[45] Although Williams, characteristically, offers no comment on the passage, Walpole's interpretation has been both upheld and attacked by other Swiftians.[46] Turning to Stella, Walpole describes Swift's journal as "a fund of entertainment. You will see his insolence in full colours, and at the same time how daily vain he was of being noticed by the ministers he affected to treat arrogantly."[47] Montagu, for his part, was "much pleased" with many of Swift's letters, correspondence being "the only sort of reading I can relish."[48] In another letter he added, "Swift's letters have ... amused me all this winter. 'Tis the kind of writing that animates me most; and I had rather read of the knaves of former days than hear of the fools of these."[49]

---

[43] Bathurst to Swift, 30 June 1730, *Letters*, II, 27; *Correspondence*, III, 400.

[44] Walpole to Montagu, 20 June 1766, *Yale Edition*, X, 218. For Walpole's close control over the publication of his own writings, see Peter Sabor, ed., *Horace Walpole: The Critical Heritage* (London and New York, 1987), pp. 3–12, and "'An Old Tragedy on a Disgusting Subject': Horace Walpole and *The Mysterious Mother*," *Writing and Censorship in Britain*, eds Paul Hyland and Neil Sammells (London and New York, 1992), pp. 91–106.

[45] *Yale Edition*, X, 219; Swift to Esther Vanhomrigh, *Letters*, II, 214; *Correspondence*, II, 430.

[46] See *Yale Edition*, X, 218n8. David Nokes suggests that the many "coffee" references in Swift's correspondence with Vanessa "probably do not refer to intercourse, but rather to a special sexually-charged sense of intimacy that originated at their first meeting at Dunstable when Vanessa spilt some coffee;" see *Jonathan Swift, A Hypocrite Reversed: A Critical Biography* (London, 1985), p. 258. The sexual charge of "coffee," which initiated Walpole's interpretation, derives from the fact that some brothels in eighteenth-century London masqueraded as coffee-houses.

[47] *Yale Edition*, X, 219.

[48] Montagu to Walpole, 12 July 1766, *Yale Edition*, X, 223.

[49] Montagu to Walpole, 16 December 1766, *Yale Edition*, X, 239.

Since abusing Swift in letters to Montagu was clearly a lost cause, Walpole turned to two other correspondents. In a letter to Horace Mann of May 1767, he again insisted on the evil of publishing "private letters, while the persons concerned in them are living," and cited the case of his friend, the Countess of Suffolk, who a year ago had "found herself in some disagreeable letters of Swift."[50] When two further volumes of Swift's correspondence were published in the following year, Walpole renewed his assault in a letter to Thomas Gray. The second volume, he wrote,

> is the dullest heap of trumpery, flattery, and folly. The first is curious indeed! what a man! what childish, vulgar stuff! what gross language to his goddess! what a curious scene when the ministry thought themselves ruined! what cowardice in such a bully! – then his libels, and his exciting the ministers to punish libels in the same breath! – the next moment generous and benevolent.[51]

Walpole's intense hostility towards Swift here is matched by other passages in his letters and journals. In his "Anecdotes Written in 1765," he cites Swift's attitude to Oxford and Bolingbroke as a prototype of insolence.[52] In a letter printed in the *Public Advertiser* for August 1767, he found a perverse way to commend Swift's and Bolingbroke's wit: they "would not have disliked to have had a few throats cut in an insurrection," but they "made their countrymen laugh, at the moment that they offered them daggers."[53] And in a similarly backhanded compliment, Walpole observed to John Pinkerton that "a style may be excellent without grace – for instance, Dr Swift's."[54]

In 1780, fourteen years after acquiring Hawkesworth's edition of Swift's correspondence, Walpole was still recoiling in disgust. In a letter to Horace Mann, he wrote:

> Last night at Strawberry Hill, I took up, to divert my thoughts, a volume of letters to Swift from Bolinbroke, Bathurst and Gay – and what was there but lamentations on the ruin of England – in that era of its prosperity and peace, from wretches who thought their own want of power a proof that their country was undone! Oh, my father! twenty years of peace, and credit, and happiness, and liberty, were punishments to rascals who weighed everything in the scales of self!

The railing continues for another sixteen lines. Pope, though "leagued with such a crew," is compared favourably to the "arch-fiend" Bolingbroke and the "malignant" Swift, but Walpole's hero, of course, is his father, with his "temperance and steady virtue, and unalterable good humour, and superior wisdom." In a lengthy postscript, Walpole turns to his father's adversaries again:

> Swift was a wild beast, who baited and worried all mankind almost, because his intolerable arrogance, vanity, pride, and ambition were disappointed – he abused Lady Suffolk who tried and wished to raise him, only because she had not power to do so ... Such were the men who wrote of virtue to one another.[55]

Mann had long been Walpole's correspondent of choice for such anti-Swift and pro-Sir-Robert ruminations. When Swift's *History of the Four Last Years of the Queen* was pub-

---

[50]   Walpole to Mann, 30 May 1767, *Yale Edition*, XXII, 524.

[51]   Walpole to Gray, 8 March 1768, *Yale Edition*, XIV, 183.

[52]   See *Yale Edition*, VII, 354.

[53]   *Public Advertiser*, 28 August 1767; *Yale Edition*, XLII, 499.

[54]   Walpole to Pinkerton, 26 June 1785, *Yale Edition*, XVI, 269.

[55]   Walpole to Mann, 13 January 1780, *Yale Edition*, XXV, 6–8.

lished in 1758, Walpole at once wrote to Mann, telling him that "Pope and Lord Bolingbroke always told [Swift] it would disgrace him, and persuaded him to burn it. Disgrace him indeed it does, being a weak libel, ill-written for style, uninformed, and adopting the most errant mob stories."[56] A few weeks later, Walpole assured Mann that Swift's *History* had "already fallen into the lowest contempt," and then expanded these remarks in the second edition of his *Catalogue of Royal and Noble Authors*.[57]

Such vituperation, however, reveals only one side of Walpole's attitude to Swift. There is an "alternative view" of Swift in Walpole's letters, which consists in part, surprisingly, of Walpole's coming to Swift's defence.[58] In a letter to Mann of June 1742, for example, Walpole remarks on Lady Pomfret's incomprehension of one of his own anecdotes, and in doing so compares himself indirectly to Swift: "The grave personage! It was of a piece with her saying, 'that Swift would have written better, if he had never written ludicrously.'"[59] Writing again to Mann in May 1760, Walpole belittles Lord Lyttelton's newly published *Dialogues of the Dead*, declaring that "he is as angry too at Swift, Lucian and Rabelais, as if they had laughed at him like all men living."[60] Thirty years later, Walpole took umbrage at Samuel Johnson's criticisms of Gray's poetry, as reported in Boswell's *Life*, and added: "The same oracle dislikes Prior, Swift and Fielding. If an elephant could write a book, perhaps one that had read a great deal would say that an Arabian horse is a very clumsy ungraceful animal."[61] Walpole was probably reacting here to Johnson's notorious remark about *Gulliver's Travels*, "When once you have thought of big men and little men, it is very easy to do all the rest."[62] It is intriguing to find Walpole seeking derogatory epithets to characterize not Swift but Swift's enemies: "the grave personage" for Lady Pomfret, "t'other noble author" for Lord Lyttelton, and "the same oracle" for Johnson.

It is also remarkable to find Walpole's correspondents linking him with Swift in various ways. Perhaps the first to do so was the Marquis de Saint-Simon, who met Walpole in 1755 and shortly after sent him a manuscript translation of *A Tale of a Tub* to annotate, polish, and correct.[63] Walpole, who evidently declined the task, was nonetheless amused, telling Richard Bentley in a letter of August 1755 "it is my fault if I am not a commentator and a corrector of the press."[64] Walpole goes on to cite some glaring errors in Saint-Simon's translation, and in doing so becomes, however briefly, a close analyst of Swift's text – a work to which he alludes nowhere else in his surviving letters.

Another unexpected association between Swift and Walpole was made in the second number of John Wilkes's weekly paper *The North Briton*, in June 1762. Writing in the voice of a patriotic Scot in order to ridicule the newly appointed prime minister Bute, himself a Scot, Wilkes declares:

---

[56]  Walpole to Mann, 21 March 1758, *Yale Edition*, XXI, 184–85.
[57]  Walpole to Mann, 10 May 1758, *Yale Edition*, XXI, 201; Walpole, *Works*, I, 430.
[58]  Welcher, "Horace Walpole," p. 47.
[59]  Walpole to Mann, 30 June 1742, *Yale Edition*, XVII, 477.
[60]  Walpole to Mann, 24 May 1760, *Yale Edition*, XXI, 408.
[61]  Walpole to Mary Berry, 26 May 1791, *Yale Edition*, XI, 277.
[62]  James Boswell, *Life of Johnson*, ed. George Birkbeck Hill, rev. L. F. Powell, 6 vols (Oxford, 1934–64), II, 319.
[63]  See Marquis de Saint-Simon to Walpole, 19 July 1755, *Yale Edition*, XL, 82–83. Walpole's reply has not survived; the translation was not published, and is not known to be extant.
[64]  Walpole to Bentley, 4 August 1755, *Yale Edition*, XXXV, 241.

We are certainly growing into fashion ... Mr Horace Walpole, in that deep book called *Royal and Noble Authors*, says we are *the most accomplished nation in Europe* ... How faithful is this masterly pen of Mr Walpole! How unlike the odious, sharp, and strong incision-pen of Swift! who has only called us *a poor, fierce, northern* people.[65]

A direct contrast is thus made between works by Swift and by Walpole: Swift's *Public Spirit of the Whigs* (1714), from which the phrase "a poor, fierce, northern people" is taken, and Walpole's *Catalogue of Royal and Noble Authors* (1758), which has a brief but surprisingly complimentary preface to a section on Scottish authors.[66] In his "Short Notes on my Life" (1779), Walpole answered at some length the charge of having flattered Scotland to gain favour with the prime minister, without, however, taking notice of the contrast made between himself and Swift.[67] A less invidious comparison is made by Hannah More in a letter to Walpole of April 1785. More contrasts the present-day corruption of English prose style with "the courtly ease of the style of Addison, the sinewy force and clear precision of Swift, and the elegant vigour of a work well known to, but not duly appreciated by Mr Walpole, called *The Castle of Otranto*." Again, however, Walpole chose not to respond to the comparison between his writing and Swift's, both of which, More declared, provided "models of good taste in their several species of composition."[68]

When his thoughts turned to *Gulliver's Travels*, however, rather than to Swift's letters or his political writings, Walpole was ready to find links between himself and his predecessor. Both his gothic novel *The Castle of Otranto* (1765) and his *Account of the Giants Lately Discovered* (1766), a satire of contemporary accounts of Patagonian giants said to be some ten feet tall, draw on the images of magnification in the first two books of *Gulliver's Travels*. Walpole himself acknowledged his debt, in letters and in the text of *An Account of the Giants*. Insisting on the veracity of his story, the putative author of Walpole's satire advises us not to "take the relation for some political allegory, or think it a new-vamped edition of Swift's Brobdignags." Unlike Swift in Book One of *Gulliver's Travels*, who shows the King's mathematicians calculating that Gulliver would require as much food as 1,728 Lilliputians, Walpole's mock author declares: "Do not go and compute by Gulliver's measures, and tell me, that a populous nation of such dimensions would devour the products of such a country as Great Tartary in half a year."[69] Ostensibly contrasting his satire with Swift's work, Walpole is, of course, using *Gulliver's Travels* to demonstrate the absurdity of travellers' tales about the Patagonians; his giants are no more real than the Brobdingnagians, or than Gulliver in relation to the Lilliputians.

In a letter of November 1782, Walpole wrote to Lady Ossory of his love of "gigantic ideas," while assuring her that he is "not going to write a second part to the *Castle of Otranto*, nor another account of the Patagonians who inhabit the new Brobdignag planet" Uranus.[70] The comment reveals Walpole's awareness of the relationship between *Otranto* and the *Account of the Giants* and of their common connection with *Gulliver*. *Otranto* is filled with Brobdingnagian appurtenances, beginning with the "enormous helmet" that dashes Manfred's son Conrad to pieces and concluding with a gigantic apparition that causes

---

65  Wilkes, *The North Briton*, 2 (1762); cited in *Yale Edition*, XIII, 37n251.

66  See *Prose Works*, VIII, 49, and Walpole, *Works*, I, 492.

67  See *Yale Edition*, XIII, 37–38.

68  More to Walpole, c. 4 April 1785, *Yale Edition*, XXXI, 224.

69  Walpole, *An Account of the Giants*, Works, II, 94, 97.

70  Walpole to Lady Ossory, 5 November 1782, *Yale Edition*, XXXIII, 364–65.

the castle walls to collapse: "The form of Alfonso, dilated to an immense magnitude, appeared in the centre of the ruins."[71]

In her article on Walpole and *Gulliver's Travels*, Jeanne Welcher observes that "Walpole's characteristic practice was to discover a parallel, usually comical or satiric, between some immediate event and a Gulliverian one."[72] To this, I would add that the event in question often involved Walpole himself. On several occasions, he writes of the Lilliputian qualities of his beloved Strawberry Hill. When the bulky Duke of Cumberland, nicknamed Nolkejumskoi by Walpole, visited Strawberry Hill in 1754, Walpole wrote to Richard Bentley: "I can't conceive how he entered it. I should have figured him like Gulliver cutting down some of the largest oaks in Windsor Forest to make jointstools, in order to straddle over the battlements and peep in at the windows of Lilliput."[73] Conversely, to characterize his reception in Paris in 1766 after the publication of his mock letter from the King of Prussia, satirizing Rousseau, Walpole depicted himself as the Gulliver of Book Two: "There was I dandled about, with my little legs and arms shaking like a *pantin* ... I thought at last I should have a box quilted for me like Gulliver, be set upon the dressing-table of a maid of honour and fed with bonbons."[74]

Although Walpole once referred to *Gulliver's Travels* as a "national satire,"[75] his letters show that he conceived of the work in imagistic rather than narrowly political terms. In addition to his preoccupation with questions of scale and size – Lilliputian being used as a synonym for delicate, graceful, and stylish, and Brobdingnagian for anything he found in bad taste – Walpole alludes to particular scenes from the *Travels:* the dispute between Big-Endians and Small-Endians in Lilliput; Gulliver the man-mountain capturing the Blefuscudan fleet; Gulliver's three-minute urinary extinction of the fire at the Lilliputian palace; and Gulliver's making a comb out of the King of Brobdingnag's shaven bristles, and a chair seat out of the Queen's combings.[76] Walpole alludes infrequently in his correspondence to the Houyhnhnms and not at all to the Yahoos; and in Book Three is concerned almost exclusively with the Struldbruggs.

The Struldbruggs are "the single Gulliverian image most cited by Walpole."[77] He first referred to himself as a Struldbrugg at the age of forty-five, remarking to his correspondent Horace Mann in valetudinarian terms that "few think themselves so old as I do at five and forty."[78] Intriguingly, Swift was only two years older when, he told Bolingbroke, "I began to think of death; and the reflections upon it now begin when I wake in the Morning, and end

---

71  Horace Walpole, *The Castle of Otranto*, ed. W. S. Lewis (London, 1964), pp. 17, 108.

72  Welcher, "Horace Walpole," p. 48.

73  Walpole to Bentley, 2 March 1754, *Yale Edition*, XXXV, 161.

74  Walpole to Anne Pitt, 19 January 1766, *Yale Edition*, XXXI, 100; *Prose Works*, XI, 118–19 (II, v, 6–7).

75  Walpole to Mason, 12 May 1778, *Yale Edition*, XXVIII, 391–92.

76  Walpole to Bentley, 6 March 1755; Walpole to Mason, 28 September 1779; Walpole to Montagu, 18 May 1748; Walpole to Mann, 6 August 1744; *Yale Edition*, XXXV, 212, XXVIII, 467, IX, 55, XVIII, 495. See *Prose Works*, XI, 49–50 (I, iv, 5), 51–53 (I, v, 1–3), 56 (I, v, 9), 125 (II, vi, 1–2).

77  Welcher, "Horace Walpole," p. 49. Welcher exaggerates, however, in stating that the Struldbruggs are "very very rarely noticed by other eighteenth-century writers." Williams's *Critical Heritage* volume contains discussions of the Struldbruggs by, *inter alia*, Lord Orrery (1752), Hawkesworth (1755), and W. H. Dilworth (1758), pp. 126, 152–53, 170.

78  Walpole to Mann, 20 December 1762, *Yale Edition*, XXII, 110, 111.

when I am going to Sleep."[79] Walpole, too, dwelt on his putative proximity to death for the remaining thirty-four years of his life. Repeatedly playing variations on the Struldbrugg theme, he depicted himself at fifty-seven as having "lived past my time ... the only one of my contemporaries with whom I began the world;" at sixty as having "long taken my doctor's degree in Strulbruggism;" at sixty-six as "very well content to be a Strulbrug, and to *exist* after I had done *being*;" and at seventy-seven as "lamenting the loss of my cotemporaries, as if the world ought to be peopled by us Strulbrugs. It would be a dull world indeed, and all conversation would consist of our old stories."[80]

In a strange and rather moving fashion, the Struldbruggs seem to have united Swift and Walpole. A letter to Mann of 1784 contains an especially revealing passage in which Walpole, "attached to Being but by few threads," Madame du Deffand, his "dear old friend," who "often said she did not understand modern French," and Swift himself are all portrayed as Struldbruggs. The passage concludes with Walpole declaring that "Swift was out of humour with many words coined in his own time – a common foible with elderly men, who seem to think that everything was in perfection when they entered the world, and could not be altered but for the worse."[81] Walpole could as well be speaking of himself. A year later, in a letter to Lady Ossory, Walpole writes:

> How you will be disappointed on receiving, instead of a letter, the reflections of a Strulbrug on his own inanity. When Swift drew the character, he did not know it – poor man! the turbulence of his own temper, and the apprehensions of his own decay, made him conceive it as a miserable condition – on the contrary it is almost a gay one.[82]

Walpole's concern here is less to explicate Swift's portrayal of the Struldbruggs than to rewrite them in his own manner: less to interpret than, in Bloomian terms, to create a necessary "misprision," a strong misreading of a work by his father's antagonist.

There are several indications in his correspondence that Walpole regarded himself as a rewriter as well as a reader of Swift. In a letter to Madame du Deffand of May 1774, he wrote of his plans for creating a pastoral in which a shepherd would speak of Jupiter, with its four moons:

> Je vais plus loin; je me suis imaginé que dans ce monde-là, tout est dans une proportion quadruple; par conséquent qu'une belle femme a quatre paires d'yeux, et ainsi du reste. Vous voyez qu'un tel système fournit plus que les pigmées, et les géants de Gulliver.[83]

Madame du Deffand, who would later tell Walpole of her low opinion of *Gulliver's Travels*, was unimpressed by the scheme,[84] whereupon Walpole took up the idea with another cor-

---

[79]  Swift to Bolingbroke, 31 October 1729, *Correspondence*, III, 354.

[80]  Walpole to Mason, 3 April 1755, 15 May 1778; Walpole to Conway, 25 June 1784; Walpole to Lady Ossory, 6 October 1794; *Yale Edition*, XXVIII, 186, 397; XXXIX, 415, XXXIV, 205.

[81]  Walpole to Mann, 1 November 1784, *Yale Edition*, XXV, 538 and n. 2.

[82]  Walpole to Lady Ossory, 7 June 1785, *Yale Edition*, XXXIII, 464.

[83]  Walpole to du Deffand, 1 May 1774, *Yale Edition*, VI, 47. For the phenomenon of eighteenth-century Gulliveriana, see Welcher's article on Walpole and *Gulliver's Travels*, and Welcher, "Gulliver in the Market-Place," *Studies on Voltaire and the Eighteenth Century*, 217 (1983), 125–39. See also *Gulliveriana*, eds Jeanne K. Welcher and George E. Bush, Jr, 8 vols (Gainesville, FL, and Delmar, NY, 1970–88).

[84]  See du Deffand to Walpole, 8 May 1774, 15 July 1780, *Yale Edition*, VI, 49, VII, 237; see also n. 2 above.

respondent, William Mason. Mason should, Walpole suggested, write an idyll, elegy, ec-
logue, or romance set in Saturn or Jupiter, with "Celias having their everything quadrupled
– which would form a much more entertaining rhapsody than Swift's thought of magnifying
or diminishing the species in his *Gulliver*."[85]

Neither Mason nor Walpole pursued this project further. Walpole had, however, already
written a miniature sequel to *Gulliver's Travels*, sent in a letter to Lady Ossory of December
1771. This story, depicting a war between giants and fairies that ends with the extinction of
both parties, is less than a thousand words in length: a Lilliput to Swift's Brobdingnagian
*Gulliver*. It contains parallels with scenes from Book One of the *Travels*, such as a giant's
holding up a fairy who fears he is going to devour her, but no direct references to Swift
beyond the title.[86] Walpole's *Hieroglyphic Tales*, published in a Lilliputian edition of six
copies in 1785, is also in part a response to *Gulliver's Travels* and to *A Tale of a Tub*. The
first of the tales, whose hero is a five-foot emperor described by his courtiers as a giant, is
told by what Kenneth Gross aptly describes as a "momentarily Swiftian narrator" who
"warns us that he will write an abusive treatise about any man who questions his information
about oviparous goats."[87] The same narrator provides a solemn preface to the collection,
longer than most of the tales, promising that one hundred thousand copies will be printed
"lest the work should be lost to posterity."[88] Another hieroglyphic tale, not included in
Walpole's edition, contains a "vast Vermilion Baboon, as [*sic*] least ten feet high ... eagerly
gazing" at the heroine's undergarments, an inverted allusion to the female Yahoo "inflamed
by Desire" for a naked Gulliver.[89]

In a letter of 1737 to Walpole, then a student at Cambridge, his boyhood friend and
fellow-student Thomas Gray declared gnomically that "crowned heads and heads *mouton-
nées*, scald heads and lousy heads, quack heads and cane heads must all come together to the
grave, as the famous Abou-saïd has elegantly hinted in his Persian madrigals."[90] Nineteen
years later, in a letter to Montagu, Walpole revised Gray's utterance so that the heads came
to disgrace instead of the grave, attributing it not to Gray's fictitious source Abou-saïd but
instead to "St Jonathan Swift."[91] Previously, in his quasi-Biblical "Lesson for the Day,"
Walpole had written: "And these things came to pass that the saying of the prophet Jonathan might be fulfilled – those that are in, shall be as those that are out; and those that are
out, as those that are in."[92] The use of Swift for purposes of mystification is appropriate.

---

[85]  Walpole to Mason, c. May 1774, *Yale Edition*, XXVIII, 160.
[86]  Walpole to Lady Ossory, 14 December 1771, *Yale Edition*, XXXII, 71–73; reprinted in Wil-
      liams, *Swift: The Critical Heritage*, pp. 189–91.
[87]  Walpole, "A New Arabian Night's Entertainment," *Hieroglyphic Tales* (1785), ed. Kenneth
      W. Gross, ARS, nos 212–13 (Los Angeles, 1982), p. v.
[88]  *Hieroglyphic Tales*, p. iii.
[89]  "The Bird's Nest," *Hieroglyphic Tales*, no pag.; *Prose Works*, XI, 266-67 (IV, viii, 6). An-
      other transcription of "The Bird's Nest" is provided by A. Dayle Wallace, "Two Un-
      published Fairy Tales by Horace Walpole," *Horace Walpole: Writer, Politician, and Con-
      noisseur*, ed. Warren Hunting Smith (New Haven and London, 1967), pp. 250–52.
[90]  Gray to Walpole, c. 12 November 1737, *Yale Edition*, XIII, 142.
[91]  Walpole to Montagu, 28 October 1756, *Yale Edition*, IX, 199.
[92]  Walpole's original version of the "Lesson for the Day" was sent to Mann in a letter of 14
      July 1742. An expanded version, including the reference to Swift, was published in *The
      Lessons for the Day* (London, 1742). See Walpole's "Short Notes," *Yale Edition*, XIII, 13,
      and *Yale Edition*, XVII, 493n15.

The creator of Onuphrio Muralto and William Marshal, the ostensible author and translator of *The Castle of Otranto*, of Xo Ho, a Chinese philosopher, and of mock letters to Rousseau from both Émile and the King of Prussia, delighted in hoaxes and reader entrapment as much as the creator of Isaac Bickerstaff and Richard Sympson.[93]

In a letter to Horace Mann of 1779 about those who "tell one lies as solemnly as Swift related his voyages to Brobdingnag and Lilliput,"[94] Walpole's ambiguous attitude to Swift – both wild beast and saint or prophet – is clearly apparent. Telling lies solemnly, that great gift for the writer of fiction, was also, in Walpole's view, the disfiguring characteristic of Swift as a political commentator. The imaginative force with which Walpole responded to both aspects of Swift gave him none of the detachment, moderation, and even-handedness that Kathleen Williams sees as essential to perceptive criticism, but it did enable Walpole to write on Swift and rewrite Swift for over fifty years, with Swiftian inventiveness, clarity, and concentration.

[93]  See the title-page of *The Castle of Otranto* (1765), Walpole's *A Letter from Xo Ho, a Chinese Philosopher at London* (1757), and his letters to Rousseau as from Émile (1766), *Yale Edition*, VIII, 117–18, and from Frederick II, King of Prussia, 23 December 1765, Frederick A. Pottle, "The Part Played by Horace Walpole and James Boswell in the Quarrel between Rousseau and Hume: A Reconsideration," *Horace Walpole*, ed. Smith, pp. 258–59.

[94]  Walpole to Mann, 11 October 1779, *Yale Edition*, XXIV, 519.

Ian Simpson Ross
*The University of British Columbia*

# Swift and the Scottish Enlightenment

ABSTRACT. Swift expressed animosity towards the Scots as a nation, but characteristically professed loving esteem for an individual Scot, Dr Arbuthnot, whose intellectual formation occurred at an early stage of the Enlightenment in Scotland. This paper discusses the love-hatred for Swift expressed by certain leaders of a later stage of the Scottish Enlightenment: Hume, Smith, Kames, Blair, Beattie, and Monboddo. A survey of their responses to Swift permits documentation of the role of these literati in the problematic admission of Swift's texts to the canon of English literature taught to university students.

Jonathan Swift could make excellent copy from his many aversions, among them the Scots, whom he roundly condemned in *The Public Spirit of the Whigs* (1714) as a "poor, fierce Northern People,"[1] avidly draining England's wealth and menacing her constitution.[2] This attack drew upon its printer a prosecution for libel, which was not pressed because censored states of the shilling pamphlet were issued, and it seems an uncensored one could not be produced in court. Nevertheless, the House of Lords petitioned Queen Anne to issue a proclamation setting a price of £300 for the detection of its author.[3] Swift made a likely story of all this in the poem "The Author upon Himself," also written in 1714, linking the episode with Anne's animosity aroused over his imprudent publication of "The Windsor Prophecy" (1711), to suggest that he was the object of a Scottish vendetta:

> The Queen incensed, his services forgot,
> Leaves him a victim to the vengeful Scot;
> Now, through the realm a proclamation spread,
> To fix a price on his devoted head.
> While innocent, he scorns ignoble flight;
> His watchful friends preserve him by a sleight.[4]

Swift's animosity towards Scotland, itself, went back to the composition of *A Tale of a Tub* (c. 1696–97, published 1704), in which it features as *Skotia*, the *"Land of Darkness,"*

---

1  *Prose Works*, VIII, 49; see also V, 294, 295, 296 *passim*.
2  See Ehrenpreis, *Dr Swift*, p. 704; more references to Swift's views on the Scots, especially in a political context, are to be found in Françoise Berrie, "Swift et l'Écosse," *Les Langues Modernes*, 62 (1968), 490–95.
3  See John Irwin Fischer, "The Legal Response to Swift's *The Public Spirit of the Whigs*," *Swift and his Contexts*, eds John Irwin Fischer, Hermann J. Real, and James Woolley (New York, 1989), pp. 21–38.
4  *Poems*, p. 164, ll. 57–62.

charged with exporting the "choicest *Inspiration*" of furious religious enthusiasm to be disploded "among the Sectaries in all Nations."[5] A basis for this charge, perhaps, lay in Swift's 1694–95 encounter with Ulster Presbyterians of Scots descent, when he was the Church of Ireland, that is, Anglican, priest, officiating at Kilroot, near Belfast. We may think of the forerunners of the Revd Ian Paisley assembling their thousands for tumid, extempore preaching and emotion-filled spiritual exercises at field meetings, contrasting with Swift reading divine services from the Anglican prayer book to handfuls of his church's communicants. It is probable that in scandalized horror at his Ulster religious rivals lies the origin of Swift's demonizing of the Presbyterians as Æolists.

It is well known, however, that after sweeping expression of hatred for groups: "all Nations professions and Communityes," Swift declared, "all my love is towards individualls." In the letter to Pope of 29 September 1725 regarding *Gulliver's Travels* (1726) which includes this declaration, Swift listed as objects of his hatred lawyers and physicians – he spared his fellow-parsons – but he continued, "Soldiers, English, Scotch, French; and the rest," in short, "that animal called man." Swift further declared he had erected his *Travels* on this "great foundation of Misanthropy," and intended to publish his book to "vex the world rather then divert it." Yet, turning to another topic, the illness of his great friend, Dr John Arbuthnot (1667–1735), and contemplating his amiable and useful qualities and virtue, Swift was prepared to write: "O, if the World had but a dozen Arbuthnets in it I would burn my Travells."[6]

Swift, so far as is known, did not acknowledge that Arbuthnot was a Scot, nor did he connect his friend's learning with a point he made in *An Essay on Modern Education* (1728), that education in Scotland was generally better than in England. This was meant to shame the English rather than praise the Scots. Far from being entirely a "*Land of Darkness*," Arbuthnot's native country could give him an effective training in mathematics, one of the primary disciplines of the sustained intellectual revolution that we know as the Enlightenment. Its early progress in Scotland can be traced, for example, from the record of Edinburgh imprints bought for Göttingen University Library. Up to the 1680s, there appeared mostly works of mind-darkening polemical divinity, supporting Swift's view of Scotland, but thereafter came a sequence of works on herb gardening relating to medical investigation, geometry, legal thought, and moral philosophy.[7] On coming to London, very likely in 1691 after the death of his father, Arbuthnot found employment for some years teaching mathematics, and in 1692 he published anonymously a little book entitled, *Of the Laws of Chance*, seemingly a part translation of a work on the application of probability theory to gaming and dicing by Christiaan Huygens (1629–95): *De ratiociniis in ludo aleae*.[8] Another anonymous publication of Arbuthnot's was *An Essay on the Usefulness of Mathematical Learning*, which appeared at Oxford in 1701. In it, Arbuthnot makes the standard Enlightenment claim that studying mathematics frees the mind from "prejudice, credulity, and superstition":

---

5   See *A Tale of a Tub*, eds A. C. Guthkelch and D. Nichol Smith, 2nd ed. (Oxford, 1958), p. 155.

6   *Correspondence*, III, 102–4.

7   See Graham Jeffcoate and Karen Kloth, *A Catalogue of English Books Printed before 1801 Held by the University Library at Göttingen*, ed. Bernhard Fabian, 3 parts (Hildesheim, Zürich, New York, 1987–88).

8   See *The Life and Works of John Arbuthnot*, ed. George A. Aitken (Oxford, 1892), p. 9.

first, by accustoming us to examine, and not to take things upon trust; secondly, by giving us a clear and extensive knowledge of the system of the world; which, as it creates in us the most profound reverence of the almighty and wise Creator, so it frees us from the mean and narrow thoughts which ignorance and superstition are apt to beget.[9]

Swift himself was suspicious of the mounting ascendancy of mathematical and scientific reasoning in his time, and satirized this development in his account of the Academy of Lagado in Part III of *Gulliver's Travels*. Arbuthnot is likely to have absorbed Enlightenment views, however, in the course of his Arts degree studies at Marischal College, Aberdeen, where a Chair in Mathematics had been occupied from 1623, and the professors introduced to their students the scientific advances of Kepler, Galileo, and Descartes, then those of Newton. Indeed, the famous "mathematical Gregories" hailing from Aberdeenshire carried on this tradition in Chairs at St Andrews and Edinburgh.[10] One of the family, David Gregory (1661–1708), became in 1691 Savilian professor of astronomy at Oxford, where his friendship with Arbuthnot was confirmed, and in 1702 he published the first textbook revealing mastery of Newtonian gravitational principles: *Astronomiae physicae et geometricae elementa.*

Arbuthnot went on to contribute to the history of satire rather than science as inventor of the figure of John Bull and co-inventor of Martinus Scriblerus. Still, in the Scottish universities, the tradition of mathematical and scientific learning he upheld continued to flourish, and the professors and their students, including famously David Hume (1711–76) and Adam Smith (1723–90), responded to Newton's call at the conclusion of his *Opticks* (1704):

> And if natural Philosophy in all its Parts, by pursuing this Method [analysis through experiments and observation followed by synthesis], shall at length be perfected, the Bounds of Moral Philosophy will be also enlarged.[11]

Paradoxically, in attempting "to introduce the experimental Method of Reasoning into Moral Subjects," as Hume acknowledged in the subtitle to *A Treatise of Human Nature* (1739–40), he was driven as a cognitive scientist to espouse that "Sceptical System," which his Common Sense adversary Thomas Reid (1710–96) correctly saw opened a "large field for Wit, Humour and Ridicule."[12] Inevitably, Hume turned to Swift for guidance in this field.

As for Smith, his profession of "moral Newtonianism"[13] led him to produce a foundation work along analytic-synthetic lines on political economy, but his career as man of letters took him from a focus on rhetoric to dealing with economics. Thus, we find him at the

---

[9]  Lester M. Beattie, *John Arbuthnot: Mathematician and Satirist* (New York, 1967 [1935]), p. 327.

[10] See Ronald Gordon Cant, "Origins of the Enlightenment in Scotland: the Universities," *The Origins and Nature of the Scottish Enlightenment*, eds R. H. Campbell and Andrew S. Skinner (Edinburgh, 1982), pp. 45–46.

[11] Sir Isaac Newton, *Opticks*, ed. I. Bernard Cohen (New York, 1952), p. 405.

[12] See Kathleen Holcomb and Charles Stewart-Robertson, "On Turning Over a New Leaf: An Old Tale of Editing," *East-Central Intelligencer*, 7, no 3 (1993), 8–10.

[13] This term was coined by Elie Halévy to describe attempts to discover a principle analogous to gravitation in Newtonian celestial mechanics to establish a "synthetic science of the phenomena of moral and social life;" see *The Growth of Philosophical Radicalism* (Boston, 1955 [1928]), pp. 3, 6–7; Smith's efforts along this line are discussed in Ian Simpson Ross, *The Life of Adam Smith* (Oxford, 1995), pp. 56–57, 126, 179, 346.

outset championing and mastering Swift's style as that of the "plain man" who has acquired reliable knowledge of the world and communicates it effectively.[14]

Hume offered criticism of Swift's style as we shall find, but Smith's praise of it was echoed by other contributors to the Scottish Enlightenment. These included their patron, Henry Home, Lord Kames (1696–1782), a judge who theorized about criticism, and Smith's successor as a lecturer in rhetoric in Edinburgh, Hugh Blair (1718–1800). Yet another Aberdeen adversary of Hume, James Beattie (1735–1823), professor of moral philosophy at Marischal College, lectured to his students and the public on aspects of style and composition. Also Lord Monboddo (1714–99), speculator about the common ancestry of apes and humanity, when inquiring into the origin of language as an aptitude developed in humanity but not in apes, seized the opportunity to comment on style. Between them, Smith, Blair, Reid, and Beattie may be said to have invented English literature as a subject for university study, and for good or ill they made Swift's writings part of the canon.[15] To be sure, Beattie also heightened the clamour against Book IV of *Gulliver's Travels* as morally unhealthy.[16] From the Scottish Enlightenment's interest in Swift, then, came a problematic legacy: keen awareness of his power as a writer, some willingness to adopt his rhetorical and expressive strategies, and yet distrust of his motives and tendencies.

The complex responses of the Scottish literati to the sign "Swift" reveal how much they were both inspired and troubled by what one critic has described as features of his texts and, we may add, his biographies: "metamorphoses, ventriloquisms, and contradictions ... [a] myriad transformations [that] thwart the basic human desire to simplify and to categorize."[17] Hume, seemingly intrigued by the scatological poetry of Swift, whom he politely identifies by the title of doctor of divinity, notes in the essay, "Of the Rise and Progress of the Arts and Sciences" (1741), that one source for Swift's anti-romantic imagery is the *De rerum naturae* (IV, 1165) of Lucretius.[18] Dealing with the issue of restraints on foreign imports in "Of the Balance of Trade" (1752), Hume remembered the intelligence sometimes shown about economics by Swift, and draws attention to one of his maxims, "That, in the arithmetic of the customs, two and two make not four, but often make only one."[19] Swift made this witty point in a 1728 pamphlet entitled, *An Answer to a Paper, Called, A Memorial of the Poor Inhabitants, Tradesmen and Labourers of the Kingdom of Ireland*.[20] His argument was that heavy duties lessened imports, hence revenue, and smuggling paid off, further reducing what was supposed to be collected by the government. This contention surfaces

---

[14]  See Adam Smith, *Lectures on Rhetoric and Belles Lettres*, ed. J. C. Bryce (Oxford, 1983), pp. 36–39. The text Bryce edited for the Glasgow Edition of the Works and Correspondence of Smith is dated 1762–63, but it is not likely that Smith made many changes from the version of 1748–51; see Ross, *The Life of Adam Smith*, pp. 128–29.

[15]  See Robert Crawford, *Devolving English Literature* (Oxford, 1992), pp. 30, 33.

[16]  See Donald M. Berwick, *The Reputation of Jonathan Swift, 1781–1882* (New York, 1965 [1941]), pp. 39–40.

[17]  Ann Cline Kelly, "The Birth of 'Swift,'" *Reading Swift: Papers from The Second Münster Symposium on Jonathan Swift*, eds Richard H. Rodino and Hermann J. Real (München, 1993), p. 18.

[18]  See David Hume, *Essays Moral, Political, and Literary*, rev. ed. Eugene F. Miller (Indianapolis, 1987), p. 128 n20.

[19]  Hume, *Essays*, ed. Miller, p. 324.

[20]  *Prose Works*, XII, 21.

again, of course, in Smith's *Wealth of Nations*.[21] Elsewhere, Hume gives high praise to Swift, or so we assume, in linking his name to the assertion, in the essay "Of Civil Liberty" (1741), that the "first polite prose we have was writ by a man who is still alive."[22]

To be sure, in a letter of November or December 1768, Hume qualifies his view of Dean Swift:

> [He is a writer] whom I can often laugh with, whose style I can even approve, but surely can never admire. It has no harmony, no eloquence, no ornament, and not much correctness, whatever the English may imagine. Were not their literature still in a somewhat barbarous state, that author's place would not be so high among their classics.[23]

This critical assessment of Swift is anticipated in a characterization of him as a commentator on English politics in *Gulliver's Travels*, which Hume offers in another essay, "Of the Populousness of Ancient Nations" (1752). He writes that Swift's satire is carried to extremes, even beyond other satirists' limits, and that it is "dangerous to rely upon writers who deal in ridicule and satyre," even though Swift had some grounds for attacking the vindictiveness of the Walpole Government.[24] Hume summed up his estimate of Swift in "Of the Balance of Trade": he is an "Author, who has more humour than knowledge, more taste than judgment, and more spleen, prejudice, and passion than any of these qualities."[25] But this negative assessment is still not the end of the story of Swift and Hume. A letter of February 1751, within a year of the publication of the *Political Discourses* (14 January 1752) just quoted, reveals that Hume wished to write in the vein of Swift:

> I have frequently had it in my Intentions to write a Supplement to *Gulliver*, containing the Ridicule of Priests. 'Twas certainly a Pity that Swift was a Parson. Had he been a Lawyer or Physician, we had nevertheless been entertain'd at the Expense of these Professions. But Priests are so jealous, that they cannot bear to be touch'd on that Head; and for a plain Reason: Because they are conscious they are really ridiculous. That Part of the Doctor's Subject is so fertile, that a much inferior Genius, I am confident, might succeed in it.[26]

Nevertheless, Hume demonstrates in his philosophical writings that he read Swift and his satiric precursors with care.[27] For example, in the essay "Of Miracles," Hume deals with the topic of what made priests "really ridiculous" in his eyes: their traffic in alleged suspensions of the laws of nature, involving attempts to found their authority on interpretations of these astonishing events. In this piece, Hume illustrates those "metamorphoses, ventriloquisms, and contradictions" so memorably associated with Swift. "Of Miracles" opens in the voice of an Anglican apologist deferring to the reasoning of grave Archbishop Tillotson subverting the claims for transubstantiation, but also those for all miracles if the reader presses the implications of what Tillotson has to say. The essay's voice shifts to calm, probabilistic reasoning, echoing the kind of discourse found in Arbuthnot's book on games of chance.

---

[21] See Adam Smith, *An Inquiry into the Nature and Causes of the Wealth of Nations*, eds R. H. Campbell, A. S. Skinner, and W. B. Todd, 2 vols (Oxford, 1976), II, 884 (V, ii, k).

[22] *Essays*, ed. Miller, p. 91.

[23] *The Letters of David Hume*, ed. J. Y. T. Greig, 2 vols (Oxford, 1969 [1932]), II, 194.

[24] *Essays*, ed. Miller, p. 414 n100.

[25] *Essays*, ed. Miller, p. 633, quoting 1st and 2nd editions of *Political Discourses* (Edinburgh, 1752).

[26] *Letters*, ed. Greig, I, 153.

[27] See Ian S. Ross, "Hume's Language of Scepticism," *Hume Studies*, 21 (1995), 237–54.

Next, we have the Pentateuch's miraculous stories examined according to the principles of the Christian rationalists.[28] This procedure reduces such episodes to a bundle of absurdities. Thereafter, the conclusion blandly insists that a "continued miracle" is required for a person to maintain faith in the *Christian Religion*. It is a dizzying performance, worthy of being linked to Swift's own *Argument against Abolishing Christianity*, surely one of Hume's literary models.

"Of Miracles" was composed in the 1730s but published first in 1748, as a section of *Philosophical Essays Concerning Human Understanding*, later (in 1758) renamed *An Enquiry Concerning Human Understanding*, and usually so named thereafter. Also in 1748, three years after Swift's death, there appeared the first volume of Mrs Laetitia Pilkington's *Memoirs*, incorporating personal reminiscences of Swift's odd humour and, at times, exceedingly bizarre behaviour, which helped to feed the biographical tradition of an unhinged, even satanic personality.[29] In 1752, John Boyle, fifth Earl of Orrery, published *Remarks on the Life and Writings of Dr. Jonathan Swift*, a book which offers some genuine criticism of its subject's writings, but consistently attacks him as "sour, envious, vain, depraved, cruel, stupidly ambitious, and so mad that his giddiness at last rendered him the 'exact image of one of his own *Struldbruggs*, a miserable spectacle.'"[30]

Between 1748 and 1751, when this dubious posthumous characterization of Swift was created, Adam Smith was prevailed on by Henry Home, an advocate later to be raised to the Bench as Lord Kames, to give free-lance lectures on rhetoric and belles lettres to students, young ministers, and lawyers resident in and around Edinburgh. These lectures proved highly successful, and Smith was elected to a professorship first of logic then of moral philosophy at Glasgow, where he repeated his rhetoric course, again to much acclaim. Successors were found at Edinburgh, among them Hugh Blair, who was appointed to a Regius Chair in rhetoric, which initiated in a formal sense university teaching of English literature and composition. George III may have lost Britain the American colonies, but perhaps he did a wiser thing in promoting English studies by his timely patronage. To be sure, it has recently been argued that Smith and Blair and Beattie and their successors pushed English literature so hard that native Scots writing was disvalued, and Scottish culture was given a vast inferiority complex. An additional point made is that the teaching of English literature reinforced the English political hegemony, and served the interests of the Hanoverian fiscal-military state, which by this time was embarked on the course of English imperialism.[31]

There is some justification for this view, and it is certainly fashionable in these days of post-colonial *angst*, but it is far too simple a version of facts and tendencies. Above all, it neglects what Smith was teaching in his lectures on composition and literary criticism, and what was widely copied in the other Scottish universities, by Blair and Beattie, for example,

---

[28]  For example, the Protestant rationalists of the later seventeenth century (Taylor, Barrow, Cudworth, Leighton) discussed by Sir Leslie Stephen in *History of English Thought in the Eighteenth Century*, 2 vols (New York and Burlingame, 1962 [1902]), I, 66–68, and their French Catholic counterparts discussed by Alan Charles Kors in "The French Context of Hume's Philosophical Theology," *Hume Studies*, 21 (1995), 221–36.

[29]  See *Memoirs of Mrs Laetitia Pilkington*, ed. A. C. Elias, Jr, 2 vols (Athens and London, 1997).

[30]  John Boyle, *Remarks on the Life and Writings of Dr. Jonathan Swift* (London, 1752), p. 19; see also Berwick, *The Reputation of Jonathan Swift*, p. 4.

[31]  See Crawford, *Devolving English Literature*, pp. 16–44.

also in the universities emerging in the American colonies such as Princeton. Smith took great pains with his own writing, and the lesson he wished to impart to his students was that writers should aim to be *perspicuous* or, as we would say, *transparent*. He had no time for the usual books on rhetoric, dwelling on a thousand and one figures of speech. He regarded that practice as "silly." Smith's own approach reveals his accurate knowledge of human nature:

> When the sentiment of the speaker [we can add, *and writer*] is expressed in a neat, clear, plain and clever manner, and the passion or affection he is possessed of and intends, *by sympathy*, to communicate to his hearer [*and reader*], is plainly and cleverly hit off, then and then only the expression has all the force and beauty that language can give it.[32]

The stress here is on the communicative, emotive force of language transacting its business effectively. Commentators have been right to see a parallel between Smith's system of rhetoric and that of ethics, in which the operation of the mechanism of *sympathy* is the basis for the formation of moral judgments:

> When we approve of any character or action, the sentiments which we feel are ... derived from four sources, which are in some respects different from one another. First, we sympathize with the motives of the agent; secondly, we enter into the gratitude of those who receive the benefit of his actions; thirdly, we observe that his conduct has been agreeable to the general rules by which those two sympathies generally act; and, last of all, when we consider such actions as making a part of a system of behaviour which tends to promote the happiness either of the individual or of the society, they appear to derive a beauty from this utility, not unlike that which we ascribe to any well-contrived machine.[33]

Setting aside speculation about the merry work Swift would have made of Smith's utilitarian "system of behaviour," as yet another example of vaunting of the "mechanical operation of the spirit" disploded from *Skotia*, discussion here will concentrate on the linguistic situation Smith was addressing in his rhetoric lectures. There was a wide discrepancy between what his Scottish auditors spoke as a dialect and standard received English, current among the upper classes in southern England and reflected in print.

Smith focuses on three writers who could be viewed as model writers of standard English by the Scots. One is Shaftesbury, who might have been thought attractive to Smith because of his affiliation with the moral sense school of philosophy founded by the noble lord. Smith dismisses Shaftesbury as "no great reasoner," however, and criticizes his style as prolix and pompous.[34] The second model writer is Sir William Temple, regarded in England from early in the eighteenth century as the "most perfect Pattern of good *Writing* and good *Breeding* this Nation hath produced."[35] In his eighth rhetoric lecture, Smith sets up an effective contrast between Temple, whom he portrays as the simple man, and that of his third model writer, Swift, whom he portrays as the plain man. Smith vindicates Swift as the best model for the Scots, even in their speculative writings on politics and morality or ethics, which he notes were taking up the attention of the men of genius in his country. This is his manner of describing the progress of the Scottish Enlightenment. What Smith finds in Swift is

---

[32] *Lectures on Rhetoric*, ed. Bryce, p. 25.
[33] Adam Smith, *The Theory of Moral Sentiments*, eds D. D. Raphael and A. L. Macfie (Oxford, 1976), p. 326.
[34] See *Lectures on Rhetoric*, ed. Bryce, pp. 57–61.
[35] Henry Felton, *A Dissertation on Reading the Classics, and Forming a Just Style*, 2nd ed. (London, 1715), p. 67.

mastery of the subject matter, consequent natural arrangement of it in the most proper order, and painting each thought "in the best and most proper manner and with the greatest strength of colouring."[36] Smith insists further that Swift can demonstrate this control in his own person or speaking through a *persona*, and with the keenest eye for the ridiculous in the objects of the plain man's scrutiny. Objections have been raised to Smith's presentation of Swift as a writer of perspicuous English on the grounds that readers have had trouble with his irony, often disagreeing about the latent meaning or meanings existing in tension with surface meaning.[37] However, this is perhaps more a matter of concern for historians of interpretation of Swift than for those who wish to learn how to write lucid, idiomatic English that expresses their intentions effectively, albeit on occasion indirectly through irony. A good example of Smith's ironic deployment of idiomatic phrasing is to be found in a maxim worthy of Swift: "There is no art which one government sooner learns of another, than that of draining money from the pockets of the people."[38]

The detailed endorsement of Swift's mastery of style in Smith's *Lectures on Rhetoric* is sustained by Kames in his influential *Elements of Criticism*, first published in 1762, and much reprinted and widely used as a college textbook on into the nineteenth century in North America.[39] Kames praised Swift's unequalled adjustment of language to subject, and his happy talent, shared with Thucydides, for making the reader an eye-witness of what is narrated, giving rise to singular "energy of style."[40] In another widely adopted textbook, *Lectures on Rhetoric and Belles Lettres*, Blair discusses, with acknowledgment to Smith, the association of Swift with the triumph of the plain style, especially in his "humorous pieces." He also upholds the tradition of Swift's difficult personality in noting that his "haughty and morose genius made him despise any embellishment [of language] ... as beneath his dignity."[41] Beattie took up the theme of identifying sections of *Gulliver's Travels* as writing that was a model of admirably simple discourse. He regarded Part IV, however, with horror:

> But when a writer endeavours to make us dislike and despise, every one his neighbour, and be dissatisfied with that Providence, who has made us what we are, and whose dispensations towards the human race are so peculiarly, and so divinely beneficent; such a writer, in so doing, proves himself the enemy, not of man only, but of goodness itself; and his work can never be allowed to be innocent, till impiety, malevolence, and misery, cease to be evils.[42]

Monboddo does not favour us with any views on the Voyage to the Country of the Houyhnhnms, but declares forthrightly that Swift has excelled in the plain style above all English authors in *Gulliver's Travels*. He takes the Voyage to Lilliput to be the best part,

---

[36] See *Lectures on Rhetoric*, ed. Bryce, pp. 41–43.

[37] See Vivienne Brown, *Adam Smith's Discourse* (London and New York, 1994), pp. 15–16.

[38] *An Inquiry into the Nature and Causes of the Wealth of Nations*, II, 861 (V, ii, h).

[39] See William Charvat, *The Origins of American Critical Thought, 1810–1835* (New York, 1961 [1936]), Chapter III; see also Ian S. Ross, *Lord Kames and the Scotland of his Day* (Oxford, 1972), p. 290; and Crawford, *Devolving English Literature*, pp. 40–41.

[40] See Henry Home, Lord Kames, *Elements of Criticism*, 5th ed., 2 vols (London, 1774), II, 348, 351.

[41] Hugh Blair, *Lectures on Rhetoric and Belles Lettres*, 14th ed. (London, 1825), p. 239.

[42] James Beattie, *Dissertations Moral and Critical* (London, 1783), p. 516; Beattie's "dissertations" or literary essays were based on his college lectures, recorded in his "Journal of Sessions," 1762–93; see Everard H. King, *James Beattie* (Boston, 1977), pp. 29–37.

"especially in what relates to the politics of that kingdom, and the state of parties there."
Perhaps discerning readers of English literature will go along with his final judgment:

> When we add … the hidden satire which it contains [on the Walpole administration], and
> the grave ridicule that runs through the whole of it, the most exquisite of all ridicule, I
> think I do not go too far when I pronounce it the most perfect work of the kind, antient
> or modern, that is to be found.[43]

If taking Swift into the canon of English literature was meant, consciously or unconsciously,
to reinforce the English hegemony, here was the admission of a Trojan horse. It is clear that
the ridicule that Swift directed at colonialism and imperialism was not lost on the author of
the *Wealth of Nations*. To be sure, Swift did not love the Scots. In the instance of Hume
and Smith, at least, they advanced his programme of requiring adroit as well as forceful,
idiomatic handling of the English language that could be understood everywhere, and sting-
ing human beings to think critically, rather than congratulate themselves on the peaceful
enjoyment of their follies.

---

[43]  [James Burnett, Lord Monboddo], *Of the Origin and Progress of Language*, III (Edinburgh,
1776), 196.

Joseph Ronsley
*McGill University, Montreal*

# Denis Johnston's Jonathan Swift

ABSTRACT. Denis Johnston had careers not only as a playwright and broadcaster, but as an academic scholar as well. In this last capacity, his major scholarly contribution was a biographical study of Jonathan Swift, one which, however, was considered too eccentric by Swift scholars to be taken seriously. Nevertheless, Johnston's interest in Swift became nearly an obsession which impinged on his own life and world view. The number of his writings about Swift is considerable, though there is an inevitable redundancy among them as he repeatedly presses his thesis. These writings were produced over a period of more than thirty years, from a radio play in 1938 to a book review in 1970: expository works in the form of several lectures, articles, and reviews, and the book *In Search of Swift*; dramatic works for stage, radio, and television. This paper is an account of Johnston's Swift experience, his motivating impulses, and the effect of that experience on him and his work. Ultimately, Johnston identified with Swift in projecting his own "savage indignation."

I am not a Swift scholar. Consequently, I feel a little uneasy over my participation in this conference, delighted as I am to be here. Not being a Swift scholar, I both enjoyed and was impressed by Denis Johnston's 1959 biographical study *In Search of Swift*. On the other hand, I understand that most of you, *being* Swift scholars, may just possibly have enjoyed it, but were *not* impressed by it. I am not entirely convinced the correct attitude here is so obvious, but it would be absurd for me to come to any biographical conclusions of my own, and in any case Swift's biography in itself is not my primary concern. I am more concerned with Johnston, and the reaction by the Swift scholarly establishment to what at least he considered his important contribution to Swift scholarship. This reaction, perhaps along with other disappointments of his life connected with the theatre and broadcasting, has contributed to a certain cynicism and bitterness that prevailed in Johnston's later life, not unlike that which characterized Swift's own old age. This is despite Johnston's very real successes in several fields of endeavour. Johnston, among other things a university teacher, clearly saw his scholarly work to be a compelling combination of original research, disciplined logical conclusions, and brilliant insights, likely to revolutionize the prevailing biographical perspective of Swift. He expected to make a considerable academic stir, and in fact had already eighteen years earlier made a minor one. The earlier one having been quite negative, however, he expected this one to be better received. It was not.

Johnston had reason to be confident in his own abilities. Before embarking on any of his various careers, he had written a dissertation for an advanced law degree at Harvard on the Anglo-Irish treaty of 1921, and in so doing satisfied his supervisor, who was to become one of the American Supreme Court's most distinguished Chief Justices. As a playwright, he had

had mixed receptions, some of his plays being highly controversial, though, disappointingly for Johnston, not so controversial as O'Casey's. He liked being provocative, but however much controversy he stirred, or did not stir, he was considered for a time by many to be the brightest new playwright talent in the Irish theatre. At this point, he left the theatre for a career in broadcasting.

Early in his new career, in March 1938, Johnston produced what was a pioneering spectacle in broadcasting, a documentary dramatization of the 1688–89 siege of Londonderry, called "Lillibulero." The programme required a year's preparation, including considerable research on an historical period that coincides with Swift's life. Then, only two months later, in June, he produced for radio the first version of his Swift play, entitled "Weep for Polyphemus," which also involved considerable historical research. Johnston's studies for the two projects overlapped, with one possibly generating the other. The Swift research may, in fact, have begun earlier. However that may be, the radio play embodied in inchoate form much of the theory that was to be developed more fully later in *In Search of Swift*.

Johnston's broadcast career, from 1936 to 1947, provided him with more satisfaction, success, and distinction than he was to know before or since. Beginning with BBC radio, he quickly moved to the infant medium of television where he helped to develop basic production techniques and in a sense actually to define the medium. During World War II, he was a BBC war correspondent, in North Africa and Continental Europe, introducing several innovations to war reporting, and after the war became the first Programme Director of BBC Television. He also wrote an artful book on his war experiences entitled *Nine Rivers from Jordan*.[1] So, with a strong sense of his own sophistication and worldliness, combined with his intellectual prowess as well as his legal and investigative reporting experience, Johnston's scholarly endeavours over Swift in the mid-1950s must have seemed to him well within his capacities. The subject was a fascinating but relatively easy challenge, and his creative work for the stage and broadcasting would allow him to give his academic production an artistic form that would make it unusually enjoyable reading for the genre.

But the fact is that Johnston had already been disappointed with the academic community's failure to take him seriously on the subject of Swift, and *In Search of Swift* is really a desperate attempt to correct matters. This book was expected to open the eyes of Swift scholars to the important revelations which he had already presented to them in various forms on several occasions over the previous twenty years. His Swift play as transcribed from radio to the stage and called *The Dreaming Dust* was produced at the Gaiety Theatre as early as 1940 by Edwards' and MacLiammoir's Dublin Gate Theatre Company, but was not published until 1954, when it was included in a book entitled *The Golden Cuckoo and Other Plays*.[2] Speaking of *The Dreaming Dust* in the introduction to that book, Johnston anticipates *In Search of Swift*:

> One would imagine that, at this distance, it is not a matter of any very great importance to suggest that Swift was a bastard. But unfortunately it involves the statement that a great many books, to which many years of study have been devoted, are at fault in their facts, and that more than one respectable tome has been written without a proper check of the original documents that it quotes. In the circumstances it is perhaps not so surprising that I have unwittingly got myself into a lot of hot water over Dr. Swift, and am unlikely to get

---

[1]  London, 1953.
[2]  London, 1954.

out of it until I have made matters worse, by writing a tome of my own – a tome studded with footnotes and terminating with a Bibliography, which, God knows, will make dull reading.[3]

This book was published five years later, though whatever else it is, most would agree it is not "dull reading."

Most would agree, that is, but not all. Frank Kermode, in his review entitled "The Dean Drank Coffee," says the book tends to be dull because of too much detail and documentation. It does seem difficult for Johnston to win. In fact, many of the reviewers do credit Johnston's painstaking research and his uncovering of many previously accepted errors. Finally, Kermode says he hopes Johnston "is right, not only because Swift deserved his coffee, but because everything that weakens the myth of his insanity helps his books to a better reading."[4]

It is not my intention to review the reviews. It is sufficient to say that the book was reviewed extensively and with considerable interest, and that the reviews were mixed, with the most serious, and ultimately the most influential, coming down against Johnston, particularly against his evidence for a January date for the death of Jonathan Swift the Elder, a date that would have made it impossible for him to be Swift's father. Other evidence and aspects of Johnston's scholarship are both praised and criticized. Johnston's speculativeness is condemned, often because it conflicts with the reviewer's own speculations. In one or two cases, it does seem that the criticism is more abusive than convincing, as in Frank Brady's "Swift: Scholarship and Fancy," in *The Yale Review*.[5] Matthew Hodgart, on the other hand, in "A Question of Paternity," has no real objection to Johnston's argument, and says that his "publication of the documents is admirably thorough," but objects to his tone, his apparently "talking crossly to himself rather than addressing the jury with the eloquence of which he is capable."[6]

Defending his endeavours in his introduction to the book, Johnston gives Hodgart the grounds for his criticism:

> For nearly twenty years I have been an unwilling target for a succession of adverse comments on a short paper that I read to the Old Dublin Society in 1941, and that subsequently appeared in the Journal of that body. And as this annoyance is a continuing one, and shows no signs of coming to an end, a man who happens to have been serious in what he said is driven eventually to make matters either worse or better by repeating his point in louder and better documented tones. As a general rule no one will ever come to one's rescue in such matters except oneself.[7]

Looking back at that Old Dublin Society paper, "The Mysterious Origin of Dean Swift,"[8] we find that it itself responds to even earlier disappointment over not being taken seriously when his thesis was artistically expressed in his 1938 radio play. In that paper he explains:

> The theory that I propose to offer as an explanation of the mystery surrounding the life of this perhaps greatest of all Dubliners is one that I embodied in a radio programme some three years ago. Although it was propounded in the most public and universal manner

---

3  *The Golden Cuckoo*, p. 16.
4  *The Spectator*, 6 November 1959, p. 639.
5  See 49 (1959), 600–2.
6  *The Guardian*, 8 November 1959.
7  *In Search of Swift*, p. ix.
8  See *Dublin Historical Record*, 3, no 4 (1941), 81–97.

known to science, no attention was paid to it whatsoever, and the whole thing was, presumably, dismissed as an invention of my own for purely dramatic purposes. Nevertheless
it was based upon several years of exceedingly interesting research in and around this City
of ours, and I am glad to have this opportunity of bringing some of the results of my
investigation to the notice of those interested in the mind that conceived *Gulliver* and the
*Drapier Letters.*[9]

As I have indicated, this paper had been preceded the previous year by *The Dreaming Dust*,
the stage adaptation of Johnston's radio play. Between the 1941 paper and the 1959 book,
the radio play was adapted for television in 1947 with the new title "Weep for the Cyclops,"
and *The Golden Cuckoo and Other Plays* was published in 1954, with its introduction and
the first publication of *The Dreaming Dust*, as one of the "other plays." In fact, Swift appears to have been approaching an obsession for Johnston, as he explored his biographical
theory in one medium after another, the only result being that in one medium he was ignored, in the other reviled. Writing in the 1954 introduction, now an academic himself, he
says with barely concealed fury:

> When originally produced on the radio – that is to say by the most universal means known
> to science, and to the largest audience possible – it produced no critical reactions what-
> soever. Nobody takes what they hear on the radio seriously, except News and invasions
> from Mars. In stage form it evoked very little more response. But then I read a short paper
> on the subject to the Old Dublin Society, which published it in its journal, at which point
> the reactions were catastrophic. I had invaded the realm of scholarship, and violent as the
> reactions of an audience may be to a Point [*sic*], they are nothing to the reactions of the
> owners of any literary Tom Tiddler's Ground, towards inter-meddlers from other depart-
> ments.[10]

So, with what to Johnston were ever more compelling arguments and evidence on the subject repeatedly being rejected, and finally not taken seriously at all, it is not difficult, for all
his urbane pretence of modesty and lofty insouciance, to imagine his frustration leading to
an almost Swiftian sense of outrage.

Not surprisingly, this outrage becomes increasingly unveiled when not even Johnston's
well documented "tome studded with footnotes and terminating with a Bibliography" is
received seriously. And nowhere is his outrage vented more clearly than in his review of
Volume I of *Swift: The Man, His Works, and the Age* by Irvin Ehrenpreis,[11] in which review,
coming four years after the publication of *In Search of Swift*, he says contemptuously:

> It is not easy to make Swift dull, and while Professor Ehrenpreis comes very close to
> performing this feat, thanks to some peculiarities in his prose, the substance of his com-
> ments on most of the Works that he has dealt with to date are both informative and help-
> ful. This applies particularly to *The Battle of the Books*, which he evidently enjoys. It is
> when he approaches the biographical snake pit that one wishes he had posted some warn-
> ing notices before inviting his students to accompany him down the primrose path leading
> to "Mr. Swift."[12]

The compliment to Professor Ehrenpreis, you will notice, is brief, mild, and sarcastic, sand-
wiched as it is between caustic criticism, which Johnston elaborates as he focuses on his own
area of painstaking research:

---

[9]  "The Mysterious Origin of Dean Swift," p. 81.
[10]  *The Golden Cuckoo*, pp. 15–16.
[11]  London and Cambridge, MA, 1962.
[12]  *The Nation*, 26 January 1963, pp. 73–76.

A sound historian might say that the best way to determine whether the residence in Dublin of Sir John Temple, Irish Master of the Rolls, during the closing years of his life, is a fable or not would be to examine the records of King's Inns, of which Sir John was a Bencher, or to make inquiries of the Dublin Corporation. Professor Ehrenpreis prefers to settle the matter by citing Professor Woodbridge of Middletown, Connecticut, who says what he thinks is "likely" on the subject, having been unaware that Sir John's signature appears continuously in the Minutes of the Inns throughout the relevant period. The reason for this preference is sophistical and is not a mere mistake. So also there are valid reasons outside a detached objectivity for Professor Ehrenpreis' views on the coming of the Swift family to Ireland, on the location of Uncle Godwin's residence, on the probable ownership of the house in Hoey's Court in which Swift says that he was born, and most significant of all, on the problem of the date of the death of Jonathan Swift, the elder. He finds evidence on all these points in books that he admires, and it is in line with what he wants to say about Swift. What he omits to mention is that there is source material which – whether he accepts it or not – tends to contradict him on all these points.

Provokingly enough, three years after Johnston's own "important discoveries" had been published in "respectable" academic form, neither his name nor his work is mentioned even in a footnote by Ehrenpreis. No one likes to be treated with the contempt this omission implies. The closest Ehrenpreis comes to recognition that Johnston ever had a word to say about Swift was to declare on the first page of his preface that the first "fable" he was going to "eliminate" was that either Swift or Stella was a bastard.[13] Actually, when it comes to it, he does not really bother to "eliminate the fable;" in fact, he never even mentions it at all. Moreover, it seems there is nothing in Ehrenpreis's biography that makes Johnston's theories unlikely. Quite the contrary. That Swift is not always accurate in his own account of events touching his life is clear. Temple's taking Swift into his family as he does, his distance from his rather dour wife after losing so many children, this combined with his amorous enthusiasms and his vanity in talking about them, Swift's mother's odd behaviour, and Stella's high standing in Temple's family, even, arguably, the extent of Swift's loyalty to Temple, all contribute to Johnston's case, at least circumstantially, and suggest that at least a refutation is called for.

Johnston's theory in regard to Stella had been entertained by others. His Swift argument was more adamantly rejected. But Ehrenpreis says nothing about either of them. Whatever mistakes he may have made, Johnston prides himself on his meticulous documentation. Ehrenpreis, so meticulous and so thorough on other matters, simply makes different assertions on this subject. Right or wrong, then, Johnston's indignant response to Ehrenpreis's "authoritative" work following so close upon his own published treatment of the subject is not surprising. Then, too, more personally, Johnston's mild anti-semitism must have further exacerbated his feelings, especially in the context of his sense of his Anglo-Irish heritage, his consequent strong feeling of kinship with Swift, and his own particular identity with St Patrick's. Certainly, Ehrenpreis's being Jewish was not the main cause of Johnston's annoyance, but it did lend additional pique. His personal territory had been violated by someone who did not belong, and who did not even pay his respects, to this rightful member of the clan.

Four years later, in 1967, the Swift Tercentenary Year, and the year of publication for Ehrenpreis's second volume, Johnston, in a contribution to a Swift celebratory pamphlet, again presses his attack against the scholarly establishment, and, by implication, against Ehrenpreis in particular:

---

[13] *Mr Swift*, p. ix.

The trouble starts between those who have written their books in the easiest way, by treating everything that they have been told as the truth, and the others [like himself], who
believe nothing that they are told until they have been to see what is to be found in the
Record Office, or in the basement of the Custom House. Nobody likes to have it shown
that he has not checked his facts properly, least of all when it may mean bringing out a
revised edition or adding a shameful page of *Errata*. So the books, once published, have
to be stood over as a matter of professional integrity, and the sceptical snoopers are either
ignored or dismissed as gossips or busy-bodies.[14]

Volume 2 of *Swift: The Man, His Works, and the Age* surely infuriated Johnston even more
than had the first volume. Recognizing the very monumental dimension and overwhelming
erudition of the book, he must have been all the more frustrated. There was still no recognition that he existed. But more importantly, it was a matter of the pot calling the kettle
black. Many of Ehrenpreis' speculative conclusions are particularly well informed, his insights sound, even brilliant, but when he discusses the reasons for Esther Johnson and Re-
becca Dingley coming to Ireland, for example, he is more speculative than Johnston ever is.
Even more striking is Ehrenpreis's account of Tisdall's marriage proposal to Hetty, where
he simply announces that "according to Swift only a single obstruction stood in the way of
his own offer to marry Mrs Johnson, and that was a determination never to marry at all."[15]
Rarely is Ehrenpreis so unquestioning. Without any previous indication of movement toward
this decision, and while he certainly questions Swift's statements elsewhere, he simply accepts
Swift's word on this subject. Ehrenpreis does, however, give reasons for this "determination"
a few pages later: "*To press my own speculations on the episode still further,*" he says,

> I may describe Swift's immediate, unthinking response to the news of Tisdall's designs on
> Hetty as elementary panic. With more pains than most men devote to choosing a spouse,
> Swift had re-created the domestic pattern which gave him the deepest comfort. As a de-
> pendent, compliant confidant, part daughter, part pupil, part mistress, Hetty was a mi-
> raculous prize. Every assistance he gave her made her more his own. He could be uni-
> formly benevolent because she must be uniformly docile. It was not conceivable that he
> should find yet another fatherless young beauty, equipped with intelligence and polite
> breeding; that he should isolate her too from her family and obligate her to the point where
> she would indulge his unspoken wishes.[16]

Ehrenpreis's analysis, speculative though it be, may be absolutely correct, but Swift appears
here worthy of a character out of Molière, or to be the "monster" he is called by one of the
women in Johnston's play. Johnston is kinder. Even more astonishing to him than this version
of Swift's behaviour, however, was the notion that Stella would be willing to play such a
role. Ehrenpreis explains Hetty's opting for spinsterhood and continuing her ambiguous
relationship with Swift as resting on the pleasure of continuing Swift's good company and
worldly associations, as well as with the general disadvantages of marriage for a woman in
the eighteenth century.[17] Whatever personal appeal Tisdall lacked, these explanations seem
to me inadequate. Spinsterhood is the least of it, when one considers Hetty's bizarre relationship with Swift. Nevertheless, it is not impossible that Ehrenpreis is right regarding
Stella as well as Swift, but his conclusions are again *entirely speculative.* Johnston could not
have been pleased to have been attacked and then rejected for his own informed specu-

---

[14]  "The Trouble with Swift," *The Dublin of Dean Swift* (Dublin, [1967]).
[15]  *Dr Swift*, p. 135.
[16]  *Dr Swift*, p. 138 (emphasis added).
[17]  See *Dr Swift*, p. 139.

lativeness, and at the same time to see Ehrenpreis' speculations on the same subject, which Johnston found preposterous, accepted with enthusiasm.

The number of Johnston's writings about Swift is considerable, though there is an inevitable redundancy among them as he repeatedly presses his thesis. These writings were produced over a period of over thirty years, from the radio play in 1938 to a book review in 1970: expository works in the form of lectures, articles, and reviews, and the book; dramatic works for stage, radio, and television.

Clearly, Johnston identified with Swift. At least, there are interesting parallels between the scholar and his subject, and it may well be that these apparent likenesses enticed Johnston to his subject in the first place. Both men unquestionably made many enemies, both real and imagined. Moreover, they both took a certain perverse satisfaction in doing so, and were more than normally paranoid and vindictive. Johnston refers to "the Dean's habit [in the *Autobiographical Fragment*] of producing facts in his old age that do not always agree with versions he had already written down."[18] Johnston himself was to do precisely the same thing. He spent his last years revising the diary he had been keeping for over sixty years, often inserting in relevant places long passages which appear to have been written at the times of the events described, but which were in fact inscribed from memory in his old age, with all the hazards to accuracy this method suggests. Johnston comments in regard to Swift's identical procedure in the *Autobiographical Fragment*, which, he says,

> has certain peculiarities that strike the eye at once. First of all, it is written in the third person, as if JS, aware of the fact that future biographers would be interested in his background and early life, was eager to give them what appeared to be some outside party's objective outline of what was to be said on the subject, and so save them from the labour of any independent research, or even of thinking up phraseology of their own ... For what, after all, could be more convenient and authentic than a man's own account of himself – always assuming that his intention is to inform us, and not the reverse?[19]

Allegedly, this was Bernard Shaw's method as well as Swift's: leaving to posterity, by means of extensive autobiographical writings, an account of things as he wished them to appear rather than as they were. Johnston, who in his youth sat at Shaw's feet, refers to this policy: "Shaw," he says in his 1954 introduction, "used to object strenuously to any independent investigation of his youth. But as soon as he saw that the enquirer was going ahead with it anyhow, he would immediately bury the writer under a mountain of voluntary information."[20] Johnston, in his own very extensive diary, his own "autobiographical fragment," certainly has "future biographers" in mind as he writes, and wishes to be as accommodating as were Swift and Shaw. In fact, Johnston's assiduous journal-keeping (a journal which he specifically directed in his will to be made freely available to scholars) suggests an imitation of Swift writing his *Journal to Stella*.

"As a man," Johnston says of Swift in his 1941 paper, "a large number of intelligent and sensitive women admired and respected him at all stages of his life, and at least two of them loved him – one of them better than life itself."[21] Johnston, even more than most men, would

---

18  *In Search of Swift*, p. 82n9.
19  *In Search of Swift*, pp. 10–11.
20  *The Golden Cuckoo*, p. 15.
21  "The Mysterious Origin of Dean Swift," p. 89.

have liked this statement to apply to himself. A passage in his diary from September 1939
seeks to justify his fascination with his subject. It is simply headed at the top of the page
with the word "Polyphemus," a reference to the first version of his Swift play. Under it, we
find the following list (the list itself being reminiscent of Swift's own list-making habit):

> Because it is of Dublin.
> Because it is of the great eighteenth century that still lives in odd corners there.
> Because it is of Saint Patrick's, with grand organ music, and a strange epitaph upon the
> wall.
> Because it has humour and guts and a queer satirical twist.
> Because it [is] about a great man who, in a way, I understand.
> Because it enshrines both the love and the hatred of love that torments me too.
> Because of the two women, both of whom appeal to me.
> Because of the magnificent ready made material.
> Because of the insoluble mystery of it all.
> Because of the Shakespearean proportions of the characters and the superb tragedy of the
> plot.
> Because it is difficult but worth while.
> Because it lightens my own darkness, for I also have loved two women at the same time,
> wished them both well and inevitably failed them both.[22]

The impersonal observations are mixed with, and ultimately dominated by, very personal
ones. It has already been noted that Johnston's investigations in the end exonerate Swift of
charges that he behaved so badly in his personal life. Johnston may have wished for a similar
kind of sympathetic understanding for his own behaviour.

Clearly, he was anxious to identify with Swift. In an "Oration delivered by Hilton Edwards from a script prepared by Denis Johnston on the tercentenary of Swift's birthday in
Saint Patrick's Cathedral, Dublin," on 30 November 1967, Johnston imagines Swift speaking out on current issues:

> Can we not hear Swift calling for the creation of a few Communist cells – dummy ones, if
> you insist, but as formidable in appearance as possible. For why, he would ask, must Ire-
> land be left out of the world-wide distribution of the American tax-payers' money? What
> have we done that we alone must pay for the equipment of our Army out of our own
> pockets. It is because we have no Communists. Let us arrange to have some as promptly as
> possible, even if we have to pay them a small fee to put up a show, before everything has
> been emptied down the drain of Vietnam, and the last available dollar has been spent on
> giving tanks and napalm to the Jews and the Pakistanis.

Perhaps the views expressed here in rather heavy-handed satire could be Swift's as well as
Johnston's, as Johnston would like to believe. The two men shared, each in his own generation, an intolerance which comprises one of the least attractive features of their characters.

Swift has, of course, been the object of interest and admiration among many of the most
important Irish writers of this century. His name has been one to conjure with, as Yeats
does so effectively in some of his greatest poems. Joyce's *Ulysses* is punctuated with Swift
quotations. And Denis Johnston's own urbane and witty, often patronizing and abusive satire
dictates that he was an admirer of Swift's, as were Oscar Wilde and Bernard Shaw. Pride in
their Anglo-Irish heritage, of which Swift was a brilliant component, contributed most vis-
ibly to Yeats's and Johnston's enthusiasm for him. Both, as well as Lord Longford, wrote

---

[22] Johnston's diaries are now held in the Library of Trinity College, Dublin.

plays about him.[23] And, aside from the play specifically about him, Swift's was one of John-ston's dancing shadows in his first play, *The Old Lady Says 'No!'* – one of the great literary voices in the play, quoted in order to provide satirical comment on contemporary Irish values.[24]

In fact, Johnston claims that it was not academic ambition or scholarly interest, but his problem as a playwright that set him off on his Swift scholarship. While his enthusiasm for Swift was already well in place in the late 1920s when he was writing *The Old Lady Says 'No!'*, Johnston tells us in his 1941 paper that he "first became fascinated by the problem of Swift after seeing Lord Longford's play at the Gate Theatre [in 1933] – a play that brought very vividly before my mind three interesting and vital characters, two women and a man, in a very peculiar and obscure relationship with each other." He goes on to elaborate, as an introduction to his paper:

> What particularly caught my attention after reading several of the published biographies was the fact that the more one read about them – the deeper one delved in an effort to reconstruct their story – the more puzzling became the problem of their collective be-haviour. It was no good explaining the matter away by saying that the central character, Swift himself, was a very unusual person and could therefore hardly be expected to act in a normal way, because unfortunately the problem of conduct did not end with Swift. It appeared that not only did the Dean require some explanation, but so also did his two women, his mother, his father, his uncle, his patron, his nurse, and his wife's duenna – in fact everybody in any way closely connected with him – a perfect nest of extraordinary people! Yet few of them gave the impression of being in any way abnormal.[25]

Yeats' Swift play, *The Words upon the Window Pane*, produced in 1934, the year following Longford's, does not clear things up, but instead makes them worse, "drawing Swift," as it does, "as a man haunted by the fear of madness and unwilling to marry on that account. "Yet," says Johnston, "there is nothing in Swift's works or correspondence to suggest any fear of insanity, least of all a fear that would prevent his marrying."[26] Yeats, in writing his Swift play, was undoubtedly much more concerned with myth-making than he was with biographical accuracy. But Johnston implies that his own fascination with the subject came to a head when he tried himself to write a play about Swift, and the matter of dramatic realism became a problem. As he says in the 1954 introduction, in his usual condescending tone when speaking of scholars out of English Departments,

> There are a great many books on Swift, and what struck me at an early stage of my research was the fact that, however satisfactory they may be to writers of dissertations in the English Departments, to a man of the Theatre, who had to make sense of the story, they were a total loss ... [A] Dramatist ... is only concerned with personal history, and ... cannot be expected to write a play without proper motivation of the behaviour that he describes.[27]

---

[23] See Yeats, *The Words upon the Window Pane* (Dublin, 1934), and Longford, *Yahoo: A Tragedy in Three Acts* (Dublin, 1947).

[24] "The Third Shadow. Dingley, pray pay Stella six fishes and place them to the account of your humble servant, Presto. Stella, pray pay Dingley six fishes and place them to the account of your humble servant, Presto. *(He laughs.)* There's bills of exchange for you!" See *Collected Plays*, I (London, 1960), p. 80. There are six speaking and dancing, un-named shadows: Yeats, Joyce, Swift, Wilde, Mangan, and Shaw. Johnston reduced the number to four while revising the plays for *The Dramatic Works*, I (Gerrards Cross, 1977), eliminating Swift and Mangan.

[25] "The Mysterious Origin of Dean Swift," p. 81.

[26] "The Mysterious Origin of Dean Swift," p. 82.

[27] *The Golden Cuckoo*, pp. 13, 14.

And in the last introduction Johnston wrote for the play, now specifically for *The Dreaming Dust*, an essay called "Period Piece," he explains:

> A character in a play has to be explained sooner or later to the player who is expected to portray it, and this is no easy task if his or her behaviour bears no resemblance to any known pattern of human conduct, or even to some convention of the stage. Yet here we have a set of characters actually taken from life, the oddness of whose conduct is inescapable, whatever their real motives may have been ... While biographers can be intimidated by authorities, playwrights are even more intimidated by the need to make sense that can be explained to a cast.[28]

In a 3 December 1947 radio broadcast dealing with the three figures, Johnston had maintained that while men tend to believe in, and adore, the sad, devoted and self-effacing but mythical, Stella, women find her at best unbelievable and at worst boring; they prefer the more real flesh-and-blood Vanessa.

Johnston puts this female cynicism into his play, as the actress playing the double role of Stella and Pride (one of the Seven Deadly Sins) angrily interrupts the action and complains of being given a part that makes no sense. (The play, I should explain, consists of a series of vignettes from Swift's life, linked by commentary among a group of actors who meet in St Patrick's Cathedral after having played in a masque of the Seven Deadly Sins. Each vignette portrays Swift as embodying a different sin, and the actors double in their roles as characters representing the Sins in the linking material and as characters out of Swift's life in the vignettes.) In the vignette just previously presented, Stella has received the letter from Vanessa asking if she is Swift's wife. At this point, breaking out of her role as Stella and returning to the present as an actress playing the Sin of Pride, she says, "I am not Stella in any sense of the word. I'm not even a credible woman. What woman in her senses would behave like this?" To which the modern Dean of St Patrick's, who has been playing Swift before the interruption, replies:

> Dean (*nervously*). Your behaviour is perfectly reasonable. A very wonderful woman.
> Pride. Perfectly reasonable!
> Dean. It has satisfied generations of biographers.
> Pride (*scornfully*). Swift's biographers – not hers. It's enough for *his* story that she should be content to live her life as his unacknowledged mistress.
> Dean. No! As his secret wife.
> Pride. That is worse! If I am your wife, why shouldn't I be recognized? Am I something to be ashamed of?

And so on, continuing to express Johnston's difficulty with accepted versions of the story. Pride says, several lines later: "If I am Stella, I must be a real woman – not a wraith invented by some biographer to explain *his* behaviour." No woman, the actress argues, could possibly behave as Swift's male biographers tell us Stella did.[29] As Johnston says, the playwright must be able "to make sense that can be explained to a cast." Johnston, whose own female dramatic characters, he has noted, tend to be "killers," becomes a former-day feminist.

At the insistence of the indignant actress, the scene moves back in time to a private conversation in the garden at Laracor, where Swift discloses to Stella that while she is Sir William Temple's daughter, he is Sir John Temple's son, hence William Temple's half-brother,

---

28   *The Dramatic Works*, I, 252.
29   *Dramatic Works*, I, 296–97. Professor Ronsley has kindly presented a tape recording of this play to the Ehrenpreis Center. Eds.

and Stella's uncle. And when Stella concludes that "it is a sin for [her] to love" him, Swift explains: "More than a sin, Hetty. It is a crime … a crime against Church and State. Do you realize what this means in a world that is filled with bitter enemies? Above our heads hangs the unspeakable charge of incest."[30] This revelation settles the matter between Swift and Stella – for a time. But what Swift does not then foresee is the complications that arise because of the sexual attractions of Vanessa, and the fact that he is not so different from other men after all.

In the scene where Stella has received Vanessa's letter, Stella reverses her relationship with Swift, becoming the wise tutor, and he rather a confused pupil. Eventually, Stella diffidently asks: "Presto, are you … after all … are you only …" And he breaks in:

> Yes, I'm only a man – just like other men! Why not? Time and again I asked myself, what before God, is the impediment? Have I wife of my own, that I must fly from her? Am I to chase after trulls and trollops all my life to keep my thoughts from honest women?[31]

For Ehrenpreis, Swift is not "just like other men." For all his recognition of Swift's human frailties and foibles in other aspects of his life, Ehrenpreis does not allow for them in the Dean when it comes to sex, and maybe he is right. While the information Ehrenpreis provides on their relationship leaves the question quite open in my mind, perhaps nothing physical did occur between Swift and Vanessa. But for Johnston, who approached Swift from the perspective of his own life experience, this does not make sense. Swift had to be as sexually vulnerable as Johnston was himself. The circumstances of Johnston's love life were of course different from Swift's. He did have two wives after all, and hardly the same moral qualms. But, like Swift's, Johnston's love life was complicated – despite the diary entry quoted earlier, it involved three concurrent women against Swift's measly two! – and caused him to have a guilty conscience, even as he rationalized his behaviour. At least in part of this dramatic outburst by Swift can be heard Johnston's plea for tolerance for himself.

Ehrenpreis's and Johnston's speculations on the subject of Swift's love life are different. Whether or not Johnston's biographical theories are correct, they are not entirely unreasonable. Moreover, they make pretty good drama, being more interesting than theories about Swift's lack of money, the surfeit of fruit, the fear of madness, or simply Swift's own eccentricity. Right or wrong, Johnston enhances Swift's humanity, and he feels a strong sense of kinship with him. In the larger picture, Johnston, like Yeats, took refuge from disappointment by joining company with Swift in projecting his own "savage indignation."

---

[30] *Dramatic Works*, I, 299.
[31] *Dramatic Works*, I, 303.

# Contributors

Michael J. Conlon teaches in the English Department at Binghamton University, State University of New York, and also serves as Faculty Master of a residential college. His recent publications address the subjects of spectacle, performance, parody in eighteenth-century English literature and culture.

Michael DePorte is Professor of English at the University of New Hampshire. He is the author of *Nightmares and Hobbyhorses: Swift, Sterne, and Augustan Ideas of Madness* (1974), and of numerous essays on Swift and other writers of the period, most recently, "*Vinum Daemonum*: Swift and the Grape."

J. A. Downie is Pro-Warden (Academic) and Professor of English at Goldsmiths' College, University of London. His books include *Robert Harley and the Press: Propaganda and Public Opinion in the Age of Swift and Defoe* (1979), *Jonathan Swift, Political Writer* (1984), and *To Settle the Succession of the State: Literature and Politics, 1678-1750* (1994).

A. C. Elias, Jr, wrote *Swift at Moor Park* (1982) and edited Laetitia Pilkington's *Memoirs* (2 vols, 1997). A frequent visitor to Dublin, he is a founding trustee of the American Society for 18th-Century Studies' Irish Research Travel Fund, and serves as exclusive North American representative for Jams O'Donnell Productions International (Indexing and Donkeywork) PLC.

Carole Fabricant is a Professor of English at the University of California, Riverside, and author of *Swift's Landscape* (1982), recently reissued by the University of Notre Dame Press, as well as numerous articles on Swift and other 18th-century subjects. She is currently working on an edition of Swift's Miscellaneous Prose for Penguin Classics.

Rudolf Freiburg holds the chair of Modern English Literature at the University of Erlangen-Nürnberg. He is author of *Autoren und Leser: Studien zur Intentionalität literarischer Texte* (1985) and of many articles on both 18th-century and 20th-century literature.

Christopher Fox is Professor of English and Director of the Institute for Scholarship in the Liberal Arts at the University of Notre Dame, Indiana. He is the author of *Locke and the Scriblerians: Identity and Consciousness in Early Eighteenth-Century Britain* (1988), and the editor of several books, including *Gulliver's Travels: Case Studies in Contemporary Criticism* (1995) and, with Brenda Tooley, *Walking Naboth's Vineyard: New Studies of Swift* (1995). He is currently working on *The Cambridge Companion to Swift*.

Brean Hammond is Rendel Professor of English and Pro Vice-Chancellor, University of Wales, Aberystwyth. He is the author of several books and articles on the Scriblerians, and other authors and topics in the long eighteenth century. His most recent book is *Professional Imaginative Writing in England, 1670-1740: "Hackney for Bread"* (1997).

Phillip Harth is Merritt Y. Hughes Professor Emeritus and Senior Member Emeritus of the Institute for Research in the Humanities at the University of Wisconsin, Madison. He is the author of *Swift and Anglican Rationalism* (1961), as well as of several books on John Dryden.

D. W. Hayton is Lecturer in Modern History at the Queen's University of Belfast, and has written widely on the political history of Britain and Ireland in the late seventeenth and early eighteenth centuries. His publications include *Penal Era and Golden Age: Essays in Irish History, 1690-1800* (1979), *British Parliamentary Lists, 1660-1800: A Register* (1995), and, most recently, *The Parliamentary Diary of Sir Richard Cocks, 1698-1702* (1996). He was recently appointed joint-editor of the journal *Irish Historical Studies*.

Ann Cline Kelly is Professor of English at Howard University in Washington, D.C. She is author of *Swift and the English Language* (1988) and of numerous articles that have appeared in *SEL, ELH, PMLA*, and *Swift Studies*, among others.

Baptized into the Church of Ireland and still active in his Philadelphia parish, Hugh Ormsby-Lennon teaches eighteenth-century studies at Villanova University. Faced by his graduate students' insistence that he reincarnates Swift, Ormsby-Lennon retorts that his own scruffiness, conversational bluntness, and reliance upon shopping bags must render every such whimsy asinine. Immersion in commonplace books notwithstanding, he has squeezed out idiosyncratic scribbles on Prague Structuralism, Rosicrucian Linguistics, Quaker Sociolinguistics, Cargo Cults, Charlatanism, and Swift's own focus upon das Dong-an-sich.

J. T. Parnell is Lecturer in English at Goldsmiths' College, University of London. His publications include essays on Milan Kundera, Salman Rushdie, Sterne, and Swift, an edition of *Tristram Shandy*, and a co-edited collection of essays on Christopher Marlowe. He is editor of "Defoe and the Novelists" for the *Scriblerian* and is currently writing a literary biography of Sterne.

Clive Probyn is Professor of English at Monash University, Clayton, Victoria, Australia. He has written and edited a number of books and articles on Jonathan Swift.

Patrick Reilly is Emeritus Professor at the University of Glasgow. His publications include *Jonathan Swift: The Brave Desponder* (1982); *"Tom Jones": Adventure and Providence* (1991); *George Orwell: The Age's Adversary* (1986); *"Nineteen Eighty-Four": Past, Present, and Future* (1989); *The Literature of Guilt: "Gulliver" to Golding* (1988); *"Lord of the Flies": Fathers and Sons* (1992).

Hermann J. Real is Professor of English and Director of the Ehrenpreis Center for Swift Studies at the Westfälische Wilhelms-Universität. In addition to being co-translator of *Gullivers Reisen* (1987), he is editor of *The Battle of the Books* (1978), and of *Swift Studies*, as well as co-author of *Jonathan Swift: "Gulliver's Travels"* (1984), and co-editor of *Proceedings of The First Münster Symposium on Jonathan Swift* (1985), of *Swift and his Contexts* (1989), and of *Reading Swift: Papers from The Second Münster Symposium on Jonathan Swift* (1993).

Joseph Ronsley is Professor of English (retired) at McGill University, Montreal. He is author of *Yeats's Autobiography: Life as Symbolic Pattern* (1968), has edited *The Dramatic Works, III: The Broadcast Plays* by Denis Johnston (1992), Johnston's *Selected Plays*, and books of essays, *Myth and Reality in Irish Literature* (1977), *Denis Johnston: A Retrospective* (1981), and *Omnium Gatherum: Essays for Richard Ellmann* (1989). He is co-General Editor of the series *Irish Drama Selections*, and has written many articles and lectured extensively.

Ian Simpson Ross is Professor of English (Emeritus) at the University of British Columbia, Vancouver. Having co-edited Adam Smith's correspondence for the Glasgow edition of his works, he went on to write *The Life of Adam Smith* (1995). He is also the biographer of Lord Kames, Smith's patron (1972). His new book, *Contemporary Responses to the Wealth of Nations*, will be published this Spring.

Peter Sabor is Professor of English at Université Laval, Québec. His publications include *Horace Walpole: A Reference Guide* (1984), *Horace Walpole: The Critical Heritage* (1987), and the Introduction to a facsimile edition of Walpole's *Works*. He has also published many articles on, and editions of, works by eighteenth and early-nineteenth-century authors.

Peter J. Schakel is Peter C. and Emajean Cook Professor of English at Hope College. He is author of *The Poetry of Jonathan Swift* (1978) and editor of *Critical Approaches to Teaching Swift* (1992).

Helgard Stöver-Leidig is Research Assistant at the Ehrenpreis Center for Swift Studies at the Westfälische Wilhelms-Universität. She is editor of *Die Gedichte Thomas Tickells* (1981) and assistant editor of *Swift Studies*. After the untimely death of Richard Rodino in 1990, she co-edited *Reading Swift: Papers from The Second Münster Symposium on Jonathan Swift* (1993), with Hermann J. Real.

Michael Treadwell is Professor of English at Trent University. In addition to numerous articles on Jonathan Swift, he has also written widely on the English book trade in the seventeenth and eighteenth centuries.

Peter Wagner is Professor of English, and Chairman of the Department of English, at the Universität Koblenz-Landau. He is editor of *Icons – Texts – Iconotexts: Essays on Ekphrasis and Intermediality* (1996), and author of *Reading Iconotexts: From Swift to the French Revolution* (1995).

# Index